# Learning From Text
# Across Conceptual Domains

# Learning From Text
# Across Conceptual Domains

Edited by

## Cynthia R. Hynd
*University of Georgia*

Section Editors:

## Steven A. Stahl
## Martha Carr
## Shawn M. Glynn
*University of Georgia*

**NRRC** National
Reading Research
Center

*A Consortium of the University of Georgia and the University of Maryland*

**LEA** LAWRENCE ERLBAUM ASSOCIATES, PUBLISHERS
1998   Mahwah, New Jersey                         London

Lawrence Erlbaum Associates, Inc., Publishers
10 Industrial Avenue
Mahwah, New Jersey 07430

Cover design by Kathryn Houghtaling Lacey

**Library of Congress Cataloging-in-Publication Data**

Learning from text across conceptual domains / edited by Cynthia R. Hynd ;
   section editors, Steven A. Stahl, Martha Carr, Shawn M. Glynn.
      p.   cm.
   Includes bibliographical references and index.
   ISBN 0-8058-2183-X (c). — ISBN 0-8058-2184-8 (p).
   1. Learning. 2. Knowledge, Theory of. 3. High school teaching.
   4. Students—Psychology. 5. Reading (Secondary). I. Hynd, Cynthia R.,
   1948–       .
   LB1060.L4242  1998
   370.15′23—dc21                                          97-43514
                                                               CIP

Books published by Lawrence Erlbaum Associates are printed on acid-free paper,
and their bindings are chosen for strength and durability.

Printed in the United States of America
10  9  8  7  6  5  4  3  2  1

# Contents

# Preface

This volume, *Learning From Text Across Conceptual Domains*, is an attempt to synthesize the understandings we have about reading to learn as a result of our work with the National Reading Research Center. Although we discuss learning at all ages, our main focus is on middle and high school classrooms—critical spaces of learning and thinking. The education of students in these classes, taken as a whole, seems inadequate if our goal is to produce readers and writers who understand, learn from, and think critically about the information in various forms of text. That goal is complicated by the fact that the amount of knowledge presented in written form is increasing, and the information we get from texts is often conflicting. It is also complicated by the fact that students have varying motivations, self-perceptions, goals, and needs that often hinder their accomplishment of our goal that they understand, learn from, and think critically about what they read. In addition, teachers, pulled by various and sometimes conflicting goals, are often hindered by the contexts in which they work. Finally, students have social, ethnic, and cultural differences that mitigate the overall effectiveness of instruction. It is vitally important that we study the instruction that helps students to be critical consumers of texts, the contexts within which that instruction is successful, the texts students read, and the students who are affected by instruction. We hope that the research in this volume increases readers' knowledge as much as it did that of the authors.

This book is written for educators of various ilks. We want it to be read by our researcher colleagues, of course. But we are concerned, as well, that this book be read by graduate students, practicing teachers, and teachers in training who are interested in understanding the issues that are central to improving students' learning from text. We hope that this book convinces these readers that the issues are complex and multidimensional, and that our understandings of one aspect of literacy is dependent on our understandings of other aspects, as well. For example, we cannot really understand why students have difficulty changing their conceptions about science unless we understand the social implications for that change and the individual and societal influences that help determine why some children become literate in science and others do not. We mean for this volume to be used in colleges and universities where students are expected to develop theoretical as well as practical understandings. We hope that this book will foster further research efforts, whether that research be a teacher's local study of his or her classroom or a large-scale study that produces generalizable understandings about learning from text. We also hope that practicing teachers will learn to consider their students in new ways, that they will see them both as being influenced by and influencing, not just the classroom, but the total fabric of the disciplines they are learning.

This book is divided into three sections. In part I, The Nature of Knowledge and Learning, we begin with three teachers' descriptions of their high school interdisciplinary program. In this program, a group of students studies English, world history, and biology as a team. The teachers, Dena Pruitt, Teri Sanders, and Michael Wayne, tie their content together, closely monitor their students' progress, and encourage similar study strategies across their courses. It is an attempt to produce some integrated understandings of content across disciplines, to engage students by making them feel part of a community of learners, and to foster the development of strategies to help students learn. If you were to ask parents and students at the school what they think of the program, they would say it is enormously successful, but the teachers know there are difficulties in reaching their goals as well as successes. The teachers describe their program and honestly discuss both their successes and failures. We use this description for at least two purposes. First, it helps illustrate some of the issues related to curriculum that must be understood if a person wants to improve learning from text. Also, it gives us a backdrop from which we can illustrate our understandings about the various aspects of learning from text that we present in the subsequent chapters.

After this description, we present two chapters. The first, What Do We Mean by Knowledge and Learning? by Cynthia Hynd and Steven Stahl, gives an overview of the theoretical notions about knowledge and learning that seem most cogent to the skill of reading to learn that occurs as a student progresses in school toward high school graduation and beyond. The second, Motivation to Read and Learn From Text by Martha Carr, Nancy Mizelle, and David Charak, discusses theory about interests, attributional beliefs, and learning goals; presents an integrated model of these aspects of motivation; and discusses ways to improve motivation from developmental, cognitive, and sociocultural perspectives. The authors take a generally developmental look at motivation, and discuss its implications for students at all ages, from kindergarten through grade 12.

Part II of this volume, How Students Learn Content Knowledge, tackles the intersection of theory and practice. In this section, the authors discuss various aspects of theories that have implications for instruction aimed at helping students learn from text. The first chapter, Four Questions About Vocabulary Knowledge and Reading and Some Answers by Steven Stahl, asks these questions: (a) What is the relationship between vocabulary knowledge and reading comprehension? (b) How many words do people know? (c) What does it mean to "know" a word? and (d) How do people learn words from context? Vocabulary knowledge is at the heart of learning from text, and this chapter unpacks the relationship between knowing words and understanding the contexts of different knowledge environments, how people learn words indirectly, and how word knowledge can be taught. The next chapter, What Is the Point? Tests of a Quick and Clean Method for Improving Instructional Text by Robert Sorrells and Bruce Britton, discusses three research studies aimed at understanding the effects of different texts on students' learning and improving those texts. The authors discuss the way in which texts can be written to enhance the development of disciplinary understandings. Bruce VanSledright and Lisa Frankes have written the following chapter, Literature's Place in Learning History and Science, which explores the effect of literature on students' understandings of their content subjects. According to theory, literature can enhance content understandings in a number of important ways. The authors discuss this theory and its practical implications, but they also present and discuss a review of the research, which is equivocal.

Cynthia Hynd and Barbara Guzzetti's chapter, When Knowledge Contradicts Intuition: Conceptual Change, discusses a problem in knowledge growth and the effect that text has in overcoming this problem. The problem is that students sometimes have deep-seated beliefs and understandings about the world that are inconsistent with what they need to learn to become immersed in a discipline. These beliefs and understandings are singularly difficult to change, and the authors discuss the role of text and other instructional and contextual influences on this change.

Lynn Anderson-Inman and David Reinking, in their chapter, Learning From Text in a Post-Typographic World, discuss the role of technology in transforming education for middle and high school students.

The chapter that follows, Making Text Meaningful: The Role of Analogies, written by Shawn Glynn, Michael Law, and Elizabeth Doster, explains the role of analogies in helping students learn topics in school. Analogies are used by textbook authors, teachers, and students to aid the understanding of complex content. Whereas the systematic use of analogies enhances learning and develops critical thinking, inappropriate analogies can lead to confusion. The authors discuss previous and new research that explores the analogies used in texts, by teachers, and by students, and provides practical information about how to construct and use well-formed analogies to enhance students' understandings.

Taken as a whole, the chapters in part II present a view of reading to learn that is multifaceted and complex. Part III, Learning Disciplinary Knowledge, places the understandings gained from these chapters within a disciplinary perspective. That is, as students move from elementary to high school and beyond, they are exposed to an ever-increasing distinction among the disciplines of science, history, English, and so on. By the time students graduate from high school, they are expected to have a fairly sophisticated understanding of not only the content embedded within these disciplines, but also the nature of knowledge production and dissemination that is characteristic of each. Thus, it is important to understand what it means to develop this disciplinary knowledge. Leigh Craft Hern, Mark Faust, and Maureen Boyd, in their chapter, Literacy, Textuality, and the Expert: Learning in the English Language Arts, discuss the view that instruction in English is aimed at helping students enter an English "Discourse Community." They explain that there seem to be three views of literacy constituting the Discourse Community: (a) literacy as adaptation, (b) literacy as a "state of grace," and (c) literacy as power. They also describe how three aspects of English classes—reading, writing, and language—are instantiated within those views of literacy. Finally, they discuss a view of learning from text that encompasses intertextuality, ideology, and expert knowledge. Maureen McMahon and Bernadette McCormack write about ways To Think and Act Like a Scientist: Learning Disciplinary Knowledge. In their chapter, they discuss what it means for a scientist to read, and how (and if) that knowledge is learned by science students.

This volume closes with a chapter by Patricia Alexander: The Nature of Disciplinary and Domain Learning: The Knowledge, Interest, and Strategic Dimensions of Learning From Subject Matter Text. Patricia discusses theory explaining the development of disciplinary knowledge, then describes the interaction of various influences in that development. In her view, these factors exist and grow in tandem, so they must all be considered if students are to learn from text.

This closing chapter provides a fitting conclusion. It reflects our common understanding, expressed earlier, that learning from text is a complex matter including student factors, instructional and teacher factors, and disciplinary and societal factors. There has never been a more crucial time for students to understand, learn from, and think critically about texts. We are in a knowledge explosion that leaves us reeling and may effectively disenfranchise those who are not keeping up. Thus, understanding the meaning of reading to learn is vital for all educators.

## AKCNOWLEDGMENT

The editor and section editors wish to thank Tom Montgomery, doctoral student at the University of Georgia, for his work in helping to compile this volume. At times, the task seemed endless, and we very much appreciate his perseverence and hard work.

—*Cynthia R. Hynd*

—*Steven A. Stahl*
—*Martha Carr*
—*Shawn M. Glynn*

# PART ONE

# THE NATURE OF
# KNOWLEDGE AND LEARNING

Knowledge becomes increasingly specialized as students go through school. The nature of the disciplines is such that different traditions for reading, research, and writing are developed. Experts in biology, for instance, value objectivity and write research reports in specialized ways. Historians value interpretation and favor the writing of narratives. As students progress, then, they become immersed in these different traditions, and it becomes more and more difficult to find linkages across disciplines. Yet, there is at least a theoretical appeal for the idea that students develop cross-disciplinary understandings by means of enhancing such skills as critical thinking and problem solving.

Beane (1995), argued that true integrated understandings are developed when students use knowledge gained from the various disciplines to solve authentic problems. For example, comprehension, learning, and critical thinking are enhanced by the study of how to solve a real-world problem such as what can be done to improve the ecology of a polluted pond. Students may need to research the history of the pond to determine how it became polluted, learn something about the chemical compositions of healthy and polluted ponds, and draw on English and political science to develop a writing campaign that ends in political action. Beane also argued that students learn history, English, and chemistry by solving problems.

Although a problem-centered curriculum is theoretically appealing, it is
increasingly resisted by teachers and schools as students move up through
the grades. A number of reasons exist for this resistance. For one thing, high
school teachers are disciplinary experts who have a stake in distinguishing
one discipline from another. It is interesting to see how teachers negotiate
a balance between their own need to develop disciplinary distinctions and
their need to provide students with interdisciplinary understandings. The
first chapter in this section, written by three high school teachers, entitled
Interdisciplinary Instruction in a Southeastern High School, describes one
group of teachers' attempt to address this balance. The type of interdisciplinary instruction described here may prove feasible for high school teachers. It is not the kind of instruction that Beane described, but teachers,
parents, and students believe that it is successful. The teachers describe their
program and discuss its strengths and weaknesses.

Chapter 2, What Do We Mean by Knowledge and Learning, discusses
the notions of knowledge and learning that are borne out in instruction and
find their place in classrooms like those described in the first chapter as
well as in more traditional classrooms of disciplines such as science and
history. Chapter 3, Motivation to Read and Learn From Text, goes into detail
about aspects of motivation that play a part in learning from texts in the
various disciplines. Motivation is the "engine" that drives cognition and is
central in the development of both integrated and discipline-specific understandings. These three chapters, taken in concert, are meant to provide the
theoretical backdrop for chapters in the next section, which discuss more
specific instructional aspects of reading to learn.

## REFERENCES

Beane, J. A. (1995). Curriculum integration and the disciplines of knowledge. *Phi Delta Kappan,*
*76* (8), 616–622.

## CHAPTER ONE

# Interdisciplinary Instruction in a Southeastern High School

Dena Pruitt
Teri Sanders
Michael Wayne
*Clarke Central High School, Athens, Georgia*

Several years ago, Teri, a world history teacher, and Betty (pseudonym), an English teacher, began a discussion that would have wide-ranging implications for the school in which they taught. They saw their ninth grade students having difficulty meeting the challenges of high school after experiencing the more supportive environment of middle school. At Clarke Central High School, high school students drop out at an alarming rate, and the rate of failure for advanced students is high, as well.

The discussion of these two teachers stemmed from the observation that most of the middle schools in their town had adopted the middle school model, in which each team of social science, English, math, and science teachers worked with the same group of students during the year. By organizing their instruction in cross-disciplinary teams, middle school teachers found it easier to keep track of student progress, reinforce ties across content areas, and give students a feeling of community and connectedness. In coming to high school, these students typically would move from an environment where they were monitored very carefully to a situation in which they had six different teachers who had no idea of any student's performance or behavior in any other classroom setting. Furthermore, students were confronted with a large physical setting and many more students than they were used to, usually of varying ages and ability levels, in one classroom.

Teri and Betty reasoned that they could provide the same benefits of the middle school model to their high school students by organizing a team. At the same time, they saw that their classes could be supportive of each other. The English teacher, for example, could reinforce some of the strategies for reading, studying, and writing needed in history. The history class, in turn, could provide a focus for reading that would give students studying literature the necessary background for the interpretive work they did.

In the next year, with the principal's blessing, these two teachers organized such a team and handpicked a group of advanced students to help them try out the concept. The idea was accepted so favorably by students and parents that the next year they added a science teacher to the mix. This team also received much positive feedback. The following year, the English teacher changed jobs and Dena replaced her. A math teacher was added also. However, too many different levels of mathematical ability in a class-room of otherwise advanced students became a logistical nightmare for the math teacher. Grouping them by mathematical ability did not allow for the mixture of students the team was striving to achieve in the other disciplines. At the end of the year, the teachers decided it was too hard to integrate mathematics, so the math component was dropped. In addition, the science teacher changed jobs, so Michael, a new science teacher, was added. This last year is the one that is now described. The team consisted of Dena, the English teacher; Teri, the world history teacher (and only original team member); and Michael, the science teacher (new to the team). (We refer to members of our Interdisciplinary Team as "we." In referring to students, we use pseudonyms.)

## DESCRIBING OUR PROGRAM

Our Interdisciplinary Team was formed in an attempt to create a "school within a school." Students advanced in the areas of English, social studies, and science are grouped into three classes that travel en masse from one study to the next. Approximately every 6 weeks, we randomly choose 10 to 12 students and rearrange their schedules within the team subjects only. This keeps an entire class of 28 students from staying together for half the school day all year long. In the beginning, students hate schedule changes, but by the end of the year they clamor for them. This shifting of students from one class to the other provides for a good mix of students and keeps them from identifying solely with one group or another.

The three classes on the team are taught in consecutive periods. This last year, the team was moved from first through third periods to fourth, fifth, and sixth periods to accommodate other disciplines such as band and foreign language. The teachers of these disciplines did not like the idea of always getting this large group of advanced students at the end of the day. Our team dreaded that year, fearing that having ninth graders take three of their hardest classes in a block at the end of the day would be disastrous. Much to our surprise, the team worked just as well at the end of the day as it had at the beginning. The students rose to the occasion and succeeded beyond our expectations.

Including a lab science on the team and keeping each class intact from one subject to the next means that class size must be kept to 28 students, which is an advantage of the team approach. Because the three periods are consecutive, the team is able to do some flexible scheduling, and we have been lucky enough to have an administration that supports those changes as long as they are in the best interests of the students. For example, 3 days a week, we have a 2-hr block in one class and see one other class. We still meet with each class the same number of minutes per week, but the block scheduling allows for extended activities (lengthy tests, group projects, videos, etc.), which are normally interrupted with the 50- or 55-min class schedule. As Ken said, "We're in there for two periods. You learn stuff like biology that you won't catch on to with less time. You get to know students better. It's more interesting, and you can do something a little different." We are also able to arrange field trips and other activities, which take place only during our three class periods. For example, during the Greek unit in world history and *The Odyssey* unit in English, the students and teachers take a walk and complete an assignment to identify types of columns and other components of Greek architecture found on fraternity and sorority houses. These half-day events do not affect any other classes, so the students do not have to worry about missing work in another class or not being permitted to go by another teacher. We have also used the three-period block for guest speakers, who come in and speak to the entire team of 84 students at once rather than making the same presentation three different times.

The three team teachers share a common planning period, which allows us to plan projects and interdisciplinary units as well as to share communication about particular students. It has also been an excellent time to schedule parent conferences, in which we make it routine to include the student. In past years, we also have managed to arrange for the entire team to have the same lunch period, because fourth period was included on the team. Again, our supportive administrators allow us to change the lunch schedule of one or more of the team teachers to ensure a common lunch time for the students. This gives us freedom to use the lunch period for everything from parties to celebrating academic successes to lunch detention for minor infractions of classroom rules. Ironically, eating lunch with the teachers becomes a social event for some students. This allows the teachers to gain insight into student attitudes, background, and so forth that they might not get in a regular classroom setting.

## DESCRIBING OUR GOALS

The first goal for the Interdisciplinary Team is to create an environment in which our students can feel safe and supported. We hesitate to use the word "nurtured," because we are not always there to make students feel good.

Once students get past the idea of being labeled, they view the team as a tool they can use to help them overcome an otherwise scary high school situation. Renee, for example, said, "The teachers are very understanding. They're not like teachers; they're like friends. They give advice. They're pretty easy to talk to." And Carolyn said, "It's like a family." The team likes to think it distinguishes between "being friendly" and "being their friends." We are not their buddies, but we do try to be approachable.

The team also strives to teach integrated units across the three disciplines so that instruction becomes more meaningful. Concepts covered in several subject areas become more concrete for students, and they are far more likely to remember material they see in more than one subject. For example, the background on Greek culture they bring from world history helps them better understand the events and relationships encountered in *The Odyssey*. For example, James, a diligent, learning-disabled student who pushed himself harder than even we intended, reported that he got more out of reading *Animal Farm* in English class because he could relate it to what he had learned about the Russian Revolution in world history. In fact, many of our students expressed appreciation for content ties across classes because it helped them to learn.

Another goal of our team is to provide some consistency in rules and disciplinary procedures among the three teachers on the team. We serve to reinforce each other and let the students know that the teachers are a team that will stick together. They quickly learn that we keep up with them, and whereas some of them never get past the discomfort of being followed so carefully, many appreciate the firmness with which we handle them. We also try to provide consistency in some types of class activities. For example, all three team teachers encourage the use of notebooks for organizational skills as well as study guides and note cards to improve study habits. Students from previous years often return later to tell us that the study techniques required by the Interdisciplinary Team benefitted them greatly in other subject areas and later years. Mary, a self-driven, gifted young lady, stated that sharing these concepts from one class to another gave students an opportunity to learn (imagine a student appreciating that) and made them want to learn more. I am not sure, however, that we always accurately convey the team concept to our students. Ken, for example, said that the team teachers were "laid back" because they had more time. We would be curious to know where he thought we got this. However, he also more correctly stated that the team teachers were able to know their students better—"know their tendencies"—and therefore they could "relate better to you."

One thing in which the Interdisciplinary Team prides itself is communication with parents. One of our team members, Teri, is especially diligent about making telephone calls home, and although the students see this as a nightmarish situation, parents deeply appreciate it. One situation from last year illustrates this—our notorious Senior Skip Day, which has trickled, to our intense displeasure, all the way down to the freshmen. Teri made it a point to call the parents of every single student who was absent from our afternoon classes that day. All of the parents who got a phone call appreciated the fact that our team cared enough to check up on their children. Some students see this as unfair. Trevor, for example, said, "I don't like the idea that teachers communicate when a student is not in class." Parents, however, are generally thrilled.

The Interdisciplinary Team also sends out progress reports twice as often as the school does during the first semester. Our first progress reports go home only 3 weeks after the school year begins, before problems are too severe to be corrected. Although individual subject teachers are certainly free to send home progress reports at any time they choose, having three acadmic subject teachers do so together sends a much more meaningful message. Parents can see immediately if their child is having difficulty in one area or if there are some study strategies that must be polished. Some students appreciate the warning. Jerry says, "I like when we get our progress reports, so we know what are grades are before report cards." The students thus know what their grades are between other grading periods, and they know what they must do to correct any deficiencies before the "real" progress reports come out.

Because of our close communication and commitment to the team concept, we are able to keep from overwhelming our students with too many tests. We constantly check with each other regarding test dates so we can plan, not only around our own tests, but those of our teammates as well. Making it a practice to schedule major tests during the double-block period means that the students will not have more than one major test on any given day. We also employ some common test-taking strategies. Our team recognizes that not all students can take a test effectively in the same environment as their classmates. It is not unusual for a student to join us for lunch and retake a test orally, proving that poor test-taking skills rather than deficient knowledge of the material caused a failing grade. Again, any classroom teacher may use the oral test option; seeing that all three team members utilize that option keeps students from being singled out or from feeling they are receiving "special treatment."

## DESCRIBING OUR STUDENTS

Students on the Interdisciplary Team at Clarke Central High School are ninth graders identified as advanced in the areas of science, English, and world history. Even so, these classes contain students with a wide range of abilities. A student identified as gifted would normally be channeled into a different program, but such a student may choose not to participate in the gifted program or the parents may prefer the structure of the Interdisciplinary Team to the gifted program. Also in that same class, there may be a student who normally would not have been placed in advanced classes, but the middle school teachers, parents, and team teachers agree that the benefits of the supportive environment found on the team outweigh the disadvantages associated with placing such a student above his or her ability. We have found that such students generally rise to the occasion and fit in well with their classmates, achieving far more than they have in an average "regular" class, which would be much larger than the team classes and would not offer the same support and encouragement. Trevor, a student from last year, serves as an example of this.

Trevor could not manage a passing grade on any of Dena's 15-word, multiple-choice vocabulary tests. She watched him make flash cards, study with his classmates, read the definitions to himself, all to no avail. He worked hard, however, to get the daily work done, putting extra effort into home-work assignments and classwork, thus overcoming the damage done by his test grades. His problems were evident not only in English class, but in world history as well. Teri knew that Trevor knew the material but had an extremely difficult time getting the information down on paper. He asked intelligent questions and could discuss concepts from lectures fluently. Teri allowed Trevor to take his first-semester exam orally after he first failed a written form of it, certain that his failure was not due to lack of study.

Trevor was never a behavior problem, but he became understandably frustrated at his own deficiences and would show off to cover his embar-rassment. We knew this and treated him with respect. Trevor thrived in our advanced classes, and we are confident that he would not have done as well outside the team. He learned by having three subjects tied together and adapted to tough teachers because we worked with him. In an interview, he said, "I like where they can talk about the same three [subjects] and talk about them in the same way. . . . I'm able to learn a little bit better because they know what they're talking about between [them]." At the beginning of the year, Trevor had an especially difficult time with biology. When asked to rate his motivation to learn on a scale of one to six, he rated his motivation to learn biology as one. However, he changed his mind as he learned to adapt and expressed it this way: "I hated it [biology] worse than English. . . . But I've gotten used to it. . . . I got a 78 on an exam, and now I'd give it a 5 'cause I've learned to adapt to him [Michael], and I've learned a lot. And I really like the animal project. I'm listening to what he says."

The students on the team are typically on track. Very few of them are over-age compared with their classmates. Yet, as with most groups of ninth graders, these students demonstrate a diversity of social skills, from the very quiet individual battling shyness to the outgoing, seemingly well-rounded teen-ager to the youth still striving for attention through acting-out behaviors.

Typical of most ninth graders, these students hate labels, even those applied to them by the Interdisciplinary Team. They abhor anything that makes them different from their classmates in "regular" ninth-grade classes. Brutally honest with each other and with their teachers, they do not mind telling each other when they look bad or act strange and they readily tell teachers when they are doing something they [the students] dislike. Part of this honesty comes from the closeness among the students and teachers that develops by being on a team. These students tell us details about their private lives that we often wish we did not know. They struggle to reconcile being liked by their peers as well as their teachers because often they see the two as being mutually exclusive. Such is the mind of a high-schooler.

Many of these students will accept a low grade rather than put themselves in an awkward situation. Kirk, for example, was discovered to have his vocabulary list on the floor in front of his desk during a vocabulary test. Wanting to give him the benefit of the doubt, Dena gave him the opportunity to come to her classroom the next morning to retake the test, but he failed to show up. During a subsequent conversation with his stepfather, Dena learned that Kirk had indeed been dropped off at school early to take the test, but rather than experience the awkwardness of facing her, he not only failed to take the test, but skipped all of his classes that day. He much preferred a test grade of zero to showing up in Dena's room to retake a test on which he had cheated. That young man had dealt with her anger on more than one occasion, but he could not face Dena's disappointment in him.

In a typical class day, positive peer pressure seems to keep most of the students focused and on task. They are generally prepared for class with books, paper, and writing utensils. Moreover, students take care of each other when one of their classmates happens not to be prepared for class. We like to think it is the team concept that compels them to take care of each other. They seem to be as interested in the entire class doing well as they are in their individual successes.

## EVALUATING OUR STRENGTHS AND WEAKNESSES

Of all our goals, we think that providing the supportive environment has been the most successful because it feeds on itself. Students respond positively to the encouragement they receive from their teachers and pass that encouragement on to their classmates. The classroom itself becomes a positive environment, and students and teachers alike can concentrate on the task at hand, which is learning. We have numerous accounts from students saying that they appreciate and value these positive experiences. Rhonda, for example, said, "I like it because we have more time to do stuff, because we have two periods, and we do more, like go on field trips, . . . and you get to know people better because you have classes with them. The teachers, they get together and try to make us understand." Heidi said, "I like it a lot. The teachers take time to know who you are and know when you have problems. They help you work on it. . . . The classes are more well behaved. In my math class, there are students who are really distracting. There's nobody like that [in the Interdisciplinary Team]."

We probably have been least successful in teaching totally integrated units because of the difficulty associated with incorporating science, English, and world history. Even concepts that do come naturally to the areas of world history and English (e.g., the Greeks) take much longer to teach in one subject than in the other. For example, Dena typically spends 4 or 5 weeks on *The Odyssey*, whereas the Greek chapter in the world history book is covered in a week and a half at the most. Even though we cannot adequately integrate our content areas to our satisfaction, the students still feel that this part of our team works well. Many students, without being explicitly asked, said that it is actually one of the most positive aspects of the team. John said, "We're doing the Russian Revolution and we just read *Animal Farm*. It deals with the Russian Revolution. . . . It teaches you—it reinforces it, sort of. You're learning it in two classes. You get more information out of it." Trevor said, "I like how they can talk about the same three things and talk about them in the same way." Jerry said, "The three teachers work [with] each other, and their [topics] coexist. One teacher can reflect on another thing. We work on the same thing in both classes. It helps you out a little bit." Katie said, ". . . like if you're learning one thing in world history, you learn part of the same thing in literature, and it makes it easier to keep up." Renee said, "That's neat [the subject-matter integration]! *A Tale of Two Cities*—it's about war, and we were talking about it in history, and in biology we're talking about germ warfare—when they used bacteria to kill people. Then you can pretty much understand it from a science, social studies, and English reading point of view, and you understand it better cause you [give it] a whole lot more attention."

Adapting a team concept to a high school situation is not without its challenges. High school teachers are typically focused on their own areas and do not have the interest or the time to become involved in any other teacher's subject matter. Even finding teachers willing to be a part of such a team is not easy. Dena entered the team in the school year 1994–1995 as team leader. Two strong team members were already in place, one of them having been with the team from its inception and the other coming in a year later. Even though Dena was the team leader, she was the one who had to adapt to the teaming concepts the others had already established, and it was not always easy. For example, when a field trip for the team was scheduled with the principal, before the other team member and Dena had even been consulted, Dena felt undermined, not as a team leader, but as a team member. The resulting friction, however, was short lived, partly because the three of us share very similar personalities. This carries over to our students as well because we tend to handle similar classroom situations in the same ways. For example, although eating in class is technically prohibited at our school, two of us have found that allowing students to snack during class actually improves the flow of instruction rather than inhibits it. Students acknowledge that we are bending the rules for them, and they appreciate the agreement between the two of us. Paradoxically, the third member of the team does not allow students to eat in his classroom, and the students adapt very well to that and accept it as a minor inconvenience.

Two of the teachers have also used the same computer program in the past, so the grade printouts for student progress reports look very similar. They are still trying to convert our third team member to use some form of computer program for grades so the students will have tangible evidence of their progress.

As mentioned, one of the established team members left the school in the year 1995–1996, and we added a male teacher to the team for the first time. Michael was young, only a second-year teacher, and tended to be less relaxed with the students than we veterans were. He had very high expectations for the students and placed what appeared to the other two teachers as tremendous demands on students' time and abilities. A very high percentage of the students had failing grades in Michael's class after only 3 weeks in school, and some of those failures stretched out to the end of the first semester. Open house was very awkward; we wanted to sing the praises of our team, and parents wanted to confront him about his high failure rate.

It turned out we had very different philosophies. Michael believed that we were coddling the students, whereas we believed we were supporting them. He believed teachers should hide their personal lives, whereas we believed in sharing them. Part of being a team member is learning how to work through our differences. During the weekly team meeting, Teri and Dena offered Michael suggestions on how to help students succeed without compromising his standards. They discussed their study tools with him and advised him how to adapt these for his own classroom. By the end of the year, Michael came to believe that the extra support was actually beneficial to students. He said, "Earlier in the year I would have said that it holds the students back in their maturity [to be more personal], but now I feel like the benefit of improved interactions makes up for the delay in progress early on in the year." As for Dena and Teri, they learned to help students see teachers who have different values as just different, not bad. They supported Michael as a team member and colleague when students questioned his approach. It took students longer to adapt to Michael, but by the end of the year a much more harmonious relationship existed, and everyone had learned to deal with other viewpoints.

Another negative associated with the Interdisciplinary Team comes from outside the team, in the perceptions and attitudes of other students and teachers. Many teachers are still a little suspicious of our motives, and we have heard it said that we "baby" our students when they just need a strong dose of reality in order to cope with high school. We maintain that by the time some students become aware of their skills to cope with the normal high school setting, the damage has been done. We do not think our students feel "babied" at all. When Dena joined the team, she had been teaching at-risk students for 2 years, and her expectations had slipped a little during that period. She is a little ashamed to admit that she was amazed at what her new students could do. The more they did, they more she threw at them. She quickly realized that these students were dedicated enough to meet any challenge she devised. She has been much happier with her teaching since joining the Interdisciplinary Team.

We have also been criticized for being too "friendly" with the students, and it is understandable why someone outside the team would view our relationships with our students that way. However, we firmly believe our students would say that our relationships with them push them to learn more, not less. Heather, for example, had to work harder than others in every class due to a learning disability, but it was her opinion that students are able to learn more when they enjoy a positive relationship with the teacher.

Even when team personnel remain the same, future directions shift from year to year. As an example, for this school year, the science department decided that all ninth graders would take physical science instead of biology, which had always been included on the team in the past. This descision means that we will need to reevaluate our integrated units and see how our three subject areas will be connected. We also want to move toward incorporating a foreign language into the Interdisciplinary Team. As an English teacher, Dena realizes that language concepts taught in two different languages become more meaningful for students. Having a foreign language teacher as part of our team would mean we could plan grammar units together and help students see the patterns that make languages more concrete.

In a perfect setting, we envision block scheduling used throughout the entire school. We have seen the benefits of using extended periods of time in the classroom, and we would like to see the whole school embrace this concept. Many of the models for block scheduling that we have examined would allow for two ninth-grade interdisciplinary teams during a single school year. One team would take mainly elective and nonteam subjects during first semester and team subjects the other semester, and the other team vice versa.

In this perfect world, the three team teachers would be linked by computer, allowing for more effective communication among the three as well as tracking attendance, keeping up with grades, and so forth. It would be ideal if the three classrooms were located near one another. At present, we are on three different floors, but having the three classrooms close together would reinforce the team concept with the students, particularly at the beginning of the year when high school itself is so overwhelming. A common area large enough for all three classes to meet for joint projects, guest speakers, team meetings, and the like would be a bonus.

We would like to see this team concept expanded to the 10th grade. Scheduling in the upper grades would become trickier because students take a greater variety of courses, but some students could benefit from that extra year of support and encouragement.

Teaching on the Interdisciplinary Team has forced us to become more flexible because we sometimes have to adjust our schedules to meet the needs of team members. We hope that we have passed this flexibility on to our students, allowing them to learn in a relaxed atmosphere, and we know that we have become better teachers because of it. We enjoy teaching, and the number of students who leave us each year saying that they enjoy learning reinforces our feeling of satisfaction with our choice to work together.

## CHAPTER TWO

# What Do We Mean by Knowledge and Learning?

Cynthia R. Hynd
Steven A. Stahl
*University of Georgia*

Our schools presumably function as ways for students to prepare for participation in society. Schools serve students and the nation well when upon completing their education, students become productively employed and can demonstrate their responsibility as citizens by engaging in activities such as voting and participating in community activities. At the core of these activities is literacy. Citizens who read efficiently, widely, and critically tend to be more productive members of society in both community involvement and work (Guthrie, Shafer, & Hutchinson, 1991).

In today's world, however, schools face unique challenges in producing such citizens. One challenge is in the development of knowledge. Traditionally, students have been seen as knowledge accumulators. As students continue their schooling, new knowledge is added to existing knowledge, so that by the time students end their high school careers, they are expected to know a broad range of basic, commonly shared information and are primed to develop expertise in a chosen field of work. Hirsch (1987) argued that this knowledge is important because a populace who knows the traditions and history of a nation and has background in science and technology is more likely to participate intelligently in democratic traditions. A shared knowledge of English literature, cultural figures, and basic science allows citizens to communicate with each other. Partly because of the information explosion, however, educational researchers and theorists debate about what is most important to teach in order to develop that knowledge. If there is too much information for everyone to learn, then what needs to be taught?

To share in a common knowledge base means that someone has to decide what that common knowledge should be. That decision is made difficult by the competing demands of special interest groups, minorities, and those with traditional Euramerican viewpoints, among others.

Thus, educational researchers and theorists debate about what informa tion is important. They also argue about whether the processes used in creating and sharing disciplinary knowledge should be emphasized over the actual knowledge that has been accumulated. For example, science education theorists disagree about whether their field should be emphasizing methods of scientific inquiry or science knowledge. On the one side, constructivists argue that teachers need to take into account students' own scientific theories and teach them ways to discover scientific knowledge using methods of inquiry. On the other side, realists argue that scientists have, through the centuries, uncovered a number of basic principles that help us understand reality, and that these principles must be taught. At the core of these debates lie some important questions. What does it mean for students to develop expertise? How do schools develop it? Is that development a viable goal for every student in every subject? These questions are crucial if we wish for students to be productive members of society.

Another challenge is that knowledge is becoming more ubiquitous, complex, and easily accessed at the same time that our tolerance for complex messages seems to be waning. Technological innovations such as the Internet have caused a proliferation of information at varying levels of quality. Perhaps for this reason, we seem to want our information in simplified form. For example, the average television sound bite of a political candidate has lessened from 25 sec to 8 sec in the last decade, and according to a Roper poll, 64% of the population gets most of their news from television (where the average story is less than 1 min), whereas only 40% of the population gets their news from newspapers (Patterson, 1995). The need for schools to educate students in selecting, comprehending, evaluating, and acting on sources of information is crucial, and more challenging today than it has, perhaps, ever been.

These challenges and others swirl around education, and their answers become more important for students as they move from elementary to high school. Yet, secondary school teachers and their classrooms seem to remain relatively untouched by the controversies. Alvermann and Moore (1991) depicted secondary education as predominated by teachers who relay factual information in ways meant to maintain control, and who do not, as a rule, engage students in critical thinking or the development of cross-disciplinary understandings. One result is a secondary education that has remained relatively stable and unchanged for decades. O'Brien, Stewart, and Moje (1995), in discussing the difficulties teachers had infusing literacy instruction into content classrooms, cited bureaucratic structures and relationships, subject matter subcultures, and occupational circumstances ("the daily grind") as factors that influenced teachers to resist changing traditional forms of teaching. Moore (1996) commented that secondary school literacy "predominantly consists of students" reproducing text-based contents in highly controlled forms" where students "generally work on getting the right answer and getting the answer right" (p. 17). Thus, high school classrooms today look very much the same as the high school classes of years ago, despite society's vast changes. Yet teachers are not passively reacting to bureaucratic and other influences. Their beliefs and goals, sometimes conflicting, play a role in how student learning is fostered. Students both are influenced by and influence that educational process as well. Their beliefs and goals, also sometimes conflicting, help to create the learning environment in every classroom. It behooves us to understand that creation.

To help ourselves untangle the processes, problems, and promises in education, we should perhaps return to the basics—what we mean by knowledge and learning. In this chapter, we review theories of knowledge and learning, discuss research that illuminates these theories, and, finally, discuss influences on both teachers and students that deter from and enhance knowledge and learning, referring often to the year-long study of the high school program depicted in chapter 1 and our work with those and other high school students and their teachers. We do not intend for our discussion of knowledge and learning to be exhaustive because the literature is too diverse and extensive to be discussed in detail. Rather, we wish merely to highlight theories that help us explain classroom interactions that affect literacy and learning.

## KNOWLEDGE

Knowledge, as it is discussed in this chapter, involves knowledge of content, processes, and contexts. Content knowledge represents a set of connected concepts that exist on a continuum from discrete to abstract. The concept of a cell is relatively discrete and concrete, for example, whereas the concept of democracy is relatively abstract. For experts, concepts exist in a richly interconnected network, and this interconnection is achieved through repeated opportunities for learning. In physics, for example, concepts about projectile motion are directly related to concepts of gravity and air resistance. To understand scientifically accepted ideas about projectile motion, one must also understand concepts related to gravity and air resistance. In history, the concept that the Vietnam Conflict was precipitated by the Tonkin Gulf Incident is connected to other concepts about causes and effects that date back to World War II and beyond. Some theorists regard related concepts as schema: conceptual sets that are easily accessed to help us interpret incoming perceptions (Anderson & Pearson, 1984). For example, we know what is expected of us in social events such as football games because we have a well-developed schema for such events.

Concepts are also multidimensional and learned over time. In fact, the more a student considers a given concept, adds to the concept, reorganizes the concept, or discusses the concept with others, the more highly connected to other concepts it becomes. Thus, the construction of richly elaborated concepts requires active thinking rather than passive observation.

There is more to knowledge, however, than the accumulation of inter-connected concepts. We view content knowledge as existing on several levels. In the ideal world, when students develop knowledge, they become familiar with topics they are taught, such as the principles of gravity. They make connections among related concepts. For example, they relate prin-ciples of gravity to principles of projectile motion. They also begin to know the domain within which these topics lie (e.g., gravity is studied in the domain of physics). Furthermore, they develop a sense of the discipline in which they are studying (science) and begin to see that, not only does this discipline encompass a number of related topics, but it also encompasses processes used to gain and evaluate knowledge, such as experimentation, peer review, and power relationships that maintain and promote knowledge. For example, when an author publishes an article in *Science*, that publication represents a statement about the power and influence of the researcher as well as statements about concepts. As students gain these levels of knowl-edge, they gain expertise. Thus, an expert in any discipline must have more than content knowledge. There must also be a knowledge of processes and contexts as part of a disciplinary tradition.

Additionally, in the ideal world, students develop a sense that ideas across disciplines are related. In reality, this knowledge is difficult to gain, given disciplinary traditions entrenched in the same system that teaches students to specialize. There is evidence, for example, that by the time students reach graduate school, they read and react to texts differently depending on their chosen discipline (Perfetti, Britt, Marron, & Rouet, 1995). Many have docu-mented the fact that academic disciplines differ in their histories, epistemolo-gies, and degree of consistency within the field (Grossman & Stodolsky, 1994; Bernstein, 1971; Schwab, 1978). These disciplinary traditions are entrenched and inhibit cross-disciplinary understandings. Yet a person's success as an expert within that discipline often means accepting and operating within these traditions. Therefore, tension exists between content knowledge and interdis-ciplinary knowledge. We explore that tension later.

**Theories of Knowledge Construction**

The source of knowledge—the actual process by which it is constructed from experience—has been viewed in many different ways by philosophers, sociologists, and educators, among others. Often, the difference is in the

way theorists view the role of society, or the social worlc
of knowledge. Many scientists believe that their scient.
luminate reality. For example, the discovery of DNA w
a fact in nature that remains relatively immune to socia
scientists engage in scientific inquiry, they search for o
commit themselves to publicizing scientific knowledge,
pressures and being skeptical about new discoveries un
rigorously tested. The rigor with which scientists discover knowledge, then,
guarantees that these discoveries are real (Merton, 1973).

*Cognitive constructivists* (Piaget, 1980), argue, however, that reality remains forever elusive. Rather, knowledge is constructed by individuals interacting with their environment and forming symbolic representations of
their interactions so that knowledge is based on how a person interprets
what he or she perceives, not what is real. What counts as knowledge is
what is useful to us. Von Glasersfeld (1987, 1993, 1995), for example, said
that scientific theories cannot be called true; they are merely useful in helping
us achieve our goals. The concept of DNA is merely a scientists' way of
describing their observations rather than an objective truth, but DNA is a
useful construct for us because it helps us to predict the physical characteristics of humans. Likewise, gravity is a useful construct because we can
use the principles to help us predict how fast something will fall. Chinn (in
press) illustrated this idea when he described two different approaches to
plant taxonomy. Researchers using the two approaches sometimes disagree
about the classification of plants, but both classification systems continue to
exist because they are both useful. One system is needed for answering
questions in evolutionary biology; the other is needed because it allows for
the quick identification of species. In the cognitive constructivists view, the
symbolic representation of one's experiences with the environment is a
relatively individual experience, but with social input. Peers, for example,
help us consider other theories and provide us with new data to consider
as we construct our personal understandings of the world.

*Social constructionists*, in contrast, believe that the social world plays a
greater role (Knorr-Cetina, 1993) than cognitive constructivists would admit.
They believe that knowledge is created through social negotiation and that
reality plays virtually no part in determining that knowledge. To most social
constructionists, there are no objective empirical grounds for deciding which
theories are better than others; it is only the social settlement of controversies
that counts. Knorr-Cetina went so far as to say that scientists do not even
study nature. As Chinn (1998) said, scientists merely "create an artificial
laboratory environment where they tinker with equipment to make things
work. Scientific reality is a human artifact."

After data are constructed in this matter, others must be persuaded to
accept the data. This is done by rhetorical arguments that move from tenuous

olidified as they are interpreted and reinterpreted in scientists' writings and presentations. For example, the original interpretation of the data may be made in a statement such as "these data suggest . . ." although a subsequent interpretation may be made in a statement such as these data show. . . ." Thus, what we come to know is always social rather than real.

Chinn (1998) offered another more balanced theory of how knowledge is constructed called *integrated constructivism*, in which nature, cognition, and society are integrated into explanations of knowledge in that social and cognitive factors interact but are constrained by nature to shape what we know. To integrated constructivists, science can create theories that at least correspond to reality (Cartwright, 1983; Giere, 1988), and although, as they believe, knowledge is always embedded in social interaction, social structures can either enhance or detract from the validity of knowledge. For instance, attention to rigorous research methods can enhance the chances that principles created by scientists more closely approximate or describe reality. Furthermore, although scientists always operate in a social context, cognition is important, as well, in the ways that individuals "represent information and use language and other means such as diagrams to convey information to each other" (Thagard, 1994, p. 641). This is the view we take in this chapter.

We should not underemphasize the role of social interaction in our understanding of the world, however. In fact, everything we know, including language, history, and science, is constructed through this interaction. For example, historians interpret important events through a social lens. While collecting data from certain time periods they themselves belong to a time period. They represent various political organizations, belong to cultural groups, and hold certain beliefs that determine the way in which they select and interpret historical evidence. For example, a Native American historian might interpret Columbus' "discovery" of America differently than traditional historians. Scientists, even though they wish to understand reality, are influenced by the way in which previous knowledge has been categorized and described, by political considerations, and by their measurement devices that have been developed under social constraints. What we learn in school is socially constructed as well. The kinds of reading experiences students have in school are determined, for example, by curriculum experts who negotiate the reading list.

## LEARNING

Piaget discussed how children's experiences are perceived and become integrated into their understandings of the world. Although he acknowledged the role of social interaction, his main concern was with the an individual's cognitive development derived from sensory information. This development included processes of *assimilation* (adding new knowledge to existing knowledge) and *accommodation* (changing existing knowledge to account for new, even contradictory knowledge). One important understanding that comes from Piaget is the importance of what a person already knows. To Piaget, you cannot learn something unless you already know it. That is, you learn something when you discover a connection between your new experiences and previous ones. This understanding has immediate and practical implications for education, in that teachers must always be aware of what sort of knowledge their students have if they wish them to learn the things they want them to learn.

## Social Influences on Learning

Vygotsky (1978) refined our understanding of the way social interactions aid learning. Through communication between people with different levels of knowledge, learners appropriate, or take on, the thinking of others at the point where their previous knowledge and any new ideas intersect: the *zone of proximal development*. The melding of new and existing knowledge represents a construction of a new understanding.

The importance of social interaction is also highlighted by theorists operating from sociocultural perspectives. According to this perspective, the social nature of learning takes place in discourse. Kelly and Green (1998) stated that "as members interact over time, they shape and are shaped by discourses (Davies, 1993; Fairclough, 1992; Fernie, Davies, Kantor, & McMurray, 1993; Gee, 1990), develop situated definitions of what it means to be a scientist, reader, writer, or group member among other roles and relationships (Brilliant-Mills, 1993; Floriani, 1993; Heras, 1993; Yeager, Floriani, & Green, 1996), and construct *local knowledge* (Geertz, 1983) that becomes *common knowledge* within the group or class (Edwards & Mercer, 1987; Santa Barbara Classroom Discourse Group, 1992a, 1992b)." In other words, there is a dynamic relationship between a person's individual knowledge and that held in common by a group. Each influences and is influenced by the other (Bloome & Egan-Robertson, 1993).

## Affective Influences on Learning

Recently, researchers have become more attuned to the affective influences that play a part in learning. Social psychologists include affective as well as cognitive constructs in their definition of beliefs because they view beliefs, attitudes, motivation, drive, desire, and emotion all as aspects of cognition (Fiske & Taylor, 1991), and educational researchers are beginning to believe the same thing. Motivation is an important concern. It is defined by Oldfather (1993) as "a continuing impulse to learn" (p. 672) and by Wigfield and his colleagues (Wigfield & Guthrie, 1995; Wigfield, Wilde, Baker, Fernandez-Fein, & Scher, in press) as including the desire for involvement, curiosity, social interaction, challenge, recognition, grades, competition and work avoidance, and belief in the importance of the topic as well as one's efficacy to achieve. Intrinsic motivations such as interest and curiosity, feelings of self-efficacy, and feelings about the usefulness of the knowledge to be learned all seem to have high associations with conceptual learning and often are described by students as contributing to their motivation. The amount of control students feel over their learning (related to self-efficacy) and social interaction are also important. For example, Oldfather (1993) found that third- and fifth-grade students were motivated by classroom environments that were respectful and responsive, allowed self-expression, focused on meaning rather than correctness, and let students make choices. When students did not feel motivated, it was because they wished for more control or felt that they were incompetent to perform the task required of them. Oldfather concluded that students' motivations were most helpful to them if they were intrinsic, but that students also needed to feel a sense that they were capable and in charge. Hynd and her colleagues (1994a; 1995) found that students in physics classes were most motivated by their intense interest in physics topics, their belief that the knowledge of physics was relevant to their everyday lives and future careers, and the belief that doing well in physics would help them meet their present and future goals. Students who reported feeling these kinds of motivations were more likely than others to learn physics concepts. Although grades were important, the students saw these as a means of accomplishing their future goals (e.g., getting into college) and not as an end in themselves.

Motivation and social involvement often interact. We (Hynd et al., 1996) asked students in the integrated curriculum group described in chapter 1 about their motivation to learn in the three integrated classes. We learned that the students perceived their motivation to be high and offered numerous reasons for their positive feelings. Three of the most often mentioned reasons were these: (a) they got to know each other better; (b) they knew and liked their teachers better; and (c) they liked the integration of content across subject matter. These three reasons for liking the integrated team were reasons not mentioned by students in traditional classes. That is, students in the traditional classes did not say that they liked their classes or were motivated to learn because of teacher–student and student–student social interaction or because the content of their classes was tied together in any way. Thus, students in the integrated program felt more connected to each other as a community of learners. The content integration also proved to be an important consideration for these students.

The feeling of community is apparently an important one for adolescents. Oldfather and McLaughlin (1993) described students' loss of motivation as they moved from an experimental, open-ended fifth- and sixth-grade class to middle school that was traditional in nature. One critical problem that students faced was their loss of the close relationship they had with their teacher. One student, for example, pointed out that her middle school teachers could not really see her as a total person with strengths and weaknesses (a good reader, but not good in math) because they saw her for only one subject. Another critical problem was that students did not know each other well. Oldfather and McLaughlin believed that *honored voice,* or the feeling that students have important things to say, depends on close interpersonal relationships. In addition to Oldfather and McLaughlin's research, Phelan, Davidson, and Cao (1992) and Turley (1994) showed in their research that students liked classrooms in which the students knew each other and their teacher well, and wanted safe, tension-free environments with active involvement in subject matter. This sense of knowing each other occurred most often in programs with blocked scheduling and a team approach (Powell, 1993). In the integrated curriculum, the teachers had borrowed the blocked scheduling and team approach from middle school models. These structural changes appeared to maintain the benefits experienced by middle school students.

## Strategic Influences on Learning

Strategies are tools that help individuals to understand and remember information. For example, the strategy of diagramming the digestive system in biology can help a student understand that system. Self-questioning and talking through the diagram can help the student remember it. Students report using a number of strategies to learn information they are motivated to learn. When we asked students in the integrated curriculum program as well as traditional students what strategies they used to help them learn, the two most popular strategies for learning were "read over" and "memorize." But students mentioned a variety of other techniques, regardless of whether they were in the integrated curriculum or a traditional program: using word associations or other mnemonics, making lists and writing down information, self-questioning, answering questions posed by family members, studying a little every day, thinking about the information throughout the day, and paying attention to comprehension and understanding. Of the 12 students in the integrated curriculum program, 6 said that they used flash cards—a method of studying reinforced by all three teachers—but no student attributed the use of flash cards to the teachers. In fact, most students said that they learned strategies through trial and error or because they had always used them. We suspect that students using the strategies recommended by their teachers did so because they were motivated to learn and were at that stage of knowledge development where the cards proved helpful to them.

Most models of strategy use include the need for students to have *procedural knowledge*: knowing how to perform a strategy; *declarative knowledge*: some knowledge of the content in which they are to use the strategy; and *metacognition*: knowing when to apply the strategy, understanding whether they are applying it effectively, and monitoring their understanding of the content as a result of the strategy (Pressley et al., 1994). Some also include motivation in the model: A student needs to be motivated in order to learn and use a strategy effectively. Two motivating goals for strategy use are understanding and self-efficacy.

Several researchers have developed integrated models of strategy use, motivation, and learning. One compelling model for those of us who study literacy in secondary schools is Patricia Alexander's model of domain literacy (Alexander, 1988, 1998). In this model, students exist at three stages of development. Alexander refers to learners in the first stage as *acclimated*. At this level, students have limited knowledge of the domain with which they are engaged; they rely on general strategies; and they have little personal investment in learning information. Because their knowledge of the domain tends to be limited and fragmented, they have a difficult time distinguishing what is important from what is not, and thus have a difficult time knowing when to use strategies and what types of strategies to use. Furthermore, their lack of knowledge means that they will have to exert considerable cognitive effort in understanding, and without deep-seated interests in the domain, their motivation for this effort may be extrinsic (grades or recognition) rather than intrinsic. A student in a high school physics class, for example, demonstrated that he was at this level when he described his strategy for studying physics as "memorization," and his motivation for using that strategy as grades. He commented that he did not see much use for understanding physics, and felt that his parents were putting too much pressure on him to learn something he did not really like. Dreher (1995) found that fifth-grade students did not use search strategies they had been taught how to use when given the task of finding information for a report. They had difficulty with the task even though they had chosen their own questions to answer. Their difficulties in applying strategies are consonant with the kinds of difficulties students at the acclimated stage seem to experience.

Some students at the acclimated stage of domain learning may find that situational interest in a certain topic within the domain sparks a deeper seated interest or an understanding of how knowledge in this domain can help them meet their long-term goals. For example, a person with plans to be a physician may come to realize that there is a physical element to the workings of the skeleton and muscle system and, hence, become more interested in physics. A student of history may take a liking to historical analysis, even though the student does not enjoy the memorization of facts, and becomes interested in the processes involved in thinking like a historian. At other times, repeated exposure to information and experiences in the domain, along with incentives and support, can impel a student beyond the initial stage of acclimation toward the next level, the competent stage of domain learning.

In the *competent* stage, students begin to understand the fundamental principles defining the domain, making it more likely that they can distinguish between important and nonimportant information. For instance, to be competent in physics, it is important for students to understand that their perceptions may not accurately account for scientific processes. In biology, they learn that understanding of systems is important because a system carries out its functions in similar ways across organisms. In history, students learn that history books relate historians' interpretations of events rather than reality, and that these interpretations are derived from a combination of primary, secondary, and tertiary sources. Students at this level are also more able to employ general strategies to help them comprehend and remember information. In addition, they may be more interested in the subject matter being studied, so they can persist in exerting effort to learn even when their situational interest is diminished. One student in world history demonstrated his being at this stage of development when he told how he liked some topics in history more than others (e.g., World War II), but was motivated to learn history because it told him a lot about how many factors act together to create important events, including people making mistakes. His strategy for studying was to focus on understanding the material, arriving in class early to discuss what he did not understand with the teacher, and asking his parents to question him about history.

The move from competence to the next level, *proficiency,* requires much more than knowledge accumulation, strategic effort, or the will to learn or achieve, and is not reached by every student. Some students develop a richly interconnected body of domain knowledge allowing them to use well-defined strategies for learning new information. These students also have an intense interest and personal investment in learning in the domain. Students may be misleading, however, as most do not reach the proficiency stage of learning until they have completed schooling and perhaps become engaged in creating knowledge for the domain and mentoring the knowledge construction of others. An educational researcher, for example, demonstrates proficiency by reading widely but efficiently, selecting and using information from reading to expand or restructure her already rich network of ideas, seeing connections across areas of interest and different fields, and contributing to her own knowledge and that of others through research and written and oral discourse. Wineburg (1991, 1994) provided another example of proficiency when he described the reading strategies of practicing historians as very different from the strategies of high school students reading history. When historians read, according to Wineburg, they *contextualize* (place what they read into a time frame, social framework, or historical era), *corroborate* (compare and contrast the work of one author with the work of others), and they *use sourcing*, that is, focus on the credentials of the author and take into account the source of the writing (e.g., whether it appeared in a textbook or as an editorial in a magazine or newspaper). These processes often are not used by high school students, who read mainly to "get the facts."

Research efforts have highlighted the differences between experts and students operating at lower levels. VanSledright and Kelly (1996) found that fifth-grade history students did not have strategies for interpreting trade books and historical novels. Rather, they confused novels with reality and read most texts in similar ways, regardless of their purpose. In a study by Stahl, Hynd, Britton, McNish, and Bosquet (1996) of students reading a variety of primary to tertiary texts about the Tonkin Gulf Incident of the Vietnam Conflict, students rarely noted the expertise of the author or the time of the writing. They reported commonalities across texts but did not report discrepancies, and they preferred the textbook version of the incident rather than primary sources. We concluded that these students, who admitted knowing practically nothing about the Vietnam Conflict, were reading to gain enough introductory information to understand the incident and may have had insufficient knowledge of the incident to think critically about it or use higher level reading strategies. In another study by Stahl, Hynd, Montgomery, and McClain (1997), students involved in both the integrated curriculum program described in chapter 1 and the traditional students, who had background information about the topic of Columbus' expeditions, showed evidence of believing new interpretations of Columbus' discoveries from a secondary source that was balanced in its viewpoints. These two studies illustrate the importance of existing knowledge and its interaction with strategy use and learning.

The three levels of domain learning described by Alexander help us understand some of the interplay between strategy use, motivation, and knowledge that come to play for a person becoming an expert in a domain.

## Conceptual Change

Up to this point, we have mostly discussed learning through a process that Piaget (1980) referred to as assimilation. That is, a student has developed a network of understandings surrounding a concept, and when something new is learned, the student adds that new understanding to the network. For example, this student may already know that Columbus discovered America, that the date he sailed for America was in 1492, and that he sailed from Spain. If the student learns, subsequently, that their were three ships—the Pinta, the

Nina, and the Santa Maria—then she or he would add this information to the network. The information fits together and is not contradictory. Rumelhart and Norman (1981) said, however, that, not only can concepts can be changed in this additive manner, referred to as *accretion*, but also through tuning and restructuring. In *tuning*, one makes minor adjustments in understanding, such as creating generalizations or clarifying the attributes of a construct. For example, if the student made a generalization that the men on Columbus' voyage showed courage or that the voyage was a large undertaking for Spain, given the period of time, then that would be tuning.

If, however, the student learned that Columbus did not really discover America, but landed on a small Island in the Caribbean, that information would be contradictory to the information learned previously. Thus, it cannot be merely assimilated. The network must be restructured in some way to allow for this new information to be added without contradiction. This process represents *accommodation* (Piaget, 1980) or conceptual change. Theorists believe that the *restructuring* is not just a replacement of one concept with another, but no one is exactly sure how that restructuring takes place. Vosniadou and Brewer (1987) refered to two types of restructuring. In some instances, they argued, conceptual change takes place in a gradual manner because of emerging relations among concepts or through the formation of a more abstract conceptual structure, referred to as weak restructuring. In other instances, the restructuring represents a dramatic shift: a significant and sudden transmutation that the authors refer to as radical restructuring.

One thing is fairly certain, however. People resist radically changing their conceptions. Studies from reading education, science education, and educational psychology point to the difficulty students have in changing their ideas about the world, particularly if these ideas seem intuitively correct and logical (Guzzetti, Snyder, Glass, & Gamas, 1993) or represent strong beliefs (Sinatra & Dole, 1998). As one physics student who refused to believe new, conflicting information about gravity put it: "There's logic and then there's physics."

Theorists have hypothesized the conditions necessary for people to change their conceptions. Posner, Strike, Hewson, and Gertzog (1982) said that a student must feel conflict between a new explaination and his existing explaination for what he observes. For the conflict to make him actually change his ideas, however, the new explanation must also appear reasonable, and it must be understood. In addition, it must provide him with a better explanation of the phenomenon he is observing than his current knowledge and convince him that it will also provide him with a better way to explain additional phenomena. In other words, the new explanation must appear fruitful.

Chinn and Brewer (1993) identified ways that students can handle incoming information that appears anomalous: (a) ignore it, (b) reject it, (c) hold it in abeyance, (d) exclude it (e.g., say that the new information is a concern of another discipline), (e) reinterpret it, (f) change their thinking in minor ways, or (g) radically change their theory. Note that in every instance but the last, the student has not truly accepted the anomalous information. The existence of many avenues for discounting new, conflicting information makes it unlikely that existing theories will be changed. This unlikelihood appears even more solidified if the existing theory is embedded in a network of other related beliefs (Hewson, 1981; Posner et al., 1982; Vosniadou & Brewer, 1992), satisfies personal or social goals, represents ontological beliefs (beliefs about the physical world; Chi, 1992), or represents epistemological commitments or beliefs about the nature of knowledge (Posner, et al., 1982).

Chinn and Brewer (1993) said that for conceptual change to take place in schools the anomalous data presented must be accurate, credible, and unambiguous. In addition, teachers need to understand students' objections to the data and be ready to challenge these objections in multiple ways. The authors also say that teachers should help students to engage in deep processing of the new information. Sinatra and Dole (in press), presenting a social–psychological perspective, backed up this idea when they said that "relatively permanent change in beliefs can come about through the deep processing of information and thoughtful weighing of issues and arguments involved in a message." (p. 9).

Finally, it is likely that conceptual change involves some affective commitment as well. Pintrich, Marx, and Boyle (1993) argued that conceptual change is often conceived in a way that is over-rational, and that goals, values, feelings of self-efficacy, and control beliefs mediate conceptual change. Conceptual change is difficult. According to these authors, students are more likely to change their notions when they are engaged in tasks with authentic and challenging goals, when they are personally interested in the topic, when they see that the information has some usefulness and importance, when they feel capable of understanding and using the information, and when they believe they have the ability to control the outcome of their efforts.

Below, we present a scenario in which conceptual change is an issue and discuss how it illustrates some of the aspects of conceptual change theory.

Bill, a Euramerican senior in a high school advanced physics class, came into his sixth period already having heard from members of the same third and fourth period class that they were to learn that a bullet shot out of a gun will hit the ground at the same time as a bullet dropped from the same height. He had two other male students in tow—one African American and the other Euramerican. He was telling them that it could not be true of a high-powered rifle. They were agreeing.

The teacher began class by placing two steel balls on an apparatus designed to drop one ball at the same time it shot the other. She had students predict what would happen, then close their eyes and listen for the balls to drop. They dropped at the same time. Bill raised his hand and said that this would not happen if you had used a high-powered rifle: The bullet that was shot would have hit the ground last because it was traveling at such high speeds and would go a much further distance. She asked the other students what they thought, and they were divided evenly in their thinking that bullets would drop at the same time or at different times because of the horizontal speed of the shot bullet. Bill reiterated his stance and said that he knew because he had spent so much time hunting with a high-powered rifle.

Over the next couple of days, the teacher (a) showed a video depicting a monkey falling and being shot by a high powered dart that was aimed at its starting position (showing that dropped things and shot things fall at the same rate), (b) explained the principle of independent horizontal and vertical motion, (c) had students calculate the rate at which both shot and dropped objects would fall, and (d) asked students to explain why they thought that gravity would "take a vacation" while objects moved horizontally. She constantly asked students what they were thinking and to explain their ideas, but she was very explicit in stating the scientifically accepted principle that the vertical motion of an object was independent of the horizontal motion and that gravity was the force that must be accounted for in a vertical direction for both a dropped and shot object.

Bill ended up believing that his teacher was right and that he had been mistaken. The reasons he gave were that his teacher had answered all of his questions and that he had talked to his father (with whom he had gone hunting) and his father had helped him understand the physics principle. After instruction, however, he still had a lingering idea that went against accepted scientific understandings. Although he now believed that a dropped and shot object would fall to the ground at the same time, he could not offer a scientifically accepted explanation. He believed that the short distance of the dropped ball and the fast speed of the shot ball canceled each other out, resulting in them hitting the ground at the same time. I asked him [the researcher] to read a refutational text at that point. This text refuted the idea that the two objects would fall at a different speed and explained that it was because objects, whether they were projected or merely dropped, would fall at a certain speed independently of their horizontal motions. It gave a reasonable explanation, given a bullet shot from a rifle that was pointed up, horizontal, and toward the ground. After reading this text, Bill scientifically explained the path of a shot projectile compared to a dropped one. He could still scientifically explain the phenomena several days later.

In this scenario, Bill held an intuitive, highly entrenched belief in an ontological phenomenon, and the belief was reinforced by his perceptual and social experiences. These influences made it likely that conceptual change would be very difficult for him, even with presentation of anomalous data that was accurate, credible, and unambiguous. On the plus side, he was vitally interested in the topic and saw the utility in understanding projectile motion (for hunting). The influence that led most to his understanding and acceptance of the anomalous data was an anticipation and refutation of his most conflictual understandings using refutational text. In other words, his objections to the data had to be met in understandable ways. A meta-analysis confirms that refutation is powerful (Guzzetti, Snyder, Glass, & Gamas, 1993).

## INFLUENCES THAT DETER OR ENHANCE LEARNING

In this chapter, we tried to present an integrated approach to learning as it takes place in schools, an approach that includes motivation, strategy use, social interaction, and cognition in students' construction of interconnected networks or "bodies" of knowledge. In our studies of high school students, we have learned much concerning what these students value about their classrooms and what they find motivating about topics. We also know what they talk about in group learning activities, what kinds of questions they ask when they are engaged in literature discussions, and what they do when faced with multiple and conflicting information. We have studied students in high-achieving classes as well as students who are enrolled in lower level classes. We present several understandings we have gained from our research. First, however, we discuss the constraints on learning that exist in high school classes.

### Constraints on Learning

Researchers have noted that motivation for learning decreases as students advance through the grades (Schiefele, 1991). In fact, many factors detract from learning as students move from elementary school into high school. High schools are different from elementary schools in that teachers, structures, and students change as the grades advance. Teachers in elementary school are generalists who have the same students in their classes for nearly the entire day. There is ample opportunity to build close relationships between teachers and students, and innovative programs are easier to negotiate. Integrating the language arts, social science, science, and math, for example, is facilitated by the fact that teachers can create flexible schedules and teach all subjects in a seamless way.

When students move to middle schools or junior high schools, the structure of classes and the characteristics of teachers change. The flexibility of scheduling is lost because teachers are subject matter specialists and students move from classroom to classroom. To counteract this loss, many middle schools adopt a model in which teams of English, social studies, math, and science teachers work with the same groups of students. They may also initiate a block scheduling system allowing students to stay in one class for longer, or in which two teachers can combine their classes for a double period. The

English and the math teacher can work to reinforce units taught in the social studies and science classes. For example, the English teacher can help students create projects and reports initiated in social studies and science classes. In this way, some integration of content is feasible, and teachers and students get to know their each other better. As Oldfather (1993) pointed out, these types of programs can ease the transition from elementary to middle school and help students feel more connected and motivated.

When students get to high school, however, they are under even more constraints. In high school, subject matter specialization is at a high level. Most often, departments based on separate disciplines determine what will be taught and how. Teachers in the disciplines may consider themselves experts in their fields more than they consider themselves expert teachers, and they adopt methods of teaching and ways of thinking about knowledge that are discipline specific. For example, the teachers in the integrated curriculum program highlighted in chapter 1 have discipline-specific goals for their students that they do not feel they can sacrifice for the sake of integration, even though they strive to integrate their curriculum . From interviews, we learned that the English teacher wants her students to love literature and be fluent writers; the history teacher wants her students to be able to see trends in history; and the science teacher wants his students to understand that similar biological systems exist across organisms. As a result of curriculum constraints, teachers beliefs about their disciplines, and structural factors, students learn to see different subjects as completely separate entities. They also see that the nature of knowledge in each subject area becomes more specialized. The loss of subjects' connectedness to each other and to students' everyday lives may reduce their motivation.

In addition, grades become part of the permanent record that students carry into graduation and postsecondary education. It is not surprising, then, to find grades more often reported as the motivation for learning than involvement and curiosity as students get older. At the same time, students are beginning to think about what they will do with their lives. They are influenced by their family, their sociocultural circumstances, their peers, their teachers, and the classroom culture (the negotiated system of attitudes, values, interactions, and activities that exist in any classroom) to develop interests and motivations in certain directions. There may be a concomitant loss of interest in other areas. Social influences often take precedence over academic ones, because students trying out adult social roles are given more freedom to experiment with them. Thus, at the same time students are expected to know more about each discipline and to be moving toward expertise, they are pulled away from engagement in the concepts of a discipline by the need for grades and social interaction as well as by the necessity of channeling their activities toward a career.

For students from low socioeconomic backgrounds, expectations of being educated are lower than for students from higher socioeconomic backgrounds. Lower socioeconomic students often report being pulled away from school by their peers and even by their parents as they enter high school. Brody et al. (1994), for instance, found that when parents had few financial resources, they were more depressed and less optimistic. Their adolescent children were negatively affected. Specifically, they were less likely to regulate their lives and their learning. This lack of self-regulation decreased their academic competence and socioemotional stability. Ogbu (1990) reported that African American students from lower socioeconomic levels often said that education was important, but placed little emphasis on the effort necessary to achieve that goal. Even though they expressed a desire to go to college and escape poverty, they were often absent and negligent in their work. Many students are placed in noncollege preparatory classes where expectations are diminished as well. In these classes, students often are expected to complete perfunctory tasks, and they may resist learning, which to them may seem irrelevant and decontextualized. O'Brien and Dillon (1997) believed that, because schools are organized and governed according to middle-class values of the larger society, diverse student populations are ill matched and become disenfranchised.

## UNDERSTANDINGS ABOUT LEARNING

In this section, we present three understandings derived from areas that have been the focus of our research: (a) social interaction is an important but confusing influence on learning; (b) integrated curriculum in high school is both problematic and promising; and (c) students need more opportunities to deal with diverse readings and forms of information.

### Social Interaction

From our studies and those of others, we now believe that social interaction has a powerful influence on students. Students do learn as a result of social interaction. However, what students learn may not always be what teachers or researchers would wish. Teachers in schools have agendas. For example, they might want their students to leave their classes at the end of the year having learned some specified content and having improved their skill at operating within the constraints of the discipline by passing tests, writing research papers, answering essay questions, or engaging in scholarly discussions about text. But students have agendas also, and these agendas can conflict with those of their teachers. For example, students might desire social status among their peers, make career plans that exclude certain classes from importance, exert the minimum effort necessary to get a grade, or wish to exercise influence over others in the class. In their social interactions with others, then, students may not be carrying out the teacher's wishes but replacing the teacher's goals with their own.

Researchers have studied the influence of group interaction, and the total picture is one of both concern and promise. Hynd, McWhorter, Phares, and Suttles (1993), for example, found that students who discussed the path of a projectile in groups of three and four actually talked each other into nonscientific concepts, and that these concepts were, then, less amenable to change than those of students who had not engaged in group discussion. In another study, Hynd et al. (1995) watched students as they engaged in group laboratory investigations. Rather than gaining scientific understandings from the investigations, the students opted for lower level task completion behaviors and got bogged down in solving mechanical problems with their research equipment. When their research findings did not go the way they expected, they often explained the differences as being due to "experimenter error" or they merely ignored the differences. That is, they engaged in some of the behaviors that Chinn and Brewer (1993) discussed when they high-lighted the reactions that scientists have to anomalous data. In our study of the integrated curriculum program, students found the social interaction between themselves, their teachers, and other students in the program to be extremely rewarding (Hynd et al., 1997). They did not relate this social interaction to learning, however, even though we observed many opportu-nities for students to engage in group learning activities. In our study of student reactions to multiple sources of information about the Tonkin Gulf Incident (Stahl, Hynd, & McNish, 1996), some students in groups had rich interactions that resulted in equally rich essays, but other students in groups had virtually no interaction, or their products were in minimal compliance with the task.

Although discussion groups have been touted as ways for students to develop deeper understandings, there is need for caution in recommending that students work together and discuss ideas in groups. For example, when Alvermann, Commeyras, Young, Randall, and Hinson (1997) wished to have high school students contemplate the gendered nature of their discussion of literature, the students in the class ended up forming solidified groups who denigrated each other. Thus, the discussion technique failed to achieve the researchers' goal. Yet, their study does illustrate the power of social interaction. Alvermann and colleagues (1995) asked middle school students what made group discussions about their discipline-related reading effective. She found that they had well-formed ideas about discussion. First, they preferred working in small groups with people they knew well and liked, without the presence of the teacher. Second, they believed it was better to focus on open-ended tasks rather than those in which the students could divide up the work and complete the task independently. Third, they liked to have some say in the topics they discussed and how they discussed them. We believe that their observations make some intuitive sense and help us to consider more effective ways to help students learn from group interactions, with one caveat. When the topic is highly counterintuitive or we wish students to change their ideas, teachers may need to become more involved.

**Integrated Curriculum**

Providing an integrated curriculum program entails combining the knowledge of several disciplines in order to foster understanding of overarching themes. Ideally, such programs have several defining features apart from the fact that different subject matters are combined for the purpose of studying a common theme (Beane, 1995). First, within a thematic area, students may be given some control over forming questions they would like to study, and they are encouraged to work in groups to answer those questions. Second, students are provided with opportunities to search for information from a variety of print and other media sources rather than from a single textbook. Third, students are taught strategies for searching, reading, organizing, and sharing information with others. Fourth, students are encouraged to use the information they find to think about novel situations and problems. Finally, students are expected to communicate their findings to others in a formal manner such as in a report. In such an environment, students should be able to form rich mental networks of ideas, engage in critical thinking, develop strategies for learning from a wide variety of sources, and maintain a "continuing impulse to learn" while engaged in social interaction.

The integrated curriculum program highlighted in chapter 1 fell short of maintaining the sort of integrated curriculum discussed here. However, teachers believed it to be the best possible alternative, given the many constraints placed on them and students in high schools. These constraints involved both disciplinary and bureaucratic considerations. As for the discipline-related constraints, the teachers operated under the weight of having to teach three separate curricula as specified in their discipline-related departments and having to prepare students for subject-matter graduation tests. Thus, although they wished they could integrate the curriculum more around problems or themes, they ended up rearranging their existing curriculum as much as they could to closely approximate themes. For example, they studied the Greeks in all three classes. The English teacher had students read *The Odyssey* to mesh with the world history teacher's unit on Greek history, and the science teacher provided students information about the contributions of Greek scientists. Students walked a city street to identify elements of Greek architecture and worked on group Olympics projects stemming from fact that the Olympics originated in Greece.

The teachers themselves had goals for learning that impeded integration. The three teachers in the program had ideas about what was important to teach about each of their disciplines, as mentioned previously. The world history teacher felt strongly that learning about each era in sequence helped students to build on their knowledge of history in a structured way, and that a sequential approach made it more likely that students would learn about events, trends, and issues in history. She liked to move her students faster through the eras than other teachers so that they could get to more modern history. The science teacher believed that he had to teach some concepts before teaching others because systems play themselves out in similar ways with different organisms, a fundamental point in biology. The English teacher was the only one who felt that she could rearrange her schedule in any significant way or change the materials she used. Even so, she still believed that teaching students to appreciate literature and feel comfortable with writing was at least as important as teaching an integrated curriculum. Thus, these teachers were constantly needing to juggle their disciplinary beliefs with their belief that an integrated approach to learning could be beneficial. Given that the teachers were subject matter experts immersed in disciplinary understandings and approaches, their conflicting feelings are not surprising.

There were also bureaucratic and structural constraints to teaching in an integrated way. Teachers had to teach their students in separate classrooms because they lacked facilities to combine students into a double period with two teachers. In addition, they lacked time to plan and carry out extracurricular duties.

With all the constraints hampering true integration, the majority of students we talked to reported that they liked the integration of subject matter because it made things more interesting and easier to learn. They also liked the connectedness they felt with their teachers and fellow students and believed that they were more motivated, competent learners than others who had not participated in such a program.

We question whether it is feasible to have true content integration at secondary levels, or whether this integration would not be perceived as diluting subject content knowledge to the point that students would not be prepared for college. Our current educational system is geared to the idea that students need to learn basic information about several core disciplines. That is, they should understand the state of knowledge in those disciplines and have some notion about how knowledge is accumulated and shared. Their disciplinary understandings become more complex as they move from elementary school to college, and in college, if not before, they assess this knowledge to determine in which area they will seek expertise. We assume that, as students grow in knowledge, they also grow in their ability to think critically about that knowledge and make cross-disciplinary ties. This is the assumption questioned by researchers who advocate an integrated curriculum. They believe that students will be more likely to think critically and act competently if they are taught how to use cross-disciplinary knowledge to develop deeper understandings.

Beane (1995) argued that a truly integrated curriculum draws from the disciplines to answer real-world problems. He said that intergrated study is not antithetical to learning disciplinary knowledge, but that students will learn subject matter information as they research ways to solve problems. After our study of the high school described in chapter 1, we believe that most secondary teachers would not agree. As subject matter specialists, they believe their increased focus in a separate discipline has led to their expertise, and they believe that a structured approach to studying their subject matter (focusing on events in sequence and systems) leads to increased understanding. We can see both sides.

One recommendation, then, is to look at other ways for developing integrated understandings that do not diminish secondary teachers' attempts to develop ordered ways of looking at a discipline. One idea, for example, is to offer an additional class for high school students that would be cross disciplinary and problem focused in nature. The class could be taught by a generalist consulting with subject matter experts, community leaders, librarians, computer experts, and others as resources on which students can draw to learn how to gather information across sources, evaluate that information, and plan and execute problem-solving actions based on their evaluations. These classes could allow both college-bound and non–college-bound students to work together in solving community problems, a model found in real-life agencies such as Habitat-for Humanity, in which needy families and non-needy volunteers work together to build houses.

Another suggestion involves developing high schools that offer students and their parents choices about which sort of curriculum to follow, integrated or traditional, then providing teachers who are teaching integrated classes more support as they restructure the curriculum, design ways to measure learning that can take the place of traditional subject matter grading, and change the schedule and physical structure of classrooms so that students are not tied to just one teacher in one class period. There are alternative schools in which current constraints have been altered in these ways. Whether all teachers and parents will embrace "schools within schools" that have a radically different structure and whether colleges will accept different systems of evaluation is open to question. Moore (1997) reported that his undergraduate students, having observed an alternative school, were unsettled. They wondered whether the adolescents were being well served in an environment that was so radically different from other school environments.

Although a truly integrated curriculum may not be for everyone, it is a viable alternative that may have the potential to foster learning. The students in our study perceived that their learning was improved when they could link ideas across different subjects. Although this finding is certainly not proof that integrated curriculum works, it does point to a promising avenue for further study.

**Access to Multiple and Diverse Forms of Information**

In a literate, modern-day society, it is vital that we have efficient strategies for accessing information to solve problems and make informed decisions. These skills lie at the heart of democracy, yet they are becoming increasingly difficult to obtain. Although it is easier to access information now than it was before the Internet and e-mail, it is harder to ferret out that which has quality and importance. Often, data exists in so many varied and conflicting forms that we find it difficult to make sense of it. In our view, we must focus a significant portion of education on accessing, evaluating, and using information if we are to develop citizens who truly contribute to the work and worth of society. Schools should require teachers to use multiple sources of information and teach students how to deal with them.

To make this point, we take the case of history. In our view, it is difficult, with a single textbook, to teach students what historians do. This difficulty, in large part, stems from the traditional format of most history textbooks. Whereas textbooks in other fields, such as psychology, often refer to the research efforts of psychologists and may even report conflicting findings, history textbooks rarely present such information. Rather, the tradition is to present the information as a story. Thus, the reader never sees the hidden activity of the historian in constructing the telling of the story.

When several texts are taken in concert, however, a teaching opportunity is present, especially when the texts contradict each other, present different information, or expose differing viewpoints of various groups. For example, we collected three texts that represented, respectively, a traditional, revisionist, and postrevisionist view of the discoveries of Christopher Columbus. The traditional text included the idea that Christopher Columbus' discoveries required great courage and brought the world closer together. The revisionist view presented the Native American perspective that Columbus was greedy and cruel, denigrating the culture of a peace-loving and prosperous people and bringing disease and pestilence to an area that was not, to the people living there, the "New World." The postrevisionist view argued that Christopher Columbus was merely a product of his time and was neither more cruel nor more courageous than other explorers. Indeed, this text said that other explorers would have discovered the "New World" even if Christopher Columbus had not, and the same subsequent events surely would have occurred. These texts, with their differing viewpoints, present opportunities for history teachers to help students engage in sourcing (who wrote the texts and where did they appear), contextualization (in what time period were they written and what was the climate in which they were written), and corroboration (how do they compare and contrast). In helping students look at these elements teachers can make the argument that these texts represent the presentation of historical facts as arguments rather than as "truth." Students can learn that history is interpreted differently by different groups at different time periods as a result of sociocultural and political conditions. Furthermore, they can construct a deeper understanding of the life of Christopher Columbus by viewing him in these contrasting ways.

In another group of texts, we presented the Tonkin Gulf Incident, a precipitating event leading to the Tonkin Gulf Resolution and, ultimately, to President Johnson's sending U.S. troops to Vietnam. The Tonkin Gulf incident actually refers to two separate times that the U.S. surveillance ships in the Tonkin Gulf believed they were being attacked by North Vietnamese vessels. Historians think, at this point in time, that the first incident really did happen, but that it was minor and dismissed by the President and his staff. They do not believe, however, based on the evidence, that the second attack actually took place. It was this second act that instigated a "limited retaliation" by President Johnson and led the U.S. Congress to pass the Tonkin Gulf Resolution, which gave President Johnson the power to act in Vietnam without a declaration of war and the approval of Congress. There is still controversy about whether or not the President was acting in good faith when he asked for the resolution to be passed, and no one is absolutely sure of what happened during the two incidents. We included a number of sources in this collection, ranging from a telegram sent by the Viet Cong to the President protesting U.S. activities in the Tonkin Gulf before the incident; an eyewitness account by James Stockdale, who was flying above the U.S. ships during the alleged second incident; an excerpt from Dean Rusk's autobiography that chronicles his and the President's actions in relation to the "attack"; the verbatim text of the Tonkin Gulf Resolution; and several essays presenting opposing viewpoints. This collection of sources presents numerous opportunities for students to engage in thinking as a historian does.

There are issues to consider, however, in the use of multiple texts. The following points were derived both from our interpretation of research findings and from our understanding of the constructivist viewpoint held by historians.

1. *Students need to be taught to think like members of the discipline.* One thing we learned from our research is that students will not, by and large, engage in thinking like historians by merely being presented with multiple texts representing differing viewpoints. Students, especially those who lack background knowledge, persist in reading to get the facts held in common across multiple texts rather than in trying to understand why the interpretation of events is different. Therefore, we recommend that students be taught what historians do.

2. *Students will have difficulty interpreting multiple texts without knowing the purpose for reading them.* Unless students understand the purpose for the presentation of multiple texts, they will have difficulty interpreting them. In our research, some students became angry because they could not understand the telegram written by the Viet Cong. If they had understood who the authors were (sourcing), the conditions under which the telegram was written (contextualization), and the authors' purpose for writing the telegram, they would have been much more capable of engaging in meaningful activity while reading. In other words, they would have known to interpret the text as a way for the author to make a point rather than reading it to get "the facts." We recommend that teachers make sure that students understand the purpose for reading multiple texts before they read them.

3. *Students are more likely to think critically about multiple texts if they have some background knowledge.* Alexander and Judy (1988), in their literature review, conclude that there is a symbiosis between knowledge level and strategic thinking about that knowledge. That is, students who know something about a topic will be more able to engage in the kind of behaviors that will help them learn more. Those strategic behaviors, in turn, will result in their knowing more about the topic. Therefore, we believe that, before presenting students with multiple readings about a topic, they should engage in learning some of the background necessary to help them interpret the multiple readings. That is, they should have an understanding of the known events and be aware that controversies exist.

4. *Sourcing, contextualization, and corroboration should be the focus of teaching.* Because these three activities were most often those engaged in by historians and, we expect, other disciplinary experts, we believe that they should be the focus of what is taught to high school students. As students pay attention to the source, context, and corroborating elements in texts, they can be helped to evaluate the veracity of certain interpretations of events over other interpretations, and to become critical consumers of multiple perspectives in other arenas besides historical ones.

5. *Students will need to be taught how to write about multiple perspectives.* In our Tonkin Gulf study, students had difficulty writing about the multiple documents. When asked to write opinion papers, most wrote generalizations without support that appeared unrelated to the texts they had read. When asked to write descriptive papers, most students failed to represent the differing viewpoints presented in the multiple documents. Although teaching students to engage in reading like a historian might help them to be better writers, we believe students must be taught to write as well.

It likely will take a great deal of time and effort to move high school students toward thinking in a constructivist manner about history and other disciplines. However, we believe the time and effort is worth it. Not only will students be better prepared to attend colleges and universities where that perspective is pervasive, they will also learn a way of thinking that should help them become more critical consumers of the often contradictory and confusing messages about vital national issues that appear in newspapers and magazines and on television. For these reasons, we urge teachers to use multiple texts and engage in other activities designed to help students adopt constructivist notions of history.

## CONCLUSION

In this chapter we discussed our notions of knowledge and learning and presented some of the ideas we have learned from 5 years of research with the National Reading Research Center, focusing mainly on our year of observing an integrated high school curriculum program. We have studied high schools because we believe that they represent key reasons why adults function in society as they do. They also illustrate the tensions felt in education. We feel tension between the development of disciplinary knowledge and the development of integrated understandings of knowledge across disciplines. We feel tension between critical thinking and knowledge accumulation. Finally, we feel tension between students' construction of knowledge through social interaction with peers and their construction of knowledge based on a teacher's strict guidance.

In an ideal world, students would learn everything we want them to. They would be compliant accumulators of disciplinary knowledge at the same time that they are persistent challengers of existing thinking through their scholarly evaluation of diverse forms of information. They would be problem solvers and activists on the basis of their richly connected networks of knowledge. They would care about their influences on society, and they would learn better ways to meet society's challenges. How do we prepare students for those challenges? In our view, a look at what happens in high schools has implications for how we view education across the grades, and we can better answer the question of how to prepare students if we consider the point at which, in high school, the tensions between seemingly conflicting goals are perhaps the most keenly felt.

## REFERENCES

Alexander, P. A. (1998). Positioning conceptual change within a model of domain literacy. In B. Guzzetti & C. Hynd (Eds.), *Theoretical perspectives on conceptual change*. Mahwah, NJ: Lawrence Erlbaum Associates.

Alexander, P. A. (in press). Stages and phases of domain learning: The dynamics of subject-matter knowledge, strategy knowledge, and motivation. In C. E. Weinstein & B. L. McCombs (Eds.), *Skill, will and self-regulation.* Mahwah, NJ: Lawrence Erlbaum Associates.

Alexander, P. A., & Judy, J. E. (1988). The interaction of domain-specific and strategic knowledge in academic performance. *Review of Educational Research, 58,* 375–404.

Alvermann, D. E., Commeyras, M., Young, J. P., Randall, S., & Hinson, D. (1997). Interrupting gendered discursive practices in classroom talk about texts: Easy to think about, difficult to do. *Journal of Literacy Research, 29*(1), 3–44.

Alvermann, D. E., & Moore, D. W. (1991). Secondary school reading. In R. Barr, M. L. Kamil, P. Mosenthal, & P. D. Pearson (Eds.), *Handbook of reading research: Volume II* (pp. 951–983). New York: Longman.

Alvermann, D. E., Weaver, D., Hinchman, K. A., Moore, D. W., Phelps, S. F., Thrash, E. C., & Zalewski, P. (1995). *Middle- and high-school students' perceptions of how they experience text-based discussions: A multicase study* (Reading Research Report No. 36). Athens, GA: National Reading Research Center.

Anderson, R. C., & Pearson, P D. (1984). A schema-theoretic view of basic processes in reading. In P. D. Pearson (Ed.), *Handbook of reading research* (pp. 255–292). New York: Longman.

Beane, J. A. (1995). Curriculum integration and the disciplines of knowledge. *Phi Delta Kappan, 76*(8), 616–622.

Bernstein, B. (1971). On the classification of educational knowledge. In M. F. Young (Ed.), *Knowledge and control: New directions for the sociology of education* (pp. 47–69). New York: Collier Macmillan.

Bloome, D., & Egan-Robertson, A. (1993). The social construction of intertextuality in classroom reading and writing lessons. *Reading Research Quarterly, 28*(4), 305–333.

Brilliant-Mills, H. (1993). Becoming a mathematician: Building a situated definition of mathematics. *Linguistics and Education, 5,* 301–334.

Brody, G. H., Stoneman, Z., Flor, D., McCrary, C., Hastings, L., & Conyers, O. (1994). *Financial resources, parent psychological functioning, parent co-caregiving, and early adolescent reading competence in rural two-parent African American families* (Reading Research Report No. 20). Athens, GA: National Reading Research Report.

Cartwright, N. (1983). *How the laws of physics lie.* Oxford: Clarendon.

Chi, M. T. H. (1992). Conceptual change within and across ontological categories: Implications for learning and discovery in science. In R. Giere (Ed.), *Minnesota studies in the philosophy of science: Vol XV. Cognitive models of science* (pp. 129–186). Minneapolis: University of Minnesota Press.

Chinn, C. A. (1998). A critique of social constructivist views of knowledge change. In B. Guzzetti & C. Hynd (Eds.), *Theoretical perspectives on conceptual change.* Mahwah, NJ: Lawrence Erlbaum Associates.

Chinn, C. A., & Brewer, W. F. (1993). The role of anomalous data in knowledge acquisition: A theoretical framework and implications for science instruction. *Review of Educational Research, 63*(1), 1–49.

Davies, B. (1993). *Shards of glass.* Cresskill, NJ: Hampton Press.

Dreher, M. J. (1995). *Sixth-grade researchers: Posing questions, finding information, and writing a report* (Reading Research Report, No. 40). Athens, GA: National Reading Research Center.

Edwards, A. D., & Mercer, N. (1987). *Common knowledge.* London: Methuen.

Fairclough, N. (1992). *Critical language awareness.* New York: Longman.

Fernie, D., Davies, B., Kantor, R., & McMurray, P. (1993). Becoming a person: Creating integrated gender, peer and student positionings in a preschool classroom. *Qualitative Studies in Education, 5,* 241–274.

Fiske, S. T., & Taylor, S. E. (1991). *Social cognition.* New York: McGraw-Hill.

Floriani, A. (1993). The construction of understanding in a sixth-grade bilingual classroom. *Linguistics & Education, 5,* 241–274.

Gee, J. (1990). *Social linguistics and literacies: Ideology in discourses.* London: Falmer Press.

Geertz, C. (1983). *Local knowledge: Further essays in interpretive anthropology.* New York: Basic Books.

Giere, R. N. (1988). *Explaining science: A cognitive approach.* Chicago: University of Chicago Press.

Grossman, P. L., & Stodolsky, S. S. (1994). Considerations of content and the circumstances of secondary school teaching. In L. Darlin-Hammond (Ed.), *Review of research in education: Vol. 20* (pp. xx–xx). Washington, DC: American Educational Research Association.

Guthrie, J. R., Shafer, W. D., & Hutchinson, S. R. (1991). Relations of document literacy and prose literacy to occupational and societal characteristics of young black and white adults. *Reading Research Quarterly, 26*(1), 30–48.

Guzzetti, B. J., Snyder, T. E., Glass, G. V., & Gamas, W. S. (1993). Meta-analysis of instructional interventions from reading education and science education to promote conceptual change in science. *Reading Research Quarterly, 28*, 116–161.

Heras, A. L. (1993). The construction of understanding in a sixth-grade bilingual classroom. *Linguistics & Education, 5*, 275–299.

Hewson, P. W. (1981). A conceptual change approach to learning science. *European Journal of Science Education, 3*, 383–396.

Hirsch, E. D. (1987). *Cultural literacy.* Boston: Houghton Mifflin.

Hynd, C., Guzzetti B. G., McNish, M. M., Fowler, P., & Williams, W. (1997). *Texts in physics class: The contribution of reading to the learning of counterintuitive physics principles.* Unpublished manuscript.

Hynd, C., McNish, M. M., Lay, K., & Fowler, P. (1995). *High school physics: The role of text in learning counterintuitive information* (Reading Research Report, No. 27). Athens, GA: National Reading Research Center.

Hynd, C., McNish, M. M., Qian, G., Keith, M., & Lay, K. (1994a). *Learning counterintuitive physics concepts: The effects of text and educational environment* (Reading Research Report, No. 16). Athens, GA: National Reading Research Center.

Hynd, C., McWhorter, Y., Phares, V., & Suttles, W. (1994). The role of instructional variables in conceptual change in high school physics topics. *Journal of Research in Science Teaching, 31*, 933–946.

Hynd, C. R., Stahl, S. A., Britton, B., Glynn, S., Carr, M., Tiller, D., Sanders, T., & Wayne, M. (1996). Observational analysis of an integrated curriculum at the high school. Unpublished manuscript.

Kelly, G. J., & Green, J. (1998). The social nature of knowing: Toward a sociocultural perspective on conceptual change and knowledge construction. In B. Guzzetti & C. Hynd (Eds.), *Theoretical perspectives on conceptual change.* Mahwah, NJ: Lawrence Erlbaum Associates.

Knorr-Cetina, K. (1993). Construction and fiction: The prospect of constructionism in the study of science and beyond. *Danish Yearbook of Philosophy, 28*, 80–98.

Merton, R. K. (1973). *The sociology of science.* Chicago: University of Chicago Press.

Moore, D. W. (1997). Contexts for literacy in secondary schools. In D. J. Leu, C. K. Kinzer, & K. A. Hinchman (Eds.), *Literacies for the 21st century: Research and practice: Forty-fifth yearbook of the National Reading Conference* (pp. 15–46). Chicago, IL: National Reading Conference, Inc.

O'Brien, D. G., Stewart, R. A., & Moje, E. B. (1995). Why content literacy is difficult to infuse into the secondary school: Complexities of curriculum, pedagogy, and school culture. *Reading Research Quarterly, 30*, 442–463.

O'Brien, D. G., & Dillon, D. R. (1997). *Promoting the engagement of "at-risk" high school students: Perspectives from an innovative program.* (Tech. Rep. No. 83). Athens, GA: National Reading Research Center.

Ogbu, J. U. (1990). Minority education in comparative perspective. *Journal of Negro Education, 59*(1), 45–57.

Oldfather, P. (1993). What students say about motivating experiences in a whole language classroom. *The Reading Teacher, 46,* 672–681.

Oldfather, P., & McLaughlin, H. J. (1993). Gaining and losing voice: A longitudinal study of students' continuing impulse to learn across elementary and middle level contexts. *Research in Middle Level Education, 17,* 1–25.

Patterson, T. E. (1995). *We the people: A concise introduction to American politics.* New York: McGraw-Hill.

Phelan, P., Davidson, A. L., & Cao, H. T. (1992). Speaking up: Students' perspectives on school. *Phi Delta Kappan, 73*(9), 695–704.

Piaget, J. (1980). *Experiments in contradiction* (D. Coltman, Trans.). Chicago: University of Chicago Press. (Original work published 1974)

Pintrich, P. R., Marx, R. W., & Boyle, R. (1993). Beyond cold conceptual change: The role of motivational beliefs and classroom contextual factors in the process of conceptual change. *Review of Educational Research, 63*(2), 167–199.

Posner, G. J., Strike, K. A., Hewson, P. W., & Gertzog, W. A. (1982). Accommodation of a scientific conception: Toward a theory of conceptual change. *Science Education, 66,* 211–227.

Powell, R. R. (1993). Seventh graders' perspectives of their interdisciplinary team. *Middle School Journal, 24*(3), 49–57.

Pressley, M., El-Dinary, P., Brown, R., Schuder, T. L., Pioli, M., Green, K., & Gaskins, I. (1994). *Transactional instruction of reading comprehension strategies* (Perspectives in Reading Research, No. 5). Athens, GA: National Reading Research Center.

Perfetti, C. A., Britt, M. A., Marron, M., & Rouet, J. F. (1995, April). *Reader's models for situations and text.* Paper presented at the American Educational Research Association, San Francisco, CA.

Rumelhart, D. E., & Norman, D. A. (1981). Accretion, tuning, and restructuring: Three modes of learning. In J. W. Cotton & R. Klatzy (Eds.), *Semantic factors in cognition* (pp. 37–60). Hillsdale, NJ: Lawrence Erlbaum Associates.

Santa Barbara Classroom Discourse Group. (1992a). Constructing literacy in classrooms: Literate action as social accomplishment. In H. Marshall (Ed.), *Redefining student learning: Roots of educational change* (pp. 119–150). Norwood, NJ: Ablex.

Santa Barbara Classroom Discourse Group. (1992b). Do you see what I see? The referential and intertextual nature of classroom life. *Journal of Classroom Interaction, 27,* 29–36.

Schiefele, U. (1991). Interest, learning, and motivation. *Educational Psychologist, 26,* 229–323.

Schwab, J. J. (1978). Education and the structure of the disciplines. In I. Westbury & N. J. Wilkof (Eds.), *Science, curriculum, and liberal education* (pp. 229–272). Chicago: University of Chicago Press.

Sinatra, G., & Dole, J. (1998). Case studies in conceptual change: A social–psychological perspective. In B. Guzzetti & C. Hynd (Eds.), *Theoretical perspectives on conceptual change* (pp. xx–xx). Mahwah, NJ: Lawrence Erlbaum Associates.

Stahl, S., Hynd, C, Britton, B., McNish, M., & Bosquet, D. (1996). What happens when students read multiple source documents in history? *Reading Research Quarterly, 31*(40), 430–457.

Stahl, S., Hynd, C., McNish, M. (1996). Group processes involved in studying multiple documents in history. Unpublished manuscript.

Stahl, S., Hynd, C., Montgomery, T., & McClain, V. (1997). "In fourteen hundred and ninety two, Columbus sailed the Ocean Blue": Effects of multiple document readings on student attitudes and prior conceptions (Report No. 82). Athens, GA: National Reading Research Center.

Thagard, P. (1994). Mind, society, and the growth of knowledge. *Philosophy of Science, 61,* 629–645.

Turley, S. (1994, April). *The way teachers teach is, like, totally whacked": The student voice on classroom practice.* Paper presented at the annual meeting of the American Educational Research Association, New Orleans, LA.

VanSledright, B. A., & Kelly, C. (1996). *Reading American history: How do multiple text sources influence historical learning in fifth grade?* (Reading Research Rep. No. 68). Athens, GA: National Reading Research Center.

von Glasersfeld, E. (1987). Learning as a constructive activity. In C. Janvier (Ed.), *Problems of representation in the teaching and learning of mathematics* (pp. 3–17). Hillsdale, NJ: Lawrence Erlbaum Associates.

von Glasersfeld, E. (1993). Questions and answers about radical constructivism. In K. Tobin (Ed.), *The practice of constructivism in science education* (pp. 23–38). Hillsdale, NJ: Lawrence Erlbaum Associates.

von Glasersfeld, E. (1995). A constructivist approach to teaching. In L. P. Steffe & J. Gals (Eds.)., *Constructivism in education* (pp. 3–15). Hillsdale, NJ: Lawrence Erlbaum Associates.

Vosniadou, S., & Brewer, W. F. (1987). Theories of knowledge restructuring in development. *Review of Educational Research, 57,* 51–67.

Vosniadou, S., & Brewer, W. F. (1992). Mental models of the earth: A study of conceptual change in childhood. *Cognitive Psychology, 24,* 535–585.

Vygotsky, L. (1978). *Mind in society: The development of higher psychological processes.* Cambridge, MA: Harvard University Press.

Wigfield, A., & Guthrie, J. T. (1995). *Dimensions of children's motivations for reading: An initial study* (Reading Research Rep. No. 34). Athens, GA: National Reading Research Center.

Wigfield, A., Wilde, K., Baker, L., Fernandez-Fein, S., & Scher, D. (in press). *The nature of children's motivations for reading, and their relations to reading frequency and reading performance* (Reading Research Rep.). Athens, GA: National Reading Research Center.

Wineburg, S. S. (1991). On the reading of historical texts: Notes on the breach between school and academy. *American Educational Research Journal, 28,* 495–519.

Wineburg, S. S. (1994). The cognitive representation of historical texts. In G. Leinhardt, I. Beck, & C. Stainton (Eds.), *Teaching and learning in history* (pp. 171–208). Hillsdale, NJ: Lawrence Erlbaum Associates.

Yeager, B., Floriani, A., & Green, J. (1996). Learning to see learning in the classroom: Developing an ethnographic perspective. In D. Bloome & A. Egan-Robertson (Eds.), *Students as inquirers of language and culture in their classrooms.* Cresskill, NJ: Hampton Press.

## CHAPTER THREE

# Motivation to Read and Learn From Text

Martha Carr
Nancy B. Mizelle
David Charak
*University of Georgia*

I just have to get it in my head, to where I can understand it in my head. I didn't understand this in my head, all this together. I have to be able to, like . . . I just read this, but I couldn't tell you what it was about. The things we just got over studying, I'm like, I was interested in that. I like social studies. I seem to do good in it, but I have to be interested in it before I get it. Because that was boring, it didn't register. (eighth-grade student interview, Mizelle, 1992, pp. 123–124)

Like this eighth grader, in recent years, society in general and educators, in particular, have come to recognize students' motivation to read and learn from text (or rather the lack thereof) as a crucial issue in education. The 1992 National Assessment of Educational Progress found that students read few pages for school work each day and read less for pleasure as they get older (Mullis et al., 1994). This is reflected in the stagnation of reading achievement scores and, of more concern, a decline in reading achievement for late elementary school age students and older African American students (Mullis et al., 1994). In a recent national poll conducted by the Universities of Georgia and Maryland College Park, teachers were asked to identify and rank problems related to literacy that warranted research. They responded that their first priority was to find ways to improve students' motivation to read (O'Flahaven et al., 1992).

The purpose of this chapter is to examine motivational states and processes that are believed to empower students to use strategies and to learn from text. We discuss the roles of four forms of motivation in reading: interest, achievement goals, attributional beliefs, and self-efficacy. Several issues related to these motivations are addressed. We examine the literature and draw conclusions where possible about the developing relationship between motivations, strategy use, and reading achievement. The literature is reviewed for information about how motivations change and how those changes may affect strategy use and achievement. In addition, the types of texts used—narrative or expository—may affect how these motivations predict strategy use and reading comprehension. Whenever possible, we contrast the impact of narrative and expository text on students' motivations, strategy use, and reading achievement.

Historically, researchers have agreed that reading involves two different processes: decoding or perception of the printed word and comprehension or understanding the meaning of the printed word. They also have agreed that understanding text is the ultimate goal of reading. Accordingly, the expert reader is defined as a rapid decoder with a large vocabulary, phonemic awareness, knowledge about text features, and a variety of strategies for comprehension and memory, whereas the novice reader often focuses on decoding single words, does not adjust his or her reading for different texts or purposes, and seldom looks back or ahead to monitor or improve his or her comprehension (Baker & Brown, 1984). The development and knowledge of various strategies and skills are crucial to students' ability to read and understand text, but the development and knowledge of strategies does not ensure the use of strategies (Paris, Lipson, & Wixson, 1983).

According to Brown, Bransford, Ferrara, and Campione (1983), a theory of learning related to academic cognition is incomplete when it considers only the knowledge and strategies necessary for efficient learning without considering such motivational factors as attributions, self-efficacy, and goals. Paris et al. (1983) asserted that motivation influences students' strategic and metacognitive knowledge in dynamic and idiosyncratic ways. Judgments are made by learners about (a) the personal significance of goals within the task; (b) the perceived utility, value, and efficiency of alternative actions; and (c) the self-management of effort, time, and knowledge so that major objectives may be reached. The decisions at each step of problem solving are crucial components of employing cognitive strategies. Effort is necessary to apply such strategies as monitoring for the effectiveness of strategies and for comprehension failures. Effort is also necessary to achieve goals for reading comprehension and for learning from text. Thus, comprehension and decoding of printed words goes beyond skills: Students must be motivated to activate skills and knowledge to make the most of their reading. Ultimately, if students are being more strategic and thoughtful in their reading, then this should be reflected in their improved reading comprehension and achievement.

These motivations will not affect strategy use and performance in the same way across the school years because of students' emerging understanding of causality and because of new task demands placed on students as they progress. For example, as students move through elementary, middle and high school, their concepts of ability and effort change. Students go from believing that effort is the only explanation of outcomes to believing that effort and ability are separate and inversely related constructs (Nicholls, 1978). Students are also faced with new tasks that may affect and be affected by motivations (Pintrich & DeGroot, 1990). For example, the task of reading takes on a new dimension, with the focus of reading shifting from primarily reading narrative text that tells a story about an event, including "who did what to whom and why" (Calfee & Drum, 1986, p. 836), to reading primarily expository text that provides information about theories, predictions, persons, facts, dates, specifications, generalizations, limitations, and conclusions (Slater & Graves, 1989). These different types of texts may elicit different motivations.

In the following four sections we discuss in more detail the research connecting motivation to reading strategy use and reading achievement. We define interest, attributions, achievement goals, and self-efficacy. Then we present the literature on the relationship of each motivation to the use of strategies and to reading achievement. We discuss developmental changes and contrast the roles of motivation in processing narrative and expository text. Finally, we point out the areas in which research is lacking and our conclusions about how each form of motivation contributes to students' ability to read and learn from text.


## INTEREST

Given the chance to choose the author he would research, Will spent hours reading books by Jack London and about Jack London. He began his project reading in the fall, even though he knew the paper was not due until spring semester.

Interest is complex in that students can have topic interest as a stable characteristic, or their interest can be motivated by the situation (Oldfather & McLaughlin, 1993; Schiefele, 1991). When students are motivated by context, it is said that they are situationally interested in a topic or task. For example, a teacher may provide a lesson or a classroom context that intrigues students and fosters their interest, but that situational interest will not be maintained much beyond the lesson or the classroom. Students can also be topically interested in that their interest in a topic exists over a period of time and is not dependent on the context. The preceding paragraph is a good example of a child who is fascinated by Jack London and his work. It is this fascination and dedication that is typical of people who achieve in adulthood (Schneider, 1993).

How is interest related to students' ability to use strategies? Students who perceive that a task is interesting or useful are more likely to use cognitive and self-regulating strategies, but this relationship is mediated by the type of text read. For example, Mizelle, Hart, and Carr (1993) found that topic interest in middle school students contributed significantly to their use of cognitive and self-regulating learning strategies when learning from expository social studies text. Head, Readence and Buss (1989) investigated the relationship between topic interest, writing ability, and summarization skills for expository text in middle school-age students. They found that although topic interest did not affect writing ability, it did affect the number of ideas generated during summarization, suggesting that when students are interested in a topic, they are more likely to put the extra effort into processing the information from text. In contrast, topic interest was not found to predict the number of strategies high school students used to process narrative text (Olshavsky, 1977). The conflicting results here could be due to the differences in the types of text being read by students. Topic interest in an expository text seems to elicit the use of strategies such as summarizing, outlining, and self-testing, but topic interest in a narrative text does not. This may be the case because an interest in an expository text elicits the use of existing strategies for learning from expository text. Students may rarely need to study or recall narrative text and, therefore, were unable to activate appropriate strategies even though they were interested in the topic.

In examining the role of interest in reading achievement, researchers have found that topic interest is related to the ability of students to comprehend expository text as observed with fifth graders (Asher, Hymel, & Wigfield, 1978) and with seventh and eighth grade students who were allowed to choose their own texts (Baldwin, Peleg-Bruckner, & McClintock, 1985). For adolescent students, topic interest also is related to the extensive reading of expository and narrative texts involving an area of interest outside of school (Bintz, 1993). For middle school-age students, topic interest is linked to reading achievement through the use of cognitive and self-regulating strategies (Mizelle et al., 1993). In Will's case, his interest in Jack London will lead him to actively process what he reads. He will rephrase information and delete information that is not central. He will compare what he reads to what he knows. Thus, his interest will motivate the use of strategies which, in turn, produce improved reading comprehension.

Topic interest does not always have a significant impact on younger students' ability to gather information from text. Research by Carr and Thompson (1995) indicated that younger students are unable to use their topical interest to improve their reading comprehension. Similarly, Townsend and Townsend (1990) found that interest had no impact on the reading comprehension of third-grade students using expository text. These results suggest that other factors may be mediating younger students' ability to translate interest into improved reading comprehension.

Although students may develop interest in reading through cooperative experiences in school (and at home), they may need to develop faster decoding and processing skills before they are able to read independently to fulfill their interests. Poor cognitive skills reduce the effectiveness of interest (Schiefele, 1992). Young children, in particular, are deficient in higher level cognitive processes such as strategies (Schiefele, 1991). As these skills develop, they will support interest and, in turn, be supported by interest. For instance, when students read for meaning, they are more likely to be interested in the passage they read (Anderson, Wilkinson, & Mason, 1991), and students who are more interested in a topic are more likely to recall more elaborate information about a topic and to be more strategic (Tobias, 1994).

The authors believe that if students are interested in a topic, they will be motivated to acquire and use metacognition and strategies as a means to learning more about the topic. In regard to reading, situational interest may get students to read a topic presented in class, but only topic interest or intrinsic motivation will keep them reading outside of class. It is unrealistic to believe that students will be interested in all of the topics they must read about in school. However, interest may propel students to read consistently and to develop and automate both reading skills and vocabulary as a function of reading for interest. For example, although Will reads primarily about Jack London in his free time, his reading still will increase his vocabulary, reading speed, and reading comprehension skills. These skills, in turn, enable students like Will to read more difficult texts because they will have better basic decoding skills and higher level strategies.

## ATTRIBUTIONAL BELIEFS

Sarah likes to read books above her grade level, but is not discouraged when she has difficulty with some words. Faced with a difficult word, Sarah repeatedly sounds out the word, asks for help, or uses the context to help her understand the word. When she is questioned about her reading, Sarah expresses a belief that her successes come from her persistence in learning new words and reading difficult texts.

Max, in contrast, reads as little as possible and sees no point in reading. He does not believe that reading will improve his skills. Instead, he believes that he just is not good at reading.

Weiner's (1985) attribution theory asserts that students search for reasons or causes for their learning successes and failures. Students most often attribute their success or failure to ability, effort, luck, others, strategy, or task. These causal attributions differ in dimensions of locus (internal or external), stability (stable or unstable), and control (controllable or uncontrollable). When students are assigned a learning task, their tendency to approach the task is determined in part by prior attributions for success or failure in a similar situation. The stability of the attribution affects students' expectancy of future success, whereas the locus and controllability of the attribution affect the students' affective reaction to success or failure. Students like Max are in good standing when they succeed because they view their successes as coming from innate ability. The problem is that success cannot be guaranteed, and when Max fails, particularly when he fails repeatedly, Max's attributions to innate ability backfire. Sarah, however, views stable ability as emerging from effort and persistence. Success can be attributed to ability. Failure, though, is not viewed as an end, but as a starting point for working toward the goal of success and higher ability.

We cannot yet clearly picture the development of causal attributions for reading, but there is evidence that attributions for reading become differentiated within the domain of reading and from other domains as students get older. Hiebert, Winograd, and Danner (1984) found that third graders did not differ in their attributions in regard to types of reading situations (evaluation of reading versus reading for meaning), but that by the sixth grade, a student's attributions varied across these two reading situations. The differentiation of attributions by domain may have cultural influences. Galloway, Leo, Rogers, and Armstrong (1996) found that British middle school-age students denomstrated more learned helplessness in English with age. That is, they believed that they had stable, low ability that they could not change or control. These beliefs, however, did not emerge in mathematics. In contrast, Ryckman and Mizokawa (1991) found that American students tended to have a more learned helpless approach to mathematics as opposed to language arts as they got older. These data suggest that culture plays a role in the development of attributions.

Research examining the relationship between students' causal attributions in reading strategy use suggests that when students feel they control outcomes, they are more likely to successfully use reading strategies (Borkowski & Krause, 1985). In addition to a belief in effort and ability, students need to know why, when, and where to use reading strategies (Carr, Borkowski & Maxwell, 1991). Metacognitive knowledge and self-perceptions of high ability also predict better performance on reading comprehension tests (Paris & Oka, 1986). Thus students such as Sarah will generate and use strategies when they believe that they can control an outcome. Max does not believe that he controls outcomes, and therefore sees no point in trying. This sense of control comes from students' interpretations of previous experiences (Schunk, 1983).

Students' attributions predict reading achievement, and this relationship increases with age (Ehrlich, Kurtz-Costes, & Loridant, 1993). For example,

Nicholls (1979) found that achievement correlated with attributions of success to ability, but was negatively correlated with attributions of success to effort or luck for fourth-grade, but not for first-grade students. Similarly, Paris and Oka (1986) found that cognitive self-perceptions about ability predicted reading achievement for 10-year-olds, but not for 8-year-olds. The development of this relationship between attributions and achievement appears to be mediated by metacognitive knowledge about strategies that is developing at the same time. When students believe that the cause of outcomes is internal and that they possess metacognitive knowledge about reading, they are likely to have better comprehension of expository text, which can be observed in older elementary school students, but not in kindergarten-age students (Wagner, Spratt, Gal, & Paris, 1989). By fifth grade, students who attribute their successes to stable causes (e.g., ability) are better achievers in reading (Marsh, Cairns, Relich, Barnes, & Debus, 1984). Young children do not differentiate between ability and effort, likely because they are not aware of individual differences in outcomes following similar effort. However, as students become aware of these differences and subsequently develop an understanding of ability as a separate construct, their emerging understanding of their own ability motivates their comprehension and achievement. Metacognitive awareness may be particularly important in helping students come to realize that they can control outcomes.

Because causal attributions are pivotal in students' academic successes and failures, much research has focused on poor readers' attributions. This research suggests that specific patterns of attributions are linked to good and poor reading achievement, and these patterns appear to stabilize over time. In general, poor readers show a learned helplessness attributional pattern, including attributions of failure to lack of ability and of successes to uncontrollable factors, whereas good readers tend to see themselves as controlling successes (Butkowsky & Willows, 1980). A poor reader does not see failure as something that can be overcome through some kind of effort whether it be practice, sounding out words, or using the context of the sentence. These poor attributional patterns, however, do not necessarily worsen as students progress through school (Kistner, Osborne, & LeVerrier, 1988), which suggests that parents and teachers are intervening when students are identified as having learning problems.

What appears to be critical for reading achievement and strategy use is students' belief that they can overcome failure outcomes through the application of skills and knowledge. Effort attributions are not as important for successful older students and good readers, who are likely to attribute success to ability. These students are well served in believing that their successes come from stable ability that has developed out of effort.

We believe that causal attributions are pivotal in the development of reading strategies and comprehension, but we do not hold that a belief in effort or high ability alone will cause students to become better learners. Students need to be given the skills and knowledge on which attributions can be made. They must be able to see how and why they can control reading outcomes, and this can only occur by providing students with basic reading skills and strategies. Furthermore, we need to know how causal attributions affect and are affected by students' experiences with narrative text. We know virtually nothing about the attributions students make related to their successes and failures in reading narrative texts. Such information would be useful in that much of the reading that students do outside and inside the classroom involves narrative texts.

## GOALS FOR LEARNING

Joseph wants everyone to know how smart he is and wants to make sure that nobody sees him fail at anything. To do this, Joseph makes a big deal out of his successes and frequently claims that he never fails anything. This approach to learning has its price because Joseph will not try anything too difficult and stops working as soon as it looks like he may fail. Joseph has performance or ego goals for achievement.

Juan seems to love learning in that he will try just about anything. Failing does not seem to deter him from trying again because he believes that if he tries enough he will eventually master the task. He does not care that much about what other kids say and seems interested in their work only because he may learn some new ways to do something. Juan has learning or task goals for achievement.

Goals for learning emerge out of students' causal attributions. If students believe that ability is controllable and changeable through effort, then they are said to have learning or task goals. By learning or task goals, we mean that students like Juan are primarily interested in gathering knowledge and mastering skills with the goal of increasing their ability or intelligence (Dweck & Leggett, 1988). They see ability as the result of effortful learning. If students, such as Joseph view ability as stable, then they will worry more about looking good, pleasing others, or avoiding hard work that would indicate low ability. These students have ego or performance goals in that they do not see ability or intelligence as something that can be improved—you either do or do not have it. Instead, effort is exerted toward a display of high ability, or avoiding a display of low ability.

Students' use of strategies and their subsequent achievement is believed to be mediated by their goals for learning and their perceptions of their competencies (Dweck, 1986). That is, students with a learning or task goal, regardless of their level of self-confidence in their ability, will persist and seek more effective problem-solving strategies when they encounter difficulty in learning because they believe that they can become intelligent even though they do not at present have the knowledge skills. This is believed to result in the development of good reading skills in that students such as Juan will view reading and study strategies as means for achievement. At the same time, students with a performance goal and a high level of self-confidence will also persist in the face of difficulty because of their confidence in their ability, not because they are interested in learning. Students with performance goals and low self-confidence, however, when faced with difficulty, will either resort to face-saving strategies such as making excuses or copying someone else's work, or they will give up. Thus, a student like Joseph will use avoidance strategies to maintain a perception of high ability.

A particular goal in a learning situation can influence the students' selection of problem-solving or learning strategies when they are engaged in reading. Students who adopt a task or learning goal use more strategies when they read from expository text than students who adopt ego or performance goals (Nolen & Haladyna, 1990). Even more importantly, task-oriented students are more likely than ego-oriented students to employ those strategies that support learning and understanding. When comparing fifth- and sixth-grade students with task goals toward learning from science text to those with ego goals, Meece, Blumenfeld, and Hoyle (1988) found that task-oriented students were more actively engaged in learning with metacognitive and self-regulating strategies (e.g., reviewing, questioning) than students with ego goals. To a lesser degree, ego-oriented students reported using metacognitive and self-regulating strategies, but they also reported using such superficial strategies as seeking help often, copying, and guessing. Similarly, Nolen (1988) found that a task goal promoted the use of deep-processing study strategies by middle school-age students in reading of expository text. Recent research by Schunk and Rice (1991) suggests that the focus of task-oriented students on self-regulating strategies as well as more complex strategies may occur because these students believe that it is important to become a better reader and to learn through the use of strategies.

The research that has been done on the role of goals and reading achievement suggests that reading achievement is not directly related to students' goals although reading achievement can be improved by orienting students toward task or learning goals (Schunk & Rice, 1991). Students' goals appear to power other motivations such as self-efficacy and reading strategy use, which, in turn, promotes good reading achievement (Mizelle et al., 1993). We do not know how achievement goals affect reading from narrative texts. Given that narrative texts are highly story-like, they may elicit more task or learning goals from students.

The nature of expository text may lend itself to ego or performance goals as the focus of reading shifts from reading for enjoyment and practice to reading for information that will be tested. The classroom context can influence students to adopt one goal over another. For example, competitive situations tend to elicit ego or performance goals (Ames, 1992). This is not to say that we should attempt to focus students on task goals by not requiring them to be tested on their knowledge gained from text. We may be able to lessen the focus on performance goals, however, by focusing on the value of learning as opposed to testing (i.e., emphasizing what has been learned and not a grade).

## SELF-EFFICACY

Sonia looks forward to her history class because she has high expectations in her ability to understand what is being read in her class. She is confident that she will be able to understand her teacher, read the text and do well on the test. Sonia has high self-efficacy in history.

In contrast, her friend, Lydie, is uncertain about her ability to understand what is being covered in the class. Lydie does not believe that she will do well on the next exam because she has not had much success in this class in the past. Lydie has low self-efficacy in history.

*Self-efficacy* is defined as "personal judgments of one's capability to organize and implement behaviors in specific situations" (Schunk, 1984, p. 48). Researchers looking at the relationships between self-efficacy and the development of cognitive skills view self-efficacy as part of a self-regulating system in which self-efficacy and metacognitive awareness work together to improve strategy use and reading comprehension (McCombs, 1986). Students who understand that their skills and knowledge have brought about improvement in reading and comprehension of text will feel more capable of reading and learning from text. Similarly, that feeling of self-efficacy will lead to efforts to improve skills and knowledge.

Regarding the connection between self-efficacy and metacognitive knowledge, when students understand when, where and why they should use reading strategies and techniques, they are more likely to feel self-efficacy and to have better reading achievement (Paris & Winograd, 1990). Students' self-efficacy also is influenced by the feedback they get about their performance (e.g., "Your summarization of the chapter on Greece was right on target. You took the time to read carefully and think about the most important parts") (Schunk, 1989). When they see themselves learning new information or improving their level of skill, students' self-efficacy improves, and this positive self-efficacy leads to skill improvement (Schunk & Rice, 1985). Thus, self-efficacy works with metacognitive awareness to increase achievement, skills, and knowledge.

Initial research examining the role of self-efficacy in students' strategy use indicates that for middle and high school-age students, self-efficacy is related to cognitive strategy use and self-regulated learning (Pintrich & De-Groot, 1990). That relationship between self-efficacy and strategy use is independent of ability (Bouffard-Bouchard, Parent, & Larivée, 1991), but there is evidence that the relationship between self-efficacy and strategy use may be mediated by other factors. For example, Mizelle et al. (1993) tested several structural equation models that included self-efficacy, interest, and goal orientation and found that a model in which intrinsic interest mediated the influence of self-efficacy as a predictor of cognitive or self-regulating strategy use was a good fit to the data.

Researchers also have found that for middle and high school-age students, self-efficacy is related to reading achievement (Anderman, 1992; Williams, 1994). The work of Shell, Colvin, and Bruning (1995) indicates that at least for students from the fourth through seventh grades the relationship between self-efficacy and reading achievement remains stable. More specifically, self-efficacy is related to middle school students' ability to learn from a social studies text (Mizelle et al., 1993) and to comprehend concepts they would encounter in an expository type text (Bouffard-Bouchard et al. 1991). Students' self-efficacy also is related to their ability to make inferences about what they read in narrative text, but not their ability simply to recognize what they have read (Salomon, 1984). For poor readers, however, self-efficacy does not predict reading comprehension of a narrative text (Ehrlich et al., 1993). These findings suggest that the role of self-efficacy in reading achievement is mediated by other factors such as basic reading skills and the task demands. They also imply that students' self-efficacy may be less important for reading achievement in younger or poor readers than in older readers. For example, Ehrlich and her colleagues (1993) believed that basic word decoding, such as word recognition, is required for reading achievement and that self-efficacy beliefs emerge out of good reading skills.

The work of Schunk and Rice (1987) indicates that providing students with information about the value of strategies increases self-efficacy and comprehension skill. Thus, teachers and parents may facilitate both strategy use and self-efficacy via feedback about strategy use. For example, telling students explicitly about how a strategy works, when to use the strategy, and when not to use the strategy will provide students with the means to be successful in their reading. Self-efficacy alone will not cause students to use reading strategies, develop basic reading skills, or improve reading comprehension and test scores. Students need to be provided with the skills and knowledge, and the connection between their use of these strategies and skills and good performance must be made by teachers and parents.

With the exception of the cross-sectional study by Shell et al. (1995), we know little about how self-efficacy may change and develop in regard to reading strategy use and reading achievement. There appears to be a stronger relationship between self-efficacy and learning from expository text than from narrative texts. Furthermore, because little research has been done on younger students, we know little about how the shift from reading primarily narrative to reading primarily expository text may affect self-efficacy and be affected by self-efficacy.

## THE SELF-SYSTEM: A MODEL OF MOTIVATION TO READ

The bulk of the research on motivation for reading has focused on the relationship between a single form of motivation and students' strategy use or reading achievement. This approach is limited in that these forms of motivation do not act independently of each other. For example, task goals predict interest as well as school achievement (Butler, 1988). As another example, students who are given more autonomy, as in selecting a text to read, are more intrinsically interested in a reading task (Alexander, Kuliko-wich, & Jetton, 1994; Pressley, El-Dinary, Marks, Brown, & Stein, 1991). In looking at single variables, we are also less able to determine which variables are more or less influential than others in predicting strategy use and reading performance. For example, Wigfield and Asher (1984) suggested that attri-butions have less influence on students' achievement motivation and that other variables (expectancies and values) have a stronger influence on stu-dents' task persistence and performance. These relationships, however, do not show up when the relationship between only one motivational variable and students' strategy use or reading achievement is examined.

Presented in Fig. 3.1 is a model developed and tested by Mizelle et al. (1993). This model was designed to explore the relationships among young adolescents' motivational processes (i.e., self-efficacy, intrinsic value, and goal orientation), their use of cognitive and self-regulating learning strategies for learning from social studies text, and their classroom grades and stand-ardized achievement test scores as measured by the Iowa Test of Basic Skills (ITBS). The model assumed that students' ability as measured by the Cog-nitive Abilities Test (COGAT) would predict their performance and mastery (task) orientation. Ability was predicted as positively related to mastery (task) goals and negatively related to performance goals. Mastery and performance orientations were predictors of intrinsic value, self-efficacy, cognitive strate-gies for reading and studying (e.g., summarizing), and self-regulating strate-gies (e.g., monitoring understanding). Self-efficacy and intrinsic value were included as predictors of cognitive and self-regulated strategy use and class-room achievement. Cognitive strategies and self-regulating strategies were used to predict classroom achievement, which in turn was used as a predictor of standardized achievement.

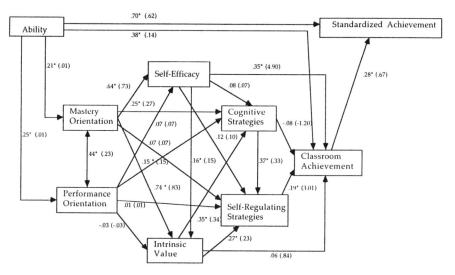

*p < .05, two-tailed.

↔ represents correlated residuals between mastery orientation and performance orientation.

FIG. 3.1. Model One. Results of LISREL VI Analysis; N = 226; chi-square 18.08,
df = 12, p = .113, goodness of fit = .98, adjusted goodness of fit index = .94,
root mean square residual = .03.

To test this model, structural equation modeling was used because it
allowed for the entire model to be tested at once, providing information
about the direct and indirect influences of these variables. Surprisingly, ability
predicted both mastery (task) and performance goals. This indicates that
middle school students of high ability can hold both types of goals. These
data suggest that teachers should not assume that because a student is doing
well, he or she is motivated by mastery or task goals.

The results of a model indicated that mastery, and to a lesser degree
performance, goals were significant predictors of students' cognitive but not
self-regulating strategy use. This is in line with prior research showing that
task goals will lead to strategy use with the goal of increasing knowledge
and that performance goals can also facilitate strategy use—frequently shal-
low strategy use. One problem with this study is that the quality of the
strategies students used was not differentiated, so it cannot be said for sure
that task and performance goals predicted a different quality of strategy use.

Mastery goals, but not performance goals, also predicted self-efficacy and
intrinsic interest. Thus, students who are motivated to learn for the sake of
learning will be more confident in future outcomes and value learning for
its own sake. In contrast, students primarily interested in looking good

(performance goals) will not value learning for the sake of learning and will be less confident in their ability to succeed on future reading tasks.

Self-efficacy predicted cognitive and self-regulatory strategies indirectly through intrinsic value. Intrinsic value did not directly predict classroom achievement, but it did predict both cognitive and self-regulatory strategy use. Taken together, this suggests that simply valuing learning or having self-efficacy is not sufficient to create good reading comprehension. Instead, students with self-efficacy will be intrinsically interested and thus will be more likely to use cognitive and self-regulatory strategies. It is the strategies that allow students to do well in class. Self-efficacy is translated into the use of cognitive and self-regulatory strategies only if students value learning.

Finally, self-regulating strategies mediated the connection between cognitive strategy use and classroom achievement. Simply knowing the steps of a strategy is not enough for its useful application in the classroom. Students need to know how to regulate strategies. For instance, they must know when and why strategies should be used. They also must be able to monitor whether a strategy is working and to know to shift strategies when necessary. All of this is information a teacher can and should include as part of strategy instruction.

Certainly, these and similar models are limited in that they do not consider other factors, such as students' existing knowledge about a topic (knowledge base), basic reading skills, and social factors that affect students' ability to learn to read and to learn by reading. Motivations can go only so far to improve reading skills and reading comprehension. A well-developed knowledge base is one factor that can both promote learning through text and the motivation to learn from text. Students need some knowledge to carry them through tough points in their reading and to maintain interest (Alexander et al., 1994). Knowledge base also has a direct impact on interest because it influences what is perceived to be important and interesting (Alexander & Jetton, 1996). A novice knowledge base can be supported by organizing text for understanding, and this also increases interest (Hamrick & Harty, 1987). Future research needs to examine how motivation changes as students move from being novices to being experts on a particular topic.

The environment of the classroom and the teacher's approaches to instruction also play a role in whether students are motivated and whether students' motivation will translate into learning. Intrinsic motivation decreases if students believe that the rewards they receive are given to them, not as an acknowledgment of excellence, but as a bribe to get them to do something (Griffith, DeLoach, & Labarba, 1984; McLoyd, 1979). Honest praise and real rewards, given infrequently but following real success, are much more motivating than a constant supply of praise and rewards given for no real reason. Related to this, students like to have some choices in what they read (Bintz, 1993). Simply allowing students to choose from a selection should increase motivation.

Furthermore, students, even poor readers, want to feel challenged. Poor readers given traditional seatwork to improve basic skills found this form of instruction to be uninteresting and irrelevant (Kos, 1991). One reason poor readers dislike simple tasks (e.g., filling in the blanks) is that they elicit more ego or performance goals in comparison to complex tasks (e.g., writing paragraphs), which elicit more task goals (Miller, Adkins, & Hooper, 1993).

Motivation to read will also be supported when students develop fast decoding and processing skills. For example, basic reading skills appear to mediate the influences of self-efficacy on reading comprehension (Ehrlich et al., 1993). For older students, interest has not been found to promote performance in nonautomated procedures such as writing (Hidi & McLaren, 1990). In addition, cognitively immature or less experienced readers may actually be sidetracked by interesting tidbits of information that are not highly relevant (Alexander, Kulikowich, & Schulze, 1994). These studies suggest that students need basic skills and knowledge in place to some degree before motivations such as interest or self-efficacy can influence achievement.

Models assuming that skills and knowledge are important at different times during development will be better able to explain the changing roles of basic skills, knowledge, higher level skills and motivation. Young students may be highly motivated to learn, but not have the skills to actualize this motivation. As students acquire skills and knowledge, they are better able to use these emerging skills and knowledge to achieve. The trick is to have students maintain their early motivation as they acquire skills and knowledge: The two can then work in concert. Paris (1988) called this the fusing of skill and will. As an example, a young child will be highly motivated to try just about anything, but this motivation is not directed through skill and knowledge and may not result in high achievement. An older equally motivated child will know how to direct that motivation by activating his or her knowledge and by using appropriate reading comprehension strategies. A child who wants to learn is one thing, but a child who wants to learn and who knows how to learn is something else. A review of reading intervention and instructional programs is presented in the following discussion.

## INTERVENTION (AND PREVENTION) TO IMPROVE MOTIVATION

Studies suggest that a child who does poorly in reading during the first year of school is likely to continue to perform poorly (Goodlad, 1984; Stanovich, 1984). For instance, Satz, Taylor, Friel, and Fletcher (1978) discovered that a meager 6% of boys who were poor readers in second grade made improvement by the end of fifth grade. Juel (1988) estimated that the probability of a child remaining a poor reader at the end of fourth grade if the child was a poor reader at the end of first grade was .88. Felton and Wood (1992) found that students with poor word identification skills in third grade were unable to improve their basic reading skills significantly by eighth grade. Furthermore, reading failure is associated with future life problems including the need for special education and retention, poor academic performance, leaving school prematurely, and poor employment outlooks (Anderson, Hiebert, Scott, & Wikinson, 1985; National Commission on Excellence in Education, 1984). These studies insist that educators must find ways either to vigorously stave off reading failure through prevention or to find interventions toward improving reading skills as soon as they are discovered. To examine the role of motivation in reading intervention and preventative instruction, we utilize Palincsar and Perry's (1995) stance that readers can be best understood from developmental, cognitive, and sociocultural perspectives.

**Developmental Perspective**

> Kerry knew that he was way behind in his reading. His primary difficulty was that he did not understand the letter–sound relationships and, as a result, could not sound out words. After Kerry had been working with his teacher and the teacher's aide using Reading Recovery, he began to understand how letters could be turned into sounds and sounds into words. Kerry read a lot of easy texts to improve his speed. As Kerry developed these basic skills, he also began to feel that he could improve his ability to read. He began to set realistic goals because he had gained confidence in himself. The combination of reading skills and positive beliefs helped Kerry improve his reading.

The developmental perspective focuses on early reading skills, or what has been termed *emergent literacy*. Perhaps because educators typically expect that students have mastered basic reading skills by the time they have reached third or fourth grade, less emphasis has been placed on developing specific programs for young adolescents who have not learned to read. The problem is that many students do reach early adolescence without adequate skills for reading and understanding text (Anrig & Lapointe, 1989; Craig & Yore, 1995). In addition to their inadequate basic reading skills, these students may come to believe that learning to read is impossible. Thus, teachers of older poor readers must deal with significant motivational problems as well as deficits in reading skills.

Examples of interventions that address the role of motivation in developing reading skills come from research on tutorials. To address the needs of these students, researchers and educators primarily have developed programs based on the specific needs of students involved (Lee & Neal, 1992; Moniuszko, 1992; Pope & Beal, 1994; Stewart, Paradis, Ross, & Lewis, 1996). The common thread that runs through programs for older students is the specific attention given to students' motivation, in particular, their intrinsic interest and their confidence or self-efficacy. Stewart and his colleagues (1996), for example, addressed student motivation by allowing seventh- and eighth-grade students to choose from a variety of fiction and nonfiction texts, to work at their own pace and spend extended periods of time reading, and to participate in a variety of response activities. The students reported that the literature-based reading program helped them to improve in their speed, fluency, understanding and remembering, overall school perform-ance, and reading out loud. They also identified the most beneficial features of the program as choice of reading material, interesting reading material, time to read, and the opportunity to practice reading.

During the early grades, instruction and intervention focus on phonological processing abilities, especially the development of the discernment of speech sounds in words, or phonological awareness. These instructional techniques have been modified to create a program developed specifically to help an eighth-grade student "gain a sense of control over print after many years of being overwhelmed" (Lee & Neal, 1992, p. 277). Reading Rescue (Lee & Neal, 1992), based on the Reading Recovery model, included reading familiar material, reading aloud to the student, taking a running record, working with words and letters, writing through language experience, and reading new material. Imbedded in this program are opportunities for students to choose interesting and relevant material to read—some written by others, some written by the themselves, and opportunities to build up the student's confidence by rereading material he or she has read before or material he or she has written. In the case of a student named David, the program resulted in progress of a student, described by his eighth-grade resource teacher as worse than any other student she had ever worked with in terms of his reading skills and comprehension strategies, to a ninth grader who was enthusiastic and no longer stressed about the prospect of reading.

Success for All (SFA), is another program designed to improve basic reading skills that is usually begun with young elementary school children, but may be useful for older students. This program is billed as a decoding and comprehension program. It focuses on intervention through, among other activities, "reading to students, engaging students in discussions of story structure and developing oral language skills", as well as "building compre-hension, thinking skills, fluency, and positive reading attitudes by integrating uses of the school system's novels or basal readers with cooperative learning, partner reading, process writing, and other components" (Ross, Smith, Casey, & Slavin, 1995, p. 779). SFA provides improved instruction for risk and nonrisk students alike through intensive individual and group instruction. Such comprehensive instruction may be of benefit to older poor readers.

The programs in the preceeding discussion above were designed to pro-vide poor readers with the basic skills and to improve motivation to read.

Normally, students' motivation to apply themselves to the task of learning to read is rewarded with a continuous improvement in reading skills. However, when students have trouble learning basic reading skills, they gradually lose confidence in themselves as learners. They do not see how they can control their actions to better their reading skills. Basic skills training gives students some control over what they read while it provides students with the resources to improve their skill. It is students' awareness of these skills and their understanding that these skills have improved their reading that restores students' confidence in themselves as readers.

## Cognitive Perspective

> Ashley was a bright fifth-grade student who would not try to learn from text because she believed she was incapable of doing so. Despite her above-average intelligence, Ashley had become learned helpless as a result of problems she had learning to read in the first grade. She still had some reading problems, but her biggest problem was the belief that she could not improve. Her teacher instituted a plan in which she made controllable attributions when Ashley encountered difficulty in reading. The teacher also gave her careful instruction in how to overcome her failures. Gradually, Ashley began to see failure as something that could be changed through the appropriate skills and strategies.

The cognitive stance conceives of reading as the active processing of text. Much credit for the focus on students' understanding of text goes to Durkin (1978–1979), who found that the teaching of comprehension skills in U.S. classrooms was almost nonexistent (Brown, Pressley, Van Meter, & Schuder, 1996). Cognitive interventions were developed in an attempt to introduce students to the strategies they must use to understand texts. These programs are generally aimed at older students and involve the instruction of comprehension strategies, such as the use of summarization. In addition, these programs are designed to motivate students by explicitly showing the value and utility of strategies that aid reading. The more students understand the value of comprehension strategies, the more likely they are to use these strategies (Schunk & Rice, 1987), the more confident they feel about learning (self-efficacy), and the more task-oriented they become (Nolen & Haladyna, 1990). In addition, because strategies are internal to and controllable by the learner, they can be acquired and successfully applied. Recent research suggests that attributing failure to poor strategy use may be particularly beneficial (Paris & Oka, 1986).

In particular, three different studies have shown the importance of combining attribution retraining with strategy instruction for poor readers (Borkowski, Weyhing, & Carr, 1988; Short & Ryan, 1984). Each of these studies found that students exposed to attribution retraining (i.e., to attribute their prior successes and failures to controllable factors such as effort, rather than to such uncontrollable factors as another person) combined with either cognitive strategy instruction (Borkowski et al., 1988) or comprehension monitoring instruction (Short & Ryan, 1984) and had higher scores on comprehension measures than students who received only the strategy training. Additionally, each group of students who received the attribution retraining maintained use of the strategy and were able to generalize its use to other situations. In the classroom, teachers can institute attributional retraining by pointing out to poor readers exactly where a mistake has been made and how to fix the problem. By pointing out where things went wrong (e.g., "you missed that word") and giving students an opportunity and the skills to deal with the problem, students will gradually begin to feel that they can overcome negative outcomes.

Teachers must be aware of students' developing motivational states and reading skills when instituting an intervention program. For instance, older students may see an inverse relationship between ability and effort. For these students, training to increase attributions to effort in success may contradict attributions to high ability (Craven, Marsh, & Debus, 1991; Nicholls, 1984; Schunk, 1983). For high achievers, the focus should be on stable ability as an outcome of effort. In addition, there is evidence that higher achieving readers comprehend more when they use their own preferred strategies than when other strategies are imposed upon them (Dole, Brown, & Trathen, 1996). Thus, students who have a repertoire of familiar and successful comprehension strategies may be hurt by strategy instruction.

Interventions to help students develop the strategies needed for processing text may also focus on issues related to curriculum and instruction (Gaskins et al., 1994; Guthrie et al., 1996). Gaskins and her colleagues, for example, found that integrating reading and writing instruction into the context of teaching science resulted in middle school students learning science content as well as the processes of learning science (e.g., stating the components of a problem, selecting appropriate reading materials, expressing in writing their understanding of science concepts, applying what they learned). Likewise, Guthrie and his colleagues (1996) implemented an integrated reading/language arts/science program that involved real-world science learning, strategy instruction, collaborative learning, and the use of trade books in the place of textbooks. The results of a year-long study indicated that third- and fifth-grade students increased in their use of learning strategies and in their intrinsic motivation.

## Sociocultural Perspective

Mrs. McCarthy's class was always game to look up information for the projects they were working on because they were able to see how these projects were connected to their everyday lives. In addition, the students in her class were enthusiastic because they were able to talk with other students about their ideas and contribute to the development of a central project. Group discussion gave them new avenues to research and encouraged them to do more reading.

The sociocultural perspective assumes that a student's participation in class is improved when there are authentic situations and reasons to utilize written language (Brown et al., 1996; Hiebert, 1994; Palincsar & Perry, 1995). In essence, the sociocultural stance dictates that "one does not attempt to break down the activities of reading and writing into component parts, but rather finds ways of supporting students so that they experience the total, meaningful activity" (Palincsar & Perry, 1995, p. 333).

It should seem evident that this perspective is part of the whole language (literature-based)–phonics (skills-based) debate. While the battle rages on concerning the side to which instruction and intervention should bow, we choose to illustrate interventions and instruction that incorporate both direct instruction of decoding skills and comprehension strategies while they provide students with the ability to read and write in a meaningful way (Hiebert, 1994). The call for combining authentic tasks with reading intervention and instruction has been a common theme in many recent instructional recommendations. For instance, Johnston and Allington (1991) charged that reading remediation should include noncompetitive, task-involving, choice-laden, instruction to increase student involvement and cooperation. Similarly, Turner (1995) found that open tasks in which students must set goals and critically evaluate what they are reading can be the strongest predictors of students' strategy use, persistence, and controlled attention. Students can be taught to be effortful and strategic when they read and write about relevant and meaningful topics. Similarly, basic reading skills can be embedded within meaningful contexts. Such interventions motivate students about reading by providing them with explicit skills, self-regulation, and attributions as well as by promoting involvement through social interactions and the reading meaningful texts in which they can make meaningful connections.

In addition to being used as an intervention, authentic tasks may become part of the regular curricula. Stahl, McKenna, and Pagnucco (1994) suggested that explicit phonics training be combined with authentic learning tasks and literature to achieve the "best of both worlds" (p. 181). These authors cite many studies suggesting that instruction about decoding can be successfully integrated into authentic literacy activities with successful results (Cunningham, Hall, & DeFee, 1991; Eldredge & Butterfield, 1986; Freppon & Dahl, 1991; Gaskins, 1994; Iverson & Tunmer, 1993; Mills, O'Keefe, & Stephens, 1990; Morrow, 1992; Turner, 1992; Uhry & Shepherd, 1990). Others have shown how instruction about strategies can also be successfully integrated into authentic literacy activities, also with successful results (Caverly, Mandeville, & Nicholson, 1995; Randall, 1996). Still others have shown how providing students with authentic, relevant learning experiences promotes greater student engagement in literacy activities (Cousin, Aragon, & Rojas, 1993; Oldfather, 1993). Teachers and other educators using authentic tasks in reading intervention and prevention can provide students with involvement, interest, and purpose in moving toward good reading skills.

In summary, we believe in the Gaskins and Elliot (1991) approach to reading instruction—be flexible. Teachers need to be flexible and creative in their approaches to improving reading skills and motivation to read. In designing classwork, teachers should include opportunities to improve motivation through instruction. They can directly motivate students by reinforcing students' beliefs that they can change negative outcomes. Teachers should also realize that success in reading is itself, motivating when students believe that the tasks are sufficiently challenging and that the success was really earned.

## REFERENCES

Alexander, P. A., & Jetton, T. L. (1996). The role of importance and interest in the processing of text. *Educational Psychology Review, 8,* 89–121.

Alexander, P. A., Kulikowich, J. M., & Jetton, T. L. (1994). The role of subject-matter knowledge and interest in the processing of linear and nonlinear texts. *Review of Educational Research, 64,* 201–252.

Alexander, P. A., Kulikowich, J. M., & Schulze, S. K. (1994). How subject-matter knowledge affects recall and interest. *American Educational Research Journal, 31,* 313–337.

American Psychiatric Association. (1994). *Diagnostic and statistical manual of mental disorders* (4th ed.). Washington, DC: Author.

Ames, C. (1992). Classrooms: Goals, structures, and student motivation. *Journal of Educational Psychology, 84,* 261–271.

Anderman, E. M. (1992, December). *Motivation and cognitive strategy use in reading and writing.* Paper presented at the annual meeting of the National Reading Conference. San Antonio, TX.

Anderson, R. C., Hiebert, E., Scott, J., & Wilkinson, I. (1985). *Becoming a nation of readers: The report of the Commission on Reading.* Washington, DC: National Institute of Education.

Anderson, R. C., Wilkinson, I. A., & Mason, J. M. (1991). A microanalysis of the small-group, guided reading lesson: Effects of an emphasis on global story meaning. *Reading Research Quarterly, 26,* 417–441.

Anrig, G. R., & Lapointe, A. E. (1989). What we know about what students don't know. *Educational Leadership, 47*(3), 4–9.

Asher, S. R., Hymel, S., & Wigfield, A. (1978). Influence of topic interest on children's reading comprehension. *Journal of Reading Behavior, 10,* 35–47.

Baker, L., & Brown, A. L. (1984). Metacognitive skills and reading. In P. D. Pearson (Ed.), *Handbook of reading research* (pp. 353–394). New York: Longman.

Baldwin, R. S., Peleg-Bruckner, Z., & McClintock, A. H. (1985). Effects of topic interest and prior knowledge on reading comprehension. *Reading Research Quarterly, 20,* 497–504.

Bintz, W. P. (1993). Resistant readers in secondary education: Some insights and implications. *Journal of Reading, 36*, 604–615.

Borkowski, J., Weyhing, R., & Carr, M. (1988). Effects of attributional retraining on strategy-based reading comprehension in learning-disabled students. *Journal of Educational Psychology, 80*, 46–53.

Borkowski, J. G., & Krause, A. J. (1985). Metacognition and attributional beliefs. In G. d' Ydewalle (Ed.), *Proceedings of the XXIII International Congress of Psychology Amsterdam.* New York: Elsevier.

Bouffard-Bouchard, T., Parent, S., & Larivée, S. (1991). Influence of self-efficacy on self-regulation and performance among junior and senior high-school age students. *International Journal of Behavioral Development, 14*, 153–164.

Brown, A. L., Bransford, J. D., Ferrara, R. A., & Campione, J. C. (1983). Learning, remembering, and understanding. In P. H. Mussen (Ed.), *Handbook of child psychology: Vol. 3* (pp. 77–166). New York: Wiley.

Brown, R., Pressley, M., Van Meter, P., & Schuder, T. (1996). A quasi-experimental validation of transactional strategies instruction with low-achieving second-grade readers. *Journal of Educational Psychology, 88*, 18–37.

Butkowski, I. S., & Willows, D. M. (1980). Cognitive motivational characteristics of children varying in reading ability: Evidence for learned helplessness in poor readers. *Journal of Educational Psychology, 72*, 408–422.

Butler, R. (1988). Enhancing and undermining intrinsic motivation: The effects of task-involving and ego-involving evaluation on interest and performance. *British Journal of Educational Psychology, 58*, 1–14.

Calfee, R., & Drum, P. (1986). Research on teaching reading. In M. Wittrock (Ed.), *Handbook of research on teaching* (pp. 804–849). New York: Macmillan.

Carr, M., Borkowski, J. G., & Maxwell, S. T. (1991). Motivational components of underachievement. *Developmental Psychology, 27*, 108–118.

Carr, M., & Thompson, H. (1995). *Interest and metacognition as predictors of reading comprehension* (Technical Rep. No. 35). Athens, GA: National Reading Research Center.

Caverly, D. C., Mandeville, T. F., & Nicholson, S. A. (1995). PLAN: A study-reading strategy for informational text. *Journal of Adolescent & Adult Literacy, 39*, 190–199.

Cousin, P. T., Aragon, E., & Rojas, R. (1993). Creating new conversations about literacy: Working with special needs students in a middle-school classroom. *Learning Disability Quarterly, 16*(4), 282–298.

Craig, M. T., & Yore, L. D. (1995). Middle school students' metacognitive knowledge about science reading and science text: An interview study. *Reading Psychology, 16*(2), 160–213.

Craven, R., Marsh, H., & Debus, R. (1991). Effects of internally focused feedback and attributional feedback on enhancement of academic self-concept. *Journal of Educational Psychology, 83*, 17–27.

Cunningham, P., Hall, M., & DeFee (1991). Non-ability grouped, multi-level instruction: A year in a first-grade classroom. *The Reading Teacher, 44*, 566–571.

Dole, J., Brown, K., & Trathen, W. (1996). The effects of strategy instruction on the comprehension performance of at-risk students. *Reading Research Quarterly, 31*, 62–88.

Durkin, D. (1979). What classroom observations reveal about reading comprehension instruction. *Reading Research Quarterly, 14*, 481–538.

Dweck, C., (1986). Motivational processes affecting learning. *American Psychologist, 41*, 1040–1048.

Dweck, C., & Leggett, E. (1988). A social-cognitive approach to motivation and personality. *Psychological Review, 95*, 256–273.

Ehrlich, M.. Kurtz-Costes, B., & Loridant, C. (1993). Cognitive and motivational determinants of reading comprehension in good and poor readers. *Journal of Reading Behavior, 25*, 365–381.

Eldredge, J., & Butterfield, D. (1986). Alternatives to traditional reading instruction. *The Reading Teacher, 40,* 32–47.

Felton, R. H., & Wood, F. B. (1992). A reading level match study of nonword reading skills in readers with varying IQ. *Journal of Learning Disabilities, 25,* 318–326.

Freppon, P., & Dahl, K. (1991). Learning about phonics in a whole language classroom. *Language Arts, 68,* 190–197.

Galloway, D., Leo, E. L., Rogers, C., & Armstrong, D. (1996). Maladaptive motivational style: The role of domain specific task demand in English and mathematics. *British Journal of Educational Psychology, 66,* 197–207.

Gaskins, I. (1994). Creating optimum learning environments: Is membership in the whole language community necessary? In F. Lehr & J. Osborn (Eds.), *Reading, language, and literacy* (pp. 115–130). Hillsdale, NJ: Lawrence Erlbaum Associates.

Gaskins, I., & Elliot, T. (1991). *Implementing cognitive strategy instruction across the school: The Benchmark manual for teachers.* Cambridge, MA: Brookline Books.

Gaskins, I. W., Guthrie, J. T., Satlow, E., Ostertag, J., Six, L., Byrne, J., & Connor, B. (1994). Integrating instruction of science, reading, and writing: Goals, teacher development, and assessment. Special issue: The reading-science learning-writing connection. *Journal of Research in Science Teaching, 31*(9), 1039–1056.

Goodlad, J. (1984). *A place called school.* New York: McGraw-Hill.

Griffith, K. M., DeLoach, L. L., & Labarba, R. C. (1984). The effects of rewarder familiarity and differential reward preference on intrinsic motivation. *Bulletin of the Psychonomic Society, 22,* 313–316.

Guthrie, J. T., Van Meter, P., McCann, A. D., Wigfield, A., Bennett, L., Poundstone, C. C., Rice, M. E., Faibisch, F. M., Hunt, B., & Mitchell, A. M. (1996). *Growth of literacy engagement: Changes in motivation and strategies during concept-oriented reading instruction* (Reading Research Rep. No. 53). Athens, GA: National Reading Research Center.

Hamrick, L., & Harty, H. (1987). Influence of resequencing general science content on the science achievement, attitudes toward science, and interest in science of sixth grade students. *Journal of Research in Science Teaching, 24,* 15–25.

Head, M. H., Readence, J. E., & Buss, R. R. (1989). An examination of summary writing as a measure of reading comprehension. *Reading Research and Instruction, 28,* 1–11.

Hidi, S., & McLaren, J. (1990). The effect of topic and theme interestingness on the production of school expositions. In H. Mandl, E. DeCorte, N. Bennett, & H. F. Friedrich (Eds.), *Learning and instruction: European research in an international context* (pp. 295–308). Oxford: Pergamon.

Hiebert, E. (1994). Becoming literate through authentic tasks: Evidence and adaptations. In R. Ruddell, M. Ruddell, & H. Singer (Eds.), *Theoretical models and processes of reading* (4th ed.). Newark, DE: International Reading Association.

Hiebert, E. H., Winograd, P. N., & Danner, F. W. (1984). Children's attributions for failure and success in different aspects of reading. *Journal of Educational Psychology, 76,* 1139–1148.

Iverson, S., & Tunmer, W. (1993). Phonological processing skills and the Reading Recovery program. *Journal of Educational Psychology, 85,* 112–126.

Johnston, P. H., & Allington, R. (1991). Remediation. In R. Barr, M. L. Kamil, P. Mosenthal, & P. Pearson (Eds.), *Handbook of reading research: Volume II* (pp. 984–1012). White Plains, NY: Longman.

Juel, C. (1988). Learning to read and write: A longitudinal study of 54 children from first through fourth grades. *Journal of Educational Psychology, 80,* 437–447.

Kistner, J. A., Osborne, M., & LeVerrier, L. (1988). Causal attributions of learning-disabled children: Developmental patterns and relation to academic progress. *Journal of Educational Psychology, 80,* 82–89.

Kos, R. (1991). Persistence of reading disabilities: The voices of four middle school students. *American Educational Research Journal, 28,* 875–895.

Lee, N. G., & Neal, J. C. (1992). Reading rescue: Intervention for a student "at promise." *Journal of Reading, 36*(4), 276–282.

Marsh, H. W., Cairnes, L., Relich, J., Barnes, J., & Debus, R. L. (1984). The relationship between dimensions of self-attributions and dimensions of self-concept. *Journal of Educational Psychology, 76,* 3–32.

McCombs, B. L. (1986). The role of self-system in self-regulated learning. *Contemporary Educational Psychology, 11,* 314–332.

McLoyd, V. C. (1979). The effects of extrinsic rewards of differential value on high and low intrinsic interest. *Child Development, 50,* 1010–1019.

Meece, J. L., Blumenfeld, P. C., & Hoyle, R. H. (1988). Students' goal orientations and cognitive engagement in classroom activities. *Journal of Educational Psychology, 80,* 514–523.

Miller, S. D., Adkins, T., & Hooper, M. L. (1993). Why teachers select specific literacy assignments and students' reactions to them. *Journal of Reading and Behavior, 25,* 69–81.

Mills, H., O'Keefe, T., & Stephens, D. (1990). *Looking closer: The role of phonics in a whole language classroom.* Urbana, IL: National Council of Teachers of English.

Mizelle, N. B. (1992). *Middle grade students' motivational processes and use of strategies with expository text.* Unpublished doctoral dissertation, University of Georgia, Athens.

Mizelle, N. B., Hart, L. E., & Carr, M. (1993, April). *Middle grade students' motivational processes and use of learning strategies with expository text.* Paper presented at the Annual Meeting of the American Educational Research Association, Atlanta, GA.

Moniuszko, L. K. (1992). Motivation: Reaching reluctant readers age 14–17. *Journal of Reading, 36*(1), 32–34.

Morrow, L. (1992). The impact of a literature-based program on literacy achievement, use of literature, and attitudes of children from minority backgrounds. *Reading Research Quarterly, 27,* 250–275.

Mullis, I. V. S., Dossey, J. A., Campbell, J. R., Gentile, C. A., O'Sullivan, C., & Latham, A. S. (1994). *Report in brief: NAEP 1992 trends in academic progress.* Washington, DC: National Center for Education Statistics, U.S. Government Printing Office.

National Commission on Excellence in Education. (1984). *A nation at risk: The full account.* Cambridge, MA: U.S.A. Research.

Nicholls, J. (1984). Achievement motivation: Conceptions of ability, subjective experience, task choice, and performance. *Psychological Review, 91,* 328–346.

Nicholls, J. G. (1978). The development of concepts of effort and ability, perceptions of own attainment, and the understanding that difficult tasks require more ability. *Child Development, 49,* 800–814.

Nicholls, J. G. (1979). Development of perception of own attainment and causal attributions for success and failure in reading. *Journal of Educational Psychology, 71,* 94–99.

Nolen, S. B. (1988). Reasons for studying: Motivational orientations and study strategies. *Cognition and Instruction, 5,* 269–287.

Nolen, S. B., & Haladyna, T. M. (1990). Motivation and studying in high school science. *Journal of Research in Science Teaching, 27,* 115–126.

O'Flahaven, J. O., Gambrell, L. B., Guthrie, J., Stahl, S., Baumann, J. F., & Alvermann, D. E. (1992). Poll results guide activities of research center. *Reading Today, 10*(1), 12.

Oldfather, P., & McLaughlin, H. J. (1993). Gaining and losing voice: A longitudinal study of students' continuing impulse to learn across elementary and middle level contexts. *Research in Middle Level Education, 17,* 1–25.

Olshavsky, J. E. (1977). Reading as problem solving: An investigation of strategies. *Reading Research Quarterly, 12,* 654–674.

Palincsar, A., & Perry, N. (1995). Developmental, cognitive, and sociocultural perspectives on assessing and instructing reading. *School Psychology Review, 24,* 331–344.

Paris, S. G. (1988, April). *Fusing skill and will in children's learning and schooling.* Paper presented at the Annual Meeting of the American Educational Research Association, New Orleans, LA.

Paris, S. G., Lipson, M. Y., & Wixson, K. K. (1983). Becoming a strategic reader. *Contemporary Educational Psychology, 8*, 293–316.

Paris, S. G., & Oka, E. R. (1986). Children's reading strategies, metacognition, and motivation. *Developmental Review, 6*, 25–56.

Paris, S. G., & Winograd, P. (1990). Promoting metacognition and motivation of exceptional children. *Remedial and Special Education, 11*, 7–15.

Pintrich, P. R., & DeGroot, E. V. (1990). Motivational and self-regulated learning components of classroom academic performance. *Journal of Educational Psychology, 82*, 33–40.

Pope, C., & Beal, C. (1994). Building pathways for at-risk students and their teachers. *Voices From the Middle, 1*(2), 3–10.

Pressley, M., El-Denary, P. B., Marks, M. B., Brown, R., & Stein, S. (1992). Good strategy instruction is motivating and interesting. In K. A. Renninger, S. Hidi, & A. Krapp (Eds.), *The role of interest in learning and development* (pp. 333–358). Hillsdale, NJ: Lawrence Erlbaum Associates.

Randall, S. N. (1996). Information charts: A strategy for organizing student research. *Journal of Adolescent & Adult Literacy, 39*(7), 536–543.

Ross, S., Smith, L., Casey, J., & Slavin, R. (1995). Increasing the academic success of disadvantaged children: An examination of alternative early intervention programs. *American Educational Research Journal, 32*, 773–800.

Ryckman, D. B., & Mizokawa, D. T. (1991). Cross-situation variability of attributions for success and failure: A cross-sectional study. *Journal of Adolescent Research, 6*, 197–211.

Salomon, G. (1984). Television is "easy" and print is "tough": The differential investment of mental effort in learning as a function of perceptions and attributions. *Journal of Educational Psychology, 76*, 647–658.

Satz, P., Taylor, G., Friel, J., & Fletcher, J. (1978). Some developmental and predictive precursors of reading disabilities: A six year follow-up. In A. Benton & D. Pearl (Eds.), *Dyslexia: An appraisal of current knowledge* (pp. 313–348). New York: Oxford University Press.

Schiefele, U. (1991). Interest, learning, and motivation. *Educational Psychologist, 26*, 299–323.

Schiefele, U. (1992). Topic interest and levels of text comprehension. In K. A. Renninger, S. Hidi, & A. Krapp (Eds.), *The role of interest in learning and development* (pp. 151–182). Hillsdale, NJ: Lawrence Erlbaum Associates.

Schneider, W. (1993). Acquiring expertise: Determinants of exceptional performance. In K. A. Heller, F. J. Monks, & A. H. Passow (Eds.), *International handbook of research and development of giftedness and talent* (pp. 311–324). New York: Pergamon.

Schunk, D. H. (1983). Ability versus effort attributional feedback: Differential effects on self-efficacy and achievement. *Journal of Educational Psychology, 75*, 848–856.

Schunk, D. H., (1984). Self-efficacy perspective on achievement behavior. *Educational Psychologist, 19*, 48–58.

Schunk, D. H. (1989). Self-efficacy and cognitive achievement: Implications for students with learning problems. *Journal of Learning Disabilities, 22*, 14–22.

Schunk, D. H., & Rice, J. M. (1985). Verbalization of comprehension strategies: Effects on children's achievement outcomes. *Human Learning: Journal of Practical Research & Applications, 4*(1), 1–10.

Schunk, D. H., & Rice, J. M. (1987). Enhancing comprehension skill and self-efficacy with strategy value information. *Journal of Reading Behavior, 19*, 285–302.

Schunk, D. H., & Rice, J. M. (1991). Learning goals and progress feedback during reading comprehension instruction. *Journal of Reading Behavior, 23*, 351–364.

Shell, D. F., Colvin, C., & Bruning, R. H. (1995). Self-efficacy, attribution, and outcome expectancy mechanisms in reading and writing achievement: Grade-level and achievement-level differences. *Journal of Educational Psychology, 87*, 386–398.

Short, E., & Ryan, E. (1984). Metacognitive differences between skilled and less skilled readers: Remediating deficits through story grammar and attribution training. *Journal of Educational Psychology, 76*, 225–235.

Slater, W. H., & Graves, M. F. (1989). Research on expository text: Implications for teachers. In K. D. Muth (Ed.), *Children's comprehension of text* (pp. 140–166). Newark, DE: International Reading Association.

Stahl, S., McKenna, M., & Pugnucco, J. (1994). The effects of whole-language instruction: An update and a reappraisal. *Educational Psychologist, 29*, 175–185.

Stanovich, K. (1984). Matthew effects in reading: Some consequences of individual differences in the acquisition of literacy. *Reading Research Quarterly, 21*, 360–407.

Stanovich, K. (1994). Constructivism in reading education. *Journal of Special Education, 28*, 259–274.

Stewart, R. A., Paradis, E. E., Ross, B. D., & Lewis, M. J. (1996). Student voices: What works in literature-based development reading. *Journal of Adolescent and Adul Literacy, 39*, 468–478.

Tobias, S. (1994). Interest, prior knowledge, and learning. *Review of Educational Research, 64*, 37–54.

Townsend, M. A. R., & Townsend, J. E. (1990). Reading comprehension of high- and low-interest reading material among Maori, Pakeha and Pacific Island children. *New Zealand Journal of Educational Studies, 25*, 141–153.

Turner, J. (1992, December). *A motivational perspective on literacy instruction.* Paper presented at the annual meeting of the National Reading Conference, San Antonio, TX.

Turner, J. (1995). The influence of classroom contexts on young children's motivation for literacy. *Reading Research Quarterly, 30*, 410–441.

Uhry, J., & Shepherd, M. (1990). Segmentational spelling instruction as a part of a first-grade reading program: Effects on several measures of reading. *Reading Research Quarterly, 28*, 218–233.

Wagner, D. A., Spratt, J. E., Gal, I., & Paris, S. G. (1989). Reading and believing: Beliefs, attributions, and reading achievement in Moroccan school children. *Journal of Educational Psychology, 81*(3), 283–293.

Weiner, B. (1985). An attributional theory of achievement motivation and emotion. *Psychological Review, 92*, 548–573.

Wigfield, A., & Ashcr, S. R. (1984). Social and motivation influences on reading. In D. Pearson (Ed.), *Handbook of reading research* (pp. 423–452). New York: Longman.

Williams, J. E. (1994). Gender differences in high school students' efficacy-expectation/performance discrepancies across four subject matter domains. *Psychology in the Schools, 31*, 232–237.

# PART TWO

# HOW STUDENTS LEARN CONTENT KNOWLEDGE

As you read these chapters you will see several influences on students' abilities to gather information from text. Student characteristics constitute one thing that affects students' ability to gather information from text. Specifically, students' interpretations of text can be influenced by their epistemological beliefs and prior knowledge. A belief that knowledge is simple, unchanging, and provided by authority will discourage evaluation of what is read. Such a belief combined with nonscientific understanding of a complex phenomenon, such as the concept of force, results in the development of nonscientific conceptions that are very difficult to alter. Students' understanding of text is also directly related to their knowledge and skill, for example, their vocabulary. Children who have a poor vocabulary read less as a result of their poor reading skills and poor motivation and, therefore, get less from available texts. Thus, teachers need to assess and consider the knowledge and beliefs students bring with them to the classroom.

The format, content, and availability of texts can also influence students' interpretations of what they read and their ability to learn from text. As you read, you will find that coherent and cohesive texts result in a better global understanding of a topic. In addition, the use of multiple texts, particularly texts that provide different information or views of a topic, can allow students to critically evaluate what they are reading. The use of analogies also provides students with opportunities to make sense out of what they are reading. Thus, the texts students read should support a critical analysis of a topic rather than present simple unrelated facts.

The following chapters also discuss several approaches to improving students' ability to learn from text. These approaches are specifically aimed at changing epistemological beliefs and changing or avoiding nonscientific conceptions. One approach is to use multiple text sources such as different accounts of a historical event or fictional accounts. The use of multiple text sources allows children to see that there are many ways to look at a topic. Another approach is to use analogies, which provide opportunities for children to learn scientific explanations of such subjects as photosynthesis, which might ordinarily be thought of in nonscientific ways. The use of refutable texts that present opposing but plausible explanations also encourages students to critically evaluate what they are reading. A common theme here is that students need to have multiple ways to approach the information they must learn.

These chapters also caution the reader in several instances. For example, teachers need to be aware that not every text is useful for altering nonscientific ideas and providing children with multiple perspectives on a topic. Some texts do more harm than good. For example, the use of fiction may motivate children to read about historical events, but these fictional accounts may provide children with inaccurate information. Related to this, teachers must critically evaluate the analogies they use to instruct children. Although analogies can be useful for instruction, a poorly chosen analogy can be more trouble than it is worth. Simply providing students with multiple texts or analogies is not enough. Teachers must be actively involved in students' interpretations of what they read.

# Four Questions About Vocabulary Knowledge and Reading and Some Answers

Steven A. Stahl
*The University of Georgia*

Since the time of Edward L. Thorndike (1917), about the time that scientific methodology was first applied to the study of human thought, psychologists and educators have studied people's knowledge of word meanings and how they relate to other aspects of human thought. Perhaps much of this interest derives from the centrality of vocabulary knowledge in so many aspects of mental behaviors. Vocabulary knowledge is related to reading comprehension, intelligence, content area knowledge, and reasoning. Much of the research conducted since Thorndike's time has centered around four questions:

- What is the relationship between vocabulary knowledge and reading comprehension?
- How many words do people know?
- What does it mean to "know" a word?
- How do people learn words from context?

Our answers to these questions will help us understand what kind of vocabulary instruction we should have if we want to improve students' comprehension.

## WHAT IS THE RELATIONSHIP BETWEEN VOCABULARY KNOWLEDGE AND READING COMPREHENSION?

The importance of vocabulary knowledge for reading comprehension would seem self-evident to anyone who has ever read a jargon-filled text then left scratching his or her head. For example, here are three sentences from an early draft of a paper written by the author:

> The findings of our study also reveal that there is nothing especially difficult about setting up a mental representation for a new lexical item as presumably children would have to do for unknown words. For example, for localist versions of connectionist viewpoints, it seems probable that one would first have to create a new lexical node before orthographic, phonological, and semantic information could become connected with it. Presumably, if instantiating a mental representation for a new lexical item was particularly difficult, we would expect to see that the development of unknown words was slower than for partial knowledge words because partial knowledge words already have an existing lexical node with corresponding orthographic and phonological features but few semantic features.[1]

To understand this paragraph, a reader must know the meanings of words such as "localist," "connectionist," "lexical," "node," "instantiating," and so on. Without that knowledge, this paragraph would be gibberish. One of the oldest findings in educational research is the strong relationship between vocabulary knowledge and reading comprehension. Evidence from correlational studies, readability research, and experimental studies all reflects strong and reliable relationships between the difficulty in a text and text comprehension (see Anderson & Freebody, 1981; Graves, 1986, for review).

But why is there such a relationship? The most obvious notion is that knowing word meanings enables or causes a person to comprehend a text containing those words. In this view, a person who knows the words can comprehend the text, regardless of any other factors. Anderson and Freebody referred to this as the *instrumentalist hypothesis*, which is shown in the following diagram:

**Vocabulary Knowledge→Reading Comprehension**

It is possible, however, to know all the words in a passage and still not make any sense of it. Consider the following passage taken from a Melbourne, Australia, newspaper:

> A hair raising century by Australian opener Graeme Wood on Friday set England back on its heels in the third test at the Melbourne Cricket Ground. Unfortunately, living desperately cost the Australians the match. Wood was caught out of his crease on the first over after lunch. Within ten more overs, the Australians were dismissed. Four were dismissed by dangerous running between creases. Two were dismissed when the English bowlers lifted the

---

[1]This was taken from a draft version of an article. I am withholding the reference out of embarrassment.

bails from the batsmen's wickets. The three remaining batsmen were caught by English fieldsmen. One was caught as he tried for a six. When the innings were complete, the Australians had fallen short of the runs scored by the English.

Even though we know words like "crease," "six," "century," and so on, this passage makes no sense unless we know about the sport of cricket. Similarly, the words in the first passage are jargon from cognitive psychology and make no sense unless you understand the grander theories being discussed. Anderson and Freebody (1981) also suggested a *knowledge hypothesis,* which suggests that word meanings themselves do not cause people to understand texts. Rather, our knowledge of words reflects our knowledge of the topic. It is this knowledge of the topic that helps us comprehend. Thus, words like "century" have specific meanings when we are talking about cricket, and it is these meanings that help us understand the text. The knowledge hypothesis states that vocabulary knowledge is related to topic knowledge, which, in turn is related to reading comprehension, as shown in this diagram:

**Vocabulary Knowledge→Topic Knowledge→Reading Comprehension**

Vocabulary knowledge is also strongly related to intelligence. In fact, Louis Terman (1916) said that if he could test only one factor to determine a person's IQ, he would use a vocabulary test. Because intelligence is also related to reading comprehension, it could be that vocabulary tests are actually measuring children's intelligence, which in turn is affecting their ability to read texts, as in the *general ability hypothesis* pictured in this diagram:

**Vocabulary Knowledge→General Ability→Reading Comprehension**

Which of these hypotheses are true? Well, in some way, all of them are. They all tell us something about vocabulary and comprehension. Vocabulary knowledge does directly affect comprehension because we do have evidence that teaching word meanings can improve comprehension. Vocabulary knowledge is certainly related to topic knowledge, as should be evident from the article about cricket. Furthermore, vocabulary knowledge is related to intelligence, although the nature of that relationship is far from clear.

For a teacher, though, the first hypothesis, that vocabulary knowledge directly affects comprehension is the most important because it suggests that teaching word meanings will improve a child's comprehension. Stahl and Fairbanks (1986) found that vocabulary instruction does directly improve comprehension, thus also validating the instrumentalist hypothesis. However, they found, further, that not all approaches to teaching word meanings will improve comprehension. Before reviewing approaches to the teaching of word meanings, though, it would be useful to discuss three other questions that illuminate instructional issues.

## HOW MANY WORDS DO PEOPLE KNOW?

At first it would seem that this question is esoteric. After all, why should we care how many words people know when our concern is to teach the words they are finding in the texts they might be reading? This question, however, is at the core of many other questions. If an average high school senior knows 45,000 different words, as in one estimate (Nagy & Anderson, 1984), then it might be impossible to teach someone all the words they need to know through direct instruction. If the estimate is closer to 17,000, as other authors have suggested (D'Anna, Zechmeister, & Hall, 1991), or even 5,000 (Hirsh & Nation, 1992), then direct teaching might play a more important role. This is especially true for speakers of other languages who are learning English.

There are two ways of looking at the question of how many words people know: looking at texts that people read and testing people. Although estimates vary widely as to how many total words there are in English (unabridged dictionaries can have between 250,000 and 500,000 entries, depending on what they allow as entries), we have good data as to the number of words in books used by elementary and secondary students. Our best estimate, taken from Nagy and Anderson (1984), is that there are roughly 88,700 word families used in books up to 12th grade. A *word family* is defined by Nagy and Anderson as groups of words chosen so that "an individual knowing one of the words (in the family) could guess or infer the meaning of the other when encountering it in context while reading"(p. 307) such as "add" and "addition," "additive," "adding," and so on.

About half of the texts we read consists of the 107 most common words. Another 5,000 words account for the next 45%, so that 95% of the texts we read consists of about 5,100 different words (Adams, 1990). The rest of the texts we read consists of the remaining 83,000 or so words. If this is so, then why do we not just teach the 5,100 most common words and not worry about the relatively rare words? The problem is that these rare words are just the words that carry most of the content of the texts. How much would one understand in a biology text dealing with the discovery of penicillin without such rare words as "penicillin," "antibiotic," "bacterium," and so on? Many, but not all, of the uncommon words have to do with the particular topic of the text. This is especially true in the content areas. Words such as "abiotic," "ecosystem," and "niche" are relatively uncommon, but also very useful.

It is useful to look at the number of words in texts students read, but this does not tell us how many words an average student knows. We do know that this number is considerably less than 88,700, but it is not clear how much less.

Early attempts varied wildly, from 17,000 to more than 200,000 words estimated as known by university undergraduates, or from 2,562 to 26,000 words estimated as known by first graders (Lorge & Chall, 1963). There are two reasons for these wildly differing estimates: different sized dictionaries used for sampling and different definitions of what a "word" is.

Even with a low estimate of 17,000 words, a researcher cannot simply ask students to define every word they supposedly should know. Even a test of 100 words is likely to be so fatiguing that the results would be off. Thus every study that estimates the number of words known uses a sample. Usually this sample comes from a dictionary, possibly the fifth word from every 40th page.

The differing estimates of vocabulary knowledge are crucial to making decisions about vocabulary instruction. Because 300–400 words per year can reasonably be taught through direct instruction,[2] the figure accepted is important in determining how to plan for vocabulary growth. If a teacher accepts Nagy and Anderson's (1984) estimate that there are 88,700 word types in English, and that students learn about half of them, this suggests that the average child learns about 3,000 words each year. (There is other independent evidence that, indeed, children do learn about 3,000 new words per year [White, Graves, & Slater, 1990].) Most of these words must come from context because that is a greater number of words than one can teach. However, if you accept a lower figure, such as the 17,000 words suggested by D'Anna et al. (1991), then it may be possible to teach all the words that a person needs to learn. This distinction is especially important in teaching English as a second language (Gouldman, Nation, & Read, 1990).

If we take a higher estimate for the number of words that children learn each year, then will contextual reading be enough for children to learn 3,000 words per year? This is a monumental task, about 8 words a day, every day, or twice that many if word learning occurs only on school days. William Nagy and his colleagues (Nagy, Anderson, & Herman, 1987; Nagy, Herman, & Anderson, 1985; Herman, Anderson, Pearson, & Nagy, 1987) have calculated that much of this annual growth in reading can come from incidental learning of word meanings from a reasonable amount of contextual reading. If, for example, we assume that a fifth-grade child reads for an hour per day (in and out of school) at a rate of 150 words per minute (a conservative estimate; see Harris & Sipay, 1990), 5 days a week, then the child will have encountered 2,250,000 words in the course of all this reading. If 2% to 5% of those words are unknown, then the child will have encountered from 45,000 to 112,500 unknown words. From other research, we know that children will learn between 5% and 10% of previously unknown words from a single reading (Nagy & Herman, 1987). This would account for 2,250 to 11,000 new words

---

[2]This is my guess, but it is also accepted by others, including Nagy and Herman (1987).

learned from context each year. Making all the estimates as conservative as possible, the 2,250 new words is close enough to 3,000 to suggest that context can be a powerful influence on students' vocabulary growth. This suggests that one of the most powerful things we can do to increase children's vocabulary is to encourage them to read as widely as possible.

However, what if we accept the lower estimate of 1,000 words per year? Although our estimates show that children usually can be taught 300 to 400 words per year (8 to 10 words per week, 40 weeks a year), with more intensive vocabulary instruction this could be doubled. Thus, we might be able to teach intensively nearly all the words an average child learns in a year through direct instruction.

What should we do? It would be hard to argue against increasing the amount of reading that children do. Wide reading not only improves children's vocabulary knowledge, but also has general effects on children's overall intellectual growth (Cunningham & Stanovich, 1991). It would also be hard to argue against providing direct vocabulary instruction. As discussed more fully later, teaching word meanings can improve children's comprehension (Stahl & Fairbanks, 1986).

## Differences in Word Knowledge

Either set of estimates to determine children's knowledge of word meaning is only an average. Averages can hide some fairly large differences in word learning. One study estimated that fifth graders learned from 1,000 to nearly 5,000 new word meanings per year (White et al., 1990). This is a fairly large spread, with the most able learners learning five times as many new word meanings as the less able learners.

One explanation for this is that good readers are more able to derive word meanings from context than poorer readers (Sternberg & Powell, 1983). But this does not seem to be the case. Studies that had students derive a word's meaning from context have found strong differences between students of high and low verbal ability (Elshout-Mohr & van Daalens-Kapteijns, 1987; McKeown, 1985). However, studies that examined incidental learning from context have failed to find such effects (Nagy et al., 1987; Schefelbine, 1990, Stahl, 1989, but see also Stanley & Ginther, 1991, who did find such differences).

The differences may lie in the tasks rather than in actual ability differences. Deriving a definition involves specific verbal skills independent of incidental learning of information from context (Snow, 1990). This task may be more susceptible to ability differences than the multiple-choice tests used in the incidental learning studies. Thus, the ability differences may affect the ability to do the criterion tasks in these studies rather than in the learning from context.

If there are ability differences in learning from context, then training children to be better at using context would also increase vocabulary. Kuhn and Stahl (in press) reviewed studies designed to teach students to be more efficient at learning from context. Failing to find evidence that children could be taught to improve their ability to derive words from context, they suggested that the differences in vocabulary growth between high- and low-ability children might be due to differences in the amount that children read rather than differences in any ability to learn from context.

Accepting the lack of differences due to ability would mean that able and less able readers acquire word meanings at roughly the same rate. Because poor readers tend to read less than better readers, the gap between good and poor readers, in absolute numbers of words read, becomes progressively greater as the child progresses through school. This is part of the *Matthew effect* discussed by Keith Stanovich (1986), who suggested that "the rich get richer and the poor get poorer" in vocabulary and other aspects of reading. That is, children who are good readers become better readers because they read more and also more challenging texts, but poor readers get relatively worse because they read less and also less challenging texts. Indeed, researchers have found large differences in the amount of free reading that good and poor readers do in and out of the school (Anderson, Wilson, & Fielding 1988). In addition, the amount of reading that children do is directly related to their knowledge of word meanings, even after accounting for intelligence (Cunningham & Stanovich, 1991). This research as a whole suggests that the differences in children's word knowledge may be due largely to differences in the amount of text to which they are exposed.

One obvious way, then, to increase the number of words children know is to increase the amount of text to which they are exposed. But the basic contradiction of the Matthew effect is that children who have difficulties in reading cannot make sense of the more challenging texts needed for growth in vocabulary.

One way of providing that exposure to new vocabulary might be in reading to children. Several studies have found that children can learn words as efficiently from having stories read to them as they can from reading stories themselves. For example, Stahl, Richek, and Vandevier (1991) found that sixth graders learned about 7% of word meanings presumed unknown from a single listening. This effect was especially pronounced among children who were lower in initial word knowledge. Although word meanings can and should be learned through listening to stories, listening can only supplement and not supplant essential practice in reading.

**Additional Problems**

Not only do poorer readers read less than good readers, but they face an additional handicap when they do read. Often content area texts add cues to a word's meaning through a parenthetical definition. However, because of the large gaps in their vocabulary, some poorer readers are unable to take advantage of these aids. For example, Schefelbine (1990) gave high- and low-vocabulary students a passage containing the sentence "Gauchos, the cowhands of South America, learned to chase the birds on cow ponies." The target word here was "gaucho," but several of the low-vocabulary students had trouble with "cowhands" as well. Misinterpreting "cowhand" as the "front legs of a cow," as one of Schefelbine's subjects did, would suggest that "gaucho" meant the same, disrupting comprehension.

Usually the text is not as "considerate" and does not provide an explicit definition (Konopak, 1988). In either case, the child with a low vocabulary faces an additional handicap. Beyond the point where such a child can compensate for not knowing a word, each additional word that is not understood, or partially or inflexibly understood, adds to the child's misunderstandings, leading the child farther and farther from the author's intended meaning (Stahl, 1991).

## WHAT DOES IT MEAN TO "KNOW" A WORD?

A question complementary to that of how many words does a person know is this one: What does it mean to "know" a word? There are a number of ways of answering this question. One way is to talk about degrees of knowledge, using Dale and O'Rourke's (1986) scale:

1. I never saw it before.
2. I've heard of it, but I don't know what it means.
3. I recognize it in context—it has something to do with . . .
4. I know it (p. 3).

Curtis (1987) found that different degrees of familiarity were necessary in responding to different vocabulary tasks. Most interestingly, only a general knowledge of the word's meaning was needed for a correct response to multiple-choice questions. Durso and Shore (1991) examined more closely the kinds of information possessed for words at each of these levels of word meaning. They found that adults possessed a surprising amount of information about both partially known and reportedly unknown words. For example, participants could choose sentences that did not violate the general semantic constraints or selectional restrictions of both partial knowledge and unknown words at a level above chance. They could also discriminate between a correct synonym and an incorrect one for partial knowledge and unknown words. This suggests that their subjects had some knowledge even of words that they reported as unknown, and that this knowledge could be used to make gross discriminations involving a word's meaning.

In addition, partially known words were found to have the advantage over unknown words. Specifically, even though subjects could not define a word fully, they could choose, at a level better than chance, between a sentence that maintained specific semantic constraints and one that did not. Furthermore, for partially known words, people were able to identify whether the words were used correctly in isolated sentences (rather than in contrasting sentences). Subjects were unable to perform either of these tasks for unknown words. Thus, implicit knowledge that people had about the meanings of unknown words was very fragile and easily disrupted by more difficult contrasts. Moreover, vocabulary instruction that provided adults with dictionary definitions appeared to particularly benefit unknown words more than partially known words (Shore & Durso, 1990).

But what is a "full and flexible knowledge of its [a word's] meaning"? The author has argued that a word's meaning contains at least two comple-mentary types of knowledge about a word: definitional knowledge and contextual knowledge (Stahl & Fairbanks, 1986; Stahl, 1991).

*Definitional knowledge* is knowledge of the logical relationships into which a word enters, such as the category or class to which the word belongs (e.g., synonyms, antonyms, etc.). This is information similar to that included in a dictionary definition. There is a form for a definition, dating back to Aristotle, in which the definition first identifies the class to which the word belongs, and then how that word differs from other members of its class. For example, *The Random House Dictionary* (1978) defines a "fissure" as "a narrow opening [class] produced by cleavage [differentiation]." There is a great deal of research showing that children cannot use conventional definitions to learn words (Scott & Nagy, 1997). Perhaps the best illustration showing the weaknesses of definitions comes from sentences children write after reading definitions. For example, note the definition and sentences for the word "redress":

1. set right; repair, remedy; *when King Arthur tried to redress wrongs in his kingdom.*

One student wrote:

The *redress* for getting well (when) you're sick is to stay in bed (Miller & Gildea, 1987).

Another student wrote for "erode" meaning "to eat out":

My family *erodes* often. (Nist, personal communication)

Such subtle misunderstandings of word meanings from definitions, al-though humorous to the native speaker, suggest that a word's meaning is not captured fully in a description of its logical relationships to other words, as in the Aristotelean dictionary definition. Instead, a word's meaning needs to be contextualized so that the learner can see how it relates to other words in conventional spoken or written context.

As an example of the need for more than definitional knowledge, consider the verb "smoke." The definition might be something like "to inhale and puff the smoke of (a cigarette, etc.)" (*The Random House Dictionary*, 1978). However, the verb "smoke" describes distinctly different actions in these sentences:

1. He smoked a cigarette.
2. The psychologist smoked his pipe.
3. The hippie smoked a marijuana cigarette.
4. The 13-year-old smoked his first cigarette.

These word usages all fit under the general definition, but the actions vary from a typical smoking action in 1 to a puffing in 2 to a deeper and longer inhaling in 3 to an inhaling followed by coughing and choking in 4. In addition, there are many impermissible contexts for "smoke." Although a person could "smoke" a burning tire, that is inhale its fumes, ordinarily we would not do that. The proper verb in that sentence might be to "burn" or some other synonym for cause to burn rather than "smoke."

These contexts are different knowledge environments, as well. Thus, to understand 4 we need to know that 13-year-olds are generally novices at smoking, and that smoking can make one cough, if one is not used to it. Similarly, to understand the words in the jargon-laden paragraph at the beginning of this chapter, a person needs to understand something about the domain of cognitive psychology and probably a bit about lexical semantics. Some words are embedded in a single knowledge domain, such as "dharma" or "jib." Most words can be used in multiple domains, but have distinct meanings within those domains. Anderson and Nagy (1991) have argued that all words are polysemous, containing groups of related meanings rather than a single meaning. These meanings have a family resemblance to each other, as in the "smoke" example earlier, but vary within contexts.

Thus, to know a word, we not only need to know the definition of the word, but we also need to understand how that word's meaning adapts to different contexts. A full and flexible knowledge of a word involves an understanding of the core meaning of a word and how it changes in different contexts. This involves exposure to the word in multiple contexts, preferably from different perspectives. Nitsch (1978) taught a set of artificial words to college students under two conditions. In the first condition, words were taught in a single context or knowledge domain. In the second condition, words were taught in multiple contexts. Subjects who received repetitions of the single context were significantly better at understanding the word in the same context, but subjects who learned the words in multiple contexts were better at understanding the words in novel contexts and better overall. Similarly, children exposed to words in multiple contexts, even without instruction, can be presumed to learn more about those words than students who see a word in a single context (Stahl, 1991).

## HOW DO PEOPLE LEARN WORDS FROM CONTEXT?

What happens when someone sees a word for the first time in a book? Consider the following paragraph, from *The Atlantic Monthly*:

> America's permanent election campaign, together with other aspects of American electoral politics, has one crucial consequence, little noticed but vitally important for the functioning of American democracy. Quite simply, the American electoral system places politicians in a highly vulnerable position. Individually and collectively they are more vulnerable, more of the time, to the *vicissitudes* of electoral politics than are the politicians of any other democratic country. Because they are more vulnerable, they devote more of their time to electioneering, and their conduct in office is more continuously governed by electoral considerations. (King, 1997, p. 42; emphasis added)

Although I had seen the word "vicissitudes" before, I did not know its meaning. From the context, one can get a general picture of what it means, something like "serendipitous changes" (my *Random House Dictionary* (1978) says "unexpected changing circumstances, as of fortune," so I was fairly accurate in my guess.)

Stahl (1991) used a connectionist model to discuss the accretion of information about a word through repeated exposures to that word's meaning in context. In Stahl's model, when a word is encountered for the first time, information about its orthography is connected to information from the context, so that after one exposure a person may have a general sense of the context in which it appeared (It has something to do with . . ."), or a memory of the specific context ("I remember seeing it in an automobile manual"), but not a generalizable sense of the meaning of the word. With repeated exposures, some nodes become strengthened as that information is found in repeated contexts, and become the way that the word is "defined." Other information found associated with the word in few contexts may recede. In a connectionist model, as information is understood, it is represented in memory through links to other information already stored.

Consider the word "vicissitudes" in the earlier context. In Stahl's (1991) model, the concept of "vicissitudes" will be linked to other concepts in the context, such as "politicians," "electorial politics," and the like, or possibly to the whole scenario presented. Because of the syntax, we know that "vicissitudes" does not directly mean "politics," but is a characteristic of politics. As the word is encountered repeatedly, it will be associated with other concepts, possibly "romance" or "getting published in academic journals," as a characteristic. (Or as one of my students' mothers told her repeatedly while growing up, "Beware the vicissitudes of life.") These become the stronger components of the concept, such as might be represented in a dictionary definition (McKeown, 1991). If the links to other concepts are not repeated, they may recede in importance. Given the core meaning of the word "vicissitudes," the fact that the subject of the essay is politics is incidental and likely would be forgotten with repeated exposures.

Under a connectionist model, word meaning would grow at a relatively constant rate, dependent on the features of the context. Thus, people would show as much absolute gain in word knowledge from an unknown word as they would from a word of which they have some partial knowledge, all other things being equal. (As we discuss later, all other things are rarely equal.) This was found by Schwanenflugel, Stahl, and McFalls (1997), who examined learning from context at different levels of word knowledge: partial word knowledge in which the students reported some general knowledge about the word and no knowledge in which students could not provide any information about the word. These researchers found that students made the same amount of growth in word knowledge from a single reading, whether they began by knowing something about a word or not. Thus, vocabulary knowledge seems to grow gradually, moving from the first meaningful exposure to a word to a full and flexible knowledge of its meaning.

An alternative to this view comes from observations of young children's fast mapping of concepts (Heibeck & Markman, 1987; Rice, Buhr, & Nemeth, 1990). Children as young as 2 years of age have been found to show appreciable learning about a concept from a single exposure. They appear to acquire superordinate information, (i.e., other category information) very quickly, and later gradually add features to their knowledge representation. Fast mapping has been demonstrated with young children (Heibeck & Markman, 1987) and children with learning problems (Rice, et al., 1990). If fast mapping is a general process, then children might be found to learn more information about unknown words than partially known words. In the case of "vicissitudes" the fast mapping would probably associate the new concept with "something characteristic of politics." This information may be enough for understanding a subsequent encounter with the word (Graves & Prenn, 1986), or even enough to answer a multiple choice question (Curtis, 1987).

## DIRECT INSTRUCTION OF WORD MEANINGS

What does this all mean for instruction? First, it suggests that if poor readers are to become good readers, they must be encouraged, cajoled, or browbeaten to read more text that contains varied and challenging vocabulary (Chall,

Jacobs, & Baldwin, 1990). Furthermore, texts designed for such readers should be considerate, providing contexts that help children learn the word meanings (Konopak, 1988). Second, direct instruction may play a more important role for such children, and direct instruction of vocabulary should be aimed toward the poorer reader in the regular class as well as in the clinic. Recall the estimate of White et al. (1990) that children learn between 1,000 and 5,000 new word meanings each year. The 300–400 new word meanings that can be taught through direct instruction can be a significant percentage of the 1,000, so that vocabulary instruction can have the greatest impact on children who are not learning as many word meanings through wide reading.

Because vocabulary instruction is an ongoing process, a teacher must be able to vary the delivery of that instruction. This involves using a variety of different approaches during the school year. Our developing model of effective vocabulary instruction suggests vocabulary instruction that (a) includes both definitional and contextual information about each word's meaning, (b) involves children more actively in word learning, and (c) provides multiple exposures to meaningful information about the word. These will be discussed below.

***Include Both Definitional and Contextual Information.*** In spite of the prevalence of the practice, using dictionaries or glossaries alone to learn word meanings does not seem to be an effective approach to learning words. Stahl and Fairbanks (1986) found that approaches providing only definitional information did not significantly affect children's reading comprehension. In contrast, methods that provided both definitional and contextual information did significantly improve comprehension. Such methods might involve providing a definition for a word and discussing how the word's definition fits into two or more sentences containing that word (Stahl, 1983), having children write and discuss several sentences for each new word, semantic mapping and possible sentences (discussed later), and so on.

***Involve Children in Actively Processing New Word Meanings.*** A second principle of effective vocabulary instruction relates to how active students are at constructing links between new information and information they already know. Children remember more information when they are performing cognitive operations on that information (Craik & Tulving, 1975). Such operations might include relating it to known information, transforming it into their own words, generating examples, nonexamples, antonyms, synonyms, and the like. Stahl and Fairbanks (1986) developed a scale of processing that is useful for evaluating vocabulary instructional programs.

*Association processing* involves the rote memorization of an association between a word and its meaning or between a word and a single context.

*Comprehension processing* has the child demonstrating comprehension of an association by reading it in a sentence or by doing something with the definitional information, such as finding an antonym, classifying words, and so forth.

*Generative processing* has the child taking the information learned and creating a new product or a novel response to the word such as creating a sentence that fully expresses the word's meaning, restating a definition in one's own words, and so on. This product could be written or oral.

Stahl and Fairbanks (1986) found that generative processing did lead to better retention of word meanings, but the effects on comprehension were not as clear. Generative processing led to improvements in comprehension only when children were given multiple exposures to different information about word meanings.

One series of studies that examined the effects of generative processing with multiple exposures was that by Beck and her colleagues (Beck, Perfetti, & McKeown, 1982; McKeown, Beck, Omanson, & Perfetti, 1983; McKeown, Beck, Omanson, & Pople, 1985). Lessons in the Beck et al. (1982) study, for example, were conducted in a 5-day cycle. On the first day, words are defined. Then, students discussed how each word is used in context. This discussion could take a number of different forms, including discussion of examples and nonexamples, pantomimes, or having students say "Yea" if the word is used correctly in a sentence or "Boo" if it is not. On the second day, after a review of the definitions, students might work on log sheets, completing sentences for each word. On the third day, students would complete another worksheet with the vocabulary words and then work on a "Ready, Set, Go" activity. This is a timed activity in which pairs of students attempt to match the words with their definitions in the shortest amount of time. This activity is repeated on the fourth day. After completion of the second "Ready, Set, Go," students are asked questions pairing two of the concepts together, such as "Can a virtuoso also be a rival?" On the fifth day, students take a posttest.

These are only examples of activities, which varied somewhat with different units. Students also completed a "Word Wizard" activity each day, in which students were given credit toward becoming a "Word Wizard" by finding examples of each word used outside of class.

This program, or variations of it, was found to significantly improve students' comprehension of texts containing taught words in a number of studies. Beck et al. (1982), for example, found strong effects of their treatment on vocabulary measures but equivocal effects on measures of text comprehension. McKeown et al. (1983) lengthened the amount of time spent on learning each word, refined the text comprehension measures, and found strong and unequivocal effects on text comprehension. McKeown et al.

(1985) compared the effects of differing amounts of encounters with each taught word and compared their extensive instruction to instruction that only required practice of definitions. They found that 12 encounters with a word reliably improved comprehension, but 4 encounters did not. They also found that their approach, which involved active processing of each word's meaning, had significantly greater effects than the definition-only approach on measures of comprehension but not on measures involving the recall of definitions.

***Use Discussion to Actively Teach Word Meanings.*** Discussion adds an important dimension to vocabulary instruction. To participate in a discussion, children must practice or prepare a response to themselves while waiting to be called on. This practiced response appears to lead to learning (Stahl & Clark, 1987). Because of the importance of each child expecting to be called upon, teachers should allow all children in the class some think time before calling on one individual (Rowe, 1974). Also, a teacher should be sensitive to his or her patterns of calling on children, and avoid just calling on the "fast" kids. If a child does not expect to be called on, the child will not practice a response. Without the practiced response, discussion is not as valuable a learning experience (Alvermann, Dillon, & O'Brien, 1987).

Discussion seems to improve vocabulary learning in general. Children seem not only to benefit from active processing encouraged by participating in discussions, but also seem to benefit from the contributions of other children. It is the experience of the author and his colleagues that children who enter a vocabulary lesson without any knowledge of a target word seem to learn a great deal from their peers, who may have partial or even fairly good knowledge of the word. We have found that in open discussions, children often are able to construct a good idea of a word's meaning from the partial knowledge of the class as a whole. For some of the words, though, we had to interject some information about the word, such as a quick definition.

**Procedures for Teaching Word Meanings**

These principles—including both definitional and contextual information, involving children actively in learning new word meanings, and using discussion—can be used to adapt existing vocabulary instruction so that it is more effective. For example, if a teacher is using materials that have students finding new words in a dictionary or glossary and writing down their definitions, a more effective adaptation might add the generation of sentences and a class discussion of sentences that students composed. The teacher might extend a lesson that involves examining the meaning of a word found in context by having students generate different scenarios that use the word or by rephrasing the definition.

These principles are useful for adapting and extending individual vocabulary learning exercises. In addition, there are a number of approaches to teach word meanings that reflect these principles. Among these are semantic mapping (Heimlich & Pittelman, 1986), semantic feature analysis (Anders, Bos, & Filip, 1984; Johnson, Toms-Bronowski, & Pittelman, 1982), and possible sentences (Bismonte, 1994; Stahl & Kapinus, 1986).

***Semantic Grouping.*** Semantic mapping and semantic feature analysis as well as the program developed by Beck and her colleagues (Beck et al., 1982) discussed earlier all chose words not randomly but in semantic groups. In Beck et al.'s program, one unit taught "people" such as "virtuoso," "novice," "hermit," "rival," "philanthropist," "tyrant," "miser," and "accomplice," another stressed "Things you can do with your arms," and so on. Some authors (Nagy, 1988) suggested that all words should be taught so that there is a common relationships among the words.

The rationale for grouping words in semantic categories comes loosely from studies of adult's knowledge of concepts, which suggests that words are stored in long-term semantic memory in networks (Collins & Loftus, 1975). In these models of memory, concepts are stored in nodes, which are connected to other nodes by various links, including logical relations. Thus, a concept such as "shark" might be connected to "fish," as well as to related concepts such as "man-eating," "hammerhead,", Jaws, and so on. One can answer questions such as "Do sharks have gills?" through one's knowledge that sharks are fish, even if one does not know for a fact that sharks do have gills. This view of knowledge as an organized, structured domain has developed into schema theory (McNeil, 1987).

If words are stored in categories, then it makes sense to teach them that way. Moreover, teaching words in semantic categories has been recommended by several different authorities (Graves, 1986; Johnson & Pearson, 1982; Nagy, 1988). However, the three studies that tested this directly found mixed results. Durso and Coggins (1986) found that some aspects of grouping led to better word learning, but only on some measures. The general vocabulary treatment used in the Durso and Coggins study, memorizing definitions, was one that had not been found effective in improving performance on comprehension tasks (Stahl & Fairbanks, 1986). Drum and Madison (1991) also found mixed results, but did not control instruction. Stahl, Buridge, Machuga, and Stecyk (1992), using materials adapted from those of Beck et al. (1982), found that children learned words equally well whether they were learned in groups or not. They suggested that children are going to draw associations among words when given rich vocabulary instruction such as that provided in the Beck et al. series of studies, and may not need to learn words in groups. This finding suggests that teachers need not choose words to form semantic groups, but can instead choose words more freely from texts, as long as they provide rich and varied vocabulary instruction for those words.

If rich and elaborate instruction is given, semantic grouping per se may not be necessary, at least in all circumstances. Semantic grouping is, however, an important component of several approaches to teaching word meanings, including semantic mapping and semantic feature analysis, which is discussed later. Furthermore, in his meta-analytic review of approaches for teaching word meanings to poor readers, Marmolejo (1991) found that approaches teaching word meanings as part of a semantic field especially suited children with low initial vocabularies. Such students may need help tying new word meanings to already existing word knowledge.

***Concept Development Approaches.*** Yet another approach to teaching word meanings comes from the studies of children's concept development. Using the model of Frayer (Frayer, Fredrick, & Klausmeier, 1969), Wixson (1986) taught children groups of words by (a) identifying the critical attributes of the word, (b) giving the category to which it belongs, (c) discussing examples of the word, and (d) discussing nonexamples of the word. For the word "prehistoric," for instance, students discussed why dinosaurs were prehistoric animals and lions were not and what prehistoric men might have worn. They recognized a definition for prehistoric ("before written history"), discussed whether stone hammers and steel hammers were prehistoric tools, and wrote a definition of "prehistoric" in their own words. Wixson found that such a procedure affected comprehension of passages containing the taught words.[3]

Schwartz and Raphael (1985) transformed this general procedure into word maps, which were used to teach children elements commonly found in definitions (Fig. 4.1). In addition to using these word maps for directly teaching new words, they intended their use to help children learn new word meanings from context. This approach does appear successful in teaching new words, but its effectiveness in helping children become better at learning word meanings from context is questionable. However, as discussed earlier, it is not clear whether any instructional approach has unequivocally improved children's learning of word meanings from context.

These techniques were chosen because of the research base that supports their use. There are other techniques, some of which might be as effective.

---

[3]Wixson also varied the placement of words in the passages and found that teaching vocabulary improved the comprehension of text portions containing the taught words. If the words taught related to a relatively unimportant section of the text, vocabulary instruction improved recall of that section, to the detriment of the main ideas.

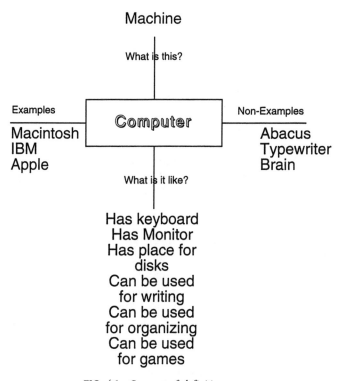

FIG. 4.1.  Concept of definition map.

Because vocabulary development is an ongoing process, vocabulary instruction is a long-term process. To avoid boredom, varied techniques need to be used. Therefore, an effective program of vocabulary instruction might include not only these, but as many other approaches as possible.

## VOCABULARY AND READING COMPREHENSION

The first question posed was how vocabulary knowledge relates to reading comprehension. Of the three hypotheses—that of the instrumentalist, the general knowledge, and the general aptitude—the first two seem to be most apt. Teaching word meanings does improve reading comprehension, but only if it is done in a way that incorporates both definitional and contextual information, engages the student actively in learning, and involves multiple exposures to meaningful information about each word. How important vocabulary instruction is depends on the estimate chosen for the number of words known by an average student. If we take the most commonly accepted figure, that an average student learns about 3,000 words per year, then the

300–400 words that are commonly taught in a school year account for 10%. If we take a smaller figure of vocabulary growth, then the number of words taught can account for a larger percentage. Either way, the greatest effect on vocabulary knowledge will come from increasing the amount of reading that children do, especially of books that contain challenging vocabulary.

The general knowledge hypothesis also captures some important understandings about vocabulary knowledge. We know that words do not have a fixed meaning, but instead contain a core meaning that adapts to different contexts. Word meanings interact with domain knowledge. In other words, word knowledge is world knowledge. Word learning should not be seen as a separate subject, but as part of the growth of other forms of content knowledge and as part of intelligent interactions with people and with texts.

Ability does not seem to play an especially important role in word learning. Researchers using an incidental learning paradigm have not found differences between students of high and low verbal ability in how they learn words from context, nor has learning from context been shown as especially amenable to instruction. Instead, it seems that a realistic source of the differences between high and low vocabulary students may be in their differential exposure to words through differing amounts of wide reading.

## REFERENCES

Adams, M. J. (1990). *Beginning to read: Thinking and learning about print.* Cambridge, MA: MIT Press.

Alvermann, D. E., Dillon, D. R., & O'Brien, D. G. (1987). *Using discussion to promote reading comprehension.* Newark, DE: International Reading Association.

Anders, P. L., Bos, C. S., & Filip, D. (1984). The effect of semantic feature analysis on the reading comprehension of learning disabled students. In J. Niles & L. A. Harris (Eds.), *Changing perspectives in research in reading/language processing and instruction* (Vol. 33, pp. 162–166). Rochester, NY: National Reading Conference.

Anderson, R. C., & Nagy, W. E. (1991). Word meanings. In R. Barr, M. L. Kamil, P. Mosenthal, & P. D. Pearson (Eds.), *Handbook of reading research* (Vol. 2, pp. 690–724). New York: Longman.

Anderson, R. C., & Freebody, P. (1981). Vocabulary knowledge. In J. T. Guthrie (Ed.), *Comprehension and teaching: research reviews* (pp. 77–117). Newark, DE: International Reading Association.

Anderson, R. C., Wilson, P. T., & Fielding, L. G. (1988). Growth in reading and how children spend their time outside of school. *Reading Research Quarterly, 23,* 285–303.

Beck, I. L., Perfetti, C. A., & McKeown, M. G. (1982). Effects of long-term vocabulary instruction on lexical access and reading comprehension. *Journal of Educational Psychology, 74,* 506–521.

Bismonte, A. R. (1994). Effectiveness of the possible sentences vocabulary strategy with middle school students in Guam. *Reading Improvement, 31*(4), 194–199.

Chall, J. S., Jacobs, V., & Baldwin, L. (1990). *The reading crisis.* Cambridge, MA: Harvard University Press.

Collins, A. M., & Loftus, E. E. (1975). A spreading activation theory of semantic processing. *Psychological Review, 82,* 407–428.

Craik, F. I. M., & Tulving, E. (1975). Depth of processing and the retention of words in episodic memory. *Journal of Experimental Psychology: General, 104,* 268–294.

Cunningham, A. E., & Stanovich, K. E. (1991). Tracking the unique effects of print exposure in children: Associations with vocabulary, general knowledge, and spelling. *Journal of Educational Psychology, 83,* 264–274.

Curtis, M. E. (1987). Vocabulary testing and vocabulary instruction. In M. G. McKeown & M. E. Curtis (Eds.), *The nature of vocabulary acquisition* (pp. xx–xx). Hillsdale, NJ: Lawrence Erlbaum Associates.

Dale, E., & O'Rourke, J. (1986). *Vocabulary building.* Columbus, OH: Zaner-Bloser.

D'Anna, C. A., Zechmeister, E. B., & Hall, J. W. (1991). Toward a meaningful definition of vocabulary size. *Journal of Reading Behavior, 23,* 109–122.

Drum, P., & Madison, J. (1991, April). *Domain-organized vocabulary instruction.* Paper presented at annual meeting of the American Educational Research Association, Chicago, IL.

Durso, F. T., & Coggins, K. A. (1986). *Semantic fields and vocabulary: Acquisition, comprehension, and production.* Paper presented at annual meeting of the Psychonomic Society.

Durso, F. T., & Shore, W. J. (1991). Partial knowledge of word meanings. *Journal of Experimental Psychology: General, 120,* 190–202.

Elshout-Mohr, M., & van Daalen-Kapteijns, M. M. (1987). Cognitive processes in learning word meanings. In M. G. McKeown & M. E. Curtis (Eds.), *The acquisition of word meanings* (pp. 53–72). Hillsdale, NJ: Lawrence Erlbaum Associates.

Frayer, D. A., Frederick, W. C., & Klausmeier, H. J. (1969). *A schema for testing the level of concept mastery* (Working Paper No. 16). Madison, WI: Wisconsin Research and Development Center for Cognitive Learning, University of Wisconsin.

Gouldman, R., Nation, P., & Read, J. (1990). How large can a receptive vocabulary be? *Applied Linguistics, 11,* 341–363.

Graves, M. F. (1986). Vocabulary learning and instruction. In E. Z. Rothkopf (Ed.), *Review of research in education* (Vol. 13, pp. 49–91). Washington, DC: American Educational Research Association.

Graves, M. F., & Prenn, M. C. (1986). Costs and benefits of various methods of teaching vocabulary. *Journal of Reading, 29,* 596–602.

Harris, A. J., & Sipay, E. (1990). *How to increase reading ability* (10th ed.). White Plains, NY: Longman.

Herman, P. A., Anderson, R. C., Pearson, P. D., & Nagy, W. E. (1987). Incidental acquisition of word meanings from expositions with varied text features. *Reading Research Quarterly, 23,* 263–284.

Heimlich, J. E., & Pittelman, S. D. (1986). *Semantic mapping: Classroom applications.* Newark, DE: International Reading Association.

Heibeck, T. H., & Markman, E. M. (1987). Word learning in children: An examination of fast mapping. *Child Development, 58,* 1021–1034.

Hirsh, D., & Nation, P. (1992). What vocabulary size is needed to read unsimplified texts for pleasure? *Reading in a Foreign Language, 8,* 689–696.

Johnson, D. D., Toms-Bronowski, S., & Pittelman, S. D. (1982). *An investigation of the effectiveness of semantic mapping and semantic feature analysis with intermediate grade children* (Program Report 83-3). Madison, WI: Wisconsin Center for Educational Research, University of Wisconsin.

Johnson, D. D., & Pearson, P. D. (1982). *Teaching reading vocabulary.* New York: Holt, Rinehart & Winston.

King, A. (1997). Running scared: America's never-ending election campaign. *The Atlantic Monthly, 279*(1), 41–47.

Konopak, B. C. (1988). Effects of inconsiderate versus considerate text on secondary students' vocabulary learning. *Journal of Reading Behavior, 20,* 5–24.

Kuhn, M. R., & Stahl, S. A. (in press). Teaching children to learn word meanings from context: A synthesis and some questions. *Journal of Literacy Research.*

Lorge, I., & Chall, J. S. (1963). Estimating the size of vocabularies of children and adults: An analysis of methodological issues. *Journal of Experimental Education, 32*(2), 147–157.

Marmolejo, A. (1991, April). *The effects of vocabulary instruction with poor readers.* Paper presented at annual meeting of the American Educational Research Association, Chicago, IL.

McKeown, M. G. (1985). The acquisition of word meaning from context by children of high and low ability. *Reading Research Quarterly, 20,* 482–496.

McKeown, M. G. (1991). Learning word meanings from dictionaries. In P. Schwanenflugel (Ed.), *The psychology of word meanings.* Hillsdale, NJ: Lawrence Erlbaum Associates.

McKeown, M. G., Beck, I. L., Omanson, R. C., & Perfetti, C. A. (1983). The effects of long-term vocabulary instruction on reading comprehension: A replication. *Reading Research Quarterly, 15*(1), 3–18.

McKeown, M. G., Beck, I. L., Omanson, R. C., & Pople, M. T. (1985). Some effects of the nature and frequency of vocabulary instruction on the knowledge and use of words. *Reading Research Quarterly, 20,* 522–535.

McNeil, J. D. (1987). *Reading comprehension: New directions for classroom practice* (2nd ed.). Glenview, IL: Scott-Foresman.

Nagy, W. E. (1988). *Teaching vocabulary to improve reading comprehension.* Newark, DE: International Reading Association.

Nagy, W. E., & Anderson, R. C. (1984). How many words are there in printed school English? *Reading Research Quarterly, 19,* 304–330.

Nagy, W. E., Anderson, R. C., & Herman, P. A. (1987). Learning word meanings from context during normal reading. *American Educational Research Journal, 24,* 237–270.

Nagy, W. E., & Herman, P. A. (1987). Breadth and depth of vocabulary knowledge: Implications for acquisition and instruction. In M. G. McKeown & M. E. Curtis (Eds.), *The nature of vocabulary acquisition* (pp. 19–36). Hillsdale, NJ: Lawrence Erlbaum Associates.

Nagy, W. E., Herman, P. A., & Anderson, R. C. (1985). Learning words from context. *Reading Research Quarterly, 20,* 233–253.

Nitsch, K. E. (1978). *Structuring decontextualized forms of knowledge.* Unpublished doctoral dissertation, Vanderbilt.

Random House. (1978). *Random House dictionary.* New York: Random House.

Rice, M. L., Buhr, J. C., & Nemeth, M. (1990). Fast mapping word-learning abilities of language-delayed preschoolers. *Journal of Speech and Hearing Disorders, 55,* 33–42.

Rowe, M. B. (1974). Wait time and rewards as instructional variables, their influence on language, logic, and fate control: Part one—Wait time. *Journal of Research in Science Teaching, 11,* 81–94.

Schefelbine, J. (1990). Student factors related to variability in learning word meanings from context. *Journal of Reading Behavior, 22,* 71–97.

Schwanenflugel, P. J., Stahl, S. A., & McFalls, E. L. (1997). *Partial word knowledge and vocabulary growth during reading comprehension* (Research Report No. 76). Athens, GA: University of Georgia, National Reading Research Center.

Schwartz, R. M., & Raphael, T. (1985). Concept of definition: A key to improving students' vocabulary. *The Reading Teacher, 39,* 198–203.

Scott, J. A., & Nagy, W. E. (1997). Understanding the definitions of unfamiliar verbs. *Reading Research Quarterly, 32,* 184–200.

Shore, W. J., & Durso, F. T. (1990). Partial knowledge in vocabulary acquisition: General constraints and specific detail. *Journal of Educational Psychology, 82,* 315–318.

Snow, C. E. (1990). The development of definitional skill. *Journal of Child Language, 17*, 697–710.

Stahl, S A. (1983). Differential word knowledge and reading comprehension. *Journal of Reading Behavior, 15*(4), 33–50.

Stahl, S. A. (1989). Task variations and prior knowledge in learning word meanings from context. In S. McCormick & J. Zutell (Eds.), *Cognitive and social perspectives for literacy research and instruction* (pp. 197–204). Chicago: National Reading Conference.

Stahl, S. A. (1991). Beyond the instrumentalist hypothesis: Some relationships between word meanings and comprehension. In P. Schwanenflugel (Ed.), *The psychology of word meanings* (pp. 157–178). Hillsdale, NJ: Lawrence Erlbaum Associates.

Stahl, S. A., Buridge, J. L., Machuga, M. B., & Steyck, S. (1992). The effects of semantic grouping on learning word meanings. *Reading Psychology, 13*, 19–35.

Stahl, S. A., & Clark, C. H. (1987). The effects of participatory expectations in classroom discussion on the learning of science vocabulary. *American Educational Research Journal, 24*, 541–556.

Stahl, S. A., & Fairbanks, M. M. (1986). The effects of vocabulary instruction: A model-based meta-analysis. *Review of Educational Research, 56*(1), 72–110.

Stahl, S. A., & Kapinus, B. A. (1991). Possible sentences: Predicting word meanings to teach content area vocabulary. *The Reading Teacher, 45*, 36–43.

Stahl, S. A., Richek, M. G., & Vandevier, R. (1991). Learning word meanings through listening: A sixth grade replication. In J. Zutell & S. McCormick (Eds.), *Learning factors/teacher factors: Issues in literacy research, Fortieth yearbook of the National Reading Conference* (pp. 185–192). Chicago: National Reading Conference.

Stanley, P. D., & Ginther, D. W. (1991). The effects of purpose and frequency on vocabulary learning from written context of high and low ability reading comprehenders. *Reading Research and Instruction, 30*(4), 31–41.

Stanovich, K. E. (1986). Matthew effects in reading: Some consequences of individual differences in the acquisition of literacy. *Reading Research Quarterly, 21*, 360–407.

Sternberg, R. J., & Powell, J. S. (1983). Comprehending verbal comprehension. *American Psychologist, 38*, 878–893.

Terman, L. M. (1916). *The measurement of intelligence.* Boston: Houghton-Mifflin Company.

Thorndike, E. L. (1917). Reading as reasoning: A study of mistakes in paragraph meaning. *Journal of Educational Psychology, 8*, 323–332.

White, T. G., Graves, M. F., & Slater, W. H. (1990). Growth of reading vocabulary in diverse elementary schools: Decoding and word meaning. *Journal of Educational Psychology, 82*, 281–290.

Wixson, K. K. (1986). Vocabulary instruction and children's comprehension of basal stories. *Reading Research Quarterly, 21*(3), 317–329.

# What Is the Point? Tests of a Quick and Clean Method for Improving Instructional Text

Robert C. Sorrells
Bruce K. Britton
*University of Georgia*

Instructional text is one of the most venerable of educational technologies, and is still among the most widely used, probably exceeded only by the blackboard. Teachers rely on the textbook to provide accurate, up-to-date information and clear explanations aided by appropriate examples, illustrations, and analogies (chap. 9, this volume) for themselves and their students. Students view the text as the voice of authority (chap. 7, this volume), and it is continuously available to them, so they can return to it again and again when the teacher and other learning resources are unavailable.

Students must be able to understand and remember what they read from textbooks, but often find them "frustratingly difficult and arcane" (chap. 7, this volume). Textbooks are widely criticized on these and other grounds. The conditions under which textbooks are produced appear to be related to their inadequacies (Tyson-Bernstein, 1988).

Many methods have been proposed to improve the learnability of textbooks, and the overwhelming majority of those methods, when empirically tested, have been found effective (Britton & Gulgöz, 1991), albeit some are a great deal more effective than others (Britton, Van Dusen, Gulgöz, & Glynn, 1989; Britton, 1996; Britton & Gulgöz, 1991; Britton & Tidwell, 1995). In evaluating the usefulness of any such methods, it is important to consider the proportion between the amount of work required to make the improvements and the amount of improvement obtained. An ideal ratio is for a small amount of easy work to produce a large improvement.

In this chapter, we report tests of a method for improving the learnability of expository texts that requires very little work but produces substantial improvements in learning from the text. Our development of the method began when we encountered Colomb and Williams' (1987) claim that all expository texts have a point, which is a central tenet around which the text is organized. From this idea, our three hypotheses emerged. First, do expert readers generally agree about the point of a text, whereas less skilled readers differ in their judgments of the point? Second, do readers who have the point of a text signaled to them recall more of that text than readers who do not have the point signaled? Finally, do readers who have the point signaled to them construct a different structure of the text, incorporating more of the important information than those who do not? If these hypotheses are supported, they suggest that identifying the point of a text and informing readers that it is the point would improve the learnability of that text.

## THE POINT

In a knowledge structure, it seems always to be the case that some of the ideas and relationships are more important than others. In an exposition of that knowledge structure, some ideas are central themes of the exposition, whereas others are illustrations of these themes, and some are transitions between themes. The ideas have differing amounts of informative content. The point of an expository text is that set of ideas that are central to and highly informative about the structure of knowledge that the text is intended to communicate. The structure of the exposition is set up around the point. This structure could be hierarchical with the point at the top, or circular with the point at the hub, or any of several other shapes, but in each case it is the point that is the nexus for the exposition's structure. Colomb identified the points of the texts used in this study by asking himself and his coworkers: if only one sentence from this text could be transmitted, which would it be? If an author wants her readers to acquire a similar structure to her own, then she should make it clear to the reader which ideas are the point. A simple means is to typographically signal the sentence that best conveys the point.

The literature supports the idea that typographical cues, such as under-lining, facilitate memory for a text, but for the cued text only (Lorch, 1989). These studies manipulate location of, amount of, and type of typographical cue (Hartley, Bartlett, & Branthwaite, 1980; Lorch, Lorch, & Klusewitz, 1995), as well as subject underlining (Johnson, 1988). These manipulations gener-ally produced better memory for cued information, whereas uncued infor-mation was unaffected. The question of interest for our study was this: What is the effect of underlining the sentence that carries the most informative content? If the point of a text telegraphs the information in that text, as Colomb and Williams suggested, then cuing the point should affect the recall of other information.

There are several hypotheses to account for the previous findings that typographically signaled information is recalled better than unsignaled information. One explanation is that there is a trade-off between memory for the signaled content and memory for the rest of the text. This trade-off suggests that more processing of the signaled information yields better recall, whereas memory for unsignaled content is unaffected, or perhaps even reduced. Lorch, Lorch, & Klusewitz (1995) manipulated the amount of underlining in three conditions: no underlining, light underlining (5% underlined), and heavy underlining (50% underlined). The subjects in the light underlining condition recalled more underlined than nonunderlined targets (a signaling effect), whereas this effect was not present in the heavy condition. In other words, when underlining was sparingly used, the cuing helped with retrieval of signaled content only, but when there was excessive underlining (50% of all words were underlined), equivalent amounts of underlined and nonunderlined sentences were recalled. The authors concluded that typographical cues lead to an increase in processing of the cued content, with little effect on the uncued content. Additionally, cuing had an effect on the underlined sentences only in the light condition, indicating that the selective effect diminished with increased underlining. It is important to note that the targets underlined were completely counterbalanced for position in the text to avoid confounding of the cue manipulation with text content.

Our study focused on the effect of underlining specific content, namely the point of a short expository passage, on its subsequent recall. Three expository texts were provided by Greg Colomb, who had identified the point of each passage along with the important themes. Experiment 1 investigated whether expert readers were better at identifying the points of the texts than less skilled readers. Experiments 2 and 3 used a between-subject design in which the experimental group received the three texts with the point of each underlined, along with directions identifying the underlined sentence as the point of that text. The control group received the nonunderlined texts in Experiment 2, and a third condition was added for Experiment 3. In this condition, a random sentence was underlined and identified as the point. All groups received instructions to remember as much of the text as possible in free recall tests. Profile analyses were conducted to assess the hypothesis that readers who have the point of a text signaled have a different structure of recall than readers who do not have the point signaled.

## EXPERIMENT 1

The first question to be addressed concerns the validity of Colomb's identification of the point, and the extent to which students are able to identify the point. If experts can agree and easily identify the points of texts, whereas students have difficulty, and if identifying the point to the student helps with subsequent recall, then a simple solution for improving expository text would be to have experts (preferably the authors) underline the various points of the text.

## Method

### Subjects

Five Ph.D. English faculty were recruited and volunteered to participate, and 12 introductory psychology students participated for credit.

### Materials

Greg Colomb provided three short expository texts. He identified the point of each text, as well as the theme related to the point. The texts varied in length and the position of the point in the text. The texts and scoring materials are in the Appendix. The titles of these texts are provided there for explanatory purposes only. The texts that participants saw had no titles.

### Procedure

All participants were given the texts and asked to underline the point after careful reading.

### Scoring

The point sentences of each text were divided into units roughly corresponding to noun-modifier propositions (adapted from Bovair & Kieras, 1985). There were a total of five units that corresponded to the points of the texts. Percentages of the units correctly identified as the point served as the dependent measure.

## Results

The expert readers correctly identified 86.4% of the points, significantly more than the students, who were right 49.5% of the time ($t_{(15)} = 3.94$, $p < .05$). One sample $t$ tests also revealed that both groups performed significantly better than chance (Experts $t_{(4)} = 9.57$; students $t_{(11)} = 8.60$, $p < .05$).

## Discussion

The experts were able to identify the points of the texts. The students, however, were less able, and had greater variance in their responses. It should be noted that the students performed well above chance on their selection of the point. Perhaps with more motivation, their performance would be better. In other words, the students were not particularly bad at identifying the point, but they were not as good as the experts.

## EXPERIMENT 2

The methods for Experiments 2 and 3 were very similar, with differences noted in the respective procedure section. The materials were the same in all experiments.

### Subjects

Twenty-nine introductory psychology students participated for credit.

### Materials and Procedure

In the three passages provided by Greg Colomb, the important themes of each was identified, as well as the point. These themes were considered to have less informative content than the point, but more than other idea units.

Each participant received a booklet with the three texts counterbalanced for order, instructions, and paper for writing down what they remembered. The experimental group had the point of the passage underlined, along with instructions that identified the underlined sentence in each passage as the point of that passage.

Participants' protocols were scored against the noun–modifier propositions.

### Scoring

The participants' free-recall protocols were examined for matches to the idea units. A match was scored as a one, and missing idea units were scored as zeros. Subsequently, for each participant, the data was recorded as a string of ones and zeros that corresponded to the order of the sentences in the texts.

The first author of this paper scored the protocols for Experiment 2, and an independent rater, blind to condition, scored the protocols for Experiment 3. Both raters scored 10% of the protocols from the other rater, and interrater reliabilities were above .90.

**Analyses.** Several types of analyses were conducted for each experiment. Measures of reading and recall time were gathered, and differences between the groups were tested. Differences between groups were analyzed by the number of point units recalled, the number of theme units recalled, and the number of other units recalled.

Profiles of the responses of each participant were also compared to investigate any differences in the pattern or structure of recall that could be attributed to the experimental manipulation. When the profiles of the participants within each group were combined, the resulting profiles indicated, for each idea unit, the percentage of participants in that group that recalled that idea unit. This percentage can be regarded as the activation level or strength of that unit in the group. If all of the participants in a group recalled a particular unit, then that unit had the maximum strength of one. Given that the groups were roughly equivalent in language skills, different patterns of activations between the groups can be attributed to the manipulated underlining of the point.

These profiles were compared in several ways. First, the mean of each profile roughly reflected the mean activation level for all of the units across all of the participants. This corresponded to the overall level of recall for each group. Second, the variability, or spread of the profile provided information about the variability of responses in the groups. If the groups were equivalent in that sense, then the variability in responses (measured in standard deviations) should also have been equivalent. Third, the correlation between the profiles of each group provided information about the similarity between the shape or pattern of the profiles. If differences in structure existed, then the correlation coefficients, along with visual inspection of the profiles, provided evidence as to the nature of those differences. The group profiles for each text were compared.

## Results

Table 5.1 shows the mean reading times and recall times for both groups. No reliable time differences for reading or recall were found.

### *Free Recall Scores*

The mean number of idea units recalled in each condition for Experiments 2 and 3 are shown in Table 5.2. Overall, the experimental group recalled, on the average, 10.1 more idea units than the control group ($t_{(27)} = 3.42$, $p$

TABLE 5.1
Means for Reading and Recall Times for Experiments 2 and 3

| Group | Reading Time (min) | | Recall Time | |
| --- | --- | --- | --- | --- |
| | Mean | SD | Mean | SD |
| Experiment 2 | | | | |
| Control | 9.08 | 3.27 | 10.53 | 4.34 |
| Experimental | 7.77 | 3.29 | 12.04 | 5.48 |
| Experiment 3 | | | | |
| Control | 9.05 | 2.56 | 15.03 | 6.62 |
| Random | 6.80 | 2.37 | 15.10 | 6.15 |
| Experimental | 7.77 | 2.14 | 17.31 | 9.14 |

TABLE 5.2
Mean Number of Idea Units Recalled: Experiments 2 and 3

|  | Experiment 2 | | Experiment 3 | | Group |
|---|---|---|---|---|---|
| Overall Recall | | | | | |
| Experimental | 42.20 | (6.75) | 36.77 | (14.50) | |
| Control | 31.10 | (10.40) | 26.00 | (9.60) | |
| Random | . . . . . . . . . . . . | | 25.64 | (9.90) | |
| Points | | | | | |
| Experimental | 3.43 | (1.48) | 3.00 | (1.62) | |
| Control | 2.41 | (.98) | 1.21 | (.80) | |
| Random | . . . . . . . . . . . . | | 1.93 | (1.14) | |
| Theme Units | | | | | |
| Experimental | 17.35 | (6.24) | 14.69 | (6.03) | |
| Control | 11.82 | (7.38) | 10.08 | (3.44) | |
| Random | . . . . . . . . . . . . | | 11.21 | (2.39) | |
| Other Units (nonpoints) | | | | | |
| Experimental | 38.7 | (6.75) | 32.86 | (13.13) | |
| Control | 28.6 | (10.40) | 23.79 | (8.14) | |
| Random | . . . . . . . . . . . . | | 24.85 | (9.67) | |

*Note.* Standard deviations are parenthetical.

< .05). To assess the question of memory for different classes of content, the data were divided into three parts: the idea units corresponding to the point sentences, the idea units corresponding to the theme sentences, and the other idea units. First, the experimental group recalled significantly more of the points than the control group ($t_{(27)} = 3.13$, $p < .05$). Second, a subset of data was analyzed for differences between the groups for recall of the important themes (as identified by Colomb). The experimental group also recalled significantly more of these theme-related units than the control group ($t_{(27)} = 2.09$, $p < .05$). Also, the differences between the groups in recall for the unsignaled content (the themes and the other units) were assessed. The experimental group recalled more of these nonpoint units than the control group ($t_{(27)} = 3.11$, $p < .05$).

### Profile Analyses

***Text 1: Context Matters.*** The profiles for both groups are shown in the top panel of Fig. 5.1. The mean recall of the experimental group exceeded that of the control group (.46 > .36). The standard deviations were identical (.27). The correlation between the two profiles was .70.

Visual inspection of the profiles revealed that the groups differed substantially in the activations of at least nine idea units. The first idea unit, corresponding to the first sentence of the passage, had an activation of .36 for the experimental group, and .69 for the control group. It would seem that the control group gave more importance to the first unit than the ex-

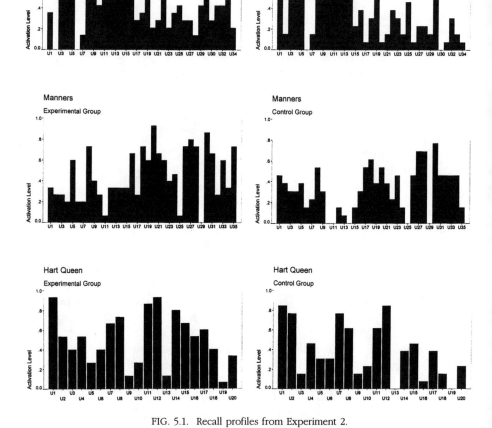

FIG. 5.1.  Recall profiles from Experiment 2.

perimental group. This could be due to a primacy effect, or perhaps the control group, not knowing the point, attributed more informative content to this unit than the experimental group, which presumably knew that the first unit was not the point. Several other units also had a higher activation for the control group (U9, U10, U11). They are details related to the opening sentences only: For a salesman, people remove shoes (U9); for a bank, people show their license (U10); and for a barber, people expose their neck (U11). These ideas support the notion stated in the first sentence that people only think they are independent.

In contrast, the experimental group had very high activations for units that corresponded to important themes and to the point (U8, U22, U33, &

34): People obey authority in a reasonable context (U8); the office experiment demonstrates that context is important (U22); in the right context, people conform to authority (33); and in the wrong context, people conform to assumed authority (34).

In summary, the experimental groups' profile reflects the relatively large activation of the ideas related to context. Context is the central idea of the point (i.e., that perceived context influences conformity). The control group, in contrast, has most of the highest activations clustered near the beginning of the passage. It seems that the control condition as a group may have attempted a strategy that was less effective than the strategy used by the experimental group.

***Text 2: Manners.*** The mean activation level of the experimental group exceeded that of the control group (.46 > .33), whereas the standard deviations were the same (.25). The correlation between the profiles was .68. The shape of the profile was analyzed to provide evidence about any difference in structure between the two groups.

Visual inspection of the middle panel of Fig. 5.2 revealed that the control group's activations were not generally higher than those of the experimental group except for units 17, 32, and 34 in which the control groups' activations exceeded those of the experimental group. Units 32 and 34 corresponded to sentences at the end of the text which refer to Erasmus, a 16th century philosopher, and unit 17 refers to the unrefined manners of the nobility. Also the control group had slightly higher activations at the beginning of the passage. Perhaps some members of this group were employing strategies such as these: "The information at the beginning is important" and "the mention of a name is important." Notice the relative lack of activation around units 12–16. In the middle of these units is the point of this passage: that manners, even unpleasant ones, make people think they are special. The profile suggests that the control group missed this idea.

The experimental group had relatively high activations around the point units, which occur in the front middle of the profile (U13 & 14), as well as around the important themes at the beginning and end of the profile. These themes relate to the type of people that use manners (e.g., distinguished, exclusive), as well as the crude behaviors that have been deemed polite by past generations (e.g., spitting on the floor). These themes highlight the point and reiterate the idea that even "good" manners may look unpleasant to others.

***Text 3: Hart Queen.*** The mean activation level for the experimental group exceeded the level of the control group (.51 > .39), and the standard deviations did not reliably differ (.27, .28). The correlation between the profiles was .82. Again, visual inspection of the profiles (see the bottom

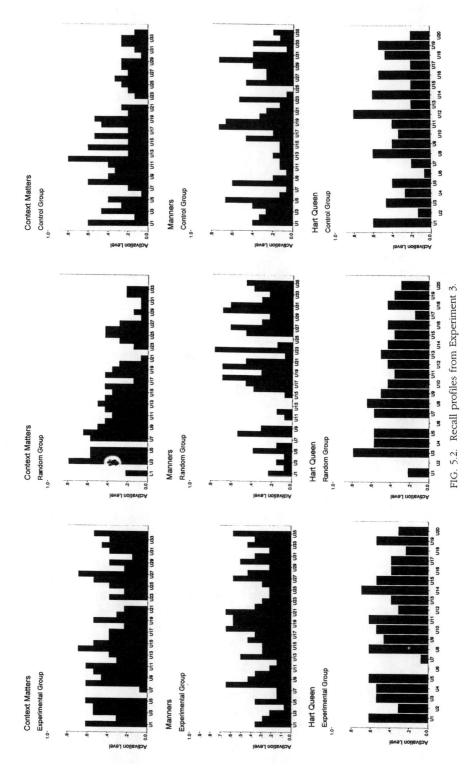

FIG. 5.2. Recall profiles from Experiment 3.

104

panel of Fig. 5.1) provided evidence for a difference in structure between the groups.

The control group's pattern of activations was biased toward the beginning of the text, which here is the location of the point. The themes of the text, however, are bimodally distributed at the beginning and end of the passage. Notice that the experimental group's activations were higher at the end of the profile than those of the control group. The point of this text is that the Hart Queen is a good ski for beginners. The reason that it is good is because it has qualities that a beginner needs such as durability (U2), versatility (U3), and flexibility (U4). Both groups had roughly equivalent activations for these units. However, the reason the Hart Queen has these qualities is its construction: The wood is molded in two sheets of steel (U14), which are wrapped in fiberglass (U15) and provide strength (U16). The activations of these units were much greater for the experimental group than for the control group.

It appears that the control group employed a strategy with this passage that was similar to that used in the other passages. Specifically, information at either the beginning of a text or at the end was recalled more often. These primacy and recency strategies may have hindered their recall, compared with strategies based on the meaning of the text, as used by the experimental group.

**Discussion**

These results demonstrate that underlining the point facilitated overall recall, and recall for unsignaled content was also increased. Knowing the point yielded a 30% improvement over the performance of the control group. Additionally, more of the more important idea units were recalled by the experimental group. This is consistent with the hypothesis that the point has greater semantic connectedness than other idea units. Its cuing may have facilitated comprehension of the text, and its subsequent retrieval may have facilitated the recall of other, less important content.

Additionally, the profile analyses gave evidence that knowing the point of an exposition influenced the structure of the subsequent recall. The structure produced by knowing the point was superior to one used by participants who had either to find the point for themselves or do without. It was superior in that it facilitated recall of more ideas in the passage.

A limitation of the profile analysis is that only the experimental manipulation was used to aggregate the groups of subjects. Even though the point was made explicit to one group and not the other, this may be an imperfect way of determining whether the participants knew what the point was. If the results of the first experiment can be generalized to this situation, we would expect about half of the control group to get the point on their own.

Additionally, some participants in the experimental group may know the point, but not what to do with it. Perhaps their recall was determined by a point of the text which is different from what the instructions told them. Some meaningful information may be lost by combining the subjects' profiles, but even this blunt instrument has proved useful.

## EXPERIMENT 3

### Method

This experiment replicated Experiment 2 and added another condition in which a random sentence was underlined and designated as the point. If the mere underlining of a sentence was responsible for the effects found in Experiment 2, then the random underlining condition would exhibit recall patterns similar to those found for the experimental group in Experiment 2. However, if the pattern of recall for the random group was similar to that for the control group of Experiment 2, then evidence would be provided that it is the semantic importance or informative content of the point that, when signaled, facilitated recall.

#### Subjects

Forty-one introductory psychology students participated for credit.

#### Materials and Procedure

All materials and procedures were the same as for Experiment 2, except that the random condition was added. In the random condition, a different nonpoint sentence was underlined for each participant. This condition was given the identical instructions as those given to the experimental group in Experiment 2.

### Results

As in Experiment 2, there were no reliable differences in reading or recall time (see Table 5.1).

#### Free Recall Scores

The mean number of idea units recalled for each condition are shown in Table 5.2. There was a main effect for condition in overall recall ($F_{(2,38)}$ = 3.80, $p <$ .05), in recall of the points ($F_{(2,38)} = 6.51$, $p <$ .05), in recall of the themes ($F_{(2,38)} = 3.80$, $p <$ .05), and in recall of the unsignaled content

$(F_{(2,38)} = 3.07, p < .05)$. Post hoc comparisons revealed that the experimental group recalled more idea units than either the random ($t_{(26)} = 2.31, p < .05$) or control conditions ($t_{(26)} = 2.30, p < .05$), which did not differ from each other. The experimental group also recalled more of the actual points than either the random ($t_{(26)} = 3.71, p < .05$) or control condition ($t_{(26)} = 2.03, p < .05$), which did not differ from each other. The experimental group also recalled significantly more of the theme-related units than either the random ($t_{(26)} = 2.42, p < .05$) or control conditions ($t_{(26)} = 2.02, p < .05$), which did not differ from each other. Considering only the unsignaled content, the experimental group recalled more than either the random ($t_{(26)} = 2.03, p < .05$) or the control conditions ($t_{(26)} = 1.78, p < .05$), which did not differ from each other.

### Profile Analyses

The profiles for the experimental, control, and random groups are shown in Fig. 5.2. Again, the activation levels for the experimental group were relatively high and consistent throughout the passages compared with the activation levels of both the control and random conditions. Although the patterns of activations for the groups in this experiment were slightly different from those in the previous experiment, the trend of the experimental group to have high activations around the point and themes continued.

The structures that emerge from these profiles are similar to those seen in the previous experiment. In general, having the point signaled led to better recall of the point, as well as better recall of the themes. The themes help explicate the point and provide a richer basis for comprehension. For example, in the *Context Matters* text, the control group had greater activation than the experimental group for the idea that people obey authority (U12). However, the experimental group had higher activation for the next unit (U13), which corresponds to the idea that context affects obedience. From this, as well as their better recall of other themes, it would seem that the experimental group had a richer understanding of what the passage was about.

## Discussion

The experimental group recalled more of the signaled idea units, and more of the unsignaled content as well. The experimental group also recalled more of the idea units related to the themes of the texts. That is, they remembered more important ideas. The resulting structure of the point with its supporting themes corresponded to better overall recall, and potentially to better comprehension. The results of the random underlining condition indicated that it was the informative content of the signaled idea unit, not the signaling per se, that facilitated recall of unsignaled units. It is also interesting to note that in Experiment 3, the control group recalled more of the actual points, as well as more of the related themes than the random group (although these differences were not significant). If this particular finding is replicated, then an argument could be made that signaling random content can be detrimental to recall.

## GENERAL DISCUSSION

Empirical evidence has been provided that knowing the point of an exposition facilitates its recall. The effect was found in three passages and replicated in two experiments with different participants. Experts were better able to identify the points of texts than students, and students benefited in their level of recall from having the point made explicit to them. The profile analyses of Experiments 2 and 3 provided a means of assessing the different structures in the protocols of groups who had and did not have the point underlined. The random condition of Experiment 3 disconfirmed the idea that mere underlining of text facilitated the recall. In fact, the slight decline in performance of the random group as compared to both other groups suggests that the underlining distracted them from constructing a more appropriate text-based structure.

Contrary to the findings in the reviewed literature, this study has demonstrated that cuing certain information, namely the point of the text, can facilitate recall of the unsignaled text. Much work has been done using typographical cueing (e.g., Lorch et al. comparing underlining and capitalization cues), but facilitation for unsignaled content has not been found in previous work. These results have been explained with either trade-off or extraprocessing explanations. The current study signaled the specific content that carries the most semantic importance and showed facilitation of other content. Furthermore, the additional content remembered was related to the themes of the texts: content that is arguably more intimately related to the point. These findings suggest that the point of a passage can somehow be better integrated into the structure of the text than nonpoint content. Knowing the point of a text can be used as a central hub connecting the other idea units into a coherent structure. Signaling the point facilitated recall, but not because of a trade-off. The experimental groups were better able to remember nonsignaled information in all conditions.

What impact does underlining the point have on students' reading of texts? Presumably, the students are attempting to construct a coherent representation of the text. If the students have low prior knowledge of the subject matter, then they are forming a novice knowledge structure out of information written by an expert. The point of a passage is presumably obvious to its author, as are the connections between points, themes, and details. By providing the student with the nexus for the discourse structure, that is, the important point according to the author, the student has a better chance to form the appropriate structure.

More research needs to be conducted on the effects of identifying the point for readers. Using populations that can be readily divided into groups that consistently get the point and those who have trouble identifying the point can help to refine our methods for improving text. Perhaps techniques can be found to diagnose readers who cannot consistently identify the points of expository passages. It is this group of readers that will benefit most from both signaling of points and instruction on how to identify the point themselves.

What do these findings tell us about how to modify textbooks to improve learning? First, we know that students, even when prompted to find the point of an expository text, tend to have difficulty, whereas expert readers do not. Current textbooks generally do not signal the point of any part of the text, so it is likely that many students do not know what it is.

Students need to know not only what the main points are, but also what part the points play in the exposition. They need to know that the point explicitly states the main idea and is connected to the main themes. Knowing the point and knowing that it was the point facilitated recall of the more important information. The participants who were not told the point had overall lower recall of the passages, and their recall structure missed important connections specified by the point. For example, the control group remembered that the Hart Queen was a good ski for beginners, and that it was strong and flexible. But only the experimental group reliably remembered the reasons that the Hart Queen was strong and flexible. The point connected the important information in a way that made it easier to recall. Textbooks need to help the student keep the point activations high. Underlining the points, along with instructions on the utility of the points, should help make textbooks less frustrating and difficult. The important information will be made more clear, and students can turn to the text for this information with little help from the teacher.

In general, textbooks need to be written in principled ways, based on our current understanding of the cognitive processes involved with understanding them. Experts write texts and novices read them. We must look for ways to make the knowledge structures encoded in the text easier for novices to reclaim. Signaling the main points throughout a text and stating their importance is one quick and easy way to improve instructional materials.The question remains as to the locus of the point's effect. These studies cannot answer whether the point facilitates recall, comprehension, or both.

These are certainly testable hypotheses. Students can be given the point at different times during encoding or recall, and comparisons of performance (such as free recall and comprehension measures) can be made.

# APPENDIX

## Context Matters

Most people think of themselves as independent souls who are not easily bossed around. And it is easy to find situations that seem to confirm that view. If you walk up to someone sitting in a bank and ask them to remove their shoes, they are almost certain to refuse. Demand that someone in a barber shop show you their driver's license, and they are unlikely to comply. If you pull out a razor in front of someone in a shoe store and ask them to lift their chin and expose their neck, chances are their response will be rude or even violent.

This apparent independence is not, however, absolute. People are quick to refuse unexpected requests from someone who has no right to make the request. Change the context so that the request makes sense and comes from someone in authority, and people become quite obedient. People sitting in a show store do not hesitate to remove their shoes when strangers ask them to. In a bank, a demand to see a drivers' license is readily obeyed. Barbers easily get people to expose their necks to bare razor blades. In the right context—when faced with someone who seems to be an authority—humans are remarkably obedient creatures.

Just how obedient people can be in the right context was shown in a series of experiments conducted at Yale University. Those participating in the experiments were told to press a switch that would administer an electric shock to another person whenever that person answered a question incorrectly. The switch was not connected to anything, and so could not really administer a shock, and the person answering the question was an actor playing along with the experiment. Nevertheless, the participants thought they really were administering a shock. Even though the participants thought there were hurting the person answering the questions and felt uncomfortable about it, they repeatedly administered shocks when told to do so by an authoritative person supposedly directing the experiment. Some participants continued to administer shocks even after the person answering the questions appeared to be in great pain.

The importance of context was demonstrated when the scene of the experiment was shifted from a lab on the Yale campus to a bare office in a run-down building downtown. In the university lab, participants reported that while they did not like administering the shocks, they felt confidence in the experimenters and were assured that a Yale experiment would be run safely and with only the best motives. Because the context made them think that the person asking them to administer the shocks was an authority, they readily obeyed. In the office, however, participants were much less willing to do as they were told. When the experiments were sponsored by an unknown organization and conducted in an unpromising location, participants reported that they did not like administering the painful shocks, that they distrusted the motives of the experimenters, and that they wanted to stop. Nevertheless, participants in the office were almost as likely to obey the instructions to administer the shocks as were the participants in the lab.

Context matters, and in the right contexts people readily conform to the wishes of a figure in authority. But even when the context is not right, in response to the instructions of someone who acts as an authority, people can be remarkably obedient.

## Context Matters (idea units; point double underlined, themes single underlined)

1. People - think (they are) independent
2. Situations - confirm
3. Demand remove shoes (bank) - refuse
4. Demand drivers license (barber shop - refuse
5. Demand expose neck (to razor) - violent/rude response
6. Independence - not absolute
7. Unexpected requests (inappropriate person) - refused
8. Context - make reasonable (authority) - obey
9. For salesman - remove shoes
10. For bank - show drivers llcense
11. For barber - expose neck
12. Authoritative context - obedience
13. (Yale) experiments - (demonstrate) context affects obedience
14. For incorrect response - press shock switch
15. Switch - not connected
16. Shockee - actor
17. Participant - believed (shock) real
18. If authoritative experimenter said shock - (participants) did repeatedly
19. (Participants) - believed (they) harmed person (in pain)
20. (Participants) - felt uncomfortable
21. (Participants) - continued
22. (Dilapidated) office experiment - (demonstrates) context is important
23. (Yale Study Participants) - confident of safety
24. (Yale Study Particlpants) - confident of (experimenters') motives

25. (Participants) - obeyed (authoritative) context
26. (Office Participants) - obedience (slightly less probable)
27. (Office Study) - unpromising location/unknown organizar.ion
28. (Office Participants) - disliked administering shocks
29. (Office Participants) - distrusted (experimenters') motives
30. (Office Participants) - wanted to stop
31. (Office Participants) - nearly as obedient as (Yale Study Participants)
32. Context - important
33. Right context - conform to authority
34. Wrong context - conform to assumed authority

## MANNERS

Visit an expensive restaurant, an exclusive club, or even a suburban dinner party and you can observe the elaborate social rituals of table manners. You'll find special forks for salads, cocktail forks for appetizers, yet other forks for dessert, not to mention all the specialized knives, spoons, glassware, and china. And you'll find just as many specialized "rules" for how to behave when using them. We tend to think of the rituals of table manners as signs of civilization, and to think that refined table manners distinguish the finer sort of people. But those who practice "good" manners have always thought that their manners made them special, even when their manners would look unpleasant to us.

In the Middle Ages, European nobility boasted of their fine table manners and talked about how manners set the nobles apart from crude peasants; but by our modern standards, these manners were not exactly refined. While dining, feudal lords drank from a finely crafted goblet: a single goblet that they passed around throughout the meal. They ate with unwashed hands, which they used to scoop food from a common bowl shared by as many as six diners. They would carefully extend a finger, keeping it free of grease for dipping into the bowls of spices and condiments. (That may be where we get the hyper-polite custom of extending the little finger while holding a spoon or teacup.) If there were bones, diners would toss them back into the common bowl once they had gnawed off all of the meat. If they had soup, they would drink it from a common bowl. If the meal was served with a sauce, diners would sip it from the serving bowl. Everyone wolfed down their food, and used the tablecloth to wipe their mouths and blow their noses; but lords and nobles would never think of spitting on the table as a peasant would—they preferred to spit on the floor.

About the beginning of the sixteenth century, there was a reform movement to improve table manners. The philosopher Erasmus published a tremendously successful book that advocated some very advanced ideas about the polite way to eat. He believed, for example, that an upper class diner was distinguished by putting only three fingers of one hand into the bowl, instead of the entire hand in the manner of the lower class. Wait a few moments after being seated before you dip into it, he advised. Finish chewing what is in your rnouth before reaching for another piece. Do not poke around in the dish looking for a good piece, but take the first one you touch. Erasmus' idea of good table manners may have been an advance, but it was far from ours. You have to wonder if our table manners might one day seem just as crude.

## Manners (idea units; themes underlined, point double underlined)

1. Visit - expensive restaurant
2. Visit - exclusive club
3. Visit - dinner party
4. Observe - social rituals of table manners
5. Find - special forks
6. Cocktail forks - appetizers
7. Forks - desert
8. Find - special tableware
9. Find - speciai glassware
10. Find - specialized rules
11. We think - manners a sign of civilization
12. We think - manners distinguish people
13. People (who practice good manners) - (think) manners make them special
14. (They think this) - even when manners look unpleasant
15. (Middle Age European) nobility - boasted fine manners
16. (Nobility) - manners distinguish them from peasants
17. (Nobility's) manners - not refined by our standards
18. Feudal lords - shared (finely crafted) drinking goblet
19. They ate- with unwashed hands
20. (They) scooped food - from common bowls
21. Extended finger - for bowl dipping
22. (Believed source of our) custom - extended little finger
23. Bones tossed - common bowl
24. Meat with sauce - dipped from servlng bowl
25. Food - wolfed down
26. Tablecloth - for wiping mouths and blowlng nose
27. Nobles - spit on floor
28. Peasants - spit on table
29. 16th century - reform of manners
30. Erasmus - book of manners

31. (He) believed - nobles use only 3 fingers in bowl (not all)
32. (He) advised - wait before dipping in
33. (Advised) - take first piece touched
34. <u>Although (Erasmus') ideas advanced - far from ours</u>
35. <u>(You) wonder - our manners will (one day) seem crude</u>

## HART QUEEN

One of the best skis for beginning skiers is the Hart Queen, which is durable and versatile, with the strength and flexibility that beginners need. The Hart Queen is designed to be used with all conventional bindings, and it works best with the Salomon Double, which is a binding especially designed for beginners. The Queen can be ordered in any of six different colors. Its construction joins tried-and-true materials with an innovative design. The core of the Queen consists of a very thin layer of tempered ash, direct from the hardwood forests of Kentucky. This core is surrounded by two outer layers that employ major innovations to provide extra strength and flexibility. For increased strength, the layer of ash has molded to it two sheets of 10-gauge steel. For increased flexibility, the two steel sheets are then wrapped with highly active fiberglass. This layered construction makes the Queen a durable ski that adapts to a variety of conditions and to the growing skill levels of the skier.

**Hart Queen (idea units: themes underlined, point double underlined)**

1. <u>Hart Queen (HQ)—good beginner ski</u>
2. <u>HQ - durable</u>
3. <u>HQ - versatile</u>
4. <u>HQ - flexible</u>
5. <u>(These are qualities) - beginners need</u>
6. (Designed) - conventional bindings
7. HQ - best with Salomon double
8. HQ - six different colors
9. Construction - tried and true materials
10. HQ - innovative design
11. Core - tempered ash
12. Ash - Kentucky forests
13. HQ - between two layers
14. Ash - molded two sheets (10-guage) steel
15. Steel - wrapped with fiberglass
16. <u>(These innovations) - provide strength</u>

17. (They also) - provide flexibility
18. Layered construction - durability
19. HQ - adapts many conditions
20. HQ - grows with skill level

## REFERENCES

Bovair, S., & Kieras, D. E. (1985). A guide to propositional analysis for research on technical prose. In B. K. Britton & J. B. Black (Eds.), *Understanding expository text* (pp. 315–362). Hillsdale, NJ: Lawrence Erlbaum Associates.

Britton, B. K. (1996). Rewriting: The arts and sciences of improving expository instructional text. In C. M. Levy & S. Ransdell (Eds.), *The science of writing: Theories, methods, individual differences, and applications.* Mahwah, NJ: Lawrence Erlbaum Associates.

Britton, B. K., & Gulgöz, S. (1991). Using Kintsch's computational model to improve instructional texts: Effects of repairing inference calls on recall and cognitive structures. *Journal of Educational Psychology, 83,* 329–345.

Britton, B. K., & Tidwell, P. (1995). Cognitive structure testing: A computer system for diagnosis of expert-novice differences. In P. D. Nichols, S. Chipman, & R. L. Brennan (Eds.), *Cognitively diagnostic assessment* (pp. 251–279). Mahwah, NJ: Lawrence Erlbaum Associates.

Britton, B. K., Van Dusen, L., Gulgöz, S., & Glynn, S. (1989). Instrumental texts rewritten by five expert teams: Revisions and retention improvements. *Journal of Educational Psychology, 81*(2), 226–236.

Colomb, G., & Williams, J. M. (1987). *Discourse structures* [Tech. Rep.]. The writing programs of the University of Chicago.

Hartley, J., Bartlett, S., & Branthwaite, A. (1980). Underlining can make a difference—sometimes. *Journal of Educational Research, 73,* 218–224.

Hynd, C., & Guzzetti, B. (1997). When knowledge contradicts intuition: Conceptual change. In C. Hynd (Ed.), *Learning from text across conceptual domains.* Mahwah, NJ: Lawrence Erlbaum Associates.

Johnson, L. L. (1988). Effects of underlining textbook sentences on passage and sentence retention. *Reading Research and Instruction, 28,* 18–32.

Lorch, R. F. (1989). Text signaling devices and their effects on reading and memory processes. *Educational Psychology Review, 1,* 209–234.

Lorch, R. F., Lorch, E. P., & Klusewitz, M. A. (1995). Effects of typographical cues on reading and recall of text. *Contemporary Educational Psychology, 20,* 51–64.

Tyson-Bernstein, H. (1988). *A conspiracy of good intentions: America's textbook fiasco.* Washington, DC: Council for Basic Education.

## CHAPTER SIX

# Literature's Place in Learning History and Science

Bruce A. VanSledright
*University of Maryland at College Park*

Lisa Frankes
*Eastern Michigan University*

Both history and science educators share common concerns regarding the importance of literature as a means of supporting discipline-specific literacy. These concerns have emerged, in part, as a reaction to the limitations that accompany the use of textbooks as the primary classroom resource. Textbooks, according to students, educators, and researchers, are sorely lacking, providing neither sufficient nor adequate information (Guzzetti, Kowalinski, & McGowan, 1992; Jones, Coombs, & McKinney, 1994; Sewall, 1988; Shymansky, Yore, & Good, 1991; Stinner, 1992).

## THE PROBLEM OF USING THE TEXTBOOK ALONE

Within science textbooks, theories, laws, and principles are presented devoid of meaningful context and asserted as authoritative truths (Martin & Brouwer, 1991; Stinner, 1992). They are not embedded contextually within the explorations that led to their creation. Consequently, scientists' thinking processes are unavailable to students as a source of understanding (Chiappetta, Sethna, & Fillman, 1993). In addition, textbooks are criticized for containing too many concepts and ideas presented superficially in a list-like manner. Finally, science textbooks are ineffective as a means of eradicating students' misconceptions and promoting conceptual change (Guzzetti, Snyder, Glass, & Gamas, 1993).

**117**

Similarly, in the history classroom textbooks are often presented as chronicles of the official truth regarding past events and their causes. In many texts a central narrative has been replaced with "mentionings" of women and minorities and brief, contextless descriptions of event after event. Thorough analysis is sacrificed for superficial coverage (Beck, McKeown, & Gromoll, 1989; McGowan, Erickson, & Neufeld, 1996; Sewall, 1988; Smith & Johnson, 1995). Perhaps most crucial, history typically is presented from one perspective within textbooks. Consequently, students have little opportunity to engage in processes of historical interpretation and source evaluation (Tunnell & Ammon, 1996; VanSledright & Kelly, 1998).

Whereas the preceding criticisms of classroom textbooks contribute to recent calls for literature-based teaching approaches, the literacy goals specific to science and history education also provide a rationale for including other types of literature in the classroom. An examination of the competencies that comprise scientific and historical literacy and how literature may be used to foster the development of these competencies provides the rationale for a literature-based approach to teaching, or at the very least, a rationale for the use of literature as a supplement to the classroom textbook.

## Using Literature to Promote Scientific Literacy

What is scientific literacy? Science educators have identified some primary themes that are central to the development of students' understanding and knowledge of science. Four primary themes are (a) knowledge of science content, including models, facts, laws, and principles; (b) knowledge of processes associated with investigation; (c) an understanding of the ways of thinking specific to science; and (d) an understanding of the complex ways in which science influences and is influenced by a particular sociocultural context (Chiappetta et al., 1993). Although textbooks have emphasized the first theme—knowledge of content—they lack sufficient information in the three other thematic areas of scientific inquiry. Literature has been advocated as one means of addressing this deficiency.

Methods of scientific inquiry have been idealized in science education to such a degree that there is little match between the actual procedures scientists employ to explore phenomena and the descriptions provided in classroom textbooks. How do scientists reason? How do actual explorations proceed? The scientific method is explicated neatly in most texts through a series of traditional procedures: A scientist examines some phenomena through the lens of theory, conceives a hypothesis, tests the accuracy of it through data collection and analysis, and develops a set of conclusions. However, this is a misrepresentation, for experimentation most often proceeds in an idiosyncratic, often patternless fashion.

Wandersee (1995) studied the research processes of 10 accomplished life science researchers to better understand how scientific knowledge develops and determined that the complexities of scientific exploration are seldom explicated. He stated: "A classroom view of science that shows scientific knowledge as a simple extension of the data collected objectively during research is clearly erroneous" (p. 650). According to Wandersee, research is driven by the goals and needs of society, and application needs are often in conflict with the desire for the pure extension of knowledge. Funding pressures require an emphasis on problem solving over theory building, and questions drive experimentation rather than theory. Scientists change aims, methods, and theories depending on the circumstances, and experimentation is thus more complex than the single storyline, sanitized version offered in texts. Through the incorporation of literature (e.g., biography, science fiction), which can describe in detail the processes of scientific exploration utilized by the scientists' themselves, students may develop an understanding of the uncertain, divergent, and nonlinear ways by which scientific knowledge develops.

Some science educators advocate incorporating a historical approach (Martin & Brouwer, 1991; Stinner, 1992; Wandersee, 1995) to science learning. Literature may serve to enliven the study of science by allowing students to view the particular historical context from which discoveries emerge. Through historical narratives students examine prevalent historical beliefs that preceded a specific discovery in order to recapitulate the original arguments leading up to new understanding. Reading about the different thought experiments of scientists and their individual struggles with revolutionary ideas provides students with insight into the tentative nature of discovery and models as sources of comparison for their own scientific thinking. Autobiographies, biographies, and fictionalized histories of scientists can serve to draw students into the personal world of the scientist and allow them to vicariously share the experience of exploration:

> Indeed, the narrative mode is essential to a science education that values the belief that students must have a personal engagement with the ideas they are to learn. Stories are our natural means of sharing in the lives of others and of more fully exploring meaning in our own. Through stories students may more successfully begin to see the subtle dimensions of science and of understanding the ways in which science, culture, and world view interact. (Martin & Brouwer, 1991, p. 708)

An accurate portrayal of science should reveal the personal, historical, and societal influences that interact to shape knowledge, for knowledge is always embedded within a cultural, human context. For example, Martin and Brouwer (1991) described how modern drama can be utilized to highlight the moral dilemmas that accompany technological advancement. In

Henrik Ibsen's play, *An Enemy of the People*, for instance, Dr. Stockman must choose between furthering his own personal economic interests or acting to protect the interests of the larger community. Martin and Brouwer provided other examples of how literature can unmask the traditional view of science as objective and value neutral, and can serve to uncover the intimate and complex connections among science, technology, and society. Introducing controversial scientific issues through literature allows students to evaluate evidence and grapple with the moral implications that scientific decision making often entails (Cross & Price, 1966).

The uses of story, then, may support the development of students' scientific literacy skills and competencies by providing a more accurate and detailed portrayal of the processes that define scientific inquiry, the historical context out of which inquiry emerges, and the values and potential moral implications that follow in the wake of any exploration. Finally, one cannot ignore the importance of engaging the imagination of students by embedding abstract laws and principles within a story of discovery, one that humanizes science and allows students to participate in the act of discovery.

**Using Literature to Promote Historical Literacy**

Historians and history education researchers (e.g., Gagnon, 1989; VanSledright, 1995; Wilson, 1991) have lamented the fact that in most classrooms the processes of historical investigation have gained little currency. Learning is still synonymous with the memorization of names and dates within the context of a unified storyline. However, historical literacy entails more:

> To be able to engage in discourse on history is to be able to do more than tell the story. One must be able to indicate, through speaking or writing, some awareness of what we call the "methods" of history. . . . We mean developing awareness that, for example, the received story is simple and distorting and that the story had to be recorded in documents of various kinds, which serve as the evidence for the story. Historical literacy also implies an appreciation that evidence counts and some sense of where evidence comes from. Without knowing the sources of evidence, students cannot evaluate the story. (Perfetti, Britt, & Georgi, 1995, p. 4)

Helping students understand history as a human enterprise, comprising the creation of causal relationships and interpretations of these relationships—constantly subject to revision—may best be accomplished through incorporating various types of literature into the history classroom. Diaries, journal accounts, newspaper articles, historical fiction, poetry, biography, and autobiography should all be included within classroom learning experiences to provide students with opportunities to engage in the methods of history. Perfetti and his colleagues (1995) advocated the strategy of comparing texts so that students become skilled at recognizing the existence of textual bias and the rhetoric of persuasion used to convey different arguments. By integrating these types of texts, the authoritative, monolithic recounting of "the facts of history" peculiar to expository textbooks may be compared with narrative accounts. For example, Tunnell and Ammon (1996) provided samples of conflicting interpretations of the Columbus story and explored how disparate storylines—Eurocentric versus Native American perspectives—may support teaching children to gather evidence and evaluate various arguments.

Contextualizing a particular set of historical events is also crucial to the development of students' historical understanding. Literature provides contextual details pertaining to a particular time period. The lives of common people—often omitted from textbook representations—are depicted in detail and serve to develop students' global understanding of the environment and time period, providing an anchor for larger events (Goldstein, 1989). Poetry and music lyrics may also be used to reflect the ethos of a particular time period and highlight the perspective and particular motivations of an individual or cultural group. Levstik (1989) claimed that literature allows students to participate in events by encouraging them to identify closely with characters. However, there is also a danger in this identification, because careful assessments of a character's actions may be jeopardized (Levstik, 1986). Using additional literary sources can help to ameliorate this concern by expanding the context in which characters' actions are considered.

Another important reason for using literature, both fiction and nonfiction, in the history classroom stems from the controversies that surround textbook development. The textbook industry, responding to market demands in a climate characterized by political controversy, seeks to appease consumers and lobbyists for special interest groups. As a result, controversial issues are often omitted, minimally covered, or distorted. For example, one recently published social studies series omitted any reference to Malcolm X and allotted only one paragraph to a description of the Holocaust (Tunnell & Ammon, 1996). It is important, therefore, to incorporate the particular perspectives of traditionally disenfranchised groups through the use of literature that presents diverse sociocultural perspectives and portrays events such as the Holocaust in an in-depth manner. Introduced to literature with protagonists from diverse cultural backgrounds, students may develop an awareness and appreciation for cultural differences, while vicariously coming to understand what it means to be a person from a minority culture in a particular time and place. Moreover, minority students may perceive that their identity is affirmed and reflected in the curriculum (Smith & Johnson, 1995).

It is crucial to select historical literature that authentically portrays the perspectives of various groups and historical figures, according to James and Zarrillo (1989), who developed a list of useful criteria for the selection of literature in the classroom that accounts for a variety of instructional factors:

1. As many selections as possible should be primary sources.
2. [Make sure that the] perspectives held by participants during the period are represented.
3. The literature should fit the variety of student reading levels.
4. Along with historical fiction, a variety of nonfiction, especially biography, should be included.
5. A careful balance must be found between enjoying the literature selected as art and using literature as data for social science analysis (p. 154).

However, according to some analysts, in using a literature-based approach to teaching history, teachers must be thoughtful in their choice of literature lest they select a text based solely on its motivational appeal and general literary quality. Alleman and Brophy (1994) voiced concerns that without an understanding of the goals of instruction and what historical literacy entails, teachers who employ a literature-based approach may inadvertently trivialize social studies purposes and content. They suggested that teachers should mediate children's learning from text by guiding them to seek more than a simple storyline and by teaching them to reason in a manner specific to history and to take a critical attitude toward texts and evidence. Levstik (1995) also echoed many of these same pedagogical strategies.

## An Emphasis on Inquiry, Evidence Use, and Habits of Mind

Many parallels can be identified between the various arguments for using literature in the science and history classrooms. Advocates of literature-based teaching approaches within each discipline promote the use of literature as a means of portraying inquiry as a human enterprise marked by uncertainty, complexity, controversy, and nonlinear development. Both emphasize the motivational beliefs of narrative and the importance of using story to contextualize experience for students (Bruner, 1996). Perhaps most central, literature use in both disciplines is viewed as a means of shifting emphases away from the traditional accumulation of static, factual knowledge in the form of memorized laws, principles, names and dates, and toward understanding the nature of inquiry, the importance of evidenced-based claims, and other habits of mind specific to each discipline. To illustrate how this might work, we take a closer look at the role literature might play in an integrated history–literature classroom. We explore in more detail the ideas we advanced in the foregoing analysis of literature's role in promoting historical literacy.

## LITERATURE IN DISCIPLINE-BASED TEACHING AND LEARNING: AN ILLUSTRATION OF AMPLIFYING HISTORICAL UNDERSTANDING

We have learned from research (Wineburg, 1991, 1994) that in the discipline of history much time is spent examining a variety of texts. Historians explore diaries and journals, public records that have survived, old newspaper reports, literary accounts, and a host of other textual sources as they hunt for clues about what happened in the past. Sometimes that past gives up its secrets unwillingly, so historians need to be diligent detectives. They must persistently search, read, sort, and prioritize; they must imagine a past in its context and decide among competing interpretations what they will believe, then document it in the histories they write. In many ways, historians epitomize the types of readers described by the reading engagement perspective of the National Reading Research Center (Alvermann & Guthrie, 1993).[1]

Ideally, students learning history also would become diligent, persistent, and tenacious detectives, hunting down, sorting, and prioritizing among the different interpretations of the past they encounter. They would learn to be skillful assessors of historical texts. Teachers would apprentice students in this process of examining texts and accounts of the past and teach them how to read with a critical, searching eye—not unlike historians. In short, students would become eager, engaged readers of history. The immediate goal would not be to produce little historians, but rather to teach—using the domain of history—the art and practice of engaged reading. The broader goal would be the transfer of what students know and can do as engaged history readers into the everyday contexts they encounter, because engaged reading is crucial to life in an information-dominated democratic society. Such a society depends on motivated, knowledgeable, interactive readers who can critically assess and evaluate their many social, cultural, economic, and political choices.

Unfortunately, students studying history across the grades typically encounter it through the textbooks criticized so forcefully by many of those analysts cited earlier. Historical literacy, they claim, is blunted by these

---

[1]Alvermann and Guthrie (1993) described highly engaged readers to be motivated, knowledgeable, and socially interactive. The engagement perspective assumes that readers should have "competencies and motivations to read for diverse purposes, such as gaining knowledge, performing a task, interpreting an author's perspective, sharing reactions to stories and informational texts, escaping into the literary world, or taking social and political action in response to what is read" (p. 2).

omniscient, univocal, consensus textbooks. Historians make a practice out of searching out everything they can possibly find on a topic before they assemble the evidence, judge its veracity, determine their interpretation of events, and collate their written accounts. Why should students be deprived of multiple sources of information about the past? Why should they be relegated to only one univocal textbook version? Herein lies the important role of literature (and journalistic accounts, diaries, journals, pictorial evidence, and the like).[2]

Literature (combined with other sources describing past events, including the textbook) can serve at least three significant purposes that, in turn, can advance students' historical understanding. First, literature can provide a sense of context. Literature written during a historical period under study can provide important clues concerning how some people thought about their worlds at the time. Placing the past in its context is an indispensable aid in constructing a carefully honed understanding of a historical period, its set of events, and its agents' motives. For example, reading Upton Sinclair's (1905/1960) *The Jungle* as they study why the federal government began regulating the food industry in the early part of the 20th century can take students into the hearts and minds of people working the slaughterhouses of Chicago in, say, 1903. Remarque's (1928/1956) *All Quiet on the Western Front* can do the same for World War I. These are but two examples of how literature, augmenting other sources, can play an important role in developing a sense of historical context, and thereby enhance historical understanding.

Second, literature can assist students as they learn to take the perspective of others. This process, like placing events in their historical contexts, is also indispensable. To one degree or another, all of us are trapped by our own present sociocultural assumptions. We tend to view history from that presentist perspective. Students are no exception. If anything, they might be more apt than educated adults to overgeneralize their presentist sense of the world to the historical past. Getting into the heads and hearts of historical agents as they make mundane and not-so-mundane decisions is crucial to the way one understands that past. Literature can serve this purpose well.

In *All Quiet on the Western Front,* we enter Paul's experience as a German soldier in World War I. We see his world from his viewpoint. We grow sympathetic to his cause, his battles, his country. For careful middle or high school readers who allow themselves into Paul's world, it becomes far less possible to overgeneralize anger and vindictiveness to all Germans, even toward those who gave us the atrocities of World War II, because they are

---

[2]For our purposes here in the context of studying history, we define literature as those types of texts that have historically embedded themes, but generally are considered fictional. Newspaper texts, diaries, journals, textbooks, and letters also could be classified as forms of literature. In what follows, we make the distinction only as a means of clarification.

toward those who gave us the atrocities of World War II, because they are permitted to assume "the other's" perspective for a time. Reading about Paul means understanding that war is hell no matter which side you are on. Good literature helps to disarm our presentism, to make us less quick to judge others by our standards.

Third and finally, literature provides for alternate interpretations of events. Even fiction can help us imagine different ways of making meaning. *The Jungle*'s author, Upton Sinclair (1905/1960), was a noted socialist, and his book was written with that perspective at its center. He took his capitalist antagonists to task in the book. The engaged reader of *The Jungle* is immersed in this alternate view, a view from the workers on the factory floor, looking up rather than down from the management on unruly, union-forming employees bent on driving companies out of business with their demands for higher wages, a view often forefronted in textbooks. Readers get the sense from Sinclair that socialism is the only salvation for his slaughterhouse factory hands. They encounter a view of the ugly underbelly of capitalism and are revolted. Univocal interpretations—those frequently presented in textbook histories—are challenged by the polyvocalizing process introduced by alternative conceptions from good historical literature. Alternative interpretations via good literature (and other sources) are crucial to awakening students to the sort of thinking required for developing deep historical understandings.

These three fundamental aspects of historical study—establishing context, enhancing perspective taking, and developing alternative interpretations—are nicely supported by the use of literature in the history classroom. But the presence of literature also serves other purposes. We now look at three—promoting reading engagement, improving reading practice, and building critical historical literacy—that are closely connected to the ways powerful, historically framed literature can challenge and motivate learning.

## Using Literature to Promote Reading Engagement in Historical Study

Anyone who has read a powerful work of literature knows that one of its main strengths lies in its ability to evoke potent emotional reactions. A hallmark of good readers, whose reading practices were systematically studied and reviewed by Pressley and Afflerbach (1995), is that they engage texts with passion and respond often with intense emotional reactions (p. 98). Powerful literature engages readers and raises the prospect that passionate, emotionally charged reading will occur.

We know from survey data (Foertsch, 1992) that engagement with reading and text drops off considerably after about fourth grade. We also know that about the same time, students in school begin to have their learning experiences more regularly filtered by expository textbooks. What better way to offset this downward slide in reading practice than to offer reading opportunities that foster text engagement through the power to produce emotional attachments such as fondness, anger, sadness, surprise, and revulsion. For example, MacKinlay Kantor's (1955) novel, *Andersonville*, holds the power to evoke this array of emotions about the Civil War. To be sure, textbook history talks of human lives lost, of the tragedy of bloodshed on the battlefields of Pennsylvania and Virginia, of the suffering endured all over the country, but *Andersonville* brings it all streaming into consciousness, causing the reader's heart to pound, throat to tighten, and soul to ache over the scenes of loss. Or one could read Margaret Walker's (1966) award-winning *Jubilee*, a turbulent and vivid account of slavery at the Civil War watershed. Motivated readers engage texts with passion, but the texts must have the power to evoke passion as well. Powerful literature, unlike the standard textbook, offers that promise—to engage by emotion and passion even less motivated readers whose school experiences have left them wondering if indeed there are reasons to study the past.

In addition to enhancing motivation and engagement, using literature in the history classroom also may make readers more expert. Experts have become good at what they do by repeatedly challenging themselves (Bereiter & Scardemalia, 1993). They put themselves in situations where the problems they must solve are difficult and the tasks demanding. Those who study the past are no exception (Wineburg, 1991). Pressley and Afflerbach (1995) extended this argument about the nature of expertise and how it develops into the arena of reading. They argued that good readers challenge themselves on difficult texts. Good literature, of the historical-fiction sort mentioned earlier, can make significant demands on readers as they work to construct meaning before, during, and after reading. These demands, if they occur at the edges of a reader's competence level, can push a reader forward to more complex levels of reading. Citing Bereiter and Scardemalia (1993), Pressley and Afflerbach (1995) observed that "experts keep pushing themselves to the edge of their competence and thus, a curriculum in which students are really being pushed to read materials that increase in difficulty as reader competence increases makes sense" (p. 112). The use of good literature in the history classroom, if chosen well and matched to challenge readers at the margin of their capacities, offers the promise of increasing reader competence as well as growth in reading engagement and motivation.

Using literature in learning about the past also has the power to enhance students' critical historical literacy. By critical historical literacy, something we alluded to in the previous section, we mean a stance one takes toward historical texts that is characterized by questioning, investigation, skepticism, and evaluation. If literature is used to augment other classroom history texts, it inevitably raises questions about the reliability and validity of interpretations. Is Sinclair's (1905/1960) socialist position in *The Jungle* a valid point of view? How accurately does he convey conditions in the slaughterhouses of Chicago given his penchant for expressing his distaste for capitalism? Does Remarque's (1928/1956) fondness for Paul, and by extension the German perspective on World War I, discredit his interpretation of the war? How does an author's position influence the nature of the account he or she creates? What is the subtext of the historical interpretation offered (Wineburg, 1991)? These are a few of the questions that those developing a critical literacy sense about history begin to ask. They interrogate texts because they approach them with initial skepticism. Historical literature in the classroom can help to expand the growth of this disposition toward literary learning.

Engaged reading via involvement with passionate texts, challenge and growth in reading competence and thus in learning, and the honing of a disposition toward critical historical literacy are three of the many benefits that accrue to learners who encounter powerful historical literature. Much promise, but can these goals be realized? Probably not without intrepid teachers and effective teaching practices.

## Implications for Teaching History

Thus far, we have suggested that the use of historical literature holds much promise for enhancing historical thinking, amplifying historical understanding, and producing more motivated, engaged, and expert readers. However, little of this occurs without astute and ambitious history teachers and teaching. With this in mind, there are three issues (among many) we raise: (a) the teaching-and-learning dilemmas created by introducing literature into the history classroom, (b) the potential pitfalls of using literature as a form of historical representation, and (c) the importance of raising questions about reliability and validity in historical study.

First, using powerful historical novels to augment textbooks and other historical sources can create tensions in the history classroom. History's story can be filled with glory and triumph. But just as easily it can be covered with mud, blood, pain, and human despair. All of these matters are related to what we are as humans. We experience joy and sorrow; we love and we bleed; we kill one another and then bask in our victory over the forces of evil. These are the makings of the drama history unfolds for us when we read. More so than textbooks, historical literature spans a greater array of emotional reactions. Literature depicts the full range of human qualities from the depths of our depravity to the pinnacles of our magnanimity. This is what makes the literature so potentially compelling to readers. Yet, herein lie several difficulties.

Literature can invoke powerful reactions among students and certainly their parents, so it must be used judiciously. Some books are simply better than others. But even some of the better, more powerful books are potentially controversial. It goes without saying that each piece of historical literature must be studied carefully before it is used. It may make sense also to forewarn students and parents about the more controversial aspects of a given selection. This warning can be couched in language that justifies the importance of the literature in terms of the many benefits and important learning results described earlier. Having thought through and developed a strong rationale about why using a particular work of literature is important (e.g., building context, fostering perspective taking, enhancing motivation to read, promoting expertise and critical literacy) can go a long way toward defusing an eruption of public reticence and suspicion.

Second, the use of literature and historical fiction in the secondary history classroom poses a concern about how it will be understood as a representation of the past. The Sinclairs, Remarques, and Walkers who offer these compelling works of historical prose are doing what good authors do: They are using contexts, settings, and people to support a theme about which they wish to write. To sustain reader interest, drama, mystery, and tension are essential. Such authors are exceptionally good at creating such drama. History is filled with similar drama but it tends to be episodic. Long mundane periods punctuate history's action. Literature authors cannot wait on history's cycles, so they generate their own tensions and mysteries, sometimes without close regard to the historical accuracy of the events they portray. Nonetheless, a story well told, no matter how fictionalized, can create the illusion of research-based accuracy. Historical fiction, as a form of historical representation, carries with it this illusion.

Students, who are perhaps unfamiliar with different types of historical representation, will need help sorting out research-based accounts from those that are fictional. Because of the engaging power of many fictional history texts, students may be tempted to think that they possess greater verisimilitude to actual events than the texts generated by historians through careful research and study of the available evidence. Students will need help in sorting out these sometimes fine-grained distinctions among texts (and often within texts also). But there can hardly be a better opportunity to learn about the nature of historical representation, the act of creating historical texts through which our view of what preceded us is filtered. These can be significant lessons, ones made possible by the introduction of literature into the classroom.

Third, using literature and confronting it as a form of historical representation in the classroom raises serious questions about evidence use and about what is considered historically valid knowledge. This is bumpy terrain. Historians frequently debate these issues without resolution. Much of the landscape is highly contested. Some historians wish to stretch the limits of what should be considered valid historical accounting, whereas others would seriously limit it to the evidence at hand. Some welcome the extensive use of the historian's imagination to fill in missing pieces in the evidence trail; others act as if there was no such thing as the historian's imagination. For some, historical fiction may be a questionable but still legitimate form of historical representation; others would relegate it to the very margins of historical respectability.

These are controversies that can benefit students who learn about them. On their way to developing profound and lasting historical understandings, deep historical thinking capacities, and acute critical literacy, students can be assisted by good historical literature. It can expand their thinking, awaken their somnambulistic reading practices, and engage their interest in historical study.

## EXAMINING THE RESEARCH EVIDENCE

From what we have suggested so far, the prospect of using literature in secondary history (and possibly science classrooms) shows great promise, with only a few manageable issues with which to be concerned. But what is the research basis for the laudatory claims made by proponents? Do the benefits stand up to the scrutiny of a circumspect research lens? These are difficult questions to answer. Very few existing studies have examined the influence and efficacy of using literature in secondary history and science classrooms. Most of the studies have been done at the elementary and middle grades. Also, many of these studies have been done by reading researchers, not science or history education researchers. The results are mixed. To provide a flavor of the range of this work, we review several representative studies.

Jones, Coombs, and McKinney (1994) conducted a study in which they compared the effects of utilizing children's books incorporated into a themed literature unit with the effects of using a textbook in an elementary social studies class. Two sixth-grade classes were taught a unit on Mexico for approximately 2 weeks. The intact classes were randomly assigned to the two treatments. One class received instruction via the school-adopted textbook, strictly following the teacher's manual, and the other was taught via five nonfiction children's books that addressed the topic through a themed literature unit. For the theme-based unit, the teachers used the strategy of (a) introducing the theme, (b) introducing each of the five books, and (c) asking the children by paper ballot to choose one of the five books to read and explore. Each student was given his or her choice of book but was allowed a 24-hour grace period for a change of mind. Five collaborative groups, ranging in size from two to seven students, were formed around each book. Each group selected a project that would be presented to the class as a means of sharing new information. Poster presentations, murals, and dioramas were possible choices. Book tests were administered at certain points for purposes of accountability. Four minilessons were also used. The unit's duration involved twelve 50-minute lessons in each class.

A pretest–posttest design was employed, using a 32-item multiple-choice test to assess achievement on the unit content. An attitude survey also was used to assess students' reactions to the books they read. Results showed that the students taught with the nonfiction children's literature showed a significant gain in achievement and exhibited a very positive attitude toward their experience when compared with the traditional textbook-taught group.

Although gains in both achievement and attitude were reported from this study, these must be interpreted with some caution. The authors (Jones et al., 1994) did not describe the nature of instruction in the traditional classroom. It is possible that the difference in teachers—their approach, strategies, and general classroom comportment—influenced the results more than the differences in texts used. It also is possible that the act of giving the students choices in the theme-based literature classroom influenced their motivation and changed their attitudes, rather than that they had used the nonfiction texts as opposed to the textbook.

In a similar study of sixth graders, Guzzetti, Kowalinski, and McGowan (1992) worked in the context of a school/university partnership in which two researchers developed, implemented, and evaluated a literature-based approach to social studies in concert with a sixth-grade teacher. They collaborated on one unit taught without a textbook, using the literature-based design. Another sixth-grade teacher provided a comparison by employing only textbook-based instruction. Citing the often-referenced criticisms of textbooks, the authors concurred with the judgments that the textbooks present far too many substantive concepts in a list-like fashion (Calfee, 1987), that they are inconsiderate of readers with respect to comprehension and readability (Armbruster & Anderson, 1984), that they frequently lack message or meaning (Sewall, 1988), and that they utilize banal content and colorless prose (Tyson & Woodward, 1989). As a result, the researchers staked their claim on the power of tradebooks to provide causal relationships between concepts and to offer readers a greater opportunity to answer their own questions through reading (Calfee, 1987). They argued that a literature-based approach helps generate an environment in which children can learn to think independently. Guzzetti et al. (1992) explained that their own observations had confirmed the affective rewards of using trade books.

The literature-based unit focused on China because of student interest and book availability. The research team gathered what they judged to be appealing trade books, fiction and nonfiction, selecting 42 titles for use in the China unit. They found that 70% of the school district's objectives for reading and 68% of its objectives for social studies could be addressed through the texts. They then developed instructional activities to meet district objectives, to foster the doing of social studies (e.g., authentic inquiry tasks), and to engage students in cooperative and purposeful activity. They first addressed prior knowledge and misconceptions by brainstorming with students about what they already knew. For example, brainstorming uncovered inaccurate understandings of China's location, topography, and geography. These results were used in structuring the unit. Each day's instruction began with a read-aloud, followed by the creation of a central question and three subcategories in columns labeled "my questions," "my ideas," and "text answers." Students generated question-and-answer books about China and compared Chinese and American folktales in an effort to appreciate both differences and similarities between the two contrasting cultures. After completing a book, students were asked to create a visual display on posterboard of the relationship between their hobbies and interests and the events in the story, or to design a character chart representing individual characters in the story. Each teacher devoted 12.5 hours to China during a 5-week period. The traditional teachers' approach was not described in any comparative detail.

To assess learning, the research team used three measures: an 88-item multiple-choice test to measure concept acquisition, the Estes Reading Attitude Assessment to assess reading attitudes, and a student rank order of their sixth-grade subjects in terms of enjoyment and importance. Each measure was given as a pre- and posttest.

Results showed a significant difference in concept acquisition, but no difference in attitudes. Analysis of covariance for the multiple-choice test revealed significant gains for the group taught using the trade books. Subject preference ratings remained unchanged across the treatment. The research team reexamined both students and data to explain lack of improvement in attitudes, especially with regard to social studies. This revealed that the students in the treatment classroom did not see the unit as social studies because a textbook was not used. The authors concluded by suggesting that their results offered some empirical support for a literature-based approach to social studies instruction. They noted that it appeared as though students could acquire more concepts and a greater understanding of those concepts through a literature-based approach than through a more traditional textbook approach.

Again, caution must be exercised in interpreting this report. The traditional classroom practices were not described, nor was a comparison made of the teachers' attitudes, pedagogical strategies, and classroom comportments. The relative differences between the teachers may have accounted for as much of the variance as did the difference in texts. A Hawthorne effect also may have played a role.

VanSledright and Kelly (1998) examined how one fifth-grade teacher made use of a standard American history textbook and also a variety of alternative texts—some of them literature based—as data sources for students who were asked to conduct research and make report presentations on North American exploration and colonization, and on the American Revolution. They observed in the classroom on the average of 3 days per week for 6 months to understand how the texts were employed and to what end. Six students acted as informants in helping the researchers develop more in-depth knowledge about (a) their attitudes toward the texts, (b) how they conducted research and distinguished among the texts as sources of historical content, and (c) the ways in which the multiple text sources influenced the development of their critical reading capacities and historical understanding. To obtain their research data, VanSledright and Kelly interviewed the students at the end of three units they observed and also asked the six to participate in a think-aloud protocol on two conflicting textual accounts of the Boston Massacre. Six salient themes emerged from the data:

1. When given the choice, students opted to use the alternative, narrative texts rather than expository textbook, said they found them more interesting, and enjoyed reading them more than the textbook.
2. Despite differences in content and prose forms used in the textbook and the alternative texts and even among some of the alternative texts, and despite showing preferences for one type or the other, students did not note that these differences might affect how the content of the books might need to be read and assessed in different ways.
3. In-class encounters with the various texts did not elicit many questions or concerns about text differences and how they can influence the adjudication of historical reliability and validity issues.
4. Authors of the texts students read did not record where they had obtained their information, further muting students' curiosity and concern about reliability and validity questions.
5. Reflecting the nature of their teacher-assigned, information-gathering research tasks, students operated from an information-quantity criterion as a key measure for assessing the value of the different books they read.
6. Despite heavy reliance on the information-quantity criterion, indications emerged from the use of a variety of text sources that several students did find the author's point of view important in making judgments about a source's credibility and could think in terms of event-modeling within historical context that historian's employ when doing their research.

VanSledright and Kelly (1998) observed that the use of a variety of sources, many of which were literature based, held much promise for assisting students in the development of their critical reading capacities and historical understanding. However, they concluded, the lack of explicit instruction in how to read the different history texts and assess them for bias, subtext, reliability, and validity while also building and working from event models as historians do, significantly constrained what they learned about history and how to go about researching the past.

VanSledright and Kelly's (1998) study was based on observations in only one classroom and interviews with only 6 fifth graders, so care must be taken not to overgeneralize the results. As with the other empirical studies, despite results that point in the direction favored by literature-based curriculum proponents, there are important questions yet to be addressed by research. One that has concerned several history education researchers deals with the potential of historical fiction literature, for example, to distort students' understandings of the past.

Levstik (1989) reported that 1 fifth-grade student, Jennifer, found the narrative prose of fictionalized historical accounts in American history more appealing than expository textbook prose because they provided a sense of wholeness and resolution. The fictional accounts also offered a moral dimension, a sense of right and wrong that was attractive to Jennifer. Levstik concluded that narrative-style history, the sort found in good children's literature, humanized the study of history and called forth a subjective reaction whereby the fictional accounts were used as a method of judging the veracity of the textbook. Levstik welcomed these results as important features of developing historical understanding in students. However, Levstik (1995), as well as Freeman and Levstik (1986), has repeatedly cautioned about the possible distortive influences that a heavy reliance on fictionalized historical literature might have. She called for classroom-based discussions of historical literature, coupled with instruction in noting how characters are fictionalized, how the overall account tends to simplify and distort the past, and how characters are often portrayed stereotypically.

After interviewing 10 students at the very end of their fourth-grade year concerning what they knew about American history, VanSledright and Brophy (1992) noted that several of these students, who had relished historical fiction accounts in fourth grade, tended to respond to interview questions about such things as the American Revolution and the age of exploration in story or narrative form. The students' accounts, though interesting and told with significant flourish, bore only partial resemblances to what historians have researched and written about these topics. In their conclusion, VanSledright and Brophy raised the prospect that the historical fiction accounts may have prompted the students to think of history as any compelling, action-laced account told about past events, without regard to evidence-use rules exercised by historians. These sorts of studies suggest reservations about the heavy use of fictional literature in history classrooms unless there is strong mediation by the teacher between student and text.

At the secondary level, two studies attempted to connect multiple-source use—including literature and journalistic representations—with the development of historical literacy and understanding. They were conducted by Perfetti and his colleagues (1995) and by Stahl, Hynd, Britton, McNish, and Bosquet (1996).

Perfetti et al. (1995) spent several years examining the cognitive psychology of learning from history texts among six University of Pittsburgh undergraduates. Their study used four texts that described the historical events involved in the United States' acquisition of the Panama Canal. They argued that historical agents' motivations, historical enabling factors, and physical causes were central to understanding the acquisition. They determined common information students had learned, individual differences in students' learning styles, the quality and quantity of information the students had learned, and what text-specific information was retained.

After this initial exploration into the students' knowledge of the Panama Canal acquisition, Perfetti et al. (1995) argued that on three points the reading of history departed from other types of narrative reading: (a) There is more to history texts than the narrative structure; (b) history stories are represented as causal–temporal event chains; and (c) events and their connections are at the core of the representation. As a result, readers must interpret and reason about both the events and the author's interpretation or argument. They concluded that the sort of reasoning required was unique to history texts. Their study then focused on this type of unique reading with the six students.

The six were above-average readers who, nevertheless, had no strong background knowledge in the subject matter of history. The texts students read varied in length, complexity, perspective, and amount of detail. The texts were read as homework, with students answering questions orally during the course of class meetings the researchers held. Students were asked comprehension and reasoning questions, and they wrote summary responses. The same six questions were asked at each meeting.

Students were able to discern author bias quickly. The researchers speculated that multiple texts may highlight the existence of bias and draw readers attention to it. This prompted them to contend that reading from more than one text facilitates learning history, as well as reasoning about it; that different texts provided different emphasis and different arguments, creating controversy and demanding that students reason about the texts; and that the value of using multiple texts was to provide students with a more flexible representation of the information contained in the texts (pp. 162–163).

Perfetti et al. (1995) suggested that using multiple texts had two primary benefits: More powerful learning results through increased attention (caused by novelty and increased access to information), and experiences with the same story being told different ways helped the reader to separate situation from textual representation, which increased the reader's ability to form distinct representations of text and situation. They ended by noting:

> Our conclusion, based on what we can observe in our studies, is simply that there is value in multiple text learning. It allows students a richer representation of the situation to be learned. It forces an awareness of texts, as opposed to situations, and it can be structured so as to focus on thinking and problem solving. History seems to be an ideal subject around which to promote the use of multiple texts and documents—and from which to develop text-based reasoning skills. (p. 189)

Stahl et al. (1996) conducted a similar study in which they employed many of the same Panama Canal texts used by Perfetti et al. (1995), and also asked their participants to read multiple accounts of the Gulf of Tonkin incident, which had led the United States to direct intervention in Vietnam. The researchers worked with high school students, whose familiarity with history was largely filtered by standard history textbooks. Stahl et al. were interested in understanding what sense students would make of multiple accounts of the same event. Their high school participants tended to miss the subtleties of meaning differences among the texts, favored the textbook because it seemed more objective to them, and were confused by the shifting viewpoints of the multiple texts' different authors. Despite these difficulties, Stahl et al. concluded that using multiple texts was central to the effective study of history. They offered the following recommendations: (a) Students should be helped to think like historians as they read multiple texts; (b) students should be taught about purposes for encountering and reading from different texts; (c) students should learn to build and draw from background knowledge of the past as they consider their reading sources; (d) the focus of teaching efforts should center on showing students how to source accounts, corroborate them against other sources, and place accounts in historical perspective; and (e) students should be taught how to write from multiple perspectives just as historians do in their work.

Thus far, this representative handful of empirical research studies has focused on history–social studies and the use of literature. Although small in number and offering only cautious optimism about the role of literature, a potentially fecund beginning has been made in attempting to understand the power literature can have in developing history–social studies literacy and understanding. Unfortunately, this cannot be said with the same sense of promise in the area of science education and literacy. Our attempts to track down empirical studies that assessed the use of literature in science classrooms produced very little. Most of these studies were analyses of textbook structures and their potential influences on students and the development of their science conceptions (Bingle & Gaskell, 1994; Guzzetti, Snyder, Glass, & Gamas, 1993; Martin & Brouwer, 1991; Stinner, 1995).

## CONCLUSION

Textbooks have been harshly castigated and literature-based approaches lauded by history and science educators equally. However, there are few studies that validate many of the positive claims advanced in this chapter. Perhaps most telling about the extant research on the role of literature in non-English classrooms is the search by McGowan, Erickson, and Neufeld (1996) of 164 articles published between 1929 and 1988, which examined the use of literature in social studies teaching. Only 4% of these were found to be research-based studies. Of those, evidence primarily supported the use of literature for the purposes of increasing knowledge acquisition rather than developing historical literacy skill. They caution that the amount of rhetoric promoting literature-based approaches far outweighs the evidence that might support these claims.

In science education, studies also show the ineffectiveness of textbooks as a means of effecting conceptual change, but few studies examine the use of literature as a means of improving classroom learning. Science educators have focused primarily on the use of interventions that involve a conglomeration of strategies such as implementation of the learning cycle, the use of bridging analogies, and the use of conceptual conflict approaches in combination with other interventions (Guzzetti et al., 1993), rather than on studying the influence of using literature alone.

It appears, then, that the case for the use of literature in the science and history classroom, while compelling, may be strengthened when research provides the evidence to support the positive claims advanced by proponents. Yet, the various theoretical rationales presented in this volume for enhancing learning through literature use signal an important advance in integrating disciplines such as the sciences and history with literary study. These rationales also can be employed to aid researchers in designing studies that might show the fruit claimed by proponents.

## REFERENCES

Alleman, J., & Brophy, J. (1994). Trade-offs embedded in the literacy approach to early elementary social studies. *Social Studies and the Young Learner, 6,* 6–8.

Alvermann, D., & Guthrie, J. G. (1993). Themes and directions of the National Reading Research Center. *Perspectives in Reading Research, No. 1.* Athens, GA: National Reading Research Center.

Armbruster, B., & Anderson, T. H. (1984). Structures of explanations in history texts or so what if Governor Stanford missed the spike and hit the rail? *Journal of Curriculum Studies, 16*, 181–194.

Beck, I., McKeown, M., & Gromoll, E. (1989). Learning from social studies texts. *Cognition and Instruction, 6*, 99–158.

Bereiter, C., & Scardemalia, M. (1993). *Surpassing ourselves: An inquiry into the nature and implications of expertise.* Chicago: Open Court.

Bingle, W. H., & Gaskell, P. J. (1994). Scientific literacy for decision making and the social construction of scientific knowledge. *Science Education, 78*, 185–201.

Bruner, J. (1996). *The culture of education.* Cambridge, MA: Harvard University Press.

Calfee, R. C. (1987). *The role of text structure in acquiring knowledge.* Final report to the U.S. Department of Education (Federal Program No. 122B). Palo Alto, CA: Stanford University Text Analysis Project.

Chiappetta, E. L., Sethna, G. H., & Fillman, D. A. (1993). Do middle school life science textbooks provide a balance of scientific literary themes? *The National Association for Research in Science Teaching, 30*, 198–220.

Cross, R. T., & Price, R. F. (1996). Science teachers' social conscience and the role of controversial issues in the teaching of science. *National Association for Research in Science Teaching, 33*, 319–333.

Foertsch, M. A. (1992). *Reading in and out of school: Factors influencing the reading achievement of American students in grades 4, 8, and 12, in 1988 and 1990.* Washington, DC: Office of Educational Research and Improvement, U.S. Department of Education.

Freeman, E., & Levstik, L. (1986). Recreating the past: Historical fiction in the social studies curriculum. *Elementary School Journal, 88*, 329–337.

Gagnon, P. (Ed.) (1989). *Historical literacy: The case for history in American education.* New York: Macmillan.

Goldstein, J. (1989). Using literature in a course on the Vietnam War. *Teaching History, 14*, 59–69.

Guzzetti, B. J., Kowalinski, B. J., & McGowan, L. (1992). Using a literature based approach to teaching social studies. *Journal of Reading, 36*, 114–122.

Guzzetti, B. J., Snyder, T. E., Glass, G. V., & Gamas, W. S. (1993). Promoting conceptual change in science: A comparative meta-analysis of instructional interventions from reading education and science education. *Reading Research Quarterly, 28*, 117–155.

James, M., & Zarrillo, J. (1989). Teaching history with children's literature: A concept-based, interdisciplinary approach. *The Social Studies, 80*, 153–158.

Jones, H. J., Coombs, W. T., & McKinney, C. W. (1994). A themed literature unit versus a textbook: A comparison of the effects on content acquisition and attitudes in elementary social studies. *Reading Research and Instruction, 34*, 85–96.

Kantor, M. (1955). *Andersonville.* New York: New American Library.

Levstik, L. S. (1986). The relationship between historical response and narrative in the classroom. *Theory and Research in Social Education, 14*, 1–15.

Levstik, L. S. (1989). Historical narrative and the young reader. *Theory Into Practice, 20*, 114–119.

Levstik, L. S. (1995). Narrative constructions: Cultural frames for history. *The Social Studies, 86*, 113–116.

Martin, B. E., & Brouwer, W. (1991). The sharing of personal science and the narrative element in science education. *Science Education, 75*, 707–722.

McGowan, T. M., Erickson, L., & Neufeld, J. (1996). With reason and rhetoric: Building the case for the literature-social studies connection. *Social Education, 60*, 203–207.

Perfetti, C. A., Britt, M. A., & Georgi, M. C. (1995). *Text-based learning and reasoning: Studies in history.* Hillsdale, NJ: Lawrence Erlbaum Associates.

Pressley, M., & Afflerbach, P. (1995). *Verbal protocols of reading: The nature of constructively responsive reading.* Hillsdale, NJ: Lawrence Erlbaum Associates.

Remarque, E. M. (1928/1956). *All quiet on the western front.* New York: Fawcett Book Group.

Sewall, G. T. (1988). American history textbooks: Where do we go from here? *Phi Delta Kappan, 69,* 552–558.

Shymansky, J. A., Yore, L. D., & Good, R. (1991). Elementary school teachers' belief about and perceptions of elementary school science, science reading, science textbooks, and supportive instructional factors. *The National Association for Research in Science Teaching, 28,* 437–454.

Sinclair, U. (1905/1960). *The jungle.* New York: New American Library.

Smith, J. L., & Johnson, H. A. (1995). Dreaming of America: Weaving literature into middle-school social studies. *The Social Studies, 86,* 60–68.

Stahl, S., Hynd, C., Britton, B., McNish, M., & Bosquet, D. (1996). What happens when students read multiple source documents in history? *Reading Research Quarterly, 31,* 430–456.

Stinner, A. (1992). Science textbooks and science teaching: From logic to evidence. *Science Education, 76,* 1–16.

Stinner, A. (1995). Contextual settings, science stories, and large context problems: Toward a more humanistic science education. *Science Education, 79,* 555–581.

Tunnell, M. O., & Ammon, R. (1996). The story of ourselves: Fostering multiple historical perspectives. *Social Education, 60,* 212–215.

Tyson, H., & Woodward, A. (1989). Why students aren't learning very much from textbooks. *Educational Leadership, 47,* 14–17.

VanSledright, B. A. (1995). 'I don't remember—the ideas are all jumbled in my head': Eighth graders' reconstructions of colonial American history. *Journal of Curriculum and Supervision, 10,* 317–345.

VanSledright, B. A., & Brophy, J. (1992). Storytelling, imagination, and fanciful elaboration in children's historical reconstructions. *American Educational Research Journal, 29,* 837–859.

VanSledright, B. A., & Kelly, C. (1998). Reading American history: The influence of multiple text sources on six fifth graders? *The Elementary School Journal, 98,* 239–265.

Walker, M. (1966). *Jubilee.* Boston: Houghton Mifflin.

Wandersee, J. H. (1995). How does biological knowledge grow? A study of life scientists' research practices. *Journal of Research in Science Teaching, 32,* 649–663.

Wilson, S. M. (1991). Parades of facts, stories of the past: What do novice history teachers need to know? In M. Kennedy (Ed.), *Teaching academic subjects to diverse learners* (pp. 99–116). New York: Teachers College Press.

Wineburg, S. S. (1991). On the reading of historical texts: Notes on the breach between school and academy. *American Educational Research Journal, 28,* 495–519.

Wineburg, S. S. (1994). The cognitive representation of historical texts. In G. Leinhardt, I. Beck, & C. Stainton (Eds.), *Teaching and learning in history* (pp. 85–136). Hillsdale, NJ: Lawrence Erlbaum Associates.

## CHAPTER SEVEN

# When Knowledge Contradicts Intuition: Conceptual Change

Cynthia R. Hynd
*University of Georgia*

Barbara Guzzetti
*Arizona State University*

| | |
|---|---|
| Janice: | There's logic, and then there's physics. |
| Joey: | Science is wrong. Science is wrong because if two objects are dropped at the same time, but one weighs more, wouldn't the one that is bigger fall faster because the force is greater? Science is not logical. |
| BG: | Can you make any conclusions about your data? |
| Joey: | I don't know. I'm not a physicist; I don't have to make conclusions. |
| Ryan: | The heavier the mass, the faster the fall because Jeremy's was the heaviest and it fell the fastest. |

In this chapter, we discuss conceptual change and its implications for high school students. Much of what we present comes from the research we engaged in as part of the National Reading Research Center. These studies were conducted in high school physics classes and in the high school integrated curriculum project depicted in chapter 1 of this volume. We begin by presenting conceptual change problems in physics. Our purpose in presenting these problems is to help readers understand what we mean by conceptual change. We then discuss theories of conceptual change and highlight the research we did that illustrates these theories, addressing the roles of instruction, textbook, motivation, and gender in conceptual change in science classes. Finally, we discuss a study of conceptual change in social science conducted with the integrated curriculum students.

## THE PROBLEM: LEARNING IN THE FACE OF DISBELIEF

The excerpts at the beginning of this chapter come from our conversations with high school students in advanced and honors physics classes. As these excerpts show, some principles that students are expected to learn contradict what their intuition would tell them and thus are difficult to grasp. In fact, many adults have difficulty with them. High school students are expected to learn these principles because they provide predictive power for observable events, though they are so basic that they have long been surpassed by more elegant explanatory theories. The following problems illustrate the types of events the counterintuitive principles can predict. Pretend you are being quizzed on the problems, and answer them as you read. We believe that, after answering the questions and reading the explanations, you will have a greater understanding of the task that faces high school students in physics classes.

1. If you were to shoot a bullet horizontally out of a gun at the same time you dropped a bullet from the same height, which would reach the ground first, the bullet that was shot or the bullet that was dropped? Why?

2. If you walked briskly forward holding a steel ball in your hand horizontally out from your body (ball facing down), then dropped the ball as you kept moving, where would the ball drop in relation to the point where you released it? Why?

3. If you dropped a steel ball from the same height at the same time you dropped a wooden ball with the same surface area, which would reach the ground first? Why?

4. If you dropped a sack of potatoes out of a second story window at the same time and from the same height as you dropped a single potato, which would hit the ground first? Why?

5. If you dropped a wadded-up piece of paper from the same height and at the same time as a flat piece of paper, which would hit the ground first? Why?

6. Describe the path of a cannon ball after it is shot horizontally from a cliff.

7. If a juggler were juggling three balls as he rode a unicycle in a forward direction, would the dropped balls fall behind, in front of, or right with the juggler as he moved? Why?

The answers to the questions are: (a) the bullets would hit the ground at the same time; (b) the steel ball would fall in front of the release point; (c) the two balls would hit the ground at the same time; (d) the sack of potatoes and the single potato would hit at the same time; (e) the wadded-up piece of paper would hit the ground first; (f) the cannon ball's path would be a parabolic arc toward the ground, moving both forward and down simultaneously. The forward speed would be constant, whereas the downward speed would be accelerating; and (g) the balls would fall right along with the juggler.

These answers are considered to be scientifically acceptable because they stem from a few common and related principles. The most counterintuitive of these principles is that all objects, regardless of mass or weight, fall at the same rate of 9.8 m/s² due to the pull of the earth's gravity. The reason is a mathematical one. Mass is 9.8 × the weight of the object. Acceleration, when no other force but gravity is present, is calculated by manipulating the formula

$$F_{(force)} = M_{(mass)} \times A_{(acceleration)}.$$

In the manipulated formula, $A = M/F$. Because the force of gravity is equal to the weight of the object, if an object weighs one pound, then $A = 9.8/1 = 9.8$. If an object weighs two pounds, then $A = 19.6/2 = 9.8$, and so on. When gravity is the only force acting on an object, it will always fall at the accelerating rate of 9.8 m/s². Note that an object accelerates as it falls. After 1 s, it will be traveling at a speed of 9.8 m/s. After 2 s, its speed will be 39.2 m/s. After 3 s, it will be traveling at a speed of 88.2 m/s.

Why is all of this counterintuitive? It is because objects do fall at different speeds. They fall at different speeds, however, not because gravity is pulling one object to earth slower than another object, but because other forces are acting on it. Another force, air resistance, for example, slows objects with large surface areas, such as the flat piece of paper. Also, if you dropped a heavy object on one foot and a light object on the other, the heavy object would hurt your foot more. It hurts more because it is heavier, not because it fell faster. Thus, the principle that all things fall at the same rate is rarely observed or noticed.

Another basic principle in the problems we discussed is that an object's horizontal motion is independent of its vertical motion. The two motions do not affect each other. To find out how far and fast an object will travel in a horizontal direction, you need to consider the Newtonian law that says objects in motion tend to stay in motion. An object propelled in a forward direction will continue to move forward at a constant speed unless it is slowed, stopped, or diverted by some other force. This idea, in itself, is counterintuitive, because objects propelled forward do slow and often stop. They stop not because their forward momentum is "used up," however, which is a common intuitive theory. Rather, they stop because of friction, an opposing force.

To find out how *far* an object will travel in a *vertical* direction, you would measure the distance between the release point and the ground. To find out how *fast* it would travel in a *vertical* direction, you would consider the principle of gravity explained earlier, that all objects fall at 9.8 m/s². Thus, a bullet shot from a gun will travel forward at a constant speed at the same time it is traveling downward at an accelerating speed. The resultant path is an arc. On leaving the gun a bullet begins to deviate downward immediately due to the pull of gravity. Gravity does not "take a vacation." It is always pulling objects toward the ground. Because gravity is pulling the bullet downward at the same time it is traveling forward, the bullet will eventually hit the ground. Moreover, because gravity is the only force acting in a vertical direction (apart from some negligible air resistance), the bullet will hit the ground at the same time as a second bullet dropped from the same height. Both bullets are being affected only by gravity (except for negligible air resistance) in a vertical direction.

The last counterintuitive idea we observed is that an object carried in some direction is in motion, even though it appears to be at rest to the person carrying it. Therefore, if you dropped the object, according to Newton's law it would continue in its forward direction at the same time it is being pulled to the ground by gravity. If a person threw balls up in the air as she moved, the balls would continue to move forward at a constant speed with her, even though they are traveling vertically up, then down. (Remember that vertical and horizontal motions do not affect each other.)

Knowing these few ideas can help individuals understand many of the physical events that happen in everyday life. Yet, students find them exceptionally difficult to learn because they do not seem logical. They also defy experience. You see objects acting in a certain way, but do not see all of the forces working on objects to cause those actions. Therefore, it is hard to imagine what effect unseeable forces such as air resistance and other types of friction have on objects. Students tend to believe that objects have a force or impetus inside them that is activated when they are put into motion, but that dissipates as it is used up. They may be confusing this notion of impetus with the idea of potential energy, when they are not related. At any rate, students' intuitive theories get in the way of their learning scientifically acceptable theories that offer them more explanatory and predictive power.

## THEORIES OF CONCEPTUAL CHANGE

Why is it important to study students' intuitive theories and how they finally learn scientifically acceptable ones? The reason is that learning them requires the student actually to change his or her existing ideas, not merely add new ideas to existing ones. We call this kind of learning *conceptual change* and regard it as a subset of learning.

## Cognitive Dimensions of Conceptual Change

Piaget (1973) said that our learning consists of two types: assimilation and accommodation. In *assimilation*, individuals connect existing knowledge to new knowledge in an additive way. If, for example, an individual already knew that the Vietnam conflict widened under President Johnson, and then learned that it widened justifiably because of the United States' retaliation for North Vietnamese aggression in the Gulf of Tonkin, that would be as-similation. The new information does not conflict with the student's existing concepts, but adds to them.

In *accommodation*, however, an individual must make adjustments to his or her existing knowledge. For example, if the same person studying the Vietnam conflict learned that the United States retaliated against aggression that likely did not even take place, then that person would have to change his or her previous ideas. Previously, the student would have been led to believe that the United States was justified in widening the war. Now the possibility would have to be considered that such justification did not exist. In the same way, it would be accommodation to learn that air resistance is the factor responsible for changing the rate of an object's fall to the ground, not the weight of the object. Researchers are not sure how this accommodation takes place, but believe it probably is not the result of a simple replacement of one concept for another. Rather, some restructuring takes place.

As mentioned in chapter 2, Rumelhart and Norman (1981) called the additive form of learning *accretion*. They also discussed two other forms of learning: tuning and restructuring. In *tuning*, one makes minor adjustments in understanding, such as creating a generalization or clarifying the attributes of a construct. For example, if a child learned that some four-legged animals are called dogs, then learned that dogs also bark, have fur, wet noses, and tails that wag, then the child would be tuning his or her concept of dog.

In *restructuring*, the resulting concepts are different from the original ones. Vosniadou and Brewer (1987) referred to two types of restructuring. In some instances, they argued, conceptual change takes place in a gradual manner as a result of emerging relationships among concepts or through the formation of a more abstract conceptual structure. They referred to this type of learning as *weak restructuring*. In other instances, the restructuring represents a dramatic shift—a significant and sudden transmutation that they referred to as *radical restructuring*, which appears to be extremely rare.

Perhaps the reason for the rarity of radical restructuring is because there are so many less mentally taxing ways for individuals to handle data that is anomalous or inconsistent with their previous knowledge. Chinn and Brewer (1993) described seven different reactions to such data. For one, students can ignore the data. An example of this reaction showed up on a student's paper. The students were asked to record the weight and times that objects fell to the ground from a third-story window. The data this student recorded showed no relation between weight and rate of fall. Heavier items sometimes took slightly longer than lighter items to reach the ground. Yet, the student wrote at the bottom of the page that heavy items fall faster than light items. To give such an answer, the student simply had to ignore the data.

As a second reaction students can actually reject the data. As one student said to the other members of the class trying to explain the scientific principles of gravity to him, "Y'all are wrong."

A third reaction holds the data in abeyance. That is, a student can decide to table the new information until more is learned one way or the other. A case in point is when Lily, a senior taking an advanced high school physics class, decided to wait to make a decision on whether what she had read about gravity was correct until she had the final word that the researchers who asked her to read it were not just conning her.

A fourth reaction excludes the data from consideration. For example, a student might say that principles of gravity are true in space but not on earth. One student we highlighted in chapter 2 considered an object fired from a high-powered rifle and excluded it from following the principles that were in force when an object was fired from a lower powered gun.

A fifth reaction is to reinterpret the data. We observed this phenomenon many times in high school physics classes. Students in these classes attributed laboratory results to human error, wind resistance (when that resistance was negligible), faulty timing devices, and sabotage. It was easy to make those attributions because they really were factors in some instances. Students were very likely to invoke them when what they observed did not seem logical.

As a sixth reaction, students can change their thinking in minor ways. That is, they can change certain parts of their theories but keep the main parts intact. The student who excluded a high-powered rifle bullet from the principles of gravity (described in chapter 2) finally did say that the bullet would fall to the ground at the same time as an object that was dropped, but he adopted a reason for this phenomenon that maintained his original theory—that an object's horizontal motion affects its vertical motion.

Finally, a student can radically alter existing conceptions, as some students did. That is, they began believing that an object's horizontal and vertical motions were tied and ended up believing that they were independent. They could use that information to explain why an object that was fired would hit the ground at the same time as one that was dropped. Note that this last reaction is the only one that represents a radical shift in understanding.

Researchers have long noted the difficulty of producing conceptual change (Hynd, McWhorter, Phares, & Suttles, 1994; Guzzetti, Snyder, Glass, & Gamas, 1993; Maria & MacGinity, 1981; Sinatra & Dole, in press). Students seem especially resistant to changing their theories if the theories are entrenched, if they represent ontological or deeply embedded beliefs that exist in a network of other beliefs, if students hold epistemologies that favor compartmentalization and memorization rather than hypothesis testing, and if they cannot access relevant background knowledge (Chinn & Brewer, 1993).

Apparently, there are several influences that affect whether change occurs for deeply held beliefs. Posner, Strike, Hewson, and Gertzog (1982) said that students must first recognize the difference between their own intuitive concept and the concept they are being asked to consider, and be *dissatisfied* with their own theory. Then, they must find the new concept *understandable, plausible,* and *fruitful* in the sense that they see the concept as useful in helping them to explain the phenomena they encounter. In other words, students must be convinced that the new concept offers them more explanatory power than their existing concept affords.

Chinn and Brewer (1993) described the characteristics of anomalous data that elicit their acceptance. They believed that the data must be (a) credible, (b) unambiguous, and (c) existent in multiple forms. Many students, for example, believe that a text is credible and will consider its arguments, whereas they may not trust the credibility of their classmates. As one physics students said in explaining why he believed what he had read: "It's a text, right?" Other ways of enhancing credibility are by demonstrating that the principle was derived from scientifically accepted experimental procedures, showing that others have replicated the findings, and allowing people to observe the results of experiments through classroom demonstrations and laboratory experimentation.

Even if the anomalous data are credible, they must also be unambiguous. If data are ambiguous, students are likely to reinterpret them to maintain their existing theories. Students are less likely to reinterpret data that are clear and observable. For example, it is hard to dispute the theory that a coin and a feather fall at the same rate, except for air resistance, when one sees the experiment performed in a vacuum.

Finally, because it is difficult for a single piece of datum to be immune to criticism, there must be multiple presentations of data, so that all methodological criticisms can be ruled out. The physics student depicted in chapter 2, for example, resisted the idea that a bullet from a high-powered rifle would fall to the ground at the same time as a bullet being dropped. After being presented with evidence in multiple forms, however, he finally accepted that interpretation. When asked why, he said that the teacher had finally met all of his objections.

## Social Dimensions of Conceptual Change

The social nature of learning appears to be important to conceptual change on a cognitive level. Vygotsky (1978) discussed the idea that new information is learned through social interaction, especially when an expert connects his ideas to those of a novice. The point of juncture is referred to as the *zone of proximal development.* During the interactions between a novice and an expert, the expert appropriates or takes on the ideas of the novice in order to frame his ideas in such a way that the novice will appropriate them as well (Leont'ev, 1981). Many good teachers, such as the ones we observed in our studies of high school classes, constantly seek to know what students are thinking. They meet their students at the point of their understandings, which was recognized by the one student who said that he changed his mind because his teacher "met all of his objections." He meant that she listened to what he thought, then changed her discussion to deal with those ideas. In addition to using an inquiry approach that introduced problems and had students discuss ways to solve them, this teacher used a particular style of teaching called refutation. In *refutation*, common ideas are acknowledged, but dissatisfaction with those ideas is sought. Teachers adopting a refutational style challenge existing ideas by carefully presenting counterevidence to students and asking students to consider that evidence. They also explicitly say what new idea they would like their students to believe, but they discuss how the new idea explains phenomena more completely than students' existing ideas. In this way, they may be meeting Posner et al.'s (1982) conditions for conceptual change. That is, they try to instill dissatisfaction with existing ideas, then explain the new idea in a way that is understandable, plausible, and fruitful.

Posner et al. (1982) based this theory on the cognitive belief that students strive to make sense of their environment (to affect closure). They later acknowledged, however, that there were also affective explanations for students' conceptual change (Strike & Posner, 1990). Motivation and context are two of the affective components of conceptual change.

## Affective Dimensions of Conceptual Change

Gilovich (1991) called motivation the "engine" of cognition, in that motivation drives one's cognitive efforts. Pintrich, Marx, and Boyle (1993) discussed how motivation is a necessary component of conceptual change because of the persistent effort such change requires. In their view, conceptual change requires selective attention, activation of prior knowledge, deep processing and elaboration of new information, problem finding and solving, metacognitive evaluation and control, and volitional control and regulation. For students to undergo conceptual change, they must first recognize that their current belief is different from the new belief under consideration. They need to understand this belief through reconciling their prior knowledge with the new information; thinking deeply about the new information by engaging in such strategies as paraphrasing or summarizing; using strategies that foster elaborate processing such as concept mapping and networking; seeing the new belief's applicability in solving problems; and engaging in metacognitive reflection. Because of the persistent effort required, volitional and self-control strategies need to be employed as well. Motivation is necessary in bringing students to utilize these cognitive processes.

Pintrich et al. (1993) argued that in schools children are not operating in the same contexts as practicing bench scientists and have a number of motivations for schooling that may be inconsistent with learning a preferred scientific explanation. For example, students uninterested in science topics may be more motivated by social rather than cognitive goals. In addition, students may be given low-level tasks; their teachers may emphasize grades over learning; or the students may lack control over learning decisions. Researchers have found that these contextual conditions inhibit motivation for learning (Ames, 1992; Brophy, 1983; Elliott & Dweck, 1988; Lepper & Hodell, 1989; Meece, 1991). Students focused on mastery or learning goals who have intrinsic interest in what they are trying to learn have been found to engage in deeper cognitive processing than students focused on ego-involved or performance goals such as goals for task completion, grades, or competition (Dweck & Leggett, 1988; Nolen, 1988; Pintrich & DeGroot, 1990; Pintrich & Schrauben, 1992).

It seems reasonable to assume, however, that students will not all have mastery learning goals, nor will they maintain intrinsic motivation for every topic in every class. Individuals' goals for everyday life lead to the acceptance of adequate explanations rather than optimal ones, whereas bench scientists have a much higher stake in seeking optimal explanations. Kruglinski, as reported by Pintrich et al. (1993), added to this idea by noting that students are affected by two epistemic motivations, each existing on a continuum.

The first motivation is one for closure, and the second, at the other end of the continuum, is for the avoidance of closure. Students may want to freeze their cognitive processing of information, deciding not to think about any more new ideas. In freezing their cognition, students must necessarily discount new information that contradicts their established beliefs. Conversely, students may opt to unfreeze their cognition by seeking new information, questioning beliefs, and trying to focus on discrepancies. Thus, having a stance open to new ideas means that a person will be more likely to undergo conceptual change.

The second motivation is for specificity or, at the other end of the continuum, for nonspecificity. That is, students either want the most desirable answer or settle for any answer. Students can quickly and effectively close their cognition by settling for any answer, or they may search longer to find the best answer before they close their cognition. Of course, these two motivations are likely to be context specific. In situations where teachers push for quick answers, students might opt to choose any answer for rapid closure.

Besides goal-orientation beliefs (for mastery or for performance goals), there are other motivational constructs that potentially help in the understanding of conceptual change. For one, students may have interests and values that influence the likelihood that they will expend cognitive effort toward change. Pintrich et al. (1993) noted that intrinsic interest may coexist with valuing a field of study for its importance to one's future career. Intrinsic interest is likely to lead to mastery goals, whereas the value placed on one's career may lead to performance goals. Yet, these interests are linked to each other in potentially important ways: Situational interests, as well, may be important.

Eccles (1983) proposed three types of value beliefs: (a) interest in a content or task, (b) belief in the utility of knowing the information or performing the task, and (c) importance or the belief that the information or task is in some way related to the individual. Hidi (1990) emphasized the idea that interest influences a student's ability to selectively attend to information, increases persistence, and aids in the acquisition of knowledge. Interested students are more likely to use elaborate processing strategies, be more metacognitively aware, seek more information, and engage in more critical thinking than students who are not interested. Sinatra and Dole (in press) reported that more elaborate processing of information is related to conceptual change representing radical rather than weak restructuring.

Although most of these types of interest depend at least partially on the individual, situational interest is under more direct control of the teacher, classroom, and task. Situational interest is the interest generated by an environmental influence, such as that of an interesting text. Beck, McKeown, and Worthy (1995) studied fourth graders' learning from text and found that they learned the most from text that was more coherent and had "voice," or was enlivened through colorful language. Others have discussed how challenge, choice, novelty, and surprise contribute to a text's interest. Presumably, texts that have these features elicit deeper processing of information and, potentially, conceptual change. There are other environmental situations as well that may influence motivation. For example, researchers have noted that offering students choices, engaging students in inquiry for the purpose of solving authentic problems, and providing a supportive social climate all are motivating to students and foster deeper processing of information (Oldfather, 1993).

A final motivational construct with implications for conceptual change is self-efficacy, which is the belief that students have it in their capability to complete the task. Although the importance of self-efficacy in learning has been demonstrated empirically (Oldfather, 1993), its relationship to conceptual change has been speculative. As with the beliefs, there are few direct links in research to conceptual change, even though the links have been made to other kinds of learning.

In summary, there are cognitive, social, and motivational theories that add to our understanding of conceptual change. In the next section, we present some of the research we have done and explain our findings in relation to these theories.

## STUDIES OF CONCEPTUAL CHANGE—INSTRUCTIONAL COMPONENTS

As mentioned previously, conceptual change is difficult, particularly if current ideas seem intuitively correct and logical (Guzzetti et al., 1993) or represent strong beliefs (Sinatra & Dole, in press). Individuals may ignore, reject, compartmentalize, exclude, or otherwise refuse data that go against their current understandings. This difficulty presents a real dilemma for both theorists and teachers. On the one hand, they believe, like Piaget (1973), that learning takes place through processes of construction. That is, individuals actively construct what they learn from the environment through assimilation or accommodation, and they do not assimilate or accommodate anything they do not "discover" for themselves, in the sense that they make the construction. In addition, Piaget said that individuals learn that which they already know. They learn at the point of intersection between their current conceptions and the information they are taking in from their senses. Given these notions, educational theorists believe that discovery learning and inquiry approaches are vital for conceptual change to take place. In these approaches, teacher- or student-generated problems are posed, and students engage in activities aimed at solving those problems. The dilemma is that students, under these conditions, may not construct what their teachers wish for them to construct. In the case of physics, for example, students may not construct accepted scientific theory through discovery or problem solving.

We have ample evidence that students do not always naturally construct the principles of motion through discovery, for example. Hynd, McNish, Lay, and Fowler (1995) observed students as they performed various experiments to discover the principles of gravity and projectile motion. In one such experiment, they dropped objects from a third-story window and timed their fall. They gathered information across teams and were asked to explain why the objects fell in the way they did. In another experiment, students used dart guns, erasers, and paper to make predictions and come up with theories about gravity and projectile motion. For example, they held a dart gun at a standard height from the floor (using an apparatus) and shot it at the dry-erase board, marking where it hit. Then they stepped back several feet, made a prediction where the dart would hit compared to the previous shot, and shot again. They then stepped back several more feet, and shot again. At the end of the three trials, they were expected to conclude that gravity pulls an object in a downward direction at the same time it is moving forward, resulting in an arc. In each case, students maintained their intuitive theories and did not change them, even when the data contradicted their theories and even when they recognized that the experiment did not go as they predicted. In other experiments, students were observed focusing on the physical aspects of completing the experiment rather than its conceptual aspects. For example, in one case, the students got so involved in making their apparatus work right that they ran out of time and ended up getting their data through trial and error rather than by completing a real experiment. In another case, students spent a full 15 min figuring out how to use the spring scale. They did the experiment, but did not discuss their findings, nor did they change their intuitive theories. Even with its quantitative data, laboratory work did not produce significant change in the students' thinking about the principles of motion in either the advanced physics classes populated by eleventh and twelfth graders or the regular and basic physical sciences classes populated by ninth and tenth graders. This evidence corroborates the example earlier in this chapter showing a student ignoring evidence to maintain an intuitive theory.

We also have evidence that students' discussions with other students may not result in conceptual change. Hynd, McWhorter, Phares, and Suttles (1992) recorded students' conversations as they discussed the theories they used to explain an object's movement if dropped by a moving person or airplane. The scientifically accepted theory is that the object keeps its forward motion as it is pulled by gravity, making an arc. Students sometimes talked other students into believing their intuitive theories, but rarely did a group construct a scientifically accepted understanding. Students who participated in discussion groups did not significantly change their ideas between pre- and posttesting. Furthermore, when the groups read text that explained the scientific theory, they were less likely to change their ideas than students who had not discussed their theories with other students. Thus, the social interaction proved powerful, but did not move students in the direction their teachers would have desired. Vygotsky would explain, possibly, that the students were all novices, and that there was no one in the group to move thinking forward.

Finally, reading classroom textbooks does not seem to affect students' learning of scientific principles. In fact, students are amazingly negative about their classroom textbooks, finding them frustratingly difficult and arcane. We asked students to evaluate their textbooks (Guzzetti, Hynd, Skeels, & Williams, 1995; Hynd, Guzzetti, McNish, Fowler, & Williams, 1997; Hynd, McNish, Lay, & Fowler, 1995; Hynd, McNish, Qian, Keith, & Lay, 1994). Students were overwhelmingly negative about them, and their negative comments centered on the content of the textbook rather than the format. Forty-four comments reflected criticism toward the content of their textbooks, citing bad examples, poor explanations, and difficult vocabulary. Only six of the negative comments had to do with the format characteristics such as whether there were headings and diagrams or whether information was easy to find. The students who actually explained the physics concepts scientifically seemed even more frustrated than other students. When the advanced students were asked to arrange the teacher, textbook, laboratory experiment, and other students in a hierarchy from most to least important to their learning, they put the teacher first and the textbook last. The next two paragraphs are the comments of two students in advanced physics who did very well in physics overall, and had learned the targeted concepts.

> *First student:* I didn't do very well on the exam simply because I wasn't here when she taught one particular, the first section about the work. I was not in class, and I read through the text, but I didn't understand, and I tried asking my friends, but they didn't explain it. And I tried doing the word problems, and I knew what the variables meant and I didn't know how to use the formulas from the book. . . . I tried looking at the text, and I couldn't find where it was.

> *Second student:* Well, I know they use words that are, like confusing . . . uhm . . . difficult words to understand. Like, in a lot of those texts that you gave us to read, I mean, it was just simple words, something anybody can understand. And that's why I liked them a lot. Because I learned something from them. I mean some of the things in here they talk about, I mean, they don't explain it, or they don't use words that everyone can understand, and a lot of new words they throw at you all at once, and it's just like, wait a minute, now I've got to go back and figure out what this meant and then, so I'll know what the next thing meant.

## STUDIES OF CONCEPTUAL CHANGE— ## THE ROLE OF TEXT

Considering Posner et al.'s (1982) argument that for people to change their current conceptions, they must be dissatisfied with them, both researchers and teachers have acknowledged the potential of refutational discourse. In *refutation*, a teacher or textbook confronts students with the inadequacy of their current conceptions and presents an alternative conception that provides more explanatory power. The message is direct and unambiguous. In this section, we deal with refutational text. However, the teachers we worked with also used a refutational style as part of their teaching. Below is an excerpt from a refutational text we used in research. We adapted this text from Hewitt's (1992) high school physics textbook, *Conceptual Physics*, by adding refutation. The refutational sentences are italicized in this version only.

> *Although people have a hard time believing it,* the horizontal component of motion for a projectile is not tied to the vertical component of motion. Each acts independently of the other. Because they both occur at the same time,

*people mistakenly reason that they must get in the way of each other, but they DON'T.* What actually does result from the fact that they both occur at the same time is that the path of the projectile is a curve. The path is a curve because the ball is being pulled downward at the same time it is moving forward. It keeps on moving forward at a constant rate, just as it would be moving if it were not dropping, and it keeps on dropping at an accelerating rate, just as it would if it were not moving forward. *The projectile's forward motion is not slowed or sped up by it's downward motion, and it's downward motion is not slowed or sped up by its forward motion.*

The multiple-flash exposure of Figure 6.14 shows equally timed successive positions for a ball rolled off a horizontal table. . . . There are two important things to notice *that people can't see* unless they look at the two types of motion separately. The first is that the *ball's horizontal (forward) component of motion doesn't change as the falling ball moves sideways.* The ball travels the same distance forward in the equal times between each flash. That's because there is virtually no forward gravitational force pulling on it. Gravity acts downward, so the only acceleration (speeding up) of the ball is downward. The second thing to note from the photo is that the vertical positions become farther apart with time. The distances traveled downward are the same as if the ball were simply dropped. *It is hard for some people to believe that the downward motion of the ball is the same as that of free fall, but this figure proves that it is.* (In the text we used, a figure followed.)

In this excerpt, the commonly held nonscientific view is refuted, and the current scientific view is explained. As can be seen, the text tells people that their current conceptions are wrong. Some researchers (but very few students) find this disquieting. We would be uncomfortable, as well, if students read this text in a classroom where science knowledge was viewed as static and the teacher did not emphasize that what is seen as accurate scientific information today may be considered naive tomorrow. In each of the classes where this text was used, however, we observed teachers often placing current scientific information within a historical context. Note what one of the students said.

> I mean you know, people thought that the world was flat for thousands of years; then all of a sudden, they discovered it's round, and we think that there are little atoms and stuff, and there is gravity. How do you know that it's true?

Although this student's knowledge of the changing forms of scientific acceptability caused her to doubt the usefulness of scientific knowledge, you can see that she has developed a sense of its fluctuating nature.

The text itself, in addition, can provide this context. Take, for example, an excerpt from another text we have used, this one adapted from an article by McCloskey (1983) in *Scientific American:*

> You may have an idea about the motion of objects that you've learned from your daily life. You may even use that idea to predict what will happen to

other objects in the same situations. But, you may be wrong—scientists have found that many people have the wrong ideas about the motion of objects. These wrong ideas include the theory of impetus people believed in before the time of Sir Isaac Newton, and some people still believe. People who believe in impetus theory think that motion must have a cause. When they can't see any reason for an object to keep going, change its direction, or stop, they decide that there must be a force inside of the object that is put there when the object is set in motion. People have called this inner force impetus. Newton showed us that impetus theory (that objects have a force inside of them) is wrong.

In this excerpt, students' intuitive ideas are compared to accepted scientific ideas that existed in a different time. Students reading this may be led to appreciate the changing view of scientific knowledge.

Refutational text appears to foster conceptual change in intended directions. Guzzetti et al. (1993) presented the results from a meta-analysis of research studying the effect of different kinds of texts on student's learning of counterintuitive ideas. In that meta-analysis, refutational text was found to be effective at increasing students' learning. Other research findings since then, from analyses of both quantitative and qualitative data, have been similar. In our most recent study of text in physics and physical science classes, for example, we found that students who read refutational text increased their learning of counterintuitive scientific information (measured by application tasks) more than students who read nonrefutational text (Hynd et al., 1997). Reading refutational text had an effect even though students also participated in discussions, listened to lectures, watched videotaped and live demonstrations, participated in experiments, and completed assignments over a 2-week period. In the regular physical science class, additionally, students who read this text before other instruction did better on a true–false posttest than students who read the text after other instruction, indicating that the text may have helped them interpret these other classroom activities in more scientifically acceptable ways. Later, we asked students to read and rate a number of texts, some of them refutational and some of them not, as to their believability, ease of understanding, usefulness, and interest level. Students consistently rated the refutational texts higher than they did other texts on all characteristics.

Why did they prefer refutational style? Here are some of the comments from students at various levels:

"There's a contrast between common people and physics." (regular physics)

"What most people think is wrong is what you think, too." (regular physics)

"It was like it was talking to me." (regular physics)

"You don't think you're stupid." (regular physics)

"While it was saying the wrong ideas, they fit how I believed." (advanced physics)

"It shows common ideas you can identify with but explains why they're wrong." (advanced physics)

"The ideas show that some points are what others think about." (advanced physics)

"It makes me feel like I'm not the only one." (advanced physics)

"It's funny. In many of the cases, I was one of the wrong ones. It explained it in a rational way." (advanced physics)

"It explained what I said that was wrong." (advanced physics)

"It explained what I believed in. It's not just me." (advanced physics)

"It makes you think twice about what you think you know." (advanced physics)

"If I thought about what it said, it would help me change my mind." (advanced physics)

"It tells you what I'm supposed to know, but probably don't, but think I know." (regular physical science)

"It's good to know that people have different theories. At least my theory was there." (regular physical science)

We take these comments to mean that the students in this study identified with people who believed the "wrong" idea, were grateful that they were not alone, and then may have paid increased attention to the more scientifically acceptable information. In other words, the text connected with students' existing levels of knowledge.

Also, students in the Southeast also preferred narrative refutational text, whereas students in the Southwest preferred expository refutational text. From interviews, we tallied 17 positive comments and 18 negative comments. Students, then, either liked or disliked the narrative style. Their reasons for liking it were related to how easy it was to understand, how they could apply the concepts to everyday life, and how they could identify with it.

Here are some of their positive comments:

"It applies to common life. It's funny." (regular physics)

"It's just like me." (honors)

"It's like Mr. William's lecture." (regular physics)

"The story was interesting. I could identify." (advanced physics)

"It has a lot to do with everyday life. The things you do have to do with physics." (advanced physics)

Students' negative comments focused on the notion that the narrative style distracted readers from the physics information, and that the story was "cheesy," "childish," and "patronizing." As one student said, "It's like a Little Caesar's Commercial. You laugh at the commercial, but you forget the product" (regular physics).

Thus, refutational texts appear to be liked by students, and our narrative refutational text appeared useful to at least some students, whereas it was distracting to others. Manipulating text in ways other than making it refutational has fostered learning. For example, Beck et al. (1995) studied fourth graders' learning from text and found that they learned the most from text that was more coherent and had "voice," or was enlivened through colorful language. Britton and Gulgöz (1991) found that students increased their learning when the ties between ideas were made more explicit, thus rendering the text more coherent. These researchers used a mathematical model to test a text's harmony, or coherence, whereas Beck, McKeown, Sinatra, and Loxterman (1991) rewrote texts based on their study of students' difficulties.

We did this as well, on the basis of students' comments about their textbooks. In addition to identifying refutational style as helpful to their understanding, students also identified other elements. They liked texts that were clear (often citing clear vocabulary as the most important element of clarity), presented real-life examples and applications, showed how the presented information was useful, gave in-depth information, and allowed students to identify with the discussion. They regarded texts as believable if they connected with things the students knew previously and seemed reasonable. The students also, by and large, thought of texts as the voice of authority. Note their comments:

"It's a text, right?" (regular physical science student)

"I have no reason not to believe this. It's in a science book." (regular physical science student)

"It doesn't seem right to me, but because it's a text, it has to be true." (advanced physics student)

"I believe what I read." (advanced physics student)

Thus, texts cause people to believe them because the information appears credible if it is "in print." We might put too much stock in this characteristic of texts if it were not tempered by findings of numerous researchers (Guzzetti et al., 1993) that certain kinds of text (e.g., refutational) affect students' learning more than other kinds.

In summary, our text studies have caused us to believe that texts can be sources of frustration and confusion, or they may be powerful sources of learning that are an important part of instruction that includes demonstration, experimentation, and discussion. Texts appear to be an important factor in situational interest and are amenable to manipulation to make them more interesting and useful. They seem to be the source of at least some motivation. In the next section, we focus on motivation and some of its other sources.

## STUDIES OF CONCEPTUAL CHANGE—THE ROLE OF MOTIVATION AND EPISTEMOLOGY

In our study of conceptual change in physics classrooms (Hynd et al., 1997), we asked students to rate the importance of education in general, the importance of learning physics, their motivation and their interest in physics, and the usefulness of physics knowledge. We framed our questions in line with the types of value beliefs that Eccles (1983) proposed: (a) interest in a content or task, (b) belief in the utility of knowing the information or performing the task, and (c) importance, or the belief that the information or task is in some way related to the individual. We asked students to rate these items on a 6-point scale, with 1 as low and 6 as high, and then to explain their ratings. We separated the students we interviewed into two groups: a group that explained our targeted physics concepts according to accepted scientific principles after a unit on projectile motion and a group that explained concepts in an unacceptable way. We found virtually no difference between low and high students in their ratings of educational importance: M (high) = 9.03, M (low) = 9.16. There were only slight differences in how students rated the importance of physics from their point of view: M (high) = 6.42, M (low) = 7.17, with students who believed more strongly in the importance of physics not doing as well in describing physics concepts. In addition, there was a difference in physics motivation: M (high) = 7.6, M (low) = 6.9, favoring the students who explained physics concepts scientifically, and a smaller difference in physics interest: M (high) = 7.25, M (low) = 6.93, favoring students who explained physics concepts scientifically. Furthermore, high students tended to talk more about physics' usefulness in terms of helping them understand current phenomena (High = 43% of comments, Low = 23% of comments) rather than in terms of preparing them for the future (High = 33% of comments, Low = 58% of comments). Students who explained concepts scientifically said they were motivated more by their interest in physics (High = 63% of comments, Low = 28% of comments) than students who did not.

These data corroborate our previous studies (Hynd, McNish, Lay, & Fowler, 1995; Hynd, McNish, Qian, Keith, & Lay, 1994). They also confirm the thinking of Pintrich et al. (1993), who said that intrinsic interest may coexist with valuing a field of study for its importance to one's future career. We found both of these reasons for motivating surfacing in both our high students and low students, although intrinsic interest was discussed more often. Thus, students were motivated by both intrinsic and utilitarian goals. They were also motivated by feelings of self-efficacy. In short, their motivations were complex. Although intrinsic interest may have been responsible for their attention and persistence (Hidi, 1990), it is possible that their more extrinsic motivations sustained them when topics became less interesting.

Regarding epistemology, Hynd et al. (1994) studied its effects in three levels of physics and physical science classes. They gave students Schommer's (1990) epistemology questionnaire and found that students who believed knowledge levels could be increased through their own efforts and that learning should be complex, not simple memorization, were more likely to change their ideas about physics in a scientific direction. These data corroborate the work of Strike and Posner (1990).

## STUDIES IN CONCEPTUAL CHANGE—
## THE ROLE OF GENDER

Numerous studies show that females are at a disadvantage in science classrooms (Bazler & Simonis, 1991; Bianchini, 1993; Tobin, 1988). Textbooks give unequal treatment to males and females through their illustrations and photographs (Bazler & Simones, 1991). Furthermore, boys often have more opportunity to engage in academic tasks and are the object of their teachers' higher expectations (Hall & Sadker, 1982; Jones & Wheatley, 1990). Finally, class discussions are dominated by males, whether or not the discussions are teacher-directed recitations or student-to-student discussions (Alvermann, Dillon, & O'Brien, 1987; Sadker & Sadker, 1985; Tannen, 1992; Tobin & Garnett, 1987).

These findings are important in considering conceptual change, just as they are important in considering other kinds of science learning. Conceptual change requires a motivation that results in persistent effort, a sense of self-efficacy, a feeling that learning the counterintuitive information is somehow important to you, and a positive interest. All of these feelings are at risk when a student feels marginalized.

Guzzetti and Williams (1996) noted that in Williams' science classes females were marginalized in both small and large group discussions. They present the following small group discussion to show how females' thoughts were discounted by males.

Jason:   Number 11 is acceleration. Number 12: Inertia is mass.
Jason:   (to researcher) What do you think?
         (Researcher declines to participate.)
Jason:   Number 13.

Betty:     Is 13 B?
Jason:     (sarcastically) Yes, Betty, you are learning. Number 14 would
           be less: 16 is B. 15 is A. Stacey, did you get B for 17?
Betty:     Isn't 18 B? Because gravity is acting.
Jason:     (interrupting) Betty, put in a number before you talk to me.
           Number 18 is C. I just proved it to you with a number: $2 = 10/5$.
           This is a democracy, the majority wins. Quit slowing us down!
Sally:     (to Jason) Why do you confuse everyone with your formulas?
Jason:     They work for everything else.
Betty:     (to researcher). No one listens to me! Gravity is acting. I put my
           answer for 18 as B. Billy and Jason put C.

Interestingly, refutational whole-group discussions may also marginalize
females. Guzzetti and Williams (1996) found gender differences in whole-
class discussions when these discussions were rewarded for refutation. Williams awarded extra points to students who could argue their viewpoint.
He also chose a "shill" to offer counterarguments that were incorrect but
reasonable. He called this type of discussion "inquiry training." Under these
conditions, most of the girls rarely spoke, although the same few females
did enter into discussions occasionally. The females who joined in were
more tentative in their statements, whereas the males made statements like,
"That's wrong, because. . . ." Students, in interviews, acknowledged gender
differences, with more females stating that they would not enter into discussions. Furthermore, when the data were reported to the class, one group
of six males, in confronting statements made by females that the boys dominated and intimidated the girls, broke out in a song of solidarity: "I don't
want to grow up."

Our interviews about refutation text in the Hynd et al. (1997) study showed
that females preferred refutational text as much as males did. Thus, whereas
refutational text seemed helpful to females, refutational discussion may not
have been. In the case of text, the emphasis is on private reflection, whereas
in discussion, it is public. In the public forum, females reported feeling
intimidated.

In nonscience classrooms, gender differences also surface but not always
in the same ways. Alvermann et al. (1997), for example, found that when
they tried to interrupt gendered discussions in a high school literature class,
not only the males, but also the females divided into solidified groups and
argued with each other about which group was superior. This certainly was
not the intended effect, and illustrates the volatile nature of classroom discussion. Social interactions, as noted previously, are indeed powerful. But
when the teacher's purpose for the discussion is to change students ideas
in a predetermined direction, the social interaction that takes place during
discussion may not proceed as desired.

## CONCEPTUAL CHANGE IN THE WORKING CLASSROOM

In the integrated classrooms featured in chapter 1 of this book, conceptual change is surely a type of learning that takes place. We did not study conceptual change in the biology class, but chose instead to focus on the programs' influences on students' learning of biology in general. Hynd, Stahl, Montgomery, and McClain (1997) did, however, study conceptual change in a history class. Nonscience studies of conceptual change are rare. Furthermore, for nonscience topics in fields like sociology, conceptual change may be different from the conceptual change that occurs in science classrooms. Students' beliefs may be derived less from one's observations of the physical world (one likely source of students' beliefs about an object's motion) and more from acculturation processes. For example, a student's beliefs about religion may be difficult to change during a classroom study of world religions because religious beliefs are bound up in the student's interpersonal relationships with family members, church authority figures, friends, and relatives.

In the Hynd et al. (1997) study, we wanted to analyze the change in students' beliefs about Christopher Columbus after reading several texts. We gave students in both the integrated curriculum world history class and the nonintegrated world history class three texts that represented three stances on Christopher Columbus.

Before reading the texts, the students' views of Columbus were positive. When asked to describe him, they said that he was adventurous, brave, and smart. They also held misconceptions about Columbus: that he was Spanish, that he landed on the North American continent, that he was the first to believe that the earth was round, and that he was regarded as a great man during his lifetime.

One text the students read presented a traditional view of Columbus, essentially the view that most students held, but it did chronicle his life in a way that could dispel students' misconceptions. Another text was a revisionist view of Columbus presenting his journey from a native "Indian's" perspective. It discussed how he did not "discover" American but landed on a group of islands to the south. It depicted Columbus as a cruel, greedy ruler who decimated the peaceful and trusting native population. The third text presented a postrevisionist view. It refuted common misconceptions about Columbus, gave a balanced view of his good and bad qualities, and concluded that if Christopher Columbus had not sailed West and changed the world, then someone else would have. These texts were presented in counterbalanced order, so that two thirds of the students read the more negative views of Columbus at any reading. We found that, under these conditions, students' attitudes about Columbus changed to become more negative, and that their misconceptions about Columbus lessened. The largest change occurred after the first reading, then stabilized after that. The postrevisionist text (a combination of *Newsweek* and *Time* articles that was also refutational) had the greatest impact on students in that it produced more negative attitudes and lessened more misconceptions than the other texts. The revisionist text with the most outright negative tone about Columbus had the least impact.

This study shows that students can change their opinions and knowledge after reading text, especially if that text is refutational. It is noteworthy because the change took place in a social science rather than a science context. Students' beliefs about Columbus, however, may not be strongly held. That is, their beliefs about Columbus may not be tied up in their views of the world nor exist in a network of other beliefs. Furthermore, students all had a wealth of background knowledge to access. Most students had studied Columbus since they were in kindergarten and were familiar with the effect his journeys had on the world. This background information may have helped them to think more critically about the information they were reading, to make judgments about the bias or reasonableness of the information they read, and to adopt cogent arguments. Chinn and Brewer (1993) noted that considerations of belief entrenchment and prior knowledge are central to conceptual change.

## CONCLUSION

Our studies, in total, illustrate that there are several key elements—personal, interpersonal, and instructional—that explain why students change their ideas. Personal attributes that account for conceptual change have to do with a student's prior knowledge, motivation, and epistemology. Students must be able to access relevant background knowledge, or learning will be difficult. In addition, if students are interested in the topic; feel that they can, through effort, learn the information; and believe that learning the information will be useful to them, they will be more likely to engage in the persistent reflection required to learn counterintuitive information.

On an interpersonal level, students who discuss their intuitive ideas with other equally knowledgeable students may have difficulty changing their intuitive views. Our attempts to influence conceptual change through student-to-student discussions were ineffective and often dominated by males. Students left together on their own to engage in laboratory "discovery" rarely were able to derive scientific principles. In the years that we have been in science and other high school classrooms, rarely have students reported "learning" from other students. We know that students learn much from each other, however. It is just that what they learn from each other may not be in line with a teacher's expectations if conceptual change is desired.

Instruction that presents credible, unambiguous information in multiple contexts appears to foster conceptual change, as Chinn and Brewer (1993) suggested. Refutational text is one form of instruction that appears to be a credible source of information to students. Such text has been shown in numerous studies to be responsible for students' learning of counterintuitive information (Guzzetti, Snyder, Glass, & Gamas, 1993; Hynd, McWhorter, Phares, & Suttles, 1994; Hynd, Guzzetti, McNish, Fowler, & Williams, 1997). Refutational text, along with clear demonstrations, discussions between teachers and students (or experts and novices), and reasonable explanations of scientific principles can convince students to change their existing beliefs.

## REFERENCES

Alvermann, D. E., Commeyras, M., Young, J. P., Randall, S., & Hinson, D. (1997). Interrupting gendered discursive practices in classroom talk about texts: Easy to think about, difficult to do. *Journal of Literacy Research, 29*(1), 73–104.

Alvermann, D. E., Dillon, D. R., & O'Brien, D. G. (1987). *Using discussion to promote reading comprehension.* Newark, DE: International Reading Association.

Ames, C. (1992). Classrooms, goals, structures, and student motivation. *Journal of Educational Psychology, 84,* 261–271.

Bazler, J. A., & Simonis, D. A. (1991). Are high school chemistry textbooks gender fair? *Journal of Research in Science Teaching, 28,* 353–362.

Beck, I. L., McKeown, M. G., Sinatra, G. M., & Loxterman, J. A. (1991). Revising social studies text from a text-processing perspective: Evidence of improved comprehensibility. *Reading Research Quarterly, 26,* 251–276.

Beck, I. L., McKeown, M. G., & Worthy, J. (1995). Giving a text voice can improve students' understanding. *Reading Research Quarterly, 30,* 220–239.

Bianchini, J. (1993, April). *The high school biology textbook: A changing mosaic of gender, science, and purpose.* Paper presented at the annual meeting of the American Educational Research Association, Atlanta, GA.

Britton, B. K., & Gulgöz, S. (1991). Interactive learning environments and the teaching of science and mathematics. In M. Gardner, J. G. Greeno, F. Reif, A. H. Schoenfeld, A. DiSessa, & E. Stage (Eds.), *Toward a scientific practice of science education* (pp. 111–140). Hillsdale, NJ: Lawrence Erlbaum Associates.

Brophy, J. (1983). Conceptualizing student motivation. *Educational Psychologist, 18,* 200–215.

Chinn, C. A., & Brewer, W. F. (1993). The role of anomalous data in knowledge acquisition: A theoretical framework and implications for science instruction. *Review of Educational Research, 63*(1), 1–49.

Dweck, C., & Leggett, E. L. (1988). A social-cognitive approach to motivation and personality. *Psychological Review, 93*(2), 256–273.

Eccles, J. (1983). Expectancies, values, and academic behaviors. In J. T. Spence (Ed.), *Achievement and achievement motives* (pp. 75–146). San Francisco: Freeman.

Elliot, E., & Dweck, C. (1988). Goals: An approach to motivation and achievement. *Journal of Personality and Social Psychology, 54,* 5–12.

Gilovich, T. (1991). *How we know what isn't so: The fallibility of human reason in everyday life.* New York: Free Press.

Guzzetti, B., Hynd, C., Skeels, S., & Williams, W. (1995). Improving physics texts: Students speak out. *Journal of Reading, 38*(8), 656–665.

Guzzetti, B., & Williams, W. O. (1996). Gender, text, and discussion: Examining intellectual safety in the science classroom. *Journal of Research in Science Teaching, 33*, 5–20.

Guzzetti, B. J., Snyder, T. E., Glass, G. V., & Gamas, W. S. (1993). Meta-analysis of instructional interventions from reading education and science education to promote conceptual change in science. *Reading Research Quarterly, 28*, 116–161.

Hall, R., & Sadker, B. R. (1982). *The classroom climate: A chilly one for women? Project on the status of women* (ERIC ED 215628). Washington, DC: Association of American Colleges.

Hewitt, P. G. (1987). *Conceptual physics.* Menlo Park, CA: Addison-Wesley.

Hidi, S. (1990). Interest and its contribution as a mental resource for learning. *Review of Educational Research, 60*, 549–571.

Hynd, C., Guzzetti, B. G., McNish, M. M., Fowler, P., & Williams, W. (1997). *Texts in physics class: The contribution of reading to the learning of counterintuitive physics principles.* Unpublished manuscript.

Hynd, C., McNish, M. M., Lay, K., & Fowler, P. (1995). *High school physics: The role of text in learning counterintuitive information* (Reading Research Report, No. 16). Athens, GA: National Reading Research Center.

Hynd, C., McNish, M. M., Qian, G., Keith, M., & Lay, K. (1994). *Learning counterintuitive physics concepts: The effects of text and educational environment* (Reading Research Report, No. 16). Athens, GA: National Reading Research Center.

Hynd, C., McWhorter, Y., Phares, V., & Suttles, W. (1994). The role of instructional variables in conceptual change in high school physics topics. *Journal of Research in Science Teaching, 31*, 933–946.

Hynd, C., Stahl, S., Montgomery, T., & McClain, V. (1997). *"In fourteen hundred and ninety two, Columbus sailed the ocean blue": Effects of multiple document readings on student attitudes and misconceptions* (Reading Research Report, No. 82). Athens, GA: National Reading Research Center.

Jones, M. G., & Wheatley, J. (1990). Gender differences in teacher–student interactions in science classrooms. *Journal of Research in Science Teaching, 27*, 861–874.

Leont'ev, A. N. (1981). The progressive construction of mind. *Cognitive Science, 5*, 1–30.

Lepper, M., & Hodell, M. (1989). Intrinsic motivation in the classroom. In C. Ames & R. Ames (Eds.), *Research on motivation in education* (Vol. 3, pp. 73–105). New York: Academic Press.

Maria, K., & MacGinitie, W. (1981, December). *Prior knowledge as a handicapping condition.* Paper presented at the annual meeting of the National Reading Conference, Dallas, TX.

McCloskey, M. (1983). Intuitive physics. *Scientific American, 248*, 122–130.

Meece, J. L. (1991). The classroom context and children's motivational goals. In M. Maehr & P. Pintrich (Eds.), *Advances in motivation and achievement* (Vol. 7, pp. 261–286). Greenwich, CT: JAI Press.

Nolen, S. (1988). Reasons for studying: Motivational orientations and study strategies. *Cognition and Instruction, 5*, 269–287.

Oldfather, P. (1993). *Students' perspectives on motivating experiences in literacy learning* (Perspectives in Reading Research, No. 2). Athens, GA: National Reading Research Center.

Piaget, J. (1973). *To understand is to invent: The future of education.* New York: Grossman.

Pintrich, P. R., & DeGroot, E. (1990). Motivational and self-regulated learning components of classroom academic performance. *Journal of Educational Psychology, 82*, 33–40.

Pintrich, P. R., Marx, R. W., & Boyle, R. (1993). Beyond cold conceptual change: The role of motivational beliefs and classroom contextual factors in the process of conceptual change. *Review of Educational Research, 63*(2), 167–199.

Pintrich, P. R., & Schrauben, B. (1992). Students' motivational beliefs and their cognitive engagement in classroom academic tasks. In D. Schunk & J. Meece (Eds.), *Student perceptions in the classroom: Causes and consequences* (pp. 149–183). Hillsdale, NJ: Lawrence Erlbaum Associates.

Posner, G. J., Strike, K. A., Hewson, P. W., & Gertzog, W. A. (1982). Accommodation of a scientific conception: Toward a theory of conceptual change. *Science Education, 66,* 211–227.

Rumelhart, D. E., & Norman, D. A. (1981). Accretion, tuning, and restructuring: Three modes of learning. In J. W. Cotton & R. Klatzy (Eds.), *Semantic factors in cognition* (pp. 37–60). Hillsdale, NJ: Lawrence Erlbaum Associates.

Sadker, D., & Sadker, M. (1985). Is the O.K. Classroom O.K.? *Phi Delta Kappan, 55,* 358–361.

Schommer, M. (1990). Effects of beliefs about the nature of knowledge on comprehension. *Journal of Educational Psychology, 82,* 498–504.

Sinatra, G., & Dole, J. (in press). Case studies in conceptual change: A social-psychological perspective. In B. Guzzetti & C. Hynd (Eds.), *Theoretical perspectives on conceptual change* (pp. xx–xx). Mahwah, NJ: Lawrence Erlbaum Associates.

Strike, K. A., & Posner, G. J. (1990). A revisionist theory of conceptual change. In R. Duschl & R. Hamilton (Eds.), *Philosophy of science, cognitive science, and educational theory and practice.* Albany: SUNY Press.

Tannen, D. (1992). How men and women use language differently in their lives and in the classroom. *Education Digest, 57*(6), 3–6.

Tobin, K. (1988). Differential engagement of males and females in high school science. *International Journal of Science Education, 10,* 239–252.

Tobin, K., & Garnett, P. (1987). Gender related differences in science activities. *Science Education, 71*(1), 91–103.

Vosniadou, S., & Brewer, W. F. (1987). Theories of knowledge restructuring in development. *Review of Educational Research, 57,* 51–67.

Vosniadou, S., & Brewer, W. F. (1992). Mental models of the earth: A study of conceptual change in childhood. *Cognitive Psychology, 24,* 535–585.

Vygotsky, L. (1978). *Mind in society: The development of higher psychological processes.* Cambridge, MA: Harvard University Press.

## CHAPTER EIGHT

# Learning From Text in a Post-Typographic World

Lynne Anderson-Inman
*University of Oregon*

David Reinking
*University of Georgia*

In 1981, Shel Silverstein published a book of poems entitled *Light in the Attic*. Among its many engaging, though slightly rebellious, poems is one entitled "Twistable Turnable Man." In the poem, Silverstein described the perfect man for our "bendable, foldable . . . easily moldable" society.

He's the Twistable Turnable Squeezable Pullable
Stretchable Foldable Man.
He can crawl in your pocket or fit in your locket
Or screw himself into a twenty-volt socket,
Or stretch himself up to a steeple or taller,
Or squeeze himself into a thimble or smaller,
Yes he can, course he can,
He's the Twistable Turnable Squeezable Pullable
Stretchable Shrinkable Man. (p. 138)

About the same time this poem was published, a revolution was occurring in the computer industry that would eventually have a profound effect on how students learn from text. With the joint inventions of the electronic circuit board and the microprocessing chip, computers were suddenly small and affordable enough to be purchased by public schools as well as individual families. What was once a machine used only by the government, large corporations, and computer science departments, became an accepted and even necessary fixture in K–12 schools and a household appliance purchased today by an estimated 40% of all American families.

With this transformation in the size and availability of computing power has come a tool of unprecedented adaptability and utility—electronic text. Like the twistable, turnable man, electronic text is exceptionally flexible. Because it is composed of electronic dots on a computer screen instead of ink on paper, electronic text can easily be altered in both appearance and function. Although impermanent in form, it can be copied and shared around the world in a matter of minutes. Because it is not constrained by the limitations of the printed page, it can be sent long distances over telephone wires and even translated quickly into multiple languages. Electronic text supports society's need for a medium of written communication that is both malleable and controlled by the user, and in schools around the country, electronic text is having an impact on both how and what students learn from text.

In this chapter we describe a variety of ways in which electronic text is substantially different from traditional, typographic text (i.e., text that has been typeset and printed on paper), and we illustrate how these differences are irreversibly altering the way students learn from and with text. In addition, we present two examples of learning from electronic text, each capitalizing on different features of this new medium. Finally, we briefly outline some questions about the role of electronic text that are likely to become important in the future.

## PRINTED AND ELECTRONIC TEXT

Conventional printed texts have a physical presence, and thus a permanence, that is both familiar and comfortable. It resides on paper or some other printable substance much as the author wished it to appear, being altered only when annotated by the reader or defaced by conditions leading to its deterioration or destruction. Printed texts do not invite change. Even readers' annotations have to be squeezed into margins that are not typically designed for such activity. Printed texts are static, passive, and noninteractive. They await an active agent, the reader, to peruse lines of alphabetic code to make sense of words and phrases. Whether the reader is successful in doing so or not is of no concern to texts or to books. Indeed, printed texts have no way of "knowing" what a reader carries away from the experience of reading. Moreover, without the use of machines designed to transform the text's appearance (e.g., copiers with enlarging capabilities), it cannot be altered to increase its accessibility or readability.

Electronic texts, by comparison, have no physical form and no permanence. Thus, they can be altered in a myriad of useful ways, both before and during the processes of reading and writing. Seven features of electronic texts are now discussed. Each feature highlights the malleability of electronic texts in the service of learning. Although these features are not mutually exclusive, labeling each feature helps to focus attention on its potential contribution to reading and learning from text.

## Modifiable

Electronic text can be quickly and easily modified to reflect an author's revisions or to incorporate a reader's annotations. Because electronic text can be easily extended, altered, or deleted, it allows writers to make corrections, update information, and insert alternative perspectives into existing documents. The same capabilities enable a reader to interact with electronic text, inserting comments to the writer or making notes for studying later. In addition, there is nothing to prevent the reader from assuming the role of author, perhaps substantially changing the original text. As suggested by Landow (1992) the flashing cursor in a word processing document is the visual manifestation of the readers' presence and therefore their capacity to alter the text being read. Clearly, the distinction between reader and writer is much less obvious in dealing with electronic text, which may have potentially positive and negative ramifications.

The capability to modify electronic texts can be especially useful when students are assigned a project that requires writing and revising. Consider, for example, the benefits of electronic text when students are asked to write a comparison essay on the literary versus historical personage of a character in one of Shakespeare's plays. Each student might first create an electronic outline listing the main ideas and supporting details to be covered in each paragraph and then turn this in to the teacher for feedback. (See Anderson-Inman, 1995, for a more detailed description of computer-based outlining as a prewriting tool.) Because the outline is produced in electronic text, the student can easily modify it to reflect the changes and improvements suggested by the teacher.

Once the outline is modified, the student uses a word processing program to create a first draft of the essay based on the outline. Both paper and disk copies of the draft essays are then exchanged with other students in the class, who make up a peer editing system designed to give fellow students more input as they revise their essays. Each peer editor might be charged with reading one or more essays and inserting comments and suggestions into the electronic versions of the text. After receipt of the peer editors' suggestions, the original student authors consider the feedback they have received and incorporate the new input as appropriate. Because the students are working in electronic text, these changes, whether small corrections or major restructuring, can be accomplished without tedious retyping. Before turning in the final product, the whole document can be checked for spelling errors with an electronic spell checker (Anderson-Inman & Knox-Quinn, 1996) and formatted to meet a teacher's expectations by using the word processor's automatic styling features. The end product is an essay that has benefited from multiple levels of input and frequent revisions, all made possible, or at least easier, because students have writing tools at their disposal that capitalize on how easily electronic text is modified.

Over the previous decade, there has been considerable interest in examining how students write with electronic text and the effects that word processing or related electronic writing tools have on the quantity and quality of student writing. Results vary considerably, reflecting such parameters as the type of writing tool used, students' keyboarding skills, intensity of instruction, and prior student experience working in electronic writing environments. Nonetheless, the better-designed studies are quite revealing. Owston, Murphy, and Wideman (1991, 1992) conducted a series of studies in which they actually observed and electronically recorded students during the process of writing with electronic text. In one study, a screen-recording device was used to record unobtrusively the text entries and revisions made by 8th grade students (all of whom had considerable experience writing in electronic environments) while writing expository papers (Owston et al., 1992). These data revealed that students vary considerably in their approach to composing with electronic text, and that they revise at all stages of the writing process. By comparing the quality of students' papers written on computer with those the same students wrote on paper, the researchers also found that papers written with electronic text scored significantly higher on all four dimensions of a holistic/analytic writing assessment scale. The authors concluded that the differences in quality were due mostly to the facilitation of the writing and revising environment provided by the word processor, and that electronic text may well encourage students to adopt different writing strategies.

## Enhancible

Electronic text can also be enhanced to include various forms of multimedia for the purposes of illustration, clarification, and reader support. Although paper-based textual materials have long used pictures and other forms of graphics to illustrate key concepts, places, or people, their inclusion in printed form is expensive and their use therefore is highly selective. In addition, because the printed page must rely solely on media that can be presented visually and in static form, there are serious limitations to how traditional text can be enhanced. Neither of these conditions exist for electronic text. It is no more expensive to embed multiple pictures in an electronic document than it is to embed one picture. Furthermore, the types of media that can be embedded in electronic texts may easily include sound, digitized or synthesized speech, animations, and full-motion video.

Anderson-Inman and Horney used the term "supported text" to refer to electronic documents in which the text has been enhanced with various types of multimedia for the purposes of expanding or improving student comprehension (Anderson-Inman & Horney, 1998; Anderson-Inman, Horney, Chen, & Lewin, 1994). The rationale for selecting this term emphasizes the goal of reading and learning from text. In supported texts, the role of accompanying multimedia is seen as secondary to this goal. In other words, the very existence of the multimedia enhancements of texts is to promote increased comprehension and enriched understanding of a text to which the enhancements are attached. Although this theoretical perspective does not undergird the design and production of all, or even most, multimedia documents, it is useful as a construct for highlighting one major advantage of electronic text: its amenability to reader support. Furthermore, much of the research on electronic text enhancements assumes this perspective.

For example, in reviewing the research on informational graphics within electronic documents, Reinking and Chanlin (1994) found a small number of studies designed to address the effects of embedded graphic aids on reading and learning from electronic text. In each of these studies, the graphics were assumed to be an adjunct to the text. For example, a series of studies by Rieber and colleagues (Rieber, 1989, 1990; Rieber, Boyce, & Assad, 1990; Rieber & Hannafin, 1988) compared student learning from interactions with a text-only presentation of information on Newtonian mechanics to learning from interactions with text accompanied by either static or animated graphics. In a related series of studies, Hegarty, Carpenter, and Just (1991) found that animations attached to electronic text were especially beneficial for students with low mechanical ability, presumably by helping them to compensate for an inability to develop an adequate visual representation from text alone.

In today's world of CD-ROM books and information on the World Wide Web (WWW), electronic text is increasingly enhanced with an impressive array of audio as well as visual media. In addition to static and animated graphics, sound and speech are frequently used to enrich and to support students' reading. An electronic book on the history of music incorporates musical excerpts from composers' works. A text on contemporary poets includes the poets reading selected poems, and a WWW page on Mexican culture includes pronunciations for Spanish terms.

Although there is little research on the efficacy of these enhancements, to the reader they feel intuitively beneficial as supports to the joint processes of text comprehension and appreciation. One exception to this dearth of research is in the study of computer speech technologies to promote fluent reading and text comprehension. For more than a decade, researchers have documented the beneficial effects of enhancing electronic text by providing poor readers with computer-generated pronunciations of unknown or difficult words or even complete passages (Elkind, Cohen, & Murray, 1993; Farmer, Klein, & Bryson, 1992; Olson, Foltz, & Wise, 1986; Reitsma, 1988).

Reading to learn in an electronic environment can be a highly interactive experience because readers are usually free to select from the various sorts of multimedia enhancements designed to enrich or improve their comprehension. While reading in electronic environments, students might alternatively elect to view an animated simulation of some complex process, hear the pronunciation of an unfamiliar word, listen to a melody as played on different instruments, and study a sculpture photographed from multiple perspectives. The text enhancements that make these types of interactions possible usually reside out of the reader's sight or hearing until selected, although they might be represented in the text by some icon or notational convention such as bold or underlined text. Whether these text enhancements are accessed is determined by a reader, thus necessitating a certain level of motivation to comprehend the text, or at least a sense of exploration. Readers who fail to exhibit these qualities are not likely to benefit from reading in electronic text environments, no matter how many quality enhancements are embedded in the text for their use (Horney & Anderson-Inman, 1995).

**Programmable**

The capabilities that allow texts to be modified or enhanced at the direction of the reader also allow the presentation of texts that limit readers' choices for the sake of enhancing their learning. In other words, electronic texts can be programmed to monitor the various contingencies associated with an individual reader's experience in reading a particular text, and to modify automatically the presentation of the text in specified ways for the sake of increasing attention to important information, stimulating deeper processing of textual material, shaping strategic reading and learning, and so forth.

A theoretical base for understanding and exploring this capability can be derived from the simple fact that electronic texts are displayed on a single computer screen instead of a sequence of pages that are freely accessible to the reader. The reader of an electronic text depends on the computer program, actually the person who wrote the program, to view more than relatively limited portions of text at one time. In this sense the computer screen that displays electronic texts is like a window through which one views the textual world (Wilkinson, 1983), or, as Daniel and Reinking (1987) pointed out, creating an electronic text involves taking into account three dimensions. In addition to the two-dimensional space that requires decisions about where to place textual material on the page or screen, a writer, designer, programmer, or developer of electronic texts must contend with a third dimension: time. That is, those creating electronic texts must decide when and under what conditions textual material will be available to a reader.

Some of the practical implications of this capability can be realized by considering a common limitation faced by many teachers who expect students to acquire content by reading independently. For example, students in a science class might be assigned to read a difficult chapter on cell division, following a study guide advising that at a certain point their comprehension will be enhanced by carefully examining several accompanying illustrations of cells at various stages of division. Unfortunately, secondary teachers who make this kind of assignment are often resigned to the reality that many students will consider their reading task easier because it includes illustrations that can be ignored. An electronic text presenting the same text and illustrations, however, could be programmed to restrict students from accessing subsequent text until they had demonstrated some attention to the relevant portions of the illustrations. Another difference, of course, is that the electronic illustrations could also be enhanced in a variety of ways not possible on paper, such as animating the stages of cell division.

L'Allier (1980) was one of the first researchers to appreciate and explore the programmable capabilities of electronic texts. He developed a computer program that modified the structure and readability of texts on the basis of a complex algorithm that took into account, among other factors, readers' accuracy and response time to questions inserted into the text. He found that high school readers identified as having reading problems and who read texts under these adaptive conditions comprehended as much as average and above average readers studying conventional printed texts that were not adapted. In the work of Reinking and colleagues (Reinking, 1988; Reinking & Rickman, 1990; Reinking & Schreiner, 1985), middle-grade readers required to access various types of assistance while reading electronic texts comprehended (a) more than students who had no assistance and (b) more than students who had access to assistance but were free to make their own decisions about what assistance they needed and when to access it. For example, Reinking and Rickman (1990) investigated the effects of mandatory versus self-selected access to vocabulary definitions. They found that students required to access definitions of difficult vocabulary words while reading passages from science textbooks comprehended more and performed better on a test of vocabulary from the passages.

Likewise, Boone and Higgins (1992) conducted multiple studies on the use of hypermedia study guides to support and extend the text comprehension of secondary students reading electronic versions of material from their social studies textbooks (Higgins & Boone, 1990; Higgins, Boone, & Lovitt, 1996; Horton, Boone, & Lovitt, 1990). In addition to other features, the study guides are programmed to control student movement through the text as a function of their responses to multiple-choice questions embedded in the document. When students answer the questions correctly, they are given positive feedback and allowed to go to the next page. When students answer the questions incorrectly, their attention is drawn to the exact spot in the text needed to answer the question correctly, and the multiple-choice question is presented again. Although the research suggests that the hypermedia study guides have a positive effect on student learning, the design of the studies makes it difficult to separate the effects of this feature from others embedded in the study guides.

The mandatory review of partially or inadequately learned information from texts has been the focus of research that illustrates how the program-mability of electronic texts may be used to alter reading and study strategies. For example, Tobias (1987, 1988) found that mandatory review of relevant portions of a text after a reader has answered an inserted question incorrectly, amplified a negative effect found in previous research investigating inserted questions in printed texts. That is, readers frequently do better on posttest items directly related to the inserted questions, but they do worse on items not directly related to the inserted questions when compared with readers who read versions of the text without inserted questions (or in this case, without mandatory review). Tobias hypothesized that during mandatory review, readers were using a "search-and-destroy" strategy that prompted them to focus exclusively on information related to the inserted question in order to avoid further mandatory review.

To test this hypothesis, and to determine if the capabilities of the computer might be used to alter readers' strategies under conditions of mandatory review, Reinking, Pickle, and Tao (1996) studied the effects of asking dif-ferent types of follow-up questions after mandatory review in electronic texts. By adding a condition in which mandatory review was followed by a new question related to the reviewed material (instead of the same question previously missed), they were able to study the effect that question type had on what students did during mandatory review. They found some evi-dence that readers receiving a new question following mandatory review of the text more evenly distributed their review time across the paragraphs they were required to review. Readers receiving the same question tended to spend a disproportionate time reviewing the paragraph that provided the information necessary to answer the missed question. This study provides an example of how the programmable nature of electronic texts has impor-tant implications for enhancing learning from texts and for shaping readers' strategies during independent reading.

## Linkable

Electronic text provides new opportunities for linking chunks of information, both within and among related materials. Expository information in printed materials is presented in specific forms and genres such as an article in a magazine or journal, an entry in an encyclopedia, a chapter in a book, or an investigative report in a newspaper. Such textual units of information are written to stand alone as distinct entities, although they may exist as parts of larger, more integrated textual units such as encyclopedias, books, and journals. Some writers (Spivey & King, 1989) have used the term "intertextuality" to emphasize how readers and writers build bridges across the boundaries that separate such distinct textual sources. Indeed, a major part of the educational endeavor at the secondary level is to cultivate increasing competence in the ability to analyze and synthesize information from separate sources into a new entity. Scholarship, whether it is a term paper written by a student or a published treatise by a seasoned academic, is exercised essentially by creating links between diverse sources of information to create a new unit for others to consider and possibly use in making their own links.

As we become more familiar with electronic texts, we grow consciously aware of the constraints that print technology imposes on this process of linking information across separate texts, and of how entirely new ways of structuring textual information might bring certain advantages to the tasks of reading and learning. Again, this realization has both theoretical and practical dimensions.

On the practical side, it is becoming increasingly obvious that the boundaries dividing printed texts into clearly identifiable units are beginning to dissolve, at least in the environments most natural to electronic texts. That is, the links between informational texts in digital form can be so fluid and effortless that there is little to reinforce their identity as separate textual units of information. The use of the WWW is clearly the best current example. At its simplest level, the WWW can be envisioned as chunks of formatted electronic text (often enhanced with graphics and sound) residing on computers around the world, all of which are connected to the Internet via phone lines and fiber-optic cables. Each "page" of a website is accessible to readers through a unique system of links, allowing for near seamless movement both within a document on the same computer or across documents on multiple computers. Each webpage may have hundreds of links to related information that can be accessed by clicking on "hot" portions of the text, typically indicated by text in color. Following these links may lead to relevant or irrelevant information about museums, professional organizations, hobbyists, news organizations, other students, scholars, and businesses around the world.

Although the WWW is only beginning to have an effect on how teachers and students seek information in schools, its use suggests enormous possibilities for transforming reading and writing in academic contexts. Until just a few years ago, for example, students doing a conventional report would go to the library and use the card catalog and various indexes to generate a list of individual sources related to their topic. They would then seek out their sources at various locations in the library, often experiencing the frustration of discovering that several key books or articles were missing or unavailable. Key information would then be written on note cards and assembled into an outline, followed by multiple drafts of a paper, and a listing of reference sources.

This conventional process can be contrasted with an analogous but qualitatively different process in seeking out information on the WWW. Instead of starting with the card catalog, students may enter key words into one or several search engines on the WWW to locate a much wider array of sources than they can reasonably use. A click of the mouse sends a student's computer zooming across cyberspace in search of any selected source. The source may or may not turn out to be useful, but determining this requires accessing the website, probably residing on a computer located at a great geographic distance. Serendipitous explorations are likely, given the diversity of sources displayed and the ease with which they can be accessed. Instead of being frustrated by finding too little information, students using the WWW for research will most likely be inundated with too much information. As students seek to determine which sources are valid and relevant, they have to screen and filter what they find, culling the best from the vast web of linked electronic text. When relevant information is found, it may be in any form: prose, illustrations, animations, speech, movie clips, and so forth. These can be cut and pasted into a student's own report or multimedia presentation. Clearly, not only are the products of students' research using the WWW likely to be different from conventional text, but so are the abilities and strategies needed to locate information, synthesize across sources, and attribute ownership.

The ease with which electronic texts can be linked has raised theoretical speculation about how textual information in digital and printed documents might be structured differently and how alternative structures may affect reading, writing, and learning (Bolter, 1991; Duchastel, 1986; Landow, 1992; Lanham, 1989, 1993; Reinking, 1994, 1995; Tuman, 1992a, 1992b). Printed texts, because they exist as distinct entities, are naturally linear and hierarchical, or, put another way, what separates textual documents is that each has a clearly defined beginning, middle, and end. Although readers may read a book in other than a linear manner (e.g., reading the chapters out of order or by stopping to read parts of another book before continuing), doing so runs counter to the way that printed documents are written and preserved. Structuring textual information in nonlinear, nonhierarchical formats using the capabilities of digital media has been collectively referred to as *hypertext* or, when the prose is accompanied by other forms of media, as *hypermedia*. Hypertexts and hypermedia are created, not only to permit readers to explore flexibly the links between nodes of textual information, but to encourage them to do so. A map showing the textual nodes of a typical hypertext and the links connecting them is shown in Fig. 8.1.

The impact that reading and writing in hypertext will eventually have on literacy activities remains to be seen. Some serious writers are exploring hypertextual fiction as a new genre of narrative for middle- and high school students (Larson, 1993), and futurists have predicted that teacher-assigned

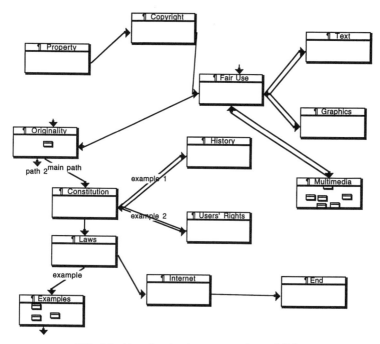

FIG. 8.1. Map showing hypertext nodes and links.

writing in hypertext will some day replace the five-paragraph essay. Such developments have important implications for reading and studying in electronic environments, for teaching and learning in schools, and indeed for defining literacy itself (Reinking, 1998).

## Searchable

Electronic text can also be searched by the computer for any desired key word or phrase. Using character recognition and algorithms for matching strings of letters embedded in the text, the computer can automatically find words and phrases that match any set of letters provided by the reader. The reader simply enters a word or part of a word, and the computer will search an entire document to find matches. If multiple electronic documents are linked together, the search can be conducted across all of them.

If a word search is conducted from within a word processing document or text file, for example, the computer will display each appearance of the word, one at a time, in the order that they appear in the document. By analyzing either the words found or the text around them, a reader can answer questions about the author's use of language or gather information about a specific topic. For example, searching for the word "learning" in this document reveals that we have used the word 53 times and in three different ways: as a verb (as in "learning from text"), as an adjective (as in "learning disabilities"), and as a noun (as in "enhanced learning"). More relevant to the educational goals of secondary students would be searching an electronic version of Hawthorne's *The Scarlet Letter*. A student, for example, might search all appearances of the word "Hester" in order to collect examples of her emotional growth under adversity and persecution. One might conversely search for all appearances of the words "Arthur" or "Dimmesdale" to explore the author's view on the destructive effects of hidden guilt.

The computer's primary role is to enhance the efficiency of the search process, although it may also increase its accuracy and richness. In a study exploring the relative speed and richness of searching an electronic version of the *Encyclopedia Britannica* (found on the WWW at http://www.eb.com:180/) with the traditional multivolume printed version, Anderson-Inman (in preparation) found that students could locate significantly more material on a given topic in a specified amount of time when using the web-based version. More important than speed, however, was the fact that searching the electronic text of the encyclopedia revealed the existence of information not located in the index.

For example, one student searched both the electronic encyclopedia and its paper-based cousin for information about Frederick Douglass, the black abolitionist born into slavery. Using the index to the printed set, the student was able to locate all three entries listed under Douglass' name in the appropriate volumes in the specified time of one-half hour. These included the main biographical article on Douglass and two references to him in other articles (one on Abraham Lincoln and one on abolitionism). Using the electronic version of the *Encyclopedia Brittanica* (accessed via Netscape on the WWW), the student was able to locate and look up the same three articles, but also found a reference to the writings of Douglass in an article on slave literature. In addition, the main biographical article contained links to four full-text electronic versions of articles or books that Douglass had written, including his autobiography. The latter was a wealth of new information because it contained not only Douglass' narrative of life as a slave, but also an introduction by contemporary William Lloyd Garrison in the form of a letter describing Douglass' work as an abolitionist. All were found under a list of "Related Internet Resources" and accessed via direct links to the Electronic Text Center at the University of Virginia. With her remaining time, the student checked out a companion volume found at the *Encyclopedia Britannica* site entitled "Spotlight: The Britannica Guide to Black History," which presented the same biographical article, but also provided a picture and a bibliography. In sheer volume of words found, either about Frederick Douglass or written by him, the contrast is startling. Not counting the duplicated article, the student found material totaling 308,407 electronic words, as compared to only 8,246 words found on paper.

## Collapsible

Because of its impermanent nature, electronic text can be collapsed and hidden from view until needed. The text feels like it is still there, but appears tucked away until the reader wishes it to re-emerge on the screen. The most common use for collapsible text is the menu bar that appears across the top of many computer screens. Such hidden menus also have been employed in hypertext documents to provide readers with lists of supportive resources or notational tools for annotating electronic text (Anderson-Inman, 1989; Horney & Anderson-Inman, 1994b). When interacting with hidden collapsible menus, the reader must click on the desired menu item to expand its options and then drag the cursor down the menu list to select an operation or feature. The primary advantage of this technology is that it can be used to provide readers with easy access to many operations without having information cluttering up the screen. This feature enables readers to navigate in, and use the features of highly sophisticated applications and complex hypermedia documents, without feeling overwhelmed or hopelessly lost.

Another useful implementation of collapsible text can be seen in electronic outlining programs. Outlining in an electronic environment has numerous advantages over outlining on paper (Anderson-Inman, 1995), not the least of which is that text under a heading or subheading can be collapsed and then expanded. Figure 8.2 shows an electronic outline in three different stages of expansion. This capacity for text to be hidden and then revealed at will has at least two useful functions. The first is to facilitate creating and working with long outlines. Because any number of subheadings and text notes can be folded up under a heading that is higher on the hierarchy, information in an electronic outline can be kept hidden from view until needed. This feature prevents endless scrolling through headings and subheadings to find some piece of information or to insert new subheadings in an existing outline.

The capacity for electronic headings and subheadings to be collapsed and then expanded also makes an electronic outlining program an ideal study tool. Students can be taught to use this capacity to test their own knowledge of the content in an electronic outline. Anderson-Inman and colleagues have developed a self-testing study strategy that takes advantage of this ability to manipulate which parts of an electronic outline are visible at any given time (Anderson-Inman, 1995; Anderson-Inman, Horney, Knox-Quinn, Corrigan, & Ditson, 1997). When using the self-testing strategy, students are taught to (a) expand a heading to reveal its subheadings, (b) study the material under a heading by asking themselves a series of questions, and then (c) hide the subheadings and test themselves to see if they can remember the information just rehearsed. If they are unsuccessful in remembering the information accurately, the process is repeated. This self-testing

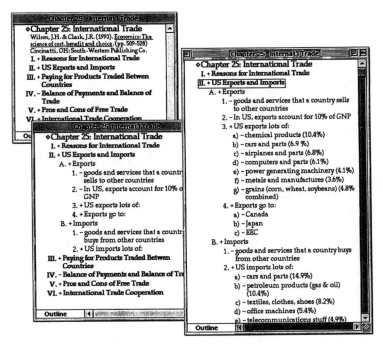

FIG. 8.2.  Electronic outline of a textbook chapter on International Trade, in three stages of expansion.

process is facilitated by the act of collapsing and then expanding the text in headings and subheadings, thus making the study task highly interactive and engaging. Furthermore, students can accurately monitor how well they are learning the material and are therefore able to predict more accurately when they are ready to be held accountable for the information in a test or some other evaluation activity.

Anderson-Inman and colleagues have conducted several studies on the use of computer-based outlining as a tool for studying material from content-area textbooks (Adams, 1992; Adams & Anderson-Inman, 1991; Anderson-Inman, Redekopp, & Adams, 1992; Tenny, 1988). The study strategy has three basic steps, of which self-testing is the last (Anderson-Inman, 1995; Anderson-Inman & Tenny, 1989). The basic procedure is to (a) create a skeleton outline of the headings and subheadings found in the chapter to be studied, (b) summarize the text by inserting key words and phrases under each heading or subheading, and then (c) self-test for understanding using the process just described. In the first study to assess the effects of this study strategy on text comprehension, Tenny (1988) found much higher comprehension of material from an American history textbook when performance under this condition was compared to the performance of the same students under a read and reread condition. Furthermore, observations of student body language indicated they were far more actively engaged while reading and studying with the computer as a "cognitive partner" (Salomon, Perkins, & Globerson, 1991) than they were on their own.

An investigation into the effects of a similar procedure on the test performance of low-achieving students in two world history classes yielded mixed results (Anderson-Inman, Redekopp, & Adams, 1992). Although some students evidenced pronounced improvement in test scores after learning to outline and self-test their understanding of text-based material, the performance of other students showed little change. This study suggests there are other factors that influence whether the strategy is effective for improving students' ability to learn from text, among them student attitude and motivation, as well as the amount of time they have to implement the strategy. Research conducted with students who have learning disabilities (Adams, 1992; Adams & Anderson-Inman, 1991; Anderson-Inman, Knox-Quinn, & Horney, 1996) suggests that not only is the study strategy effective for this population, but that computer-based studying can be conducted in a special education pull-out setting (e.g., a resource room) as a way of impacting student performance in general education classes.

## Collaborative

Electronic text can be used to provide readers and writers with a shared space for communication and construction of textual documents. Traditionally, writing has been private and solitary. It is hard to imagine more than one person working on the same typewriter at the same time, or people simultaneously taking pens and pencils to a single piece of paper. Reading too is usually private and solitary. However, it is possible to design electronic reading and writing environments in ways that facilitate collaborative literacy activities. Networked computers running software that allows simultaneous access to multiple users is called *groupware.*

Anderson-Inman and Knox-Quinn (Anderson-Inman, Knox-Quinn, & Tromba, 1996; Knox-Quinn, 1995; Knox-Quinn & Anderson-Inman, 1996) described the use of one such program, *Aspects* (Group Logic, 1994), for collaborative writing and notetaking. Knox-Quinn (1995), for example, explored collaborative story writing using *Aspects* in a networked computer laboratory as a follow-up activity to reading and discussing Joseph Cambell's *The Hero With a Thousand Faces.* Students, writing in anonymous pairs and communicating only through a shared space on their respective computer screens, worked on the same document simultaneously, jointly negotiating the story line and character development. Students' responses to the collaboration were positive, and they requested that this activity continue. The instructor's response was also positive, indicating surprise about the animation of the laboratory while students were writing and about the quality of their social interactions, which was a distinctly different scenario from the usual isolation of writing assignments.

The collaboration that is more natural to writing and reading electronic texts can also be used to enhance students' content-area literacy by supporting notetaking during in-class presentations and discussions. Anderson-Inman and Knox-Quinn have been investigating the use of networked notetaking as a strategy for assisting secondary and postsecondary students with disabilities who have difficulties taking notes in class (Anderson-Inman, Knox-Quinn, & Tromba, 1996; Knox-Quinn & Anderson-Inman, 1996). Each student is paired with a notetaker, and both are given laptop computers wirelessly connected by the use of infrared devices. Using the same collaborative writing software, the notetaker and student are able to construct class notes simultaneously, as well as communicate via a "chat box" that supports ongoing tutoring. Results suggest that having a real-time model for good notetaking results in students being able to take better notes on their own. This in turn affects their abilities to recognize key vocabulary and comprehend material from their textbooks, resulting in improved performance on class tests.

The Internet also has fostered collaboration through e-mail and bulletin board discussion groups often called "list-servs." E-mail has proven to be a major stimulus for collaborative writing. The text of a draft document can be easily and quickly shared with a writing partner, even when that partner is halfway around the world. The partner can make alterations and additions, then return the document just as easily and quickly.

The Internet also supports collaborative writing projects of larger groups, often in "real time." Anderson-Inman, Knox-Quinn, and Tromba (1996) described two types of environments in which participants are engaged in writing at the same time on the Internet: synchronous chat programs and multiuser simulated environments called MOOs. The first type can be used to foster "freewheeling chats" (Jody & Saccardi, 1996) among many people from geographically diverse locations. Because the communication mode is electronic text and not speech, there is a permanent record of each Internet-mediated conversation. Synchronous chat programs benefit the writing and learning process when the synergy of group brainstorming or discussion is needed for a project involving people who cannot get together in person.

For joint writing projects, MOOs are richer environments because they can present writers with a virtual world in which to work or a fantasy world to write about, and they offer educators a way to design teaching spaces to fit specific instructional goals and prompt specific types of collaborative writing. Daedalus MOO, for example, is a virtual classroom for users of the Daedalus Integrated Writing Environment (DIWE), providing students from geographically distant schools a place to work together on collaborative writing projects over the Internet. The newest generation of MOOs, called WebMOOs, now incorporate graphics and sounds from the WWW to make the virtual worlds more visually interesting and realistic.

## IMPLICATIONS FOR LEARNING FROM ELECTRONIC
## TEXT: TWO EXAMPLES

Because of its unique characteristics, electronic text has potential to have an impact on how students learn from text, as well as on what they learn from text. It may also have an impact on how they communicate or share what they have learned from text with others. These effects may transform the activities and roles of teachers and students. In this section we present two examples from many that might be selected to illustrate what may be early evidence of this promised transformation. These examples also illustrate the type of research questions that will need to be addressed in order to understand and guide the use of electronic texts for reading and learning.

### Example One: Reading to Learn
### From Electronic Books

Electronic books have the look and feel of traditional books, but may also benefit from many (or all) of the characteristics of electronic text outlined previously in this chapter. Electronic books are increasingly available to teachers and students, usually on CD-ROM, and cover almost any subject relevant to the secondary curriculum. The WWW is a growing medium for developing and distributing electronic books and has the advantage of providing worldwide access. Figure 8.3 presents a page from an electronic book on CD-ROM entitled *Edgar Allan Poe: Selected Works.* Figure 8.4 is a page from an electronic book in the Virtual Bookshelf (Island Multimedia, 1997) on the WWW. (For a more complete discussion of selecting and using electronic books with secondary students, please see Anderson-Inman & Horney, 1997.)

Describing what students do when they read electronic books has been the focus of several studies conducted by Anderson-Inman and Horney (1993; Anderson-Inman, Horney, Chen, & Lewin, 1994; Horney & Anderson-Inman, 1994a, 1995; Horney, Anderson-Inman, & Chen, 1995). Using electronic books with varying degrees of sophistication, they have investigated how and when students access the types of text enhancements and supportive resources available to them and also how students combine their resource use into strategies for comprehending what they are reading. This research leads to the following general observations about student use of electronic books:

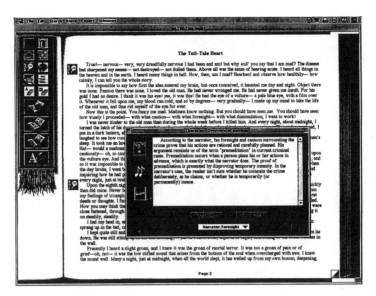

FIG. 8.3. Page from an electronic book on CD-ROM, *Edgar Allan Poe: Selected Works* (Poe, 1996).

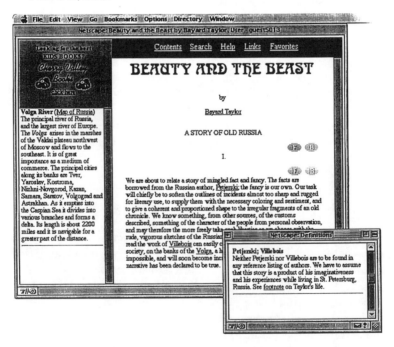

FIG. 8.4. Page from an electronic book on the World Wide Web, *Beauty and the Beast* (Virtual Bookshelf at http://www.islandmm.com/).

1. Students adopt different patterns of interacting with electronic books.

2. Students' interaction patterns are influenced by numerous factors, some of which seem to reside in the student or the educational environment, and some of which are related to the characteristics of the electronic book.

3. Students' interaction patterns change over time, as they acquire more experience reading interactive text and more familiarity with the features available to them.

4. Some interaction patterns are counterproductive to learning and may require specific interventions, either internal or external to the program.

5. Reading electronic books is more time consuming than reading printed books, especially when students access the resources embedded in the text to support their reading comprehension and acquisition of information.

6. Students who use electronic books productively have improved reading comprehension and increased learning of related content-area material when compared to their performance with printed texts.

7. Productive use of electronic books can be enhanced by providing students with clear expectations for reading and training in how to use the book.

8. Most students enjoy reading electronic books, and that enjoyment seems to increase with continued use. However, a few students find reading electronic books to be less enjoyable than reading printed books, primarily because they must use a computer.

From their investigations of electronic books, Anderson-Inman and Horney developed a taxonomy for text enhancements and supportive resources that can be integrated into electronic books for the purpose of promoting comprehension and enriching understanding (Anderson-Inman & Horney, 1997, 1998). Their taxonomy, which follows, illustrates how research may guide educators in selecting or using electronic texts:

1. *Translational resources:* The purpose of translational resources is to provide the reader with an alternate form for words or phrases that might be problematic. The translation might be into simpler language (e.g., a synonym, definition, or paraphrase), into another language (e.g., Spanish or American Sign Language), or into speech (e.g., synthesized or digitized pronunciations). Translational resources are particularly helpful if the reader does not have strong literacy skills or is not a native speaker of the language in which the electronic book is written.

2. *Illustrative resources:* The purpose of illustrative resources is to provide the reader with examples, illustrations, or comparisons to some concept or

set of concepts. Although illustrative resources can be in the form of more text, they may take advantage of the multimedia nature of electronic books and appear as graphics, animations, or sound. Illustrative resources also help students who lack strong literacy skills, and can be used to promote a greater in-depth understanding of unfamiliar concepts and processes.

3. *Summarizing resources:* The purpose of summarizing resources is to provide an overview of the text's structure, content, or major features. This overview might be presented to a reader as an outline (e.g., a table of contents with each title linked to its appropriate page in the text) or in graphic form (e.g., a concept map of key ideas in the document or a timeline of major events). It is helpful if the summarizing resource also provides access to the parts of the document being summarized, thus serving as a navigational aid.

4. *Instructional resources:* The purpose of instructional resources is to prompt student learning by guiding the way they interact with the text. For example, questions might be embedded in the text to help students assess their comprehension; tutorials might be provided to teach students how to access the book's features; or assignments might be included to promote information synthesis. Instructional resources in electronic books are usually included to help students study the material more in-depth or over a longer time.

5. *Enrichment resources:* The purpose of enrichment resources is to augment the main body of text with material that is related, but not actually necessary for comprehension. Enrichment resources can be of any media, and multiple enrichment resources might be attached to any single concept or chunk of text. For example, enrichment resources for the text of the Gettysburg Address might be a photo or drawing of Lincoln at Gettysburg, a sound clip of someone reading the speech, and an analysis of its rhetorical features. None are essential to understanding the speech, but all might augment the reader's appreciation or enhance motivation.

6. *Notational resources:* The purpose of notational resources is to enable students to support their reading by such activities as recording observations, summarizing main ideas, or marking parts of the text. Actions often fostered in electronic books for these purposes include marking pages, tagging and saving favorite photographs, writing annotations or margin notes, taking notes in a notebook, and highlighting text with color.

7. *Collaborative resources:* The purpose of collaborative resources is to promote the process of joint construction of meaning when reading from text. Electronic books that support file sharing allow readers to communicate back and forth over a local or wide area network while reading the same book. This enables discussions while reading and even joint work on comprehension activities.

8. *General purpose resources:* General purpose resources support the content of an electronic book with information that is relevant to, but never designed to be, a part of the book. A good example of a general purpose resource is the full text versions of Frederick Douglass' writings available to readers of the web-based version of the *Encyclopedia Britannica* from the Electronic Text Center at the University of Virginia's website. These electronic text materials exist for a multitude of reasons, but if linked to an electronic book, they provide a useful and enriching extension to the book's content.

## Example Two: Synthesizing Information With Electronic Study Tools

Learning from text often requires students to synthesize information gathered from multiple sources. The expectation that such synthesis will occur usually underlies requests by teachers that students write a research paper or report on some topic relevant to the curriculum. Students are expected to locate multiple sources related to a topic, extract information from each source pertinent to a paper's thesis, and then synthesize this information into a final product that is both original and representative of the students' under- standing. Teachers hoping to promote interdisciplinary understanding will often assign topics that require searching sources from multiple disciplines and synthesizing information across conceptual domains.

Research by Anderson-Inman and colleagues at the Center for Electronic Studying suggests that many students have considerable difficulty with the expectations just outlined. They are often hesitant to separate information from the context in which it is presented, and they frequently are immobilized by the need to construct a product that reflects how they have turned that information into a representation of their personal understanding and knowl- edge. In short, students often express a fear of thinking for themselves, or rather, a fear of putting the results of their thinking into print. This fear leads to unoriginal papers using borrowed phrases and sentences to present a compilation of details as opposed to a personal synthesis.

To address this difficulty, Anderson-Inman and colleagues have investi- gated the effects of providing students with computer-based tools for gath- ering, organizing, and synthesizing information in preparation for writing a paper or report. Two types of tools have been explored: computer-based outlining programs and computer-based concept mapping programs (An- derson-Inman, 1995; Anderson-Inman, Knox-Quinn, & Horney, 1996; An- derson-Inman & Zeitz, 1994). Both types of programs provide students with a flexible vehicle for recording the information they find while searching through multiples sources for relevant material. In an outlining program, the information is recorded as headings and subheadings; in a concept-mapped program, it is recorded as nodes and links. The advantage of recording information in an electronic environment is that the tools are infinitely expansive, details can be inserted anywhere in the outline or concept map, and the environment expands to accommodate the new material.

Another advantage of outlining and mapping software is that it helps students to state information in their own words. Outlines and concept maps encourage brevity, and to achieve this, students must pick out key words or rephrase content into text capturing the essence of the information to be recorded. The need for brevity helps students to separate a main idea from supporting details, thus enabling students to insert supporting details derived from multiple sources under the same heading. Under normal circumstances, this level of semantic analysis is difficult for students to do, and is probably the reason why students often resort to borrowing the arguments and synthesized ideas of the experts they are reading. Because the electronic tool supports this process of decontextualization, students are more willing to engage in it.

Software tools for studying also support and promote information manipulation, leading students to synthesize the ideas and facts they have gathered and recorded. Electronic environments such as outliners and concept mappers are ideal for this type of information manipulation because they enable text to be expanded and contracted; headings and subheadings to be inserted, deleted, or rearranged; and even whole sections to be dragged to new places or copied to multiple locations. The software tool becomes a "cognitive partner" (Salomon, Perkins, & Globerson, 1991), helping students think in new ways about the information they have gathered. The experience of imposing a new structure on someone else's ideas or a new spin on details gleaned from numerous sources is often intellectually stimulating for students. Moreover, the papers they write after engaging in this task of information manipulation reflect a more personal process of knowledge construction and ownership.

Thus, using electronic tools for information manipulation and synthesis promises to provide important new options for helping students of varying abilities to process and organize information and to write better research papers. Indeed, that has been the experience of researchers at the Center for Electronic Studying (Anderson-Inman, Knox-Quinn, & Horney, 1996).

## A FINAL WORD

As these two examples illustrate, the use of electronic texts has important implications for the future of reading and learning in schools. Considering what those implications might be requires first an awareness of the unique features of electronic text, particularly in comparison to more traditional typographic text. In this chapter we addressed that first step by presenting several characteristics of electronic text that we believe are especially relevant to reading and learning from text-based material. Identifying these characteristics provides a conceptual framework that sets the stage for the next step: considering the potential implications of electronic texts for teachers and students in today's schools. It is crucial to ask how electronic text can be used to enhance reading and learning given current educational contexts and practices. In other words, how can an understanding of electronic text contribute to the development of new options for helping students to be more successful in learning with text given the demands created by existing or emerging models of instruction? Electronic books and tools for synthesizing information, discussed in the preceding section, are but two examples of how that question might be answered. Moreover, as we have shown throughout this chapter, empirical evidence is beginning to accumulate that, under certain conditions, electronic texts can enhance the conventional goals associated with reading to learn in our nation's schools.

However, more difficult-to-answer, and ultimately more important, questions remain: Do electronic texts and their increasing prevalence contribute to, perhaps even demand, a fundamental transformation of conventional instruction? More specifically, does their existence require a reconceptualizing of the role of text in instruction? Will alphabetic prose no longer be the "organizing spine" of texts as Lemke (1998) has argued? That is, should we begin to assume that helping students to become literate means adopting broader conceptions of literacy, conceptions that encompass skills in reading and interpreting a broad range of media or symbolic modes of expression? (Cognition and Technology Group at Vanderbilt University, 1994; Flood & Lapp, 1995.) What strategies will readers need for locating and processing information in digital environments? What kind of instruction and learning will emerge in schools if students have unlimited and immediate access to information from diverse sources? Will the textbook survive? What will happen to conventional understandings of concepts such as intellectual property, copyright, and plagiarism (Reinking, 1996) when digital information is easily shared and modified, and when reading and writing become more naturally collaborative?

In this chapter we did not directly address these and similarly consequential questions related to reading and learning from text, but we have hinted at their relevance. We believe such questions will acquire increasing relevance as we move beyond the horizon separating long-standing conceptions of reading and learning from printed texts and into an era that McLuhan (1962) and others have referred to as a post-typographic world (Ong, 1982). The evidence that we are crossing a threshold from a world dominated by print to one dominated by digital media is increasing. Literacy in general, and learning from text in particular, are not likely ever again to be as they were. The portent of crossing that threshold cannot be overestimated.

## ACKNOWLEDGMENT

We wish to acknowledge the contributions of Dr. Mark A. Horney, Research Associate at the Center for Electronic Studying, who has helped elucidate the distinctions between printed and electronic texts identified in this chapter.

## REFERENCES

Adams, V. (1992). *Comparing paper-based and electronic outlining as a study strategy for mainstreamed students with learning disabilities.* Unpublished doctoral dissertation, University of Oregon.

Adams, V., & Anderson-Inman, L. (1991). Electronic outlining: A computer-based study strategy for handicapped students in regular classrooms. In J. Marr & G. Tindal (Eds.), *Oregon conference monograph 1991* (pp. 86–92). Eugene, OR: University of Oregon.

Anderson-Inman, L. (1989). Electronic studying: Information organizers to help students study better, not harder: Part II. *The Computing Teacher, 16,* 21–29.

Anderson-Inman, L. (1995). Computer-assisted outlining: Information organization made easy. *Journal of Adolescent and Adult Literacy, 39*(4), 316–320.

Anderson-Inman, L. (in preparation). *Finding and accessing research materials: A comparison of electronic and paper-based strategies.*

Anderson-Inman, L., & Horney, M. (1993). *Profiles of hypertext readers: Case studies from the electrotext project.* Paper presented at the annual meeting of the American Educational Research Association (AERA), Atlanta, GA.

Anderson-Inman, L., & Horney, M. (1997). Electronic books for secondary students. *Journal of Adolescent and Adult Literacy, 40*(6), 486–491.

Anderson-Inman, L., & Horney, M. (1998). Transforming text for at-risk readers. In D. Reinking, L. Labbo, M. McKenna, & R. Kieffer (Eds.), *Handbook of literacy and technology: Transformations in a post-typographic world* (pp. 15–45). Hillsdale, NJ: Lawrence Erlbaum Associates.

Anderson-Inman, L., Horney, M. A., Chen, D., & Lewin, L. (1994, April). Hypertext literacy: Observations from the ElectroText project. *Language Arts, 71,* 37–45.

Anderson-Inman, L. A., Horney, M. A., Knox-Quinn, C., Corrigan, W., & Ditson, M. (1997). *Computer-based study strategies: A manual for teachers.* Eugene, OR: Center for Electronic Studying.

Anderson-Inman, L., & Knox-Quinn, C. (1996, March). Spell checking strategies for successful students. *Journal of Adolescent and Adult Literacy, 39*(6), 500–503.

Anderson-Inman, L., Knox-Quinn, C., & Horney, M. A. (1996). Computer-based study strategies for students with learning disabilities: Individual differences associated with adoption level. *Journal of Learning Disabilities, 29*(5), 461–484.

Anderson-Inman, L., Knox-Quinn, C., & Tromba, P. (1996, October). Synchronous writing environments. *Journal of Adolescent and Adult Literacy, 40*(2), 134–138.

Anderson-Inman, L., Redekopp, R., & Adams, V. (1992). Electronic studying: Using computer-based outlining programs as study tools. *Reading and Writing Quarterly, 8,* 337–358.

Anderson-Inman, L., & Tenny, L. (1989, May). Electronic studying: Information organizers to help students study better, not harder: Part I. *The Computing Teacher, 16*(8), 33–36.

Anderson-Inman, L., & Zeitz, L. (1994, May). Beyond notecards: Synthesizing information with electronic study tools. *The Computing Teacher, 21*(1), 21–25.

Bolter, J. D. (1991). *Writing space: The computer, hypertext, and the history of writing.* Hillsdale, NJ: Lawrence Erlbaum Associates. (Also available as hypertext computer program)

Boone, R., & Higgins, K. (1992). Hypermedia applications for content-area study guides. *Reading and Writing Quarterly, 8*(4), 379–393.

Cognition and Technology Group at Vanderbilt University. (1994). Multimedia environments for developing literacy in at-risk students. In B. Means (Ed.), *Technology and education reform: The reality behind the promise* (pp. 23–56). San Francisco, CA: Jossey-Bass.

Daniel, D., & Reinking, D. (1987). The construct of legibility in electronic reading environments. In D. Reinking (Ed.), *Reading and computers: Issues for theory and practice* (pp. 24–39). New York: Teachers College Press.

Duchastel, P. (1986). Computer text access. *Computer Education, 10,* 403–409.

Elkind, J., Cohen, K., & Murray, C. (1993). Using computer-based readers to improve reading comprehension of students with dyslexia. *Annals of Dyslexia, 42,* 238–259.

Farmer, M. E., Klein, R., & Bryson, S. E. (1992). Computer-assisted reading: Effects of whole-word feedback on fluency and comprehension in readers with severe disabilities. *Remedial and Special Education, 13,* 50–60.

Flood, J., & Lapp, D. (1995). Broadening the lens: Toward an expanded conceptualization of literacy. In K. A. Hinchman, D. J. Leu, & C. K. Kinzer (Eds.), *Perspectives on literacy research and practice: Forty-fourth Yearbook of the National Reading Conference* (pp. 1–16). Chicago: National Reading Conference.

Group Logic. (1994). *Aspects* [Computer software]. Arlington, VA: Group Logic Inc.

Hegarty, M., Carpenter, P. A., & Just, M. A. (1991). *Diagrams in the comprehension of scientific texts.* In R. Barr, M. L. Kamil, P. Mosenthal, & P. D. Pearson (Eds.), *Handbook of reading research: Vol. 2* (pp. 641–668). New York: Longman.

Higgins, K., & Boone, R. (1990). Hypertext computer study guides and the social studies achievement of students with learning disabilities, remedial students, and regular education students. *Journal of Learning Disabilities, 23,* 529–540.

Higgins, K., Boone, R., & Lovitt, T. C. (1996). Hypertext support for remedial students and students with learning disabilities. *Journal of Learning Disabilities, 29,* 402–412.

Horney, M. A., & Anderson-Inman, L. (1994a). Students and hypertext: Developing a new literacy for a new reading context. In D. Wray (Ed.), *Literacy and computers: Insights from research* (pp. 71–77). Cheshire, England: United Kingdom Reading Association.

Horney, M. A., & Anderson-Inman, L. (1994b). The ElectroText project: Hypertext reading patterns of middle school students. *Journal of Educational Multimedia and Hypermedia, 3*(1), 71–91.

Horney, M. A., & Anderson-Inman, L. (1995). Hypermedia for readers with learning impairments: Promoting literacy with electronic text enhancements. In K. Hinchman, D. J. Leu, & C. K. Kinzer (Eds.), *Perspectives on literacy research and practice: Forty-fourth Yearbook of the National Reading Conference* (pp. 448–458). Chicago: National Reading Conference.

Horney, M. A., Anderson-Inman, L., & Chen, D. T. (1995). *Analysis of interactive reading strategies in a hypertext reading environment.* Paper presented at the annual meeting of the American Educational Research Association, San Francisco, CA.

Horton, S., Boone, R., & Lovitt, T. (1990). Teaching social studies to learning disabled high school students: Effects of a hypertext study guide. *British Journal of Educational Technology, 21,* 118–131.

Island Multimedia. (1997). *The virtual bookshelf.* Available at http://www.islandmm.com/islandmm.

Jody, M., & Saccardi, M. (1996). *Computer conversations: Readers and books online.* Urbana, IL: National Council of Teachers of English.

Knox-Quinn, C. (1995). Authentic classroom experiences: Anonymity, mystery, and improvisation in synchronous writing environments. *Computer Writing, Rhetoric and Literature* [Online], *1*(2). Available at http://www.cwrl.utexas.edu/~cwrl/v1n2/v1n2.html.

Knox-Quinn, C., & Anderson-Inman, L. (1996). *Collaboration and connectivity: Using laptop computers and wireless networks to enhance student performance.* Paper presented at the annual meeting of the American Educational Research Association, New York.

L'Allier, J. J. (1980). *An evaluation study of a computer-based lesson that adjusts reading level by monitoring on-task reader characteristics.* Unpublished doctoral dissertation, University of Minnesota, Minneapolis, MN.

Landow, G. (1992). *Hypertext: The convergence of contemporary critical theory and technology.* Baltimore: The Johns Hopkins University Press.

Lanham, R. A. (1989). The electronic word: Literary study and the digital revolution. *New Literary History, 20*(2), 265–290.

Lanham, R. A. (1993). *The electronic word: Democracy, technology, and the arts.* Chicago: University of Chicago Press.

Larson, D. (1993). *Marble springs* [Computer software]. Cambridge, MA: Eastgate Systems.

Lemke, J. (1998). Multimedia literacy: Transforming skills and schools. In D. Reinking, M. McKenna, L. Labbo, & R. Kieffer (Eds.), *Handbook of literacy and technology: Transformations in a post-typographic world* (pp. 283–303). Mahwah, NJ: Lawrence Erlbaum Associates.

McLuhan, M. (1962). *The Gutenberg galaxy: The making of typographic man.* Toronto: University of Toronto Press.

Olson, R., Foltz, G., & Wise, B. (1986). Reading instruction and remediation with the aid of computer speech. *Behavior Research Methods, Instruments and Computers, 18,* 93–99.

Ong, W. (1982). *Orality and literacy: The technologizing of the word.* New York: Methuen.

Owsten, R. D., Murphy, S., & Wideman, H. H. (1991). On and off computer writing of 8th-grade students experienced in word processing. *Computers in the Schools, 8*(4), 67–87.

Owsten, R. D., Murphy, S., & Wideman, H. H. (1992). The effects of word processing on students' writing quality and revision strategies. *Research in the Teaching of English, 26*(3), 249–276.

Poe, E. A. (1996). The tell-tale heart. In *Edgar Allan Poe: Selected works* [CD-ROM]. Lothian, MD: CIT/ Bookworm. (Original work published 1843)

Reinking, D. (1988). Computer-mediated text and comprehension differences: The role of reading time, reader preference, and estimation of learning. *Reading Research Quarterly, 23,* 484–498.

Reinking, D. (1992). Differences between electronic and printed texts: An agenda for research. *Journal of Educational Multimedia and Hypermedia, 1*(1), 11–24.

Reinking, D. (1994). *Electronic literacy* (Perspective in Reading Research No. 4). National Reading Research Center, University of Georgia, University of Maryland.

Reinking, D. (1995). Reading and writing with computers: Literacy research in a post-typographic world. In K. A. Hinchman, D. J. Leu, & C. K. Kinzer (Eds.), *Perspectives on literacy research and practice: Forty-fourth Yearbook of National Reading Conference.* Chicago: The National Reading Conference.

Reinking, D. (1996). Reclaiming a scholarly ethic: Deconstructing "intellectual property" in a post-typographic world. In D. J. Leu, C. K. Kinzer, & K. A. Hinchman (Eds.), *Literacies for the 21st century: Research and practice* (pp. 461–470). Forty-Fifth Yearbook of National Reading Conference. Chicago: The National Reading Conference.

Reinking, D. (1998). Introduction: Synthesizing technological transformations of literacy. In D. Reinking, M. McKenna, L. Labbo, & R. Kieffer (Eds.), *Handbook of literacy and technology: Transformations in a post-typographic world* (pp. xi–xxx). Mahwah, NJ: Lawrence Erlbaum Associates.

Reinking, D., & Chanlin, L. J. (1994). Graphic aids in electronic texts. *Reading Research and Instruction, 33,* 207–232.

Reinking, D., & Pickle, J. M. (1993). Using a formative experiment to study how computers affect reading and writing in classrooms. In D. J. Leu & C. K. Kinzer (Eds.), *Examining central issues in literacy research, theory, and practice, Forty-second Yearbook of National Reading Conference* (pp. 263–270). Chicago: The National Reading Conference.

Reinking, D., Pickle, M., & Tao, L. (1996). *The effects of inserted questions and mandatory review in computer-mediated texts* (Reading Research Rep. No. 50). Athens, GA: National Reading Research Center.

Reinking, D., & Rickman, S. S. (1990). The effects of computer-mediated texts on the vocabulary learning and comprehension of intermediate-grade readers. *Journal of Reading Behavior, 22,* 395–411.

Reinking, D., & Schreiner, R. (1985). The effects of computer-mediated text on measures of reading comprehension and reading behavior. *Reading Research Quarterly, 20,* 536–552.

Reitsma, P. (1988). Reading practice for beginners: Effects of guiding reading, reading while listening, and independent reading with computer-based speech feedback. *Reading Research Quarterly, 23,* 219–235.

Rieber, L. P. (1989). The effects of computer-animated elaboration strategies and practice on factual and application learning in an elementary science lesson. *Journal of Educational Computing Research, 5,* 431–444.

Rieber, L. P. (1990). Using computer animated graphics in science instruction with children. *Journal of Educational Psychology, 82,* 135–140.

Rieber, L. P., Boyce, M. J., & Assad, C. (1990). The effects of computer animation on adult learning and retrieval task. *Journal of Computer-Based Instruction, 17*(2), 46–52.

Rieber, L. P., & Hannafin, M. J. (1988). Effects of textual and animated orienting activities and practice on learning from computer-based instruction. *Computers in the Schools, 5,* 77–89.

Salomon, G., Perkins, D. N., & Globerson, T. (1991). Partners in cognition: Extending human intelligence with intelligent technologies. *Educational Researcher, 20*(3), 2–9.

Silverstein, S. (1981). *Light in the attic.* New York: Harper & Row.

Spivey, N. N., & King, J. R. (1989). Readers as writers composing from sources. *Reading Research Quarterly, 24,* 7–26.

Tenny, J. L. (1988). *A study of the effectiveness of computer-mediated and rereading study procedures.* Unpublished doctoral dissertation, University of Oregon, Eugene, OR.

Tobias, S. (1987). Mandatory text review and interaction with student characteristics. *Journal of Educational Psychology, 79,* 154–161.

Tobias, S. (1988). Teaching strategic text review by computer and interaction with student characteristics. *Computers in Human Behavior, 4,* 299–310.

Tuman, M. C. (1992a). *Word perfect: Literacy in the computer age.* London: Falmer Press.

Tuman, M. C. (Ed.). (1992b). *Literacy online: The promise (and peril) of reading and writing with computers.* Pittsburgh, PA: University of Pittsburgh Press.

Wilkinson, A. C. (1983). Learning to read in real time. In A. C. Wilkinson (Ed.), *Classroom computers and cognitive science* (pp. 183–199). New York: Academic Press.

Zeitz, L., Horney, M., & Anderson-Inman, L. (1992). Empowering students with flexible text. *The Computing Teacher, 19*(8), 16–20.

## CHAPTER NINE

# Making Text Meaningful:
# The Role of Analogies

Shawn M. Glynn
Michael Law
Elizabeth C. Doster
*University of Georgia*

Throughout history, exemplary teachers have used analogies to introduce new concepts to students (Hesse, 1966; Hoffman, 1980; Oppenheimer, 1956; Thagard, 1992). The analogies serve as initial models, or simple representations, of the concepts. It is not surprising, therefore, that contemporary teachers and textbook authors use analogies to introduce concepts. They frequently preface their explanations with expressions, such as, "Similarly," "Likewise," "Just as," and "That is comparable to." These expressions are all ways of saying to students, "Let me give you an analogy."

This chapter describes the role of analogies in text learning and presents new research on the Teaching-With-Analogies Model (Glynn, 1995, 1996). The purpose of this model is to provide teachers and textbook authors with guidelines for constructing analogies and strategically using them to build on what students already know.

The Teaching-With-Analogies Model is particularly appropriate in *integrated curricula* (Beane, 1995; Shoemaker, 1991) in which concepts are meaningfully connected across disciplines. In integrated curricula, teachers and textbook authors make a special effort to help students build "conceptual bridges" within and among disciplines. Analogies are powerful tools for building these bridges.

## ANALOGIES ARE EXPLANATORY TOOLS

Authors of textbooks often use analogies when introducing key concepts (Glynn, Britton, Semrud-Clikeman, & Muth, 1989). Teachers frequently capitalize on these analogies and incorporate them into their lesson plans

(Treagust, Duit, Joslin, & Lindauer, 1992). When an author has not used an analogy, teachers frequently create their own (Thiele & Treagust, 1991).

Often teachers and authors are unaware that they are using analogies—they do it automatically—and sometimes, the analogies may do more harm than good (Gilbert, 1989; Thagard, 1992; Treagust et al., 1992). That is because teachers and authors, lacking guidelines for using analogies, sometimes use them unsystematically, causing students to form misconceptions.

Before discussing analogies further, it would be helpful to examine some analogies found in science, mathematics, and social studies textbooks. In the following sections, three typical analogies are presented.

### A Cell Is Like a Small Town

For example, DiSpezio, Linner-Luebe, Lisowski, Skoog, and Sparks (1994) drew an analogy when they introduced the *cell* in their middle school textbook, *Science Insights*. They compared the cell to a small town:

> Imagine a small town or city. What are some of its parts? There are roads, factories, schools, and houses. There are power lines and telephone lines. Each person has a special job to do. Each building has a special use. All the people, services, buildings, and other structures work together to make the town function properly.
>
> A cell is like a small town or city. The different parts of a cell have special jobs. Each part helps the cell carry out its life processes. Each part helps to keep the cell working properly. Like the parts of a town must work together, the parts of a cell also must work together to live. . . . In a town, the mayor and city council make important decisions about the workings of the town. They govern the town. In a cell, the nucleus governs the cell. The *nucleus* is the control center for most of the cell's activities. (pp. 78, 80)

### An Equation Is Like a Scale

Buffington et al. (1985) drew an analogy when they introduced the concept of an equation in their middle school textbook, *Merrill Mathematics*. They compared an equation to a scale:

> Bob Gaultney uses a scale to weigh vegetables at his market. Suppose the scale is balanced and he adds weight to one pan. Does the scale still balance? What happens if he adds the same weight to each pan? Does the scale still balance? Equations are like scales in balance. If you add the same number to each side of an equation, an equivalent equation results. (p. 152)

## A Ziggurat Is Like a Skyscraper

In the middle school textbook, *The World: Past and Present* (Harcourt Brace Jovanovich, 1991), an analogy was drawn between a Ziggurat and a sky-scraper:

> In a Sumerian city one structure was noticeable over all others. The Ziggurat towered above the noisy city almost like a modern skyscraper. Reaching to the heavens, some Ziggurats stood as tall as 70 feet (21.3 m). . . . Sumerians had none of the tools or machinery that are used in construction today. They were careful builders, however. Brickmakers formed mud bricks that were all exactly the same size. After they were dried, the bricks were transported to the building site and set in place with bitumen (buh-too-muhn). Bitumen is a thick, sticky, black substance that is used today to pave roads. Reeds were braided together and used to bind the building in much the same way that builders today use steel cables. (p. 34)

## GUIDELINES FOR ANALOGIES

As the preceding examples from science, mathematics, and social studies texts suggest, analogies are explanatory tools used by textbook authors in all the content areas. Unfortunately, the authors' analogies are often ineffective, failing to facilitate students' text learning (Gilbert, 1989). That is because authors, lacking guidelines for using analogies, sometimes use them unsys-tematically, causing students to become confused (Thiele & Treagust, 1994). The distinctions between a target concept, features of the concept, examples of the concept, and an analogy become blurred in students' minds. One solution, of course, would be to advise authors not to use analogies in textbooks. That would be unrealistic because authors, like all human beings, are predisposed to think analogically, and they will use analogies, consciously or unconsciously, during explanation (Lakoff & Johnson, 1980; Piaget, 1962). The better solution is to develop guidelines for constructing and using analogies in textbooks. These guidelines are part of the Teaching-With-Analo-gies Model. These guidelines enable authors to construct effective analogies that help students activate, transfer, and apply relevant existing knowledge when learning from text. These guidelines also enable teachers to extend the authors' analogies or to construct analogies of their own.

The Teaching-With-Analogies Model is based on a constructive view of text learning (Glynn & Duit, 1995). In the following sections, this view is described and questions about the role of analogies in text learning are answered. Then, the Teaching-With-Analogies Model and current research on the model are discussed.

## MEANINGFUL TEXT LEARNING: A CONSTRUCTIVE VIEW

Meaningful text learning is the process of integrating new knowledge with existing knowledge (Glynn & Muth, 1994; Holliday, Yore, & Alvermann, 1994; Hynd & Alvermann, 1989; Hynd, McWhorter, Phares, & Suttles, 1994; Mayer, 1989). Students should not be viewed as human video cameras, passively and automatically recording the knowledge "transmitted" by teachers and textbooks. On the contrary, students actively construct their knowledge when learning meaningfully. They challenge the complex concepts they encounter in text, struggle with them, and try to make sense of them by integrating them with what they already know.

Complex concepts are the rule rather than the exception in science (e.g., photosynthesis), mathematics (e.g., function), and social studies (e.g., inflation). To learn such concepts meaningfully, students should learn them *relationally*, not by rote (Glynn, Yeany, & Britton, 1991). That is, students should learn concepts as information networks rather than as lists of facts. When learning becomes relational rather than rote, it becomes meaningful. It also becomes interesting. Like playing with an erector set, the process of joining new knowledge to existing knowledge intrinsically motivates students.

Studies of experts and novices (Anderson, 1993; Chi, Glaser, & Farr, 1988) have shown that experts are experts, not just because they know more facts than novices, but because their knowledge exists in the form of interrelated networks. The construction of conceptual relationships enhances an expert's working memory and long-term memory performance. Because the expert's knowledge is relational, it is easily stored, quickly retrieved, and successfully applied.

Unfortunately, a student's knowledge is all too often learned by rote. The result is a system of knowledge that is easily forgotten and is not readily transferable to new, related situations that the student may encounter. Meaningful learning requires that students' existing knowledge be taken into account, not ignored. Teachers and textbook authors need powerful instructional methods to help develop novices into experts. *Concept mapping* (Novak, 1990) is one such method that facilitates the learning of relationships within a conceptual network. But what about relationships among different, but in some ways similar, conceptual networks? How can teachers and authors develop such relationships and use them to bridge conceptual networks? Analogies can help students to build these bridges between existing knowledge and new knowledge.

## ANALOGIES: QUESTIONS AND ANSWERS

In this section, the questions that teachers and authors often raise about analogies are answered. The answers contain important background information for successfully using analogies in instruction.

## What Is an Analogy?

An analogy is drawn by identifying similarities between two concepts. In this way, ideas can be transferred from a familiar concept to an unfamiliar one. The familiar concept is called the *analog* and the unfamiliar one the *target*. Both the analog and the target have *features* (also called *attributes*). If the analog and the target share common or similar features, an analogy can be drawn between them. A systematic comparison, verbally or visually, between the features of the analog and target is called a *mapping*.

An abstract representation of an analogy, with its constituent parts, appears in Fig. 9.1.

## How Do Analogies Facilitate Text Learning?

An effective analogy puts new ideas into terms already familiar to students, thus bridging concepts and promoting the transfer of ideas. An analogy drawn by an author or a teacher between a concept covered earlier in a text and one covered later is particularly effective because there is some assurance that the earlier concept is familiar to every student. Analogies of this kind are frequently drawn by Paul Hewitt (1987), the author of the popular high school text, *Conceptual Physics*. For example, Hewitt explains the concept gravitational potential energy in chapter 8 and uses it again in chapter 33 to introduce students to the concept electrical potential energy:

> Recall from Chapter 8 the relation between work and potential energy. Work is done when a force moves something in the direction of the force. An object has potential energy by virtue of its location, say in a force field. For example, if you lift an object, you apply a force equal to its weight. When you raise it

---

### ANALOGY

----------------------

:

ANALOG compared with TARGET

| : | | | : |
|---|---|---|---|
| Feature | " | " | Feature |
| 1 | " | " | 1 |
| 2 | " | " | 2 |
| 3 | " | " | 3 |
| n | " | " | n |

---

FIG. 9.1.  An abstract representation of an analogy with its constituent parts.

through some distance, you are doing work on the object. You are also increasing its gravitational potential energy. The greater the distance it is raised, the greater is the increase in its gravitational potential energy. Doing work increases its gravitational potential energy.

In a similar way, a charged object can have potential energy by virtue of its location in an electric field. Just as work is required to lift an object against the gravitational field of the earth, work is required to push a charged particle against the electric field of a charged body. (It may be more difficult to visualize, but the physics of both the gravitational case and the electrical case is the same.) The electric potential energy of a charged particle is increased when work is done to push it against the electric field of something else that is charged. (pp. 501–502)

Ideally, an analogy effectively drawn between two concepts will help students transfer their existing knowledge to the understanding, organizing, and visualizing of new knowledge. The result is often a higher order, relational understanding: The students see how the features of a concept fit together and how the concept in question connects to other concepts. Students thus will be more likely to generalize their understanding to a superordinate concept, such as that of potential energy. They also will be more likely to transfer their understanding to other instances of the superordinate concept, such as elastic potential energy and chemical potential energy, and see the similarities among different examples of potential energy, such as a lifted stone, a charged battery, a drawn arrow, and an unstruck match.

## What Makes an Analogy Effective?

It is possible to draw a good analogy on the basis of one or a few features, but analogies tend to become more effective as the number of similar features shared by the analog and target increases. For example, teachers and textbook authors have traditionally used a camera as an analog to describe the structure and function of the human eye because the two concepts share so many similar features. Consider the following excerpt from Hewitt (1987):

> In many respects the human eye is similar to the camera. The amount of light that enters is regulated by the *iris*, the colored part of the eye which surrounds the opening called the *pupil*. Light enters through the transparent covering called the *cornea*, passes through the pupil and lens, and is focused on a layer of tissue at the back of the eye—the *retina*—that is more sensitive to light than any artificial detector made. . . . In both the camera and the eye, the image is upside down, and this is compensated for in both cases. You simply turn the camera film around to look at it. Your brain has learned to turn around images it receives from your retina! (pp. 450–451)

The analogy between the camera and the eye is a powerful one because the analog and the target share many features of a common concept. The camera is an effective analog, however, only when students are familiar with its many features, especially those related to its internal structure. Hewitt ensured his students' familiarity with the features of the camera by explaining its components in a section entitled "Some Common Optical Instruments" that preceded the section on "The Eye."

Regardless of how many features are shared between an analog and a target concept, teachers and textbook authors should ensure that students are familiar with the features of the analog before they attempt to draw an analogy. This may be done using pictorial analogies where possible, providing a clear description of the relevant analog features and, in the classroom setting, questioning the students concerning aspects of the analog before mapping the shared features.

## Can Analogies Cause Misconceptions?

Analogies are double-edged swords. They can hinder as well as help learning. When stretched too far, analogies lead to misconceptions. For example, the analogy discussed previously between the camera and the human eye breaks down with respect to focusing. A camera is focused by changing the distance between the lens and the film, whereas a human eye is focused by the cornea and the ciliary muscle around the lens. If teachers or authors do not point out this difference when drawing the analogy, then students might form a misconception. The best solution to this problem is to adopt guidelines for using analogies.

## TEACHING-WITH-ANALOGIES MODEL

One source of guidelines for constructing analogies is the Teaching-With-Analogies Model (Glynn, 1991; Glynn, Duit, & Thiele, 1995; Harrison & Treagust, 1993; Thiele & Treagust, 1995). These guidelines were developed from task analyses of the analogies used in science textbooks by exemplary authors, such as Hewitt (1993).

A *task analysis* is "the process of breaking down an instructional task to determine its essential components and the relationship of those components" (Goetz, Alexander, & Ash, 1992, p. 337; see also Ryder & Redding, 1993; Wiggs & Perez, 1988). A task analysis of how experts perform a cognitive task leads to a representation of the experts' knowledge and, eventually, to a model of the task that includes the operations carried out in the performance of the task. For example, a task analysis of expert writers led Flower and Hayes (1981) to a model of competent expository writing, a model that has subsequently played an important role in the instruction of novice writers. Likewise, task analyses of science textbooks and exemplary teachers have led to guidelines on how to use analogies effectively. The guidelines, applied to the camera–eye analogy described previously, are these:

1. Introduce the target concept (i.e., the human eye).
2. Remind readers of the analog concept (i.e., the camera).
3. Identify relevant features of the target and analog (e.g., lens).
4. Map similarities (see Fig. 9.2).
5. Indicate where the analogy breaks down (e.g., focusing).
6. Draw conclusions (e.g., about accommodation).

Although the guidelines were developed from science texts, they are broad enough to apply to content area texts in general. These guidelines are currently being used to construct analogies in studies of science text learning.

## CURRENT RESEARCH ON ANALOGIES IN TEXT

Glynn and Takahashi (1997) recently completed a study to determine if adding an elaborate analogy to a science text could enhance middle school students' learning of a major concept. The study focused on middle school students because important conceptual foundations for learning science are established in the age range of 10 to 14 years. The children progress from concrete to abstract thinking and begin to develop initial "mental models" of major science concepts. These initial models often take the form of analogies.

An elaborate analogy was defined as one with both graphic and text components that integrate and map key features from an analog to a target concept. The elaborate analogy was constructed following the guidelines in

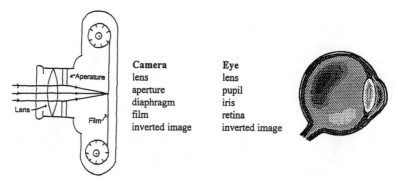

FIG. 9.2. An analogy is drawn between a camera and the human eye.

the Teaching-With-Analogies Model. The role of the analogy was to map a familiar, concrete schema (conceptual structure) onto a new, but in some ways similar, schema, thereby making the new schema more memorable. In this section, an overview of the text-learning task, the findings, and the implications of this study are discussed. The complete manuscript, currently under journal review, is available from the authors.

## Text Learning Task

Sixth graders and eighth graders read either a standard, control text about the cell or an analogy-enhanced version. The 1014-word control text was adapted from a unit on cells in a leading middle school textbook, *General Science* (Alexander et al., 1989). In the analogy-enhanced version, the standard text was enhanced by the inclusion of an analogy (Table 9.1) (Fig. 9.3) that compared the target concept, the cell, to an analog concept, a factory.

The animal cell was selected as the target concept because it represents a complex conceptual system that includes many interrelated, features (e.g., membrane, nucleus, and cytoplasm). Also, the cell plays a fundamental role in middle school students' understanding of life processes.

After text study, to examine the students' awareness of analogies, the students were asked if the cell reminded them of anything. It was expected that the students in the analogy-enhanced condition would be reminded of the factory analogy primarily, whereas the students in the control condition

TABLE 9.1
Text Component of the Factory-Cell Analogy

You might think of a cell as a tiny factory that takes in raw materials, performs many tasks, and makes products. Different people in the factory work at machines doing different jobs. Likewise, each part of the cell has a special job. Together, the parts keep the cell working properly. Here are some similarities between factory parts and cell parts:

| *Factory* | *Animal Cell* |
|---|---|
| 1. Restricted entrance/exit | Membrane |
| 2. Control center | Nucleus |
| 3. Air inside the factory | Cytoplasm |
| 4. Production machines | Protein-making ribosomes |
| 5. Inside delivery and storage | Endoplasmic reticulum |
| 6. Packaging and outside delivery | Golgi apparatus |
| 7. Power Generators | Mitochondria |

Think carefully about each of the above similarities and study the illustration. But remember that this factory-cell analogy, like all analogies, breaks down in places. For example, the membrane envelops the entire cell and has many tiny openings, whereas a factory has only a few entrances in specific locations. In general, however, if you remember how an animal cell is like a factory, it will be easier for you to remember the cell parts and their functions.

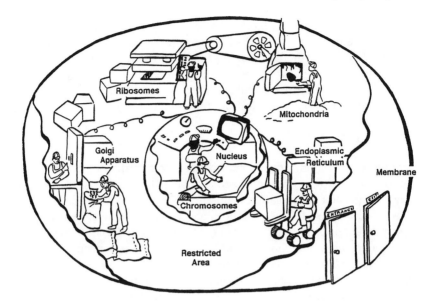

FIG. 9.3. Graphic component of the factory–cell analogy. Copyright © 1997 Shawn M. Glynn.

would be reminded of either various "spontaneous" analogies or no analogy. The students also were administered a recall test that listed the seven major cell parts discussed in the text and asked the student to explain (in writing) the function of each.

### Students' Analogies

In the analogy-enhanced condition, almost all of the eighth and sixth graders thought of analogies for the target when asked if "it reminded them of anything," with the majority being reminded of the factory they had read about. In the no-analogy control condition, almost all of the eighth graders thought of analogies, on a variety of topics (Table 9.2), but only a minority of the sixth graders thought of analogies. One explanation for this finding is that some of the sixth graders simply lacked the content-area knowledge they needed to generate effective analogies. But another explanation is also possible. It may be that some of the sixth graders had the content-area knowledge to construct analogies, but not the "metacognitive awareness" to strategically do so.

In a review of the development of strategy use in children, Pressley and McCormick (1995) concluded: "When given a memory task, students often fail to use a memory strategy that they could use if given a small amount of instruction about how to apply the strategy to the task in question" (p.

TABLE 9.2
Samples of Eighth Graders' Responses to the Question,
"What Does a Cell Remind You Of?"

---

Anne's *human body* analogy: "The function of a cell reminds me of the function of the entire body. All the parts work together to make the whole function successful."

Ricky's *clock* analogy: "The way a cell works reminds me of a machine because everything works almost like a clock works."

Jenny's *hospital* analogy: "The cell reminds me of a hospital. You have many people (organelles) that work together to help you and your body."

Robert's *society* analogy: "The way the cell parts work together in order to help the cell reminds me of society since everyone is different and has different jobs in life, but have common goals to fulfill of life, love, and the pursuit of happiness."

Laura's *rain-and-rock cycles* analogy: "Sort of like the rain and rock cycles because they never end and because something is always happening."

---

*Note.* These students were in the no-analogy control condition. For readability, the students' spelling and punctuation errors have been corrected.

29). Thus, it may be that some of the sixth graders in the present study could have constructed analogies if they had been taught how to do so. This is certainly a promising direction for future research; however, caution is advised. If the sixth graders in question are not developmentally ready to learn an analogy-construction strategy, they might learn it by rote, and be unable to apply it in other situations.

The variety of the spontaneous analogies was remarkable. Most of these analogies were based on commonplace concepts in the students' daily lives. The students' spontaneous analogies were quite reasonable in most cases because they described systems with functional, interacting parts (e.g., the human body, a hospital, and society). Beyond this, however, the spontaneous analogies were rather rudimentary. Only a small number of them mapped out the corresponding features between the analog and the target, and none of the spontaneous analogies mapped as many features as the elaborate analogy, even when "a factory" happened to be chosen as an analogy.

## Text Retention

The findings indicated that the analogy facilitated students' recall of cell–part functions both immediately after text study and 2 weeks later. Moreover, the students rated the analogy-enhanced text as more understandable than the standard text. Thus, the findings supported this hypothesis: By mapping features of the relatively concrete, familiar analog onto the more abstract, less familiar target, the analogy presumably acted as a mediator and made the corresponding features of the target more understandable and memorable.

Although both eighth graders and sixth graders benefited from the elaborate analogy, the sixth graders benefited more. The sixth graders' relative level of cognitive development most likely accounted for this difference. Sixth graders are often in a transition between concrete, intuitive thinking, and more abstract, reflective thinking (Carey, 1985; Kuhn, Amsel, & O'Loughlin, 1988; Lawson, 1993; Metz, 1995; Piaget, 1964). The analogy provided both a conceptual foundation and a bridge to understanding the relatively abstract, less familiar target concept.

**Practical Implications**

The findings of this study support the use of analogies in middle school textbooks. The elaborate analogy in this study was crafted to perform the Teaching-With-Analogy operations for students: Introduce the target; remind students about the analog; identify relevant features; map similarities; indicate where the analogy breaks down; and draw conclusions. These operations provided a blueprint for constructing an elaborate analogy about the cell. These operations are equally well suited for explaining many other relatively complex science concepts (e.g., the atom, the human eye, and an electric circuit) that are routinely introduced to students in the middle grades. By following these operations, the textbook author can increase the likelihood that an analogy will be productive. If an analogy is not used carefully, it can be counterproductive, causing students to form misconceptions. For this reason, the students in this study were warned that the factory analogy, like all analogies, breaks down in places (e.g., a factory has only a few entrances, whereas a membrane has many tiny openings). This warning was apparently effective because no analogy-based misconceptions (e.g., the "floor" of the cell) were detected in the recall of students who received the elaborate analogy.

**Theoretical Implications**

The findings of this study suggest that analogies play an important role in the meaningful learning of science text. The students' adoption of the elaborate analogy and their generation of spontaneous analogies represented efforts to connect familiar schemas with new ones—these were efforts to make learning meaningful. Meaningful text learning is, after all, relational and constructive in nature, not rote (Glynn & Muth, 1994; Holliday, Yore, & Alvermann, 1994; Mayer, 1989). It involves integrating existing knowledge with new knowledge to develop mental models that function as explanatory tools. For middle school students, carefully crafted analogies can serve as initial mental models. As the students develop cognitively and learn more knowledge, they will adopt more sophisticated models.

# FUTURE RESEARCH:
## STUDENTS GENERATING ANALOGIES

The research described in this chapter focused on how teachers and textbook authors can construct effective analogies to help students comprehend textbook concepts. Future research will focus on how students can interpret, criticize, and extend analogies provided by authors and teachers. A modified form of the Teaching-With-Analogies Model, called the Learning-With-Analogies Model, is being developed for use in an integrated curriculum.

An integrated curriculum represents an ideal environment for students' analogical reasoning. In such an environment, students can easily be encouraged to connect concepts within and among disciplines. Students also can be encouraged to be autonomous learners, taking increasing responsibility for building their own bridges across conceptual domains.

In an integrated curriculum, text study of a key concept could be followed by lively class discussions in which analogies are analyzed by students who have been taught the Learning-With-Analogies Model. These discussions could help students to connect concepts in different conceptual domains and, at the same time, help the teachers to diagnose misconceptions the students might have.

For example, students might be asked to compare the structural and functional parts of an animal cell to the structural and functional parts of a city. When students compare a cell to a city, they construct meaningful connections among features of the two concepts (e.g., the nucleus is like the mayor; the endoplasmic reticulum is like a network of streets; the mitochondria are like power companies). These active comparisons promote meaningful learning. Because this analogy, like all analogies, breaks down at various points, it provides teachers with opportunities to assess the real depth of students' conceptual understanding.

It is important that students realize that all analogies break down at some point. Students should realize that analogies are like double-edged swords, with the potential of facilitating comprehension and, at the same time, creating misconceptions.

Students could use a Learning-With-Analogies Model as a guide when constructing their own analogies from scratch, without prompting from teachers. For example, a student seeking an alternative to the city analogy for the cell might compare the cell to a hospital, as a student did in the Glynn and Takahashi study (1997) (see Table 2).

In conclusion, students' own analogies can be more meaningful than those provided by teachers and authors because the students draw on their own knowledge to construct them. Furthermore, students who construct their own analogies can learn in a more interdisciplinary fashion, particularly in an integrated curriculum.

## ACKNOWLEDGMENT

The work reported herein was prepared with partial support to the first author from the National Reading Research Center (NRRC) of the University of Georgia and University of Maryland. It was supported under the Educational Research and Development Centers Program (PR/AWARD NO. 117A20007) as administered by the Office of Educational Research and Improvement, U.S. Department of Education. The findings and opinions expressed here do not necessarily reflect the position or policies of the National Reading Research Center, the Office of Educational Research and Improvement, or the U.S. Department of Education. An earlier version of this chapter was published as an NRRC instructional resource.

## REFERENCES

Alexander, P., Fiegel, M., Foehr, S. K., Harris, A. F., Krajkovich, J. G., May, K. W., Tzimopoulos, N. D., & Voltmer, R. K. (1989). *General science: Book one.* Morristown, NJ: Silver Burdett & Ginn.

Anderson, J. R. (1993). Problem solving and learning. *American Psychologist, 48,* 35–44.

Bean, J. A. (1995). Curriculum integration and the disciplines of knowledge. *Phi Delta Kappan, 76,* 616–622.

Buffington, A. V., Graening, J., Mahaffey, M., Stoeckinger, J. H., Garr, A. R., Halloran, P. P., O'Neal, M. A., & Vannatta, G. (1985). *Merrill mathematics.* Columbus, OH: Merrill.

Carey, S. (1985). *Conceptual change in childhood.* Cambridge, MA: MIT Press.

Chi, M. T. H., Glaser, R., & Farr, M. J. (1988). *The nature of expertise.* Hillsdale, NJ: Lawrence Erlbaum Associates.

DiSpezio, M., Linner-Luebe, M., Lisowski, M., Skoog, G., & Sparks, B. (1994). *Science insights.* Menlo Park, CA: Addison-Wesley.

Flower, L. S., & Hayes, J. R. (1981). A cognitive process theory of writing. *College Composition and Communication, 32,* 365–387.

Gilbert, S. W. (1989). An evaluation of the use of analogy, simile, and metaphor in science texts. *Journal of Research in Science Teaching, 26,* 315–327.

Glynn, S. M. (1991). Explaining science concepts: A Teaching-With-Analogies Model. In S. M. Glynn, R. H. Yeany, & B. K. Britton (Eds.), *The psychology of learning science* (pp. 219–240). Hillsdale, NJ: Lawrence Erlbaum Associates.

Glynn, S. M. (1995). Conceptual bridges: Using analogies to explain scientific concepts. *The Science Teacher, 62*(9), 25–27.

Glynn, S. M. (1996). Teaching with analogies: Building on the science textbook. *The Reading Teacher, 49,* 490–492.

Glynn, S. M., Britton, B. K., Semrud-Clikeman, M., & Muth, K. D. (1989). Analogical reasoning and problem solving in science textbooks. In J. A. Glover, R. R. Ronning, & C. R. Reynolds (Eds.), *A handbook of creativity: Assessment, theory, and research* (pp. 383–398). New York: Plenum.

Glynn, S. M., & Duit, R. (1995). Learning science meaningfully: Constructing conceptual models. In S. M. Glynn & R. Duit (Eds.), *Learning science in the schools: Research reforming practice* (pp. 3–33). Mahwah, NJ: Lawrence Erlbaum Associates.

Glynn, S. M., Duit, R., & Thiele, R. (1995). Teaching with analogies: A strategy for constructing knowledge. In S. M. Glynn & R. Duit (Eds.), *Learning science in the schools: Research reforming practice* (pp. 247–273). Mahwah, NJ: Lawrence Erlbaum Associates.

Glynn, S. M., & Muth, K. D. (1994). Reading and writing to learn science: Achieving scientific literacy. *Journal of Research in Science Teaching, 31*, 1057–1073.

Glynn, S. M., & Takahashi, T. (1997). *Middle school students' recall of analogy-enhanced science text.* Manuscript submitted for publication.

Glynn, S. M., Yeany, R. H., & Britton, B. K. (1991). A constructive view of learning science. In S. M. Glynn, R. H. Yeany, & B. K. Britton (Eds.), *The psychology of learning science* (pp. 3–19). Hillsdale, NJ: Lawrence Erlbaum Associates.

Goetz, E. T., Alexander, P. A., & Ash, M. J. (1992). *Educational psychology.* New York: Merrill.

Harcourt Brace Jovanovich, Inc. (1991). *The world: Past and present.* Orlando, FL: Author.

Harrison, A. G., & Treagust, D. F. (1993). Teaching with analogies: A case study in grade-10 optics. *Journal of Research in Science Teaching, 30*, 1291–1307.

Hesse, M. B. (1966). *Models and analogies in science.* Notre Dame, IN: University of Notre Dame Press.

Hewitt, P. G. (1987). *Conceptual physics.* Menlo Park, CA: Addison-Wesley.

Hewitt, P. G. (1993). *Conceptual physics* (3rd ed.). Menlo Park, CA: Addison-Wesley.

Hoffman, R. R. (1980). Metaphor in science. In R. P. Honeck & R. R. Hoffman (Eds.), *Cognition and figurative language* (pp. 393–423). Hillsdale, NJ: Lawrence Erlbaum Associates.

Holliday, W. G., Yore, L. D., & Alvermann, D. E. (1994). The reading–science learning–writing connection: Breakthroughs, barriers, and promises. *Journal of Research in Science Teaching, 31*, 877–893.

Hynd, C. R., & Alvermann, D. E. (1989). Overcoming misconceptions in science: An on-line study of prior knowledge activation. *Reading Research and Instruction, 28*(4), 12–26.

Hynd, C. R., McWhorter, Y., Phares, V., & Suttles, W. (1994). The role of instructional variables in conceptual change in high school physics topics. *Journal of Research in Science Teaching, 31*, 933–946.

Kuhn, D., Amsel, E., & O'Loughlin, M. (1988). *The development of scientific thinking skills.* Orlando, FL: Academic Press.

Lakoff, G., & Johnson, M. (1980). *Metaphors we live by.* Chicago: University of Chicago Press.

Lawson, A. E. (1993). The importance of analogy: A prelude to the special issue. *Journal of Research in Science Teaching, 30*, 1213–1214.

Mayer, R. E. (1989). Models for understanding. *Review of Educational Research, 59*, 43–64.

Metz, K. E. (1995). Reassessment of developmental constraints on children's science instruction. *Review of Educational Research, 65*, 93–127.

Novak, J. D. (1990). Concept mapping: A useful tool for science education. *Journal of Research in Science Teaching, 27*, 937–949.

Oppenheimer, R. (1956). Analogy in science. *American Psychologist, 11*, 127–135.

Piaget, J. (1962). *Play, dreams, and imitation in childhood.* New York: Norton.

Piaget, J. (1964). Development and learning. *Journal of Research in Science Teaching, 2*, 176–186.

Pressley, M., & McCormick, C. (1995). *Cognition, teaching, and assessment.* New York: HarperCollins.

Ryder, J. M., & Redding, R. E. (1993). Integrating cognitive task analysis into instructional systems development. *Educational Technology Research and Development, 41*, 75–96.

Shoemaker, B. J. E. (1991). Education 2000 integrated curriculum. *Phi Delta Kappan, 72*, 793–797.

Thagard, P. (1992). Analogy, explanation, and education. *Journal of Research in Science Teaching, 29*, 537–544.

Thiele, R. B., & Treagust, D. F. (1991). Using analogies in secondary chemistry teaching. *Australian Science Teachers Journal, 37*(2), 10–14.

Thiele, R. B., & Treagust, D. F. (1994). The nature and extent of analogies in secondary chemistry textbooks. *Instructional Science, 22,* 61–74.

Thiele, R. B., & Treagust, D. F. (1995). Analogies in chemistry textbooks. *International Journal of Science Education, 17,* 783–795.

Treagust, D. F., Duit, R., Joslin, P., & Lindauer, I. L. (1992). Science teachers' use of analogies: Observations from classroom practice. *International Journal of Science Education, 14,* 413–422.

Wiggs, C. L., & Perez, R. S. (1988). The use of knowledge acquisition in instructional design. *Computers in Human Behavior, 4,* 257–274.

# PART THREE

# LEARNING DISCIPLINARY KNOWLEDGE

In this section, the authors look at learning from text from within disciplines such as English, science, or history. The research methodology, forms of writing, type of knowledge that is valued, and means to power and authority are shared within a discipline, and, while ties across disciplines exist, efforts to understand these ties are relatively rare. There is sometimes controversy within a discipline about research methodology, what counts as knowledge, and what forms of writing are appropriate, but experts who share a discipline understand those controversies, while those outside of the discipline may not. Thus, disciplines exist as separate entities. As students move through high school and beyond, their immersion in these disciplines accelerates. This acceleration is fostered by three factors: the way high schools and colleges are structured—by discipline; the way teachers are trained—as discipline experts; and the way knowledge is disseminated—history texts are written as narratives of events, biology books as descriptions of processes, and so on. These distinctions between disciplines are at once facilitative and problematic. They are facilitative in the sense that teachers and students focus on subject matter in depth, and can build upon previous understandings. They are problematic because they inhibit cross-disciplinary ties. Students may believe they are uninterested in one discipline because they may be unable to tie that body of knowledge to others for which they show interest. Or they may be discouraged from serious study of a discipline because of the narrow forms of communication (e.g., science texts may be seen as arcane and obtuse).

There are three chapters in this section. It begins with a chapter by Hern, Faust, and Boyd, who address disciplinary concerns about learning to read as an expert in the English language arts. Next is a chapter by McMahon and McCormack, who describe the disciplinary concerns of students using science texts as they learn to think and act like scientists. The last chapter is by Alexander. In her chapter, Alexander attempts to show how students' strategies, knowledge, motivations and interests are interwoven as they become engaged in disciplinary learning. It is with this chapter we end the book.

## CHAPTER TEN

# Literacy, Textuality, and the Expert: Learning in the English Language Arts

Leigh Craft Hern
Mark Faust
Maureen Boyd
*University of Georgia*

Think back to your twelfth-grade English class. Do you remember your classmates, your teacher, the books you read? What about the reading and writing assignments? What did it mean to "do" English in that classroom? Now think of your other English classrooms—eleventh grade, tenth grade, ninth grade. How were all these classrooms similar? How were they different? Of one thing we can be sure, as a student of the English language arts, you used reading, writing, speaking, and listening in various contexts for a variety of purposes. The claim that a common discourse community governs (or ought to govern) the practice of the language arts across schools and grade levels is the subject of some debate that we will consider in this chapter.

To begin, we define *Discourse* as formal, orderly, and extended expression of thought about a subject. Those who share common patterns of discourse in their use of written and spoken language comprise a *Discourse community*. In the academic world, experts disagree about what and how thoughts are to be expressed and who should be allowed to express them. Although these debates tend to be played out at the macro level of Discourse practice, we argue that the micro level of practice—discourse with a little "d"—in English language arts classrooms should not be ignored by anyone concerned about teaching and learning from texts.

Generally speaking, the structure of language arts curricula in secondary schools reflects the tripartite division of the subject at universities into literature, composition, and language study. The question of whether this division indicates different strands within a single Discourse community calls into question our understanding of what we mean by a Discourse community, including what constitutes membership in one community or another. This uncertainty is by no means negligible insofar as it affects the development of language arts curricula at all levels as well as our ability to define criteria for acknowledging expertise within the field of language arts.

## WHAT IS THE DISCOURSE?

Being able to read and write the words of a text means little if that ability cannot be used to participate in a desired Discourse community. That participation depends on developing competence in carrying out the various functions of the Discourse (Gee, 1990, p. 293).

In secondary schools, the way curriculum is divided into subject areas—science, mathematics, English language arts, and so on—is a manifestation of academic Discourse communities. The operation of smaller, local discourse communities that arise in specific learning contexts, for example, classrooms, assignments in and for the classroom, and discussion groups (O'Brien, Stewart, & Moje, 1995) governs the access to membership in any of the Discourse communities. These smaller discourse communities are groups of individuals "bound by a common interest who communicate through approved channels and whose discourse is regulated" (Porter, 1986, p. 38). With few exceptions, where academic disciplines are concerned, the primary responsibility for defining the "common interest" and regulating the discourse of those seeking membership in the larger Discourse community lies with classroom teachers.

In this chapter, we discuss factors influencing the gatekeeping role played by classroom teachers in the English language arts. We begin by pointing out disagreements among leaders in the profession over the defining characteristics of English study as a Discourse community. Uncertainty at the macro level gets played out in various ways at the micro level of classroom instruction as teachers interpret what "experts" seem to be saying about the goals and purposes of the language arts as a curricular requirement. Then we offer an alternative view that attempts to position teachers, themselves, as experts, shaping discourse communities within their classrooms and schools. From this perspective, a Discourse community exists as identifiable sets and subsets of questions, and concerns the understanding that enables members to learn from texts and contribute to an ongoing conversation.

As a subject of study, American schools and colleges require all students to study the English language arts, and many students achieve a high degree of competency as users of the English language. This does not mean necessarily that everyone who experiences success in language arts classes thereby becomes an expert or expects to become an expert in the dominant Discourse community represented by his or her teachers. Many take English simply because it is required. Taking a class you enjoy, however, can be an altogether different experience, so volition is a part of the desire to become an expert like the classroom teacher. An important question we address concerns the status of teachers as experts. Usually, you can claim expert status when you understand the focus of the Discourse, can acquire and create knowledge for and within the Discourse, and use existing authority relationships to further the Discourse. Today, it is abundantly clear that, within English language arts, disagreement at the macro level has resulted in widespread confusion among local discourse communities where the actual criteria for membership are defined and entry level access to the larger Discourse community is either granted or denied.

## DISAGREEMENT AMONG EXPERTS ABOUT LITERACY

The Dartmouth Conference (1966) marks a defining moment in the debate over what ought to be the focus of the English language arts, a debate that traditionally has been sometimes congenial and sometimes quite heated (Elbow, 1990). The focus of and definitions of competency within the Discourse community are largely determined by the theoretical stances of those who have established themselves as "experts" within the Discourse (e.g., Beach & Anson, 1992). Yet, consensus does not exist among the experts as to exactly what "English" is. This lack of consensus at the highest levels of the profession is magnified by smaller discourse communities in which students undergo the process of becoming members of a somewhat ill-defined Discourse community.

Generally speaking, students are introduced to the dominant Discourse by viewing it through the lens provided by their classroom teachers, whose theoretical stances are grounded in their own literacy beliefs as determined in turn by their interpretation of those they deem to be "experts" (see Fish's interpretive communities, 1980). Interpretive assumptions about what constitutes literacy in the English language arts influences the practice of the classroom teachers, but in an inconsistent and unpredictable fashion.

In American schools, English as a subject area is in large measure defined by what classroom teachers deem will constitute literate behavior. Individual teachers often are influenced by county- and/or state-sponsored curriculum guides (another source of "expert" opinion) that attempt to offer a vision of what someone will be able to do after successfully mastering the English curriculum (e.g., students will be able to communicate effectively in a business letter; will be able to name, discuss, and critique the elements of fiction in a short story; or will be able to analyze critically a writing of fiction). These local efforts as well as others sponsored by national organizations such as the recent National Council of Teachers of English and International Reading Association

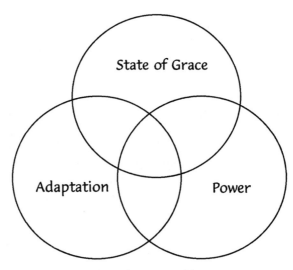

FIG. 10.1.   Three views of literacy.

(NCTE/IRA) Standards (1996) for the English language arts attempt to limit, and to some extent standardize, the definitions of literate behavior available to classroom teachers. Insofar as these efforts have succeeded, they have done so by blurring the boundaries separating three distinct, historically developed views: individual functional literacy (literacy as adaptation); individual cultural literacy (literacy as a "state of grace"); and community social literacy (literacy as power) (Scribner, 1988). Yet in the blurring of the boundaries, finite literate behaviors can characteristically belong to one or more views (Fig. 10.1).

**Literacy as a "State of Grace"**

Literacy as a "state of grace" is the oldest of the three views (Scribner, 1988). People enjoying the educational pursuits of technologies, colleges, and universities defined this tradition (Robinson, 1988) because their social class allowed them the leisure of education while other adolescents worked in family businesses or hired out. The concept of a cultural literacy, a literacy that gives one "thinking" abilities by the close study of literature, is the root of literacy as "salvation." One can be "saved" from the dull pursuits of merely a functional literacy if one studies literatures under the guidance of experts who populate the high schools and universities. This stance originates in the American Puritan tradition of schooling under the influence of postrevolution France, in which mass education was conceived as a means of "saving the poor cousins" from their illiterate ways (Robinson, 1988). Literacy as a "state of grace" implies that studying, writing, and talking about literature imbues you with a common American "culture." (For arguments on multiculturalism, see Sleeter & Grant, 1994.)

## Literacy as Adaptation

Just after World War I with the onset of mandatory school attendance into the adolescent years, public education set its goal of individual literacy. Each person completing school was expected, at a minimum, to read and write as competently as a fourth grader. According to this view, functional literacy is defined as the ability to adapt to and cope with the demands of one's community (Hunter & Harman, 1979) and to be capable of writing and reading well enough to compete for economic sufficiency (Robinson, 1988, p. 246). Such concepts of functional literacy drive curriculums concerned with mastery of basic reading–writing–communication tasks. These literate behaviors tend to be the mastery tasks of "low-track" students. Yet functional literacy was just that—concerned with functioning—and school tasks that supported such a literacy did not include varied readings or writings beyond those tasks.

## Literacy as Power

The third view of literacy, and in recent theoretical discussions possibly the most powerful view, is community social literacy. Here, literacy becomes a tool of the community to help transform perceived inequities in society through education and engagement of its youth (Scribner, 1988). Very few, if any, public schools engage in transformative literacy practices, given that in the last 50 years, schools have been institutions bent on perpetuating the power structure (Apple, 1979; Freire, 1985; Giroux, 1988). This view of literacy openly acknowledges its social and political nature, in which the goal is to bring about a more egalitarian and democratic society.

None of the three literacy views necessarily excludes the others. Experts acknowledge their differing stances within the larger Discourse community, and quite often documents such as the NCTE/IRA Standards employ features of them all. The existence of differing definitions of literacy and literate behavior needs to be acknowledged as a defining characteristic of the larger Discourse community that sets the agenda for teachers working to sustain smaller discourse communities in their classrooms. In any given secondary school, you will find teachers referring to common curriculum objectives. Certain objectives receive more weight and credibility, which reflects a teacher's beliefs and perspectives, shaping the nonexpert into a member of a particular classroom discourse, a discourse contrastive to other classrooms. Do you remember the differences between your high school English class-rooms? Those distinctions cannot all be placed on the shoulders of content and personality. Your teachers began to shape your knowledge of the Discourse by choices they made. In this way, you moved through a county's curriculum to find that the Discourse of English is comprised of parts, and that not every teacher valued each part equally. Although this may have caused you some discomfort as you moved from class to class each year, you learned how to participate in the new discourse community, reshaping your view of English and of literacy. Competing theories of textuality further complicated the patterns of discourse from one classroom to the next.

## DISAGREEMENT AMONG EXPERTS ABOUT TEXTUALITY

Historically, English curriculum has been constructed around three strands of the language arts: literature, composition, and language study. What students do in these strands has looked different across the years as educational pedagogies changed with learning theory, but the strands themselves have remained fairly consistent. Some of the debate that surrounds the discipline of English arises because college professors (and consequently classroom teachers) choose to focus on one of the three stands for individual study. In fact, professors of literature, composition, and language study at the university level tend to represent distinct discourse communities within the larger Discourse community (Keller-Cohen, 1994). Actual classroom practice is often dominated by a particular stance derived from one of the three strands, although teachers rarely will deny that the remaining two deserve at least some attention. Nonetheless, most students are exposed to a highly limited view of the Discourse community as a whole. Competing definitions of literacy (see earlier discussion of literacy) serve only to complicate the picture for teachers and students. At the center of this discensus lies what teachers understand about the construction of texts.

What counts as text and how a text is created are not simple questions. The question "What is a text?" can elicit a variety of legitimate responses from a traditional notion of written words to a particular representation of life experience to an author's or reader's cultural stance and discourse. Recent literary theory has tended to complicate the idea of written word or code as text. Traditional literary theorists usually focus on "literary" texts: novels, stories, poems, essays, or dramas. Response theorists, such as Rosenblatt (1978), distinguished between the printed text—what the author offers to the reader—and the "transacted text or poem"—a weaving of the reader's "past experiences and present personality." Lately, scholars have broadened the idea of text to include a wide range of modes, genres, and media forms (Beach, 1993; Langer, 1995; Lemke, 1992; Scholes, 1989). What happens locally in a particular discourse community will depend not only on a teacher's stance toward what constitutes literate behavior, but will depend as well on that teacher's view of textuality. Generally speaking, the Discourse community of English language arts allows three distinct points of departure for discussing textual power: reading texts, writing texts, and language texts. Because these texts parallel the three strands of English language arts, the reading, writing, and speaking tasks that create texts can overlap (Fig. 10.2).

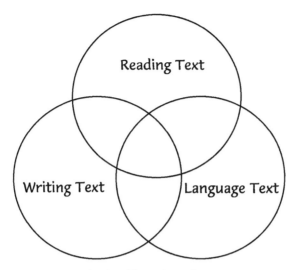

FIG. 10.2. Three views of texts.

## Reading Texts

The phrase, reading text, describes the outcome when an act of reading is understood to involve some sort of collaboration between writer and reader (Barthes, 1974; Langer, 1995; Scholes, 1989) resulting in a unique, momentary understanding of a written text that can be remembered and endlessly reexamined. The co-creation of a reading event (text) is a complex process; "making meaning" involves at least one reader, written words ascribed to at least one writer, and the context of the reading event. As soon as the attempt is made to define the terms reader, written words, and so forth, then the complexity of "text construction" becomes apparent. Individual teachers do define those terms, implicitly if not explicitly, as they go about the business of conducting discussion, making assignments, and evaluating students. In doing so, they position themselves within the Discourse community. For example, teachers working through any one of the three literacy views would assign reading materials and construct assignments that would support their interpretations of that view:

| View of Literacy | Examples of Reading Material |
| --- | --- |
| *Adaptation* | Vocabulary-Building Stories |
| | Technical/instructional writing |
| | Conventionally structured genres |
| *State of Grace* | Traditional Literary Canon |
| | Cultural artifact of dominant group |
| *Power* | Social-Consciousness Books |
| | Open/closed text |

When teachers emphasize literature instruction, their stance toward textuality determines what will and what will not count as a valid reading text.

## Writing Texts

Writing texts are created when we give written form to our meanings. Although prose or fiction can be meaningful for the writer of the work and may be meaningful for a reader of the work, it does not necessarily follow that the work will be meaningful or create knowledge for the specific discourse community. To create knowledge for the specific discourse community, "students need to learn to extend themselves into the commonplaces, set phrases, . . . and necessary connections that determine 'what might be said' and constitute knowledge" within the academic discipline (Bartholomae, 1988, p. 278). They must attend to the audience of the community and indeed write more for it than for themselves. Within that process of creating knowledge for the discourse community, the valuing of the teacher (the usual audience in the classroom) can shape the form and content of the writing. Here again, an adherence to a literacy view guides the types of assignments that a teacher chooses to develop for her classroom.

| View of Literacy | Examples of Writing Activities |
| --- | --- |
| *Adaptation* | Filling in Forms |
| | Letters, resumes, business communications |
| | reports, summaries |
| *State of Grace* | Literary Analysis |
| | Cultural artifact of dominant group |
| *Power* | Critiques of Social Relevance |
| | Action plans for community reform |

## Language Texts

Language texts, "utterances" (Olson, 1988), are created in dialogic conversation either with ourselves or with others in the discipline. For Olson, utterances are "informal language statements" (p. 176), so these texts exist as the conversations of the classroom and, it could be argued, as the inner speech of the individual. When a teacher enacts ways of discussion in her classroom, she provides acceptable ways of talking about the Discourse, helping to shape the form and content of the metadiscourse—the discourse about the Discourse.

| View of Literacy | Examples of Discourse |
| --- | --- |
| *Adaptation* | Parts of Fiction |
| | Grammar, punctuation, usage |

| | |
|---|---|
| *State of Grace* | Expert Opinion |
| | Literary competence |
| | Individual response statements |
| *Power* | Socratic Argument |
| | Textually constructed subject |

Inviting students to participate in this activity creates language texts that can be examined, teased apart, and reconstructed within the developing text of the self (Scholes, 1989). The conversations can be student directed (small and large group), teacher directed (lecture and initiate-response-evaluate), or a mixture of both. Through participation, students may choose to incorporate or ignore new knowledge and, in doing so, shape their stances within the community. The contexts in which those conversations occur usually involve an expert of some kind—a professor, a teacher, a more knowledgeable peer—and within that structure, a student's discourse may be marginalized, shaping the nonexpert in specific ways.

Depending on the expert's view of literacy and intertextuality, conversations between and among the domains may not occur. All three texts described so far in this discussion can be found in most classrooms. However, they are often dealt with in isolation from each other. As noted earlier, a teacher's experience of schooling shapes her beliefs and preferences of the three strands (Lortie, 1975). Nonexperts are indoctrinated into this triad because the strands are taught separately in the primary school as writing, reading, and grammar. By high school, all three appear in classrooms as activities that constitute "doing English." Those students who wish to become part of the Discourse community learn from the three texts that are created almost as by-products of classroom activities. However, it is in the interaction (intertextuality) of the texts that meaning is created and knowledge is critiqued by the experts. Yet if we shape and are shaped by experts, how do we become competent in a discourse community, and who decides when we are competent?

## COMPETENCE IN ENGLISH

"Reading is always, at once, the effort to comprehend and the effort to incorporate" (Scholes, 1989, p. 9). If we are in the process of becoming members of a discipline, then "to comprehend" and "to incorporate" what counts as disciplinary knowledge becomes the objective of our study. Learning from our texts is all a part of the overall process that supports the comprehension and incorporation of knowledge.

### Reading as a Process to Gain Disciplinary Knowledge

Gaining disciplinary knowledge normally begins in a classroom of some type, whether it is the school building of western cultures, the talk between caregiver and child, or the interaction of text and reader. The cogent factors in a learning relationship are an "expert" and a "nonexpert," in which an expert is someone who has discourse knowledge derived from experience and is knowing as a result of extensive practice. As a student moves through educational experiences and chooses to become a member of Discourses, then the process most often relied on for comprehension and incorporation is reading: reading literature texts, reading composition texts, and "reading" language texts.

## Reading Literature Texts

How we read literature, or for that matter what even counts as literature, is currently contested. Questions that ask about literary theory, role of the reader, and role of the teacher are continually defined and redefined in a discourse community as the community engages in reading activities. Even so, the teacher's model of literacy will determine what materials are allowed in the classroom to count as literature, and even the teacher's selection can be constrained by curriculum, resources, and censorship issues. The specific purpose of reading for and in the classroom reflects the teacher's view of literacy. Is it to gain functional knowledge, to foster an appreciation of great books, or to confer power on an individual or group? Furthermore, if the literature is contained within a single discipline, who decides which literatures we read? Those seeking access to a discourse community allow the literature selections of a disciplinary member to shape their knowledge of the discipline, until the nonexperts gain an ability to shape the discipline and create the literatures that eventually shape other nonexperts.

## Reading Composition Texts

Composing within the discipline and reading our self-selected compositions, or being the first reader of our compositions, lends a particular reflection to disciplinary knowledge. If reading literature shapes our understanding of the past and the present of the discipline, then writing possibly gives shape to our understanding of the future (Scholes, 1989). Therefore, as the first readers of our own compositions (i.e., literatures), we simultaneously are shaped by and shape our understanding of the discipline. Yet composition requirements imposed by an expert can narrow the types of writing experienced by the nonexpert. These narrowings distort a nonexpert's view of the community and writing as well.

## Reading Language Texts

Conversations that occur in discourse communities can become the site at which intertextual practices are made public. If conversations can be considered "texts," then they can be "read." Meaning can be made of them

(Scholes, 1989). Perhaps conversation texts are more readily shaped by and also shape the creation and critiquing of disciplinary knowledge because they are created with others, or even the self. Within a classroom, experts rigorously regulate discussion practices by providing immediate feedback (implicit and explicit) on the quality and quantity of the nonexpert talk.

The processes of reading literature, composing texts, and studying language within the discipline are not completely independent from each other. To comprehend and incorporate disciplinary knowledge, we build on what we know. We impose intertextual events that are central to the learning process on the current subject. Intertextual events have been described as "intertextuality," most commonly defined as "the process of making connections between current and past texts, of interpreting one text by means of previously composed texts" (Short, 1992). We are convinced that this concept is central to the process of creating and critiquing disciplinary knowledge. Such intertextual events are processes that rely on teacher and student co-construction of a more immediate discourse community. Learning is influenced by the teacher, the students, and the context, as well as by the content of the intertextual connections, the sum total of the interdependencies just discussed.

## INTERTEXTUAL CONNECTIONS

The term *intertextuality* implies "the insertion of history (society) into a text and of this text into history" (cited in Fairclough, 1992, p. 270). Many discourses have appropriated the concept of intertextuality and have transformed it to reflect more accurately the processes used for the critique and creation of specific disciplinary knowledge (Beach, 1993; Hartman, 1992; Lemke, 1992; Scholes, 1989; Short, 1992). However, there are commonalities across the definitions of intertextuality: the idea of chains (Fairclough, 1992), links (Beach & Anson, 1992), or intertexts (Lemke, 1992), in which texts are influentially connected to one another. Connecting new texts to old and current texts is a simplified example of cognition—a process of how students learn. Although the intertextual connections may not be explicitly seen and certainly are unique to the individual, students still learn from texts by imposing these types of connections. For example, the activity of reading a literature text in common in the classroom can become the basis for discussions that create multiple language texts and writing activities that create separate writing texts. During those discussions and writings, intertextual connections are imposed and brought to light by the students as they reference established personal, cultural, and Discourse knowledge in the activities.

In coming to understand Discourse knowledge, nonexperts participate in intertextual events that presume the nonexpert has an interest in the concepts presented (Scholes, 1989). These events usually occur in the social interaction as a linguistic process between experts and nonexperts (Bloome & Egan-Robertson, 1993). Experts often "consciously and systematically help (nonexperts) construct a range of intertextual relationships among events that support particular ways of engaging with texts, communicating with others, and constructing text (Lin, 1994, p. 396). Also, these nonexpert constructions allow the expert to judge the nonexpert's grasp of the knowledge, thereby giving or denying access to the larger Discourse community, while maintaining the nonexpert's membership or participant status in the more localized discourse or classroom community.

Thus, critically evaluating disciplinary knowledge has two facets: the nonexpert's evaluation and the expert's judgment of that evaluation. The expert judgment is not rendered in a sterile, culture-free, ideology-free environment. Such judgments are delivered in the form of comments embedded in a specific and tangible social context. How intertextual connections are made is thus a social construct. The appropriateness of what is constructed—the rules and norms of the discourse community—and the ways in which meanings are built—how texts are juxtaposed—are all intertextual processes. An intertextual relationship is proposed, recognized, acknowledged, and imbued with social significance to the discourse community (Bloome & Egan-Robertson, 1993). What the expert allows and encourages from the nonexpert, however, is not necessarily an overt or conscious process.

## IDEOLOGY AND EXPERT KNOWLEDGE

How intertextuality is constructed is perhaps not so much a matter of perspective as a function of what is acknowledged by the discourse community. Constructing intertextual links is a way of making meaning, but what meaning is recognized in the classroom establishes the structure for the accepted making of meaning. In attending schools—public, private, parochial, college, university—nonexperts are subject to the influences of teacher ideologies. What an expert chooses or does not choose (implicitly or explicitly) to count as texts—her theoretical stance—helps to co-construct knowledge in the classroom, as does nonexpert stances of what happens or should happen within the discourse community. "In exchanging texts . . . they are creating a shared intertextual meaning" (Beach & Anson, 1992, p. 335). Yet when these two stances are incommensurate, the nonexpert may marginalize herself or become marginalized within the structure of the intertextual events.

## IDEOLOGY AS A STANCE

How are these stances created? The social construction of identity both within and without the discourse community influences the nonexpert's ideology: "the body of ideas and beliefs common in a society or culture that controls how we as participants in the society or culture view the world and understand our place within it" (Nodelman, 1996, p. 292). Furthermore, through the intertextual processes of learning, the expert has been shaped by and has shaped the literacies that "count" in the discourse community. If we are socially constructed into particular ideologies, and those ideologies operate intertextually with readings, writing, and discussions, then experts can develop "stances" within the discourse community. Here stance is defined "as a reader's orientation or frame for responding to a text that reflects a certain set of attitudes or critical strategies" (Beach, 1993, p. 164). Any expert can change her stance to view disciplinary knowledge differently than before. She can use a "classroom teacher" stance or a "feminist" stance or a "feminist classroom teacher" stance. The stances provide a theoretical frame through which we view our disciplinary knowledge. When stances are shared and intertextual processes are employed, we have discourse communities engaging in the creation and critiquing of content knowledge. This brings us back to the question of how the experts, including classroom teachers, view the discipline.

## ROLE OF THE EXPERT

The teacher is generally assumed to be the expert in the classroom. This needs to be recognized in discussions about the ongoing formation of the larger Discourse community. We have been arguing that the classroom discourse community is shaped in complex ways by the ideologies of the expert teacher and co-constructed with the nonexpert students. Teachers need to be aware of the power they wield that privileges particular ways of knowing and learning. Teacher ideologies shape what is recognized as knowledge in the immediate discourse community.

We want to view the role of the teacher as expert, as one of helping students acquire multiple ways of working with literature, writing, and language texts. If the expert teacher is rigid in her view of literacy, then the materials presented and activities developed will address only the specific view the teacher endorses. Expert teachers need to acknowledge the intertextual process by which we all learn and the influence of ideology on her theoretical stance(s). Rather than threatening the Discourse community, conflicts about literacy and textuality become critical in the gatekeeping role. Discussions of different ways of knowing and making meaning can add to the learning process while at the same time including and incorporating the members' ways of knowing and promoting an understanding of diversity. Local discourse communities are situated social learning communities co-constructed by the actions and interactions of members. What the participants bring to the community and how they are received shape the learning context and emerging relationships between expert and nonexpert. The actions of the expert teacher are consequential to what counts as learning (Short, 1992). Perhaps, then, the expert's role is to make the nonexpert aware of the conflicts within the larger Discourse community (Graff, 1990), to help the nonexpert "try on" stances and participate in many small discourse communities, while engaging in the appropriate intertextual practices of the broad Discourse community.

Even though the discourse community is co-constructed by both expert and nonexpert, the expert has social and political power (Boyd, 1996). This power is maintained in part by the nonexpert's desire to participate in the discourse community, and possibly to become an expert of the broad Discourse community (Scholes, 1989). If so, then the expert has a responsibility to the nonexpert to represent the Discourse community in all its conflicts. If the conflicts within the Discourse community are to be made explicit to the nonexpert, then experts must represent themselves as collectivity—voices more similar than disparate—and not as individual experts (Graff, 1990). They will need to articulate to the nonexpert their stances and the relationship of these stances to other stances and the Discourse community.

These collective representations become problematic when the expert speaks from a particular model of literacy, articulating that model as the only path to membership in the Discourse community. Experts must therefore become less enchanted by "the jargon of individuals and coteries than about the intelligibility of the larger disciplinary conversation" (Graff, 1990, p. 5). Experts need to become comfortable with conflict and, indeed, must teach the conflicts to the nonexperts.

## CONCLUSIONS

Learning from a text can occur individually, but those wishing to become experts, or at least members of a Discourse community, must do so through the intertextual connections found in the local discourse communities. The academic pursuit of only one of the texts does not provide a rich textualization of Discourse knowledge. For example, a student may read every book authored by Charles Dickens, but that will not make her a member of the English Discourse community. Learning from multiple texts by participating in the creation of language and writing texts allows the student some understanding of the questions and concerns that drive the conversation among experts.

People are "experts" when they understand the focus of the Discipline, can acquire and create knowledge for and within the Discipline, and use existing authority relationships to further the Discipline. However, historical conflict in the Discourse community constrains the focus of the Discipline, and most experts choose stances that do not acknowledge other stances within the Discourse. Reading processes and intertextual practices work to establish a nonexpert's competence in the filed, yet that competence is subject to the stance-driven or ideological judgments of an expert that constrains the acquisition and creation of knowledge for the Discourse. Relationships established in the Discourse community are social, political, co-constructed, and often incommensurate with the culture or worldview of the nonexpert, which also constrains the use of existing authority relationships.

Although wanting to be a member or participant of the Discourse community, engaging in appropriate intertextual practices, and participating in many local discourse communities certainly builds toward your expert status, such status is never guaranteed. What is the hope in this pursuit? Why would you wish to pursue such study? Perhaps your answer is because it is something that shapes and is shaped by your identity. The process of becoming an expert is a part of your identity that will in turn shape and be shaped by other nonexperts. For example, it is often the case that students who feel they have done well in their English classes and find their perceived role of the teacher as something attractive will follow a degree in English or English teaching.

Individuals elect to participate in discourse communities when they know their contributions are valued. Respect for the nonexpert who is willing to participate in the creation of texts then becomes a function of the expert's gatekeeping process. An expert that implicitly and explicitly acknowledges a nonexpert's creation of reading, composition, and language texts avoids a more narrow view of the discourse community. Classrooms in which alternative forms of discourse are representative of the Discourse community build a complexity of literacies and text. To prepare nonexperts to participate in the Discourse, experts should avoid being impositional. Teachers should avoid setting students up to believe that the Discourse conflicts are fields of battle meant to be won. Intertextual practices give a much more realistic view of the Discourse community as one in which the experts do not agree. Thus, they engage in the creation and critiquing of discourse texts, and they willingly participate in discourse communities that value their contributions.

## REFERENCES

Apple, M. (1979). *Ideology and the curriculum*. Boston: Routledge & Kegan Paul.

Barthes, R. (1974). *S/Z*. Translated by Richard Miller. New York: Hill & Wang.

Bartholomae, D. (1988). Inventing the university. In E. R. Kintgen, B. M. Kroll, & M. Rose (Eds.), *Perspectives on literacy* (pp. 273–285). Carbondale: Southern Illinois University Press.

Beach, R. (1993). *A teacher's introduction to reader-response theories*. Urbana, IL: NCTE.

Beach, R., & Anson, C. M. (1992). Stance and intertextuality in written discourse. *Linguistics and Education, 4*, 335–357.

Bloome, D., & Egan-Robertson, A. (1993). The social construction of intertextuality in classroom reading and writing lessons. *Reading Research Quarterly, 28*(4), 305–333.

Boyd, M. (1996). Negotiating classroom culture. *TESOL in Action, 10*(3), 13–16.

Elbow, P. (1990). *What is English?* New York: Modern Language Association.

Fairclough, N. (1992). Intertextuality in critical discourse analysis. *Linguistics and Education, 4*(3–4), 269–293.

Fish, S. (1980). *Is there a text in this class? The authority of interpretive communities.* Cambridge, MA: Harvard University Press.

Freire, P. (1985). *The politics of education.* South Hadley, MA: Bergin & Garvey.

Gee, J. (1990). *Social linguistics and literacies: Ideology in discourses.* London: The Falmer Press.

Giroux, H. (1988). *Schooling and the struggle for public life: Critical pedagogy in the modern age.* Minneapolis: University of Minnesota Press.

Graff, G. (1990). How to deal with the humanities crisis: Organize it. *ADEBulltein, 95*, 4–10.

Hartman, D. (1992). Intertextuality and reading: The text, the reader, and author, and the context. *Linguistics and Education, 4*, 295–311.

Hunter, C. S. J., & Harman, D. (1979). *Adult illiteracy in the United States.* New York: McGraw-Hill.

Keller-Cohen, D. (Ed.). (1994). *Literacy: Interdisciplinary conversations.* Cresskill, NJ: Hampton Press.

Langer, J. A. (1995). *Envisioning literature: Literary understanding and literature instruction.* New York: Teachers College Press.

Lemke, J. (1992). Intertextuality and educational research. *Linguistics and Education, 4*, 257–267.

Lin, L. (1994). Language of and in the classroom: Constructing the patterns of social life. *Linguistics and Education, 5*, 367–409.

Lortie, D. C. (1975). *Schoolteacher: A sociological study.* Chicago: University of Chicago Press.

National Council of Teachers of English and International Reading Association. (1996). *Standards for the English language arts—For the profession, by the profession: A guide for discussion.* Urbana, IL: NCTE and IRA.

Nodelman, P. (1996). *The pleasures of children's literatures* (2nd ed.). White Plains, NY: Longman.

O'Brien, D. G., Stewart, R. A., & Moje, E. B. (1995). Why content literacy is difficult to infuse into the secondary school: Complexities of curriculum, pedagogy, and school culture. *Reading Research Quarterly, 30*(3), 442–463.

Olson, D. R. (1988). The bias of language in speech and writing. In E. R. Kintgen, B. M. Krull, & M. Rose (Eds.), *Perspectives on literacy* (pp. 175–189). Carbondale: Southern Illinois University Press.

Porter, J. E. (1986). Intertextuality and the discourse community. *Rhetoric Review, 5*(1), 34–47.

Robinson, J. L. (1988). The social context of literacy. In E. R. Kintgen, B. M. Krull, & M. Rose (Eds.), *Perspectives on literacy* (pp. 243–253). Carbondale: Southern Illinois University Press.

Rosenblatt, L. (1978). *The reader, the text, the poem.* Carbondale: Southern Illinois University Press.

Scholes, R. (1989). *Protocols of reading.* New Haven, CT: Yale University Press.

Scribner, S. (1988). Literacy in three metaphors. In E. R. Kintgen, B. M. Krull, & M. Rose (Eds.), *Perspectives on literacy* (pp. 71–81). Carbondale: Southern Illinois University Press.

Short, K. (1992). Researching intertextuality within collaborative classroom learning environments. *Linguistics and Education, 4*, 313–333.

Sleeter, C. E., & Grant, C. A. (1994). *Making choices for multicultural education: Five approaches to race, class, and gender* (2nd ed.). New York: Merrill.

## CHAPTER ELEVEN

# To Think and Act
# Like a Scientist: Learning
# Disciplinary Knowledge

Maureen M. McMahon
Bernadette B. McCormack
*University of California, Davis*

In a culture increasingly pervaded by science, mathematics, and technology, science literacy requires understandings and habits of mind that enable citizens to grasp what those enterprises are up to, to make some sense of how the natural and designed worlds work, to think critically and independently, to recognize and weigh alternative explanations of events and design trade-offs, and to deal sensibly with problems that involve evidence, numbers, patterns, logical arguments, and uncertainties. (American Association for the Advancement of Science [AAAS], 1993, p. xi)

These few sentences are found in the Introduction of *Benchmarks for Science Literacy* (AAAS, 1993). On reflection, there is great importance to be found in these lines because they imply that understanding science is greater than the learning of science facts. There is basic agreement among science educators that the traditional science curriculum is indefensible. Teachers are being called on to link science in the schools to the modern world, the welfare of the individual, and the welfare of society (Hurd, 1991). How can educators go about unveiling the world of science and offering entrance to this realm for all students? If there is to be a discussion around the notion of secondary school students learning what it means to think and act like a scientist and beginning to understand the structure of the domain called science, then surely what is happening in today's science classrooms and among today's science teachers must first be brought into focus.

Some outstanding things happen in science classrooms today, even without national standards. But they happen because extraordinary teachers do what needs to be done despite conventional practice. Many generous teachers spend their own money on science supplies, knowing that students learn best by investigation. These teachers ignore the vocabulary-dense textbooks and encourage student inquiry. They also make their science courses relevant to student's lives, instead of simply being preparation for another school science course. (*National Science Education Standards*, 1996, p. 12)

According to the preceding quote, the traditional teaching of science is changing in classrooms where extraordinary teachers empower themselves to broaden and enlarge the notion of science. These teachers are dismissing the decontextualized 3-inch-thick science textbooks and lecture teaching modality for a more meaningful, relevant, inquiry-based student-centered learning approach.

However, what do these few changes to tradition really mean? Should a secondary school science experience simply mean less reading and more laboratories? Less writing and more hands-on investigation? Less historical science background and more present-day science breakthrough information? Will these changes allow students to more readily understand and enter the world of science? Science curriculum reform efforts (AAAS, 1993; National Research Council [NRC], 1996) argue for a more robust reform with higher science expectations for America's children. To give the best answer to these questions, it is prudent to critically explore the daily world of a scientist and the person called a "scientist" who lives and works within this realm.

On examination, it can be seen that a scientist is an extremely complex being with an intricate professional and personal life. Even after only quick scrutiny, it becomes evident that a scientist is more than the stereotypic white-coated disheveled male genius who lives in his laboratory mixing chemicals and making magic potions. Contrary to popular belief, scientists spend their professional lives engulfed in many activities over and above time spent in a laboratory. In fact, much of their time is spent reading, writing, and delivering oral presentations. A successful scientist must be a good reader, writer, and speaker as well as a sound researcher. Lectures and books cannot simply be replaced with current facts and hands-on investigations as an answer to meaningful science education reform. According to Manzo and Manzo (1990), the stated goals of science education now include understanding self, appreciating technology, preparing for college, advancing modern culture, and understanding local issues. They state, as well, that the typical science curriculum contributes naturally to growth in reading, and that the characteristics of the mature reader strongly resemble and are compatible with those of a "scientifically literate" person as defined by the National Science Teachers Association (NSTA):

The scientifically literate person has a substantial knowledge base of facts, concepts, conceptual networks, and *process skills* which enable individuals *to continue to* learn and think logically. [emphasis added] (Manzo & Manzo, 1990, p. 398)

On the basis of these beliefs, it is wise to orchestrate the construction of a science education learning environment that facilitates the understanding and viewing of the integrated complete life of a scientist and the professional domain of science. Only in this way can all facets of science disciplinary knowledge be learned.

The reader will find nested in the remainder of the chapter an introduction to science-based integration in the schools and an annotated journey through an integrated curriculum designed to offer students a chance to walk in a scientist's shoes through a 9-week project-based experience. Special attention is given to offering extensive examples of curriculum pieces with detailed guidance regarding the facilitation of the literacy skills needed to become successful learners in this nontraditional learning setting. Traditional roles of student and teacher as well as conventional understandings of "science" are strongly challenged in this integrated learning environment. By way of each example scenarios the authors hope to convey throughout this chapter that students need information, guidance, and assistance from as many sources as possible. Moreover, the critical importance of the role the teacher plays in guiding and assisting students in interacting successfully with texts, as part of the process of *thinking and acting like a scientist*, is stressed.

## SCIENCE AND INTEGRATION IN SCHOOLS

Imagine a high school in which sophomore students find themselves learning about world history and cultures, public speaking, statistics, energy and natural resources, and practical industrial arts. Realistically, this could be an average high school student's schedule anywhere in the United States. The student's day is composed of social studies, English, mathematics, science, and practical or cultural arts courses. Each class traditionally meets 45 to 90 minutes per day in a classroom where a single teacher facilitates the learning of a single-focused subject area. Often, there are no connections created for the students between content domains because rarely are there any connections made between the teachers of the various disciplines. Enter the idea of interdisciplinary teaching and integration!

Integration is not a new idea. John Dewey (1938) himself described school as a place in which a child should learn about the world experientially (Posner, 1995). He supported the notion that school needed to be real and relevant for children, a place where real-world problems and issues could be tackled, and certainly not a place centered around nonintegrated discreet academic content domains. But for the schools of the 20th and 21st centuries, integration is a challenge. Present school structure, teacher education, and conventions have left many educators without the tools and confidence to unite the disciplines for a fuller and richer learning environment for today's students. Rather than proposing total school and curriculum restructuring, we offer in this chapter a model for slow and planned restructuring and integration from within the current school framework. From a science teacher's point of view, it is necessary only to begin viewing the world of science and scientists as part of a larger world that includes humanities, politics, culture, arts, and mathematics. To understand the disciplinary knowledge area of science is to understand the integrated realm of scientists and the global world in which they work.

On the basis of this premise, an integrated scenario slowly unfolds throughout the remainder of this chapter that could be used within a secondary science course to offer students a full opportunity to explore the processes used to gain, create, and critically evaluate knowledge as well as view the relationships and professional responsibilities all fully operational within what scientists understand as science discipline knowledge. Melded into the scenario are examples and associated theoretical and practical arguments for the important integration of reading, writing, and presentation skills into the natural learning of science.

## SCIENCE-BASED INTEGRATED SCENARIO

Energy and Natural Resources is a broad topic taught and learned within a typical one-semester secondary general science course. In years past, many teachers divided this 9-week unit into energy subtopics and methodically covered each natural resource and its related type of energy. No attempt was made to forge any connections beyond relevant science content, vocabulary, and understanding. Adopting an integrated approach to the teaching of this unit will significantly change the structure and design of the curriculum as well as the roles of both the teacher and the students.

Within the new approach students are posed with the task of taking on the roles of teams of energy scientists from nations all over the world. As the teacher explains the daily professional responsibilities of a scientist, the challenge thrust on these participating students unfolds. As representative groups of scientists from nations circling the globe, it will be each student team's tasks to learn about their selected country's history of natural resources, types and processes of energy use, and reasons for their type of energy selections. On the basis of this knowledge, the teams will move toward discussions of alternative energy sources that may prove more efficient, more cost effective, and less environmentally hazardous for possible use in their representative countries in the future.

As groups of energy scientists, the students will be challenged to write a grant proposal to fund the building and study of a scaled pilot model of their country's selected alternative energy source. Subsequent to funding, the teams will investigate, design, craft, and study their models for harnessing energy. All results will be organized and shared in both written and oral form at the end of the 9-week unit as a mock Global Alternative Energy Summit is convened to share scientists' knowledge, understandings, and beliefs from around the world. This integrated approach differs greatly from the typical conventional high school science approach to the study of energy and energy alternatives. Whereas the traditional curriculum includes textbook reading, the posing of questions and answers, structured laboratory work, and minimal writing, the integrated approach incorporates all of the following:

- Reading and interpretation of historical texts and documents
- Study of conflicting beliefs and facts found in competing texts
- Interpretation and construction of tables, graphs, maps, figures, photos, and diagrams
- Electronic search and retrieval of information via the Internet
- Writing of a structured protocol scientific grant proposal
- Reading and analysis of scientific technical and research reports and papers
- Team problem solving and decision making based on scientific facts, historical precedence, and cultural beliefs
- Student-centered design and implementation of a scientific model and research study
- Writing of a scientific research paper based on personal research
- Preparation and delivering of a scientific talk with associated technical visuals

Collectively, these challenges offer the students a comprehensive view of what it means to work in the realm of science. Issues of culture, history, literacy, numeracy, problem solving, decision making, and scientific professionalism are all interwoven with science content to construct a global view of science disciplinary knowledge.

## SCIENCE AND READING

Many of the scientist's roles as well as the preceding student-integrated science-based tasks include a primary focus on reading and making meaning from text. Accordingly, it is necessary to take time to discuss the association of these two domains before delving into specific curricula examples. Manzo and Manzo (1990) stated that the skills in reading and science are parallel and mutually contribute toward supporting the growth of a learner. However, these researchers did suggest that there are often problems students encounter in their reading of science materials, which may include:

- Inadequate background information
- Misconceptions about the physical world
- Inconsiderate (assumptive, inadequately explained or technically overwhelming) text
- Difficult esoteric terms

The first problem mentioned was *inadequate background information.* Students reading science texts often lack the background information (content schema) required to comprehend text (Yore & Shymansky, 1991). If students do have adequate background knowledge to comprehend text (assimilation), the issue often becomes one of activating that schema. However, if students do not have the necessary background information to fill in the gaps as they read (instantiation of schema), they are thus unable to create new understanding (accommodation). The work of Royer and Cable (1975) dealing with science-based texts points to the importance of building on what students already know when introducing new information. They state that we should not present students with materials they are cognitively ill-prepared to encounter. In their research they found that text containing concrete referents increased the comprehension of subsequent related reading and facilitated transfer of information. Text concreteness may also be related to how well students are able to visualize or make mental images of what they are reading, which in turn is related to the ability to activate appropriate schema. Looking at interaction regarding natural phenomena, Schmidt, De Volder, De Grave, Moust, and Patel (1989) found that "activation of prior knowledge through small group discussion of a problem can be a successful instructional strategy for bridging the gap between what is already known or can be inferred about a subject and new information to be learned" (p. 617).

The second problem is related to the first, but here students have *misconceptions,* or inaccurate information about the world, and therefore read science texts with an inaccurate schema. Osborne and Freyberg (1985) suggested that students frequently construct and hold more than one understanding of a science concept. Often they have an in-school understanding and a competing real-life understanding. These inaccurate or misconceived science schemata are resistant to change. In fact, these misconceptions may be more difficult to change than inadequate schemata are to build. In other words, students reading science text with the alternate schema may have a more difficult time in coming to a full, accurate understanding than those with little or no schema on a topic. Alternative schema may be worse than little or no schema (Lipson, 1982). Another related problem is a phenomenon that occurs when students think they understand, but do not; they experience an illusion of knowing (Bransford, Stein, & Vye, 1982). They have not become strategic, active readers who are able to assess their own level of text comprehension accurately, and therefore cannot help themselves learn from texts. The goal is to assist students in becoming aware that there are universal principles affecting human comprehension and memory that involve experiencing the effects of "precision training." These researchers state that students are actually very receptive to this idea of the need for precision.

The third problem, *inconsiderate texts*, is not so much about what a student brings to the text, but what the text brings to the student in terms of physical cues and helping features (external structure) and how well written or rhetorically well organized texts are (internal structure). Frequently, science texts are stocked with foreign vocabulary and unique semantics and syntax, as well as odd sentence structure and grammatical frameworks (Yore & Shymansky, 1985; Yore & Shymansky, 1991). Some texts have an external structure that facilitates reading, whereas others offer few physical/visual cues to readers. However, well-formatted texts are of little use to students who do not know how to employ the helping features of these texts. The conventions written into science texts, particularly technical reports and research papers, greatly facilitate comprehension by way of external structure. However, here content schema and vocabulary (difficulty in handling esoteric terms) can become problematic. These points are taken up in detail later in the section on Reading Technical Reports.

Some texts are better written and more easily understood than others. Their internal structure is organized and written in a way that facilitates comprehension. Again, students need to know what these structures are, how they can be recognized, and the way ideas and relationships are connected. They must be able to recognize main ideas and details as well as those connectors or words that signal relationships between them. These exercises are best accomplished with students using actual texts with which they practice identifying relationships and how they are marked in texts and then explaining the major relationships in some form, possibly an outline, semantic map, concept map, diagram, or model (Kaplan & Shaw, 1983; Novak & Gowin, 1984). When good readers approach reading, they look for these major thought relationships, aware that texts are organized in particular ways, for example, incorporating problem–solution, cause–effect (which have many of the same connectors and markers), description, sequence, and comparison–contrast. Some of these discourse types are better organized than others and therefore more easily recalled (Meyer & Freedle, 1984).

What are the implications of this for teachers? The goals of teachers should include having students become independent readers who can understand various types of texts by recognizing their structure and organization, and who then can produce these types of texts themselves. Moreover, through their reading and participation in associated inquiry activities, students

should progress in their understanding of science concepts and the global
world of science. These goals are achieved through a process, which for
students is gradual, approximate, socially contextualized, and guided by
teachers or more competent peers. Researchers (Resnick, 1991; Roth, 1993)
have found that students are supported in their strategy development and
use when they are encouraged to cooperate and instruct one another in
content-based problem solving. Students must come to understand that
meaning construction is a process of transaction between reader and text
(Rosenblatt, 1989), and that meaning is not found in the words themselves,
but in thinking about what the words mean. Rosenblatt refuted the notion
that certain types of texts (e.g., scientific texts or literary texts) necessarily
evoke a particular reaction or result in a particular outcome. Each reader is
experiencing the interaction with the text on the basis of individual intentions
and stance, which may fall on a continuum from efferent to aesthetic and
involve the purpose for which one is reading. The teacher's job is to assist
students in meaningful purposes and to strategically scaffold instruction
through modeling, practice, and interaction so that students eventually acquire the academic and aesthetic skills necessary to read and write effectively.
Metacognitive skills are key in students helping themselves to learn from
texts and to bridge the gaps that may exist between the ideas, content, and
relationships they are studying and their own knowledge, interests, attitudes,
cultural background, language ability, and reading proficiency (Jacobs, &
Paris, 1987; Vacca & Vacca, 1996). Science teachers are in an excellent
position to reinforce deep cognitive processing as well as critical thinking
and reading skills. Good readers differ from poor readers primarily in the
type of training they have received (not in any neurological functioning),
so teachers must offer students training in the attention and mental processing skills they need to become good readers (Whimbey, 1980).

Finally, the issue of *inadequate teacher preparation* must be addressed. At
the secondary level, content teachers generally have the training and background necessary to teach the sciences, whereas elementary teachers often
lack this content training. Conversely, secondary teachers often lack information and training in language and literacy (Yore, 1991). This proves problematic if science teachers are to address reading issues. Regardless of discipline
and diverse backgrounds, all teachers must be both language and content
teachers because it is through language that content and disciplinary knowledge is acquired. Teachers must have information about how to help students
activate or otherwise acquire background knowledge and how to interact with
texts. This involves modeling and explicit teaching of awareness about what
one already knows, about what one does not know, as well as awareness
about how one might come to know that which is currently unknown.

All of this is grounded in schema theory and metacognition. The two
types of schema relevant to our discussion, of which teachers and students

must be aware are: (a) content schema or background knowledge and (b) text schema or knowing how to interact with texts, which involves understanding that texts have both internal and external structure. Additionally, teachers must understand how to guide students in their selection of resources and in the organizational process of doing literary and scientific research. Vacca and Vacca (1996) offered the following procedures for guiding student research. Students must have enough structure to give them (a) a problem focus, (b) physical and intellectual freedom, (c) an environment in which they can obtain data, and (d) feedback situations to report the results of their research and guide the writing process. These authors reminded teachers that they must teach, model, and encourage an awareness of strategy use. This is achieved by explicit teaching of research skills including notetaking, summarizing, and annotating and by constant practice and evaluation in the classroom. The authors also added that students need to develop study systems that work for them, that they can use with confidence and ease. Often these systems are not those transmitted to students as formulas, but rather those that evolve for individual students through interaction and practice over time.

Reading as a cognitive process has been widely researched, whereas the social and cultural factors related to literacy have been less investigated by reading researchers and theorists. Reading in its entirety is an incredibly complex phenomenon, and it is therefore understandable that researchers would choose to focus on one aspect at a time. However, looking at the interactions of variables is important. Meeks (1987), for example, developed a model of affective metacognition in reading and stated that these two variables—affect and metacognition—cannot be meaningfully separated because they are so deeply interwoven. We must be aware of the multifaceted nature of reading and what that means for teachers. Often, the problem is that traditional reading and writing training comes at the expense of and is offered in place of the other ways of knowing and expressing themselves that students bring with them to school. However, it is possible for teachers to use the language and knowledge students already have while teaching "schooled" ways of doing things, for example, gathering and reporting data and using metacognition (Heath, 1983; Heath & Magnolia, 1991). Moll, Amanti, Neff, and Gonzales (1992) demonstrated how teachers can successfully utilize and incorporate students' cultural literacy and background knowledge, termed "funds of knowledge," into the curriculum. Hammond (1997) explained how a commitment to utilizing cultural funds of knowledge forms the basis of a curriculum to teach science to children and adults in what is a powerful and effective way of promoting literacy and biliteracy by means of culturally appropriate pedagogy. Researchers in education and related fields have called for a confluence of insider and outsider knowledge together with research knowledge and local knowledge (Goldenberg & Gallimore, 1991). We have seen the positive effects of including indigenous knowledge or cultural funds of knowledge in agriculture, technology, literacy, and science education. Across disciplines, the valuing and use of indigenous and cultural knowledge is increasingly recognized as a form of mental and economic decolonization. More commonly though, we have seen the negative effects of not recognizing and valuing sociocultural knowledge. Often within western science, characterized by positivism, there is a prejudice against indigenous knowledge or folk wisdom as being inaccurate and imprecise, a characterization that is often inaccurate (Williams & Muchena, 1991). However, as reform efforts in science education continue to grow, the integration of culture and multiculturally diverse literature into the learning of science is becoming more commonplace.

Language, reading, and writing are fundamental units within the domain of science. It is through language that ideas are communicated and hence hold primary importance in the life of a scientist. As teachers move into the integrated student challenge, they should notice the significance that language, reading, and writing play in fully understanding the realm of science and the person we call a scientist who works in this world.

## DISSECTING THE INTEGRATED
## SCIENCE-BASED CHALLENGE

As the integrated student challenge is slowly unveiled, we divide the challenge into the sections that follow. Within each section the science content and skills, the literacy skills, and the elements of integration are emphasized and discussed. Important considerations and issues for teachers are also accented. This eight-step integrated challenge is designed to be implemented successfully by one teacher in a secondary science classroom over one 9-week cycle or grading period.

### Looking at Old Data: Interdisciplinary Historical Perspectives

#### *Reading and Interpretation of Historical Texts and Documents*

When investigating a research subject or phenomenon, scientists generally study what has been researched by others before designing and carrying out their own investigation. This important first step of looking at old data may involve reading and interpreting many different types of historical texts and documents, which in turn requires many different reading and critical thinking skills on the part of the reader. The team of students role-playing as energy scientists from Great Britain set out to gather historical data on the use of coal in Britain. The students quickly encountered information on the following topics, which may be placed within these disciplines:

***Social History.*** Topics addressed include the labor movement, coal mining villages, child labor, health, and safety. These are found mainly in the form of nonfiction texts and include such things as songs, autobiographies, and photo histories, which facilitate understanding of historical time and place.

***Political Economist.*** The study of coal's importance to the Industrial Revolution in Great Britain and the impact of England's wealth and strength around the world is critically evaluated.

***Literature.*** For example, D. H. Lawrence's *Women in Love*, written in 1923, includes a chapter entitled the "The Industrial Magnate." Lawrence was the son of an impoverished coal miner, and his fictional accounts have their base in his personal experience.

***Geology/Geography.*** Type and numbers of mines are studied: how, where, when, and how much coal was produced? Where were the major coal deposits and how were the various types of coal formed? Reading includes many maps, drawings, and diagrams.

***Scientific and Mathematical Measurement.*** Topics include the standards of weight and measure used for coal mining in England through the years. Conventions and standards change over time. Students must know this information in order to meaningfully compare figures over time.

***Archaeology/Anthropology.*** Coal use, technology, tools and labor, and the first historical records of coal mining are topics found in this category. Mining changes over time (e.g., from human beasts of burden to machines) are discussed.

***Chemistry and Historiography.*** Topics include the origins of coal, content knowledge of chemistry of compounds, and early beliefs about the origin and makeup of coal. These topics highlight how scientists do not operate in a vacuum: Early beliefs about coal origin were based on peoples' beliefs about the origin of the universe.

***Economic/Environmental Effects of Burning Coal.*** Students weigh costs and benefits of using coal, then and now. They investigate how technology has changed over time and how using coal has become less polluting and more efficient.

This example reinforces the point that real-life investigation and problem solving require multiple literacies and multidisciplinary domain knowledge, which often result in a team approach to solving the problem under investigation. For students to evaluate the past, then the present and future of coal in England critically, they must first understand the historical times in which the documents they will encounter were written. Understanding the importance of coal mining in England to the Industrial Revolution and the effects of that revolution on the rest of the world involves understanding cause–effect relationships on many levels and across many disciplines. A true understanding in this case would come only from an integrated analysis. Martin and Brouwer (1991) supported the notion that stories and historical documents, necessarily of an integrated nature, add the human element to the understanding of science and reduce the often unnecessary complexities of the domain.

Teachers assist students in seeing these relationships by providing structures for extracting information and organizing it mentally and graphically. When students in this group are at the point of studying present and future uses of coal, they become interested in asking and knowing the following:

Why was coal chosen historically as Britain's main source of energy?

What problems are associated with burning coal?

What are the possible solutions to those problems?

What costs and benefits are associated with each possible solution?

How can using coal as an energy source become more efficient and less polluting?

For each of these questions, the teacher asks students to decide on the best ways to find, organize, and display answers. When students cannot find effective ways of doing this, the teacher asks a number of questions to help students pinpoint what information they need, what they already know, and how they can find out what is unknown. The teacher helps them find and retrieve appropriate sources of information and guides their study of these sources. Additionally, the teacher helps students construct various graphic organizers that assist them in their organization of information and ease in recognizing relationships. This student-centered technique is supported by the research of Alvermann and Moore (1991).

For the preceding question about costs and benefits, one teacher suggested that the students look at this as a set of "If . . . then" propositions. The students designed the following graphic organizer and were able to fill it in with the information they had gained from researching the first few questions in the preceding series.

Possible Energy Solutions: What Costs and Benefits Are Associated With These Solutions?

|  | *If* | *Then* | *Costs* | *Benefits* |
|---|---|---|---|---|
| 1. | Sulfur removed | | | |
| 2. | Coal burned more efficiently | | | |
| 3. | Pollutants trapped | | | |
| 4. | Gasified and used with fuel cells | | | |

Most of the "If . . . then" propositions were generated from the historical information the students were able to glean from old texts and documents. However, much of the cost–benefit information was obtained from a chemistry text, a "new-generation" text entitled *ChemCom: Chemistry in the Community* (for a critical review of this text, see Posner, 1995, pp. 274–303), and from EPA documentation via the Internet. The graphic organizer assisted the students in structuring both their information search and the organization of their findings.

Although learning is an individual event, much of the strength and basis for learning is social (Alexander & Knight, 1993). In dealing with historical documents and unfamiliar texts, the teacher can facilitate the use of strategies through modeling and group discussion. Directly, the students begin to see a breadth to the domain of science frequently missing from a traditional school science experience. Historical accounts, stories, government documents, and even the Internet become sources of science background knowledge and understanding. Teamwork and cooperation start to take the place of individual responsibility and competition. The students' beliefs about what it means to study science begin to be challenged. These new beliefs are more fully tested as the students move into the next step and encounter discrepancies within science documents.

## Looking at Old and New Data: Contrasting Information

### Study of Conflicting Beliefs and Facts Found in Competing Texts

While gathering background information, students often come across conflicting data. The student-energy scientist team role-playing as Russians experienced this problem as they gathered information on nuclear energy and the Chernobyl nuclear power plant disaster. In this case, the Chernobyl nuclear disaster is used as an example of contrasting and competing old and new data, where politics are a confounding variable. Moreover, time is a variable that also plays an important role in this contrasting data controversy. Aside from the immediate deaths from the effects of radiation exposure, the long-term effects can only be known over time.

Another major problem of comparing data in this case is the secrecy around the accident based on the Soviet policy at the time of trivializing or minimizing natural disasters. After the accident, the Soviet government issued only a four-sentence statement and failed to mention that the disaster happened close to the heavily populated city of Kiev. Even this announcement came only after increased levels of radiation had been reported in Scandinavia. The news failed to state exactly what had happened or when and if there were causalities or health risks. A second Soviet report about a day later said two persons were dead and four towns in the area had been evacuated. This sketchy information was all that the world was given for one of the worst nuclear disasters in human history. A week after the disaster *The Boston Globe*, in the Science and Technology section, carried a story entitled "Dose and Type Determine Radiation Effects" (Lehman, 1986), containing information reportedly given by Dr. Henry Royal, assistant professor of radiology at Harvard Medical School. This highly readable, informative piece details for the lay reader the difference between radiation exposure and contamination, different types of radioactive isotopes and their effects, and information about the kinds of background radiation to which most of us are constantly exposed. The writer ends the article with the following paragraph:

> While background radiation may contribute to the normal cancer rate, the effect has not been proved. For nuclear power regulations as well as research, scientists assume that no radiation is safe—that there is some risk, primarily more cancer, with any radiation exposure. But relatively brief exposure to several times background radiation, as occurred in Europe after the Chernobyl accident, probably means only a minutely increased risk of cancer, Royal said. (p. 42)

In the January 1997 issue of *Discover* magazine, an article entitled "Ten Years After" (Stone, 1997) detailed the long-term effects of the nuclear accident at Chernobyl. The disaster has allowed scientists to conduct large longitudinal studies and gather new information on radiation's genetic effects. Findings published in 1996 show that humans and wildlife living near the disaster suffered genetic damage that was the passed to the next generation, and that the rates of thyroid cancer in children in parts of Ukraine, Russia, and Belarus are as much as 30 times higher than before the Chernobyl explosion. It has long been known that the radioactive isotope Iodine 131 is absorbed by the thyroid gland. However, the article states that it is the longer lived radioactive isotopes like Cesium 137 that settle into soil and water and become a major threat to health. The article goes on to present information on the shuffling of "junk" DNA due to radiation. These data present an opportunity to show the kinds of skills required in thinking like a scientist: the facts do not clearly show cause and effect, but there is a very strong correlation.

It is recognized that students need guidance and practice in acquiring and refining research skills. Learning to find information is itself a skill and includes a body of knowledge with which students must become familiar if they are to participate successfully in the kind of integrated project presented in this chapter. Research skills are not something one casually gathers, but given good teaching, time to practice accessing information and guidance in finding, evaluating, and selecting which materials are most useful for the project in question, students can, over time, acquire these skills. The most important elements here are guidance in finding materials and time devoted to collaboratively evaluating them for particular purposes.

While researching their topics, students encountered various types of information, requiring a variety of reading and critical thinking skills including recognizing point of view, distinguishing fact from opinion, and logically supporting an argument or hypothesis with different kinds of data, including facts and examples. While searching for journal, magazine, and newspaper articles on the Chernobyl topic, students found articles stating opinions, articles containing highly technical and scientific information, and articles in which the two are combined. They were also confronted with scientific articles containing conflicting data and results due simply to time of publication. Students encountered texts of oral language, speeches, lectures, or transcripts of radio show interviews. They came across one piece that referred to uranium as "poison fire," another in which nuclear energy was portrayed as one of the safest, cleanest sources of energy, and one promising that nuclear energy would be "too cheap to even meter." Something as seemingly subtle as whether what happened at Chernobyl is referred to as an incident, an accident, a disaster, or a catastrophe gives insight into the writer's point of view. Similarly, in reading current events or social science documents, students might find the same individuals or groups referred to as either freedom fighters or terrorists, depending on the author's perspective. It is also important for students to learn to form their own opinions when that does not mean disrespecting or disregarding those of others.

This example highlights some of the reading and critical thinking skills as well as content knowledge students need to analyze academic discourse, which includes distinguishing fact from opinion, supporting facts with evidence, seeing cause and effect, distinguishing between correlation and cause, understanding the writer's position and stance, and gathering domain knowledge about science (radioactivity), politics (of the Soviet Union at that time), and the history of questionable nuclear use in this country. According to Norris and Phillips (1994) in their article on interpreting pragmatic meaning from text, students would profit greatly from reading-strategy instruction that assists in interpreting authors' inferences, opinions, and intentions in text.

These authors continue by arguing that it is the responsibility of all science teachers to view themselves also as teachers of language, and in so doing, to develop classrooms in which students are encouraged to be engaged readers, thinkers, and speakers about the science they encounter through print and other forms of media.

**Research Literacy Skills: Visuals and Electronic Searching**

*Interpretation and Construction of Tables, Graphs, Maps, Figures, Photos, and Diagrams*

***Electronic Search and Retrieval of Information Via the Internet.*** The group of students investigating Denmark found that their adopted country has the most successful wind energy program in the world. They set out to discover why and how wind energy came to prominence in their country. They learned that after the energy crisis of the 1970s, many Scandinavian countries made a commitment to more energy self-sufficiency, which depended less on imported fuels and more on domestic, renewable sources of energy such as that provided by the wind. They found that Denmark is exceptional in several ways, notably in its potential for wind energy. They discovered, too, that government incentives to promote wind energy in Denmark have resulted in major developments in wind technology, including two experimental, 600-kilowatt wind machines and a test station for wind turbines. They were surprised to discover that by 1986 Danish turbines supplied half the amount used in California, and by 1991, 45% of the world's wind power. The students learned about the importance of test stations to ensure reliability and progress in wind technology and the reasons why Danish turbines have had so few technical setbacks. Students in this group also studied about the new Danish demonstration project to test offshore wind potential by building offshore windfarms (adapted in part from Gipe, 1995; Grubb & Meyer, 1993; Schmid & Palz, 1986).

After a brief Internet refresher session led by their teacher, the Danish student energy scientists began searching the World Wide Web for windmill information. Traditional library sources provided a great amount of information (Gipe, 1995; Rosenberg, 1993), but the students sought to find the most recent developments in harnessing the wind as a renewable resource. They hypothesized that they might find this highly specialized timely data on the Information Highway, and they were correct. The team encountered photographs of various wind energy converters from traditional to modern, which they were able to classify by type of converter (horizontal, vertical, cross-wind, pitch, stall-controlled, etc.). They also found many models explaining concepts involved in wind energy, such as:

- Wind mechanics (solar energy, Corolis force, etc.)
- Wind to energy conversion
- Relationship of wind, motion, and thrust
- An airfoil
- Airfoil-type windmill blade

Moreover, these students encountered the European Community Wind Atlas, which contains detailed assessments of wind resources throughout Europe and maps of each European Community country depicting the geographical distribution of five classes of wind energy as well as five different topographic conditions for each class. Additionally, they examined a computer simulation study of integration of wind energy in power systems and the potential for wind penetration on utility grids. Finally, the team even found blueprints of the latest designs in windmill technology with complete design specifications and suggestions for optimal efficiency.

This scenario is presented to highlight some of the other literacy skills students must acquire: the ability to interpret, study, and understand, as well as produce diagrams, models, simulations, photographs, and maps of many sorts. Visual aids such as the ones noted in this section are important devices for aiding student comprehension (Pressley, Johnson, Symons, McGoldrick, & Kurita, 1989). It is necessary for teachers to facilitate students using visual aids to begin organizing and summarizing textual information. Many of the windmill visuals were so intricate and specific that they provided many needed details omitted from the accompanying text. In fact, these visuals became the basis for many of the initial decisions the Danish student team would eventually make when designing and building their windmill model later in the integrated challenge. Interpreting visuals is a much needed skill and useful strategy in understanding complex science text and abstract ideas.

After the students unearthed the many technical and cultural pieces of Denmark's wind-energy program, they tackled the search for the answer to their question about how Denmark came to have the most successful wind program in the world. They discovered that it involved a government commitment to support research and implementation of renewable energy technology. In the next step we address the issue of support and funding through the process of writing a scientific grant.

## Grant Writing

### *Writing of a Structured Protocol Scientific Grant Proposal*

The first three steps focus on research skills and information retrieval and analysis. Students now undertake the next step in the process of thinking and acting like a scientist—grant writing. Grant writing is a valuable skill for scientists, and indeed for researchers across disciplines. The authors are not implying that the only scientific research worthy of inquiry is that which receives major funding. We are, however, aware that due to a lack of funding many important scientific research questions go unstudied and are never addressed. From a pragmatic perspective we see the ability to procure funding as a necessary and important skill that allows much scientific study to be done (regardless of one's position regarding this reality). Students should understand the role of funding, and we believe this information will empower them. Part of a scientist's life includes the reality of economics and politics. Unless understood, these areas can become gatekeepers as a person ventures further into the realm of science.

In terms of literacy, the grant writing stage is an important writing component of the research process. In this step students learn to write persuasively for a specific audience, using a particular register. However, we propose the final grant writing step be done after some practice, which may come as first preparing the grant proposal information for a younger audience. Initially, students write the grant draft with the purpose of offering it as a "how to" model for next year's group of students doing the same project. They can present it orally to these younger students who are unfamiliar with the concepts, vocabulary, and processes involved in the grant, which will require simplification and distillation of the main ideas.

After this initial round conducted for an audience of younger peers, the grant proposal is rewritten for the final target audience of professional scientists and funders. Naturally, this final draft is more elaborate, detailed, and technical than that written for the first audience. Offering students excellent models and the opportunity to write for their peers as an initial step in the writing process supports the students in their needs for stages of attainable success. Palincsar and Brown (1984) found that peer support and adult modeling of successful interaction with text increases student comprehension and self-esteem. Moreover, Howard (1988) suggested that the writing process should be used to increase comprehension. If students are offered an opportunity to write in order to articulate their ideas, learning and comprehension increase. We recommend a process approach to all of the writing in this project, but particularly in this step.

The student team from the United States submitted a grant proposal for funding to develop geothermal energy in the United States. Grant writing is a genre unto itself. It is technical, specialized, and imbued with conventions of many sorts. The types of tasks and writing required for grant writing are somewhat generalizable, and the specific contextual example of geothermal energy was used to contextualize the process and the genre. We offered the following examples to illustrate the types of knowledge students must have to successfully complete this task. The framework used is from an actual grant application publication used in the State of California (1996). It is crucial for students to be provided with many models before they attempt this type of writing. Students must understand the specialized language and style required in grant writing and the importance of writing for a specific audience. Completing each of the following major grant components requires particular skills and knowledge. We have chosen to highlight Part B: Project Goals and Actions as an example of the requisite functional language and content knowledge that is also part of thinking and acting like a scientist.

Grant Application Components and Process: Geothermal Program

A. General Information (used for screening)
B. Project Goals and Actions (used to evaluate application)
C. Project Task Description
D. Project Management Structure and Personnel
E. Task by Task Budget
F. Cash Flow Projections (expected net energy cost savings)
G. Credit Information
H. Authorizations

Project Goals and Actions (Part B)

This part contains the criteria used for evaluating and screening the grants. A task analysis shows that students must be able to demonstrate the following successfully:

1. Represent a reasonable funding request relative to overall costs and consideration of short- and long-term benefits
2. Promote geothermal energy development or demonstration by
   • Creating a commercial product or process that will save energy or money
   • Including technology transfer activities to help others use project results
3. Help remove technical, economic, environmental, and/or institutional barriers to geothermal energy use
4. Reduce the use of nonrenewable energy resources by
   • Substituting geothermal for nonrenewable energy sources
   • Increasing efficiency of geothermal use
   • Shifting or leveling electricity loads to enable more efficient use of existing power plants and resources
5. Mitigate negative impacts to air and water quality, noise levels, wildlife, vegetation, and visual esthetics, or improve public or worker health or safety

6. Create economic benefits for the public by
   • Improving job opportunities, tax revenues, or other economic factors
   • Stimulating small business competition (particularly in alternative energy development) as well as local employment
   • Creating or expanding export markets for energy technologies
   • Reducing capital or operation/maintenance costs

It is clear that this type of task requires numerous types of literacy, content knowledge, and language skills including numeracy and budget analysis; functional language of describing, analyzing, explaining, persuading, comparing, and defining; domain expertise and the ability to understand and write for an audience using the appropriate language register (in this case highly technical, but at the same time requiring aesthetic appreciation). This is the kind of task that obviously is best achieved through a multidisciplinary or team approach in which individual areas of expertise and skills (i.e., multiple intelligences) are shared through a common process and purpose with all learners contributing and benefiting. Indeed, thinking and acting like a scientist has come to reflect this type of collaborative venture as opposed to the more independent, competitive model of scientific work of an earlier era, in part because of the complexity and multidisciplinary nature of the question that scientists today attempt to answer. Remember, the purpose of the grant writing stage is not to create expert student grant writers, but to offer the students a more complete view and experience of the professional life of a scientist. With this in mind, student teams should be encouraged to be creative and confident while working on their grant proposal. The aim is for students to experience success in accomplishing a team challenge containing many tasks very foreign to typical school classrooms. Creating budgets, cost-benefit analysis tables, and needs assessments will probably be foreign activities for most students. Simply offer the students ample models (from the library or Internet) and encourage them to use their resources and collected information to tackle the charges presented them. Where data is unknown, support them in using their skills of estimation and assist them in using their prior related knowledge to solve new problems.

After this grant writing stage, the students are at the midpoint of the integrated challenge. If teacher modeling and support has been strong, the students should be feeling very confident and excited about what they have accomplished so far and about where they are headed within each of their respective country teams. Internal motivation should be high. The students have traveled a great distance in their learning of science and in their learning of what it means to think and act like a scientist.

It is wise at this point in the challenge to take some class time for update and discussion. Facilitate a review of the students' many accomplishments. The student teams have learned a great deal about their selected countries;

have found historical documents and literature that have unveiled scientific understandings and beliefs through time; have delved into government documents to search for facts and figures; have searched the Internet for timely data, diagrams, photos, and information; have been confronted with conflicting scientific text accounts based on politics, culture, and date; and finally, have been challenged to synthesize all of this information in the process of compiling and authoring a grant proposal. Through all of these activities their literacy skills have been supported and used greatly.

Teachers should take this opportunity to have the students reflect on this experience. What are their current beliefs about science and scientists? Have student opinions changed and why? How do the students feel about the literacy skills employed within the integrated challenge so far? What are students finding as the most positive and most negative parts of the integrated experience? Do students feel they could use additional support in any one area in order to feel a greater level of success? Student self- and group reflection allows them opportunity to contemplate their learning and share their feelings with their peers and with their teacher. It offers the chance to have value linked to student thoughts about the learning process. After this sharing process is conducted, it is wise to provide time for refocusing on the remainder of the integrated student challenge. On the basis of all their synthesized and collected background knowledge, data, and understandings, the student energy teams can now embark on the second half of the integrated challenge. It begins with the reading of technical reports.

**Reading Technical Reports**

*Reading and Analyzing Scientific Texts:*
*Conference Proceedings, Technical Papers,*
*and Research Reports*

Reading and producing technical texts is another type of literacy, requiring yet another set of skills. These processes are featured in the next step in the research process. The language of technical reports is often what makes reading technical reports most difficult.

Technical language tends to be domain and topic specific, and much scientific language is universal, having its roots in Latin and Greek (Yore & Shymansky, 1991). Technical vocabulary can be learned, or its meaning can be guessed or implied from the context. Together with guessing from context (and with bilingual students using cognates), a strategy that benefits students in all disciplines is learning vocabulary skills that involve word morphology. For example, the following sentence is taken from a solar energy report discovered by the students role-playing as energy scientists from Colombia: "The design process for developing the prototype passive solar house was based on integrating bioclimatic evaluation, microclimate modification, shape, orientation and envelope materials analysis."

Such language can present a serious "decoding" problem. Students may utilize bottom-up reading strategies that include decoding a word by finding its various morphological parts, identifying the meaning of those parts or morphemes, and reconstructing the word. The first unfamiliar word in this sentence may be "prototype," which can be broken into its constituents— proto and type. Others for which the same strategy can meaningfully be applied are "bioclimatic" and "microclimate." Chances are that students know or can guess the meanings of the roots and their prefixes. Of course, syntax also conveys meaning.

In this case, the students know that "envelope" is not a noun, the ordinary usage of this word. They know that it is modifying another word or words because of its order in the string of words (syntax), which thus facilitates meaning (semantics). However, comprehension is not necessarily derived from the sum of known words. If students must constantly resort to these microprocessing strategies, they may have their working memory taxed to the point that they are often readers with poor reading speed and poor comprehension. For this reason, it is important for readers of scientific, technical, and often unfamiliar text to be provided with as much information as possible before reading so that they can activate or build the schema needed for making meaning while reading (Pearson & Spiro, 1982). Awareness of text organization and structure can increase a reader's comprehension considerably. Thus, the inherent structure of technical reports offers good news for readers.

Technical reports have built-in scaffolding structures that help make them accessible to readers. These include their physical layout and external structure, their formulaic nature, their inclusion of abstracts, and their visual displays. The external structure and outline of technical reports are fairly transparent. Usually, headings, titles, and subtitles are clearly delineated and marked in the text by the use of bold print, spacing, italicizing, underlining, and numbering. A second aid in reading technical reports is knowing that they are highly formulaic—from the abstract to the findings and conclusions. This formula projects a blueprint that aids comprehension and allows readers to utilize "good reader" psycholinguistic strategies—predicting, hypothesizing, and confirming—while reading. A third major aid for readers of technical reports is the abstract. A well-written abstract provides a preparatory set, activates background knowledge, and acts as an advance organizer for the reader.

Awareness that technical reports have these built-in scaffolding structures, together with proper guidance and assistance from teachers or peers, allows students to read at a higher level and understand much more than they may have been able to comprehend without such training and assistance. In Vygotskian terms, such awareness moves them closer to reading within the "zone of proximal development."

Technical reports usually contain visual information that puts technical language into charts, diagrams, models, or other visual forms to aid comprehension. However, some charts and graphs, especially those containing complicated statistical data, often are not so easily understood, and their interpretation requires specific knowledge and acquired skills. The role-playing student team from Colombia read technical reports about energy in their country as they prepared to do their own research and present their own data at the upcoming Global Energy Summit. The technical report used as an illustration here is titled "Computer Aided Solar House Design Made of *Guadua* in Bogota, Colombia" (Lozano & Chalfoun, 1995). The *external structure* or physical layout of the five-and-a-half page technical report on passive solar housing in Colombia follows this form:

Abstract, 1. Introduction, [Maps of Colombia, in relation to the continent and Bogota to the equator], 2. Climate Characteristics, [Diagram of typical house floor plan and cross sectional diagram of same], 3. The Row Housing Case Study, 4. Thermal Characteristics [Drawings (2) of row housing], 5. Computer Energy Analysis [Printout of computer basecase file], 6. The Suggested Material—*Guadua* [Drawing (3) of wall construction and elevation], 7. Thermal Performance Prediction [Diagram of plan of *Bajareque* wall section], 8. Cost of *Guadua* Material [Diagram showing ratios of wall materials and a table summarizing energy consumption results], 9. Conclusions, and finally, References.

In a technical report such as this, language is concise and text is compartmentalized. Each section is spaced, numbered, and underlined, and all are relatively short—from one to several paragraphs. The report contains a total of 13 visual representations: two maps, one chart, nine drawings or diagrams, and one half page of computer printout data. Of course, the type and number of these visuals are a function of the topic and methodology of the report in question. The domains of this particular report include computer-assisted design of passive solar architecture using indigenous building materials, thus justifying and explaining the use of nine architectural drawings. The *content knowledge* required to understand this report includes a conceptual understanding of how passive solar systems work as well as how and why a computer program would be used to help design structures. This in turn requires an understanding of the key variables and their interaction—in this case, construction and climate.

This step offered students a chance to delve into the technical, highly specific language of scientific documents and reports. They were challenged by the language, but assisted by the structural framework and visual aids in the writings. Once again, the students' views of the daily life of a scientist are stretched as they come to understand the kinds of reports and writings scientists must produce. In the next step students continue discovering the limitless boundaries of the science domain as they experience how important cultural understanding is to informing science and scientists.

## Science and Cultural Understanding

### *Team Problem Solving and Decision Making Based on Scientific Facts, Historical Precedence, and Cultural Beliefs*

Conceptual, domain, and schema knowledge, together with text reading and vocabulary strategies are not sufficient for fully understanding and critically analyzing technical reports. In Freirean terms, reading the word is not necessarily reading the world. In the integrated scenario presented, students are studying how and why energy is produced and consumed differently in different parts of the world. These cases highlight not only the importance of thinking like a scientist in the traditional sense but also that of thinking like a social scientist. By looking at the past, present, and future of energy, students study the cultural practices of peoples. To think critically about energy and appropriate, sustainable energy options, students must possess a certain *cultural literacy*, which allows them to make good judgments. In the case presented here, energy advisors choose to use local, sustainable, cheap, abundant sources of energy that have social and economic benefits for the end users, who importantly, might also be the producers.

Multidisciplinary knowledge is required to effectively carry out the tasks set for students by this project. Students must understand not only the geography and science of natural resources and energy use, but also the sociocultural politics surrounding these issues. In another published technical report taken from the same 1995 solar conference as the preceding Colombian example, the authors included the following quotation from the great Dalai Lama:

> Finally Figure 12 shows the saying of the great Dalai Lama Tenzin Gyasto: "May all sentient beings, one self and others, find constant happiness through love and compassion associated with wisdom." And with this wisdom the design of the solar dispensary has been accomplished. (Ahmed, Rittelman, & Kingman, 1995, p. 188)

This technical report on a solar dispensary in Tibet has two end pages containing 14 tables, charts, and drawings. The last figure of the paper contains a copy of the Dalai Lama's written words as shown in the preceding quote, testifying to the relative importance of the evidence or data in this case. The reader and those working in Tibet must appreciate this worldview (one not characterized by western secularism) as well as the country's history and present reality in which politics are deeply entwined with religious issues, beliefs, and struggles for autonomy.

In this example, science and culture are forever united. As the students move on to the experimentation and design phase of the integrated challenge in the next step, teachers should remind students to continue their consideration of cultural implications as they begin to make important scientific decisions.

## Scientific Exploration Through Experimentation and Investigation

### *Student-Centered Design and Implementation of a Scientific Model and Research Study*

In conjunction with reading and analyzing technical reports and conference proceedings, the role-playing student teams design, build, and test a scaled model or computer simulation of the type of renewable energy harnessing source they have selected for their countries. This is the hands-on investigative piece of the integrated project. In a traditional science classroom students would be given a laboratory recipe format and all the supplies needed to conduct an investigation around the topic of alternative energy use. In this scenario the student teams are challenged to make decisions and move forward on the basis of all their research and data collected to this point in the project. All the information they have gleaned from print, electronic, and video media is used as a foundation for planning and decision making during this stage of the process. It is here that the students often realize some fruits of their labor. Historical, cultural, technical, economic, and political pieces of information are all reviewed and discussed in order to make a sound and defensible decision for their representative countries. Ownership and responsibility for decisions begin to become part of the student's experience.

Many questions surface during this stage of the integrated process. These questions should come from the student teams, but it is the teacher's responsibility to facilitate the initial thinking and asking of such questions:

- Do we have enough background on the history and culture of this country to make a decision about energy?
- Do we have enough information about the economics of the country to know if it is feasible?
- Will the government and people of this country support our decisions?
- Did we budget enough in our grant proposal to fund our pilot project?
- Do we have enough technical knowledge to proceed with the building and testing of our pilot model or simulation?

After generating questions such as these, the teams rally to move forward with their plans. This often means that some members of the team will return to the first sections of the integrated process to find important missing information while others continue to plan and design possible pilot models.

Once the issues in question are resolved among all team members, then plans, designs, and testing procedures for the pilot model are finalized. Much as the team had to conquer difficulties in reading and interpreting documents of all types, they too have to overcome the challenge of designing and carrying out a sound scientific investigation. Team dynamics and problem-solving skills are put to the test. Such skills of experiment design are not often fostered in traditional science classrooms because the laboratory directions are usually printed in advance. To do an experiment, students need only follow directions. In this scenario, however, the team must not only design the alternative energy harnessing machine, but also a scientifically sound experiment to test it. The teacher can support the students in achieving success at this stage by facilitating a discussion on variables and experimental expectations. Teams will all choose unique alternative energy sources, model machine designs, and experimental routes. However, in all cases the teams should aim to test their ideas and collect data around which future decisions regarding their country's selected energy source will be based.

This stage of the scenario allows the students time to revisit the text and video media they searched out and retrieved during the initial sections of the challenge. Time for analysis and synthesis of ideas is given the students while a further challenge of a hands-on investigation and experimentation is posed. The breadth of what it means to think and act like a scientist is enlarged to even greater proportions as the students grapple with the complexities of this stage. Students now begin to recognize that understanding the domain of science means becoming involved in the constant interplay between language, culture, history, economics, politics, and science. This all leads up to the last step of the integrated challenge in which the student teams will organize and present their findings during a mock Global Energy Summit Conference.

### Presentation of Data Across Three Modalities

#### *Written, Oral, and Visual Communication*

In prior sections of the thinking and acting like a scientist integrated process, we argue for helping students acquire the ability to write for a particular audience using whatever language is most effective for the task and audience in question. In this final step students are assisted in recognizing and utilizing the kind of multimodal-communicative competence required of those who present data in various forms. Scientists regularly attend conferences, seminars, and symposia where they and their colleagues present the data and findings of their work. At these meetings scientists are required to present their information in many forms: written research papers, visuals or graphics, or oral presentations.

An acceptable oral presentation does not include reading one's written paper, a practice that lacks the animation and spontaneity required to capture most audiences. Oral presentations run the gamut from very formal to rather impromptu. The important point is that students need to have the ability to communicate in all of these modes in order to effectively and successfully function in the academic world at large, and in the world of science in particular.

As was the case with grant writing, these skills require numerous models and much practice. Data presentation is the culminating stage at which all of the skills, knowledge, and information amassed up to this point are synthesized and applied in several forms. Deciding how best to organize and present this information is itself an important and acquired skill. Not only does it involve knowing how to interpret data, but also how best to display it (e.g., knowing when it is best to use a pie chart, a line graph, or a bar graph). Computers obviously can help students not only gather, analyze, and present information in many forms, but also allow them to share their information with others—another student, an entire class, or anyone across the globe with access to the Internet or e-mail.

Written papers are permanent and formal artifacts designed to hold up over time. Conventions of scientific writing must be understood—empirical evidence supported by facts and data regarded as valid, not opinions or emotional arguments—largely because of the importance attached to the replicability of scientific research. In highlighting the differences between written and spoken data presentation, it should be emphasized that the written data is generally much more formalized (e.g., little or no use of the pronouns "I," "we," or "my colleagues and I" because referring in writing to oneself as the doer of the research has traditionally been taboo). The passive voice is often invoked (e.g., experiments were performed, data were analyzed, and it was discovered) as opposed to the active voice often used in an oral presentation (e.g., "When we did the experiments and analyzed the data we were surprised to find . . ."). Oral presentations can and should be adjusted to increase their usefulness for the target audience. Conversely, written papers often contain a degree of detail that would not be appropriate nor effective presented orally. Rather this information would be referenced only and described in more general terms, possibly by highlighting findings, implications, or conclusions. Visual displays often are confined to just the facts or highlights. These are used to convey visual information that can stand on its own and be comprehensible without further oral or written clarification, or that can be used to emphasize, add detail, or enhance an oral or written presentation. Visual information may be presented in bulleted, outline form and as various types of charts, graphs, diagrams, photographs, or any combination of these. In visual displays, as with abstract writing, students must be capable of identifying the main ideas, concepts, and overall importance of their information and be able to distill this down into a minimum of text.

In this phase of the integrated process of thinking like a scientist, each student group presents its overview of the past, present, and recommended future use of energy in its chosen country. The focus of the latter is on sustainability and those renewable sources of energy that are most appropriate for a particular region. Costs and benefits, including those costs (human and environmental) not normally included in more traditional cost/benefit energy scenarios, are considered. In this final step students are presenting data to their classmates as scientists would to their colleagues.

In our scenario all students have gained deep understanding of one country's energy practices. The Global Alternative Energy Summit provides an authentic purpose for students to share what they have learned in their groups with those in all other groups, resulting in a more comprehensive view of energy practices around the globe. The sharing of stories and information is an educative, enlightening experience for all students in which the fruits of their learning and labor, shared and appreciated, contribute to the learning and edification of all students.

The following are hypothetical sample excerpts from data presentations by students role-playing a case study of biogas electricity in the village of Pura, India. The excerpts illustrate three modalities: written, oral, and visual (adapted from Rajabapaiah, Jayakumar, & Amulya, 1993).

MODALITY: Written TASK: Writing an Abstract

A useful source of energy is biogas, which is an approximately 60/40 mixture of methane ($CH_4$) and carbon dioxide ($CO_2$), produced by the anaerobic fermentation of biomass materials such as bovine wastes, which are readily available in the case described, Pura village in south India. Since 1987, the traditional system of obtaining water, lighting and fertilizer in Pura village has been replaced with a community biogas plant electricity generation system. The technical, managerial, and economical aspects of this are the subject of this paper. A comparison of the traditional and present systems shows that households benefit in all areas—obtaining water, illumination and fertilizer—and therefore enjoy improved hygiene and greater convenience at relatively low cost. (pp. 787–815)

MODALITY: Oral TASK: Meeting Target Audience Objectives

In closing, I would like to offer you, my fellow colleagues, the following cautionary advice. In the case I've presented here today, the community biogas plant is sustained by the coming together of individual and collective interests. Noncooperation with the community plant results in a heavy individual price where access to water and light are cut off by one's fellow villagers. This is a great loss compared to the lesser advantages of noncooperation and non-contribution to collective interests. Nonetheless this happens on a somewhat regular basis, each time requiring a form of intervention or mediation. Energy planners like ourselves must understand the social and cultural dynamics of operating any energy system, especially a decentralized, collective plant like the one in Pura village, where the main operating problems are social, rather than technical. This is not to say that decentralization and community-based, collective utilities are not recommended for rural areas; in fact their social and economic benefits far outweigh their costs.

MODALITY: Visual TASK:   Presenting Data Visually: Diagrams, Flow Charts, Tables, Graphs, and Text

**Diagrams.**   One diagram shows an overview of the existing community biogas plant system. This diagram uses labeled boxes and arrows to show relationships (spatial and interactive) between resources and outcomes. A second diagram shows elevation and a sectional view of the plant itself.

**Tables.**   Tables include statistical information on the community, including number of households, cattle population, and energy consumption. Another set of tables includes information about the biogas plant operation, including number of operating hours, average fuel consumption, and capital costs as well as operating expenditures and income.

**Charts and Graphs.**   A *flow chart* is chosen as the most appropriate and comprehensible presentation of visual information concerning the operation of the dual fuel engine at the plant. It lists operation checks and instructions for which both "okay" and "problem" outcomes result in different instructions for the next step. Following this is a 3-by-5-celled troubleshooting chart showing a series of possible problems and their respective causes and remedies. A *line graph* is used to show variation in the unit costs of energy during the working hours of the plant, and a *pie chart* is used to show the percentage components of the cost of electricity from the biogas system.

**Text.**   Bulleted text is an effective means of communicating ideas visually. In this case students chose to present their major conclusions in the form of 10 sentences, one line each. These included, for example, increased self-reliance, improved quality of life and health with regard to illumination and water, and the establishment of a youth training program for operation and maintenance of the plant.

How do we cultivate these multimodal competencies in students? How do we teach the student skilled at writing technical, academic papers to present the same information orally in an interesting, animated, yet professional manner, and to make good decisions regarding what to present and how best to convey various kinds of information? Conversely, how do we help the student whose professional presentation is made in the same colloquial, vernacular language characteristic of close interpersonal communication? How are these bridges built, these skills learned, these "languages" acquired?

Traditionally the court trial model was adopted to teach scientific data presentation skills. Students have generally been offered these models from television, video, and movies. However, the trial model conveys the message that students must defend their data. This is inaccurate. Students must learn to answer questions only about their own work and only insofar as they understand it. They must be able to say what they did and why and how they did it. At no time should they feel the need to draw more meaningful conclusions, or to confirm or deny whether or not there are other, possibly even better, methods to address the same research questions or alternate implications. Role-play can be used to act out various question and answer scenarios in which intellectual confrontation and even debate are acceptable and encouraged.

These interactive communications take place on many levels, from friendly discussions in offices, classes, and labs to whole audiences asking questions of a presenter or panel. If a video of scientists presenting their research is used with students as a means of providing models, we offer one cautionary caveat: The information should be personalized and socially contextualized. In her research on this topic, McMahon (personal communication, March 1995) found that even scientists chosen for their renown, and whose research was in the high-interest category, could not hold students' attention when the oral report was presented in a technical manner devoid of a personalized story. This finding held across gender, race, and topic of presenter. Indeed, oral presentation is necessarily a two-way interaction between the presenter and the audience. Audiences must be "drawn in," and, as all good journalists know, this means human, emotional involvement. The role of affect cannot be underestimated in science any more than in any other discipline. We make memories most readily for those things that are emotionally charged for us. However, the positive affect must come from a human desire to share a story or experience rather than to make an emotional appeal to an audience for an investment in the research. Students must understand this distinction as well.

All of the preceding eight steps offered the students and teacher an opportunity to experience the integrated world of a scientist over an extended period of time. Students' experiences led them to include literature, culture, history, government, economics, and politics in the realm of science. Their experiences also added the important skills of reading and writing to the list of laboratory and science processing skills needed in the everyday life of a scientist. Not only was the domain of science enlarged in the students' eyes, but their content knowledge also was increased as the integrated scenario progressed. On a need-to-know basis the students were motivated to seek and find the information they needed to learn and achieve success in the challenge. This all led to the final phase of the integrated scenario: the mock Global Energy Summit Conference. In this culminating event the students continued their role-playing of energy scientists from around the world as they presented their countries' energy use history and plans for the future.

## GLOBAL ENERGY SUMMIT:
## OUTCOMES AND SYNOPSES OF PRESENTATIONS

The cultural and scientific literacy that students acquired throughout this process was exemplified and displayed at the Global Conference on Energy Alternatives where each student group of energy scientists presented its findings and recommendations: the results and application of the knowledge and critical thinking skills learned and honed throughout this process of thinking and acting like a scientist. The following are synopses of presentations given by students representing Ethiopia, The People's Republic of China, and Great Britain. These synopses are offered here as closure to this process so that the reader has a sense of information synthesis and outcomes as presented by student teams in the culminating integrated activity.

The student team from Ethiopia chose biomass from eucalyptus plantations as a future source of energy for their country. Eucalyptus, an exotic plant introduced almost a century ago, causes few serious ecological problems in Ethiopia. Eucalyptus is often thought of as ecologically undesirable because it can prevent ground vegetation from growing and thereby contribute to erosion. But in Ethiopia this has not been the case because it has been planted on barren, deforested highlands where it has reduced erosion and could be helpful in reintroducing native species to those areas. Forest cover in Ethiopia went from 40% in 1900 to 2.7% in 1985 with the present reforestation rate at approximately 100,000 hectares a year. Students learned important lessons from this case: both present and past conditions and solutions must be considered in making decisions. This is a case in which eucalyptus, often considered an undesirable plant, is a most appropriate choice under present ecological conditions for reforestation and biomass because it is well adapted to highland soil and climate, is unpalatable to livestock, and can be used for fuelwood and construction (adapted from Hall, Rosillo-Calle, Williams, & Woods, 1993, pp. 593–651).

The student team from The People's Republic of China offered a historical account of energy use in their country and chose to continue the use of hydropower in China where approximately 100,000 hydropower plants have been built over the past 30 years. However, the group recommended mainly small-scale projects using relatively simple technology in which all equipment, construction materials, and labor are obtained locally. Each proposed plant should be judged on a case-by-case basis, in which the criteria for suitability include the following environmental and social considerations:

Human populations: issues of disappropriating land, relocating people, and compensating owners for their lands. (For one proposed Chinese dam project, an estimated 1,400,000 persons may be displaced. A World Bank review identified involuntary resettlement as the major problem surrounding dam construction worldwide.)

Climatic effects: Large bodies of water affect local climate; generally, the greater the body of water, the greater the effects.

Impact on plant and animal life.

Impact on the river: aquatic ecosystems, water quality, and sedimentation.

Incorporation of socioenvironmental dimensions into planning.

Economic and financial issues.

The team recommended continuation of the country's policy of communal construction, management, and consumption of hydropower, allowing each station to be responsible for its own profits and losses. In recent years a pilot rural electrification program involving 100 selected counties has been undertaken to provide power for cultural/educational programs, domestic use, farm processing, agriculture/livestock, and industrial production (adapted from Moreira & Poole, 1993; Xiong, 1990).

The team from Great Britain, a country whose past energy practices relied heavily on coal, chose to recommend the use of wave energy in the future, building on the wave technology currently available. They highlighted Osprey—Ocean Swell Powered Renewable Energy—as the "wave of the future." Although the Osprey unfortunately sank, it offers valuable information for scientists, engineers, and energy planners in Great Britain as well as those interested in such technology around the world. The team was encouraged rather than defeated by the Osprey experiment because they understood how developments in science and technology require diligence in trial and error, approximation, refinement, and adjustment to new ways of thinking and doing things, which are what ultimately result in the success that often comes after a long series of unsuccessful trials. Perseverance and the ability to delay gratification are characteristic qualities of scientists and all those whose pursuits are carried out incrementally and often without numerous external rewards.

Following the oral presentations of the student teams, there was an opportunity for all students to view each team's work during an informal scientific poster session. The teacher facilitated a discussion before the poster session that encouraged the students to generate and ask questions of their peers during their perusal of the posters. Written papers were also available at each of the role-played country locations. Students were expected to read and review each team's papers in preparation for debate and discussion as the 3-day Summit Conference continued. During the 3-day Conference, there was much room for creative planning. In using this paradigm, it is wise if the teacher reflects on the goals of the integrated challenge and includes a time for realization and sharing of each goal with the students. In this model the teacher offered the second day of the Conference as a time when each of the student teams would display their pilot machine or simulation for harnessing energy. Time was allotted for demonstration, data sharing, and dialogue between teams. Many discussions of economics, culture, and politics surfaced during the conversations and explanations of team decisions. The third day was designed as a day for questions, answers, opinions, and reflection. As is true with scientific meetings, there must be time for interaction and communication if scientists are to learn from each other. The teacher can facilitate this interaction in small or large groups, depending on time and resources.

## CONCLUSION

Our goal has been to show how the process of thinking and acting like a scientist both promotes and requires multiple literacies: social, cultural, scientific, and text based. All are essential for both academic and real-world success. Real-world problem solving involves authentic tasks in which motivation to learn from texts is driven by the desire to answer the questions and solve the problems posed. This most often requires a multidisciplinary approach that involves countless skills and strategies including questioning, guessing, hypothesizing, testing, classifying, describing, defining, comparing, analyzing, and synthesizing information. Scientific thinking is a habit of mind to which critical thinking is the key factor. Critical thinking is necessary for effective participation in a democracy. By writing this chapter we hope to raise questions not only regarding reading skills and literacy but also about what constitutes science and who in our culture and schools is encouraged to think like a scientist. We hope our global energy integrated project has served as an example of how the use of a thematic unit draws on multiple literacies and crosses disciplinary boundaries.

Although the specific content knowledge and necessary reading strategies may differ by project, the skills of focusing, questioning, finding and evaluating information, reading critically, and acquiring cultural literacy are fundamental to successful learning in any domain. In science specifically, focusing on these skills within an integrated setting allows students entrance into the real world of science. Students are offered the opportunity to walk in a scientist's shoes as they traverse an entire experience from the planning to the presentation of investigative findings. As individual and group needs arise, students are internally motivated to seek, find, and analyze information in order to progress through the challenge and propel their project and team forward.

This shift in curriculum also requires a shift in teaching and learning. The roles of both the teacher and students must be reconceptualized. Teaching becomes a matter of teachable moments rather than large group lectures or interactive question and answer sessions. The teacher's modeling of questioning and dialogue is critical in guiding students to find answers, ask further questions, and reconcile contradictory information. Through the modeling of strategies teachers offer students opportunities to learn in new ways. Over time, students do learn to ask and answer questions and facilitate their own learning. They are motivated to learn through having a purpose to learn. In our global energy project, it was first a need to understand a country and its people. In achieving this, the students were able to move on toward understanding how the science of energy use can be understood within each country's many complexities.

Through this integrated challenge, acting and thinking like a scientist is something each student experiences in a personal way. Science disciplinary knowledge is enlarged to include not only science content, but also cultural, social, historical, political, and economic features of the context under study. The notion of a scientist is augmented to include a well-rounded person who spends much of her time reading, writing, and speaking with others about her work. Most important, the students experience the learning of science as a challenging, invigorating, exciting interdisciplinary enterprise attainable by all who are engaged in trying.

## REFERENCES

Ahmed, S., Rittelman, P., & Kingman, K. (1995). Solar powered dispensary in Tibet. In R. Campbell-Howe & B. Wilkins-Crowder (Eds.), *Twentieth national passive solar conference* (pp. 185–190). Boulder, CO: American Solar Energy Society.

Alexander, P. A., & Knight, S. L. (1993). Dimensions of the interplay between learning and teaching. *Educational Forum, 57*, 232–245.

Alvermann, D. E., & Moore, D. W. (1991). Secondary school reading. In R. Barr, M. L. Kamil, P. Mosenthal, & P. D. Pearson (Eds.), *Handbook of reading research: Vol. II* (pp. 951–983). White Plains, NY: Longman.

American Association for the Advancement of Science (AAAS). (1993). *Benchmarks for science literacy.* New York: Oxford University Press.

Bransford, J., Stein, B., & Vye, N. (1982). Helping students learn how to learn from written texts. In M. Singer (Ed.), *Competent reader, disabled reader: Research and application.* Hillsdale, NJ: Lawrence Erlbaum Associates.

Dewey, J. (1938). *Experience and education.* The Kappa Delta Pi Lecture Series. New York: Collier/Macmillan.

Gipe, P. (1995). *Wind energy comes of age.* New York: Wiley.

Goldenberg, C., & Gallimore, R. (1991). Local knowledge, research knowledge and educational change: A case study of early Spanish reading achievement. *Educational Researcher, 20,* 2–14.

Grubb, M., & Meyer, N. (1993). Wind energy: Resources, systems and regional strategies. In T. Johansson, H. Kelly, A. Reddy, & R. Williams (Eds.), *Renewable energy: Sources for fuels and electricity* (pp. 157–212). Washington, DC: Island Press.

Hall, D., Rosillo-Calle, F., Williams, R., & Woods, J. (1993). Biomass for energy: Supply prospects. In T. Johansson, H. Kelly, A. Reddy, & R. Williams (Eds.), *Renewable energy: Sources for fuels and electricity* (pp. 593–651). Washington, DC: Island Press.

Hammond, L. (1997). Teaching and learning through Mien culture: A case study in community-school relations. In G. Spindler (Ed.), *Education and cultural process: Toward an anthropology of education.* Prospect Heights, IL: Waveland Press.

Heath, S. B. (1983). *Ways with words: Language life and work in communities and classrooms.* Cambridge, MA: Cambridge University Press.

Heath, S. B., & Magnolia, L. (1991). *Children of promise: Literate activity in linguistically and culturally diverse classrooms.* Washington, DC: National Education Association.

Howard, V. A. (1988). Thinking on paper: A philosopher's look at writing. In V. A. Howard (Ed.), *Varieties of thinking: Essays from Harvard's Philosophy of Education Research Center* (pp. 84–92). New York: Routledge, Chapman & Hall.

Hurd, P. D. (1991). Why we must transform science education. *Educational Leadership, 49*(2), 33–35.

Jacobs, J. E., & Paris, S. G. (1987). Children's metacognition about reading: Issues in definition, measurement, and instruction. *Educational Psychologist, 22,* 255–278.

Kaplan, R., & Shaw, P. (1983). *Exploring academic discourse.* Rowley, MA: Newbury House.

Lawrence, D. H. (1937). *Women in love.* New York: The Modern Library.

Lehman, B. (1986, May 12). Dose and type determine radiation's effect. *Boston Globe,* p. 42.

Lipson, M. (1982). Learning new information from text: The role of prior knowledge and reading ability. *Journal of Reading Behavior, 14,* 243–261.

Lozano, M., & Chalfoun, N. (1995). Computer aided solar house design made of "guadua" in Bogota, Colombia. In R. Campbell-Howe & B. Wilkins-Crowder (Eds.), *Twentieth national passive solar conference* (pp. 191–196). Boulder, CO: American Solar Energy Society.

Manzo, A., & Manzo, U. C. (1990). *Content area reading: A heuristic approach.* Columbus, OH: Merrill Publishing.

Martin, B. E., & Brouwer, W. (1991). The sharing of personal science and the narrative element in science education. *Science Education, 75,* 707–722.

Meeks, J. (1987, May). *Toward defining affective metacognition.* Paper presented at the International Reading Association, Anaheim, CA.

Meyer, B., & Freedle, R. (1984). Effects of discourse type on recall. *American Educational Research Journal, 21,* 121–143.

Moll, L., Amanti, C., Neff, D., & Gonzales, N. (1992). Funds of knowledge for teaching: Using a qualitative approach to connect homes and classrooms. *Theory Into Practice, 31,* 132–141.

Moreira, J., & Poole, A. (1993). Hydropower and its constraints. In T. Johansson, H. Kelly, A. Reddy, & R. Williams (Eds.), *Renewable energy: Sources for fuels and electricity* (pp. 73–119). Washington, DC: Island Press.

National Research Council (NRC). 1996. *National Science Education Standards.* Washington, DC: National Academy Press.

Norris, S. P., & Phillips, L. M. (1994). Interpreting pragmatic meaning when reading popular reports of science. *Journal of Research in Science Testing, 31*(9), 947–967.

Novak, J. D., & Gowin, D. B. (1984). *Learning how to learn*. New York: Cambridge University Press.

Osborne, R. J., & Freyberg, P. (1985). *Learning in science: The implications of children's science*. London: Heinemann.

Palincsar, A. S., & Brown, A. L. (1984). Reciprocal teaching of comprehension-fostering and comprehension-monitoring activities. In L. B. Resnick, J. H. Larkin, & R. C. Anderson (Eds.), *Cognition and instruction*. Hillsdale, NJ: Lawrence Erlbaum Associates.

Pearson, P. D., & Spiro, R. (1982, May). The new buzz word in reading is schema. *Instructor*, 46–48.

Posner, G. J. (1995). *Analyzing the curriculum*. New York: McGraw-Hill.

Pressley, M., Johnson, C. J., Symons, S., McGoldrick, J. A., & Kurita, J. A. (1989). Strategies that improve children's memory and comprehension of text. *Elementary School Journal, 90*, 3–22.

Rajabapaiah, P., Jayakumar, S., & Amulya. (1993). Biogas electricity: The Pura village case study. In T. Johansson, H. Kelly, A. Reddy, & R. Williams (Eds.), *Renewable energy: Sources for fuels and electricity* (pp. 787–815). Washington, DC: Island Press.

Resnick, L. B. (1991). Shared cognition: Thinking as a social practice. In L. B. Resnick, J. M. Levine, & S. D. Teasley (Eds.), *Perspectives on socially shared cognition* (pp. 1–20). Washington, DC: American Psychological Association.

Rosenberg, P. (1993). *The alternative energy handbook*. Lilburn, GA: Fairmont Press.

Rosenblatt, L. (1989). Writing and reading: The transactional theory. In J. Mason (Ed.), *Reading and writing connections*. Boston: Allyn & Bacon.

Roth, W. M. (1993). Heisenberg's uncertainty principle and interpretive research in science education. *Journal of Research in Science Teaching, 30*, 669–680.

Royer, J., & Cable, G. (1975). Facilitated learning in connected discourse. *Journal of Educational Psychology, 67*, 116–123.

Schmid, J., & Palz, W. (1986). European wind energy technology. *Solar energy R & D in the European community, Series G, Volume 3*. Dordrecht, The Netherlands: Reidel Publishing Company.

Schmidt, H., De Volder, L., De Grave, W., Moust, J., & Patel, V. (1989). Explanatory models in the processing of science text. The role of prior knowledge activation through small group discussion. *Journal of Educational Psychology, 81*, 610–619.

State of California. (1996). *Grant application for geothermal program*. California Energy Commission, Sacramento, CA.

Stone, R. (1997, January). Ten years after. *Discover*, 62–63.

Vacca, R., & Vacca, J. (1996). *Content area reading*. New York: HarperCollins.

Vygotsky, L. (1978). *Mind in society*. Cambridge, MA: Harvard University Press.

Whimbey, A. (1980). *Intelligence can be taught*. New York: Dutton.

Williams, D., & Muchena, O. (1991). Utilizing indigenous knowledge systems in agricultural education to promote sustainable agriculture. *Journal of Agricultural Education, 3*, 52–57.

Xiong, S. (1990). Small hydropower developments in China: Achievements and prospects. *International water power and dam construction*, October, *42*(10), 27–31. Sutton Surrey, England: Reed Business Publishing Group.

Yore, L. D. (1991). Secondary science teachers' attitudes towards and beliefs about science reading and science textbooks. *Journal of Research in Science Teaching, 28*, 55–82.

Yore, L. D., & Shymansky, J. A. (1985). *Reading, understanding, remembering and using information in written science materials* (ERIC Document Reproduction Service No. ED 258 825).

Yore, L. D., & Shymansky, J. A. (1991). Reading in Science: Developing an operational conception to guide instruction. *Journal of Research in Science Teaching, 2*(2), 29–36.

# The Nature of Disciplinary and Domain Learning: The Knowledge, Interest, and Strategic Dimensions of Learning From Subject Matter Text

Patricia A. Alexander
*University of Maryland*

In training a child to activity of thought, above all things we must beware of what I will call "inert ideas"—that is to say, ideas that are merely received into the mind without being utilized, or tested, or thrown into fresh combinations (Whitehead, 1929/1957, p. 1)

Throughout this volume, educational practitioners and researchers from diverse backgrounds have offered an extensive look at text-based learning. This exploration has examined the nature of knowledge and learning both from a cognitive orientation (Stahl & Hynd, chapter 2, this volume) and from a motivational perspective (Carr & Mizelle, & Charik, chapter 3, this volume). Further, these contributors have considered how learning occurs for particular tasks (e.g., vocabulary development or mental models) and in specific domains (e.g., Holliday or Wineburg).

As the epilogue to these invaluable inquiries, I want to weave together several threads that have appeared in various chapters. My goal is to weave these threads into a tapestry that depicts a journey toward competence in academic disciplines or domains—a journey highly dependent upon the knowledge and experiences that reading affords. Although they come in varied shades and textures, these threads include: (a) learners' knowledge base; (b) their interests, goals, and investment in the enterprise of learning; and (c) their efforts at strategic processing or self-regulation. In addition, as the opening quote from Whitehead (1929/1957) suggests, deeper conceptual understanding through text arises when the student's journey has a clear destination—such as domain competence—that makes each step in that journey more purposeful and meaningful.

Over the past 4 years, I have been engaged in a series of investigations into the nature of domain learning. Through these studies and my own instructional experiences, I have come to believe that our picture of learning can be greatly enhanced when we cast its separate and powerful elements into a coherent model. Rather than pay homage to knowledge, interest, and strategic processing individually, such a model would allow us to delve into the intimate and combined nature of these basic forces. In the end, what we hopefully possess is a cross-disciplinary/cross-domain understanding of learning from text. Examining text-based learning with this integrative eye allows us to extract certain developmental patterns that appear to persist whether we are learning biology, history, or physics. It may be helpful to think of these developmental patterns as the paths that individuals can follow in their journey from novice to competent or expert learner in any discipline or domain.

## WHAT CONSTITUTES A DISCIPLINE OR DOMAIN?

From an individual perspective, the journey toward competence or expertise in any discipline or domain is a long-term, often lifelong, process. From the moment of birth, and perhaps even from the moment of conception, we begin the process of formulating a conceptual understanding of the world in which we live (Alexander, in press-a). Over time, some of these conceptual understandings become aligned with other related concepts that are viewed as aspects of socially constructed fields of study (i.e., disciplines or domains). When this consolidation begins to occur, individuals can be said to have the rudiments of disciplinary or domain knowledge (Alexander, 1992; Alexander, Schallert, & Hare, 1991; McGonagill, 1995). Stahl, Hynd, Glynn, and Carr (1996) described a similar phenomenon when they spoke of the formation of "richly interconnected sets of concepts and relations among concepts" (p. 142)—what they refer to as content knowledge.

For instance, as a young child, I understood that the bright, round object in the sky is what those around me called the sun. Not only was my conceptual knowledge of the sun limited at this age, but it was also very unscientific and unexamined. Later, I learned more about this heavenly sphere as part of my education both in and out of school. Simultaneously, I learned more about my own planet and about other bodies and forces that exist in the universe. Likewise, I began to sense the relationship between and among these concepts. As this process transpired, my conceptual knowledge of sun, in effect, became part of an emerging body of scientific knowledge in the domain of astrophysics. Piaget (1929, 1930), Vygotsky (1934/1986), and others (e.g., Gardner, 1991) have provided rich descriptions of this transformation in one's knowledge base from *spontaneous* or nonscientific notions to *scientific* or formal concepts. Moreover, this transformation is a critical dimension in what constitutes the development of a discipline or domain knowledge for an individual. Whitehead (1929/1957) talked about this development of competence as the "rhythmic character" (p. 27) of human growth that needs to be matched by the "rhythm of education" (p. 15).

## Defining Parameters

Because I intend to speak to the nature of text learning in relation to disciplines and domains, it is important to explicate what I believe constitutes these realms of knowledge. Specifically, as we progress through this discussion, I at times talk about disciplines and domains as bodies of knowledge that exist outside the individual in the form of an acknowledged and accepted corpus of knowledge. Thus, when I talk about history or biology as fields of study that individuals may pursue, I am speaking in terms of this abstract, external body of knowledge. At other times, however, I discuss the state of knowledge within the individual relative to that established corpus. For instance, I have described an individual's development of domain knowledge as progressing across three stages—acclimation, competence, and proficiency/expertise (Alexander, 1997b, in press-b)—each represented by quantitative and qualitative differences in learners' subject-matter knowledge.

Although different interpretations of what constitutes disciplines and domains exist in the literature (Hirst, 1974; Phenix, 1964a), I use these terms under certain assumptions. First, both disciplines and domains, in my estimation, fall under the rubric of subject-matter or content knowledge. This means that disciplines and domains represent the consolidation of knowledge around core principles or precepts associated with recognized fields of study (Matthews, 1994; Stahl et al., 1996; West & Pines, 1985). These core principles and precepts are typically negotiated by those judged as experts within that discipline or domain, and are subsequently authorized or sanctioned through sociocultural practice (Phillips, 1987, 1995).

Currently, within educational practice, it is popular to talk about interdisciplinary instruction or programs (Maurer, 1994; also chapter 1, this volume). However, it is not always evident that these innovative programs are based on the careful delineation of core concepts and principles that relate the targeted disciplines. That is, rather than representing a configuration of instruction around shared concepts or principles central to each of the related fields, many of the presumably interdisciplinary curricula are more accurately orchestrations of the curriculum around similar topics or chronologies (McGonagill, 1995). As various contributors to this volume have articulated, it is not enough to use certain disciplinary knowledge and procedures in the instruction of another, as when historical methods are applied in the study of biology. If students are ultimately to think and function as a biologist or as a historian, then the integrity of those disciplines must be maintained even as we attempt to integrate them. It is also not clear what educators might mean when they describe such subject-matter areas as band or social studies as disciplines. Certainly, most educational theorists would view the term "discipline" as an unsuitable moniker for these academic courses of study (Phenix, 1968; Schwab, 1964).

Second, even more than the term "discipline," the word "domain" has been variably applied in the research literature. For instance, some researchers refer to topics within areas of study as domains (Hasselhorn & Körkel, 1986; Walker, 1989). Within the domain of astrophysics, for example, there are a multitude of topics for which individuals may or may not possess relevant knowledge (e.g., black holes, singularities, or quantum mechanics). For this reason, I have attempted to make distinctions in my writings between topic knowledge and domain knowledge (Alexander, Kulikowich, & Schulze, 1994a, 1994b; Alexander, Pate, Kulikowich, Farrell, & Wright, 1989). Further, in the expert/novice literature, investigations have been conducted on such "domains" as waitressing, typewriting, and chess that do not seem well linked to underlying disciplines (e.g., Chi, Glaser, & Farr, 1988). To avoid this confusion, I have restricted this discussion to academic domains, thereby maintaining a focus on schooled subjects that have a more direct and evident link to disciplinary knowledge.

In addition, some theorists and researchers have made clear distinctions between disciplines and domains of knowledge (Bazerman, 1985; Phenix, 1968; Schwab, 1964), whereas others appear to use these terms almost interchangeably. Hirst (1974; Hirst & Peters, 1971), for example, sorted existing knowledge into empirical, mathematical, philosophical, moral, aesthetic, religious, and historical/sociological disciplines, which he viewed as distinctly different in nature and form. Established fields of study, in Hirst's judgment, draw differentially from these underlying disciplines. For instance, the field of reading may draw from empirics, in terms of its syntactic or graphophonemic structure. When we consider the beauty or the captivating nature of texts, we are likely considering the aesthetic dimensions of reading. When we look at the content of narratives, expositions, or their sources (VanSledright & Frankes, chapter 6, this volume), we may be surveying the influences of the historical/sociological disciplines in the field of reading.

Viewed in this manner, disciplines are essentially the taproots or the fundamental realms of knowledge from which multiple domains of study emerge (Hirst, 1974; Hirst & Peters, 1971). In this regard, I concur with Hirst's approach to identifying disciplines, even though I would categorize these disciplines differently to include the traditional areas of history, literature, science, and mathematics. As a way of demonstrating this relationship between disciplines and domains, Foshay (1962) stated that disciplines must have three essential elements: a domain, a set of generalizations or guiding rules, and a history. Thus, in the discipline of science, we may identify the domain of biology, which we can further dissect into such branches as microbiology, human biology, genetics, and immunology.

Whether you hold to Hirst's disciplinary taxonomy or another in the literature (Brent, 1978; Foshay, 1962; Schwab, 1964), disciplines and domains remain formalized bodies of knowledge. That is to say, what we call a discipline or domain cannot be achieved purely from everyday, pedestrian experiences, but must be acquired, in some measure, through systematic instruction. This is true because disciplines and domains entail a certain abstraction from direct evidence of physical experiences or occurrences, particularly as one begins to achieve some level of competence. We see this abstraction in Hynd and Guzzetti's (chapter 7, this volume) discussion of counterintuitive understandings in the domain of physics. Indeed, to reach competence in certain fields, such as physics, one must be able to set aside lay theories that seem perfectly adequate and sound in the face of everyday experiences. It might also be argued that expertise in any discipline or domain makes similar demands on the learner for abstraction and generalization. Further, this abstraction and generalization cannot occur without the orchestrated (i.e., formal) pursuit of knowledge (Gagnon, 1989; VanSledright, 1996; Wilson & Sykes, 1989).

Overall, I see this issue of abstraction as important in understanding how students are capable of achieving competence or proficiency in any discipline or domain. Sir Karl Popper (1972) offered a thought-provoking depiction of the relationship between abstraction and disciplinary understanding in terms of three worlds of objective knowledge. In World 1, our understanding is bound to the physical or concrete realm. In essence, what we understand is captured in the act of touching, seeing, hearing, or smelling. Within World 2, knowing moves beyond the physical, concrete world and into the mind. In short, knowledge is our interpretation or construction of the physical. For example, I no longer need to touch, see, or smell a dog to know it. I can contemplate or conjure "dog" in my mind as a result of direct experiences. On the basis of Popper's description, educators focus much of their energies in classrooms on this secondary world, centered on the understandings that students build in their minds as an outcome of the learning experiences they are afforded (Bereiter, 1994).

For disciplines and domains of knowledge, such as literacy, science, history, or mathematics, individuals can travel to yet another dimension of knowledge—World 3. It is within this realm that ideas themselves become objects of thought. It might be said that experts spend relatively more of their professional time functioning in this third world than those who are still on the road to competence. Thus, when individuals theorize, problem solve, or generalize, as contributors have done throughout this volume, they operate in this third world. To warrant the classification of a scholarly discipline, in Popper's judgment, those associated with it must function principally within

World 3. Thus, a high level of abstraction must exist for any field to qualify as a discipline.

Even though I find Popper's treatise on the three worlds metaphorically useful in distinguishing disciplines and domains from other forms of knowledge, I do not subscribe wholly to his objectification of knowledge. Instead, I would argue that much of the knowledge base that constitutes academic disciplines and domains, and thereby these disciplines and domains, themselves, is socioculturally constructed (Phillips, 1995). This perspective places me theoretically between Popper and radical constructivism. That is, whereas Popper tends to objectify virtually all knowledge, radical constructivists seemingly question the existence of any objective reality and tend to speak of all knowledge as relative, sociocultural constructions (von Glaserfeld, 1991). For my part, I hold that there are, indeed, objective realities that can be known in some way or to some degree. For example, however we choose to label them or regardless of our capacity to understand or explain them to others, there are certain phenomena (e.g., gravity, molecular structures) that exist. Still, such realities represent only a small segment of any body of disciplinary or domain knowledge, and the way we come to know them, and certainly the manner in which we communicate their essence and value, are socioculturally determined.

There are two additional assumptions that underlie my perspective throughout this discussion. First, because knowledge is always in the process of becoming, disciplines and domains are in perpetual formation. Consequently, we must fight the tendency to treat any field of study as solidified, certain, or complete. All bodies of knowledge, including disciplines and domains, are dynamic and highly speculative. Even those we honor as experts in a discipline or domain know only some measure of knowledge relevant to their fields. Second, there are important distinctions between disciplines and between domains that are reflected in the way these bodies of knowledge are taught and learned (Alexander, 1992). Thus, we can describe mathematics as rather well structured in terms of its defining principles, and more algorithmic in regard to problem-solving strategies. History, however, might best be cast as more ill structured and more dependent on heuristic strategies for problem solving (Spiro, Coulson, Feltovich, & Anderson, 1994; Spiro, Feltovich, Jacobson, & Coulson, 1992.)

## Positioning Literacy Within the Discipline/Domain Continuum

What about the area of study on which this volume is based—literacy? Does literacy or its recognized components of reading, writing, listening, and speaking fit within the parameters I have established for disciplines or domains? What supportive role does learning from text play in the development of one's disciplinary or domain knowledge in other fields?

I am probably on safe ground in classifying literacy, including reading, as a domain of knowledge. Not only is literacy a formalized field of study, but there is also a degree of consolidation around guiding principles and a level of abstraction in the body of knowledge that are typically incorporated in the study of literacy. Of course, it may be argued that the nature of reading instruction in many K–12 classrooms may obscure the principles that serve to define this domain for some learners. For this reason, these school-aged learners may never come to see the richness of the domain of reading. In contrast, if we hold to the criterion that disciplines must be the roots from which domains arise, then it seems unlikely that the composite domain of literacy or reading itself, warrants this classification. Rather, it is more likely that literacy in general and reading in particular are domains of knowledge that also contribute significantly to the individual's acquisition of disciplinary knowledge in other realms, including history, science, and mathematics.

Certainly, if we consider the way that reading and related language arts are taught in school, it reinforces my supposition that literacy constitutes a domain of knowledge. For example, the acquisition of fundamental reading skills is stressed in the early elementary grades. For the large percentage of children, the basic procedures required to make sense of written language can be acquired with assistance from more knowledgeable others (e.g., teachers or parents) within a relatively few years. After that initial learning, these core understandings can be enriched and expanded, in part to facilitate development of students' disciplinary and domain knowledge in other fields, as well as to allow for the pursuit of the aesthetic.

In this volume, we see ample evidence of this focus on reading (especially on learning from text) as a necessary tool for building one's disciplinary or domain knowledge. Individuals who become captivated with text-based learning as a field of study, in and of itself, likely will have to wait until undergraduate or graduate school to find the mechanisms available to pursue expertise in this subject-matter domain. Until that time, the application of reading as an avenue to becoming learned in other fields or as a means of being aesthetically engaged will dominate their school experiences, especially after the primary grades.

To understand how literacy, and more specifically learning from text, aids in the development of disciplinary and domain knowledge, I want to return to the three dimensions I believe are requisite for growth from acclimated or novice learner to someone with competence and perhaps even expertise in academic arenas: subject-matter knowledge, individual interest, and strategic abilities.

## READING AS KNOWLEDGE SEEKING

Regardless of the discipline or domain, there is no way to attain a modicum of competence without acquiring a foundation of relevant subject-matter knowledge. In short, a person cannot be competent in science, history, or mathematics without an appropriate foundation of scientific, historical, or mathematical knowledge (Ball, 1993; VanSledright, 1996). Further, given the manner in which subject-matter information is recorded and transmitted in today's world (Alexander, Murphy, & Woods, 1996), there is little hope of acquiring this foundational knowledge base without the ability to decipher and interpret written language (Alexander & Knight, 1993). That is to say, much of the established corpus of knowledge that marks the boundaries of disciplines and domains exists in written form. Thus, without an ability to learn from text, the prospects of becoming competent (to say nothing about expert) in any discipline or domain are dismal.

Even the movement afoot to convey content via multimedia does not circumvent the power of text processing in the acquisition of subject-matter information (Alexander, Kulikowich, & Jetton, 1994). Although the nature of reading within information technologies may be more nonlinear than we typically ascribe to traditional texts (Spiro et al., 1992; Spiro & Jehng, 1990), processing text remains crucial nonetheless. Indeed, it might be argued that the demands of learning from nonlinear text in the years and decades to come will be even more exacting on individuals who are not competent at text processing or who find themselves operating in an unfamiliar discipline or domain.

The paradox of the relationship between reading effectiveness and subject-matter knowledge is readily apparent. When students open a book for the purpose of acquiring conceptual understanding in disciplines or domains, it will be those students who already possess a greater and more cohesive body of relevant knowledge in that content area who will come away from the experience better informed (Alexander & Murphy, in press; Anderson, Pichert, & Shirey, 1983; Anderson, Reynolds, Schallert, & Goetz, 1977; Piaget, 1929). The Matthew Effect (Stanovich, 1986) remains alive and well on this journey toward competence in academic fields. One reason that the rich get richer in learning from discipline-specific or domain-specific texts is because these individuals can make more informed decisions about what constitutes relevant (versus trivial) and important (versus unimportant) content. They can, in essence, separate the wheat from the chaff when it comes to written text (Alexander & Jetton, 1996). The presence of a cohesive body of disciplinary or domain knowledge also serves as a framework during text processing, decreasing the cognitive demands on informed readers and increasing the efficiency of knowledge acquisition.

Of course, understanding how to use the structure of the text as a signal to more or less important information can assist the learner in various ways (Kintsch & van Dijk, 1978; Meyer, 1975; Taylor & Beach, 1984). However, reliance on structural importance alone is likely insufficient to ensure that students will make reasoned attentional decisions as they study (Alexander, Jetton, Kulikowich, & Woehler, 1994). For instance, many of the texts that students are called on to study: (a) are not well structured with regard to key concepts; (b) present incorrect or outdated information; or (c) place undue emphasis on interesting but tangential content. In addition, some of the most central concepts for a topic or a domain are treated only superficially within the text, or a knowledge of them is simply assumed (Beck, McKeown, & Gromoll, 1989), leaving the weakly informed reader at a significant disadvantage. There is also evidence that the concepts emphasized in classroom discussions or on teacher-made tests do not always coincide with the structurally important content in students' textbooks or other written materials (Jetton & Alexander, 1997; Schellings & van Hout-Wolters, 1995; Schellings, van Hout-Wolters, & Vermunt, 1996).

In our research, my colleagues and I (Alexander & Kulikowich, 1991, 1994; Alexander, White, Haensley, & Crimmins-Jeanes, 1987; Garner, Alexander, Gillingham, Kulikowich, & Brown, 1991), along with others (Garner, Gillingham, & White, 1989; Wade, 1992; Wade & Adams, 1990; Wade, Schraw, Buxton, & Hayes, 1993), have found that some of the literary devices inserted into text to aid readers (e.g., analogies, enticing details, or personally involving information) do not always have the desired effect on study learning. Indeed, this research suggests that such devices often have more facilitative effect on those individuals with higher levels of relevant subject-matter knowledge, and may actually distract attention from relevant, albeit dry, content for others.

The work on extended text analogies, what Glynn, Law, and Doster (chapter 9, this volume) referred to as *elaborate* analogies, serves as a case in point. When high school and undergraduate students came to demanding scientific texts with some grounding in the topic or domain (Alexander & Kulikowich, 1991), they could better use the available analogies as scaffolds for deeper processing and better recall. For those students with little or no background knowledge of the topic, however, the text without the supporting analogy was remembered better. This finding suggested to us that the analogy appeared to add complexity to the reading for low-knowledge readers, becoming, in effect, just more information for the student to process and remember. For this reason, I applaud the guidelines that Glynn et al. (chapter 9, this volume) provided for enhancing the effectiveness of extended or elaborate analogies, particularly their admonition to develop the target concepts first, before highlighting the supporting analogy.

Even in those cases where readers come to the task of learning from text with well-honed reading abilities and an adequate framework of subject-matter knowledge, the learning situation can often be far from optimal. For example, one of the dilemmas I have witnessed is the tendency in certain classrooms to treat learning from text as an obligatory venture of answering someone else's questions (e.g., teachers' or textbook authors'), rather than as an opportunity to explore a discipline or domain of knowledge for the sake of answering one's own questions (Alexander, 1997a). When students have the chance to "knowledge seek," they are given greater autonomy within the learning environment. As such, they may well view learning from text as an avenue for their personal fulfillment rather than as an unwanted assignment demanded of them. The parameters for such a knowledge search, of course, can vary depending on the skill and background of the students. However, I believe that any student of any age or ability can be allowed greater freedom to seek knowledge through text and should be supported in her efforts.

Ongoing research has shown that learners can become meaningfully engaged in the reading of informational text and motivated to learn in content-area classrooms (Guthrie, McGough, Bennett, & Rice, 1996; Stahl et al., 1996). To engineer this transformation to engaged and motivated learners, educators should consider alternative approaches to learning about text in schools. Specifically, when students are engaged in the process of learning how to read, there is far more emphasis on reading narration than exposition. The familiarity, attractiveness, predictability, and other characteristics of narration serve to justify its usefulness as an ally in early reading instruction. Beyond its role in reading skill development, narration has been strongly linked to the aesthetic. Teachers are urged to set aside their inclinations toward efferent (information-getting) approaches to text in favor of an aesthetic response, which Rosenblatt (1978) described as losing oneself in the story or as having a lived-through experience.

There is absolutely nothing wrong with assuming an aesthetic stance in the act of reading (Many & Wiseman, 1992; Rosenblatt, 1938/1995, 1978). However, there is also no reason why the process of knowledge seeking (a phrase I prefer to "information-getting") should be relegated to a subordinate or undesirable role. Such a preferential orientation may lead teachers to view the act of learning from text as an unsatisfying or unmotivating endeavor, when the opposite may well be the case. One simple way to avoid this misconception about learning from text is to introduce more exposition during the learning-to-read phase of reading development, while simultaneously incorporating more knowledge seeking through multiple forms of text in other subject-matter areas (VanSledright & Frankes, chapter 6, this volume). Finally, teachers should provide opportunities for students to pursue topics or questions of personal interest within all classes—a point I elaborate in the following discussion of self-exploration.

## READING AS SELF-EXPLORATION

What is it that makes some individuals persist in their journey toward disciplinary or domain knowledge, while others falter or resist? Why do some students seem eager to engage in learning from text in certain fields, while their peers must be prodded or cajoled? What can be done to make the experience of learning from text in any field more enticing for students? These are fundamental questions that many educational researchers and practitioners have been asking for as long as there have been seemingly disengaged or unmotivated learners. In effect, where does interest and subsequent engagement in learning originate? To address this question, I want to explore three related areas: interest, goals, and self-determination.

## Learner Interest

Although there are many forms of interest discussed in the literature, there are at least two that have been found to play a crucial role in learning from text: individual interest and situational interest (Hidi, 1990; Schiefele, 1991). These two different forms of interest can have different impacts on students' development of conceptual understanding.

*Individual interest*—or what is also called personal interest—is the enduring and absorbing involvement often associated with one's vocations and avocations (Alexander, 1997b; Alexander & Jetton, 1996). In addition, individual interest is linked to students' goals and self-identities (Alexander, 1997a). For instance, it is quite possible that readers of this volume have this type of interest in the study of literacy or text-based learning. Similarly, the youngster who cannot get enough information on dinosaurs is probably displaying her individual interest.

As these illustrations suggest, personal interests touch the cognitive and affective nature of the learner in deep and lasting ways (Alexander, in press-b). Further, this form of interest seems most in keeping with Dewey's (1913) endorsement of motivating from within, and is most likely to result in the active pursuit of experiences and knowledge relative to that interest. In our research, my colleagues and I (Alexander, Jetton, & Kulikowich, 1995; Alexander, Kulikowich, & Schulze, 1994a, 1994b; Alexander, Murphy, Woods, Duhon, & Parker, 1997) found that an individual's personal interests are strongly tied to their subject-matter knowledge and to their subsequent academic performance. In particular, Alexander et al. (1994a) found that students with more discipline or domain knowledge (e.g., immunology or astrophysics) reported higher levels of interest in even more demanding expository text. It was also the high-knowledge/high-interest readers who learned more from these subject-matter texts, as evidenced by their recalls.

In contrast to these abiding interests, we have all experienced a temporary or fleeting sensation caused when something in our environment intrigues us or arouses our attention (Reynolds, 1992). This form of interest has been characterized as *situational interest* (Hidi, 1990; Schiefele, 1991; Schraw & Dennison, 1994), which not only has limited duration, but is also tied to the immediate situation or context (thus, its name). Those who attempt to create captivating texts or produce enticing advertisements understand the power of situational interest. Sometimes, and for reasons we do not fully understand, these typically momentary glimmers of interest can have a more lingering effect. Our attention is not only captured but held (Mitchell, 1993), and may even become the seeds of personal interest. Rarely, however, do these occasions of situational interest remain from one context to the next or transform into personal interests. Their influence, however strong, remains short-lived. Still, when we characterize a text as "interesting," we are generally describing how situationally interesting we find it to be.

However, what factors in text actually result in situational interest? This is the empirical question that Schraw and his colleagues (Schraw, 1995; Schraw, Bruning, & Svoboda, 1995; Schraw & Dennison, 1994) have been investigating. Currently, Schraw et al. (1995) have identified several contributors to situational interests in texts: ease of comprehension (i.e., how easy it is to remember), cohesion (i.e., its organization and clarity), vividness (i.e., whether it includes exciting or vivid details), engagement (i.e., how thought provoking or timely it is), emotiveness (i.e., whether it evokes strong emotions), and prior knowledge (i.e., how familiar the reader is with the content). In the view of Schraw et al., texts with more of these qualities should be more interesting than texts with fewer.

What effects do these forms of interest have on learning? As I have already stated, those with the benefit of a personal interest in a given discipline or domain have an advantage when it comes to learning from relevant text. For one thing, those with a deep-seated interest in the topic have less need to read texts infused with attention-getting or enticing content. To illustrate, Garner et al. (1991) found that individually interested readers preferred to read texts with fewer personally involving details. However, these situationally interesting features were found to be important for readers who were not already personally invested in the topic or domain being studied.

Still, there can be a downside to situational interest. For one thing, the segments that pique interest or arouse attention in text are not always those associated with information that is structurally important or academically relevant (Garner et al., 1991; Garner et al., 1989; Wade et al., 1993). The negative effects of this highly interesting, but relatively unimportant, content have been documented in the "seductive detail" research. What this research suggests is that educators must be cautious in their attempts to motivate students to ready by trying to make text interesting. Rather, they should work to maintain readers' attention on important information in text and help students find the interest in the text's central concepts. Although teachers certainly should seek to interest students in the subject at hand, it would be better if they found some connection between students' deeply held interests and pertinent textual content (Dewey, 1913; James, 1890; Jetton & Alexander, 1997a). Under the best conditions, a student with an abiding interest in a particular discipline or domain is afforded the opportunity to pursue that interest by means of a well-crafted text. This text, which is considerate, coherent, colorful, and accurate, feeds the student's desire to know more about a personally relevant subject. The very experience of engaging the text may not only enrich the student's existing base of relevant knowledge, but it also may serve as the catalyst for future exploration.

## Learner Goals

The ideal learning environment would not only engage an individual with personal interest in the reading of quality text, but would also include a student with a goal of learning from that text (Ames, 1992; Dweck & Leggett, 1988). There are many reasons why students undertake the task of learning from text. As cognitive and motivational researchers have shown, these differential performance goals can have a strong impact on how and what students learn (Ames & Ames, 1985, 1989; Pintrich, Marx, & Boyle, 1993; Pintrich & Schrauben, 1992). Therefore, in this discussion it is worthwhile to consider the influence of goals on text-based learning.

Meece and Holt (1993) described three clusters of goals that capture students' actions, which include learning from text. One cluster, *task-mastery goals*, encompasses the individuals' desire to learn or master the content or task before them. In another category, *ego-social goals*, students are more concerned with demonstrating a high level of ability or with pleasing others (e.g., teachers or parents) than with deepening their understanding. Finally, according to Meece and Holt, there are those students who manifest *work-avoidance goals* or a focus on avoiding academic tasks such as learning from text, or on getting those tasks done with minimal effort. It is not very likely that students with work-avoidance goals will gain much from the task of learning from text, regardless of the quality of the written materials. At the bottom line of these varied goals is this reality: Students who set out to become more informed and more knowledgeable will generally benefit more than those students who are just there to make themselves look good, please others, or get the task done. This should be the case regardless of the quality of the text or the demandingness of the task.

## Self-Determination and Agency

*Self-determination*—and the related construct of autonomy—is a label that Deci (1992) applied to activities that learners undertake with a "full sense of wanting, choosing, and personal endorsement" (p. 44). According to Connell (1985), these constructs represent choice in the initiation, pursuit, and regulation of an activity. Thus, the student who becomes captivated with Stephen Hawking and decides to read more on grand unification theory, or the high-schooler who follows up a trip to Gettysburg with readings on the Civil War is demonstrating self-determination. Even those occasions when students are presented with a text or a task by someone else, such as the teacher, they may still feel that they are active agents in their own learning. In such cases, they are operating with a sense of *agency* (Deci & Ryan, 1985, 1991; Dworkin, 1988; Ryan, 1993). Students in a history class, for example, may be given assignments to read about different inventions during the Industrial Revolution. Within this framework, one student decides to focus her efforts on inventions related to transportation, using both written and video materials. This young woman has demonstrated agency in her learning.

Of course, it is unrealistic to assume that students can fully exercise self-determination or autonomy in all that they do. Nor can we expect that students will be free to function as totally independent agents within the classroom, any more than teachers can be expected to actively instruct students who are unwilling to learn. Students and teachers must negotiate and compromise their personal agendas from time to time as members of the classroom community (Bandura, 1989). Yet, students and teachers can work at becoming sensitive to the opportunities for self-determination and agency that exist in their everyday learning environments. The justifications for seeking occasions for self-determination and agency include enhanced academic performance.

For example, in her research in social psychology, Amabile (1983, 1990) reported that more creative, positive outcomes result when even young learners feel that they have some autonomy or control in the learning process. For these individuals, doing a task for its own sake is what they find rewarding and stimulating. The mistaken step of offering some external reward for these children's participation in the initially self-rewarding task had the negative effect of diminishing its inherent value for them. Deci (Deci & Porac, 1978; Deci & Ryan, 1985; Deci, Valleran, Pelletier, & Ryan, 1991) came to a similar conclusion in his research on self-determination and agency.

In several recent studies, my colleagues and I have been faced with the reality that much of the process of learning from text truly remains within the individual's control (Alexander & Dochy, 1995; Alexander, Murphy, Guan, & Murphy, in press). That is, teachers may require students to read or "learn" about difficult, provocative, or counterintuitive concepts (e.g., principles of falling bodies or evolution of the species). However, teachers cannot make their students change their deeply held understandings or beliefs (Alexander, in press-a; Pintrich et al., 1993). The chapter by Hynd and Guzzetti (chapter 7, this volume) brings these challenges of conceptual change to the forefront.

As successful instructional programs (Bereiter & Scardamalia, 1989; Brown & Campione, 1990; Brown & Palincsar, 1989; Cognition and Technology Group at Vanderbilt, 1990) have shown, teachers can foster students' active, self-directed learning by creating meaningful and stimulating learning environments. These environments afford students the opportunity to define their academic goals, to pursue their interests, to experience self-determination, and to take responsibility for their learning (Corno & Rohrkemper, 1985; deCharms, 1968; Zimmerman & Martinez-Pons, 1986, 1992). Similarly constituted, the classroom environment can offer occasions for students to establish their own goals, initiate their own knowledge searches, or build their own interpretations as they read both exposition and narrative. Certainly, the act of learning from text can be an illuminating, if not an aesthetic, event when it is personally relevant, self-directed, and well constructed (Csikszentmihalyi, 1990).

## READING AS STRATEGIC PROCESSING

When the rich literature on learning strategies is examined it becomes clear that the role of strategies in learning has been significant to literacy researchers. Perhaps this is so because much of the early strategy research centered on text-based processing (Alexander & Murphy, in press), or perhaps it is because so many of the procedures fundamental to good reading are general cognitive and metacognitive strategies (Pressley, Borkowski, & Schneider, 1989). Still, one of the hallmarks of competent performance in any discipline or domain is the ability to function skillfully and strategically in that field. Yet, there are important similarities and differences between skills and strategies that deserve attention in this discussion, especially given the widespread use of these terms in educational materials.

First, among their similarities, both skills and strategies can be described as forms of procedural knowledge (Chi, 1985; Paris, Lipson, & Wixson, 1983; Ryle, 1949). That is, whether we are talking about step-by-step algorithms, such formulas in mathematics, or whether we are describing the rather general procedures or heuristics so common to reading and other literacy tasks, we are essentially dealing with "how to" (i.e., procedural) knowledge.

Second, the skills and strategies for acquiring, remembering, organizing, or transforming information, as well as the ability to monitor and regulate one's performance, are prerequisites for any level of competent performance in any academic field. This latter ability to self-monitor or self-regulate is a particular case of strategic processing that has been explored under such related labels as metacognition or executive control (Borkowski, Carr, & Pressley, 1987; Brown, Armbruster, & Baker, 1986; Garner, 1987; Garner & Alexander, 1989) and self-regulation (Schunk & Zimmerman, 1994; Winne, 1995; Zimmerman, 1989).

A third aspect that skills and strategies have in common is that they can vary in terms of their generality. That is, skills or strategies sometimes are broadly applied, meaning that the same skill or strategy can be used in many disciplines or domains (e.g., history or mathematics) or with very diverse tasks (e.g., analyzing historical documents or conducting a scientific experiment). In the literature, these broad-application procedures are referred to as general skills or strategies (Alexander & Judy, 1988; Glaser, 1984; Weinstein & Mayer, 1986). However, some of the procedures used in certain disciplines or domains do not have this wide "transportability." Instead, we find that these helpful procedures are greatly limited to only certain academic fields or even to particular learning tasks. We refer to this class of procedures as domain-specific or task-limited skills or strategies (Glaser, 1984; Pressley, Goodchild, Fleet, Zajchowski, & Evans, 1989).

My ability to parse a text segment into idea units or a young reader's ability to determine the meaning of a word from the surrounding context by using a particular heuristic represent likely instances of these domain-specific or task-limited strategies in literacy. In some cases, we see domain-specific or task-limited skills or strategies as particularized forms of general skills or strategies. For example, mnemonic strategies are highly versatile aids for remembering important content in many fields. In reading, one variation of this strategy is keyword mnemonics (Levin, 1981; Pressley, Levin, & Delaney, 1982), which is a procedure suggested for the recall of unfamiliar vocabulary. An even more limited use of the mnemonic strategy is the well-worn F-A-C-E, used to recall the spaces on the treble clef.

Despite their apparent similarities, however, there is at least one critical difference between skills and strategies that is frequently overlooked in discussions of these terms. This distinction pertains to *automaticity* or *intentionaltiy* of use on the learner's part (Alexander et al., 1991; Garner, 1987). In essence, skills are procedures that have been honed to a level of automaticity, resulting in fluid and efficient performance. For instance, skilled readers typically decode or reread segments of text without awareness that they are engaged in those activities. Under these typical circumstances, such cognitive procedures, which are basic to reading, are seamlessly performed without exacting much in the way of cognitive capacity. It makes sense, therefore, that one goal of literacy education is to maximize fluid performance by providing ample opportunities for students to develop these essential literacy skills.

These same cognitive procedures, however, take on a different character when readers encounter barriers to full or deep comprehension or are called on to perform an uncommon or nonroutine task. At such times, learners must consciously and with effort draw upon their repertoire of general and domain-specific procedures to bring the task to fruition. When this evocation occurs, we can say that the learner is engaged in *strategic processing*. Suppose our skilled reader comes across a particularly troublesome word that disrupts reading processing. He then consciously analyzes the sound–symbol relationships in the word and compares the resulting production against his available word corpus in hopes of discovering a match. Finding none, he (a) purposefully evaluates the importance of the word to overall understanding of the text segment, (b) ascertains its minor role in meaning-making, and then (c) moves on in his reading with the intention of (d) looking up the unknown word later. In this instance, our student recognized that his understanding was incomplete (i.e., self-monitoring) and drew upon his repertoire of cognitive strategies to assist his performance. Many other terms have been used in the literature to mark this kind of planful and effortful engagement including problem-solving, critical thinking, or reasoning (Bereiter & Scardamalia, 1989; Ennis, 1985, 1989; Nickerson, 1989).

In the research on strategic processing, we have recently moved beyond simple questions such as whether general or domain-specific strategies are more important in learning (Alexander & Judy, 1988; Alexander & Murphy, in press). Research energies now focus on more complex questions such as when, where, and for whom certain strategies are more effective for learning and development than others (Harris & Graham, 1996; Schoenfeld, 1988). For instance, it may be that the quantity and quality of strategy use changes as the student moves from acclimated or novice states of learning to more competent or expert levels in a given discipline or domain. The studies I have undertaken (Alexander & Judy, 1988; Alexander, Murphy, Woods, Duhon, & Parker, 1997), as well as the work of others (Hasselhorn & Körkel, 1986; McCutchen, 1986), support such a prediction.

Variations in strategic behavior have also been reported for readers when the task they are given is complex or novel (Baker & Brown, 1984; Schmeck, 1988). Further, researchers have determined that students' problem-solving efforts are enhanced when they are afforded a chance to discover or personalize strategies for themselves, or when they are part of a learning community in which strategic effort is recognized, supported, and rewarded (Ceci & Bronfenbrenner, 1985; McCombs, 1988; Paris & Winograd, 1990). Yet, as Garner (1990) noted, students often function in environments where the conditions leading to this discovery of, instruction about, or support for strategic learning are not readily apparent. For this reason, strategic processing deserves specific attention within instructional environments. However, it is important that such attention does not take the form of contrived or isolated strategy instruction. As Wagner and Sternberg (1984) determined in their review of thinking programs, such unnatural and disembodied treatment of strategies offers few long-term benefits for students.

Finally, there is a need to examine the relationship that apparently exists between strategic processing of text and motivation. It would appear that the defining characteristics for strategies (i.e., that they are intentionally and effortfully applied) make their association with motivation almost undeniable (Alexander & Murphy, in press; Pintrich et al., 1993; Wigfield & Eccles, 1992).

Still, at present, we understand far too little about what drives individuals to behave strategically and how learners come to choose one strategic path over another. Much more needs to be known about this intricate relationship between strategies and motivation.

## CONCLUDING THOUGHTS

My overarching goal in this chapter was to conclude this volume's exploration of learning from text in conceptual domains by considering two broad topics. First, I gave some thought to what it is that marks a field of study as a discipline or a domain. Related to this theme, I posed the question of whether literacy, and more particularly reading—as the fields to which learning from text pertains—represent disciplines or domains of knowledge. On the basis of analysis, it is my position that literacy and its subcomponent of reading are not only domains of knowledge, but also essential fields for achieving competence in other disciplines and domains. That is, without the keys needed to unlock the doors to knowledge found in the pages of subject-matter texts, it is unlikely that students will ever be able to enter the realm of competence in any discipline or domain. Instead, these students will remain the slaves to others' interpretations of what has been written, and they will never experience the exhilaration that can come from the pursuit of knowledge or the quest for expertise.

Second, I highlighted three dimensions of learning from text that I believe are necessary for those who hope to reach this state of competence in disciplines or domains: knowledge, interest, and strategic processing. In reading the other contributions to this volume, I saw evidence of these dimensions throughout. That is, there seems to be much agreement among researchers in text-based learning that students who construct a richer more coherent foundation of relevant knowledge, who possess a true interest in the subject at hand, and who come to the task of reading with a desire to learn and a sense of self-determination and agency in their learning are more likely those who will thrive on the journey toward competence. As guides on this journey, we must do all we can to understand the terrain that lies before these learners, and we must provide them with the support and the opportunities to make that journey as successful and fulfilling as possible. Surely, we will gain as much from this adventure as they.

## ACKNOWLEDGMENT

I thank P. Karen Murphy for her helpful suggestions on an earlier draft of this work. Send correspondence to Patricia A. Alexander, Department of Human Development, University of Maryland, College Park, MD 20742; e-mail, pa34@umail.umd.edu.

## REFERENCES

Alexander, P. A. (1992). Domain knowledge: Evolving themes and emerging concerns. *Educational Psychologist, 27*, 33–51.

Alexander, P. A. (1997a). Knowledge seeking and self-schema: A case for the motivational dimensions of exposition. *Educational Psychologist, 32*, 83–94.

Alexander, P. A. (1997b). Mapping the multidimensional nature of domain learning: The interplay of cognitive, motivational, and strategic forces. In M. L. Maehr & P. R. Pintrich (Eds.), *Advances in motivation and achievement* (Vol. 10, pp. 213–250). Greenwich, CT: JAI.

Alexander, P. A. (in press-a). Positioning conceptual change within a model of domain literacy. In B. Guzzetti & C. Hynd (Eds.), *Theoretical perspectives on conceptual change*. Mahwah, NJ: Lawrence Erlbaum Associates.

Alexander, P. A. (in press-b). Stages and phases of domain learning: The dynamics of subject-matter knowledge, strategy knowledge, and motivation. In C. E. Weinstein & B. L. McCombs (Eds.), *Skill, will, and self-regulation*. Mahwah, NJ: Lawrence Erlbaum Associates.

Alexander, P. A., & Dochy, F. J. R. C. (1995). Conceptions of knowledge and beliefs: A comparison across varying cultural and educational communities. *American Educational Research Journal, 32*, 413–442.

Alexander, P. A., & Jetton, T. L. (1996). The role of importance and interest in the processing of text. *Educational Psychology Review, 8*(1), 89–122.

Alexander, P. A., Jetton, T. L., & Kulikowich, J. M. (1995). Interrelationship of knowledge, interest, and recall: Assessing a model of domain learning. *Journal of Educational Psychology, 87*, 559–575.

Alexander, P. A., Jetton, T. L., Kulikowich, J. M., & Woehler, C. (1994). Contrasting instructional and structural importance: The seductive effect of teacher questions. *Journal of Reading Behavior, 26*, 19–45.

Alexander, P. A., & Judy, J. E. (1988). The interaction of domain-specific and strategic knowledge in academic performance. *Review of Educational Research, 58*, 375–404.

Alexander, P. A., & Knight, S. L. (1993). Dimensions of the interplay between learning and teaching. *Educational Forum, 57*, 232–245.

Alexander, P. A., & Kulikowich, J. M. (1991). Domain-specific and strategic knowledge as predictors of expository text comprehension. *Journal of Reading Behavior, 23*, 165–190.

Alexander, P. A., & Kulikowich, J. M. (1994). Learning from physics text: A synthesis of recent research. *Journal of Research in Science Teaching (Special Issue on Print Based Language Arts and Science Learning), 31*, 895–911.

Alexander, P. A., Kulikowich, J. M., & Jetton, T. L. (1994). The role of subject-matter knowledge and interest in the processing of linear and nonlinear texts. *Review of Educational Research, 64*, 201–252.

Alexander, P. A., Kulikowich, J. M., & Schulze, S. K. (1994a). How subject-matter knowledge affects recall and interest on the comprehension of scientific exposition. *American Educational Research Journal, 31*, 313–337.

Alexander, P. A., Kulikowich, J. M., & Schulze, S. K. (1994b). The influence of topic knowledge, domain knowledge, and interest on the comprehension of scientific exposition. *Learning and Individual Differences, 6*, 379–397.

Alexander, P. A., & Murphy, P. K. (in press). The research base for APA's learner-centered principles. In B. L. McCombs & N. Lambert (Eds.), *Issues in school reform: A sampler of psychological perspectives on learner-centered schools*. Washington, DC: The American Psychological Association.

Alexander, P. A., Murphy, P. K., Guan, J., & Murphy, P. A. (in press). How students and teachers in Singapore and the United States conceptualize knowledge and beliefs: Positioning learning within epistemological frameworks. *Learning and Instruction*.

Alexander, P. A., Murphy, P. K., & Woods, B. S. (1996). Of squalls and fathoms: Navigating the seas of educational innovation. *Educational Researcher, 25*(3), 31–36, 39.

Alexander, P. A., Murphy, P. K., Woods, B. S., Duhon, K. E., & Parker, D. (1997). College instruction and concomitant changes in students' knowledge, interest, and strategy use: A study of domain learning. *Contemporary Educational Psychology, 22,* 125–146.

Alexander, P. A., Pate, P. E., Kulikowich, J. M., Farrell, D. M., & Wright, N. L. (1989). Domain-specific and strategic knowledge: Effects of training on students of differing ages or competence levels. *Learning and Individual Differences, 1,* 283–325.

Alexander, P. A., Schallert, D. L., & Hare, V. C. (1991). Coming to terms: How researchers in learning and literacy talk about knowledge. *Review of Educational Research, 61,* 315–343.

Alexander, P. A., White, C. S., Haensly, P. A., & Crimmins-Jeanes, M. (1987). Training in analogical reasoning. *American Educational Research Journal, 24,* 387–404.

Amabile, T. M. (1983). *The social psychology of creativity.* New York: Springer-Verlag.

Amabile, T. M. (1990). With you, without you: The social psychology of creativity, and beyond. In M. A. Runco & R. S. Albert (Eds.), *Theories of creativity* (pp. 61–91). Newbury Park, CA: Sage.

Ames, C. (1992). Classrooms: Goals, structures, and student motivation. *Journal of Educational Psychology, 84,* 261–271.

Ames, C., & Ames, R. (Eds.). (1985). *Research on motivation in education: The classroom milieu* (Vol. 2). San Diego: Academic Press.

Ames, C., & Ames, R. (Eds.). (1989). *Research on motivation in education: The classroom milieu* (Vol. 3). San Diego: Academic Press.

Anderson, R. C., Pichert, J. W., & Shirey, L. L. (1983). Effects of reader's schema at different points in time. *Journal of Educational Psychology, 75,* 271–279.

Anderson, R. C., Reynolds, R. E., Schallert, D. L., & Goetz, E. T. (1977). Frameworks for comprehending discourse. *American Educational Research Journal, 14,* 367–381.

Baker, L., & Brown, A. L. (1984). Metacognitive skills of reading. In P. D. Pearson (Ed.), *Handbook of reading research* (pp. 353–394). New York: Longman.

Ball, D. L. (1993). With an eye on the mathematical horizon: Dilemmas of teaching elementary school mathematics. *Elementary School Journal, 93,* 373–397.

Bandura, A. (1989). Human agency in social cognitive theory. *American Psychologist, 44,* 1175–1184.

Bazerman, C. (1985). Physicists reading physics. *Written Communication, 2,* 3–23.

Beck, I. L., McKeown, M. G., & Gromoll, E. W. (1989). Learning from social studies texts. *Cognition and Instruction, 6,* 99–158.

Bereiter, C. (1994). Constructivism, socioculturalism, and Popper's World 3. *Educational Researcher, 23*(7), 21–23.

Bereiter, C., & Scardamalia, M. (1989). Intentional learning as a goal of instruction. In L. B. Resnick (Ed.), *Knowing, learning, and instruction: Essays in honor of Robert Glaser* (pp. 361–392). Hillsdale, NJ: Lawrence Erlbaum Associates.

Borkowski, J. G., Carr, M., & Pressley, M. (1987). "Spontaneous" strategy use: Perspectives from metacognitive theory. *Intelligence, 11,* 61–75.

Brent, A. (1978). *Philosophical foundations for the curriculum.* Boston: George Allen & Unwin.

Brown, A. L., Armbruster, B., & Baker, L. (1986). The role of metacognition in reading and studying. In J. Oransanu (Ed.), *Reading comprehension: From research to practice* (pp. 49–75). Hillsdale, NJ: Lawrence Erlbaum Associates.

Brown, A. L., & Campione, J. S. (1990). Communities of learning and thinking, or a context by any other name. *Contributions to Human Development, 21,* 108–126.

Brown, A. L., & Palincsar, A. S. (1989). Guided, cooperative learning and individual knowledge acquisition. In L. B. Resnick (Ed.), *Knowing, learning, and instruction: Essays in honor of Robert Glaser* (pp. 393–451). Hillsdale, NJ: Lawrence Erlbaum Associates.

Ceci, S. J., & Bronfenbrenner, U. (1985). "Don't forget to take the cupcakes out of the oven": Prospective, memory, strategic time-monitoring, and context. *Child Development, 56*, 152–164.

Chi, M. T. H. (1985). Interactive roles of knowledge and strategies in the development of organized sorting and recall. In S. F. Chipman, J. W. Segal, & R. Glaser (Eds.), *Thinking and learning skills: Research and open questions* (Vol. 2, pp. 457–483). Hillsdale, NJ: Lawrence Erlbaum Associates.

Chi, M. T. H., Glaser, R., & Farr, M. J. (1988). *The nature of expertise.* Hillsdale, NJ: Lawrence Erlbaum Associates.

Cognition and Technology Group at Vanderbilt. (1990). Anchored instruction and its relationship to situated cognition. *Educational Researcher, 19*(6), 2–10.

Connell, J. P. (1985). A new multidimensional measure of children's perceptions of control. *Child Development, 56*, 1018–1041.

Corno, L., & Rohrkemper, M. (1985). The intrinsic motivation to learn in classrooms. In C. Ames & R. Ames (Eds.), *Research on motivation in education: The classroom milieu* (Vol. 2, pp. 53–84). New York: Academic Press.

Csikszentmihalyi, M. (1990). *Flow: The psychology of optimal experience.* New York: Cambridge University Press.

deCharms, R. (1968). *Personal causation: The internal affective determinants of behavior.* New York: Academic Press.

Deci, E. L. (1992). The relation of interest to the motivation of behavior: A self-determination theory perspective. In K. A. Renninger, S. Hidi, & A. Krapp (Eds.), *The role of interest in learning and development* (pp. 43–70). Hillsdale, NJ: Lawrence Erlbaum Associates.

Deci, E. L., & Porac, J. (1978). Cognitive evaluation theory and the study of human motivation. In M. R. Lepper & D. Greene (Eds.), *The hidden costs of rewards: New perspectives on the psychology of human motivation* (pp. 149–176). Hillsdale, NJ: Lawrence Erlbaum Associates.

Deci, E. L., & Ryan, R. M. (1985). *Intrinsic motivation and self-determination in human behavior.* New York: Academic Press.

Deci, E. L., & Ryan, R. M. (1991). A motivational approach to self: Integration in personality. In R. Dienstbier (Ed.), *Nebraska symposium on motivation, 1990* (pp. 237–288). Lincoln, NE: University of Nebraska Press.

Deci, E. L., Valleran, R. J., Pelletier, L. G., & Ryan, R. M. (1991). Motivation and education: The self-determination perspective. *Educational Psychologist, 26*, 325–346.

Dewey, J. (1913). *Interest and effort in education.* Boston: Riverside.

Dweck, C. S., & Leggett, E. L. (1988). A social-cognitive approach to motivation and personality. *Psychology Review, 95*, 256–273.

Dworkin, G. (1988). *The theory and practice of autonomy.* New York: Cambridge University Press.

Ennis, R. H. (1985). Critical thinking and the curriculum. *National Forum, 65*(1), 28–31.

Ennis, R. H. (1989). Critical thinking and subject specificity: Clarification and needed research. *Educational Researcher, 18*(3), 4–10.

Foshay, A. W. (1962). Discipline-centered curriculum. In A. W. Passow (Ed.), *Curriculum cross-words* (pp. 66–71). New York: Teachers College Press.

Gagnon, P. (1989). *Historical literacy: The case for history in American education.* New York: Teachers College Press.

Gardner, H. (1991). *The unschooled mind.* New York: Basic Books.

Garner, R. (1987). *Metacognition and reading comprehension.* Norwood, NJ: Ablex.

Garner, R. (1990). When children and adults do not use learning strategies: Toward a theory of settings. *Review of Educational Research, 60*, 517–529.

Garner, R., & Alexander, P. A. (1989). Metacognition: Answered and unanswered questions. *Educational Psychologist, 24*, 143–148.

Garner, R., Alexander, P. A., Gillingham, M. G., Kulikowich, J. M., & Brown, R. (1991). Interest and learning from text. *American Educational Research Journal, 28,* 643–659.

Garner, R., Gillingham, M. G., & White, C. S. (1989). Effects of "seductive details" on macroprocessing and microprocessing in adults and children. *Cognition and Instruction, 6,* 41–57.

Glaser, R. (1984). Education and thinking: The role of knowledge. *American Psychologist, 39,* 93–104.

Guthrie, J. T., McGough, K., Bennett, L., & Rice, M. E. (1996). Concept-oriented reading instruction: An integrated curriculum to develop motivations and strategies for reading. In L. Baker, P. Afflerbach, & D. Reinking (Eds.), *Developing engaged readers in school and home community* (pp. 165–190). Mahwah, NJ: Lawrence Erlbaum Associates.

Harris, K. R., & Graham, S. (1996). *Making the writing process work: Strategies for composition and self-regulation.* Cambridge, MA: Brookline.

Hasselhorn, M., & Körkel, J. (1986). Metacognition versus traditional reading instruction: The mediating role of domain specific knowledge on children's text processing. *Human Learning, 5,* 79–90.

Hidi, S. (1990). Interest and its contribution as a mental resource for learning. *Review of Educational Research, 60,* 549–571.

Hirst, P. H. (1974). *Knowledge and the curriculum.* London: Routledge.

Hirst, P. H., & Peters, R. S. (1971). *The logic of education.* New York: Humanities Press.

James, W. (1890). *Principles of psychology* (Vols. 1 & 2). New York: Holt.

Jetton, T. L., & Alexander, P. A. (1997). Instructional importance: What teachers value and what students learn. *Reading Research Quarterly, 32,* 290–308.

Kintsch, W., & van Dijk, T. A. (1978). Toward a model of text comprehension and production. *Psychological Review, 85,* 363–394.

Levin, J. R. (1981). The mnemonic '80s: Keywords in the classroom. *Educational Psychology, 16,* 65–82.

Many, J. E., & Wiseman, D. L. (1992). The effect of teaching approach on third-grade students' response to literature. *Journal of Reading Behavior, 24,* 265–287.

Matthews, M. R. (1994). *Science teaching: The role of history and philosophy of science.* New York: Routledge.

Maurer, R. E. (1994). *Designing interdisciplinary curriculum in middle, junior high and high school.* Boston: Allyn & Bacon.

McCombs, B. L. (1988). Motivational skills training: Combining metacognitive, cognitive, and affective learning strategies. In C. E. Weinstein, E. T. Goetz, & P. A. Alexander (Eds.), *Learning and study strategies: Issues in assessment, instruction, and evaluation* (pp. 141–169). San Diego, CA: Academic Press.

McCutchen, D. (1986). Domain knowledge and linguistic knowledge in the development of writing ability. *Journal of Memory and Language, 25,* 431–444.

McGonagill, B. K. (1995). *Defining, developing, and modeling interdisciplinary curriculum.* Unpublished doctoral dissertation, Texas A&M University, College Station, TX.

Meece, J. L., & Holt, K. (1993). A pattern analysis of students' achievement goals. *Journal of Educational Psychology, 85,* 582–590.

Meyer, B. J. F. (1975). *The organization of prose and its effect on memory.* Amsterdam: North-Holland.

Mitchell, M. (1993). Situational interest: Its multifaceted structure in the secondary school mathematics classroom. *Journal of Educational Psychology, 85,* 424–436.

Nickerson, R. S. (1989). New directions in educational assessment. *Educational Researcher, 18*(9), 3–7.

Paris, S. G., Lipson, M. Y., Wixson, K. K. (1983). Becoming a strategic reader. *Contemporary Educational Psychology, 8,* 293–316.

Paris, S. G., & Winograd, P. (1990). Dimensions of thinking and cognitive instruction. In B. F. Jones & L. Idol (Eds.), *How metacognition can promote academic learning and instruction* (pp. 15–51). Hillsdale, NJ: Lawrence Erlbaum Associates.

Phenix, P. H. (1964a). *Realms of meaning: A philosophy of the curriculum for general education.* New York: McGraw-Hill.

Phenix, P. H. (1964b). The architectonics of knowledge. In S. Elam (Ed.), *Education and the structure of knowledge* (pp. 67–93). Chicago: Rand McNally.

Phenix, P. H. (1968). The use of disciplines as curriculum content. In F. L. Steeves (Ed.), *The subject of curriculum* (pp. 1–16). New York: Odyssey.

Phillips, D. C. (1987). *Philosophy, science, and social inquiry.* Oxford, England: Pergamon.

Phillips, D. C. (1995). The good, the bad, and the ugly: The many faces of constructivism. *Educational Researcher, 24*(7), 5–12.

Piaget, J. (1929). *The child's conception of the world.* Totowa, NJ: Littlefield, Adams.

Piaget, J. (1930). *The child's conception of physical causality.* New York: Harcourt, Brace.

Pintrich, P. R., Marx, R. W., & Boyle, R. A. (1993). Beyond cold conceptual change: The role of motivational beliefs and classroom contextual factors in the process of conceptual change. *Review of Educational Research, 63,* 167–199.

Pintrich, P. R., & Schrauben, B. (1992). Students' motivational beliefs and their cognitive engagement in classroom academic tasks. In D. Schunk & J. Meese (Eds.), *Student perceptions in the classroom* (pp. 149–183). Hillsdale, NJ: Lawrence Erlbaum Associates.

Popper, K. R. (1972). *Objective knowledge: An evolutionary approach.* Oxford, England: Clarendon.

Pressley, M., Borkowski, J., & Schneider, W. (1989). Good information processing: What is it and what education can do to promote it. *International Journal of Educational Research, 13,* 857–867.

Pressley, M., Goodchild, F., Fleet, J., Zajchowski, R., & Evans, E. D. (1989). The challenges of classroom strategy instruction. *Elementary School Journal, 89,* 301–342.

Pressley, M., & Levin, J. R., & Delaney, H. D. (1982). The keyword mnemonic method. *Review of Educational Research, 52,* 61–92.

Reynolds, R. E. (1992). Learning important information from text: The role of selective attention. *Review of Educational Psychology, 4,* 345–391.

Rosenblatt, L. M. (1978). *The reader, the text, the poem: The transactional theory of the literary work.* Carbondale, IL: Southern Illinois University Press.

Rosenblatt, L. M. (1995). *Literature as exploration.* New York: Modern Language Association. (Original work published in 1938)

Ryan, R. M. (1993). Agency and organization: Intrinsic motivation, autonomy, and the self in psychological development. In J. Jacobs (Ed.), *Nebraska symposium on motivation* (Vol. 40, pp. 1–56). Lincoln, NE: University of Nebraska Press.

Ryle, G. (1949). *The concept of mind.* London: Hutchinson.

Schellings, G. L. M., & van Hout-Wolters, B. H. A. M. (1995). Main points in an instructional text, as identified by students and their teachers. *Reading Research Quarterly, 30,* 742–756.

Schellings, G. L. M., van Hout-Wolters, B. H. A. M., & Vermunt, J. D. (1996). Selection of main points in instructional texts: Influences of task demands. *Journal of Literacy Research, 28,* 355–378.

Schiefele, U. (1991). Interest, learning, and motivation. *Educational Psychologist, 26,* 229–323.

Schmeck, R. R. (1988). Individual differences and learning strategies. In C. E. Weinstein, E. T. Goetz, & P. A. Alexander (Eds.), *Learning and study strategies: Issues in assessment, instruction, and evaluation* (pp. 171–188). San Diego: Academic Press.

Schoenfeld, A. H. (1988). When good teaching leads to bad results: The disasters of "well-taught" mathematics courses. *Educational Psychologist, 23,* 145–166.

Schraw, G. (1995, December). *Toward a model of situational interest in prose learning.* Paper presented at the annual meeting of the National Reading Conference, New Orleans, LA.

Schraw, G., Bruning, R., & Svoboda, C. (1995). Sources of situational interest. *Journal of Reading Behavior, 27*, 1–17.

Schraw, G., & Dennison, R. S. (1994). The effect of reader purpose on interest and recall. *Journal of Reading Behavior, 26*, 1–18.

Schunk, D. H., & Zimmerman, B. J. (1994). *Self-regulation of learning and performance.* Hillsdale, NJ: Lawrence Erlbaum Associates.

Schwab, J. J. (1964). Structure of the disciplines: Meanings and significances. In G. W. Ford & L. Pugno (Eds.), *The structure of knowledge and the curriculum* (pp. 6–30). Chicago: Rand McNally.

Spiro, R. J., Coulson, R. L., Feltovich, P. J., & Anderson, D. K. (1994). Cognitive flexibility theory: Advance knowledge acquisition in ill-structured domains. In R. B. Ruddell, M. R. Ruddell, & H. Singer (Eds.), *Theoretical models and processes of reading* (pp. 602–615). Newark, DE: International Reading Association.

Spiro, R. J., Feltovich, P. J., Jacobson, M. J., & Coulson, R. L. (1992). Cognitive flexibility, constructivism, and hypertext: Random access instruction for advanced instruction for advance knowledge acquisition in ill-structured domains. In T. M. Duffy & D. H. Jonassen (Eds.), *Constructivism and the technology of instruction* (pp. 57–75). Cambridge, England: Cambridge University Press.

Spiro, R. J., & Jehng, J. C. (1990). Cognitive flexibility and hypertext: Theory and technology for the nonlinear and multidimensional traversal of complex subject matter. In D. Nix & R. J. Spiro (Eds.), *Cognition, education, and multimedia* (pp. 163–205). Hillsdale, NJ: Lawrence Erlbaum Associates.

Stahl, S. A., Hynd, C. R., Glynn, S. M., & Carr, M. (1996). Beyond reading to learn: Developing content and disciplinary knowledge through texts. In L. Baker, P. Afflerbach, & D. Reinking (Eds.), *Developing engaged readers in school and home community* (pp. 139–163). Mahwah, NJ: Lawrence Erlbaum Associates.

Stanovich, K. E. (1986). Matthew effects in reading: Some consequences of individual differences in the acquisition of literacy. *Reading Research Quarterly, 21*, 360–407.

Taylor, B. M., & Beach, R. W. (1984). The effects of text structure instruction on middle-grade students' comprehension and production of expository text. *Reading Research Quarterly, 19*, 134–146.

VanSledright, B. A. (1996). Closing the gap between school and disciplinary history? Historian as high school history teacher. In J. Brophy (Ed.), *Advances in research on teaching* (Vol. 6, pp. 257–289). Greenwich, CT: JAI.

von Glaserfeld, E. (1991). *Radical constructivism in mathematics education.* Dordrecht, Netherlands: Kluwer.

Vygotsky, L. (1986). *Thought and language* (A. Kozulin, Trans.). Cambridge, MA: MIT Press. (Original work published in 1934)

Wade, S. E. (1992). How interest affects learning from text. In K. A. Renninger, S. Hidi, & A. Krapp (Eds.), *The role of interest in learning and development* (pp. 255–277). Hillsdale, NJ: Lawrence Erlbaum Associates.

Wade, S. E., & Adams, R. B. (1990). Effects of importance and interest on recall of biographical text. *Journal of Reading Behavior, 4*, 331–351.

Wade, S. E., Schraw, G., Buxton, W. M., & Hayes, M. T. (1993). Seduction of the strategic reader: Effects of interest on strategies and recall. *Reading Research Quarterly, 28*, 93–114.

Wagner, R. K., & Sternberg, R. J. (1984). Alternative conceptions of intelligence and their implications for education. *Review of Educational Research, 54*, 179–223.

Walker, C. H. (1989). Relative importance of domain knowledge and overall aptitude on acquisition of domain-related information. *Cognition and Instruction, 4*, 25–42.

Weinstein, C. E., & Mayer, R. E. (1986). The teaching of learning strategies. In M. C. Wittrock (Ed.), *Handbook of research on teaching* (3rd ed., pp. 315–327). New York: Macmillan.

West, L. H. T., & Pines, A. L. (1985). *Cognitive structures and conceptual change.* New York: Academic Press.

Whitehead, A. N. (1957). *The aims of education and other essays.* New York: Macmillan. (Original work published in 1929)

Wigfield, A., & Eccles, J. (1992). The development of achievement task values: A theoretical analysis. *Developmental Review, 12,* 265–310.

Wilson, S., & Sykes, G. (1989). Toward better teacher preparation and certification. In P. Gagnon (Ed.), *Historical literacy: The case for history in American education* (pp. 268–286). New York: Teachers College Press.

Winne, P. H. (1995). Inherent details in self-regulated learning. *Educational Psychologist, 30,* 173–187.

Zimmerman, B. J. (1989). A social cognitive view of self-regulated academic learning. *Journal of Educational Psychology, 81,* 329–339.

Zimmerman, B. J., & Martinez-Pons, M. (1986). Development of a structured interview for assessing student use of self-regulated learning strategies. *American Educational Research Journal, 23,* 614–628.

Zimmerman, B. J., & Martinez-Pons, M. (1992). Perceptions of efficacy and strategy use in the self-regulation of learning. In D. H. Schunk & J. L. Meece (Eds.), *Student perceptions in the classroom* (pp. 185–207). Hillsdale, NJ: Lawrence Erlbaum Associates.

# AUTHOR INDEX

# SUBJECT INDEX

## A

Acclimation, 24
Accommodation, 21, 26–30, 143–145
Accretion, 27
Active processing, 85–86
Adaptation, literacy as, 215, 217, 218
Affective dimensions, *see also* Motivation
    of conceptual change, 146–149
    of learning, 21–23
Analogies
    definition, 196
    effectiveness, 198–199, 271
    as explanatory tools, 193–195
    guidelines, 196
    in integrated curriculum, 193
    Learning-With-Analogies Model, 205
    misconceptions caused by, 199
    research on, 200–205
    in science texts, 194–195, 197–198, 204
    students' analogies, 202–203, 205–206
    Teaching-With-Analogies Model, 193, 195, 199–200
    text learning, role of, 196, 197–198
    text retention, role of, 203–204
Aspects program, 179–180
Assimilation, 21, 26
Association processing, 85–86
Attributional beliefs, 49–52
Audio and visual media, 169–170
Authentic tasks, 64
Automaticity, 278
Autonomy, 275–277
Avoidance goals, 275

## B

Beliefs, *see* Epistemology
*Benchmarks for Science Literacy*, 227

## C

Charts and graphs, 255
Cognitive constructivism, 19
Collaboration, electronic environments, 179–181
Composition texts, 220
Comprehension, 95–115,
    relations with vocabulary, 73–76, 90–91
Comprehension processing, 86
Computer-based mapping, 185–186
Computer-based outlining, 167–168, 177–179, 185–186
Computers, *see* Electronic text
Concept mapping, 196
Conceptual change, 26–30, 139–161,156–157
    *see also* Learning; Motivation
    accretion, 27
    affective dimensions, 146–149
    cognitive dimensions, 143–145
    conditions for, 27–28, 144–145
    discovery learning in, 149–150
    discussion, 150–151, 157–158
    epistemology, relation to, 157
    gender, 157
    in history, 159–160
    instructional components, 149–158
    intrinsic interest in, 148, 156

# THE PREVENTION

# AND CONTROL

# OF DELINQUENCY

# THE PREVENTION
# AND CONTROL
# OF DELINQUENCY

*Robert M. MacIver*

**AldineTransaction**
*A Division of Transaction Publishers*
New Brunswick (U.S.A.) and London (U.K.)

Library of Congress Catalog Number: 2007025975
ISBN: 978-0-202-36160-4
Printed in the United States of America

Library of Congress Cataloging-in-Publication Data

MacIver, Robert M. (Robert Morrison), 1882-1970.
    The prevention and control of delinquency / Robert M. MacIver.
        p. cm.
    Includes bibliographical references and index.
    Originally published: New York: Atherton Press, 1966.
    ISBN 978-0-202-36160-4
        1. Juvenile delinquency—Prevention. I. Title.

HV9069.M263 2007
364.36—dc22

2007025975

# *Preface*

Having been engaged for nearly six years in a close-up study of the agencies in New York City concerned with juvenile delinquency—police, courts, departments of correction, health, welfare, supervising bodies including the Youth Board, detention houses, public and private custodial institutions, settlements, special schools and educational programs, charitable organizations, research agencies—I came to the conclusion that much of this great system of services was ineffectual in coping with a growing and perplexing problem. There were some admirable "residential treatment centers," some well-organized departments, and some devoted workers, but there was a lack of overall strategy, a failure to get down to the roots of the problem. This was broadly the conclusion arrived at by my research colleagues, too, while I was directing the City of New York Juvenile Delinquency Research Project. We made a considerable number of specific recommendations, some of which were acted upon. On the whole there have been some welcome developments recently, not only in the area we studied but also in other areas across the country. There is still, however, a great need for the application of the knowledge we now possess as a guide to an inclusive strategy of delinquency control.

I was therefore happy to welcome the opportunity presented by a grant from the National Institute of Mental Health to undertake a broader study, seeking to provide a perspective on the problem as a whole, the conditions under which delinquency occurs more frequently and less frequently, the groups most affected by it, the causes to which the higher and lower incidence are attributed, and the consequent strategy that research and experience have shown to be most effective in dealing with it. I appreciate the courtesy of N.I.M.H., which readily permitted me to postpone my work and finish it in installments when important obligations of another kind made it difficult or impossible for me to carry on as I had originally agreed. My grateful acknowledgment is also owed Miss Jeanette Gevov, who had been a researcher during my work for New York City and who did effective work as my assistant by collecting, organizing, and preparing reports on recent developments across the country in the areas covered in Part Three of this study.

I have not sought to give an exhaustive or detailed account of the numerous developments discussed in Part Three. This book is intended to state a problem and its setting so as to derive from this analysis directions for effective action in the various areas and various stages and types of delinquent behavior. It gives a concrete description of the more important devices and experiments that are now being developed and practiced. It should therefore be serviceable to organizational leaders and workers, to educators and planners active in this field, and generally to students in the social sciences.

*Robert M. MacIver*

# Contents

# Part One

## THE ASSOCIATED

## CONDITIONS

# 1

# *The Statistical Picture*

In this study we offer a perspective on juvenile delinquency as it has developed in this country and seek to show how our present knowledge bears on the question of its prevention and control. There is an extensive literature on the subject, the most significant contributions being scattered through various learned and professional journals and government reports. Many variant or conflicting explanations are put forward to account for the continuing increase in the amount of delinquency as measured by statistical indices, and more than a few divergent proposals are made as an answer to the problem. Many agencies, both public and private, are directing their energies and contributing considerable sums of money to remedial methods. Nevertheless, there are no significant indications of any general improvement. In this writer's experience, much of the official treatment of delinquents is still little affected by the findings of the research that has been devoted to the subject.

The statistical record is certainly alarming. Practically every year it shows a further increase in the proportion of delinquency. In the United States between 1948 and 1957 juvenile court cases more than doubled, whereas the youth population ten through seventeen years increased during the period by only 27 per cent. Between 1940 and 1961 court cases increased 400 per cent. The phenomenon is by no means peculiar to the United States. In Britain in 1962 delinquency was statistically twice as high for boys and three times as high for girls as it was before the First World War.[1] Western Germany reports an increase of 39.2 per cent in "convicted juveniles" fourteen to eighteen years old between 1951 and 1957, Eastern Germany an increase of juvenile offenses of 96.3 per cent for the same period.[2] Austria reports an increase of 68 per cent in "convicted juveniles" fourteen to eighteen years old between 1951 and 1956. Finland shows an increase of 61.7 per cent in its juvenile offenders fifteen to seventeen years old. Sweden reports between 1950 and 1956 an increase of 210 per cent of juveniles under fifteen years "suspected of criminal behavior." Switzerland shows an increase in the various cantons.

Public concern has been aroused particularly by the headlines reporting gang "rumbles," stabbings, shootings, and vandalism. It is impossible to derive any precise measurement of the volume of delinquency or of the actual increase that may have occurred. The various indices we employ—police arrests, court appearances, juvenile delinquency adjudications, institutional commitments—are all affected by changes in socioeconomic conditions, by the number of delinquency petitions from non-police sources, by the available space in the institutions to which delinquents are committed, by changes in methods of reporting cases, by changes in the number and in the character of juvenile courts, by developments in the voluntary welfare agencies, and even by the degree of public concern over the amount of juvenile delinquency.

The statistics are nevertheless significant as probable indicators of a trend. If arrests of juveniles in New York City more than tripled between 1950 and 1959, it is reasonable to conclude that some of the increase in the amount of delinquency is real, not merely statistical. A Children's Bureau report calculates that as many as 12 per cent of all juveniles have been cited at least once for court appearance between their tenth and seventeenth birthdays. And we must bear in mind that much delinquent behavior escapes the notice of the authorities.[3]

A clear indication that the volume of delinquency has definitely increased over recent years is that really serious offenses, assaults on the person, shootings, stabbings, and other felonies, have grown roughly in proportion to the number of minor offenses. Such offenses are less likely to be unreported, negotiated out of court, or ignored because of influence or otherwise. We must therefore conclude that conditions in our society, conditions bearing especially on the morale of our youth, have increased the tendencies to delinquent behavior. It is true that adult crimes have also increased at least as much. This fact has an important relation to youthful crime, but one comment must suffice here. When delinquency becomes habitual in a significant proportion of the young, it can be inferred that many of these young persons will graduate into adult criminality. On any accounting the situation is grievous and calls not simply for greater efforts and larger expenditures by our agencies, public and private, but even more, as we hope to show, for the development of a concerted strategy, based on the experience we have gained and on the findings of research.

Apart from those we have suggested, there is yet another reason why we must depend on broad estimates rather than on accurate measurements to assess changes in the volume of juvenile delinquency. Delinquency is a category that includes a large assortment of behavings, ranging from the merest pranks of high-spirited or adventurous youngsters to wanton crimes. It contains certain activities that are not legal offenses for adults: truancy, running away from home, insubordination to parents, endangering the health or morals of oneself or others (at least as this phrase is sometimes interpreted). Obviously so vaguely inclusive a category admits a great deal of discretion in the designation of youths as delinquent; according to the attitude of officials and the temper of the public the recorded amount of delinquency may fall or rise apart from any intrinsic change in the behavior of the young. Another important factor is the increase in traffic offenses, many of which consist in temporary "borrowing" of cars or motorcycles, illicit use of cars, and so forth. In the United States in 1961, traffic offenses constituted 27 per cent of all juvenile court cases.

Most youngsters at some time commit acts that can legally be designated delinquent. It is essential therefore to distinguish between the sporadic mischievousness of the young and the growing habit of delinquent behavior. Judges have the responsibility of making this distinction before they designate a youth as delinquent. They should also possess the capacity to diagnose the different types of delinquent behavior, though with crowded court calendars and the lack of training of some judges, this desideratum is too frequently lacking.

Skill in diagnosis is important at every stage in dealing with delinquency, which is by no means a simple or uniform malady. Various types are differently evoked, differently developed, and call for different approaches to treatment. It is no more possible to prescribe the same treatment for the different problems of delinquent youth than it is for different diseases. Without careful diagnosis we cannot hope to provide effective treatment or give the requisite aid and guidance. In our study of delinquency in New York City we were constantly impressed by the need for more careful screening before treatment. During that period (1958–1961) we found screening to be inadequate on all levels: by the police in their discretion to arrest, or to warn the offender and his parents, or to refer the case to an appropriate agency; by the courts in the process of adjudication and of disposition; by the probation division in the manner in which its members attempted to deal with their cases; by the institutions to which more serious offenders were committed; by the schools in their guidance and referral services, and also in their relegation of troublesome children to special schools or special classes; and by the welfare institutions in their programs of individual guidance and group therapy.[4]

If we are to control juvenile delinquency and redirect misguided youths we need a better understanding of their troubles and their responses to them. We need, in a word, an informed, concerted, and well-directed strategy. A main purpose of our study is to reveal this need and to offer suggestions for such a strategy.

# 2

## High-Delinquency and Low-Delinquency Areas

There is delinquency in all areas. It is always a question of degree. Charts and maps for New York City prepared under the writer's direction showed an irregular gradation in the number of delinquency cases between the highest and the lowest ranking areas. The gradation might well be more regular and less steep were it not for the advantage the better areas have in keeping their errant children from police notice, and from arrest when they are noticed.

Even in the finest residential areas we have occasional reports of wanton damage and riotous behavior by rampaging youth. A flagrant case followed a debutante party in Southampton, Long Island, on August 31 and September 1, 1963, when a mob of youths broke into a nearby beach house and proceeded to break things up, smashing windows and causing considerable destruction within the house. Four of the twenty or so youths involved were tried for vandalism, and acquitted. In 1965 a party of three hundred youths was invaded by the police as they were celebrating in an old house on the outskirts of the fashionable resort of East Hampton, and a number of them were held on charges varying from disorderly conduct to the possession or sale of narcotics. The Westchester Council of Social Agencies made a study of juvenile delinquency in some commuting areas and found the rates alarmingly high. A similar report comes from a commuter town in Connecticut. Obviously our official statistics present us with a somewhat one-sided picture of the situation. Since well-to-do parents are able and usually ready to make monetary reparation for vandalism and destruction by their children, such acts are likely to escape the courts.

Conditions in areas of relatively lower delinquency but in which there has also been some increase in delinquency, present a different problem from high-delinquency areas. In the latter we reasonably infer that the differential conditions, say, between high- and low-delinquency areas of a great city not only are correlated with the volume of delinquency but also are causally related to it. This conclusion will be pointed up in Part Two of this study. In areas of low delinquency the difference between present figures and the lower ones of earlier years is susceptible of several different explanations.

In the first place, it may be due to changes occurring specifically in the affected areas. Take, for example, the increase of delinquency in small towns. We could consider the impact of an increase of mobility, or of the stronger influence of big-city culture through television and other media of communication. The cultural urbanization of rural and small-town life might diminish the distinctive morality formerly bred in these latter areas, especially among the young. We would expect then that the towns in the hinterland of great cities would be more affected, and if a study of the relative increase in delinquency in the nearer and the more distant regions supported that conclusion the evidence would be important. We do not, however, know of any such study.

In the second place, the increase in delinquency in relatively low delinquency areas might be distributed very unequally and thus be attributable to special factors in the areas of greater increase. It is conceivable, for example, that commuter areas may have a higher tendency to juvenile delinquency, because of the father's absence from home during the whole day and sometimes the evening, or because of factors related to this mode of living. On the other hand, there is certainly evidence that some ethnic groups, especially where they are somewhat insulated by a thoroughly inculcated religious orthodoxy, tend to have lower delinquency rates while others have relatively high ones, so that the ethnic composition of an area would make a difference in the statistics.

In the third place, the relative increase shown in areas of lower delinquency may be due to the changing temper of the times everywhere. This interpretation would find a common ground for the over-all increase in juvenile delinquency in so many countries besides our own. For uncounted millions the decencies and usages of civil life were, during a long period of strain and anxiety, suspended and exchanged for the ugly necessities of killing and ravage. It was not to be expected that when that period ended people would resume their former modes of life and social attitudes. The experience of an age of unparalleled violence left its legacy of unrest, unbalance, and the confusion of morals. People were habituated to the lawlessness that goes with violence, and this has been reflected in the emphasis on violence presented through the media of mass communications—television, the movies, and the comics. The elders who have taken part in or lived through warfare are affected by their experience and this in turn is communicated to their children. Today we are confronted with the danger of another great war, which this time would obliterate total populations and destroy the civilization mankind has built through the ages. In such an atmosphere the sense of social cohesion is loosened, family ties are weakened, there is a general lowering of regard for spiritual and religious values. Crime increases, and juvenile delinquency climbs to new summits.

This type of explanation, with its various overtones, would not override the more special considerations that may account for the higher delinquency in areas subjected to particular pressures or disabilities, but it would, it is claimed, account for the over-all increase in every type of area. In Part Three we shall endeavor to sum up the case for this approach to the problem of causation.

Meanwhile we point out that not only in our high-delinquency areas but in all kinds of environments there occur the conjunctions of conditions that evoke or develop the more deep-seated maladjustments of youth. We have suggested that the volume of delinquency among upper-class youth is relatively greater than the statistics indicate—not only because the delinquency is more easily concealed and more frequently compounded, but also because the greater resources of the offenders can direct it into channels that do not directly bring it under the control of the law.

High delinquency occurs in areas of squalor and sheer poverty, with all the concomitants we have been indicating. If more delinquency is bred there, it is because all the young people in such areas are subjected to adverse conditions under which many of them are unable to accommodate themselves to lawful ways. In more favored areas many children find this accommodation relatively easy, but others, through a combination of unfortunate upbringing with a mental make-up that yields to the resulting vexations and disturbances, become no less maladjusted than those children of the slums. Two factors may be singled out as particularly important in conducing to delinquency in middle-class areas. One, which may be found in all areas, is the lack of home guidance or wise discipline—whether the failure be due to harsh treatment, the "spoiling" of the child because of inadequate restraint on wayward tendencies, neglect, or lack of affection. The importance of this factor has been brought out in many studies, and most notably by the Gluecks,[1] though their stress on it may not allow sufficiently for the environmental pressures that tend to disrupt family relationships. This subject will be examined more fully in a later section.

The other factor that looms up most significantly in middle-class areas is the pressure of the operative social code on resistant youth. By the operative code we mean the prescriptions inculcated by the values that rule everyday life. We distinguish it from the formal code of morality that prescribes the general rules of right behavior. The latter code is accepted, taught, and preached—and practiced within the limits of social decency. But it is the operative code that prescribes the strategy of living and tends to be followed even when it involves infractions of the formal moral code. Public pronouncements and exhortations to follow the formal code seem to be discounted compared with the inside pressures toward pursuit of the values of the operative code.[2] Foremost among these values, at least in the average middle-class circle, is the estimation of success, success in making good in business, in a career, in the more lucrative professions, in the process of "rising in the world."

There are always, however, deviant youths, who want to go their own way, perhaps to devote themselves to such unlucrative pursuits as art or music or drama, or who deride the cherished values of the business world, or who drift into becoming "playboys." Sometimes in these situations the tensions arising in the home are heightened by neurotic or temperamental tendencies in the youth, who may then resort to delinquent habits.

The young people of middle-class or upper-class neighborhoods are no more immune than those of the slums from the behavior problems or psychic disturbances that may result in confirmed delinquency, especially when they do not receive the wise guidance and skilled treatment that might redirect their aggressiveness or waywardness into more constructive activities. Well-to-do parents, no less than poor parents, may fail to understand their children's problems. In many instances, perhaps particularly with the commuting class, they see less of their children than do slum parents. Some crucial situation, such as an unfortunate sexual experience or a school failure or a foolish debt incurred by the youth, may trigger the fatal collision between parent and child that ends in the latter's dedication to rebelliousness and the total rejection of authority. Occasionally the press reports a serious crime committed by a youth—or youths—who seemed to have every advantage of fortune, revealing a glimpse of some deep disorder beneath the surface. The most famous of such cases was that of Leopold and Loeb, who out of prurient curiosity and unmitigated sadism murdered a child. With every gift of position and intelligence these two had escaped the discipline and lacked the guidance that might have averted the tragedy.

There is no class distinction in the need for watchful guidance in a spirit of affection. The crucial situation that marks the parting of the ways between an honorable or a delinquent career occurs in every environment. We were impressed a number of years ago by a report on a confirmed delinquent who had been a handsome and happy youngster, well-behaved and successful at school. In an accident at play the point of a knife pierced an eye, and the resulting disfigurement preyed on his feelings so that he became morose and withdrawn, lost interest in his work and play, and ended as an adjudged delinquent. One could but surmise what a difference it might have made if some sympathetic and understanding counselor had been with him through the time of crisis.

### High Delinquency Areas—
### The Complex of Residence and Residents

A considerable amount of research has been devoted to the conditions associated with delinquency, both the conditions under which individual cases occur and those of areas in which the volume of delinquency is high or above average. Since individual cases are excessively variant and often quite complex, we shall consider at this stage the latter line of inquiry, especially as it throws considerable light on the former.

There is everywhere a marked disparity between the amount of juvenile delinquency recorded in the various areas of cities, and the highest volume is nearly always found in the poorest sectors. This fact raises two preliminary questions. In the first place, every area combines two major constituents: the physical environment itself, with its housing conditions, its amenities or lack thereof, its higher or lower rental values, and so forth; and also the demographic aspect—the characteristics of the groups who inhabit it, their wealth or poverty, their social status, their ethnic derivation, and so on. Should we then attribute the higher or lower delinquency rates to one or to the other of these factors, or again to the combination of the two? Has either factor priority over the other as an explanation of the delinquency level?

Different answers have been given. We shall pay special attention to these questions in Part Two, when we face the problem of causation.

In the second place, we must ask whether the statistical disparity itself is a genuine index of the relative volume of delinquency in the higher delinquency areas, or is it at least in part a reflection of the greater risk of detection and police arrest and partially also of the treatment and process of adjudication after arrest? There is no doubt that the chances of detection are greater in poor areas where the playground is usually the street and the meeting place the street corner or the candy store. Chances of arrest are greater where parents are not influential, where the youth may be subject to police discrimination (so many in the poorer areas today are Puerto Ricans or Negroes), where he has no one to plead his case in court, or, since most juvenile cases are conducted without legal defense, has parents who are unable to present an effective argument on his behalf. We must therefore discount any pretension that the statistical disparity is a true differential of the actual amounts of delinquency prevalent in slum areas and in well-to-do areas respectively. It must be remembered again that quite a considerable volume of delinquency everywhere escapes police notice, and the chance of escaping is better in the more secluded retreats of well-to-do youngsters.

Nevertheless, the actual preponderance of juvenile delinquency in low-income neighborhoods is well confirmed by various studies. We take as example a recent study by Reiss and Rhodes.[3] They took a base population of 9,238 white boys aged twelve and over, registered during the 1957 school year in a public, a private, and a parochial school of Davidson County, Tennessee. A delinquent was identified as a boy adjudged delinquent before the Davidson County Juvenile Court. The study showed that the delinquency rate increased as one moved down the line from high to low IQ and from "white collar" to "blue collar" occupations. The disparity is greater for serious than for petty offenses, and considerably greater also for truancy, so often associated with delinquent tendencies. It is a reasonable assumption that under any conditions the more serious offenses are less likely to be overlooked or condoned than the petty ones. The only charge for which the "white collar" rate was higher than the "blue collar" was traffic offenses, for pretty obvious reasons. Another significant fact brought out by the Reiss-Rhodes study is that "the delinquency life-chances of *all* status groups tend to be greatest in the lower-status area and in the high-delinquency areas."

Incidentally, as these authors point out, the evidence just cited is adverse to the theory that juvenile delinquency of the more pronounced sort is a factor or an aspect of "lower-class morality" or "lower-class culture," whether as spontaneously bred within it, or as due to the ineffective effort of lower-class youth to live up to "middle-class norms"—conclusions with which we shall be concerned in a latter part of this study.

Everywhere, seemingly, there is more recorded delinquency in the lower-class areas, but this again is too broad and heterogeneous a bracketing to serve our inquiry. Further analysis shows that high incidence is concentrated in particular localities or pockets of the large city, while some lower-class areas show about average delinquency, and a few distinctly less than average. In certain higher-status areas, including some newer suburbs of great cities, delinquency is well above average for that type of area. What therefore is significant is not the broad attribution of greater delinquency to lower-class areas as such but the discovery of the delinquency-breeding conditions characterizing areas where delinquency is most rife.

The pockets of high delinquency within a larger urban area offer us an important approach to the study and understanding of youthful delinquency as a whole. The disparity between the rates for these areas and for others is usually sustained over long periods, in spite of the mobility of their populations. It would therefore seem reasonable to assume that the differential response of youth to the conditions existing within these areas is due, at least in part, to the impact of these conditions on their attitudes, habits, and aspirations. However, the populations of the high-delinquency areas are characteristically groups of in-migrants coming from backgrounds very different from that of the city, and the evidence we possess indicates that in their previous environments the young people did not exhibit any comparable tendency to delinquency. A study of the activities of delinquency-prone youth in high-delinquency areas may thus throw some light on the state of mind that, even though evoked under very different conditions, leads young persons elsewhere to be defiant of authority and disposed to resort to illegal ways.

When we seek to understand the disparity between high-delinquency and low-delinquency areas we must realize that the social pathology indicated by high delinquency is one aspect of a vital situation characterized not only by squalid and congested living conditions but also by other sociopathological features. The public has been too much disposed to regard juvenile delinquency as a gratuitous expression of youthful wrongdoing, something to be corrected simply by more discipline, more severe penalties, more vigorous action by the police and the courts. When, however, we appreciate the manner in which the high-delinquency areas are correlated to various other social evils that obviously call for a different approach, we should see how deeply such delinquency is rooted in a matrix of serious social maladjustment affecting youths and adults alike. Even less helpful is the occasional demand that the parents be penalized for the offenses of their offspring. Clearly something more fundamental than "mere correction" is necessary, even if we still attach some importance to that mode of treatment.

## Sociopathological Concomitants

Evidence from many sources indicates an association between high delinquency and other social maladies, but we shall here concentrate on the results of an intensive study in the City of New York made by its Juvenile Delinquency Evaluation Project under the direction of the writer.[4] We compared the delinquency rates of the thirty health center areas of the City with a series of indices of health disabilities and related conditions, and with another series for economic disabilities. We had thus nine variables in all, as follows: admissions to New York State mental hospitals, terminations of psychiatric clinic cases, active tuberculosis cases, infant mortality, out-of-wedlock live births, public assistance cases (all relief cases coming under the New York City Welfare Department), aid to dependent children (Federal-State programs to aid widowed or divorced mothers), home-relief cases (a State-City relief program for cases that do not qualify under the standard categories of the Federal program), together with a composite Health Department Index combining four categories; cases of children for whom no dental care was reported, relative prevalence of tuberculosis, percentage of total births to ward patients who had no private physician, and gonorrhea cases.

The outstanding fact was that delinquency rates showed throughout a remarkable concomitant variation with our nine other indices. There were minor exceptions and discrepancies. The indices for admissions to mental-health hospitals and for termination of psychiatric clinic cases showed some spotty non-conformities with the other seven indices; a few areas showed higher ratings for delinquency than for most of the other variables. But the trend to co-variation between delinquency and all other indices was significant, and the three areas that headed the delinquency index were at or near the top of all the other indices.

Evidently we have here a vicious circle of troubles. Morbidity in all its forms is somehow associated with high delinquency, though we cannot yet assume any direct causal relationships, and delinquency in turn is closely associated with other socio-psychological phenomena. We have then the alternative hypotheses that the initiation of the vicious circle lies in one or in the combination of, say, two, of the associated factors, or else that behind them all there is some fundamental condition that is the prime mover of the whole series. Once set going, the vicious circle may sustain itself by mutual interactions, with the continued support of the fundamental condition itself. We may look for the fundamental condition in the slum environment occupied by the people suffering from these evils. Certainly high-delinquency areas are almost invariably slum areas, areas of excessive populational congestion, characterized by a substantial percentage of dilapidated dwelling units, uncared-for and deteriorating, in official terms "substandard and insanitary," and lacking in park and playground facilities, where nothing but abject poverty meets the eye.

This hypothesis receives considerable support when we examine, as we shall proceed to do, the manner in which this type of slum environment creates, under the comparative stresses of American society, extremely difficult problems for the young people reared within it. Such an environment is a serious handicap, thrusting back and then dulling the aspirations initially stimulated by the mores of more prosperous neighborhoods around them.

## The Physical Environment and the Group Culture

Important as the impact of the physical environment is, it offers no adequate explanation of the social phenomenon appearing within it. A Chicago school of sociologists used to point out that successive groups of immigrants, of different background and ethnic origin, exhibited a similar tendency to relatively high delinquency when they occupied in turn the same physically deteriorating areas of the city—the "zones of transition" where industrial invasion disrupted residential neighborhoods. It must be remembered, however, that these successive groups have usually been disprivileged and rather destitute entrants, unused to the life and ways of the large city, subject to exploitation, disorganized, and exposed to social and economic discrimination. Thus we cannot impute the resultant social phenomena to the physical environment alone, and closer examination always reveals some differences of response by incoming groups of different cultural backgrounds. Each group brings with it its own predispositions, habituations, folkways, and problems. These characteristics undergo modifications under the strains of the new environment, the influence of which is usually much stronger on the young. Southern Negroes settling in a northern city enter with long-established habituations to American traditions. Their language and their general culture are those of their new home, except for minor variations developed during their segregated existence in the South. They have had lifelong relations with white Americans, even if these have often been unfavorable ones. Puerto Ricans, on the other hand, enter the same type of environment with a very different cultural experience, are for the most part unfamiliar with English, and quite unversed in the ways of our urban society. In New York City they dwell in the same kind of physical environment as the southern Negroes, often side by side in the same neighborhood, but we see some indications that their response is in some respects rather different from that of the latter group. They show less tendency to aggressive group protests, seem rather more likely to take refuge in escapist accommodations, and are more prone to narcotic addiction.

In sharp contrast to both these groups are the rigidly orthodox Hasidic Jews, who settled in Williamsburg, an area of Brooklyn where they live with Puerto Ricans and others. The Hasidim reject all contacts with the Puerto Ricans and indeed with all other groups, including an older Jewish group that has gradually been moving out of the neighborhood. They carry with them powerful indoctrinations and bring up their children under the most rigorous and exclusive training in the faith. They have a profound conviction of their own moral superiority and of the unique rightness of their doctrine, with its elaborate rituals and ceremonial observances, with its distinctive and peculiar requirements of dress and demeanor. They have succeeded in keeping the majority of their youth almost untouched by the influences around them, and among other features of this group is a low rate of juvenile delinquency. Similarly, for a long period the Chinese community in a small crowded area in Manhattan, living in its own way and cherishing its own usages in the midst of a community that was wholly indifferent and alien to it, exhibited a remarkable absence of juvenile delinquency. There are indications, however, that under the slow permeation of outside influences some tendency to delinquency has now developed.

Clearly, then, the ethos, standards, and social cohesion of the groups migrating into our congested city areas affect their responses to the new conditions and are a determinant of the degree of resistance they exhibit to the disadvantages and pressures of the physical environment. The examples of effective resistance we possess strongly suggest that two great social bulwarks against the breakdown of youthful morale within an adverse environment are, first, the group's conviction of its own values, of the superiority of its standards, making it in large measure proof against the frustrations and confusions of life in an alien and unpropitious situation, and second, an authoritative family system which inculcates these values in the young from their earliest years. One great danger to which most of our inmigrant groups are exposed is the rankling insecurity that comes from a sense of inferiority, or of imputed inferiority.

An interesting sidelight on the effect that the strength of a group's values and standards has on the behavior of its members in an adverse environment is available in records of the hideous Nazi concentration camps. A young sociologist, Paul Neurath, son of a distinguished Viennese scholar, spent many months interned in one of these camps. He surreptitiously made careful notes on the different ways the various classes of victims behaved under the brutal and degrading treatment they received. In this preoccupation, he explained, he himself found some respite from the continuous horror of the situation. It was easy to spot to which of the rejected classes any individual belonged, since each of the seven or eight categories of prisoners wore a differently colored badge. The categories included political prisoners of the Gestapo; professional criminals; vagrants and others who had gotten into trouble with the Nazi social agencies; unacceptable emigrants who had been brought back to Germany or for some reason had returned of themselves (these were mostly Jews); "race polluters" (also mainly Jewish); homosexuals; and Jehovah's Witnesses. Dr. Neurath's evidence showed that the groups with the strongest sense of group identification and group standards were the ones that best resisted the disintegrating effects of their treatment, that were least liable to break down under it.[5] Highest in the list stood the wearers of the blue triangle, Jehovah's Witnesses, a group animated by the absolute conviction that God was at their side. They refused to break down and only among them were there no suicides. They were followed in ranking by the socialist-communist groups. Lowest on the list were the wearers of the black triangle, the vagrants and those who had got into trouble on their jobs or had not kept their employment—a group officially designated the "asocial."

The conditions experienced by most of the groups that have migrated to our great cities, who come to better their lot and start on the lowest economic level, have been such as to undermine the assurances and aspirations of the members of their groups, especially the young members. Lacking cohesion, disorganized, their former ways of life disrupted because of their inability to adapt to the new conditions, their value systems deranged by conflict with the values of the surrounding community, unappreciated and discriminated against, they struggle against considerable odds for some kind of integrity, and the amount of juvenile delinquency is a register of the degree in which they are unsuccessful. The history of New York City, with its successive waves of in-migrants, shows that the newest arrivals have always lacked adequate protection against the stresses and handicaps of the slum environments which the additional congestion caused by arrival inevitably worsened. It was so with Jewish groups, Irish groups, Eastern European groups, and Southern Italians. Now it is the turn of the southern Negroes and the Puerto Ricans. Now it is these who suffer from disorientation, and this disorientation is intensified by the prejudice and discrimination they encounter from the older established residents. Groups that are economically insecure are thus rendered socially insecure as well, and the morale of the young is too severely tried.

### The Pressures of the Environment on Social Relationships

With these considerations in mind, we can now briefly consider some adverse influences on youthful morale specifically arising from slum environments. The observations that follow are primarily the result of the writer's own experience with children and families exposed to these conditions, though they are borne out by many other studies.

In the first place, the sheer congestion of slum life is adverse to the aspirations of youth. Opportunities of every kind are restricted or lacking. The crowded family gives the youth no place of retreat, no quiet in which he can prepare his homework for school, no privacy. There are no books, no pictures that matter. There is seldom anyone with whom he can discuss his problems. For release he must go out to the street; in cold weather he crowds into the candy store. Often he has no outlet for his energies except in noise-making, rowdiness, and mischievous pranks.

It is symptomatic of his situation that he often finds the street more pleasant than the home. There are no influences around to teach him good manners or good speech. So, when he goes into the school, he already carries a handicap with him. His teachers speak a different language. He is unfamiliar with their type of teaching. He misses much of what they would teach and vainly tries to conceal the fact. His background, his upbringing, are all against his success. The teacher is likely to conclude that he has little learning capacity and tends to treat him accordingly. He is labeled as low IQ. He is often mechanically passed along from grade to grade, learning very little in the process.

The children of slums suffer multiple disadvantages in their schooling. Except for some dedicated ones, the better teachers naturally prefer to be placed elsewhere. The low standards, and perhaps even more the fact that the children seem unresponsive and sometimes are rowdy or troublesome, make most teachers unwilling to stay in slums if they can possibly find other positions. The schools are populated mainly by the children of the in-migrant groups. If the pupils are Puerto Ricans, they have little facility with the English language. In consequence they miss much that they are taught and are usually retarded in reading, the most serious of all retardations. The southern Negroes, the other large migrant group, are an equally bad case. Their education before their arrival in northern schools has usually been deplorable. Where, as in various neighborhoods, they constitute the majority of the school population, there is a momentum of helplessness and inertia in the face of schooling requirements. Sometimes they come to school having had too little sleep during late wasted nights at home or on the street, or they arrive burdened with the troubles from which their parents are suffering. They have already learned that they are the objects of discrimination, and nothing is more calculated to depress their ambitions as well as their prospects.

Failure in school, from whatever causes, has not only a numbing effect on youthful aspirations and on the chances of a career, it is also associated with the formation of habits and attitudes adverse to morale. Retardation leads to truancy and truants become school drop-outs. It breeds frustration and the tendency to rebel against authority. In New York City schools, reports show only 62.4 per cent of those who entered the ninth grade in 1951 were graduated in due course from academic high school; only 37.6 of vocational high school students were graduated.[6] The drop-out rate for boys was even higher, only 59 per cent graduating from academic high school and 34 per cent from vocational school. Most of the more disturbed pupils go to vocational high schools if they continue school at all, and they begin dropping out in a steady stream from the outset.[7]

The significance of these figures is registered in the delinquency statistics. Many of the children who appear before the juvenile courts are charged with chronic truancy in addition to other offenses, and truancy itself is often the first stage in the process that leads to persistent delinquency. The high correlation between school retardation and delinquency has been shown in a number of studies.[8] It is significant also that reading retardation has been found to be correlated with some of the other environmental and sociopathological conditions we have shown to be characteristic of the high-delinquency areas.[9]

The school is next to the family as a determinant of the outlook of the young and their consequent life-chances. And when trouble at school is combined with troubles within the slum family, these conditions interact, each tending to magnify the effect of the other and increasing the likelihood of delinquency. The environmental and sociopathological troubles disturb the life of the family and make it less congenial to the young. The relations between parents and children are in grave danger of being impaired. Rifts develop more easily, and often enough the parents (or one of them) take the wrong ways of dealing with the situation. It is not only in the "broken family" that home life is imperiled, but also and not less in the family that has suffered some demoralization under the impact of a complex of troubles. Even in happier circumstances the concord of parents and offspring is subject to tests that it may not be able to withstand. In the much more difficult and trying conditions of life in high-delinquency areas, it would certainly not be surprising if failure occurred more frequently.

To some students of the subject, juvenile delinquency is the consequence of bad family upbringing, and certainly no one can dispute the great role played by the early formative influences of the family and the kind and degree of training provided within it. The Gluecks have made the relations between parents and children and the "cohesion" of the family the basis of their predictive scale. The limitation and defects of this scale have been sufficiently pointed out; in any event what is called the cohesion of the family may be disturbed or disrupted both by forces operating from without the family and by crises within it for which the family itself cannot be held responsible. Young persons generally have a resilience that can resist many adverse influences, and it is preferable to regard the development of delinquent tendencies as caused by a complex of disturbing conditions. The transition from mere occasional or sporadic acts of delinquency to a confirmed bent toward delinquent behavior is frequently triggered by some crucial event—a gross disillusionment, a rebuff, a stigma, or whatever it may be. But this is a subject we must follow up in Part Two.

Besides the home and the school there is the street. The

clutter and frequent uncongeniality of the home lead young people to spend all the more time on the street, where what they see and hear is often harsh and ugly. They fall in with others of their kind. They have no sandlots or open spaces or available playgrounds where they might employ their energies in zestful games. They are on the lookout for something to do, and the most aggressive or "acting-out" member is likely to make himself the leader and induce the others to join him in exploits that often enough take on a law-breaking character. The group of boys who under other conditions would form a team becomes a street-corner gang. The education provided by the slum street is no training in manners or in morals.

The only place many of these boys feel at home is the street, where they can act and feel like themselves among their own kind. The school is unpleasant and discouraging—though there are now some happy exceptions. The home is troubled, often depressing, sometimes quarrelsome. What alternative have they? But the street is a place of dangers. It is a hang-out of undesirable characters. A drunkard staggers along, and may arouse the cruelty of untamed youth who take advantage of his incapacity. A bully or a homosexual or a dope peddler may accost them. One of the boys may have a brother in a neighboring gang and give the others ideas about following this lead into illicit adventures. If the boys are Negroes, they may get into trouble with Puerto Ricans, or vice versa. There may be other "alien" groups—Irish, Italian, Polish, or Jewish—who jeer at them or harass them. The street breeds more hate than love of one's neighbors.

Though the street is the inevitable resort of boys in slum areas, it is far from being either a pleasant or a desirable alternative for the facilities they lack. Much of the time it is uncomfortable because of bad weather, forcing the boys to huddle in alleys or hallways or to crowd into candy stores or other refuges. When they do gather in a knot on the street, the police are likely to tell them to move or scatter. They may be charged with "unlawful assembly." They come to regard the police as their natural enemies. One way or another they are liable to get into trouble and in consequence they come both to fear authority and to lose respect for it, an attitude that is conducive to evasive law-breaking.

Brought up in such surroundings, the boys are ill prepared to meet the demands of the future. There are two ways in particular in which their present condition and the attitudes it breeds tend to jeopardize their future welfare. In the first place, their growing interest in sex creates a problem. What they learn about it on the streets, from older boys and in casual conversations among themselves, is usually coarse, indecent, and ugly. Even little boys indulge in bawdy language; it is a sign of youthful manlinesss. The more decent girls of the neighborhood do not consort with the boys on the street. The occasional girl who does is likely to have a tendency toward promiscuity and to be ready to proceed with one or more of them to a dark alley or roof. There is no real companionship and little enough pleasure in these casual relationships, illicitly snatched in drab and degrading situations. They constitute an unhappy preparation for genuine love-making and the more enduring satisfactions that might follow.

The second danger to their future well-being is related to the first. Backward or retarded in their schooling, they are ready to abandon it as soon as possible, often before they reach the age prescribed by law. In this way and in others they are unprepared for steady employment. In our time it is hard enough even for the better equipped slum boys to find jobs. Their manners and modes of speech, often their race or ethnic origin, are against them. So, at an age when it is peculiarly dangerous to live precariously in enforced idleness, these youths, dulled in their aspirations and frustrated in their hopes, drift toward a blank future.

It should be sufficiently clear from these abbreviated comments that in itself the physical environment in which a high rate of delinquency prevails has a seriously adverse affect on the life chances of the young people growing up in it. While many somehow are able to overcome its worst dangers and become decent members of the community, these areas remain breeding grounds for delinquency and no salvage measures can do more than partially mitigate their perils.

In short, only the thorough rehabilitation of these areas, along with the creation of opportunities for the proper equipment of their youth as responsible adults, can effectively meet the present challenge of the slums.

# 3

## The Psychic Conditions

"How does it happen that some young people living in the same family environment as the delinquent . . . are able to refrain from anti-social contact?" This was the question asked by William Healy and Augusta F. Bronner in their distinctive and path-finding volume *New Light on Delinquency and Its Treatment*.[1] They focused attention on the psychology of delinquency, whereas earlier study of high-delinquency areas was in a narrower sense sociological—concerned, that is, with relating the incidence of delinquency to the conditions of the inclusive social environment, the neighborhood or urban area. It was obvious enough that within this social milieu there must be more intimate conditions to account for the fact that so many youthful residents even of the worst areas, did not become delinquent. Healy and Bronner found the differential factor in the family situation. It was mainly for them a matter of the sociopsychological adjustments of youth to familial relations within the broader context of the higher-delinquency environment.

There is certainly a convincing volume of evidence to confirm the Healy and Bronner position that the lack of sustaining close relationships of affection and trust between parent and child in the latter's early years is a delinquency-provoking factor of first importance. These authors maintained that where the parent-child tie was emotionally strong, a basis of satisfaction was constructed on which a pattern of socially acceptable habits and attitudes would in all probability be built, notwithstanding the adverse pressures of the inclusive environment. The rapport established between parent and child, even if the parent were not intrinsically worthy, made possible an adjustment that could override adverse influences from without. Along these lines, which many later writers have followed with variations, our authorities filled a lacuna and thus revised previous imputations of delinquency primarily to the physical environment and its impact on youth. Observe, however, that the new approach still placed the emphasis on environment—on the nearer and differential environment of the family situation.

This solution, however significant, was by no means the last word. It was criticized on two grounds. In the first place, it was claimed that the evidences submitted could not themselves bear the total weight of so absolute a conclusion. Queries were raised about the representativeness of the selected sample, composed of 105 delinquents and 105 nondelinquent siblings—all referral cases from the courts to diagnostic or guidance units attached to these courts. The preliminary court selection of the cases might render them unrepresentative of the court cases as a whole. Beyond this, however, the study could not answer a more far-reaching question. When our authors concluded that over 90 per cent of the delinquent cases exhibited grave discontent or extreme disturbance caused by their family experiences or life circumstances, the question still open was how far psychic deficiencies, congenital or a result of early neglect, maltnutrition, or physical damage of some kind, may have weakened resistance to unfavorable experiences. We note that 13 per cent of the sibling controls were also reported to have exhibited mental stress and disturbances. Did these then have a greater capacity to withstand the delinquency-provoking experiences to which the others succumbed? May there not be a gradient of capacity for social adjustment under stress that involves not only the experiential history of the individual but also his psychological make-up and the circumstances attending its early development?

It is important to observe that these qualifications in no way invalidate the findings of Healy and Bronner and of the many other researchers who have similarly reported on the relation of early home experiences to the presence or absence of delinquency. However, other causative factors must be reckoned with if we are to approach a fuller understanding of why some young persons become delinquent and others do not. Causation is a many-sided affair; other approaches than the psychological and the sociological have something to contribute to the solution of the complex problems of prevention and treatment. For practical purposes it is important to know that in a very large number of cases the lack of a strong emotional tie between parents and children evokes delinquent tendencies in the child. This understanding opens the way for more intelligent treatment and gives leads for more hopeful efforts in prevention. But certainly in a considerable number of cases remedial help can be sought from the pediatrist and the specialist in neurotic and psychosomatic ailments. And there are of course particular categories, such as the psychotic and the mentally deficient, for which only specialist treatment can be of much service.

Other professional groups have also found the roots of delinquency in the near environment—in the family and the early upbringing of the child. This approach is pre-eminently that of the psychoanalysts. They agree generally with most psychologists, social psychologists, and psychiatrists in emphasizing disturbances that occur in the early socialization of the child. The psychoanalysts are distinctive, however, in the role they assign to unconscious motivation, to the suppressed "instincts" of childhood that find expression in neurotic anxieties and wayward behavior. The human infant is at first an animal directed to the satisfaction of its animal instincts. It is asocial and becomes socialized as experience and indoctrination exercise control over the purely "instinctive" nature. If this process is successfully carried out, the "ideal ego" or the "superego," at first very weak, develops and takes over. But failures occur in the process and the superego may remain weak. The suppressed desires take their revenge in various ways, delinquency being one of them.

An early leader in the psychoanalytic interpretation of delinquency was the Viennese psychoanalyst, August Aichhorn, who set up his own home for delinquents. He found in the frustrated yearning for love and affection the basis of delinquent behavior, and he believed that a system of persistent, friendly, permissive care was best calculated to bring about readjustment. For Aichhorn a large part of the problem is the enabling of the delinquent to achieve "identification" with the therapist. He claimed that the results achieved by his institution were excellent.

Aichhorn's work had considerable influence, and it has been followed up by promising experiments in treatment along the lines he pioneered. A notable example was Fritz Redl's Pioneer House, which took a group of extremely difficult boys and found that they responded well to treatment, showing an increased capacity to deal with their problems. Pioneer House, however, was closed before, in Redl's judgment, the experiment was completed.[2]

In other experiments less favorable results were reported. An example of the latter kind was the experiment in "milieu" therapy along Aichhorn's lines undertaken with a group of girls at Hawthorne–Cedar Knolls residential center. (A thorough investigation of the conditions under which one experiment succeeds and another fails might prove revealing.)

The psychoanalytic viewpoint has influenced many investigators who would not class themselves as adhering to the psychoanalytic school. The emphasis on the importance of the conditioning the child receives in its earliest years, not least in infancy, is widely accepted, and psychonalytic concepts such as "superego" and "transference" are used somewhat freely. There is, however, a primary distinction between the viewpoint of psychoanalysis and that generally held in other disciplines. The psychoanalyst regards delinquency as the expression of natural instincts which are normally brought under control in the socialization process. Sociologists and psychologists, on the other hand, commonly regard delinquency as the reaction of the child to conditions that deny him primary psychic or emotional satisfactions, thus creating or at least evoking antisocial attitudes. From this viewpoint, delinquents are made so, whereas to the psychoanalyst they are born so. If the latter viewpoint is taken we might find some kind of contradiction in the permissive modes of treatment many psychoanalysts have approved.

In the main, it is to the psychological researchers we must turn for our knowledge of the differential mental characteristics that underlie delinquent behavior. A good deal of knowledge on the types of malfunction, the area of disturbance, that result in juvenile delinquency, has been advanced in the studies of Fritz Redl. Psychologists are particularly concerned with the processes of personality growth and with the influences on personality development that evoke deviant forms of behavior. Some psychologists have given special attention, as Healy and Bronner did, to the role of deprivation and frustration in childhood and to the variant reactions to those conditions that depend on differences of mental or constitutional type. Psychological studies of personality changes at the outset of puberty and through adolescence are serviceable for the understanding of delinquency that manifests itself in the early teens. Another type of psychological inquiry has been the classification of personality types, but while it is convenient to make broad distinctions, the total personality is so complex and has so many aspects, there are so many combinations of attributes of varying degrees of strength as well as so many changes in the course of a life history, that every classification has its problems and none has become authoritative. This statement is also applicable to the various classifications of the delinquent personality.

For practical purposes, we need some simple *ad hoc* classifications, especially to screen cases prior to disposition and treatment. In looking through the intake records of certain institutions, the writer was struck by the frequency with which the term "disturbed" appeared, usually qualified by adjectives such as "very," "emotionally," "severely." So vague and inclusive a term has no diagnostic value. It might even be applied to delinquents who are reasonably well adjusted within the delinquent associations, though causing considerable disturbance otherwise. It is certainly applied both to delinquents who are chafing under the restraints imposed on them and to those who are suffering from a deeper-seated mental trouble. A clarification of the common vocabulary of those who work with delinquents is certainly needed.

One or two terms have become fairly well defined, among them "psychopathic." One definition, offered by William and Joan McCord, is: "The psychopath is an a-social, aggressive, highly impulsive person who feels little or no guilt and is unable to form lasting bonds of affection with other human beings."[3] The typical delinquent psychopath is full of unreasoning hostility; Fritz Redl described his psychopathic boys (our appellation, not his) as "the children who hate." The identification of this type (with its several varieties) is well confirmed in studies by Robert Lindner, Kate Friedlander, R. D. Rabinowitch, Lauretta Bender, and others. Many of these studies insist on the role of early rejection, emotional starvation, or brutal treatment in evoking the psychopathic features. "In study after study," say the McCords, "emotional deprivation appeared to have precipitated a psychopathic personality structure." This conclusion does not preclude the existence of congenital or constitutional mental disorders, glandular irregularities, or even initial psychic tendencies that may develop as a result of emotional shock; but the cases that have been recorded of successful treatment indicate that a socializing therapy can be applied with rather good prospects of success. The interdependence of bodily and mental functioning within the organism is so intimate that we can learn only from tested experience how far one or another therapeutic approach is of avail.

From the psychopathic type we must distinguish the psychotic. When we speak of the psychotic we imply a more deep-seated mental disorder, probably rooted in congenital mental defect, though, as in the schizophrenic, it may not reveal itself in the earlier life history. The psychotic has persistent delusions, cannot grapple with reality, and lives in the clouded world of a distorted imagination. He is often beset with anxiety and in some form of trouble, with a sense of shame or guilt, in which respect he is markedly different from the typical psychopath. Nor is he likely to be responsive to the therapeutic processes that have already been applied with some success to the psychopath.

Before leaving the subject of classification, let us cite a division proposed by Albert J. Reiss, Jr., which has attracted considerable interest since its publication in the *American Sociological Review* (December 1952). The article is entitled "Social Correlates of Psychological Types of Delinquency," and we might at the outset raise a question about that title. We doubt whether we should speak at all of "psychological types." If the phrase implies a classification of types of delinquent behavior on a psychological basis, almost all classifications are in terms of personality traits and thus could be called psychological, while in this particular classification the terms belong to the special approach of the psychoanalyst. But this initial cavil has nothing to do with the merits of the classification. It is a significant departure from other modes of classification, for Reiss suggests interesting correlations between delinquency types and types of environment.

The classification is threefold. The first category is that of the "relatively integrated" delinquent. He is pretty much in command of himself and "in all probability will become a mature, independent adult." He is a normally capable person, who can behave perfectly well when it suits him, and his lack of morals does not imply serious personal demoralization. The second category comprises delinquents with "relatively weak ego controls." It contains highly insecure persons with low self-esteem, and also highly aggressive and hostile youngsters. Both are unstable, having weak associations with their fellows, erratic, suffering from a sense of strain, with no clear standards of behavior. The third category contains "defective superego" delinquents. These have failed to make the code of the larger society their own, to "internalize" it, and thus have no qualms of conscience over their transgressions. They pay little regard to instruction and have poor records in every respect, usually drifting into whatever chance unskilled employment is available.

The first type, we are told, is usually found in the less desirable residential areas, in families that show little place mobility and are stable, respectable, conventional. The youth himself is not troublesome at school, usually attains high school level, and then finds regular employment. His offenses are mainly burglary and larceny, the stealing of automobiles being characteristic. He gets into trouble with the police and the court at a later age than do the other two types.

The "weak ego" type is usually found in well-established residential areas, but comes from a family that frequently moves from place to place. The parents, usually native-born, are not separated but their relationship is marked by serious conflicts; they tend to disregard conventional standards. The child is likely to be a habitual truant, but of average scholarship. He differs from the other two types in his low concern for peer-group association. He gets into trouble at a very early age. His characteristic offenses are wanton destruction and flouting authority.

The "defective superego" type is characteristically found in the poorer, dilapidated, urban areas. The family is not mobile. It is often broken, with parental conflict where both parents are present, and usually includes many children who lack any proper control and easily get into trouble. Truancy is very common, and police and court troubles begin at an early age.

We have spelled out this distinctive set of correlations between delinquency types and environmental factors because it suggests various lines of study that might considerably refine our understanding of the relation between delinquency and both the nearer and the more inclusive environments of the delinquent. The correlations themselves are based on an analysis of the court records of 1,110 white male probationers of the Juvenile Court of Cook County, Illinois, for 1943 and 1944. The data on which the study drew were compiled by psychiatric social workers and psychiatrists of the Institute for Juvenile Research, and the second and third categories were so classified by IJR psychiatrists.

This kind of seminal study leaves us with a variety of question marks. To the outsider the line between the "weak ego" type and the "defective superego" type is not clear, and he may not be sure that the actual decision to put delinquents into one or the other category is sufficiently authoritative. There might, for example, be a tendency to classify a candidate as "defective superego" because he comes from a broken home and is a gang member and lives in a deteriorated area and did not complete his grade school education. But all these symptoms may be related to special conditions, and they are not themselves definitive of a "defective superego." We assume that the classification was made with scholarly care; our point is that, when the correlates which appear to be associated with a type are much more specific and well demarcated than the type itself, the problem of classification has unusual risks. Our main conclusion is that Dr. Reiss has in a most suggestive way exposed an hypothesis concerning the different aspects and forms of delinquency responsible to different social and physical environments.

Standing apart from those who relate the various manifestations of delinquency to differences in mentality or personality, is a small group which finds in the "body type"—the physical constitution—a basis for classifying mentalities that in turn gives clues to delinquent tendencies. A pioneer in this field was William H. Sheldon, but his work was eclectic and somewhat confused, and was ruled out of court in a devastating critique by the leading criminologist, Edwin H. Sutherland. The subject, however, was taken up by the indefatigable Gluecks in their volume entitled *Physique and Delinquency* (New York, 1956). They limited their claim to the proposition that some of the mental traits associated with delinquency are also associated with a particular type of physique. The "mesomorph" type, the athletic, tough, strong-bodied frame, appears to have a greater tendency to delinquency than the other two types. Such tentative conclusions are not without interest, but they do not offer much that is serviceable either for the understanding or for the control of delinquency. From time to time someone discovers a correlation between some physiological differentia and the proneness to delinquency. A physician attached to an important medical institution once showed the writer a series of photographs that revealed a divergence between the formation of the knee joints of a group of delinquents from that characteristic of the age group in general. The evidence was there, for what it was worth, but it was not, so far as the writer knows, supported by wider investigation.

To sum up, we have sought in this first part to survey the nature of the problem posed for all who endeavor to understand why delinquency is more incident to some groups than to others, to some localities than to others, under some modes of nurture and conditioning of youth than under others. Obviously, there is a great amount of further research required in order to trace more accurately the processes and conditions that affect the standards and values and attitudes of the young as they respond to their life circumstances. The growing boy or girl is subject to influences from a continually changeful system of interactive environments: the physical neighborhood, the home, the circle of acquaintances, the special experiences of the individual, and the pervasive modes of communication that convey the temper of the times and the doings and sufferings of other people. To the complex impact of this system, as particularized in the individual situation, the youth responds according to his innate disposition and his previous conditioning.

It will then be the task of the second part of this report, in reviewing the whole problem of causation, to analyze the evidence back of the different incidences of delinquency in comparable situations, in order to arrive at some conclusions respecting the relative significance of particular control factors. This in turn will lead to Part Three, where we examine the application of such controls to the prevention and to the treatment of delinquency.          *

We have reached a point at which certain conclusions have become sufficiently clear, as follows:

1. In the high-delinquency areas there are present, to a greater extent than in other areas, environmental conditions and responsive modes and habits of living that in conjunction evoke in youth a sense of frustration, a balking of energies and ambitions, with consequent tendencies to resort to legally forbidden activities by way of substitution or compensation.

2. While a majority of the young in these areas are suffi-

ciently resistant or adaptable to carry on or to find a way to surmount these obstacles, others are more sensitive, more prone to rebelliousness, or more seriously maladjusted to the conditions imposed on them, conditions that even in high-delinquency areas vary considerably in their character and the severity of their impact. It is among the latter group that the *habit* of delinquency is most frequently developed.

3. The *focus* of the clash between youthful wants and aspirations and the resistant conditions is normally the family circle, though influences from the larger environment may stimulate or accentuate it.

4. In lower delinquency areas strains and tensions, again usually focusing in family relations, are for some youth powerful enough to evoke a similar rebelliousness, with a consequent tendency to delinquent behavior.

5. The over-all increase in juvenile delinquency must be attributed to pervasive influences arising from broad changes in the condition of our inclusive civilization. The deep disturbances created by wars and the aftermaths of wars have brought about changes in attitudes, weakening the sense of security and making inroads into our value systems. Directly or indirectly through the effect on parents and elders and through the media of communication, acculturation of the young has been affected. The manner and degree in which this educational change has taken place for different groups and in different countries is a difficult subject for exploration, but we may assume that it has weakened the acceptance of authority, induced more of a skeptical attitude, and made the susceptible more familiar with violence and more inclined to resort to it under stress.

### Note on Departmental Approaches to Delinquency

In the preceding section we sketched the approaches of different departments of scholarship to the study of delinquency. There has been controversy over the respective importance of the sociological, the psychological, the psychiatric, the psychoanalytic, and the genetic modes of interpretation. Such controversy, however, is on a minor level, mostly incident to the roles of practitioners of different affiliations in schools and other institutions concerned with delinquents. Sociological classifications of delinquents are usually on a somewhat different basis from psychological ones and quite distinctly different from psychoanalytic ones. All may be equally relevant and equally good, but one can certainly quarrel with the assumption that any one basis is definitive as against the others. As we have been insisting, delinquency is a phenomenon that is the result of the impact of a conjuncture of diverse conditions on susceptible youth. The individual is not merely a sociological or a psychological or somatic being. Any trained investigator should be able to distinguish and report on the environment and the overt symptoms. Any intelligent school teacher should be able to identify the signs of trouble in the pupils under his supervision. Sociologists, psychologists, social psychologists, and anthropologists, out of a common interest in the processes of group formation and cohesion, have all studied the delinquent gang. The report of any such study contains very little to indicate whether it was made by a sociologist, or, say, an anthropologist, except perhaps that either one may use the particular jargon of his school. Differences of interpretation often seem as wide between members of the same discipline—between two anthropologists such as Margaret Mead and Ernest A. Hooten—as between two members of different disciplines. Academic departmental lines are intrusions and embarrassments when the object of study is a many-aspected social phenomenon. They also cause trouble and an unrealistic division of labor in the treatment process, but we shall leave that subject for later consideration.

# Part Two

## LEADS TO

## CAUSATION

# 4

## Statement of the Problem

A phenomenon so widespread as juvenile delinquency and one arousing so much public concern and evoking so many agencies and programs to deal with it inevitably leads to numerous explanations. Nearly everyone who comes into contact with it is ready to tell us its cause or causes, as well as what should be done about it. Besides these popular offhand interpretations there are the more responsible contributions of professional researchers. The studies of the latter have been of great service in advancing our understanding of the problem, but there are nevertheless among them various divergent and uncoordinated viewpoints. Since to the educated outsider the whole subject must appear confusing, we begin our discussion with a series of comments aimed at presenting the issue in a proper focus.

### The Limits of Causal Inquiry

We do not ask: What is the cause of delinquency? To ask why any delinquency occurs is like asking why human nature is what it is. We are not concerned with the occasional delinquencies in which practically every young person indulges at some time or another. Our interest is in the processes and experiences that lie back of the *habit* of delinquent behavior. Our interest lies not in the act of delinquency but in the delinquent. Nor do we look for an answer that would explain why any individual youth becomes a delinquent. The full investigation of the causation of delinquency in an individual case would mean the most intimate comprehension of his heredity, his mental makeup, his early experiences, his relationships with the family, the school, the playground, the neighborhood—a comprehension that is rarely, if ever, possible to attain. We do have some excellent studies of the history and background of individual delinquents—for example, in Bruno Bettelheim's *Truants From Life*—but, enlightening as these are, we cannot be sure they tell the whole story. Besides, no one life history is the same as any other.

Instead, research into causes must be directed to the discovery of significant relationships between delinquency and other phenomena. We begin by asking for correlations, the concomitance of delinquency with situations or conditions which will show that where delinquency is more prevalent or less prevalent other factors are at the same time more prevalent or less prevalent. We relate the variable of delinquency to other variables and then seek to probe into the association between the concomitant variables, framing hypotheses concerning a possible connection and finding methods of testing them. This statement is of course very obvious. We have much statistical evidence regarding variations in different localities, for different groups, at different times. What we are seeking is the reasons for such variations. As with nearly all causal investigations in the social sciences, the object is to understand why the more or the less: the more here, the less there; the more now, the less then; the more under some specified conditions, the less under others.

On this basis we are confronted with the two major types of questions already mentioned. One—the outstanding question— is how to account for the constantly increasing volume of juvenile delinquency, as evidenced by statistics of police arrests, court adjudications, youthful felonies, institutional commitments, FBI reports on crime and delinquency, and so forth. It is no doubt impossible to discover what proportion of the statistical increase is due to circumstances other than an increase in the actual amount of delinquency—the greater number of reporting agencies, the development of juvenile courts, increased police attention to youthful offenses, greater public concern, and more attention in the press. Since all authorities seem agreed that such adventitious considerations are quite insufficient to explain the recorded increase, as year after year it continues to rise, we have here a most challenging problem.

The second type of question, which has some implication for the first, is addressed to the marked disparity in the incidence of delinquency for different areas, classes, and groups within the community. The study of these differentials is of first importance alike for the understanding and the control of delinquency. Moreover, questions along these lines are fully amenable to direct investigation and have already been pursued with a considerable degree of success, whereas for the first type of question our usual research procedures are of little avail. We are dealing here with broad trends affecting the civilization of our time. We must surmise that growing up in today's world is subject to wide-ranging influences that have an unsettling effect on the mind of our youth, and our conclusions on this theme can hardly admit of total verification.

## The Polarities of Causation

The ancient question, how far is heredity responsible and how far environment, is raised in discussions of delinquency as of many other problems. We have been considering the conditions existing in the high-delinquency areas. The areas in question, the slum environment, have certainly some responsibility for the prevalence of delinquency in them. If they were abolished and their residents given decent housing, along with aid in adapting themselves to the new environment, we cannot doubt that delinquency would be reduced. Moreover, since amelioration of living conditions is within the power of the urban authorities, the onus for the prevalence of delinquency must rest with these, and with the citizens who are unwilling to support a campaign for the abolition of the slums. If we say that the residents of the slums are themselves responsible, we are giving a specious excuse for the avoidance of an obligation. If we say that the "bad seed"

is the root of the trouble, we are complacently ignoring the flagrant evidence of the role played by the environmental conditions
on the youth subjected to them.

On the other hand, we cannot hold the unfavorable environment wholly responsible. Large numbers of young persons who
are brought up in the slum environment do not become delinquents. Can we then account for the nondelinquents in the slum
environment by attributing their immunity to better heredity?
Obviously the problem is not so simple. We may find some evidence that the family life of the nondelinquents was on the
whole more stable, that the father or the mother or both took
more care of the children, showed more affection toward them,
exercised more reasonable discipline over them. But the differential behavior of such parents cannot be purely assigned to their
superior stock. They too were bred under particular conditions
and underwent particular experiences. The formative influences
of their upbringing would certainly have something to do with
the manner in which in turn they brought up their own children.
Indoctrinations, social influences of all sorts, and personal experiences mold the native plasticity of the human mentality in
ways beyond the reckoning.

There have been some attempts—as in the study by Healy
and Bronner—to take contrasting pairs of siblings and compare
their respective life histories. Various factors were found to
characterize the delinquents as contrasted with the nondelinquents. In the Healy and Bronner study some 27 per cent of the
delinquents had had many or severe illnesses, as against less
than 8 per cent of the "controls." Some 24 per cent of the delinquents showed neurotic or psychotic deviations; only 2 per cent
of the "controls." Was the difference due to heredity? Hereditary
differences are frequent often in children of the same parents,
since the combinations of genetic elements are always variant.
But environment is also at work. Even the age differential between two children in the same family means a significantly different environment for each.

It should be obvious, then, that we can never demarcate the
precise roles of heredity and environment in determining the

social behavior of the young. The relation of the two is woven from birth, from before birth. There is, for example, significant evidence that stresses and worries affecting the mother during pregnancy can have an adverse effect on the emotional development of her child. There is no assignable beginning. Children inherit from parents and remoter ancestors. All life long we are responsive, in whatever degree, to changing environments. The process is wholly continuous. Moreover, we all help to make our own changing environments, with every decision we take. Heredity and environment are both inconceivably complex, and the union of the two in any individual case is a pattern that shows no seams.

In short, heredity and environment belong to the category of polarities. Life cannot exist or develop without environment, without the particular kind of environment to which the particular kind of life is more or less adapted. Wherever the environment changes, life changes too. Wherever life exists it modifies in some respect its environments. There is this difference, however, that over the relatively short period the living being is the prime mover, the dynamic agent in the more important changes in the relationship. For the strategy of remedial action we should therefore concentrate on producing the desirable environmental change, as in the abolition of slums. While preventive care and remedial treatment are important, so long as these areas of squalor and congestion exist they will continue to breed delinquency.

## The Multiplicity of Factors

A major difficulty in arriving at causal connections between delinquency and the phenomena we find to be associated with it is that there are so many phenomena and that they fall into such diverse categories. We can, of course, find out the closeness of the correlation between delinquency and any other particular phenomenon within a given context, but there is often considerable variation in other contexts. Some associated phenomena may be closely correlated because they in turn are correlated with some third phenomenon. We find, say, a close correlation in certain urban areas between the amount of delinquency and the amount of tuberculosis; this may have no direct significance for our purpose, since tuberculosis is most often found in the dilapidated abodes of sheer poverty, a general characteristic of these areas. But the fact that many kinds of sociopathological conditions manifest themselves in these areas may have some significance, since such conditions contribute to the pressures and tensions that promote delinquency. We may learn, to take a finding from Bernard Lander, that areas of Baltimore in which there are large numbers of both whites and Negroes have higher delinquency rates than areas in which one group or the other is a small minority. This correlation may well be significant, but only if it can be related to adverse reactions in the relationship of the two groups under these conditions.

In Part One we reviewed various conditions characteristic of high-delinquency urban areas, on the general assumption that the differential conditions accompanying high delinquency rates are somehow, in some of their aspects, prejudicial to decent law-abiding behavior on the part of the young, tending to breed attitudes conducive to delinquency. We distinguished three broad ranges of such differential conditions: the physical environment of certain urban areas, the socioeconomic milieu of the groups which inhabited such areas, and the mental-emotional characteristics of some of the youth, as distinct from others living in the same area. Within each range variants occurred which affected the correlation with delinquency. For example, a socioeconomic group with a quite distinctive culture—say, a highly orthodox group with continuous and rigorous indoctrination of the young —can inhabit the type of area associated with high delinquency and still not exhibit the delinquency rate characteristic of the area. We also noted that the nearer social circle of the family may be such as to counteract the adverse influences of the neighborhood life or, on the other hand, accentuate their impact.

These illustrations highlight two aspects of the research problem. In the first place, the causal efficacy of any factor or of any complex of environmental factors depends on its relations to other factors or to a complex of conditions existing on a different level. In other words, to comprehend the differential delinquency of any area we must take into account the accommodation between the physical environment and the socioeconomic conditions, along with the cultural background of the inhabitants, and to get closer to the problem we must include also the nearer familial environment of the exposed youth and then the innate and acquired psychic attributes that help us to distinguish delinquents from non-delinquents.

In the second place, we must not think of the causes of delinquency as a series of social forces each of which has its own unit efficacy, greater or less, so that when a sufficient number of them combine they produce a corresponding amount of delinquency. A single factor, or any particular combination of factors, has *by itself* no implications for the causation of delinquency. All the conditions and surroundings of sheer poverty may be present and yet may be remarkably free from delinquent tendencies. It is the *interaction* of conditions as together they bear on some *particular* type of mentality that determines the development of delinquent tendencies. The response that takes the form of habitual delinquency is a manifestation of human nature that is no sense abnormal.

The delinquent attitude is not suddenly evoked by the conjunction of conditions at any one moment, but develops through a series of stages, through the persistence or the successive impact of influences adverse to a law-abiding way of life. The process may be hastened or slowed. It may be hastened by some shock that makes a deep impression on a young person—say, by a punishment the boy regards as wholly unfair, by a special act of brutality on the part of a father, by a sudden realization that the youth is not "wanted," or even by an accident such as a facial disfiguration. Such acts may be said to trigger a tendency, confirming it against counter tendencies, marking the parting of the ways. Any such act may prick through the resistance of youth, and the emotional revulsion contains a new note, a note of defiance—something more than a mere feeling of rebelliousness that subsides when the irritating situation is forgotten. The new note is a vindication of the outraged personality, a repudiation of responsible authority, the recognition of an approaching struggle for new self-assertion, a rift between the youth and his immediate world. The rift will widen into alienation unless some drastic change takes place. On the other hand, a timely release from brooding tensions, a new association, the guidance of some trusted person may effectively reverse a delinquent tendency, and be also a parting of the ways, before it is too late. These considerations suggest the total inadequacy of any interpretation that attributes delinquency to the impact of a single factor or series of "factors."

## The Significant Factors

It is unwise, as we have seen, to depend in a causal inquiry on the correlation of factors, or, say, on the number of factors correlated with delinquency in a particular situation. A correlation is for the student a question mark calling for analysis as to its relevance, if any, to a problem. What is specially important, instead, is to look for factors that provide significant leads toward at least a partial solution for the problem.

Among these significant factors must be included those we have designated as "trigger" factors. Let us take, for example, the case of a family where the father and mother are badly at odds. The father is a ne'er-do-well and out of a job; the mother is so beset and hard-worked that she gives little attention to her six children, except in the numbing effort to feed and clothe them. The oldest boy, thirteen, is messy and moody. Because of home pressures he cannot attend to his schooling, for which he is reasonably well qualified. He cherishes a smoldering resentment against it all, but manages to carry on. Then one day the father, finding him in the way, angrily pushes him around. The boy answers back with temper, whereupon the father beats him mercilessly. It is the trigger act. The boy changes direction and his new hatred of authority leads him toward a delinquent career.

Most children are by nature conformists. A long process of disillusionment, the constant beat of balking circumstances, may gradually undermine this tendency. Sometimes, there is a crucial situation that breaks down the defenses; and only then will the various associated conditions—family disorganization, school retardation, destitution—conspire to confirm the attitude that a critical personal experience has evoked. It is the spur to a changed motivation that counts, whether it be a sudden shock to the integrity of the personality, or a series of repeated blows that destroys the resistance weakened by the first, or the persistent pressure of untoward conditions bearing down on a mentality that can no longer endure the weight. Much depends on the youth's own values in relation to the values of his own peer group; much on his innate strength of character in pursuing his resolves; in any event, the turning point from conformity to delinquency will be reached by more young people where adverse conditions are more sustained and more frequent, as in high-delinquency areas.

The concept of the critical factor is often employed in another sense, in which one particular condition is claimed to be the paramount cause of delinquency. Sometimes the condition is so broad that it is nothing less than a bracket for a whole system of conditions—"social disorganization" is an example—and therefore the attribution is unhelpful. A somewhat more specific condition frequently considered paramount is the "broken home." "Broken homes"—that is, homes in which one parent is missing, especially while the children are quite young—figure in the life stories of enough delinquents to indicate that this condition is important. Healy and Bronner, for example, found that out of 4,000 delinquents they identified in Chicago and Boston about 50 per cent came from broken homes.[1] But the broken home usually associated with delinquency is mostly found in high-delinquency areas and suffers from various other conditions adverse to the well-being of the children. It is usually, in other words, a factor in a complex that as a whole is unfavorable to the upbringing of children. Moreover, the fact that the home is broken may itself be explained, in part at least, by the presence of these other adverse conditions. Desertion, for example, is in some neighborhoods a not infrequent occurrence in families already rife with troubles. In a later section, incidentally, we describe a situation in which a home from which the father was missing, seemed to play no part whatever in the evocation of delinquency.

Critical factors are resorted to also for the *prediction* of delinquency, as indicators of a type of disturbance very often associated with habitual delinquency. In this type of approach there is danger of confusing two senses of the term "prediction." It may refer to an overt or easily discernible aspect of the condition it identifies, as, for example, a particular kind of rash indicates a particular type of disease; or it may refer to a signal, or harbinger, or concomitant of a phenomenon of which the indicator is not an aspect nor in any way a determinant. Many of our popular weather indicators are of the latter type. When the gulls fly over the land, it is supposed to indicate a storm; when the sunrise is red, it is the "shepherd's" warning. Some of the proposed indicators of delinquency take the form of a rather elaborate scale, consisting presumably of actual determinants. The well-known Glueck prediction scale falls in this category.

The factors designated by the Gluecks for this purpose are a series of interfamily relationships: the role played by the father in maintaining discipline, the mother's supervision, the affection for the child shown by each parent, and the cohesiveness of the family group. This scale has occasioned much discussion, mostly critical. Some serious technical defects have been pointed out, and the significance of the percentages of accuracy claimed has been correctly challenged. We do not regard any scale of this type as particularly useful for purposes of prediction. The factors are usually not clear-cut. In the Glueck scale they sum up to little more than one—family cohesiveness—which is itself a whole system of relationships, and no easier to assess than the more obvious signs of disturbance in a child. Such cohesiveness depends on many conditions, some of which certainly lie outside of the family circle. The great importance of the family life is very properly stressed by the Gluecks. But many forces from the environment impinge on the life of the family and have their significant share in making it what it is. It has been suggested that for multiproblem families the causes of their trouble lie more within than outside the family, but this too is a quite dubious proposition.

There is still another sense in which we may speak of critical factors. Of the multitude of conditions associated with a relatively high incidence of delinquency, some are so bound up with others that they cannot be regarded as independent correlates; some may be incidental; some may be merely consequential; and some may be products of the same complex of conditions from which delinquency arises. Through statistical devices we can in a measure determine which of various correlated factors are clearer indications of the presence of delinquency, and which are better indicators of the delinquency rate.

An illustration offered is in Bernard Lander's *Towards an Understanding of Juvenile Delinquency* (Columbia University Press, 1942). He concluded that in a mixed area the percentage of non-whites and the percentage of home ownership were indicators almost as effective as a much larger number of variables taken together. Where the percentage of home ownership was relatively high, delinquency rates were low. This conclusion was for the city of Baltimore and could not be generalized without similar research in different types of cities. More broadly, Lander concluded that two clusters of characteristics sufficed to account for almost all the covariation of factors, these being "socioeconomic status," referring to factors indicating educational level and housing conditions, and "anomie" (his term for far-reaching social disorganization) correlated with the percentages of Negro population and those of home ownership and delinquency itself. His most drastic inference was that low economic status was not significantly related to delinquency unless it was accompanied by the demographic factors spelling "anomie." Lander's study aroused considerable interest and some constructively critical comments.[2] He is now engaged in a follow-up study of larger scale, covering Baltimore and two other cities in different parts of the country, in which he plans to include several additional factors for the determination of the presence of "anomie."

To conclude, the statistical study of the correlations of delinquency with a variety of other conditions or factors can take us only a part of the way to understanding of the causation of delinquency. We shall see later in Part Two that any particular area of the environment of youth—the home, the school, the playground, the street—may be the focus or the spur of the kind of disturbance and disorientation that is likely to result in delinquency. The young grow up with a set of expectations and aspirations that are relative both to their indoctrinations and to the situations within which they are bred, and the conditions that defeat these expectations and aspirations vary accordingly. Delinquency is the similar response of disgruntled or defeated youth to a particular collocation of circumstances that provoke deep-seated resentments and rebellion. Always we must get down to the impact of conditions on the mind of youth. The *motivation* of delinquency must be understandable before the quest for causation can end.

Influences emanating from the outside, adverse conditions of the locality, thwartings and maladjustments in the home, school frustrations, unhappy associations, untoward circumstances of any sort—except so far as they are counteracted by constructive influences, together make their impact on the minds of the young, who in turn respond according to their particular capacities and limitations. Experience alone can teach us which conjunctures of conditions in varying environments are most prejudicial to the development of a well-ordered life for the growing child. Already we have sufficient evidence to enable us to use this experience far more effectively than it has been as yet, both for preventing and for checking delinquent tendencies. This evidence is the basis for the strategy considerations we develop in Part Three.

### Causation and Treatment

In our judgment a decided weakness in many of the programs, not least the official programs, directed to the treatment of delinquents is the fact that they are not geared to the on-going researches of various kinds—sociological, psychological, and psychiatric—that are increasingly throwing light on the nature and problem of delinquent behavior. Treatment programs are too often not armed with the skills needed to cope with the difficult task of rehabilitation. We point out elsewhere the great need for better screening of cases, for better understanding of the problems of the young, for special attention to the early stages of trouble. It has been too often assumed that the treatment of delinquents is a matter of common sense, or good will, or proper discipline, and very few attempts have been made to test the assumption by a follow-up of the treatment. But such inadequate records as we possess indicate that the results are far from satisfactory.

It is sometimes asserted that study of the causation of delinquency does not provide solutions to the problems of prevention and of reform; that such solutions are more likely to be found through experience on the job, through trial and error; that the cure of a disease is often found when the cause is still unknown. The last statement, however, is at best incomplete and may be quite misleading. In some areas, including medicine, cures or solutions of problems have been discovered even where the specific causal connection is unknown. The discovery of various antibiotic drugs is an illustration. But such discoveries were preceded by research that revealed the role of viruses in the causation of disease and the counteracting effects of various bacterial agencies. In medicine vast efforts are devoted to the etiology of disease, and in cancer and heart disease, for example, with already significant results. The chances of the discovery of a cure are immensely advanced if we can reach down to the causative factors. Even an intermediate link in the causal chain can be most important for treatment or prevention. Such was the discovery of the relationship between malaria and the anopheles mosquito.

What is especially important for treatment is the study of the background of the delinquent. We must learn, on the one hand, his previous experiences: his relationships at home; the difficulties, thwartings, misadventures he has met at home, at school, with his associates; the influences that have worked on him; and, on the other hand, the characteristic attitudes he has developed under these conditions, his rationalizations of his behavior, his outlook on life. From this knowledge we can broadly place him in some category, and we have already enough information from research and experience to appreciate what are the most hopeful approaches to a program of treatment. Research is constantly revealing the interrelations and interdependences of conditions —in other words, the causal connections between them. In the light of this knowledge, in the spread of this knowledge, lies our best hope for more effective treatment and more well-grounded efforts toward prevention—especially prevention of the development of those early tendencies that may ripen into confirmed delinquency.

# 5

## Social-Class Theories
## of Delinquency

The greater prevalence of youthful delinquency in the poorer urban areas has long been made a subject for study and interpretation. Some earlier studies, such as those of the Chicago school of "social ecologists" and especially of Shaw and McKay,[1] laid stress on the relationship of delinquency to the physical environment and produced statistical evidence to show that the areas of highest delinquency were those transitional areas in which industry was encroaching on residential districts and housing was becoming dilapidated. The successive groups which occupied such deteriorating areas were alike characterized by high delinquency rates. It is noteworthy that each of these successive groups were bodies of in-migrants, entering at a very low economic level. Later studies pointed out some other characteristics of areas in which high delinquency rates prevailed; such was the case, for example, where disprivileged groups, notably Negroes, had made an initial entry into congested districts and met with resistance from the earlier residents.

Other scholars were more concerned with the association between the prevalence of delinquency and the social or class level. In their well-known "Yankee City" studies, Warner and Lunt dwelt upon the association of high delinquency with lower social class.[2] They defined the class level by a composite index, including occupational status, place of residence, educational back-

ground, and housing conditions. The basis of classification is not
wholly satisfactory. It may serve reasonably well as a general
indicator of social class differentials, but it is inadequate as a
criterion of delinquency ratings. We suggest that the two factors
which in combination are most closely associated with delinquency are urbanized poverty and ethnic or racial discrimination. The grounds for this conclusion have already been stated
and will be further developed as we proceed. Such other factors
as occupational status, educational standards, type and place of
residence are mostly consequential on these two.

Other formulations attribute the prevalence of delinquency
to the impact of the prevailing value system of a total society,
the beliefs and practices that are operative, if not openly acknowledged, within it. The young are attuned to follow the example set by their elders and those who are more limited in
their opportunities or less competent in evasion get into trouble,
though they may be no more delinquent than, say, the shrewd
officials of a big corporation who succeed in flouting the legal
code. This is the position taken by writers like Milton Barron.[3]
The view that children imitate the ways of the fathers is of
course an old and reasonably respectable sociological doctrine.
It is broadly acceptable, but quite inadequate to explain the
varieties of behavior or the changing values of successive generations. The growing youth is exposed to conflicting or competing
values, and often enough is resistant to or restive under some
of the indoctrinations of his breeding. The theory fails to take
into account the impact of differential environments and of
changing situations on the young, for in one important sense the
environment of every group is different and the situation of
every new generation differs from that of its predecessor. The
theory is too wholesale, and entirely lacking in subtlety.

Within the same general context two recent theories call for
more detailed examination, since they are sponsored by highly
competent students of the subject and contain some important
insights. The differences between the two are also significant.
Albert K. Cohen[4] maintains that the high delinquency rate is
largely due to the baffled aspiration of lower-class youth to rise

to middle-class status; whereas, according to Walter B. Miller, the lower-class culture spontaneously generates among its young a "delinquent subculture."[5] These positions are reminiscent of the viewpoint of the Chicago "ecologists" who held that the character of the urban area in which lower-class youth were bred put pressures on them which explained the higher delinquency rate.

Cohen, the leader in this newer line of interpretation, holds that lower-class youth are caught in a vise between the way of living and the philosophy of life characteristic of their own class and the influences exerted by the middle-class conditions and attitudes to which they are in one way or another exposed. They lack the means, the habituations, and the training to realize their aspirations to this higher status. The values current in their own class—the easy spending of whatever they make, the lack of industriousness, the uncalculating aggressiveness of manner—are contrary to typical middle-class ways. Frustrated in their ambitions they fall back with a kind of revulsion to the values of their own class. They react with hostility to "middle-class norms" and to the assumptions of superiority of middle-class youth. Cohen regards a certain wanton and aimless brutality exhibited by some delinquents as a violent repudiation of middle-class standards. They seek for status in illegitimate ways, ganging up to assert their own internal status.

Some features of Cohen's theory are certainly significant and give a lead to further advances in the interpretation of delinquent behavior. He emphasizes the effect of frustration, of baffled aspiration, of the falling back on illegitimate means to enhance the quest for status within a peer group in an unpropitious environment. He provides good insights and fine descriptions concerning the undirected or nonutilitarian character of youthful gang behavior, which is in marked contrast to the operation of the adult gang. Various students of the subject have followed and developed Cohen's viewpoint. Cloward and Ohlin have recognized that youth subject to the stresses and lacks emphasized by Cohen may react in a variety of ways, in response to different situations or "opportunity structures," and specify three particular reactions.[6] The first or criminal-minded type seeks illegitimate means and devious associations for immediate profit, hoping to make a killing. The second, the conflict gang, corresponds to Cohen's group, concerned with "rep"—status attained through fights and toughness. The third is the withdrawn or "retreatist" type, shuffling along for the snatched pleasures of the moment, getting by and keeping out of trouble when they can, and resorting to escapist devices, dope and drink and sexual indulgences. Another line of classification of the types of deviant behavior has been proposed by Robert K. Merton.[7] Most relevant here is what he styles "behavioral ritualism" in which the deviant, rejecting some aspects of his social milieu and overconforming to others that fit in with his interests, retreats, along with fellow deviants, into special institutionalized activities adapted to the lesser rewards available to him.

Walter B. Miller's interpretation of the role of lower-class culture in the evocation of delinquent behavior is in one respect diametrically opposed to Cohen's. For Miller it is not the baffled aspiration to middle-class status that sparks the retreat into a delinquent subculture; instead, the lower-class culture spontaneously generates the delinquent type in two closely related forms, the adolescent street-corner group as portrayed by William F. Whyte in *Street Corner Society* and the more aggressive law-violating gang. Such delinquency is regarded as primarily an unlawful way of achieving lower-class values. The delinquent subcultures are geared to the "focal concerns" of lower-class life.

The focal concerns specified are trouble, toughness, excitement, belonging, status, fate, autonomy. This congeries of preoccupations strikes us as a curious and rather capricious selection, especially when presented as characterizing a particular social class. Miller speaks of them as issues which command widespread or persistent attention and a high degree of emotional involvement, much more than they do in the middle-class society. Why not, to try another selection, economic security, good jobs, a woman at his service, better living conditions, children that grow up to support their parents?

Miller goes on to explain how these focal concerns, especially status and belonging, are built into the behavior system of the young and are given a special direction within the delinquent gang.

The first concern mentioned, trouble, is highly ambivalent in his formulation. It has a different significance for men, women, and children respectively. They all want to keep out of trouble, especially with officials or authorities. But under certain conditions there is also a certain status-conferring distinction in getting into trouble. This prestige element is cultivated in the system of the gang.

We do not feel it is necessary to enlarge on the problems posed by Miller's theory, especially as much of our critique of Cohen is also relevant here. We find much merit in Miller's description of the pressures and impulses that operate in the gang setting. But his descriptions of lower-class concerns are highly selective and needlessly generalized, and the contrasts he finds between the dominant standards of lower-class and of middle-class society are overdrawn and inadequately corroborated. He makes excessive play of some features that may be found sporadically but by no means universally in lower-class society. For example, he dwells considerably on the "female-based" household of lower-class society. It is true that in high-delinquency areas the family is not infrequently broken, or the father out of work or inadequate. But in some of these areas the family is, broadly speaking, patriarchal rather than matriarchal. This is usually the case in Italian sectors and to some extent among Puerto Ricans. As for the contrast with middle-class society, might we not with at least equal plausibility call the middle-class suburban family "female-based" since the father commutes to the city and returns in the evening, sometimes carrying the load of his office into his home and hoping that the mother has settled the problem of the children for the day?

Various aspects of the theories associated with Miller and Cohen have been subjected to an effective critique by a number of sociologists.[8] While these theories have been stimulating and provocative of further research and while they have certainly directed attention to a very significant feature of delinquency problems—the baffled urge of youth for recognition, belonging, status, we hold that they without warrant attribute this feature to the "culture" or the "mobility" or to the low estate of a particular social class. It is with this casual imputation that we are mainly concerned here. In the first place, we find the categories "lower-class culture" and "middle-class culture" somewhat misleading, when used to contrast two different ways of life. In lower- or working-class neighborhoods the amount of recorded delinquency is certainly higher than in more prosperous areas. But there is quite considerable variation among lower-class neighborhoods in amount of delinquency. While studying some tables reporting indices of economic and social conditions in New York City, the writer was struck by the seemingly anomalous position of one Health Center district in Manhattan. Its socioeconomic rating was the third lowest of all the thirty Health Center districts of the City, but its delinquency rating was in the median range and in our indices of social pathology it was also far superior to the high-delinquency areas.

When, however, we examined the figures for ethnic origins in the various districts this particular one proved to have quite a low proportion of recent in-migrants, who consist mainly of Puerto Ricans and Southern Negroes. This finding is entirely in accord with the evidences we present in the text which show that in interpreting delinquency differentials we must look at the specific conjuncture of environmental and demographic factors characterizing a particular area, and not rely on broad and elusive distinctions such as that between lower-class and middle-class culture.[9]

Cohen makes much of the statistical fact that the police and court records show a preponderance of cases occurring in the lower-class areas, but, as we have already pointed out, the statistics are unduly unfavorable to the people of these areas. If, as we have argued, the actual volume of delinquency should be represented as a gradient as we pass from the groups least affected to those with the heaviest incidence, the ground for any identification of delinquency as a class phenomenon is removed. Delinquency occurs in every area, among the youth of every social class, to an extent sufficient to refute the charge that it stems from the "culture" peculiar to a lower social class. If it occurs in greater volume in many lower-class areas there are conditions which cannot properly be called "cultural" that predispose to it. Cohen cites as supporting his thesis a study made by W. C. Kvaraceus. Kvaraceus has certainly shown a strong bias toward Cohen's position but from the study in question we draw a different conclusion. What the "overwhelming majority" of families of delinquent children have in common, said Kvaraceus, is poverty. While there may be some exaggeration in this statement, the association of poverty with higher delinquency rates seems beyond doubt. Is poverty then a cultural attribute? It is not a condition preferred or desired by the poor; quite the contrary. They are habituated to living in poverty and must adjust their behavior to that condition. Because of this necessity, certain culture traits develop, but these do not constitute their culture or even constitute its major characteristics. Even if they did, they still would not necessarily imply any special proneness to delinquency. The earth is still inhabited mostly by poverty-stricken peoples, but we have no grounds for saying that most of them show high delinquency rates. It is where poverty is accompanied by various special conditions, for which the poor cannot possibly be regarded as chiefly responsible, that high delinquency rates prevail.

Delinquency is highest in the deteriorating and overcrowded areas into which in-migrant groups, generally subject to some form of ethnic or racial discrimination, have penetrated, causing a shifting of some part of the earlier populations. The in-migrant groups usually come from more rural areas, are not well adjusted to urban living, arrive without resources or special skills, and during the first generation after their arrival are particularly helpless in alien surroundings and are subject to various forms of exploitation. They have delinquency rates out of proportion to the rest of the population. To attribute their swelling delinquency statistics to the vain efforts of the young to achieve middle-class status does not provide any adequate explanation. There may be no cited evidence of high delinquency in their previous culture—that of the Puerto Ricans is an example. We must therefore find the answer in the conjuncture of unfavorable conditions. It would be a needlessly roundabout conclusion to call the discontent and frustration of the young under these conditions a revulsion, a "reaction formation," resulting from their failure to attain "middle-class status."

It was in the kind of in-migrant area we have just described, in a district of Boston, that Miller made the studies on which he based his theory, and he himself has admitted that his description mainly applied to such "residual lower-class groups." But this limitation surely disqualifies the attribution of certain delinquency traits to a lower class as such, to its "culture," or even to an aspect of its culture. The youth of these impoverished in-migrant groups thrust into urban slums suffer in a particularly high degree from a complex of adverse factors, in their home life, in their schooling, in the pressures of their whole environment. Their expectations, stimulated by the influences deriving from the ambient American environment with its emphasis on "getting on," "rising in the world," even beyond the youthful aspirations characteristic of young people everywhere, are frustrated. The resulting response varies according to the particular youth's temperament, training, or special situation; it may be a kind of resignation, a defiant repudiation of the values that cannot be achieved, a makeshift acceptance of lesser opportunities, a belligerent struggle against what is deemed gross discrimination or neglect or abuse—the variations are endless.

In reacting in any of these ways, these young people—allowing for the difference in the mode of expression—are only doing what youth of any class do when their ambitions or expectations are continuously thwarted and they find themselves thoroughly disgruntled with the conditions that defeat them. The ensuing disorientation or alienation may stem from many different situations and may express itself in many different forms. It may be traceable primarily to excessive or arbitrary discipline or to lack of discipline, to family neglect or mistreatment, to a feeling that one does not belong, to persistent failure of any kind, or even to sheer accident. Delinquency exists in all social classes, and is statistically most prevalent where conditions are such as to evoke attitudes of rebellion, defiance, or, broadly speaking, alienation in a larger proportion of the youthful population. There can be little doubt that the in-migrant groups of ethnic minorities are those most exposed to such conditions.

Under these conditions many youth feel frustrated, certainly, and some of them resort to illegitimate means to relieve their frustration. But their frustration is more directly explained when one learns how and why they are retarded in school, how they feel cramped in the promiscuous environment of one-room or two-room homes and are often at odds with parents who are too ignorant to help them or to understand their problems and who themselves are often bewildered by their own troubles, and when we realize that they have exchanged the congenial friendly neighborliness of the poor communities from which they migrated for the distracting confusion of an urban slum.

Within the urban community the youth of the poor and the youth of the middle class have not such different viewpoints, standards, and aspirations as to create a cultural gulf between them. In the city the neighborhood sense is weakened by mobility, by the mixed character of most neighborhoods, by the many channeled influences of the city as a whole. But the poorer youth read pretty much the same school texts as do those of the middle class; they are taught the same American history; they are subjected to the same American traditions and frequently enough are ready to absorb them. They like pretty much the same comics, watch the same TV programs, and go more or less to the same movies. They have the same love of the same games and they have similar youthful yearnings, similar stirrings and misgivings about sex, though the differences of situation make some differences in resulting relationships. The youth of the middle class gang up in groups and go in for mischievous pranks that not infrequently contain an element of delinquency. They have, however, better life-chances, since their parents have more means to provide these. Their mode of life consequently diverges from that of lower-class youth. The aspirations of middle-class adolescents become geared, most likely, to social rewards and material success, and in the process of seeking these their habits and outlooks become increasingly different from those of that portion of the lower class who live in the slum areas. Another consideration is that these areas tend to harbor down-and-outs, misfits, and such resourceless persons. Adult crime is more frequent than it is in more well-to-do neighborhoods, and the example is more easily followed by susceptible and frustrated youth.

These are broad considerations, but more specific evidences also discredit the attribution of delinquency to some inclusive culture complex characteristic of the lower-status society as such. Some significant statistical evidences, for example, are offered in a recent study by Reiss and Rhodes,[10] on the basis of which the authors conclude that "there is no simple relationship between ascribed social status and delinquency." One of their findings is that the low-status boy who lives in a high-status area has "almost no chance of becoming a delinquent,"—less chance, indeed, than the high-status boy of the area. "The more the lower-class boy is in a minority in the school and residential community, the less likely is he to become a delinquent." On the other hand, a high-status boy living in a low-status area has a greater chance of becoming delinquent than his fellow living in a high-status area. Such findings would certainly seem to conflict with the Cohen doctrine that the pressure of middle-class norms on lower-class boys accounts for their high delinquency rates.

What further inferences can we draw from these and other corroborative findings? Obviously they illustrate the influence of an environment on the behavior of those exposed to it. But they also strongly imply that certain features of an environment are peculiarly significant for the morale of the young. In the higher-status environment the low-status youth still lives with his lower-status family and we have some evidence that suggests he consorts with his status peers in the area. Is his lowered delinquency rate then to be attributed to the greater opportunities and outlets for his energies that a higher-status neighborhood affords? Is it because he goes to the same schools and shares the same social occasions with higher-status youth and thus is encouraged to maintain aspirations for the future that certain conditions of low-status neighborhoods discourage? There are various possibilities here that call for further exploration.

To attribute a particular phenomenon within a social area to its "culture" seems to us to be in any event a quite dubious and unenlightening assertion. In the first place, the term "culture" is a kind of total bracket for all the manifestations of a society, including the phenomena in question. Many sociologists refuse to draw any distinction between a "culture" and a "social system," and those who seek to differentiate them have not succeeded in gaining any wide acceptance. Aside from that, the phenomenon in question, delinquency, cannot be regarded as a norm of the culture, since the majority of young persons within it are not classified as delinquents. At most, we could assume only that the lower-class culture made the young somewhat more exposed or susceptible to delinquent tendencies, and even that assumption must be qualified, since the lower-class group is not responsible for the physical environment and we know that the environmental conditions of overcrowding and consequent promiscuity, as well as the lack of opportunities, must share the blame. Finally, Cohen's explanation for the resort of the low-status group to gang delinquency—that it has in some degree accepted and "internalized" middle-class standards—seems unnecessary in view of all the frustrations that beset the young in getting along in urban slum environments of our great cities, in getting along at school or with their disturbed or disrupted families, in seeking employment, in fulfilling the normal aspirations of boys of any class.

# 6

# *Conclusions on the Relation of Culture and Delinquency*

We have seen that a number of variant theories have recently been developed which have broadly attributed the prevalence of delinquency, in general or in particular social areas, to the prevailing "culture," in effect to the society itself. The values or goals acceptable to the culture or the social milieu are such, it is claimed, as to be directly or indirectly evocative of delinquency in the young. Of course all behavior of any kind within a society can be attributed to the character of that society. It is then equally responsible for the nondelinquency of the great majority as for the delinquency of the minority. What explains everything explains nothing. We may select certain broad aspects of a society or a culture and conclude that these are favorable to the development of delinquent tendencies. We may take, for example, the mobility characteristic of American life, whether geographical or social ("vertical"), or the plurality of moral and religious codes, or the "loosening of family ties," or the emphasis on financial success, or the prevalence on TV broadcasts of scenes exhibiting crime and violence, or all of these together. We may be justified in regarding these conditions as predisposing to delinquent attitudes, but even so there are multitudes of young persons who do not appear to be seriously affected by them, and moreover, we have to set against such factors those that may on the other hand be conducive to the inculcation of decent citizenship.

In short, what we must know to interpret the incidence and the volume of delinquency, and certainly in order to combat it effectively, is, first, the differential conditions of the narrower areas where the delinquency rate is highest and then the further differentials that apply to the youth in these areas who actually exhibit delinquent habits. These further differentials are the family relations, the school relations, and the neighborhood relations of the affected youth. With these leads we reach finally the particular mentality of the youths themselves—their temperaments, their emotional make-ups, their psychological traits, as these respond to the special predisposing conditions of their new environment and its particular setting for themselves. We will still be far from the full knowledge of why any individual youngster became delinquent while others, perhaps his own siblings, did not, but we will possess reasonably adequate information as to why so many of these youngsters did take to delinquent ways.

The present tendency to attribute the prevalence of delinquency to the impact of the whole "culture" of a society or of a particular class or group is so widespread that some further comments on it may be in order, especially since it often carries the implication that only by wholesale reformation of our value system can we do much about preventing delinquency or reducing its volume.

We question particularly the sharp demarcation of a lower-class value system (or morality or culture) from that generally accepted or pursued by other classes within the total community, and the concomitant stress on the exceptional amount of delinquency it is presumed to engender. We dispute the further assumption that there is a homogeneous lower-class culture or morality, characteristic of all sorts and conditions of people who may be assigned to this lower class.

Let us examine these counts in turn. Walter B. Miller speaks of a "lower-class culture" as a cultural system in its own right, with an integrity of its own, with a characteristic set of practices, focal concerns, and ways of behaving that are meaningfully and systematically related to one another rather than to corresponding features of middle-class culture.[1] We have already disputed the relevance to lower-class culture of the rather curious list of "focal concerns" he assigns to it. The lower class, meaning the class distinguished particularly by its low income level, is not homogeneous. Its delinquency rate varies markedly according to the environmental conditions in which its members are placed. Lower-class residents in small towns in New England and in the West, in some mining villages, in certain urban pockets do not, on any evidence we have, exhibit delinquency rates approaching those of, say, Bedford-Stuyvesant or central Harlem in New York City. Lower-class in-migrants to urban slums exhibit higher delinquency rates than the same groups did prior to this migration. Different environments have a significant relation to life chances and to attitudes. The youths of groups subject to discrimination usually have inferior educational advantages and career opportunities. We have no reason to assume that the lower class is inherently less law-abiding than any higher class. The response to the denial of opportunities, taking the form of rebelliousness and resort to illegitimate means, is a natural human response not limited to any class.

One of the disadvantages of the unduly sharp demarcation of cultural or social lines is that it prevents a proper estimation of the differences that do distinguish groups—income groups, class groups, religious groups, ethnic groups, and all others. Differences exist everywhere within an area of common living, and so do likenesses. Difference and likeness combine in endless ways, creating congenialities and aversions of every description. The more insulated or exclusive a group is, the greater will be its characteristic differences from those of the environing community. Under some conditions, where seclusion from the rest of society is marked or complete, we may properly speak of a subculture. A ghetto becomes a subculture in time, as does a certain type of monastery, or a prison for criminals with lengthy sentences. But the term is not appropriate to a social class which is exposed to the same kind of schooling, the same media of communication, and numerous other forms of contact within the one larger society.

We turn to our second count. The delinquency recorded against lower-class youth is not different in kind but only in degree from that in higher economic groups; in fact we have sufficient reason to believe that official statistics tend to overestimate the disparity between lower and higher economic groups in the prevalence of delinquency. We have already offered some evidence tending to discount the sharper differentials of the official statistics, but a further illustration may be given here. One study, covering a rather large sample of Western and Midwestern high-school-age youth and using a measure of reported delinquent behavior instead of the official figures of police and courts, actually found no significant differences in the amount of delinquency of boys and girls of different socioeconomic levels.[2] We cannot doubt that the actual volume of delinquency is greater under certain circumstances, as in our great cities, for some markedly disadvantaged lower-class groups, but there too we have reason to believe that the differential is not nearly as steep as the official figures indicate. We must definitely reject Miller's thesis that "lower-class culture" has its own value system that predisposes its youth toward delinquency in a quite special way.

We cannot regard the delinquency figures for various city slum areas as an indication that there is a homogeneous lower-class culture. We cannot accept the view that a lower economic class exhibits motivations and aspirations distinctively different from those of the more prosperous classes. All want the same kinds of things within the limits of their respective circumstances. These bloc theories of culture exaggerate differences that are more attributable to differential environment than to inbred differences of values. If we want to get to grips with the problem of youthful delinquency we must think instead of eliminating slum conditions with their concomitant disadvantages and handicaps of the young, and meanwhile of providing aid, direction, and opportunity for the more vulnerable youth of such areas before delinquency habits are formed or confirmed.

### Delinquency as the Repudiation of Culture

The subjective and insecure grounds of the culture-bound theories of delinquency may perhaps be inferred from the fact that the two leading exponents whose views we have been examining offer quite contradictory interpretations of it. For Cohen it is not the lower class itself that breeds delinquent tendencies but the unsuccessful attempt to pass beyond it, to rise out of it into middle-class society and its contrasting culture. For Miller, on the other hand, it is within the lower-class culture that delinquency is fostered, by the very nature of its "focal concerns."

Alongside of these doctrines we may place the view that confirmed delinquency implies a total rejection of the values sustaining the society. These values are not those of any particular group, but of the society as a whole. Thou shalt not rob, thou shalt not damage the property of thy neighbor, and so forth. These injunctions are not the code of a group; they are fundamental prescriptions common to civilized society. The confirmed delinquent rejects them. In other words, he puts himself outside the code. He is at odds with society. He is in a state of "anomie," a term first popularized by the French sociologist, Emile Durkheim, to signify rulelessness.

We have seen that a characteristic attitude associated with habitual delinquency is a sense of frustration, rebellion, alienation—alienation from the ways of the home, from the requirements of the school, from the prescriptions of authorities who intervene to punish the delinquents or to try to reform them. They add at odds with their society. "Anomie," however, is too strong a term to express accurately their state of mind. They break laws without compunction (many "respectable" people do the same when they can get away with it safely), and they go further in exhibiting a dislike and hatred of authority, disregarding obligations which the large majority of the young respect. But there are limits to their lawlessness. They observe some rules, and in their gangs they follow a rather strict code of their own, with its appropriate loyalties.

Robert Merton has accordingly described the attitude as "modified anomie," a condition in which culturally prescribed goals are pursued by "anomic" means, illegitimate because either unlawful or morally taboo. The characterization is neat and the term "modified anomie" might be acceptable, but the reference to "culturally prescribed goals" may be misleading. Are the ends sought by the habitual delinquent properly designated as culturally prescribed, and if so, in what sense? Is it the ends or the means that are culturally prescribed? The ends delinquents usually pursue are simple ends, ends that youth everywhere seek, irrespective of particular cultures. They want more liberty, less control by elders or authorities, more recognition, more affection, more congenial peer associations, certain material objects within reach but which they can attain only by filching, certain pleasures, such as riding in cars, which they miss but are tempted to seize illegally. Some of these ends they seek to gain by illegitimate means, others by setting up their own organizations in order to obtain within them a substitute for the recognition, status, and freedom otherwise denied them.

Moreover, the means they employ, whether illegitimate or legitimate, are not calculated or intended to secure what we usually think of as specifically cultural ends. We think of American culture as geared to success, to rising in the world through the acquisition of wealth, to the entrance of the young into colleges and universities which open the road to higher status—in general, to material prosperity. But delinquents only exceptionally pursue these goals. The illegitimate means they adopt are sporadic and undirected to any end beyond an immediate gratification. Their petty filching is mostly bravado, prank, something to show the others, an incidental response to easy opportunity. Their rowdyism gets them nowhere except into trouble. The only regularized resort to illegitimate means, if we except the minority case of the narcotic addict, is to defend, in the name of status, a most unprofitable claim. It is the gang's defense of its "turf" against the invasion of the members of another gang, leading to "rumbles" with their danger to life and limb and the likelihood of police arrest. Such illegitimate activities are no more designed to advance a career than are the legitimate contests of schoolboy athletics.

The lack of "access to legitimate means" is made much of in some recent theories of delinquency, and this obvious feature of slum life is certainly provocative of delinquency. But the effect is not designed to remove the cause. Poverty, the peculiarly cramping poverty of the city slum, is a major reason why slum youth cannot compete effectively with the youth of better neighborhoods in the scramble for the "good things of life"—poverty as a lack of capital for enterprise, but, even more, poverty as blocking in multiple ways the educational and social preparation well-to-do youths enjoy, poverty as debarring slum youths from the associations the well-to-do possess with influential persons who give them promising jobs, poverty as inculcating certain modes of speech, mannerisms, and habits that are taboo in higher economic circles. No illegitimate means available to the disprivileged youth can serve as a substitute for the means they lack. The illegitimate means to which they resort are no equivalent, bring no comparable rewards; they are at best an unhappy makeshift, a very partial release from the frustrations they feel. Only in so far as society reforms the conditions and makes accessible the legitimate means, will these youths be able effectively to pursue "culturally prescribed goals."

# Salient and Crucial Situations in the Causation of Delinquency

We have referred to certain "trigger" events that can mean the parting of the ways, decisive occasions that upset the uneasy or unstable equilibrium of a youth who up to that point has been "going straight," though subjected to strains or harassing restrictions or failures. Such an event may be, for example, a jarring rebuff, some treatment that seems to the youth grossly unfair, the loss of a mother in a time of trouble, or personal disfigurement resulting from an accident or a disease such as acne. Prominent among such precipitating situations are happenings that mean a loss of "face," the realization that one has been rejected or does not belong with peers or within the family circle. The "outcast" feeling especially is the kind of disorienting experience that leads to confirmed delinquency.

The crucial situation may not be a single event but the climax of a series of frustrations or disappointments, the breaking point before the turning point. An instance of this is offered sometimes when a boy who has been doing poorly at school and behaving not too well otherwise becomes definitely a school drop-out. The die is cast, and the new situation makes easy the road to confirmed delinquency.

We have spoken of the crucial situation as precipitating the downward turn, but we should recognize also that a timely intervention may mean a turnabout in the opposite direction. A

wise counselor at the right moment, a bit of friendly aid in a
time of trouble, a considerate parent who honestly probes to the
root of a misunderstanding between himself and his boy, may
inaugurate a change of outlook that can lead to a new direction
of behavior. There are many vulnerable youth, suffering disturbances and tendencies beset by grudges and fears, whose
future depends on what is done to them and for them at this
crucial stage. Here, indeed, is the greatest field for preventive
treatment against the development of delinquency.

In the following paragraphs we characterize certain ways in
which, within the major areas of youthful experience, critical or
crucial situations develop.

### The Family Circle

Since the family is the primary and almost universal locus
for the upbringing of the young, there is naturally a large amount
of literature dealing with its role in that respect. In a very broad
sense it might be claimed that any serious tendency to delinquency in the young can be attributed to family upbringing, but
only in the sense in which the development of all kinds of tendencies, for better or worse, are at least to a degree dependent on
what happens in the family. We shall here endeavor merely to
indicate certain critical situations in family relationships that
may determine whether a particular child goes straight or develops attitudes conducive to delinquency.

There are various family conditions that are repeatedly the
source of delinquent behavior. We hear much, for example, of
"broken homes," and the records of institutions for delinquents
frequently show a disproportionate number of children who
come from such homes. No doubt a broken home, with only one
parent to aid and guide and support the children, can be quite
detrimental to a child's welfare, but we must remember that the
youthful inmates of institutions come mostly from homes which
have other serious defects. Desertion is not infrequently the
cause of a broken home, and it by no means follows that the
presence of the kind of father who is ready to abandon his

family obligations bodes any good to the children. The charge is sometimes made that the children of working mothers are more liable to become delinquent, but various studies have shown little or no basis for it.

What is of much greater importance in the upbringing of children is the type of relationship established in the earliest years between parents and children. The first learning, the first contacts with what we call reality, the first indoctrinations come from the parents. The actual content of what is instilled and the viewpoints concerning people or the meaning of things, are very often dissolved in the process of growing up, by subsequent experiences and by what the child learns at school, from the media of communication, and from the give-and-take of social contacts. What endures much more firmly, striking more deeply into the child's being, is the habits he forms and the manner in which he expresses his relations to others. Just as the toilet training he receives in the nursing stage stays with him for life, so certain primary attitudes, confirmed by appropriate habits, tend to be incorporated in the personality. Here, in these earliest years, is the first critical stage in the child's development. The discipline of these years is a character-molding factor. The spirit in which discipline is conveyed, if it is conveyed at all, whether it is sympathetic and understanding or peremptory and harsh, all affect the extent to which the discipline is accepted and integrated or resented and in the course of time rejected.

Other critical situations may arise from the vicissitudes of schooling, where family direction and encouragement may prove decisive. These situations will be considered in the section which follows. Here we briefly refer to two other situations in respect to which the relation between parents and children becomes critical.

The first is the onset of puberty. On the whole, parents, at least in countries that have puritanic traditions, are peculiarly awkward in the way they instruct their children on this subject. Some evidence suggests that mothers are wiser with girls than fathers with boys. In any event, occasions occur that lead to bitter dissensions in the home, discussions which can start a train of troubles.

The other critical situations center round the choice of a career. Parents are frequently unable to understand that their children are not made in their own image. They want them to take up the parental interests and pursuits. Fathers on one social level want their sons to enter their own business or their own line of business; on another social level they are ambitious that their sons should rise in the world. Such desires are natural and proper enough, but when children insist on following their own road, when, for example, the son of a successful businessman is set on becoming an artist, a clash may occur that results in the youth's alienation from the family.

The types of parent-youth dissension we have mentioned become critical situations when family cohesion is loose, as is not infrequently the case. As the young are growing up, in the diversity of relationships and conflicting demands, the family scene is not unlikely to be a somewhat troubled one. This is the time when differences in early training and inculcated discipline bear their respective fruits.

It has long been recognized that family cohesion is much stronger in some groups than in others, and that juvenile delinquency is definitely less frequent where family cohesion is marked. It is not so well recognized that even in groups where family cohesion is weak, in the sense that the husband is none too faithful to his marriage vows but an authoritative value system is inculcated in the home, the delinquency rate is also likely to be low. The modes of training the young may differ, but all types emphasize respect by the young for their parents and elders, and the early indoctrination insists on some primary values that enshrine this attitude of respect. In a considerable majority of Jewish homes, for example, early training of this type, including the value of family cohesion, is the rule. In the traditional Chinese home, again, respect for family obligations is the very center of all ethical training. In the Mexican family, particularly in the less urbanized areas, the father is recognized as the source of authority, and whatever the relations between father and mother, respect for both and for elders in general is instilled into the children from the first. In other respects, the doctrinal upbringing in these three types of families is very dissimilar, but the common inculcation of a disciplined respect for parents is sufficient to insure a comparative absence of serious delinquency in the young. In families of these types, differences or clashes or rifts that in many American families would become trigger situations are overridden by the presence of fundamental loyalties.

From this point of view the traditional Mexican family, which is found with variations in other parts of Latin America, has a rather special interest. The roles of the father and mother are sharply differentiated. The male is the home authority, the female is the housekeeper. Both have their respective responsibilities. The mother is expected to be very "feminine" and self-effacing, but this by no means implies that she is weak or yielding in relation to the children. She can be quite authoritative in her appropriate field. The father may be somewhat careless about his marital relations, but because of the demarcation of roles that fact does not break up the family union, and even if the children become disillusioned about their father or actually afraid of him, his authority is still respected and their need for affection is satisfied through the much-enduring mother.[1]

One significant aspect of the Mexican situation is that broken families are considerably more frequent, at least among the lower class, than in the United States, as is shown by the 1950 census of Mexico, but under such conditions the traditional value system is maintained by the mother and respect for authority seems to endure in the children. Thus we find that in the traditional Mexican family neither the prevailing abject poverty nor the fact that the family is broken is conducive to much delinquency. The conclusion would appear to be that when the young are brought up from their earliest years within a clear-cut value system that sets a high premium on the authority of the elders the tendency to juvenile delinquency is low.

In sum, if one ventured to reduce to the simplest terms the

element of family training that is most essential as a safeguard against the development of delinquent attitudes, it would be the inculcation in the child of a *sense* of obligation. When this lesson is learned in the earliest years, clothed with the doctrinal authority of the elders, it is likely to endure and to remain a guide of life, no matter to what extent the young enter new areas of experience and follow new ways.

## The School

Next in importance to what the family does for or to the young is what the school does for or to them. The school can be to the child a long stretch of drudgery and boredom, or a mixed experience of plodding work and joyful play, or a place where habits of learning are formed and new incentives aroused, or a not unpleasant refuge from the unhappiness of a wretched home. What happens through the years of growing up at school is always in the longer run crucial. How important it is for the future of the young is flagrantly illustrated by what happens when the school fails—though the failure is by no means always attributable to the school itself. The relation between drop-outs and delinquency is now a subject of great concern. The record is most revealing. "In 1952, 61 per cent of all delinquents between 8 and 17 years of age were not enrolled in school. . . . Ninety-five per cent of the 17 year olds adjudged delinquents were recorded as school drop-outs; 85 per cent of the 16 year olds. . . . Three out of five delinquents are school drop-outs."[2]

Other reports show that seriously retarded pupils have a much higher proportion of delinquency than pupils who make average or better grades.[3] The frequency of retardation is highly correlated with the slum conditions under which high delinquency rates prevail. School retardation is a link, effect and cause, in the vicious circle within which so many slum-bred children revolve. Education with adequate guidance, especially if well directed in the earliest school years, is a powerful agency to enable the youth to break out of the circle.

Critical schooling situations may occur at any stage from

the nursery school to the end of schooling. The initiation to school learning can itself be so unfavorable as to be traumatic. On the other hand, the very early redirection of offensive habits or of negligent attitudes can have an enduring effect that might be much harder to achieve at a later stage. The teacher can easily spot deficiencies that a parent, either through negligence or fondness, may fail to perceive or else to correct. Rifts with the parents may develop because the child is given a bad report, and the parents may take quite the wrong way of dealing with the situation. A school year with a dull or sarcastic or unsympathetic teacher may generate a lasting distaste for schooling, or the introduction to a new teacher who is stimulating and sympathetic may awaken an interest that grows stronger with the years. In fact, the most important lesson a training institute could offer to the prospective teacher would be to inculcate a realization that the first requisite of teaching is the ability to awaken interest and incentive in the pupil. Again, the bullying of a sensitive youth by a young ruffian may lead the former to play truant, with a train of consequences. Finally, for a brooding retarded pupil any school mishap or grievous home relationship or discouragement may be the breaking point at which the youngster becomes a drop-out. The school, as we show more fully in Part Three, has a great role to play in guiding the young, discovering the early signs that point to disturbance or maladjustment or disaffection and seeing that these receive the necessary attention and services, and thus above all preventing the development of tendencies that may mature into habitual delinquency.

## The Peer Group

Delinquency, according to one viewpoint, is as much a matter of intimate association with a group engaged in this behavior as is the spirit of neighborly service engendered in a well-knit group of Boy Scouts. The delinquent tradition which continues to thrive in the slum neighborhoods of large urban centers, according to Cohen, offers a solution to the problems of the new entrants into a gang culture.[4] The choice for attachment to a gang may have as many underlying reasons as there are individuals. A boy may choose his group for the sense of belonging and security that he derives from being with those of similar racial or ethnic background. Another may join a gang to avert being attacked by its members. For some boys the attachment to a delinquent gang helps to mitigate feelings of anxiety growing out of uncertainty about parental affection. Or a deep unconscious wish to be apprehended in order to expiate some fancied guilt may lead them into a delinquent gang.[5]

Cohen points out that "the human personality is a complex system with many roles, many activities, many aspirations and many problems. The delinquent gang provides an outlet for those who share a common core of problems." Since the delinquent gang is a joint enterprise where satisfaction is shared the implication is that the sheer accessibility to other children who have kindred problems may play an important part in the decision to join one. Once the delinquent subculture exists, it may very well tip the scale in favor of participation by a boy as a solution to his other problems as well.[6]

Another line of inquiry, as espoused by Ohlin and Lawrence,[7] is concerned with interactions directed to changing the delinquent's mode of coherence to a deviant value system and thus opening new opportunities that would lead away from violence.

As one means of early intervention in order to stall recruitment of junior member gang groups by older gangs, the Henry Street Settlement in New York established a predelinquent gang project for boys aged eight to thirteen. The goal was to prevent the "development of new gangs by weaning them away from the older gangs."[8] The group work program was aimed at detaching the young from gangs through the help of a skilled group worker. Parents, too, met to consider the situations affecting their children and learn how to provide greater regularity and order in their lives. The director states that "when the adults close ranks and stand together, the very ground these children travel from home to various parts of the neighborhood became more solid."[9]

In presenting a composite picture of youth for whom work

programs have meant an intervention in delinquent gang activity, the portrait of Charles emerges from the experiences of Mobilization for Youth. An eighteen-year-old drop-out, Charles left school in the tenth grade and had been a member of a bopping gang since he was thirteen, participating in the usual gang fights. His gang membership provided his only meaningful peer relationships. He was cynical, distrustful, and pessimistic about life. His pattern of coping with authority was "to play it cool." He had held three different jobs for an average of two months each, as a delivery boy, messenger, and factory floor boy, quickly losing interest in each job.[10]

At Mobilization for Youth he was enrolled in a building-maintenance work group which performed a variety of tasks for nonprofit agencies in the community. After seven months he was advanced to an on-the-job training program. The work groups of the program are structured to cut across ethnic, economic, and gang lines. The dominance of the goal of the work task itself provided motivation and opportunity for forming working relationships with strangers. In a number of the work groups, hostile gang groups were able to work out non-aggression pacts.

The work foreman was extremely important to Charles as a person requiring adherence to work regularity and as a male personality who was strong, fair, competent, and not to be "taken in." Charles began to see that "playing it straight" was neither so difficult nor so dangerous. Now that he worked, his mother's annoyance with his spending and his late rising hours was abated and she encouraged him in this new role. The work group introduced a new set of connections into his life. He found that his ties to some of his friends who were not working were weakened, since he had less time to be with them and their interests and concerns were no longer so similar to his. The older group thought he had "sold out," but having come under the influence of a new system of expectations, values, and behavior patterns, he felt a stronger bond with the work group. Since the work group is made up of neighborhood youth he is spared feelings of guilt and isolation.[11]

The Youth for Service program in San Francisco, developed by the American Friends Service Committee, achieved notable success in averting nearly all the gang rumbles it attempted to stop. In two respects Youth for Service has achieved results aspired to by many agencies. First, the program was successful in attracting the boys it intended to reach. At one time the large majority of participants were believed to have been "official delinquents" and members of San Francisco's toughest gangs. Second, the agency's Inter-Club Council was successful in keeping the participation of many juvenile gang leaders and proved an effective preventive against gang rumbles.[12]

A Central Harlem Street Club Project was conducted under the auspices of the Committee on Street Clubs of the Welfare Council of New York City. A series of gang wars was the impetus for the formation of the project. The street club workers in the project worked with the gang boys to gain their acceptance and influence their group values. A major aim of the project was to establish a procedure which would constrain the group from participating in antisocial behavior provoked by their "exaggerated need for status," their conception of the importance of being "tough," and their feeling of being in a "jungle." Participation in constructive programs under the guidance of the worker resulted in a lessening of such aggressive behavior as gang fighting and stealing. Reefer smoking, drinking, and gambling still went on. However, many boys did gain a new confidence through learning to make their own decisions and plans and to carry out responsibilities. Some of their negative attitudes toward adults declined and they began to take a more active and constructive interest in their neighborhoods.

# 8

# *The Over-all Increase*
# *of Delinquency*

Nearly all the serious research concerning the present delinquency situation has been directed to the relatively greater increase in some situations and under some conditions in comparison with others. There are obvious reasons why this should be so. In the first place, the high-delinquency areas, and generally the situations in which the volume of delinquency has risen sharply, attract more attention and call more immediately for preventive or remedial service. In the second place the techniques of the researcher are readily applicable to situations that yield specific correlations between the phenomenon under study and other variables, but when we are dealing with a phenomenon exhibiting itself under a great multiplicity of variant conditions over a very wide range, the problem of research is not only much more difficult but also one that is less susceptible of clear-cut conclusions.

While scholars have shied away from the larger problem, popular opinion offers its diversified verdicts freely in the broadest terms. It attributes the general increase to the decay of morality, the falling away from religion, the materialism of the times, the corruption of political life, the freedom allowed modern youth and the general slackness of family discipline, the general habituation to violence accentuated by the exhibits of television, movies and comics, and the press, and finally to the insecurities and uncertainties generated by modern conditions and climaxed by the hazard of nuclear armaments in the hands of rival powers.

Obviously, we cannot directly trace the impact on youth of any or all of these conditions. The few more positive characteristics included in the list, particularly the influence of the movies and of television, have been the object of careful research, but very few definite conclusions have been reached. We cannot, however, dismiss these imputed causes on that account. The temper of the times must surely in some way register in the minds of the young.

Some modes of attribution sympathetically regarded by a number of scholars appear to us highly dubious. Society, a social historian once wrote, is the cause of crime—not some features of society but society as a whole. This is a truism that leads nowhere. In one meaningful sense, of course, society is the cause of crime, since there is no crime except where laws exist, and the code of laws is a social creation. It can also be said that the character of crime depends on the specific character of a society. You don't find a "black market" except where society through its government restricts the free sale of particular goods. People are not arrested for being out late at night unless there is a curfew, and nobody is put in prison for speaking against the government in a genuine democracy.

A somewhat more sophisticated form of the above-mentioned approach is the view that crime and delinquency are outcomes or by-products of the society's cultural values. In its usual form this doctrine assumes that delinquency is responsive to the examples or models set by parents and elders in general.[1] It may be the consequence of imitation, or of indoctrination, or of habituation to the mores prevalent in the society.

While no doubt the example of the elders has an important influence on the young, this whole mode of explanation is seriously defective. In the first place it offers no answer to our question concerning the general increase in delinquency. Aside from that, it gives a quite excessive role to imitation, the following of the model set by elders. Many youngsters react from the ways of the parents, and everywhere youthful peer groups associate and develop attitudes and form habits of their own. The difference between the generations is in a changeful society as noticeable as their resemblance. Moreover, for the areas of high delinquency—areas mostly of squalor and destitution—it would be extremely rash to conclude that the high rate is due to imitation. As we have already sought to show, the conditions of life in such areas breed tensions and frustrations with which the more susceptible youth are unable to cope, with the consequence that they tend to resort to delinquent ways. While down-and-outs, including the more ineffective type of criminal, gravitate to these areas, there is ample evidence that a large proportion of the residents where children get into trouble with the police are by no means the "models" these youngsters imitate. From personal experience the writer can testify that this conclusion held true for one high-delinquency neighborhood, largely inhabited by in-migrant Puerto Ricans, in which he organized a study.

The doctrine that the delinquency of the children reflects the delinquent attitudes of ther parents takes a number of forms. There is the straightforward hereditary theory of causation, the theory of the "bad seed." The classical illustration is the famous history of the Jukes and the Kallikaks, whose offspring over several generations were shown to be in so many instances criminals or ne'er-do-wells or feeble-minded.[2] There is the viewpoint that the "multiproblem" families are an enclave of their own, breeding their own kind. No one disputes the importance of heredity, but the more we learn about it the more we discover the variability of the stock. And we certainly must not discount the impact of environment. So long as the Jukes breed in a slum environment subject to the depressing influence and unwholesome example of their parents, we have no right to conclude that heredity alone is responsible for the behavior of the descendants. The trouble with all such theories is that they refuse to recognize the complex interplay of conditions from which social phenomena result.

At the other extreme from the hereditary doctrine there is the broad principle that parents one way or another are respon-

sible for the sins of the children. The onus may be placed on the
parents' failure to educate the children through disregard, neglect, or lack of proper discipline, or on unduly harsh discipline
and excessive pressures on the children to meet the standards of
achievement demanded by the parents. Again there can be no
question that many parents are at fault in the upbringing of their
children. Bernard Shaw had a point when he remarked that the
only occupation for which no training is required is parenthood.
But the influence of bad home training may be offset in a measure at least if the parents have the affection and respect of the
children. And of course there are various other factors that
determine the future of the child—school influences, peer-group
influences, religious influences, timely guidance from a trusted
counselor, and so forth. The record shows also that some children, including a number who later attained to fame, have reacted strongly against an evil or unhappy home environment,
eschewing the ways of the parents.

None of the above-mentioned theories offers a logical explanation of our present problem, the over-all increase in the
volume of delinquency not only throughout this country but
across many other countries as well. The only way they could
be directed to this end would be on the assumption that events
or developments brought about by the older generation cause
greater disturbances, tension, or disorientation in the younger
generation than in the generation responsible. If, for example,
delinquency is more prevalent in large cities and in industrialized
areas, then the growth of industrialization would show an increase in delinquency in the next generation. The aftermath of
war has also some association with the increase of crime and
delinquency. We have not seen any attempt to follow up the
general theory here indicated, but it is plausible and may well
have some relevance.

Our own conclusions respecting the over-all increase of delinquency may be summed up as follows. From numerous studies
we learn a great deal about the attitudes broadly characteristic
of delinquent youth. We know the types of disturbances, the
stresses and strains, that prompt a revulsion from indoctrinated

ways; that provoke a rankling resentment, and often enough a rebelliousness against the established order as embodied in parents, teachers, and the official guardians of the law; that induce in some a certain restlessness, bravado, and aggressive push for status, and in others sullen withdrawal from participation in social ongoings or feelings of hopeless disorientation and lack of direction. A certain amount of delinquency is of course generated in other ways, through some conjunctures of conditions bearing on susceptible youth. Although for a relatively small number delinquency comes naturally, without inward strain, being nurtured by delinquent parents, it is most conspicuous where youth are subjected to thwarting circumstances that block and distort youthful aspirations. Such is the situation in our high-delinquency areas. And in areas where conditions are far less depressing, situations which put the young under severe strain can still occur. Delinquency might result, for example, from the impact on a sensitive child of family rifts and the domination of first one parent and then the other.

In general our evidence suggests that, so long as children are anchored in a system of relationships which provides the affection they need, commands their respect, and gives them room for expansion, they can for the most part take in stride the rank suggestions of some of the things they see and hear and read. The broad influences of the times are not likely to bite so deeply that young people will be jolted into delinquent ways on that account alone. The impact of changes in the daily life—increased mobility, social insecurities due to automation or other technological developments, any increase in the competitive struggle, any new conditions that tend to disturb old habituations or old beliefs—would certainly be of more direct importance. Such changes would be calculated to heighten tensions that are provoked by other circumstances. They could, in particular areas, make the differences that overcome the edgy resistance or weak equilibrium that some young people would otherwise maintain, causing some of those who not so long ago might have remained law-abiding to yield to additional stress. Such a changed situation might, moreover, be brought to bear indirectly through the influence of the changed conditions on parents and on the family life.

Since such new influences are not localized or confined to specific groups, their pervasive impact could explain the increase of delinquency beyond any national frontiers. It is widely believed, not without some grounds, that our civilization of today is peculiarly unsettled. The manner in which this unsettlement reaches into the world of the young, aggravating the difficulties of the transitions and readjustments that growing up imposes, might well be made the subject of broad-based inquiry.

Our conclusions here have had to be stated in this tentative fashion because the over-all problem has not received the scholarly attention it deserves. Every generation is reared in a different atmosphere from that of the preceding one. Even English "public school" boys, for all the pride of tradition, read different books, discuss different things, and respond differently to old usages in each succeeding generation. Sometimes the difference in atmosphere becomes especially marked because of far-reaching social changes or abrupt disturbances of the social order. Such changes have occurred in the lifetime of both the previous and the present generation. The convulsions of war and the transformations of ensuing peace have greatly affected every nation in the world. Everywhere youth faces new situations and new problems. It is no easy task to assess the influence of these changes on the minds of the young, but it should be by no means insuperable. Such an assessment would require comparative studies in various countries, on a cooperative basis. It would involve studies of the informal education of the young, of the various modes in which they adjust themselves to the life of the family, to the preparation for a career, and to the traditional standards of their elders. It would seek to probe their sense of values and their expectations and such differences as these might reveal between the outlooks of the younger and of the older generation, distinguishing the findings for various categories of the population. Comparative studies of the attitudes and rationalizations of delinquents of different classes and different countries could also throw some light on the issue.

Significant indications might also be derived from the recordings of a series of "bull sessions" so conducted that the youths attending them would feel free to express themselves with complete candor.

The many-nationed program sketched above would require extensive planning and rather substantial funds. But the reasonable chance that it would help to solve a problem so pressing and so important for the direction of the great amount of energy and resources devoted to this field would be eminently worthwhile. Without guidance of this sort we will be forced to remain in the twilight of conjecture.

# 9

## *Summation*

Any social phenomenon so disturbing and so widespread as the more serious forms of juvenile delinquency is bound to arouse a great deal of speculation and a certain amount of research regarding its causes. Relatively little has been done, however, to clarify the problem. We have many conflicting theories, ranging from simple unchecked assumptions to the variant conclusions of practitioners and theorists representing different disciplines. The subject is still in a state of confusion.[1] In Part Two we have endeavored to analyze the issue, to point out the limitations of some current theories, and to present what we hope is a consistent interpretation of the problem.

An initial difficulty is the fact that the term "cause" is used in several different senses. It may refer to the particular conjuncture of conditions, to the situation that as a whole is different from other situations and thus evokes the differential phenomenon in question. Within this total situation there may be some factors that increase or diminish the range of the phenomenon. We dealt with this subject broadly in Part One, where we distinguished the conditions associated with high delinquency rates and sought to show that they were relevant, especially when we included the "psychic conditions" associated with delinquency in the lower-delinquency areas.

In the second sense of the term, "cause" refers to some particular factor that, when brought into relation to an appropriate set of conditions, evokes the phenomenon. We say, for example, that a carelessly flung match was the cause of a forest fire or that a spark was the cause of an explosion. So we have discussed the "trigger factor" or the "precipitant" that upsets an uneasy or unstable equilibrium and is decisive as a determinant of a course of action.

In the social sphere we can speak of cause in a third sense. We call negligence, for example, a cause—the failure to perform some act that would have prevented an accident or injury or loss. This is cause as responsibility. It may mean either performing an act or some program of action which we were obligated not to perform or failing to perform one which we were obligated to perform. In this broad sense we may say that some responsibility for delinquency rests on those officials or agencies that knowingly fail to take the available steps for its prevention or control. Likewise we say that a father is responsible for his son's delinquency if, being delinquent himself, he initiated his son into delinquent ways, or, again, if he is supine or careless in the training of his child. Responsibility, we observe, can be greater or less according to the circumstances.

Most problems of social causation concern not the presence or absence of a phenomenon, but the more or the less, the multiplicity or scarcity of the phenomenon, the manner and extent of its distribution. This fact introduces several complications into the search for the cause. It makes it less likely that we can find clean-cut wholly definite answers. Thus in the environment most prolific of cases of delinquency we find that a majority of young people are not delinquents; and, when we further take into account the type of mentality that in such an environment is prone toward delinquency, we still find others with similar mental attributes who are unaffected in this direction. Getting down to the precise causation of individual cases is therefore not feasible, and we must be content with the conclusion that under stipulated conditions a quite considerable incidence of delinquency is highly probable. This, however, is a sufficient guide to preventive measures and gives us a lead for the application of remedial services. This is the subject that will occupy us in Part Three.

When we are concerned with the greater or smaller incidence of delinquency over a very wide area, when, as at present, we are faced with a general increase in its incidence over at least a great portion of the civilized world, then the problem of causation becomes much harder to investigate. The "less" in this situation is the tendency to delinquency in a previous period over this wide range, the "more" is the incidence over that range today. Comparisons of conditions then and now are obscured by the multitude of variant changes over so vast a terrain. The only lead comes from the knowledge, based on more specific comparisons and some general considerations, that an increase in tensions and pressures and a weakening of convictions and of the sense of security are conditions that tend to weaken the spirit of law-abidingness and the belief in authority and thus to promote delinquency.

# Part Three

## STRATEGIC

## APPLICATIONS

# 10

*Broad Considerations on Strategy*

In Part One we reviewed the various social, environmental, and psychological conditions that characterize areas with higher and lower incidences of youthful delinquency. We noted in particular that distinctively high rates of delinquency are generally found in close correspondence with high rates of other socio-pathological phenomena, such as economic dependence, infant mortality, admissions to mental hospitals, psychiatric clinic cases, insanitary housing; all these in turn being associated with slum conditions in our great cities. In other words, very high delinquency was itself a symptom of a serious total maladjustment of a population to the mode of existence in which it found itself, a situation determined in the first instance by squalid poverty and usually aggravated by social discrimination. The superficial judgment that the people themselves, the families living under these conditions, are to blame is irrelevant, even if it were well founded. We don't refuse to treat people for their diseases because these have resulted from their own neglect or carelessness or folly. Effective remedial treatment is important for the welfare of the community as a whole as well as for the victims of disease. *We can conclude that so long as such breeding grounds of delinquency remain, relatively high delinquency will endure.*

Important as this consideration is, it deals with only one aspect of a many-sided problem. Even in the areas of worst delinquency there are large numbers of young people who do not become delinquents under the pressures and deprivations of their social and physical environment. We saw, moreover, that the probability that a youth growing up within that environment will become delinquent depends not only on the character of the specific family life he shares but also on the specific mental make-up of the youth himself. Everywhere there are significant variations in conditions and in the response of youth to them. The same statement holds of course for youth in lower-delinquency areas. Delinquency is a mode of response to pressures and to incitations that develop in every area of society. Susceptibility to delinquency is highly variant both in degree and in type.

In Part Two we sought to draw some conclusions respecting the causation of delinquency. We regarded the fact that high-delinquency areas are high-rated also for a whole series of socio-pathological conditions characterizing urban slums as bearing out the conclusion that the delinquency in question is not to be attributed to a natural tendency inherent in the ethnic groups involved, but rather to the strains, handicaps, and family troubles to which their young people are exposed. Obviously this points to a different mode of treatment than would be applicable if we regarded it as due primarily to the cause as moral obliquity or the "bad seed." To understand the incidence of delinquency as it varies in different situations we must get down to the conjuncture of predisposing conditions that affects the respective reactions of youth of diverse mentalities. While it has long been recognized that certain conditions—the inadequacy of family relations and of family disciplines, the pull of youthful associations, the frustrations that balk ambitions and aspirations, and so forth—are conducive to delinquency, we must recognize also that the degree to which young persons resist or respond to them, the alleviations and the acerbations of these influences, the character of the breaking point that changes predisposition to commitment, are endlessly variant.

In keeping with these findings, we analyzed and criticized the various theories that offer a bloc explanation of high-level delinquency by attributing it to the "culture" of a lower social class or to the impact of middle-class standards on lower-class mores. For the same reasons we reject any theory that lays predominant stress on any one of a series of interdependent factors, whether on heredity, somatic structure, very early conditioning, or social environment. In every situation there are conditions which predispose and also conditions that in varying degrees counteract or negate the predisposing conditions. Under the worst environmental conditions a large proportion of the young do not become habitual delinquents. Recently there has been increasing evidence of the amount of delinquency in well-established families; perhaps here too we would find that below the surface of respectable well-being discord and maladjustment not infrequently lurk, or parental evasion of and disrespect for law sets a bad example.

While we cannot in our theory of causation assign predominance to any one of a number of interdependent factors, for purposes of strategy we must lay particular stress on the conditions that are more amenable to control. If the conditions are really interdependent, our ability to deal with any of them may suffice to arrest or counteract the resort to delinquency. Obviously, the physical environment (say the city slum) and certain unfavorable features of the social environment, such as the lack of opportunity, training, guidance, or protection, can be changed, controlled, or compensated for.

The considerations advanced in Parts One and Two lead us to certain more specific conclusions with respect to strategy. Actually many of these conclusions can be derived from common sense and from experience, but they are reinforced by the researches discussed in Part One and by the reflections on causation adduced in Part Two.

1. The prevention of delinquency is more feasible, less costly, and more promising than later efforts toward rehabilitation.

Every effort should be made to improve our programs of rehabilitation, but fewer would need them if we had more regard for prevention. There is practically universal agreement that the earlier we can bring guidance, protection, care, and therapy to those who show signs of needing this help, the better will be the results. Yet, although there has been some real progress in the last few years, we still expend the greater part of our available resources on rehabilitation programs that unhappily have had only rather disappointing results. Moreover, much of the preventive work is inadequately directed and is not followed through.

We need in the first place to broaden some prevailing conceptions of what a genuine program of prevention involves. The provision of opportunities for ball games and dance parties and club quarters and so forth is certainly desirable and salutary, but it reaches only to the outskirts of preventive work. The problems of troubled or difficult youth are too complex and deepseated to be solved that way. We may broadly distinguish three types of service that have greater significance.

First, there are the broad-based educational services that do not limit instruction merely to a routine curriculum in the three "r's" but are calculated to spur incentive, to awaken the mind to a rich world of opportunity, to reveal the values of the good life, and to upbuild morale to face life's problems. Such education is not to be thought of as merely preventive, as a safeguard against getting into trouble, but as the positive preparation all youth need. Nor is it a service by any means exclusive to the school; the home, the church, agencies of various kinds have important roles to play in it, but they can do it only as far as they understand the problems of the young and the approaches without which no teaching is effective. In this area the more particular function of the school is to stimulate the live interest of the pupil in the process of learning by reaching out to whatever capacities or aptitudes he may possess. Unhappily, in much of our schooling this role is very imperfectly fulfilled, and the consequences are more serious than we generally recognize.

Furthermore, the majority of school children do not proceed to college, and therefore it is incumbent on the school to prepare its pupils not only for the business of being citizens but also for their working life, training them in the basic requirements of accuracy, clear observation of details, concentration of attention, the fundamental qualities necessary for any kind of effective operation. In our present-day society many teen-agers on leaving school face the threat—and the fact—of unemployment, without prospect of a career. Nothing could be more demoralizing, and the community, in cooperation with the school, can and should take whatever steps are necessary to ensure that employment, really useful employment, is found or made for them and that they are trained to take it. Besides its other advantages such a policy becomes a very important means for the prevention of delinquency.

One of the most hopeful developments at the present time is the increasing recognition that the young in poverty-stricken areas must be trained in the kind of skills that are potentially within their range and are adapted to changes in the labor market. The fact that the percentage of unemployment among these youths is about twice as large as that among young people in general is sufficiently indicative of the educational and social handicaps from which they suffer. The training must be thorough and realistic. With the advance of automation hard manual tasks are at a discount but opportunties in a variety of service jobs and those using minor mechanical skills are likely to increase. The school should be geared to provide more of this preparatory training than it usually does, in addition to the specially established community provision under the new poverty-area programs.

Anything that increases the range of opportunity, especially for the poor and disprivileged, or helps develop in the young a sense of belonging, of effective membership within the community (and in this connection the reduction of ethnic or racial discrimination is of prime importance), serves as a safeguard against youthful delinquency.

The second type of significant service is concerned with preventive measures specifically directed to those young persons who are in immediate need of guidance and protection. These are requisite for all youth in high-delinquency areas and for near-delinquents and incipient delinquents wherever they can be found. This type of direct service has been curiously slow to be undertaken and developed, even though both common sense and the testimony of authorities emphasize the advantages of early treatment, before habit and associations confirm the tendency to delinquency and before the teen-ager has come to regard authority with enmity. Few thoroughgoing projects of this kind have been undertaken. The writer, as director of the City of New York's Juvenile Delinquency Evaluation Project, was enabled with the assistance of the President of the City Council and the Mayor, to establish one in a high-delinquency neighborhood of the South Bronx. We were able to find a number of young persons who were beginning to get into trouble and who otherwise might well have escaped notice. Some boys came and asked us to provide a leader for their group, since otherwise they might have been drawn into some trouble-making gang. Our contacts with neighborhood volunteers, with neighborhood churches and schools, revealed how ample was the opportunity and how great the need. Unfortunately, the program ceased to exist in the form in which we had envisioned it when we finished our commission from the City, too soon for its methods to be tested and its results evaluated.

Two major foci from which this type of early prevention program can be conducted are the neighborhood and the school. The lines of a neighborhood program—the neighborhood being here understood to be the narrowest urban area that can be readily distinguished as possessing or potentially possessing some demographic characteristics of its own—are clearly established. Such a program needs in the first place a small professional staff to be located in the neighborhood: a director, one or two child-welfare specialists and community organizers, and a research worker. These will enlist neighborhood volunteers and a neighborhood committee to help in a secondary program for the discovery of vulnerable youngsters and to provide first aid and arrange for follow-ups, to make referrals where therapy is needed and see that the referrals are carried through, and so forth.

2. The rescue of delinquent or near-delinquent youth cannot be effectively undertaken unless those who are assigned to

this service are properly qualified by training and experience, possessing also the attributes of character that enable them to understand the diverse problems of troubled or disturbed youngsters.

With some notable exceptions, the tendency still prevails in the official service to assume that anyone with a firm hand and a modicum of training can cope with the emotional and social problems of the young. It is assumed that while the higher-ups, the real professionals need special training and competence, the people who work "at the face," so to speak, who are in most direct touch with youthful offenders, can get along all right with less. The policeman, in whose discretion it lies, within limits, to warn the youth or to see that a report is made out for parent or guardian or to make an arrest, often has quite inadequate training for the job. Not infrequently he adopts rough and ready methods, sometimes with needless harshness. The arrested youth may be placed in detention prior to court appearance and may find detention an unhappy and stigmatic experience. Then he comes before a judge. The adjudication that follows may be decisive for his future. The judge, who has the discretion to dismiss or discharge the case, to place the youngster on probation, or to commit him to an institution, is a political appointee. He may have little comprehension of the problems of the young and generally has an overcrowded calendar, which may cause him to make a rather hasty decision.

If the juvenile offender is placed on probation, he is presumptively under the charge of a probation officer. Probation means that the offender is being given an opportunity to make good. He needs guidance, counsel, protection, new associations. But very frequently the function of the probation officer is no more than to see that he keeps out of trouble, which means only that no new law violation is recorded against him. Of all the major services rendered to delinquents this one is often enough the most perfunctory and unsatisfactory, and in many areas the probation officer lacks the standing and the training his task demands.

If the offender is committed to an institution, he enters a

situation in which he mixes with other offenders and since they
are all chafing at the restraints of confinement a spirit of rebellion is rife and tends to frustrate the best efforts of the staff. The
institution finds it difficult to secure adequate "cottage parents"
(with whom the inmate spends much of his time), or guards
who sympathize with the policies of the institution, or even
counselors who are sufficiently qualified and willing to work
under these difficult conditions.

What we have said in the preceding paragraphs is a broad
assessment of a general situation, based on considerable evidence and on the writer's own experience. But there are notable
exceptions—services, programs, and institutions that are admi-
rably meeting the many problems they encounter, and some
others that are making progress in that direction. There are
police departments that maintain a well-equipped and well-
trained youth division. There are some highly qualified and devoted judges. There are a few probation systems that achieve
high standards, and others that strive to do so in spite of inadequate resources. There are a number of custodial institutions
for juveniles that are admirable of their kind, doing all they can
to fulfill a difficult and often baffling service. On every level we
find some workers who are dedicated and competent. But the
over-all improvement of our programs for delinquents will remain halting and sluggish until there is a much wider practical
recognition that the everyday tasks of those who work with or
for disturbed and troubled youngsters require high qualities of
mind and heart and that therefore *the status, standards, and
salaries of these workers must be raised.* At the time of writing
a new illustration of the failure to recognize those facts has come
to our attention. The New York State Judicial Conference has
organized a review of the conditions and ratings of the probation
services within the City. It has been the practice to put the
qualifications and salaries of the probation officers of the superior courts well above those of the courts that deal with juveniles
and adolescents. A group that should know better has appealed
to the Conference to maintain the differential, the assumption
being that probation work with juveniles is less demanding and

less important than that with adult offenders. Nothing could be further from the fact.

3. Officials appointed to organize or administer antidelinquency programs, whether under public or private auspices, should themselves be familiar with the problems of youth and should be in a position to keep in touch with developments in treatment and with the results of research.

4. The over-all planning of a city's programs and policies concerned with the control of delinquency, and more broadly with youth problems, should be administered by a special supervisory and planning unit of high competence, located within the city government in a position where its recommendations will carry most weight—preferably within the office of the Mayor.

The reasons back of our last two conclusions are obvious enough. The fuller significance and the practical application of the four conclusions we have stated will be presented in the remainder of this work.

# 11

## *The School*

The great majority of children spend approximately twelve formative years in school, presumably under the watchful eyes of
trained educators. The school cannot educate these children
unless it makes them receptive to education, unless it awakens
incentive and aspiration in them, unless it guides them over the
distractions, disturbances, and inertias that block the educational
process. While this statement holds for schools of every kind, it
has a special significance for schools that serve the disprivileged,
the children of groups subject to discrimination and prejudice,
those who come from uncultured homes, those whose native
language is other than the English, in short, those who are in
any way educationally disadvantaged. Today in the United States
one out of every three children comes from a low-income
family.[1] The percentage has been increasing and present fore-
casts indicate that it may rise still higher.

There is ample evidence that these children need special
training and guidance. There is convincing evidence that they
are not receiving it in any adequate way. Tests given in grade
schools or specific areas show an almost normal distribution of
intelligence for such children in the first and second years, with
a regular decrease in mean scores year by year until in the ninth
grade the once "normal" group had become the "retarded"
group.[2] The same type of regression is shown on test scores in
reading and other subject-areas. Relatively few children of these

"minority" groups complete academic high school courses and fewer still ever enter college.

The bearing of these factors on the future well-being of the child and in particular on his proneness to delinquency is surely obvious. It has been estimated that about 20 per cent of the school population suffers from emotional disturbances sufficiently marked to require intensive personal or small-group guidance and that about 10 per cent is in need of clinical treatment.[3] Some evidence of the schism between the child and the school is revealed in the fact that in 1952, 62 per cent of all delinquents between eight and seventeen were not enrolled in school. Truancy is not necessarily a precursor of delinquency, yet almost every delinquent has truanting on his record and 25 per cent of all delinquents have been identified as chronic truants. Retardation, with all it implies in the blighting of prospects and in its association with truancy, contributes also to delinquency proneness—and we have very good reason to believe that retardation itself is by no means solely or even mainly due to innate incapacity for learning.[4]

*Our first conclusion, then, is that the educational guidance problem of difficult and troubled children has been sadly underestimated in most school systems of our large cities, where the need for such guidance is greatest.* But a new awareness of the need is already spreading across the land and new programs and experiments to meet it are springing up. A poll of 1400 elementary and secondary school principals showed a growing emergence of these new patterns.[5] We shall briefly indicate the various lines along which these new programs are proceeding.

First, there are programs designed as a breakaway from the old system of moving omnibus classes from grade to grade, without regard for individual capacities and often without consideration of the readiness of some pupils for entrance to a higher grade. One plan is to organize tracks (fast, average, slow, remedial) for the grouping of pupils within grades, on the theory, which is still subject to examination, that pupils do better when they compete with pupils of relatively equal ability. Another, revolting against the elementary school tradition of having every subject taught for most of the day by a single teacher in the same room, has the children move from room to room to be taught various subjects by more specialized teachers. A third plan gives a team of teachers joint responsibility for the instruction among them of, say, 200 pupils. A more revolutionary system uses ungraded schools in which youngsters advance in one or another subject according to their ability. This approach, first tried out in Milwaukee some twenty years ago, presumably gives both the slower learners and the quicker the opportunity to learn at their own speed without undue criticism and without the sense of frustration.[6] The Norwalk School Improvement Program provides transitional classes for children who are backward because of socioemotional difficulties, and a considerable variety of programs offering special counseling, remedial reading, guidance for potential drop-outs, and compensatory aid for educationally disadvantaged children.[7]

Many schools adopt the principle of dividing the pupils in any grade into sections according to IQ or performance record. Usually the low IQs and the slow learners are placed in smaller sections, each numbering perhaps 15 or 20 pupils—a very proper consideration. There are obvious advantages in the procedure, but also some disadvantages. The latter can be partly met where special care is taken to transfer children from lower to higher categories when they show signs of improvement. But further exploration of the method is called for. In some systems "special service" schools are used for highly disadvantaged pupils or more generally for those who live in slumlike areas where initially the children have, for the most part, cultural, economic, and social handicaps.

The combination of teaching, guidance, and discriminating attention to individual needs might very well, as experience has already shown, be provided not only for obviously disadvantaged pupils but for all. It was this consideration that led the New York City Board of Education to inaugurate its well-known Higher Horizons program.[8] A demonstration guidance project in a racially integrated high school has shown how minority-group children of previously mediocre achievement could, given special attention, reach higher academic standards. The results as recorded were very convincing, some of these children rising to the top of very large classes. Higher Horizons, organized at the junior high school level for all the children in the selected grades and now including grades 3 to 5 in the elementary school, provides special class guidance and small-group counseling, "inspirational" talks from business leaders and professional people, trips to places of interest, information about occupations and prevocational instruction, conferences with parents, and efforts to enlarge the cultural experience of the pupils. An interesting feature of the experiment is the number of contacts the pupils make with others besides the school teachers, including volunteers, assistant college students, as well as various types of professionals. This is a wide-flung system of operations, and there are some grounds for believing the content is spread too thin, as the endeavor has been made to include more and more schools within the program. But the value of the principle has been established beyond question.

Another program under the auspices of the New York City Board of Education, one of particular significance, is the All-Day Neighborhood Schools.[9] These schools are situated in the most depressed and deteriorated areas of the city. In addition to the regular teaching staff a group of specially qualified teachers, usually six for each elementary school, and generally a community coordinator as well, is in attendance from 11 A.M. to 5 P.M. During school hours the members take charge of groups of pupils who need special coaching or guidance. From 3 to 5 P.M. they direct "clubs" of pupils, one for each grade, for supervised play, the clubs being composed of children selected because on one ground or another they particularly need to be looked after. During the play period a psychologist as well as the teacher keeps a watchful eye for signs of emotional disturbance or other behavior difficulties. In the evenings the schools are open for meetings with parents or for discussions with neighborhood officers. In various ways the schools thus live up to their name as all-day centers for neighborhood service. In addition they endeavor to make good the cultural deficiencies of the youngsters, practically all of whom come from deprived homes. The special merits of these schools, which are somewhat more expensive to operate, have not received the amount of recognition and support accorded to the Higher Horizons program.

Finally, under the New York City school system, after-school study centers have recently been established in some 230 schools situated in impoverished areas, mostly in elementary schools but including also some academic and vocational high schools. The objective is to provide disadvantaged youngsters a further opportunity to remove, through group and tutorial instruction, their educational lags.

### The Role and Status of the Teacher

We have been specifying some of the distinctive programs that are being directed to the clamant need for more, and more effective, guidance and remedial service in the educational process. But for educational efficacy something else is clearly needed. The service a teacher can render depends on the qualifications of the teacher himself—even more, we venture to say, than on the programs he is called on to administer. It is also, in some measure, dependent on the freedom of the teacher to devote his time as fully as possible to the prime business of teaching.

Let us consider the second point first. The teacher is burdened with a variety of professional and nonprofessional duties. With large classes he has problems of gaining attention, maintaining discipline, and looking into special cases, absences, and the details of a variety of children's problems. He—more frequently she—has a plethora of forms to fill out, records to keep, exercises to check over, materials to prepare, as well as school-housekeeping chores. Together these occupy a considerable portion of the teacher's working time. There is too little left to attend to or even observe the learning difficulties of individual children. The result is mass education.

One experiment to alleviate this situation has been the enlistment of trained teacher aides, as tried out, for example, in the Bay City schools under the lead of Central Michigan College.[10] Preliminary reports showed a higher achievement level for the classes in which the plan was tried out. There is, however, some controversy over the merits of the plan, and at best it can be only a palliative. In-service training courses and workshops for instruction in guidance procedures in dealing with troubled or refractory children are very important and should be expanded and developed, since the average teacher is by no means competent to deal with the very difficult problems they pose.

The overcrowding of the schools and the shortage of teachers demand far more thoroughgoing remedies. There is an active shortage of teachers, to the extent that substitutes for regularly certified teachers often have to be employed, but more fundamental is the matter of the status and standards of the teaching profession as a whole. There are some excellent and devoted teachers and there are some really fine schools with strong leadership. But it is abundantly clear that, in spite of recent improvements and the valiant efforts some school boards are making, the status of the profession is too low and the salary rates do not compare with those of other professions. School teaching is the least regarded of the greater professions, and its practitioners have the least control over their conditions of work. We need more and better schools and we need more and better teachers, but this primary need, on which the welfare of our youth so largely depends, cannot be satisfied until the value of the teaching service is more fully realized by the community as a whole. Something can be accomplished by far-reaching changes in the training demanded for the profession, and on this point we are in agreement with the admirable study by Dr. James Conant.[11] Since it is not, however, within the province of this report to develop the subject, we shall be content to point out why this matter is so important for the prevention of juvenile delinquency.

### Delinquency and the Educational Process

We saw in Part One that high delinquency rates are strongly correlated with sociopathological factors and inferior health conditions, a complex that is characteristic of slum poverty. We must also remember that high delinquency is correlated with low school ratings, considerable reading retardation, truancy, and leaving school early largely by dropping out. Add to this the consideration that it is the disadvantaged and discriminated-against ethnic and racial groups who are mostly the victims of this total complex of evils.

The educational aspects of this complex are the ones that concern us here. The complex itself will endure as long as the slum environment and the conditions that create it continue to exist, but much can be done in the meantime to improve the life chances of the young people of these areas, especially if remedial steps and new opportunities are provided for them at an early enough age. Here is where the role of the school is of signal importance.

The conclusions of many researchers converge to show how greatly the life chances of children are affected by their educational deficiencies. They also show that in many cases these deficiencies are associated with emotional or mental disturbances as well as with the handicaps of poor earlier schooling and with the cultural poverty of the children's families. *These facts make it abundantly clear that to give such children a proper educational opportunity the schools must provide thorough-going guidance programs and incentive programs.*

The evidence for the relation of educational backwardness with delinquency is ample. In our Juvenile Delinquency Evaluation Project we found that the pupils in the special schools for disturbed or refractory children ("600" schools) were retarded in reading some 4 or 4½ years.[12] When one considers that average reading standards in our schools are themselves often far from adequate, this means that these children are practically illiterate. The same conclusion holds for the majority of juveniles who are committed to institutions. In the Quincy, Mass. public school it was found that 17 per cent of the pupils in special classes for very low IQ children and 31 per cent of the group designated as "slow learners" were known to the court.[13] Fabian recorded that 83 per cent of a sample of delinquent and pre-delinquent children had reading disabilities.[14] Roman reported that 84 per cent of the cases carried by the treatment clinic of Manhattan's children's court were severely retarded in reading. Many more studies could be cited as revealing the same correlation.[15]

The statistics on drop-outs offer further confirmation. As of the end of June 1955, of all inmates under the age of 25 who were under sentence in Federal courts only 6 per cent had completed high school.[16] The delinquency rate among Seattle drop-outs was reported as being twelve times that of those who stayed on in school, while in Bridgeport it was eight times as great.[17] Various other evidences point in the same direction. It is clearly indicated also (1) that a much higher percentage of drop-outs belonged to immigrant minority groups, Southern Negroes in Northern cities and Puerto Ricans; (2) that a larger proportion of these youth fail to find employment in their upper teens; and (3) that unemployed drop-outs figure most frequently in our delinquency statistics.

We have already noted that emotional disturbances are frequently associated with delinquency. Such disturbances may well arise from or at least be accentuated by failure at school. Retardation is apt to evoke feelings of inadequacy and frustration. To drop out is itself a confession of failure. Truancy cuts off the pupil from the prospect of a career, leads to bad associations, and creates fear and dislike of constituted authority. Many backward children develop a sense of alienation from schooling that is a prelude to further troubles. It is entirely likely that these unsatisfactory school relationships contribute to insecurity and its attendant evils. To whatever aspect of the whole complex of the causation of delinquency we turn we find the same vicious circle in operation. The school, though sometimes contributory to it, can also be a potent means of breaking it.

## Some Special-Objective Programs

Much of the service the school can render in the prevention of delinquency is at the same time beneficial to all school children. This applies, for example, to guidance programs, whether specifically for educational guidance or for behavioral or vocational guidance, and also in considerable measure to reading instruction. Special remedial reading courses are necessary for those whose reading ability is abnormally low. It is our conviction, based on considerable experience, that reading standards are generally far too low, and *that much more attention should be given in teacher training and in curricular adaptations to raise the over-all level of this most essential instruction.*

Among more specialized programs we place first and foremost that of *early identification of problem children.* Programs of this type are still far too few. It is the most obvious of principles, but in this field one is tempted to say the least regarded, that the earlier any trouble is located and diagnosed the greater the chance that treatment will effect a cure. Most commonly recognized is the "acting out" youngster who is noisy and fractious. But there may be serious maladjustment gnawing at children who are recessive and introvert or at most sulky. It requires patience and skill to discover the problems of children, and teachers no less than guidance counselors should be taught the symptoms. Discovery is, of course, only the beginning; it must be followed by early care. The principal of a New York City school once told the writer about one or two students who in later years were involved in felonies. She said she reported the matter early in the elementary school history of the cases, but the only action taken was a filed report, with no follow-up, indicating minor adjustment difficulties. This, we should add, happened a decade ago, and important developments have taken place in this school system since then. The kindergarten and first years of elementary schooling represent the stage at which identification of trouble should begin, as has been pointed out, for example, in a study under the Santa Barbara school system, and as leading authorities, such as Dr. Marion Kenworthy, have insisted.

New York City a few years ago inaugurated an early identification program for kindergarten and the first three grades, with emphasis on the second grade. It is significant that first-grade teachers indicated that from 85 to 90 per cent of the children given attention had both learning problems and social or emotional problems, reading difficulties being most apparent.[18] Another program for the elementary school, the junior guidance program, provides special classes through grades 2 to 6 for disturbed children who fail to respond to classroom teaching. Attached to the program are full-time counselors and therapists. Specially trained teachers are also provided. The counselors focus on the relation of parents to children, since so often the disturbance of the child has its root in the home situation.[19] In still another program therapeutic play groups (led by specially trained guidance counselors) are set up and function as a guidance service to a limited number of elementary schools.[20]

New York City has developed also a special type of school for children with whom the regular school claims to be unable to cope. The objective was to place these children under special teachers, to surround them with special guardianship, and to provide a training program adapted to their behavioral and educational troubles, in the hope that a number of them could be restored to the regular schools. In the early stages the experiment was not successful, except as a means of "containing" incorrigibles. None went back to the regular schools, and relatively little progress of any kind was registered. Screening for admission was by no means satisfactory. More recently, under a change of management and enough critical recognition of the deficiencies of the system, some distinct progress has been made. A new assessment of them is now being planned.

The antipoverty program under the auspices of the Office of Economic Opportunity holds good promise of new developments in the raising of the educational level of disprivileged children, since nothing can do more to abolish poverty than the removal of educational deficiency combined with equal opportunity to utilize educational advancement. One promising new program of this kind is Operation Headstart, as initiated under the New York City Board of Education. In the summer of 1965 this program was inaugurated for preschool children suffering from disabilities and educational lags. The first effort met with various difficulties, on the one hand delays in making appropriations and on the other inadequate methods of discovering the appropriate children and developing the program. Nevertheless, the reception of it was very encouraging and no less than 23,000 children received a beneficial initiation. Experience has been gained and the effort is to be continued. One definite good was that it brought backward or untrained parents into new, helpful relations with the schools, to which for the first time they had ready access. Similar service can be and is being rendered by some day-care programs, which might very well be brought into close relation with Headstart and indeed with the whole range of community services for the very young.

Some school systems do not regard special classes as an answer to the problem of difficult children. Thus the Union Free School District No. 16 at Elmont, Long Island,[21] depends rather on special teachers and on providing extra periods of art, music, physical education, and so forth, adapted to the particular needs of individual pupils. Exceptional children are grouped for programs housed outside the school, at some convenient location within the community. For the individual coaching and guidance involved, the regular teaching staff was not sufficient, and a number of mothers in the community were selected as volunteer aides, working in close contact with the school district psychologist, physician, and psychiatric consultant. The assumption is that selected but not special trained persons, when duly oriented and supervised, can be of effective help in meeting the need some children have for one-to-one relationships within the teaching process. The degree of success that attends this effort will deserve careful study.

We turn next to *programs to rescue drop-outs*. We use

the word "rescue" advisedly. To take a drop-out back to school, under the power of the law, may be worse than futile, it may be harmful. The writer recalls an occasion when he met a judge of a children's court just after he had finished his day on the bench. He looked melancholy and on being asked what troubled him replied, "I have just sent a lad back to school and I know it was a bad thing to do." The youth in question was fifteen years of age, had come to dislike school and was troublesome there. He had dropped out, falsified his age to get a job, and was driving a truck, giving most of his earnings to support his mother and generally behaving well. It was useless to force schooling on an unwilling youth at that age, where he merely wastes his time in resentful restraint. The majority of drop-outs in the city in which this case occurred belong to in-migrant groups, Negroes, Puerto Ricans, and Mexicans, who for various reasons find it difficult to feel at home in public schools, a fact which incidentally raises another problem besides that of drop-outs as such.

Actually the drop-out rate has been decreasing over a number of years, but we can take little comfort from that fact. Not only does it remain true that considerably more than a fourth of the children entering school never graduate from high school, while a probable tenth do not finish the eighth grade, but also the chances for employment for ill-educated and semi-illiterate teen-agers are much more bleak than they used to be. With the mechanical advancement of our industrial system the demand for unskilled labor is greatly restricted and whole categories of unskilled jobs are being done away with. This fact has special significance for the in-migrants—Southern Negroes, Puerto Ricans, Southern Appalachian whites, Latin Americans—who come to urban areas with the cultural and socioeconomic conditioning of rural life.[22] Schooling should be, but frequently is not, adapted to preparing them for different conditions of living and of employment.

The two primary factors in the situation are the holding power of the schools—in other words, their ability to retain the pupil population in school until graduation—and the preventive means that can be employed to retain greater numbers. It would

appear from an intensive federal project instituted in 1962 that
in the thirty years preceding this investigation the holding power
of schools generally has increased for pupils from the fifth grade
through to graduation.[23] Gratifying as this is, it also throws a
dismal light on the previous situation, since the number of drop-
outs is still a serious problem. This drop-out rate is highest in
large cities and rural districts. In cooperation with eighty-nine
secondary schools in New York State the New York City Bureau
of Guidance conducted a holding-power project between 1952
and 1960. While its identification of probable drop-outs was
reasonably accurate, its proposals for reducing the drop-out rate
did not go very far. The schools with lower drop-out rates were
also more successful in efforts for further improvement.[24] However, the schools with fewer drop-outs were situated in the
better residential areas, and this obvious fact simply accentuates
another obvious fact—that the family situation is itself a potent
determinant of the drop-out problem. We have some evidence
that the responsibility rests not so much with family pressure on
the youth to add some earnings to the family budget as with
the lack of standards and the low level of aspiration characterizing so many families that have become inured to living in the
squalor of the slum. The family attitude conspires with the retardation and consequent alienation from school that for reasons
already mentioned the youth of these families are not unlikely
to experience, and the drop-out is the consequence. Some
studies speak of new "techniques" to retain children in school,
but the pedagogical resort to techniques is out of focus here. On
the one side, the teacher must endeavor to understand the problems of vulnerable youth and adapt this teaching to what they
can take, seeking always to stir their incentive to learn. On the
other side, the family must be aided, encouraged, and instructed
so that it cooperates with the school in its endeavor to educate
the pupil. Neither task is an easy one.

We have touched here on the third of the special problems of
the school, *that of the preparation of the pupils for their working life.* If the school is to educate the child to become an effective member of society or, if you prefer, to develop his poten-

tialities as a human being, it must prepare him for the workaday world, the changeful world of our times. In doing so it must take realistic cognizance of the aptitudes, conditions, and needs of different pupils. The task will differ somewhat for school populations of different areas. But there is a common core of instruction that all students need, no matter what their abilities or their backgrounds. This is not so much a question of subject matter as of approach. Every pupil needs to be taught to be observant, to make clear distinctions, to report accurately, to notice the way things are patterned. Such training is useful for all jobs, from the lowest to the highest, and with such training a young person can advance to the extent of his ability. Every pupil has some aptitude, some latent interest that intelligent instruction can evoke. Some respond readily, with others patient work is necessary to arouse interest. This consideration should be the basis of the vocational guidance that a large number of pupils need.

Some efforts are being made in this direction. The career guidance project in the New York City schools arose out of concern in the junior high school division for potential drop-outs, pupils whose adjustment to schooling was very poor and who also often had emotional and behavioral difficulties.[25] The project embraces thirty junior high schools distributed over four boroughs and concentrates on restoring the confidence and incentive of children who have experienced a long series of failures and frustrations. Already the program is claimed to have paid off in better attendance, improved attitudes and behavior, better study habits, and more desire to learn. An older out-of-school youth guidance center program for senior teenagers in New York City has in the past two years been making special efforts to reach drop-outs; it provides opportunities for vocational training and personal guidance.[26] It reports some success in enrolling drop-outs in evening school programs or in full-time training in technical schools, radio and television schools, nursing schools, and business schools. Both the above-mentioned programs are in process of being evaluated.

One type of enterprise in finding employment is illustrated

by an arrangement the Newark, New Jersey, schools have made
with a large department-store chain. All the stores of this chain
make employment available, as job vacancies occur, to suitable
high school juniors and seniors who are likely to leave school or
have already dropped out. It is a condition of employment that
the youth remain in school and maintain satisfactory grades.
After graduation the youth is eligible for a special training program in the retailing business, which includes such trades as
carpentry, painting, baking, typing, policing, advertising, cooking and dietetic work, as well as clerking.[27]

Various other programs designed to combine job training
with actual induction into the business world could be cited. For
example, there is the Chicago program, with support from the
Ford Foundation and Carson Pirie Scott Company. An experiment headed by a professor of landscape architecture at the
University of Pennsylvania employs teenagers to build playgrounds, the youth corps involved having been granted "first
demolition rights" on renewal projects. The Detroit job-up-
grading program under the auspices of the schools and the
Youth Service Counsel provides temporary employment for
drop-outs in a variety of concerns, with some prospect of more
permanent positions. The Rockland County, New York, public
school system has been distinctly forward in planning for the
various needs of its pupils and its employment-training program
is a good example. Training is to a large extent done on the
actual job. Student carpenters, plumbers, and sheet-metal workers build houses and youth centers and work on school proper-
ties. They have even built a hospital for crippled children. Cooks
prepare banquets. Beauty-culture students work for paying
clients. Moreover, the program has received full cooperation
from local trade unions. Union members have counseled students, helped some get jobs, and found qualified teachers for the
training process. The unions have even given considerable financial help and have offered union initiation fees as prizes for successful students. A preapprenticeship experiment is being undertaken under a Brick Masonry Joint Apprenticeship Committee.

High school students showed enough capacity to lay brick and tile true to the line to prove that by school-leaving age they were fit to enter regular apprenticeships.

So effective a liaison between school and job is exceptional and though it sets an excellent example it would not be feasible under less favorable conditions. The policy of combining work experience with schooling, for youths who are not qualified or not minded to proceed to college, is one that deserves wide experimentation, as H. Dillon has pleaded in his book, *Work Experience in Secondary Schools*.[28]

If we look at the problem of post-school employment as a whole, we must conclude that its magnitude is growing and that, although some promising initiatives are developing, far greater and more coordinated measures are needed if it is to be met to any important extent. The school has its own primary role but the concerted efforts of the community, as well as of local, state, and federal governments are also required. In the community, the private employer all the way down to the householder, can be activated to provide additional temporary jobs for youths, for there are always tasks that remain to be done and opportunities that are not taken. The municipality can utilize drop-outs and other unemployed teenagers to do some needed jobs. For example, cities have neighborhood conservation and urban renewal projects, but often enough these accomplish only a fraction of what needs to be done. There is still much more to be done in the training and organizing of unemployed youth to help the restoration process in their own neighborhoods—most of them live in the dilapidated deteriorating areas. Some state governments and the federal government have training programs for teenagers, domestic Peace Corps programs, programs of financial aid, and so forth.

The problem is worthy of every effort that can be made to solve it. Unemployment is highest in the teenage group and is twice as high among the disprivileged minority groups. The costs of inaction or inadequate action are extremely serious. An unemployed youngster loses aspiration, loses incentive, loses hope, and drifts too often into criminal ways. There is no waste that can compare with the waste of the promise, the vitality, and the spirit of youth.

Our concern here is with what the school can do. The changes in the industrial system are spurring our schools to fill a role of preparation for the world of work that in the past has been given too little attention. Our vocational schools serve a purpose, particularly in the training of technicians, but they by no means meet the present need. Under some conditions the system established in the Rockland County schools might, with some further developments, suffice. But, in our great cities where the unemployment of youth has the worst consequences, another approach is more feasible and is imperatively needed.

In our Juvenile Delinquency Education Project (Final Report No. 3) we advocated a branching of the school curriculum into two divisions applicable to pupils around the age of fourteen.[29] Students who show the necessary attributes and are for the most part likely to go on to college or to professional schools of any kind would carry on with a regular academic curriculum. Students who show relatively little interest in or aptitude for academic learning would enter a work-experience division. Both types of students would attend the same schools, and care should be taken to avoid the suggestion that any stigma is attached to entrance into the second division. There might, however, be some schools in which the great majority of the students would belong to the first division, in which case arrangements might be made to locate the minority elsewhere.

Most of the less advanced and more school-shy pupils would go into the second division, which would be equipped with the tools and mechanisms of a variety of trades, and the first task of the teacher would be to discover the respective attitudes and inclinations of the entrants, for it is an exceedingly rare youth who has no work-play interest of any kind. The academic part of the curriculum would be related to the kind of job to which the youth was assigned. Often enough the practical need to know better in order to do better creates an interest in acquiring the necessary knowledge. The school would help to place the pupils in jobs when they finished school, and would maintain contact with many kinds of business for this purpose, as well as to arrange for part-time jobs in the process of learning.

As things are at present, considerable numbers of teenagers in the later years of schooling regard school as a grievous compulsion. When they do not break away altogether they merely waste their time and develop resistances and frustrations. At a meeting of school superintendents at which the writer was present it was agreed that up to 25 per cent of school youth over fourteen get little or no benefit from their schooling. Training that would prepare a future for them would be more congenial and at the same time would help to evoke or revive an incentive for remaining in school that now is wholly lacking. A recent Secretary of Labor proposed that the states should extend the period of compulsory schooling to the age of eighteen. This proposal is in our judgment highly dubious—after seventeen those who are going to college or professional schools should be ready to go, and for the others it would mean an additional year of boredom and revulsion. If the proposal were to be considered at all, it should apply only to those of the work-experience group who remained unemployed.

## Summation and General Recommendations

The school is the only agency specifically organized to impart the knowledge and the skills required to equip a child for the business of adult living and also for participation in the scientific and cultural heritage of mankind. It is no substitute for other agencies that also are engaged in the upbringing of the child—the family, the church, the peer group, and the agencies of communication—but it provides training by a professional staff working continuously over many years and is often the only agency with the opportunity and presumably the qualifications to observe with unprejudiced eyes the troubles, the problems, and the needs of the child.

Hence its importance, not only in the teaching but also in the guidance of youth. Its function is to educate, but to fulfill that function it must endeavor to remove the roadblocks to education that fall within the competence of the teachers and to refer to professional therapists those other disturbances that lie beyond his competence.

Bearing these considerations in mind we regard the following recommendations as expressions of some primary obligations of the school system.

1. Since the earlier the child's learning problems are observed, recognized, and treated the better the chance of overcoming them, every school should establish a thoroughgoing early-identification program, beginning with kindergarten. Such a program might indeed be extended with considerable advantage into the preschool programs that are now developing.

2. All teachers should be trained, in their preparation for teaching or in in-service training, to identify problem children and to provide preliminary help and guidance through sympathetic understanding of their needs.

3. All schools should have available specially trained guidance counselors to whom more difficult cases should be referred.

4. To make this service possible, classes should, whenever possible, be limited to twenty or twenty-five pupils, and for particularly refractory or difficult groups to fifteen.

5. A far more intensive effort is essential for the proper instruction of disprivileged groups, particularly the in-migrant groups in urban centers, in order to help them adjust to the conditions of city life and overcome the educational deficiencies of their background. This is of high importance for their future as citizens and directly to prevent their lapsing into delinquent habits.

6. In substandard poverty-stricken urban areas the school cannot operate effectively as an educational agency unless it becomes a neighborhood institution, cooperating with the families of the area and the local welfare organizations and providing special services for the children in order to equip them for schooling. No less imperative is the need to anticipate the likelihood that certain pupils will become drop-outs, and to give special consideration to their needs and their

difficulties, and to stimulate their families through friendly contacts to encourage them to remain in school.

7. For older pupils who have either no interest or too little ability to incline them to continue with the regular academic curriculum, it is eminently desirable that the school have a division providing work-experience courses directly related to the types of jobs on which they have a reasonable chance of being employed.

8. The schools in this country cannot rise to the high demand and challenge involved in the education of the young, and in the special and individual guidance that is the best assurance that children will overcome their difficulties and not fall into delinquent ways, unless the community comes to their aid and enables them to raise their standards, the qualifications required of teachers, the salary rates, and the whole status of the profession.

# 12

# *Inclusive Neighborhood and Community Programs*

Since delinquency on any scale stems from a complex of conditions, programs that view the problem as a many-sided one and attack it concertedly from different angles deserve special consideration. The number of such programs now in process of development reveals the growth of a better understanding of the causes of delinquency. An additional spur to this more intelligent approach is the spectacle of massive riots by Negro youth in the slums of Los Angeles, New York, and other cities, creating serious damage, loss of life, and grave disturbances of the public order. Whatever immediate incitements may have touched off these explosive outbursts, they could not have occurred except for the pent-up anger and misery of a population suffering grievous ills and rankling from a sense of social injustice. We have already insisted that so long as ghettolike slums exist the frustration of the youth inhabiting them will find an outlet in delinquency. At the same time much can be done to rescue the youth of such areas by providing for them the aid, training, equipment, and work opportunities available to more fortunately placed youths. Such programs must be organized and developed on a neighborhood or district basis, in order to achieve the necessary close-up relationships with the group, but it is for the larger community to provide the major resources and to ensure that they are applied with due regard to the needs and interests of the group they serve.

The lack of comprehensive planning to meet the problems of troubled and disoriented youth has been a main weakness in the strategy of delinquent prevention. Different agencies have sought to deal with it, each from its own viewpoint, without coordination. Many family service agencies have limited their effectiveness because they have not viewed the family as a whole, have not dealt with the often difficult relationships between parents and youth or have not reacted to the background troubles of youth that disturb these relationships, or have followed some particular social-work methodology that narrowed their approach.[1] A review of twenty-one selected social programs showed that ten followed a group-work method and six a casework method, while only two were oriented to an all-around approach.[2]

### Employment-focused Programs

Some of the newer, more inclusive programs focus round one particular objective but include various others, realizing that the initial aim can be reached only by dealing with a whole series of impediments that block its achievement. Foremost among these are programs geared to providing work-opportunities for disprivileged youth. Unemployment is exceptionally high among this group, and those who are employed have for the most part casual and badly paid jobs that lead nowhere. They lack incentive because there's little to hope for and whether they become sullen or rough-riding they are alike in danger of becoming demoralized and delinquent. Whatever else may be done to help such youth is not likely to be effective unless they are given some assurance of a future, something to occupy their time that promises betterment and advancement. Work opportunity is therefore a primary requisite. But this implies realistic training, new contacts and associations, the removal of educational deficiencies, some instruction in manners and in modes of speech, recreational facilities for their free time, not infrequently better living conditions, temporary support, work-training programs, and aid in placement. Work opportunity becomes the focus of a comprehensive program.

The most extensive of such programs is being developed under the Manpower and Training Act, which concentrates on the training of youth in areas where there is considerable youth unemployment, the congested urban areas of Chicago, St. Louis, Detroit, Washington, Los Angeles, Boston, Milwaukee, New York, and other cities. The youth enlisted under this program range from sixteen to twenty-two years of age. Various government agencies combine in the development of the training program. The older youth receive allowances up to $20 per week, and the public employment offices devote themselves to the placement of those who have completed their training in some particular trade or skill.[3]

A good example of a local program largely focused on employment is the New Haven Manpower Program, a major area of the all-around system of welfare projects presided over by that city through Community Progress, Inc. While it offers a unified service of training, guidance, and general aid for those who are in need of vocational education, education in industrial arts, apprenticeship opportunities, and so forth, working in close cooperation with a considerable variety of agencies, it also has special services for those with serious educational deficiencies and for the counseling of out-of-school youth, disprivileged minority-group youth, and unemployed youngsters generally. It operates on the neighborhood level, with the aid of neighborhood services, and plans to give the schools a central place in the community life. Associated with it is a retraining committee made up of leading employers and educators who provide retraining facilities geared to the special conditions of the New Haven labor market. Besides furnishing specific training in many fields, the program is also concerned with the broader educational qualifications so often lacking among the unemployed and the unskilled, and finally it gives some consideration to the social problems of the out-of-work, including the problem of delinquency.[4]

Among its various operations New Haven takes particular note of the need to provide leisure-time activities. On the basis of a four-year study jointly sponsored by the Citizens Action

Commission and the Community Council of Greater New Haven a project has been formulated which includes clubs and lounges and entertainments, as well as general recreation facilities, and also counseling services especially directed to delinquent and out-of-school youth. These provisions will be set up, with the aid of neighborhood volunteers, in neighborhoods where the need is greatest. The whole project is remarkably thorough and well designed. The addition of leisure-time facilities for teen-agers is no mere frill; such facilities can be a significant factor in the redirection of the activities and energies of disoriented and delinquent youth.

No city has realized more effectively than has New Haven the fact that insulated attacks on individual problems within the complex of urban slum conditions that cramp the energies and distort the aspirations of youth are likely to be futile, over-weighted by the pressures of the environment and the habits and attitudes they engender. New Haven has apparently succeeded in embracing within an integrated plan not only the resources available in the city itself but also contributions from the state as well as a program for families in public housing provided by the Department of Health, Education and Welfare. If the execution of this embracing project is worthy of its planning it could become a model for the treatment of our most grievous urban ills. The much-needed coordination of welfare services is also beginning to be recognized and pursued in a number of other cities, including Chicago, with its Joint Youth Development Program; Oakland, California, with its Inter-Agency Project; St. Louis with its Gateways for Youth; and Boston with its three multi-service centers.[5]

## School-focused Programs

The school is an obvious neighborhood institution around which a broad plan of local welfare services can be organized. It plays an important role in many inclusive programs, not least in the New Haven one. In fact, it is merely for convenience of classification that we place here some of the major developments of inclusive community service. Some schools or school systems have independently provided services for the families of their pupils; others have broadened their in-school services to help make good the social and cultural deficiencies of pupils in deteriorated neighborhoods. The All-Day Neighborhood Schools of the New York City Board of Education are an admirable example of the first type of service and the Higher Horizons program falls into the second type.[6] Those engaged in developing guidance programs of schools in various areas have realized that they must work with the families of their pupils if they are to deal at all successfully with the problems that interfere with the children's education. The Ford Foundation has launched various programs to develop extra school-based services, such as remedial training and expanded guidance facilities in difficult schools.

In the Chicago Joint Youth Development Program the role of the school is pivotal in a program that includes also a wide range of community services, health, housing, employment, recreation, law enforcement, etc. Specific projects are being formulated to meet the need of localities and of special problem groups. Neighborhood activities will center around the neighborhood schools. A lookout is to be kept for signs of behavioral disturbance and vulnerability to juvenile delinquency. The school doors are open to citizens who can drop in at any time and present their problems. Short-term counseling is to be immediately available, and long-term counseling for those who have serious troubles will be provided through a special unit. Demonstration projects of various kinds are under consideration, and special efforts will be made to bridge the departmentalization that has so often obstructed the efficiency of the various services.[7]

Another school-oriented program is in progress in the Benneker elementary school district of St. Louis. Its primary objective is to stimulate the children of this impoverished, predominantly Negro area to better scholastic achievement. This endeavor called for cooperation by various social and philanthropic organizations. It has required a revision of attitudes among teachers and principals who needed a new approach to the potentialities of their retarded pupils, as well as special training for social workers employed in the schools. And it has called regular meetings with parents to discuss their problems, to aid them in their troubles, and to enlist their help in the effort to raise the sights of the children. Thoroughgoing support from the whole community is essential, if the school is to accomplish its vital but sometimes apparently impossible function of educating the children of our depressed urban areas.[8]

## Inclusive Regional Programs

For convenience we place here some broad-based projects that take for their province a distinctive urban area, considerably larger than a neighborhood, in which a high rate of delinquency is but one of a crowding number of social ills. The most notable of such projects are Haryou-Act, located in central Harlem, and Mobilization for Youth, covering the Lower East Side of Manhattan.[9] Both operate on quite a large scale and possess funds which enable them to carry on an unusual number of concerted activities. But each has various characteristics peculiar to itself.

Haryou-Act (Harlem Youth Opportunities Unlimited in conjunction with Associated Community Teams) is confronted with what may well be the most aggravated concentration of social troubles to be found in any urban area of the United States. In this Negro ghetto long-time exploitation and discrimination are being met with the aroused passions of a bewildered population in whom the new urge for liberation has largely replaced an old apathy. Of all the Health Center districts in New York City, Harlem stands highest in the indices for sociopathological factors, for health afflictions, for economic deprivation and dependence, and for juvenile delinquency. Narcotic addiction is an increasing threat in the area. A heroic enterprise will be required to convert its wretched housing and hemmed-in congestion to decent living conditions.

Haryou has to gear its manifold activities to conditions that make its every operation more difficult. For example, in its educational work it cannot be content merely with advancing programs for raising the standards of the school pupils. It must press for the reconstruction and renovation of the schools themselves, while there is also much controversy over the question whether and how Harlem pupils should be redistributed within the greater school system. More directly, it is faced with the excessive retardation and the inefficient previous schooling of so many of these children. To meet these problems it has set up a system of preschool preparation and intensive measures for remedial work to make up educational backwardness, as well as a special academy for the sixteen-to-seventeen group, and practical and cultural workshops of various kinds. In this endeavor it is receiving considerable support from City and State authorities. It has also become a special beneficiary under the Federal Anti-Poverty Program.

Again, Harlem not only has a high proportion of youthful delinquents and parolees returning from the custodial training schools, but also is an area to which certain undesirable characters, including dope peddlers, gravitate. Incidentally, there is some reason to suspect that the Negro youth is less protected than the white youth and more liable to arrest for minor offenses. There is a strong sentiment in the area that the police for the most part are particularly harsh with Negroes caught in any trouble. Whatever degree of justification there may have been for this feeling in the past, it is satisfactory to know that the police authorities are now seeking to establish better relationships. This is certainly an area in which the young are exposed to particular dangers and need a helping hand at every turn. To meet this situation Haryou-Act has devised various expedients, including a Cadet Corps and an Adult Volunteers Corps. Efforts are made to enable the young to associate with good citizens and to give them training in citizenship. There is also a special arrangement to give young people released from institutions the protection and friendly support which they need at the stage of their return. Since unemployment is abnormally high among urban Negro youth, vocational training and job placement are given special consideration.

Among the crowding troubles of the area is the final resort of drug addiction. To counter this a special project has been devised which includes, on the one hand, a drive on dope peddlers and the centers of distribution of narcotics, and, on the other, facilities for detoxification and rehabilitation in a fully equipped upstate institution. The provision of after-care—often desperately lacking—is a special concern, in an effort to protect former addicts and integrate them with the life and work of the community.

The Harlem program is a remarkable enterprise, but it has been beset by formidable difficulties, conflicting interests, and galling reminders of the gulf between plans and achievements. There is also the stubborn problem, which is mainly beyond its power, of eliminating slum conditions over a large area which has been allowed to deteriorate to the lowest point and which is further blocked by social resistance to the free movement of Negroes into other residential areas.

Haryou has from the very beginning encountered serious embarrassments because of conflicts between local controls, direct or indirect, and the program directors and operative staff. The first director resigned after a few months, the second after a considerably longer period of frustrating experience. At the time of writing Haryou is again in a crisis, owing to charges of lax bookkeeping and other complaints, which an official committee is currently assessing. It would be peculiarly unfortunate if so vital an enterprise, in an area where the need for it is maximum, an enterprise on a scale never achieved before and one with adequate financing, were to be mutilated by power struggles and its promise to inaugurate a new era for the people of Harlem and its grossly unregarded youth defeated.

Our second example, Mobilization for Youth, presents some striking contrasts to the Harlem project.[10] It is situated in a less desperate area, the Lower East Side of Manhattan, an area that has been changing considerably with the influx of Puerto Ricans and other in-migrant groups. This area is a troubled one, with many social problems, including gang fighting and a rather high delinquency rate. But it has better local resources than has

Harlem, including several superior social settlements, from one of which, Henry Street, the project was initiated, and an effective Lower East Side Neighborhood Association. The project has accordingly received highly competent support and neighborhood cooperation. It has strong financial resources, the major amount coming from several federal agencies, with very considerable City aid as well as a grant from the Ford Foundation. While in a broad way it serves the whole area, it is oriented primarily to the provision of opportunities and amenities for the young and is especially concerned to aid in the prevention of delinquency. The success it may register in the latter respect should be a good index of the success of the whole program.

More explicitly than most projects in this field, Mobilization for Youth has formulated its philosophy and its plan of operation.[11] In the first place it holds the lower economic group to be grossly underserved by the voluntary welfare agencies in general. A recent study of family agencies has shown that they provide more service to those with high school and college education than to the less well educated. In other words, where the need is greatest, the service is least. Part of the reason is that the poorer and less educated are less prepared to communicate their problems and seek assistance. They feel ill at ease in dealing with agencies which seem remote from them, whose staffs have a language unlike their own ways of speech, and which frequently require the filling in of complicated forms. MFY endeavors in its own servicing to bridge this gap. It sets up, wherever feasible, organizations of its own, Youth Job Centers, the Youth Adventure Corps, its Neighborhood Service Center, its Training Department, with rooms for meetings, coffee shops, and so forth.

Within its wide range of projects, MFY gives training for work opportunities a central place. It has its own workshops, where it trains youths in carpentry, masonry, painting, cooking, waiting at tables, sewing and the making of children's clothes, clerical and office work, automobile repairs. It uses a Shell Oil station, and places trainees at Beth Israel Hospital as aides and orderlies. The importance of these operations may be better realized when we learn that approximately 50 per cent of its clientele are Puerto Ricans and the Negro enrollment runs from 25 to 30 per cent. These are the youths who have the greatest difficulty in finding work, whose education has been least advanced, and who lack the practical training for decent jobs. In the earlier stages between 15 and 20 per cent dropped out of the program, but careful counseling brought half of these back. For those with special disabilities, physical or mental, special therapy is sought.

On-the-job training is being provided, on a subsidized basis, as an expedient for skill-upgrading. Employers are paid up to $30 a week for the trainees so that the latter may be paid the standard labor rate. This program, however, has been questioned, because of reservations about its effectiveness. One issue is whether the schools should not provide work-training programs rather than academic ones for older youngsters in grades 7 to 9, who otherwise might be wasting their time at school or becoming drop-outs. In our JDEP report on New York City Schools we made a plea for this proposal.

Through a variety of expedients MFY endeavors to deal with the people on their own terms, eschewing the jargon of social work and communicating in the language of the folk. It seeks to make its neighborhood associations as autonomous as possible. It employs indigenous personnel in a large variety of staff positions, as visiting homemakers, parent-education aides, case aides, group leaders, coffee-shop managers, and others. Its meeting places are homey—you can walk right in from the street and you don't need an appointment. It consults youthful attitudes and styles in providing leisure-time recreations and facilities. Its Adventure Corps, for example, has some of the trappings of a military outfit, with drill and banners and parades.

The professional staff keeps a watchful eye on operations but intervenes as little as possible. It sets standards and directions and allows room for trial and error on the part of the local associations. Obviously, it is responsible for the management of the funds that make the associations possible but it encourages self-help in the community. In short, it wants to make the community feel that the new facilities and services are their own and that all are working together for the future of the community's young people.

In spite of its manifest services, MFY's policy of allowing the groups it serves to give free vent to their attitudes, complaints, and reactions to existing conditions has brought it into serious trouble. Some small element of its clientele, using the facilities of MFY, circulated damning indictments of the *status quo*. There was a hue and cry, with charges that MFY was fostering subversives. We agree that the organization might have been more alert to control such manifestations, especially in view of the temper of the times. There were also complaints of extravagant expenditures. Both charges appear to have been grossly magnified, but there was danger that this signal and pioneering enterprise would be undermined by the violent attacks of those who do not understand either the fine service it is rendering or the clamant need for it. However, some new controls were established, and MFY appears now to be developing and improving its range of service.

Both Haryou and MFY have received substantial new grants under the Federal Anti-Poverty Program and will thus be in a position to broaden considerably their range of operations.

The three types of community-oriented programs we have thus far considered by no means exhaust the ways in which such programs can be instituted or organized. Any particular social objective for the welfare of youth can be broadened into a range of operations that takes on a community character. Any social institution or movement can make itself a center that plans and coordinates an integrated series of many-sided social activities. The logic of service prompts all-round programs, since the achievement of any one objective, such as the reduction of juvenile delinquency, involves remedial activities in a variety of directions. A project may begin with, say, the provision of recreation or entertainment, but its directors will soon find that the youth thus served have many problems that interfere with its efforts. The focus of community service may thus be a playground association, a neighborhood house or settlement, or a police precinct.

Again, the coverage of the program may not be a region or larger community but a small neighborhood. A program on this lesser scale is feasible with quite limited resources and may serve as a pilot project for a series of similar programs. Various attempts have been made to set up such neighborhood centers. The writer was responsible for the planning of one in a high-delinquency neighborhood in the South Bronx, New York City, while he was director of the City's Juvenile Delinquency Evaluation Project. As our investigation proceeded, we were more and more impressed with the fact that while large sums were being spent on the rehabilitation of conscious delinquents, with at best only a modicum of success, very little was being done to reach incipient delinquents and "vulnerable" youths, at the stage where the chances of reform or change of direction were far greater. Accordingly, with some additional funds received through the intervention of Abe Stark, then President of the Council, we chose a fairly well-demarcated neighborhood and planted within it a small professional staff. The inhabitants were organized through a neighborhood committee and neighborhood volunteers were enlisted. A beginning was made in the enlistment of block captains who would be in a position to report on any youngsters who needed our aid, counsel, or support in any way. We established excellent relations with the South Bronx Community Council, with the neighborhood public schools, and with various neighborhood welfare agencies, while a church in the neighborhood was especially cooperative. We found quickly, however, that the cordial support of the people of the neighborhood was more readily secured if we sought to serve them in other ways. The great majority were Puerto Ricans, recent in-migrants, who were without experience in dealing with officials. They sought our help when they had complaints about housing violations or trouble with the Department of Welfare, or schooling difficulties, and so forth. We set up quite a variety of services—for young mothers, for children in need, for after-school play facilities, for pupils whose English was inadequate. As a result we won their confidence and were freely consulted about troubled or difficult children. Not infrequently children themselves came to us with their problems. Our little professional group situated in the neighborhood became integrated into the neighborhood.

## Comments and Conclusions

The strategic advantage of a unified centrally directed program over a series of separate single-objective operations, one devoted, say, to delinquency, one to health problems, one to employment training and placement, and so forth, should be obvious, especially in dealing with neighborhoods or groups suffering from serious handicaps. If delinquents are our primary concern, we have to do something about their schooling, about their associations, about their home life, about their opportunities for jobs, and sometimes about their health conditions. If unemployment is the problem we are attacking, obviously the chances of decent employment depend on training in the appropriate skills, a respectable general education, decent manners, good work habits, and the ability to get along with others. We could go further and say that every single welfare objective is advanced by advances made in all other welfare objectives. Every gain in one direction sustains a gain in other directions. If, for example, you improve the probation system, some youngsters will receive the friendly counsel and aid and new associations they badly need, which may save them from being institutionalized, may mean the restoration of family relationships, may mean they make better grades at school, may mean they are referred for some health service, and so forth. A beneficent cycle of changes may be substituted for a vicious circle.

The integration of the various operations of an inclusive community program, so that they are all geared together with adequate understanding among the various areas of operation, is a task calling for high capacity and expertise in the director. In some cases, irrelevant considerations in the choice of a director or the unwillingness to search for and adequately compensate effective leadership has militated against the success of community programs that otherwise were well designed.

The various community programs we have described are

mostly in the initial or developing stage. They cannot therefore be evaluated at present by the only sure test, that of actual results. We have suggested that integrated programs have the potentiality of much greater impact on the many-sided problems of youth, and it is therefore of high importance that continuing research be built into them, leading up to final evaluations. Some of these programs are taking steps in this direction. The Chicago program, for example, contemplates a series of studies to analyze the direct impact of its various operations and also to interpret the significance of its united attack. New Haven plans to test the working of the actual techniques it employs in the several areas, the effect of the coordination of operations on the quality and effectiveness of service, and the relative availability of qualified workers in various social welfare fields.

In sum, the following are our conclusions respecting the strategy of inclusive programs.

1. Since delinquency, like many other social ills, takes various forms and results from the combined impact of a complex of adverse conditions, the attack on it should also be many-sided, the different lines being geared into an integrated program.

2. The locus of operation should be the neighborhood, to assure close relations between the people and the operating staff, and the whole field of action should be a reasonably well-demarcated region.

3. A many-sided program is likely to gain in concentration and efficacy if it gives a central place to some one important problem, say education for employment (social as well as academic and technical), and if it can focus its activities in each neighborhood around an appropriate school or community center.

4. The experience of Haryou and Mobilization for Youth emphasizes the need that such major regional organizations, financed from governmental and private sources, be actively supervised by a highly qualified body, composed of welfare specialists, social scientists, and area representatives. Such a body should not be empowered to prescribe policies and methods of operation but should make evaluative comments

and suggestions and would be able to defend the organization against unwarranted attacks. It would also be desirable that a small committee of research experts be employed part time to keep in close touch with program developments, assess results, and make proposals to the director for operative improvements.

# 13

## *The Police*

The police constitute the first line of defense against juvenile delinquency. As such and as the petitioners in the cases of four out of five young persons referred to the juvenile courts, the police largely determine the extent to which the behavior deviations of young people in any community will be officially registered. About one million children a year are estimated to have contact with the police. More than three times as many juveniles under the age of eighteen as appear before the juvenile courts of the country come to the attention of police agencies, according to a United States Children's Bureau estimate. This is more than eight times the number placed in detention and ten times the number put on probation by the courts.[1]

The police officer may resort to one of several alternatives with troublesome children. He may deem a warning sufficient or he may decide upon a referral to a juvenile court or a community agency. In some communities responsibility for the redirection of the less serious offenders is personally assumed by the officer. The individual officer's discretion and training and the availability of alternative services for the young persons' care will largely determine his decision in the exercise of the responsibility assigned to him by the community. His individual discretion to warn, apprehend, detain, or refer a child to juvenile court considerably governs a police officer's decision within the dictates of official regulation.

Most of the cases handled in the initial contact appear relatively simple. The majority come to the police department's official attention only once, for a curfew violation, pilfering, bullying, or a prank, for instance. Quite often this will be the family's only contact with the police department in a lifetime. Whether this contact is well advised or rough and shabby is most important in creating an attitude toward police authority.

While a sizable proportion of police referrals probably arise from community complaint, Alfred J. Kahn points out that in New York City an overwhelming majority of the non-arrest cases referred to the Investigation Unit come through the police.[2] More alleged delinquents and children in trouble have their first official contact with the Police Youth Division than with all other agencies put together. More than half of all children reported to the New York City Youth Board in 1955 were known to the Juvenile Aid Bureau of the Police Department. There are comparable findings in other cities. About 30 to 40 per cent involve only a precautionary letter, and a third are referred to the parents following home investigation. Of the remainder, many have previous records and are handled in the courts or in social agencies. In New York City about 2,000 new referrals to court and social agencies emerge out of some 34,000 non-arrest cases annually.

Various sources bring juveniles to the notice of the police, including complaints from outside observers who witnessed some violation or made some direct surveillance. A study by G. A. Mitchell disclosed that the bases on which officers of the Youth Bureau of the Detroit Police Department decided, during an initial contact with a boy on the street, whether to handle the case formally or informally were somewhat loose.[3] If the family seemed to the officer to be interested in the boy and if the home was neat, the case tended to be handled informally. Children of "above average" intelligence had a good chance of being referred to an agency. If a boy was respectful to the officer and cooperative he stood a good chance of being released. A boy large for his age was regarded as a likely trouble-maker. "I refer most big boys to court," said one officer.

The police officer's role in this respect is to distinguish between the offender for whom a warning is sufficient and the more serious delinquent. To do so, he should have some understanding of the problems and troubles of children. In addition to information about juvenile court law and protective obligations in neglect cases, he should have enough knowledge of social agencies and community resources to direct people in need or in trouble. He should be instructed in the rights of young people during the questioning and other phases of investigation and in the conditions under which resort to detention facilities is desirable.

The activities of the police in dealing with juveniles should center round a specially trained section of the police department—its bureau for juveniles. The average policeman is not qualified to deal on his own with troublesome children, and the nature of his task in contact with criminals tends to develop attitudes that are not propitious for such dealings. All policemen should certainly be given a general training in the way to handle children, but with the scale of the police force such training can only be of a screening character. The special youth unit should be quite distinct. Its members should be selected on a different basis, from young persons with special aptitudes. In the New York City juvenile bureau and some others most of the members have college degrees in relevant subjects. In some areas police training for juvenile work is done in collaboration with colleges and universities. This important development is exhibited in the Federal Bureau of Investigation's educational activities at the National Police Academy, which has inaugurated preservice police training programs, pioneered by August Volmer and now regularly scheduled at nearly a dozen colleges and universities. Another significant example is the Delinquency Control Institute under the direction of the School of Public Administration at the University of Southern California, which is regarded as having a quite effective impact in California generally, as well as in other western states.[4]

The Police College now established under the aegis of the Board of Higher Education for the instruction of the New York City police force is also a signal advance beyond the earlier

Police Academy. But in most communities, except for a few great cities, police provision for dealing with the young is wholly inadequate. The imperative importance of such provision is better appreciated if we realize that the function of the police is not only to suppress law-breaking but to prevent it. And when dealing with youngsters the preventive function is paramount. Sir Robert Peel, who in the early nineteenth century reorganized the London police force (who are called "bobbies" to this day), maintained that the primary responsibility of the force is to prevent crime and public disorder, not simply to arrest the criminal. The police guard children when crossing streets to school, bring the young ones home when they stray and direct and warn children in various situations. It is their task also to direct and warn them away from law violation, and since they are usually the first officials who are in contact with children, they have unusual opportunties to perform this essential service. But to do so they need to be educated in the ways and needs of children as well as in the requirements of the law.

All cases of young persons who show signs of having serious problems or of being seriously disturbed or difficult, and all in which there is a record of previous offenses, should be referred from the regular police to the special youth unit, and all police-men should be instructed in the symptoms that call for the service of a trained youth staff. It should indeed be a general principle that, wherever feasible, the special youth police officer is called at an early stage to dispose of and to process juvenile cases. This special unit should decide whether a case should go directly before the court or whether some preliminary pro-gram of investigation or referral is requisite.

Not only should the training of the youth bureau personnel be distinctive but so should their social responsibilities. Their mission should include the patrolling and inspection of places and premises that attract youth, and especially juvenile hang-outs of dubious character. They should take the lead in estab-lishing, for the police in general, good working relationships with welfare agencies and civic associations. Saul Bernstein, in his recent survey, *Youth on the Streets,* found that the part played by the police juvenile bureaus was of primary importance in the maintenance of good understanding between the police and the social agency workers with whom they come into contact.[5] The cooperation of welfare agencies with the police and vice versa can be highly advantageous to both.

Of no less significance is the cooperation between the police and the schools. The particularly difficult or disturbed pupils who give so much concern to teachers are not unlikely to come also to the attention of the police, and the teachers can provide a far more intelligent report on them than outsiders or even members of the children's families can give. Such information is more significant if it is conveyed to policemen who have the requisite training, and that for the most part means members of the juvenile bureau. A close working relationship between the police and the school can be the means of avoiding serious errors in treatment.

An illustration is provided from a report on police-school liaison in Flint, Michigan.[6] During the period 1958–1959, in the area where the liaison program was operating, only one out of every 280 public school students was involved in a crime, as compared with one in every 36 such students outside the area. In the city as a whole there were 200 repeaters, whereas in the program district there were none. Even making allowance for the diverse conditions of the various city districts this was a remarkable showing.

The need for concentrated service on the part of the police juvenile unit in areas where there is tension between different ethnic groups has been highlighted by recent happenings in a number of large cities. Frequently in such areas open conflict between opposing groups is initiated by undisciplined youths or again by youths seething with anger against what they regard as gross injustice or discrimination. There are also not infrequent outbreaks that are triggered by resentment against what is regarded as needless violence or brutality on the part of the police, especially when they are seeking to make an arrest. So far has this spirit spread in certain areas in New York City that even the action of the police in arresting a youth who has committed a serious offense may cause a riot. Recently this attitude has been so pronounced in Puerto Rican areas that the police authorities have instituted a special program designed to give the police who move in these areas a more friendly and sympathetic relation to Puerto Ricans. A party of police were even sent to Puerto Rico to help improve this understanding. From first reports the program would seem to have been beneficial.

Negroes are particularly prone to the belief that the police treat them with more roughness and lack of consideration than they show to other groups. Certainly some very bad outbreaks of violence have occurred in the course of police contacts with Negro youth. One of the worst and most sustained riots in Harlem was caused by the fatal shooting of a youth who was forcefully resisting a police arrest. Since the policeman in question was exonerated by the police authorities after a hearing of the case, the event gave impetus to a demand that charges of police brutality or violence be heard by a civilian body.

The New York City Police Department has recently become much concerned over the hostile attitudes so frequently manifested by Negro and Puerto Rican groups toward the police, and is making concerted efforts to remedy the situation, both through police training and through the education of the public concerning the problems faced by the police. To advance this policy the Police College is preparing, under a Ford Foundation grant, a police training film, dealing primarily with the relations between the police and the community.

Members of the juvenile bureau could be especially helpful in spotting locations of rising tensions, probing the causes of tensions, recognizing the incitements that trigger youth uprisings, and reporting to the authorities. They would enlist the aid of strategically located persons, including school teachers, community workers, and Negro leaders, and they themselves would be more effective in dealings with the youthful disturbers than the regular police are likely to be. Their role would be not to substitute for the regular police but to cooperate with them.

Another activity entrusted to the police calls for both understanding of youth problems and knowledge of the capacities of available social agencies. This is the matter of referrals, especially referrals in cases where the offense is deemed not to require, in the first instance, court handling. We have observed that many cases referred to agencies are never followed through. The agency may be already overloaded. Sometimes a perfunctory home call is made and receives no response and the case is marked "closed." Often the final comment on the agency record is simply "did not cooperate."[7] The selection of an agency should be discriminating and the communication with it fully informative, and there should always be a follow-up to find out what, if anything, has been done. The trained juvenile unit officer is best qualified to undertake this task.

Again, since a large number of juvenile offenses result directly or indirectly from gang associations, the juvenile officer can play a special role through his knowledge of the ways and attitudes of the various kinds of gangs. While the reaction of gang members to the regular police is one of fear and strong aversion, the juvenile officer has a better chance of bringing influence to bear on them. When a whole group of gang members is apprehended—sometimes merely on the charge of "unlawful assembly," sometimes because an offense was committed by one or more members of the group—he is better able to distinguish the guilty members from those who went along simply because of gang allegiance or pressure.

To sum up, since juvenile offenders are distinguished from adult offenders under the laws that set up courts for juveniles, since they are not, except under very special circumstances, regarded as criminals but as wayward youth who need protection, treatment or rehabilitation, the investigation of their cases should also be distinctive: it calls for a particular police division or bureau composed of persons specially trained for the purpose. Experience has shown that such persons are better qualified than the regular police to assess problems of youth and to make recommendations on the disposition of cases. To take one example, in our Juvenile Delinquency Evaluation Project for New York City we studied the court disposition over one year (1955) of the cases that came before the court through the regular police and those that were brought before it by the Juvenile Aid Bureau of the Police Department. Of JAB arrests 24.8 per cent were discharged or dismissed by the Children's Court of that period, as compared with 39.3 per cent of those arrested by the regular police department as a whole.[8] This at least suggests that the screening process of the juvenile officers was more effective, a conclusion that was corroborated by other evidences.

Not infrequently the juvenile bureau is inadequately equipped and undermanned. The service they do or can render is often not properly recognized by the police hierarchy, though there are some fine exceptions. In one situation we studied, the juvenile bureau was a kind of detached body, and there was little if any opportunity for a service career within it. The Children's Bureau's standard calls for a scale of not less than 5 per cent of the total police force and the possession of divisional status.

### Conclusions

1. All "beat" policemen should be given instruction not only in the laws and regulations that apply to juveniles but also concerning the types of trouble characteristic of youthful offenders and the manner in which the police should deal with them. They should be taught, with illustrative cases, under what conditions arrests should be made and when specified alternative procedures are to be adopted, as well as when to refer cases to the special juvenile unit.

2. All cities of any scale should have a police bureau or division, well-equipped and adequately manned, to deal with the many cases of troubled youth that come to the attention of the police. Its members should be selected for their ability to establish effective relationships with the young and their capacity to understand and deal with youth problems. In smaller police systems some specially selected policemen should be appointed for this service. There should also be a continuing and comprehensive in-service training program for youth officers.

3. Wherever possible, members of the juvenile unit should be called in to assess and report on the cases of all young people exhibiting serious problems who come to the attention of the "beat" policemen, and they should also be given a

special mission to deal with troublesome gang situations and with situations where youthful groups are fomenting trouble.

4. The juvenile unit should be given full opportunity to maintain close contact with the social agencies to which referrals are made, with the families of trouble-making children, and with the schools.

5. The police on the beat should be carefully trained to show a friendly attitude to the public, especially in areas inhabited by minority or disprivileged groups. The exhibition of bias and intolerance or needless roughness not only alienates the community and discourages public cooperation, but also provokes hostile demonstration and dangerous incidents. The police are the guardians of the people. That is the face they should show to the community.

# 14

# *The Court*

The juvenile court, said Roscoe Pound, is the greatest forward step in Anglo-American jurisprudence since Magna Charta.[1] It might well have seemed so when one considers the degrading, cruel, and inherently stupid treatment that once was meted out to young people in the name of justice. The new court rejected their treatment as criminals and instead saw them as wards of the court who needed protection, guidance, training, and rehabilitation. It was to be nonpunitive. The offenders before it would have no stigma, no damning record. The findings were to be secret or at least confidential. No reporters could publicize their cases or exhibit their photographs. The only consideration before the court was how best it could assure, within its means, the future welfare of the juveniles.

But in the rough and tumble of political life the shining principle becomes somewhat tarnished. Juvenile court judges are often appointed without regard to their particular qualifications for this special task. The calendars are crowded and the harassed judge has not the time to give the cases before him the careful consideration they may need. The evidence presented by the police officer and the probation officer is often casual, hearsay, superficial, and sketchy. The parents who must appear in court with their offspring are unused to this situation and often tongue-tied or bewildered. Sometimes they are Spanish-speaking, their English is faulty or lacking, and no interpreter is at hand.[2] Counsel is rarely present, although the parents have the right to ask for legal aid. Appeals are rarely made from the court adjudication, since the process is slow and expensive. If the offender is adjudicated, the case may be discharged, often with a warning or some advice from the judge, or the judge may resort to one of two main forms of disposition—probation or commitment to an institution, either a state training school or a custodial institution under private or religious auspices. Probation, which is the resort in a majority of cases, has been in most areas a grossly underdeveloped service, conducted by inadequately trained personnel carrying too heavy caseloads. Custodial treatment carries a serious risk and should not be imposed if a feasible alternative is available. Some judges resort to it with too little consideration, and the courts generally have been slow to recognize the need for diagnostic centers, to which difficult cases could be referred to make advisory reports on disposition.

Most of the nonadjudicated cases are simply dismissed, without any referral, though in some areas of the country they may be put on unofficial probation.

During the period in which we studied the New York City Children's Court (since then incorporated into the Family Court), some 50 per cent of all cases appearing before the judge were either dismissed or discharged. The considerable percentage of cases thus treated in courts across the country, especially in the larger cities, is a sufficient indication that the initial screening system or intake process is either inefficient or is not given enough authority to do a proper job. Some judges hold that it is a salutary experience for a naughty child to confront the court, but this is questionable. In any event with calendars already crowded, the present procedure prevents the judge from giving more serious cases the attention they deserve.

Since probation is the main form of disposition, there is all the more reason why this much neglected service should be given the development of which it is capable. What is needed, in brief, is (1) more efficient recruiting of trained personnel, with adequate salaries to attract them; (2) limitation of the caseload to not more than perhaps 40 cases during any one period; and (3) reorganization of the probation office staff so that it is regarded as a professional service. These are prerequisites for the proper fulfillment of the two main functions of the probation officer: to provide the judge with a discerning report on the youth's background and living conditions and thus to aid him in making the most desirable disposition, and to guide the youth entrusted to his charge into law-abiding habits and associations.

In broad outline, such is the general situation with juvenile courts today. There are some admirable juvenile court judges, and there are a few juvenile court systems that have highly qualified presiding judges. But the general lack of recognition that for this special function judges need special qualifications, the congested court calendars, the lack of adequate screening prior to court appearance, the fact that in most jurisdictions judges spend only part of their time on the juvenile court bench, and the rotation of the job over a panel of judges, all militate against any adequate accomplishment of the great objective for which the juvenile court was designed.

## The Desirability of Separating Adjudication from Disposition

There has been considerable questioning of the propriety of the prevailing system which leaves it exclusively to the judge to determine the action to be taken with the adjudicated delinquent. The decision may be crucial for the whole future of the juvenile. For some the commitment to an institution may be in effect a condemnation to a criminal career. Others need special therapy or other service. The judge has not the time and often enough not the knowledge to understand the needs or the various complications of troubled youth. Two alternative methods have been advocated and in some cases have been put into operation. One would entrust the disposition, after the judge has adjudicated the youngster as delinquent, to a specially qualified body. As Professor Alfred Kahn has put it, "It should be possible to devise an administrative structure that permits appropriate delegation of disposition choices to technical specialists without affecting the judge's role as an adjudicator or separating him from the knowledge of the consequences of his decisions."[3] The other method is to have attached to the court a diagnostic center, composed of appropriate experts, to which problem cases would be referred for an advisory report on disposition, leaving the verdict to the court. Both alternatives have the additional advantage that any authority assigned such a task would be very conscious of the inadequacy of the disposition facilities available to the court in most areas and would take a lead in the effort to provide treatment centers, supervised residential facilities, foster homes, short-term testing or diagnostic centers, and other substitutes for the old-style "training school."

A Youth Correctional Authority Act was designed and approved by the American Law Institute as a model for the improvement of the disposition of cases. It calls for a youth authority to which the task would be entrusted. An act along the lines of this model was adopted by California and in one form or another the model has since been followed by four other states—Minnesota, Wisconsin, Texas, and Massachusetts.[4] A few more states, including New Jersey and New York, have made some changes in the same direction.

Under the California plan the court decides whether the adjudicated delinquent can be placed on probation (which, incidentally, is better developed there than in most states) or otherwise left in the community for treatment, or requires placement in some type of institution.[5] In the latter event he is generally put under the direction of the Youth Authority. The processing begins with four to six weeks at a reception center, after which the treatment decision is made. On that basis the youngster may be released on parole or sent to a substitute home or to one of the many specialized treatment centers or camps, unless a mental institution is indicated. The Authority is also empowered to create places of detention, training-for-employment centers, and so forth, to the extent to which funds are available.

## New Facilities for Adolescents

The upper age limit for juvenile court jurisdiction ranges from sixteen to eighteen and exceptionally up to twenty-one. It has tended to be raised as a result of official recommendations. In New York State, where the official juvenile must be under sixteen, some special provisions are made. Minors between sixteen and nineteen may be designated "youthful offenders" with the consent of the judge after investigation, provided the charge is not a crime punishable by death or life imprisonment. In that event they are treated somewhat along the lines of juvenile court procedure. The Wayward Minor Act made it possible to adjudicate as "wayward minors" adolescents between the ages of nineteen and twenty-one, for certain not too well-defined moral offenses, so that they could be placed on probation or committed to a reformatory for a period not exceeding three years. Several large cities maintain special courts for adolescents, in which procedures are geared to the objective of social rehabilitation.

The extension of certain juvenile court procedures to adolescents must be regarded as preferable to handling them in regular criminal court fashion. More effective recognition and treatment of adolescent problems would also result if special courts were more generally established for the hearing of adolescent cases, as is already done in three cities. The moral and social difficulties of adolescents are often of a different kind from those of juveniles. For this reason we regard the approach of the California Youth Authority as having special advantages. The Diagnostic Center at Menlo Park, New Jersey, and the Diagnostic Center at Madison, Wisconsin, are also well worthy of consideration.

A step in the same direction is the New York State Reception Center at Elmira. All convicted offenders between sixteen and twenty-one years of age are remanded to this center, which makes a careful investigation of the adolescent's problems, attitudes, and capabilities and on this basis decides to which of a considerable variety of institutions he should be sent. The Center is particularly concerned that the offender get whatever training he needs—not least, efficient and appropriate work training—and that every effort be made to find him a decent job when he leaves his institution.

### The Family Court and Its Adjuncts

An insulated juvenile court has many limitations and defects. Often it cannot deal with the whole problem of the juvenile before it. Frequently, for example, there is neglect as well as delinquency. If neglect includes a parent's lack of support, that would probably go to a different court altogether. Or, if an issue of paternity arises, that again comes under the jurisdiction of a different court. Aside from such special situations, the problem of delinquency is a family problem in every sense.

The answer is the family court, dealing with domestic issues of all kinds. Cincinnati has had such a court for over thirty years; another good example is the Municipal Court of Philadelphia. New York State, after a long period of gestation over the integration of a highly segmented system of courts, has established a state-wide Family Court. Within this court the loose procedures of the former Children's Court have been tightened, with proper rules for admissible evidence and other safeguards to protect the legal rights of children. Among the provisions are a system of law guardians for children, easy methods for hearings to reconsider past orders or proceedings, and reasonably easy appeals from Family Court decisions.[6]

Moreover, the inclusive Family Court is in a stronger position for the interaction of the various services within its ambit. These services include the intake procedure, the adjustment bureau, the probation system, and the court clinic. Previously the connections among these were loose and ineffective. The intake process has often been poorly equipped and without sufficient status, unable to carry through an effective pre-investigation and screening procedure. The probation service has too often been poorly equipped, underpaid, lacking the qualifications its function called for. Good working relationships between the probation officer and the judge, or between the clinic staff and the probation officer, were often lacking. The clinic attached to the court was inadequately staffed, was slow in reporting back on cases, and was sometimes regarded by judges as failing to give them clear leads for a disposition. No doubt such defects might have been remedied to a degree within the limits of the juvenile court, but in the wider supervision and extended authority of the Family Court the opportunity is greater and the need more obvious. Under the leadership of Judge Florence Kelley, the Family Court has been developing in efficiency and range of service. At the same time there remains within the unified court system the tendency for its various sections—The Juvenile Term, the Family Offense Term, the Support and Conciliation Term, and so on—to act in a kind of quasi-independence.

An illustration of the potentialities of pre-investigation and screening was provided in an experiment under the auspices of the New York City Children's Court.[7] With the aid of a mental health team, a consultative process was set up, involving the probation department as well as the judge. During a six months' experimental period 1000 cases came under consideration. In a majority of these, the consultation sufficed to identify the nature of the problem investigated, for all concerned. Other cases called for more comprehensive diagnostic assessment. This service has been a source of great stimulation both to the intake department and the probation department.

The new probation service at intake has developed more recently in a very promising manner. Judge Justine Wise Polier testifies: "The achievement at intake in adjusting cases of children alleged to be delinquent or in need of supervision has already improved the whole picture in detention of children pending disposition. Among other contributing factors are the sharp drop in the number of delinquent children brought before the court on new petitions, the definite restrictions under the new law on the length of time the court may remand such children pending disposition, and the expansion of state facilities for children needing placement."

Judge Polier points out, however, that "for reasons that are not clear and require careful study, the new probation service at intake has been far more effective in cases where the child is alleged to be delinquent or in need of supervision than where a charge of neglect is lodged against parents. For the first six months of 1963, there was a decrease of 37 per cent in the number of children brought before the court on new delinquency and in-need-of-supervision petitions."[8]

In only a very few regions is any effort made to relate the

probation system to a diagnostic clinic. Another example is that of the Santa Clara County Juvenile Court, which has organized a psychiatric clinic to work with the probation service.[9] A main objective is to avert, through the union of the two services, the separate functioning that may well lead to further disorganization for an already disunited family.

## *Summation*

Across the whole country much more needs to be done to make the juvenile court a fully efficient and cooperative agency within the network of services on behalf of youth. The court has a distinctive role. At a certain state in the delinquent's career the court has the crucial task of deciding whether he needs to become its ward and, if so, what form of treatment should follow. But it cannot properly perform this task unaided. The insulated self-sufficient juvenile court is an anachronism. The court itself has not the time or the experience to assess the complex problems of youth and their relation to the youth's family and environment. Both prior to and after court hearings, screening, consultative, and follow-up services are necessary if it is to fulfill the mission the community has entrusted to it. The following conditions we regard as primary.

1. Judges serving in juvenile courts should have special qualifications appropriate to their function. Some system should be adopted that would rule out patronage or other political ground for their selection. A list of candidates might, for example, be prepared by a bar association or other qualified body, the specific choice between them being made by the relevant municipal or state authority.

2. The intake system should be adequately equipped and qualified to investigate and screen out the cases that do not need to come before the court. In doing so, it should maintain close relations with the probation department and the diagnostic center where the latter exists. An effective intake service can relieve the judge of many needless hearings and enable him to concentrate more on those cases that require careful consideration.

3. The probation system, as the major and most promising of the resources available to the judge for disposition of cases, should be adequately staffed to permit the limiting of the caseload so that the probation officer has sufficient time and opportunity to give careful attention to the needs of every probationee, should be provided with a salary schedule adequate to attract fully qualified officers, and should be constituted as a professional service, with its own organization and a degree of autonomy.

4. Even where there is a superior probation service the judge can only exceptionally possess the requisite information and the expert comprehension of the adjudged delinquent's problems to determine the best mode of disposition. It is therefore highly desirable that the court have available a diagnostic center to which the more difficult cases would be referred for investigation and advisement. A psychiatric clinic does not suffice, since for many cases the skills of the clinical psychologist, the sociologist, the pediatrician, and the child welfare specialist are needed.

5. A promising type of over-all organization is a state youth authority to which adjudged delinquents would be committed for disposition. Such an authority should be empowered to utilize the available agencies, including educational and medical as well as correctional, and to create and develop needed facilities. It should have its own professionally staffed diagnostic center.

6. The socialized procedure of the juvenile court should be extended, so far as feasible, to adolescents up to the age of twenty-one.

7. Since the problem of delinquency is not detachable from a complex of problems concerning both the delinquent and his family, the juvenile court will operate with greater efficiency if it is integrated into the system of an inclusive family court.

# 15

## *The Custodial Institution*

The number of children in New York State adjudicated delinquent and placed in public or private institutions increased from 1500 in 1949 to more than 3100 in 1962. However, in 39 counties of less than 100,000 population a substantial decrease (30 per cent) has occurred in the past five years. It would certainly be desirable to discover the reason for this disparity. In the larger cities the situation has been growing steadily worse.

While in 1949 less than half of the children committed in New York State went to state institutions, 80 per cent of those committed in 1962 went to state training institutions. In fact 95 per cent of the thirteen-year increase has been absorbed by these state-operated systems. Although voluntary institutions continue to play an important role in the development of services available to children in trouble, the major responsibility for institutional care now lies with the state training schools.[1]

Approximately 350 institutions in the United States serve children adjudicated delinquent. Of these one is a federal training school, 132 are state training schools (68 for boys, 50 for girls, 14 coeducational), 52 are county or city training schools, 11 are state reception diagnostic centers, 29 are forestry camps, and 135 are schools under private auspices. The public institutions accommodate approximately 36,000 delinquent children at any one time (and about 72,000 in the course of a year), while the private schools house approximately 10,000. The average age of the training school student nationally is close to 16 but the range is from under 10 to over 18 depending on state statute and policies. Seventy-five per cent are boys; two-thirds are white; 15 per cent have been in training schools before. Forty per cent of the institutions house over 200 children each (in fact, 15 institutions have capacities of 300 to 399 and 12 house over 400). More than half have capacities for more than 150 children. Many are overcrowded and are operating well beyond official capacity.[2] More than one-third of the training schools are housing more than the number of juveniles for whom they were designed.[3]

The custodial institution for juvenile offenders raises many questions. What is the rationale for commitment? How effective are the institutions as a means of rehabilitation? What should be done to improve their effectiveness? Into what different types do they fall? When are alternative methods of treatment preferable?

## Types of Custodial Institutions

Custodial institutions may be broadly distinguished as those under public auspices, generally known as state training schools, and those under private auspices. Unlike institutions under private auspices, whether religious or philanthropic, the state institutions cannot pick and choose those inmates they regard as appropriate for their service. They are under obligation to admit, with few exceptions, the heterogeneous youngsters assigned to them. Both public and private institutions do a kind of internal selection, since both divide the inmates among a series of cottages, in which they spend the night under the charge of "cottage parents." The number in each cottage varies from an average of about twenty or less in the better-equipped institutions to an extreme of eighty. Some institutions under private auspices have led the way in the development of an all-round professional staff. On the average there is one full-time staff member (including educational and treatment officials, administrative, operational, and maintenance staff) for every 2.6 juveniles, but even so, as has been pointed out in some research studies, the staff members cannot cope adequately with the various needs of the diversity of youngsters under their charge.

The staffing of training schools has always been a problem. The quality of service that the care and treatment of difficult children demand is hard to recruit and harder to retain. Many of these schools are remote from urban areas, since they require considerable space and are not welcomed by the communities near which they might want to be located. While the more rural locations may have certain advantages, they create difficulties in securing the professional staff they need, especially as the conditions of life are arduous. Moreover, the salaries are often lower than are available elsewhere. Consequently the turnover is high, the median length of service for full-time staff employees being three years. Key staff vacancies often remain unfilled for considerable periods. Qualifications consequently have to be reduced to secure the necessary quota. This comment applies to teachers, psychologists, social workers, psychiatrists, and others, although some devoted staff members are of high quality. Few training schools have a full-time psychiatric service and some none at all. Perhaps the most difficult staffing problem for directors of training schools is finding "cottage parents." The juveniles spend more time under their charge than they do with any other members of the staff. The objective is to obtain the services of mature persons—preferably a husband and wife for each cottage—who understand the problems of children. But these desiderata are hard indeed to attain, and few are found who are really qualified for their difficult and exacting task.

Forestry schools and farm schools for delinquents may be considered varieties of state training schools. In some instances the differences are only secondary, since farming or market gardening is frequently an occupation for the youth in regular training schools, and forestry may have a relatively minor role

in schools designated as forestry. Forestry schools properly so
called probably have advantages for a select group of youngsters, but for the urban-bred population who constitute the great
bulk of adjudicated delinquents the evidence suggests that they
are by no means appropriate. Youngsters who have some feeling
for country life and work in the woods probably benefit and in
the forestry environment may feel less the chafing sense of custodial restraint. But further studies are needed to determine
the degree of success these institutions achieve.

There are certain differences between state institutions and
those under private auspices. In the first place the latter are
selective and put strict limits on their total intake. Thus they do
not reach the size of some of the very large state institutions.
The young under their care are somewhat more homogeneous,
so that treatment programs can be better concentrated. They
often refuse to accept highly disturbed delinquents, arsonists,
and others who show dangerous tendencies. They tend to have a
larger proportion of professional workers. We may distinguish
those under religious auspices, since they tend to select youth
whose families belong to the faith the institutions represent and
they lay more stress on religious training. Many of these institutions are under Roman Catholic auspices, with a few under
Jewish auspices. The private institutions not under the auspices
of a particular religion tend to be somewhat more experimental
in their modes of treatment. Those we have personally studied
in the New York area, going under the name of "residential
treatment centers," have shown considerable readiness to try
out various approaches to meet their insistent problems.[4] Institutions such as Wiltwyck and Children's Village—and also
Hawthorne–Cedar Knolls, which is under Jewish auspices—
proved to be excellent examples of their kind. If their success
is still quite limited we find in this fact some corroboration of
our contention that custodial institutions should be resorted to
only when it is imperative, to protect the public and the child
himself, to place the youth under custodial care.

We leave for later consideration certain smaller and more
specialized residential centers as well as the "halfway houses"

usually located in cities as temporary supervisory abodes particularly for youths discharged from the larger institutions.

## The Basis of Institutional Commitment

Now we turn to our critical questions. First, how are commitments to institutions made and on what grounds? When a youngster is adjudged delinquent by a court, the main alternatives at the disposal of the judge are to put him on probation or to send him to an institution. It is presumed that those committed are the "hard core" of delinquent children who have been in trouble several times and have failed to respond to warnings and to neighborly services. The majority have been on probation previously without showing any improvement. We have, however, pointed out that probation services often provide only nominal or quite perfunctory supervision and are of little or no benefit to the probationees. Some are committed who have no previous records but have been arrested for felonies of a type that cause serious concern. Some are committed, however, because their delinquency is associated with bad home conditions, and the judge feels that, for lack of better alternatives, it is desirable to remove them from home and place them under custodial care.

We may regard the preceding statements as the rationale of judicial commitment. But actually when we examine cases with any care we find no clear line of principle underlying the most serious decision the judge has to make—that is, to commit a youngster to an institution. Joseph H. Louchheim concludes from his study of commitments that the decision is based on expediency rather than on social planning.[5] In our own study of the commitment practices in New York City we found strong evidence indicating that the decision to commit to an institution is often made without adequate consideration of the nature of the case. As Louchheim states, a large number of young people are committed after their first court appearance, and a very considerable number without their having had contact with community resources.

Increasing commitments and pressures from the courts have led to the creation of additional public institutions. At least part of the reason, as Alfred J. Kahn points out in a study conducted for the New York State Department of Welfare, is that the judges could find no more appropriate recourse available. New York and some other states are now making efforts to provide such alternatives as halfway houses, foster homes, and urban group residences.

*Were adequate alternatives available, it would be sound strategy on the part of the juvenile courts to limit to the absolute minimum (a consideration we shall presently explore) the number of cases committed to large institutions such as our present state training schools.*

We should distinguish here between two types of alternatives. One is a variety of small residence, with a more homelike attitude, specialized for the different needs and problems of the young. Children who suffer mainly from neglect should not be mixed with children who have confirmed delinquent habits. Children suffering from physical handicaps or ailments should be treated in some form of hospital or hospital department where they can receive the treatment they need. Children who exhibit particularly dangerous tendencies—arsonists, nonstatutory rapists, sadistically violent children—should be segregated from other delinquents and given particular care under qualified experts, as should children who exhibit psychotic or other mental disturbances. We must always remember that the function of children's courts is not to punish, that they are not criminal courts, but are expressly set up to assure that children will receive the care, treatment, or therapy their particular problems demand.

The other type of alternative consists of directive and protective supervision, as well as therapeutic treatment, which does not require the removal of the youth from his own home environment. The most important resort of this kind is probation, which, with an adequate staff of really qualified probation officers, could be most advantageously employed for many cases that are now committed to institutions.

## The Case Against Institutionalization

The reasons we believe that institutionalization should be avoided whenever possible are particularly relevant to large-scale institutions such as the great majority of our present state training schools, but they also apply, to some degree, to all types of institutions that remove children from the home environment.

In the first place, the institutional setting is for the young delinquent an alien one that militates against his responsiveness to even the best and wisest treatment. Technically, the institution is a place where the youth is sent for friendly guidance and training, but for the youth himself it is a prison, a punishment. He is cut off from all familiar associations. He is under restraints that he bitterly resents. He lives with other youths who are equally resentful, and his only friends are those who inspire him with hostility to the authorities who have him in their charge. His relationships fall within the range of a one-sex, one-age society, among the disadvantages of which is its effect on the sexual attitude of the inmates. We must remember that these youths have, perhaps more than others of their age, associated with "girl friends" in their home environment. There is considerable evidence that the system encourages homosexuality. This is as true of the institutions for girls as of those for boys.[6]

The second count is directly associated with the first. It is the simplest principle of social behavior that likes gang up with their likes against unlikes. So do the rebellious inmates of these institutions, just as do the inmates of prisons. But for these youthful delinquents the effects are more serious. The staff is seeking to instill socialized attitudes. To frustrate the intentions of the staff, to evade the rules, at most to comply with tongue in cheek, is the natural response of the inmates. The tougher boys dominate the others. They bully the weaker and any who are minded to comply with institutional requirements. We have some evidence that entering boys are more amenable and sometimes more desirous of making a good adjustment within the institution than the same boys after they have been initiated into the mores of the institutional "subculture." Some institutional administrators tend to accommodate themselves into a kind of acquiescence with these mores within the limits that permit a degree of "coexistence."[7] One investigator, Seymour Rubenfeld, asserts that a fuller recognition of the character of the inmate society could open up a new dimension in the development of rehabilitation techniques.[8] A fuller recognition of the needs and conditions that are responsible for inmate resort to underground resistance would probably avoid mistakes and frustrations on the part of the staff, but how much more it could achieve is debatable. The youthful underground is analogous to the kind of street gang to which so many of its members have belonged and carries on the gang's characteristics so far as institutional conditions permit. In the institution, where there are no distracting outside influences on gang members, ruthless control is all the more assured.

Howard W. Polsky's study, *Cottage Six,* offers a realistic appraisal of the operation of the inmate subculture inside a first-rate residential treatment institution.[9] He points out that every boy found it necessary to adopt the values and patterns of the subculture, regardless of the system of treatment including clinical therapy. Not only was the subculture the dominant force in the life of the boys but it was potent enough to evoke a kind of covert and unwitting support from the staff itself. The removal of "key" boys did not appear to modify its effectiveness in the least. The subculture has its own social system which stabilizes and unifies its pathways. Polsky's findings have led the institution in question to make the cottage as a whole and not the individual boy the basic unit of treatment, taking into account the nature of the experience the boys collectively share. How effective this recent change of approach will be remains to be seen.

The third reason for our viewpoint is the evidence of recidivism. Various studies of children's courts, as Bloch and Flynn point out, indicate that as high as 60 to 80 per cent of the inmates of state training schools fail to make good within five years or more after discharge.[10] Mannering reported that 41 per cent of those discharged from the Wisconsin School for Boys failed within the year and 50 per cent within two years.[11] We have a variety of other figures for various institutions, but we do not cite them because they cover relatively short periods or depend on an inadequate sampling. The fact is that there has been very little serious research into the extent of recidivism. Considerable expense is involved and thorough research covering a period of years is necessary. Many of those who have been in institutions disappear from view, and it is hard to find those who have moved to another address or left their home city. One reasonably good indication, however, is the number of parolees from institutions who were recommitted. For parolees under the supervision of the California Youth Authority the figure cited over a number of years is around 45 per cent, while an additional 24 per cent were discharged from parole "under suspension," usually because the responsibility for the youth was transferred to another agency. We cannot assume that the parolees who are not convicted of further offenses can therefore be regarded as "successes," since it is a well-recognized fact that a considerable number of law violations are either not reported at all or the perpetrators are not discovered. On the other hand, there are a few instances in which the rate of recidivism reported is much lower. Thus Berkshire Farms Training School in New York State reported a "success rate" of 75 per cent for boys over 15½ years and 53 per cent for those under 15½ years.[12] Part of the explanation in this instance may be the fact that this school had an excellent official who was particularly helpful in caring for and finding employment for the boys discharged from the institution.

Our conclusion agrees with that of other investigators including Jerome Laulicht and Herbert Bloch, that the results of training school experiences are discouraging. Nor can we attribute this situation to the inefficiency of the institutions themselves. Not only do they work under considerable handicaps but many of their inmates are the most serious and confirmed delinquents with whom the courts have to deal. The fact that so many of them come up for adjudication without having previously received any proper care or treatment constitutes a strong indictment against a system that gives relatively little attention to the need for early care and guidance for vulnerable children and those beginning to exhibit delinquent tendencies.

There is another important reason why our custodial institutions so often fail in their mission of rehabilitation, and that is the inadequacy of after-care. The transition from the guarded, relatively regimented, remote and alien life of the institution to the youth's own neighborhood, with its new freedom and its associations good or bad, is a crucial experience. The parolee is suddenly faced with difficult problems. Whether he goes back to school or is old enough to seek employment, he has a count against him. He is under suspicion, a marked youth. His old gang welcomes him back. The line of least resistance, together with his burning desire to exert his regained freedom, leads him back to his old haunts and his old ways. If, as often enough happens, he cannot find a job, what is left for him but to drift into a criminal career? This is the time when above all he needs assurance, friendly protection, and aid in making a living. But often enough he is dumped out of the institution bus to find his own road with only the most casual supervision. The U.S. Senate Delinquency Subcommittee reported in 1958 that after-care was one of the most vulnerable aspects of the entire anti-delinquency effort.

One condition that has retarded the provision of after-care is the lack of any clear decision as to whose responsibility it is. Actually the institutions themselves have been most active in seeking to secure it, but their resources are usually quite inadequate for this additional service. Some of it has been supplied through State, local, and private welfare agencies. But very much remains to be done, and in many states mighty little is done in comparison with the need. The new youth employment policies, combined with the whole antipoverty program of the Federal Government, give promise of meeting an important part of this need. Nothing is more essential for the youth who is discharged from an institution than to be assured of a decent job, or, if he is not yet ready for one, to be provided under good auspices with the training that will qualify him for one. The institutions themselves are recognizing the need to train their inmates realistically for their working life, but usually they cannot do much more than initiate the work-training process. In other ways also the superior institutions do all they can to facilitate the transition from the more cloistered life to that of the youth's neighborhood. Children's Village, for example, has a terminal period during which every aspect of the returnee's relationship with the neighborhood is explored, including school recognition, job placement, family acceptability and alternatives where necessary, membership in a community center, church affiliation, if any, and so forth.[13] For the same purpose, the State of California has set up a liaison procedural plan to provide, after the youth leaves, an individualized social service, employment opportunities, family assistance and guidance, and general supervision.[14] North Carolina also, on a statewide basis, has made plans for after-care, with various types of aid through the transition period.[15]

A final reason why some alternative to institutionalization should be preferred wherever feasible is that the alternatives are considerably less costly. The annual maintenance cost per inmate in our major custodial institutions runs from $3500 to around $7500. There is, besides, the large capital outlay required for the extensive grounds and numerous buildings such institutions require. A tenth of the total annual cost of one such institution could pay for great and much needed developments in the probation services of the community.

## Some New Types of Institutions

Custodial institutions will always be necessary. There are youths who must, because they are too dangerous, too uncontrolled, too vicious to be at large, be segregated for a period from their society while they are young enough to admit the hope that under training they may still be rehabilitated. It is therefore highly important that this difficult service be under the charge of the most qualified as well as the most devoted staff that can be procured, and that the programs themselves be as appropriate and efficient as expert research can devise. Our best institutions now experiment with "milieu" therapy, group therapy, art therapy, and as much clinical treatment as they are able to provide, following the lead of such residential treatment centers as Wiltwyck and Hawthorne–Cedar Knolls, but they can give intensive treatment to only a small proportion of the inmate population, which is constantly changing.

Besides such institutions there are a few that break new ground and point up some developments which may be of moment for the future. One type is represented by the Highfields Group Center in New Jersey; another is known as the "Provo experiment." Both types offer substitutes for the large walled all-containing custodial systems.[16]

Highfields is a compact institution containing about twenty boys at any one time. It has these special features: employment of the boys away from the institution, thus enabling them to have regular contacts with the outside world, followed by group inter-action sessions in the evening. The work supervisor takes the boys each morning to some relatively near-by state hospital, where they are assigned specific jobs under the direction of hos-pital employees and the oversight of the work supervisor. They work in the storehouse, the garage, the butcher shop, the linen room, the farm, or wherever they may be needed. The work supervisor is concerned with the problems the boys may exhibit in their working habits and job relationships.

Of considerable significance are the group interaction get-togethers, a kind of "bull session" but under unobtrusive direc-tive guidance, an initiation to a process of social accommodation, testing out the attitudes of the inmates and exploring their de-fensive or hostile reactions. As the sessions proceed the boys are posed with alternatives between which they are to decide, be-tween the old way of life and a new way. The boys are at cross purposes, some more responsive, some resistant. Cliques are formed. The attainment of some form of group solidarity is at issue. Many of the youths become clearly aware that if they are to find a place in free society, they must change their attitudes and their modes of behavior.

In the final stage there is some probing of the problems of individual members, the therapist confining himself to a minimum of guidance. The members review their interrelations at Highfields and their home-ground relationships, their own past and present behavior. The whole process is free from formality. It is geared to evoking in the youth himself a new awareness of his own behavior as he learns to see it through the eyes of others and discovers that there are better ways to cope with his own problems.

The preceding is a very sketchy summary of the Highfields approach. There is nothing authoritarian about it. Its rules are simple, and they are enforced through the imposition of extra duties on the violators, though boys who are wholly unamenable are returned to court for an alternative and more forbidding disposition. The length of stay is normally about four months—much less than the average elsewhere. The combination of steady daily work of a normal kind outside the institution combines with the evocative evening sessions, in which each member of a relatively small group is given full freedom to find a way to express himself in his relation to others, to create a favorable atmosphere wholly unlike any these youth have known before.

The test of recidivism is pretty well met, and Highfields, unlike some institutions, has endeavored to test in this way the results of its work. A comparison in this respect made between Highfields and the state reformatory at Annandale shows that recidivism rates of Highfield boys were substantially lower and their rates of adjustment to social life considerably higher for one year to five years after discharge.[17] We must, however, remember that Highfields received a relatively selected group, those whom the court regarded as cases appropriate for this institution. But when comparable samples from the two institutions were taken, Highfields still had a very much better showing.

Highfields has certainly challenged some of the assumptions on which most custodial institutions for youths are conducted. Is there any advantage, and is there not some disadvantage, in retaining boys or girls for periods ranging from eight months to two and sometimes even three years—aside, that is, from quite special cases? Highfields appears to do better within a period of three to four months. Highfields is so run that it needs a considerably smaller staff in relation to the number of inmates than do most institutions, and for that and other reasons operates at a considerably lower per capita cost. It is a small-scale institution; its rules are simple and relatively few; it has no formal orientation period, no elaborate testing; it offers the boys a full working day outside of the institution, in contact with ordinary working people. All these differences, in addition to its special type of group therapy, raise significant questions regarding the whole process of institutionalization.

Our second exhibit is the Provo experiment with its focus at Pinehills, Utah.[18] It was organized and is directed under the auspices of the juvenile court, as proposed by an advisory council of laymen and professionals. Its officials are deputy probation officers appointed by the court. It is planned for habitual offenders, fifteen to seventeen years old, excluding psychotics and highly disturbed youth. In a number of respects it resembles the Highfields plan. There is no formal structure, no testing, no clinical diagnosis. The weight of important decisions is placed on the youth themselves. The group is small, no more than twenty being permitted at any one time. The key principle is that of group interaction. A regular job is prescribed, and if a boy has already a full-time job he is allowed to continue at it. The stay at the institution is not very different from that at Highfields, being usually from four to seven months. But one important difference is that the youngsters remain at home and are taken by automobile to Pinehills.

The first objective is to weld the group into a coherent whole. It is up to the group to develop a system of attitudes and mores that directs its members away from the delinquent habits of the outside groups they had associated with. The pressure on them is intended to involve them in their new group and to have it set up its own set of antidelinquent mores. The youths are free to devise situations in which they have to make their own decisions. If a boy refuses to become involved he comes under attack from the boys who are. Moreover, he knows that if he is recalcitrant he becomes a candidate for a reformatory. All the boys know that their release depends on their exhibiting a sense of involvement. It is, however, more the behavior of the youth when outside the group—a matter on which information is generally available—than his behavior within it that is made the test of his acceptance of the group-spirit and of his readiness for release.

The boys are thus taught to look to themselves for a way out of their problems. The authorities do not try to be pals with the boys. They are instigators of a group process, not regular participants in it. They do, however, apply various sanctions against any boy who fails in due time to engage in the process, ranging from docking his pay to sending him to prison for a week-end, and in the last resort to returning him to court for another and less agreeable disposition. The emphasis is put on the rejection of delinquent values through group interaction and on the establishment of good work habits. The newer boys are prompted by the older ones. The finding of employment for the boys is a permanent task of the authorities.

A careful effort is made to evaluate the results of this treatment, intended to cover a period of five years. Two types of control groups provide a basis for assessment, one a similar group of offenders who are placed on probation and the other a comparable group who are sent to the Utah Industrial School. The conclusions of this comparative study were not yet available at the time of writing.

Finally, we should note that the cost per youth under the Provo system is about one-tenth what it would have been had he been sent to a regular reformatory.

## Group Residence Programs

We have spoken of the imperative need for after-care in the difficult transition period experienced by youth on their discharge from institutions. It remains to take account of a device that has an institutional aspect but at the same time is intended as a means of transition to the ordinary life of the community—a device frequently described as a "halfway house." For many returnees the group residence is an excellent solution of the problem of transition. It allows them the freedom of a social life within and outside the residence. They are looked after and have their immediate needs met. They have counselors and advisers, but they are no longer under guard or subject to an authority who tells them what to do. Some residences provide job training or opportunities to secure it, as well as help in job placement, a highly important consideration. These residences are eminently suitable for those who cannot without peril be returned to a bad home or directly to their old environment, and some youths need the associations and the moral support of this kind of residential club to make good as parolees. We have in mind one case: a boy who had a poor and broken home life, drifted into delinquency, and after a time in a training school was paroled to a foster home with no success. Two other foster home placements were equally unsuccessful. But when he was tried out in a group residence in Manhattan he responded well and has ever since continued to make good. Now married and continuing in his original employment he is attending college classes in the evening.

A much greater development of these group residences is needed. For many thousands of young persons being returned to our cities every year such residences might make all the difference between downfall and a new more hopeful existence.[19] A considerable expenditure is required, but the cost per annum is still only about half that of the institutional training they have received, and might often make the difference between a wasted expenditure for the stay in the institution and a real social gain. The results of group residence appear to be good in a fairly high percentage of cases, though further investigation is desirable. The British probation hostels, in which the probationer voluntarily agrees to remain for a year, have won favor as being suitable for properly selected youngsters. Several states, including Wisconsin, New York, and Ohio, have already developed a number of such residences and contributed useful information on the conditions and the modes of operation that prove most expedient. Municipalities, welfare agencies, training schools, and residential treatment centers have also set up a small number of such residences.

### The Planning of Institutional Facilities

It is of high importance that our authorities break away from the uniformity of large-scale unspecialized institutions for delinquent youth. The case is already clear for the advantage of small-scale compact institutions housing twenty or thirty young persons where they can establish closer relations with a small staff, and where the danger of a rebel underground is minimized. Such small institutions make specialization possible; children who suffer from neglect more than from a confirmed habit of delinquency need no longer be housed with those who have a thoroughly bad record. We have considerable evidence from state training schools that these schools are compelled to accept children suffering from physical handicaps, specific health problems, or mental ailments that call for specialized treatment which they cannot provide. We have been informed by a competent authority in a hospital for psychotics that disturbed young persons who should not be so classified are admitted there. Intake records designate many varieties of problem children under the broad categories "disturbed," "highly disturbed," "mentally disturbed," and often no more authoritative classification is made before commitment. All such misplacements, which may have very serious consequences, could be avoided with a properly differentiated system of small-scale institutions.

*To secure that end it is essential, on the one hand, that each state have an expert body, or a special committee of the over-all authority responsible for state institutions for delinquents, to plan and put into effect the setting up and organization of these institutions, and, on the other hand, a diagnostic clinic under a Youth Authority or attached to the relevant courts with the function of assigning cases to appropriate institutions in all instances where the judge decides that institutional commitment is re-*

*quired.* Should such a body conclude that some alternative to institutional treatment is preferable, it would advise the court to that effect.

## Summation and Recommendations

The present institutional system for the treatment of adjudged delinquents raises many questions and is the subject of considerable controversy. What types of juveniles need the drastic remedy of institutional treatment? What types of institutions are proper for different forms of delinquent behavior? How should the length of stay be determined? No ready answers are available, aside from the fact that we have as yet no great variety of institutional types. Here, as elsewhere, conclusions are handicapped by the fact that far more has been done to provide reasonably good if still inadequate institutions than to develop the alternative modes of disposition, and particularly the major alternative of probation. Until the function and the potentialities of probation are better realized and fulfilled no meaningful study of the respective success or failure of the two alternatives will be possible.

It is generally agreed that when there is a manifest hazard either to the community or to the juvenile in leaving him in his home environment, some form of institutionalization is desirable. But relatively little has been done to differentiate institutions so that the various categories of young delinquents are respectively provided with the kind of institution and of therapy best suited to their needs.

Our conclusions respecting strategy may be summed up as follows:

1. In view of the handicaps of institutional living, it should not be imposed where there is a reasonable chance that probation or other treatment that does not remove the juvenile from his home environment can be effective.

2. The hazard of institutionalization can be reduced by the establishment of small-scale institutions admitting closer and more informal relations between inmates and staff. Such institutions have also the very great merit that they can be

specialized for the different needs of the various categories of problem children.

3. Neglected or homeless juveniles, especially the younger ones, unless their offenses are particularly serious, should not be sent to training schools or similar institutions, but to householdlike shelters or foster homes. Juveniles suffering from physical handicaps or mental troubles should be assigned to special treatment centers equipped for the therapy they need.

4. Much experimentation is desirable in planning diversified institutions and also in determining the length of residence and the conditions of release. Such planning should be conducted through a specially qualified arm of the state or other authority responsible for the control and prevention of delinquency.

5. The period of transition from the institution to the community is a particularly important one, in which the returnee needs neighborly counsel, help in forming new associations, job training and employment opportunities. Without such after-care any benefit he may have received from institutional treatment may be wholly dissipated. For some parolees group residences or "halfway houses" are very serviceable. The whole matter of after-care calls for much fuller examination and provision than it has generally received.

# 16

## Treatment Systems

While any service for the control or prevention of delinquency might be broadly called "treatment," the term is more specifically applicable to concerted programs under professional guidance. Recently a considerable number of such programs have been developed, with varying emphases and approaches. Of those the most promising recognize the complexity of the conditions directly associated with delinquency and endeavor to deal with the various aspects of the problem, considering the whole background of the youth under observation—not only their attitudes but also their family situation, their health, their associations, and so forth.

The datum is a delinquency habit, sufficiently confirmed to require remedial or preventive intervention. This habit has its particular history in each case; that history needs to be studied, and to do so effectively rapport must be established with the youth and as far as possible with his family. The task is one that calls for much patience and skillful probing on the part of the professional staff.

In carrying out such a program the workers tend to classify the youths under treatment into different categories. The formulation of such typologies is a significant and characteristic feature of recent researches and, usually in a looser way, of the procedures of the treatment staff. Usually the categories are defined along psychological or psychoanalytic lines. Although clear demarcations between the projected types seem impossible to make, they may still give useful leads for treatment purposes. There is not and does not appear likely to be any authoritative classification. Moreover, it is risky to use the classifications for purposes of prediction. A good warning is provided by an eight-year follow-up of a school population rated at the age of fourteen by use of the Minnesota Multiphasic Personality Inventory.[1] Seventy-one cases coded as nondelinquent which turned out delinquent were characterized generally as coming from the most seriously disturbed homes. Also included in the follow-up test were seventy-one cases coded as delinquent which actually were found nondelinquent. These were compared on the one hand with an equal number of cases in which the prediction of delinquency proved to be accurate and a similar number coded as nondelinquent who remained so. The third group was presumed to be wedded to a delinquent subculture. Whatever the categories used, the predictive test is obviously an unsafe ground on which to select for treatment. An incidental finding deserves notice— of recorded delinquents at the age of nineteen only 22 per cent were found to have committed further delinquency by the age of twenty-three.

## Two Primary Considerations

This follow-up test, one of the few thoroughgoing ones we have, confirms a conclusion on which we have already insisted. It is of primary importance that all vulnerable young people be detected at the earliest possible stage and given special care, guidance, protection, and, if need be, therapy. Under "vulnerables" we include not only children who have shown incipient delinquent tendencies but also those who are subjected to unhappy family situations or who are forming associations that may lead them into delinquency. Wherever there is disturbance or instability in the young, early remedial aid, under wisely sympathetic direction, can be vital for future well-being. But for the most part this lesson has still to be learned.

While specific typologies remain problematic, some simple correlations are clearly established. In the first place, the intra-

family experience of the youth is crucial. The association between delinquency and the neglect, indifference, or harsh or arbitrary attitude of parents, the lack of reasonable discipline or the
pampering of a child's every whim, is of paramount importance.
Where the home offers no social anchorage for the child, he becomes disoriented, disturbed, adrift. He manifests it by being
withdrawn and sullen, or aggressive with a tendency to seek
satisfaction in illicit ways. He becomes susceptible to dangerous
promptings. For a child thus rendered vulnerable, the pressures
of poverty, accidents, or misfortunes, or other untoward circumstances, or the association with other rebellious youth can easily
turn the scale to the formation of delinquent ways.

This conclusion is wholly or partly supported by many studies
of the subject, including those by the McCords, Wattenberg,
Wolberg, Slocum and Stone, and the New York City Youth
Board.[2] A recent English study presented significant evidence to
the effect that in poor neighborhoods the determination of delinquency is home-centered, not neighborhood-centered. The bad
neighborhood triggers the susceptibility created by experiences
in the family.[3]

If we accept this conclusion it by no means implies that the
adverse environment of the slum is not a significant factor in the
causation of delinquency. The pressures of poverty within—
fraying tempers and the stultifying of simple desires—are reinforced by the meanness and squalor without, which in turn
offer no decent outlets for youthful energies. The high delinquency rates of such areas are a measure of the extent to which
susceptibility to transgression, usually engendered within the
family, is confirmed by life under slum conditions.

The initiating significance of the family is suggested by another finding from the English study mentioned above. This gave
evidence that families living in relative isolation in low-delinquency areas exhibited the delinquency rates characteristic of
high-delinquency areas. The interpretation of this finding calls
for further study, and it would be important to discover how far
it is corroborated by other researchers, but the assumption is
tenable that when a family lives in near-isolation from its neigh-

bors it has peculiar characteristics or special problems that may well lead the children to break away in revulsion or rebelliousness.

A second important consideration is that anything that interferes with or interrupts the process of child development can induce a train of consequences that may lead to delinquent ways. Such an event may happen in the nursery, in the playground, in the school, on the street, as well as in the home. To the sensitive child any accident may be traumatic. It may be a change of residence, where the child cannot adapt to the new conditions. The school is not infrequently the starting point of a series of troubles, occasioned by the inability to get along with a teacher, the failure to make the grade, perhaps evoking angry reproaches from a parent who fails to understand the child's problem, or the bullying of a bigger boy. With older youth the break may come because a parent insists that the son prepare to enter his father's business whereas the youth is determined to become something else, say an artist or a scientist. There are also situations in which the driving ambitions of a father or mother spur the child to try to achieve beyond his capacity or his energy, bringing tensions that lead to rebelliousness.

The two major considerations we have dwelt on could well be the premises on which a treatment system is based. They suggest the importance of acquiring an understanding of the history of the youth under treatment. The investigator must be able to put himself in the position of the young, to see the world with their perspectives.

This is not easy. It demands much skill and patience and devotion on the part of the investigators. To restore the disturbed balance or establish a new one requires the felicity of the artist as well as the competence of the trained worker. Across the country numerous programs of treatment are now in operation. We have a record of 143 communities in which programs for problem-beset families have been set up.[4] Some of them are still in the planning stage. Some of them employ the traditional casework approach. Some focus treatment on limited objectives, such as teaching homemaking skills or budgeting efficiency. It is a promising movement, but it remains questionable whether many of these programs are thoroughgoing enough to come to grips with the complexity of the problem. Few of these projects employ clearly defined measurement scales. Still fewer use control groups or have any adequate plans for a follow-up accounting.

### Some Ground-Breaking Treatment Systems

We shall accordingly confine our review to certain well-directed and well-organized programs. One of these is the Hyde Park Youth Project in Chicago, an attempt to provide and test a coordinated approach to the treatment and prevention of serious youth troubles.[5] The neighborhood in which it is based is one in which the majority of families are above the poverty level, so that the problems to be met are directly intrafamilial or interpersonal. Of the 266 families involved, half the referrals came from the school, one-fifth from the police, and a small number through the Hyde Park Neighborhood Club. The problem of "reaching" the families for the initial diagnostic and treatment-planning stage appears to have been successfully met in a large proportion of the cases, and only a small percentage of the cases thus reached withdrew from the program prescribed. To supply whatever help seemed needed the available resources of the community were scouted and mustered. The planning appears to have been supervised with care, and the ratings recorded a not inconsiderable degree of success, with 15 per cent rated as showing "substantial improvement" and 38 per cent "some improvement."

An interesting development has been proceeding at the Wiltwyck School for Boys, one of the residential treatment centers that accepts boys committed from the New York City Domestic Relations Court.[6] The form of treatment is family therapy. (The same principle—that the problem of the youth is intimately related to and may be dependent upon the problem of the parents—is also appreciated by other treatment systems, for example the California Community Treatment Project.) It is recognized that the alienation of young people from their families, the absence of trust, the sense of having no haven is a deprivation that may bite deeply into morale. In earlier clinical work at Wiltwyck it was found that a large percentage of the parents of these boys had abdicated or were unqualified to perform the task of bringing up their children. A frequent result was that the family siblings became a subgroup on their own, following their own devices and the rough manners of the street. To restore some sense of family cohesion and to re-establish some intrafamily responsibility were the major aims of the program, and it has been undertaken with much discretion and careful and patient planning. To assist in the process the fullest aid, financial and other, was sought from the available public services. Practical approaches have been utilized to stimulate a focus of leadership within the family, to instruct in the management of the family budget, and to prepare and train the teenagers for the role of being a support to the household.

A particularly promising experiment in treatment has been inaugurated under the auspices of the California Youth Authority.[7] It is designed to study the feasibility of substituting an intensive community program for the traditional state training school system. It takes selected Youth Authority wards directly from a reception center to a community treatment center. This program, which already shows promise, could be of signal importance as supplying a preferable alternative to the risky and costly expedient of training-school custody.

The program is designed to provide different treatment for various defined types of delinquents. To enable the case work to be effective and sufficiently intensive, the average worker is given only eight cases. The communities involved were reluctant in the beginning to reaccept trouble-making youth who had recently been taken out of them for the good of all concerned and thereafter to participate in the rehabilitation process. But through a good public relations policy and the offer of special inducements the difficulty was largely overcome.

Diagnostic preparation is followed by a wide range of services, with counseling, tutoring, and group therapy adapted to diagnostic indications. Very considerable use is made of foster homes, and there are discussion groups for foster parents as well as for natural parents. Special efforts have been made to control the behavior of wards returned to the schools, since half of all the cases had given disciplinary trouble there.

The history of one such case may be cited briefly to show that wise coaching backed by the necessary discipline can sometimes succeed.[8] Tommy, aged thirteen, when committed to the Youth Authority, was being considered for permament exclusion from school, where he had frequently been defiant, malicious, and quarrelsome. After various conferences with school authorities he was given "one more chance." The understanding was that any infraction whatever would immediately send him to detention. Tommy tested the situation right at the start by "sassing" a teacher, forthwith followed by a week's detention. Tommy was so weak in internal controls that this resort was considered the appropriate one for his type. During the next six months only two rule infractions occurred, each immediately followed by a return to detention. The school authorities were much impressed not only by the vigilance of the authority's agency but also by the improvement in Tommy's behavior. The story, so far as we now have it, ends with the statement that Tommy is still frequently called into the school office but mostly now for commendation.

One conclusion which the Youth Authority's committee reached may have an important bearing on the crucial question of how far intra-community treatment is feasible and preferable as an alternative to custodial institutionalization. The conclusion was that not a single case in the experimental group was unsuitable for treatment in the community. Some of the wards who looked like being the worst cases (mainly very low-maturity youths) proved to be more amenable to the treatment than some of those rated as high maturity cases.[9] The infantile, querulous, complaining type proved remarkably susceptible to a system which provided strong controls over behavior combined with comfort, good food, and continuous patient tolerance of fumbling and abusiveness. Nearly all in this category required placement in carefully selected foster homes and almost daily contact with the community agent. The degree of success achieved with such cases and the unexpected emotional growth some of them exhibited were beyond the staff's expectations; in fact there was an impression that some of the 25 per cent regarded as ineligible could have been treated successfully under the program.

Most of those under treatment for six months or more showed a decrease in the frequency of misbehavior, and even more of those in the program for more than a year. The experimental cases had an average of forty-seven months per failure in the community while the control group averaged twenty-six months per failure.

The committee in charge divided the cases into three major categories—low maturity, middle maturity, and high maturity—but it also defined a series of delinquency subtypes and became convinced that this classification held good for differential treatment. The responsiveness to treatment varied with all nine subtypes, but the numbers under consideration in each were too small to make the statistical evidence very significant. The distinctions between subtypes, while competently formulated, raise some interesting problems that are too complex to be examined here. The staff, it should be noted, was enthusiastic about the contribution to successful treatment made by the differentiation into subtypes.

We regard this experiment under the California Youth Authority, a body which has been otherwise forward in antidelinquency programs, as the most promising lead in the strategy of rehabilitative treatment. It is one that might well be studied and followed by other states.

## The Treatment of Drug Addiction

There are some special behavior problems that call for entirely distinctive modes of treatment. It is a significant age-old fact that when a form of behavior is offensive to the prevalent moral code the treatment has been almost universally to punish the offender, to resort to forcible suppression. This has been true for alcoholics, narcotics addicts, prostitutes, and homosexuals. A famous legislator of ancient Greece prescribed a double penalty for those who committed misdeeds under the influence of alcohol, first the penalty for the misdeed and second the penalty for being drunk. Only in very recent times has there been any recognition that mere punishment does not cure and may well aggravate the trouble, and that the only hope lies in skilled research into methods of treatment that can restore the "patient" or at least alleviate the condition so that he has a chance to live a more normal life again among his fellow men.

We shall consider here the question of treatment for only one of the problems mentioned—that of narcotics addiction, which rather recently has taken on an alarming association with juvenile delinquency. It is a practice that is fraught with a peculiar danger for those who yield to it. There are numbers of young delinquents who grow out of their rebelliousness and wildness as they find a steady job, become sufficiently interested in a girl to want a permanent attachment, and thus recognize the necessity of earning a decent living. There are others who, when caught young enough, benefit from well-designed treatment and reform. But the drug addict is caught in the vise of his habit and without the most careful treatment cannot break it off. He is its prisoner throughout a life of degradation and wretchedness.

The drug addict becomes much less inclined to go rioting around or commit wanton offenses. His offenses are mainly the consequence of his addiction, of his desperate need to obtain by any possible means the funds that will enable him to satisfy his daily craving. This may account for the decline in gang wars in recent years, especially in areas where there is considerable evidence of the resort to narcotic drugs. The slave of the habit ceases to be gregarious.

There are two ways in which young people are drawn into this snare. One is as a drastic form of escapism, a respite from the burden of failure and deprivation and the bleakness of an opportunityless future. It is significant that drug addiction is more commonly found among poverty-stricken youth who are also discriminated against, Puerto Ricans and Negroes, for example. The other way is for "kicks." Here the use of drugs is likely to begin at juvenile parties where marijuana cigarettes are smoked. If that habit takes hold, the next step is to graduate to heroin or an equivalent, and the trap begins to close. Recent reports show that drug addiction has made inroads in several relatively prosperous areas. Addition can become, as a federal narcotic agent put it, "an infectious disease."

The treatment of narcotic addicts, adult or juvenile, has been so far mostly an unhappy affair. Addicts have been consigned to hospital wards, special hospitals, detention houses, or prisons—arrests usually are made when, as is so frequently the case, the addict has been charged with theft or robbery and associated offenses. Cut off from his drug, he passes through a period of dire suffering but at length may emerge detoxified. It is then that he most needs support, protection, care, and some kind of a job. But these needs have seldom been filled, and as a result he reverts to his old habits and associations.

Only very recently has this problem been given any thorough consideration and study. Some significant experiments are being made. There is increasing realization that addiction in itself should not be regarded as a matter for penal action, but as one for therapeutic measures. There are signs of progress, but the strategy of treatment is still somewhat controversial and the record of success has been low.

Two approaches are being explored and the prospects of real advancement are promising, especially when the two are combined. One is the establishment of rehabilitation centers with intensified supervision, constant experimentation, and background research. A good example is the California Rehabilitation Center. Most of the addicts are there under a law prescribing civil commitment, since the addiction takes such hold that they would not remain through the treatment except under compulsion. The program has met with some success, with fewer than the average number of relapses. It is significant that 80 per cent of the men under treatment had started the narcotic habit before the age of twenty. A newer program is that of Daytop Lodge, under the probation department of the Supreme Court of New York State, a "halfway house" for addicted probationers, in a beautiful setting at the opposite pole from the prison environment. Testing procedures are being developed and applied and the rehabilitative potentialities of therapy programs explored. Another and apparently quite remarkable experiment is the institution of Synanon at Santa Monica, California, which maintains a sort of tribal society for addicts, a system made possible by the strong *pater-familias* quality of its founder, Chuck Dederich. The evidence suggests that within the society a healthy drug-free spirit prevails. As with the other experiments mentioned, a longer period of exposure to the conditions of the outside world is needed before the degree of success achieved can be evaluated.

The second approach is through experimentation with drugs that may counteract the craving for heroin. Here quite important results have already been registered, especially with methadone, which seems to defeat the narcotic urge. Even if the substitute becomes habit-forming, the new habit appears from investigations thus far to be much less deleterious, costly, and dangerous than the old one.

While there is thus more promise than before for the rescue of the addict from his imperative craving, the way out of the deep cave of addiction is still hazardous and hard and long. Here as elsewhere primary stress must be laid on preventive measures. The insidious danger of the narcotic drug should be presented as realistically as possible. Attempts to prevent the use of narcotics by stopping the illegal traffic have in large measure been defeated by the ease of concealment and the great profits reaped by the gangsters who control the illicit market.

### Concluding Observations on Strategy

As we review the variety of treatment programs now being developed in various parts of the country we are impressed by the manner in which modern developments in sociology, child psychology, psychoanalysis, and medical science are beginning to be reflected in them. Let us consider some of these developments and their relation to the more significant advances in the treatment procedure.

In the first place, good authorities have long held, and are more clearly demonstrating, through recent studies[10] that the earliest years of the child's upbringing within the family are the most crucial for the development alike of his morale and his potential IQ. Where the family sustains the child's basic trust, giving him self-confidence and self-reliance as well as the assurance of unity with the only society he knows, the chances are good that he will win through to success. An opposite picture is that of a child deprived of cultural advantages, brought up in demeaning squalor, perhaps as a member of a race subjected to gross discrimination and denied the opportunities other groups possess. Under such conditions the chances are that a sense of inferiority will destroy trust, numb aspiration, and stultify effort.

Obviously, then, what is done for and to the child at this very early stage will have a deeper affect on him than later treatment is likely to have. The lesson is particularly important both for the formation of his attitudes and the arresting of dangerous tendencies. Prevention is much easier, as well as much better, than cure. This lesson is still insufficiently heeded, but there are some signs of its being recognized. Henry Street Settlement, on New York City's Lower East Side, set up a pre-delinquent gang project designed to detect early symptoms of gang behavior in younger groups, which worked with them and their parents to wean them away from the influence of the older gangs.[11] The Settlement believes that through its intensive efforts it has helped uncommitted peer groups to achieve status in socially acceptable ways and has enabled parents to take a more enlightened interest in their children and thus to acquire more influence with them. The five groups in this after-school program ranged in age from eight to thirteen. Another project of similar character, a pre-teenage delinquency prevention program, is conducted under the auspices of the United Neighborhood Houses of New York City, the program being operated by nine member institutions situated in high-delinquency areas.[12] We need programs of a constructive preventive nature ranging all the way down to the nursery school.

Another established finding of sociological and sociopsychological research is that the majority of delinquent acts involve the participation or the influence of the youthful group, whether or not it takes the form of an established gang. This conclusion has been in evidence since the earlier studies of Breckenridge and Abbott, Healy and Bronner, Thrasher, Shaw, and various others. The presence of the group tends to neutralize internal conflicts, to lessen the embarrassment of a sense of guilt. It provides an alternative bond of security and belongingness when the youth finds himself at odds with the authoritative society. At the same time it becomes a barrier against influences brought to bear on him for his reform or rehabilitation.

Consequently there is a growing tendency to make the group the unit of treatment or therapy. We saw how in the Provo and Highfields experiments group guidance was primary and it has been prominent in the treatment systems we have described in the present chapter. It has also been extended to programs for parolees. In the difficult task of dealing with gang members it has proved the only effective method. The worker must make himself welcome within the relative intimacy of the gang, participant and helpful in its legitimate activities. Only by being accepted can he hope to redirect its more dangerous tendencies; only so is he likely to influence the attitudes of its individual members. This has been the experience of the New York City Youth Board and of the California Youth Authority. In his work with gangs in Boston, Miller found that while an effective worker will succeed in reducing the illegal operations of the gang, violations begin to increase after the announcement of his impending departure. One impediment to success is that a worker usually remains with a particular gang for only two or three years, and consequently can achieve only a limited redirection of the gang's interests and activities.

The importance of dealing with people in the total setting in which they function may be illustrated from another mode of treatment, distinguished as "milieu" therapy.[13] A continuity of specially adapted service within a particular environment is provided for a group of which the members exhibit some serious ailment, physical deficiency, or mental imbalance. The setting permits relatively free expression of antisocial or otherwise undesirable traits. The youth is confronted steadily and gently with the meaning and consequences of his behavior, as a means of assisting him to overcome these tendencies and to develop in time some behavior skills. Particularly significant applications of this method have been developed by Fritz Redl and his colleagues, by the Orthogenic School of Chicago, and by the McCords in their work at Wiltwyck Residential Center.[14] These have demonstrated that a rewarding degree of success can be achieved with groups of psychopathic youth, a category that had previously been regarded as beyond the scope of treatment.

## Summation

1. The development of a considerable number of treatment programs under which a concerted effort is made to understand and deal with youth troubles in their relation to life conditions, family relationships, and other associations is definitely an advance in dealing with problems of delinquency.

2. In this development some progress has been made in the diagnosis of delinquency types and the screening of cases for differential treatment.

3. There is still rather frequently a lack or inadequacy of provision for the testing of progress as the work proceeds, and particularly for follow-up research to assess over two or three years at least the behavior of those who have been under treatment by comparison with that of an appropriate control group. This is still the most serious lack in the whole field of research on delinquency prevention and control.

4. The success of a treatment program depends primarily on the quality of the service. It calls not only for a variety of

cooperative professional skills but also for considerable experience, patient devotion, and fine discretion. For so important an objective no consideration of finance, proximity, or associations should be allowed to interfere with the endeavor to obtain the ablest available personnel.

# 17

* * *

# *The Over-all Planning of*
# *Anti-Delinquency Programs*

As the volume of delinquency has increased, more services have been and are being provided for its control and prevention. These services have grown up sporadically and more or less independently. They are spread out over numerous agencies, public and private, and the public ones are distributed over several main city departments, while the states and the federal government are also actively concerned. On every level of service the question of integrated planning arises. The problem is complex and the need for some kind of coordination is imperative. In an earlier chapter we pointed out how any given service is more effective when it is linked up with other services and may be wholly negated unless it is supported by these other services. The lack of integrated planning means discontinuity and the dissipation of energies and funds.

Let us look more specifically at the need and the problem. A disturbed youth may be put under good guidance but unless something is done at the same time to change his relationship with his family and his family's relationship with him, the value of the guidance may be lost altogether. A youth may learn to form good habits in a custodial school for delinquents, but if he is not provided with after-care in the form of protection, temporary assistance, and help in finding a job, the benefit may be purely transitory. Delinquency is the result of the accumulation of unfavorable conditions, and if treatment is limited to one or more of these conditions, the others may balk its efficacy.

Similar conditions apply to the series of stages through which a youth proceeds when a charge of delinquency is brought against him. The case may go first to the police, to be followed by detention and then, after the adjudication of the court, he may be put on probation. At every stage, some screening and diagnosis are necessary but there may be no consistency in the process. The police screening decides whether the youngster is warned, referred to some welfare agency, or arrested. The court screening decides whether he is dismissed, discharged, put on probation, or sent to an institution. Are the police sufficiently trained, sufficiently in touch with the procedures of the court, to decide whether a case should be brought before the court? Does the judge know enough about the case to make the best decision for the welfare of the youth and is he sufficiently in touch with the nature of the institution to which he may commit the youth? Obviously, a close relationship between these stages of service is eminently desirable.

If this statement holds for the treatment process, it is certainly no less valid for the prevention of delinquency. Delinquency cannot be effectively prevented if attention is centered solely on children who already show delinquent tendencies, important as it is to deal with these. An effective system for the prevention of delinquency should be available to all children and will be no less valuable for those who have no delinquency taint than for those who have. In its functioning the school has a large part to play, but so has the family, the church, and all the other agences attempting to provide opportunities for youth. Again, children who are particularly vulnerable or who are already showing signs of delinquent tendencies should be a concern of the neighborhood as a whole, and the neighborhood should be organized under professional leadership to discover such children, with the aid of the schools and welfare associations; otherwise they are likely to be neglected and uncared for until it is too late to arrest the formation of delinquent habits.

In light of these considerations, let us look at the problem of coordination as it affects the great city. We shall take New York City as our main illustration, since we have had occasion to give it special study. Like all great cities, it has a number of departments offering particular services for the young—the departments that deal with health, mental health, welfare, recreation, and correction. It has various agencies concerned with housing, urban renewal, foster care, day centers; its Board of Education has provided and developed a multitude of services for guidance—social, educational, and vocational.

The Youth Board is the city's major agency for anti-delinquency planning and the coordination of services, but for various reasons it has usually understood the function of coordination in an extremely limited sense. This board also has two other functions: contracting special services to private agencies concerned with the welfare of children in trouble, and an operating service concerned with street clubs for work with gangs, multiproblem families, and other activities.

While the Youth Board has contributed some important advances in particular areas and has itself filled some gaps in the city's operative services, it has never undertaken the major task of supervision and presumably was not expected to do so. Instead, it has established a rather loose liaison with various departments of the city and on the whole has been more concerned with the fulfillment of its other functions. It did not possess the status required to undertake full-scale coordination. In any event, whether the broad planning and integrating of closely related services should be conjoined with other functions is questionable.

A further problem has been that other bodies are also engaged in planning operations. The City Administrator's Office has had the special function of surveying and making reports on the efficacy and the interrelation of particular services. The Department of Welfare, in its turn, has been active in the expansion of a variety of services for health and social betterment. Again, the Community Council of Greater New York has been active in the consideration of a wide variety of city services, and its Regional and Neighborhood Planning Board has been concerned with the promotion of coherent local and regional associations. The Council, which has an elaborate structure, represents the major voluntary agencies of the City, with members of some City departments on it. Typically, in modern cities, a plethora of agencies arise to meet growing demands but little consideration is given to assuring that they will work together effectively.

The need for some kind of over-all supervision is further indicated by what has been happening to the two major enterprises recently set up within the city to provide all-around opportunities and services for the greatly disadvantaged youth of the city regions in which the projects are located. We refer to Haryou-Act and Mobilization for Youth. Such organizations should have ample freedom to devise their own plans for the exploration of the needs of the people they serve, to encourage these people to express in their own way their grievances and complaints, and to stimulate them to develop self-help while they are being ministered to by the workers for the projects. But such projects are liable to rouse objections from particular interest groups, political or economic. Moreover, they receive considerable financial contributions from both public and private sources and may be challenged to justify the way these funds are used. If they were under the aegis of a broad-based supervisory authority, they would possess a degree of security they otherwise lack. It is not unreasonable to suppose that if the two programs in question had been under the guardianship of a fully competent top-level unit responsible for the supervision and coordination of youth services, they would have been protected against unfair attacks and at the same time would be in less danger of giving grounds for such attacks. The kind of supervisory unit we have in mind would not interfere with the programs and policies of any responsible enterprise, but would make sure that it worked in proper relationship with sponsors, supporters, and city authorities.

The type of planning unit would vary with conditions but certain considerations are essential. The unit should be composed of persons of recognized standing and wide experience in endeavor to see that they are given full opportunity to establish the area of youth welfare, including persons who have shown high capacity in administration, citizens recognized for their broad and generous outlook, and one or two leading scholars. It would not carry on any direct operations of its own in the delinquency field, but would be full time devoted solely to over-all planning and supervision. It would enter into negotiations with the city's various agencies to develop policies to bridge the gap that so often exists between more or less autonomous city agencies. It would promote standards of service and would see that the conditions of service are such as to attract properly qualified personnel.

The planning unit, if it is to be effective, must be placed at a high level of government, say, within the Mayor's executive office. It would not undertake to control individual agencies but would use its influential position to assure their cooperation.

Such a planning unit should have attached to it a research group which would be in direct touch with the programs and operations of the various agencies in order to make recommendations for any necessary improvements, and also keep abreast of the studies being made in the field and bring to the attention of the planning unit any findings that might have a bearing on programs.

In the light of experience and research, the planning unit would seek to establish priorities and to promote policies that would bring them into effect. To give an illustration, a much neglected aspect of our present services is the failure to concentrate on *directed* prevention. By that, we mean those services that discover and give timely guidance and aid to those young persons who are beginning to fall into delinquent ways and who are particularly vulnerable because of their family situation or the tendency to truancy. At this early stage, the chances of rescuing such children are much greater than they are when habits of delinquency have been formed and confirmed.

Finally, the planning unit would take cognizance of the manifold services being rendered by voluntary agencies and would effect cooperation with official agencies.

While the need for the integration of programs may be greatest in the big city, with its multitude of agencies, public and private, it is also important in the state. On the state level, there is often a commission on crime and delinquency, or a council of community services, which has some general supervisory responsibilities. Some states—California and Minnesota, for example—have adopted the youth authority approach as a means of centralizing certain functions of delinquency control and treatment. The mechanisms for coordinating delinquency services vary greatly from state to state. In most states, however, there remains a considerable need for the more effective integration of state, regional, and municipal service.

Finally, on all levels of government, from federal to local, resources and programs are being provided to cope with the problems of youthful delinquency. The federal government has been greatly expanding its services to this end, especially since the establishment in 1961 of the President's Committee on Juvenile Delinquency and Youth Crime. In the same year, Congress passed its Juvenile Delinquency and Youth Offenses Control Act. Following up these initiatives, there are now important federal groups for training programs, special educational programs, many-sided programs for youth employment, and the recently established broad-based antipoverty campaign. The Department of Health, Education, and Welfare, along with its Health Institutes, has been active in furthering these developments.

These programs give new resources for states and localities, and this means an expansion of youth services all down the line. They call also for a redesigning of earlier services and for new liaisons between federal and state and between state and local activities in the field. To give fuller effectiveness to these new resources and opportunities, to avoid waste and overlapping and inefficiency, over-all planning is more imperative than ever before, both to assure the linkage between the different levels of public authority and to establish coherence and unity of effort within the operative programs of city and state alike.

# Notes

## Chapter 1

1. As reported by the British Home Secretary, January 1963.
2. The figures for the various European countries are taken from the United Nations Bulletin, *New Forms of Juvenile Delinquency* . . . , August 1960.
3. R. Perlman, "Delinquency Prevention: The Size of the Problem," (Washington, D.C.: U.S. Department of Health, Education, and Welfare), 1960.
4. The inadequacies of screening and the imperfections of diagnosis contribute to the lack of accuracy characteristic of delinquency statistics. We must never assume that official statistics in this area are at best more than rough approximations. One particularly serious defect is the unknown relationship between detected and undetected delinquencies, which probably is highly variable under different conditions and in different areas. For an able and learned discussion of this and other problems of delinquency statistics, see Isidor Chein, *Some Epidemiological Vectors of Delinquency and its Control* (New York University: Research Center for Human Relations), 1963.

## Chapter 2

1. Sheldon and Eleanor T. Glueck, *Unraveling Juvenile Delinquency* (Cambridge, Mass.: Harvard), 1950, and other works.
2. Among studies that bear out this conclusion we may cite Robert J. Havighurst and Hilda Tobin, *Adolescent Character and Personality* (New York: Wiley), 1963, and Margaret Mead, *And Keep Your Powder Dry* (New York: Morrow), 1965.
3. Albert J. Reiss, Jr., and Albert L. Rhodes, "Delinquency and Social Class Structure," *American Sociological Review,* October 1961.
4. Final Report No. 2, 1961.
5. Study presented as a dissertation for the Ph.D. degree at Columbia University. It was written under the direction of the present writer.
6. "A Five Year Study of Early School-Leavers," *Guidance News,* NYC Board of Education, March 1957.

7. "Students and Their Progress in the '600' Day Schools," NYC Juvenile Delinquency Evaluation Project, Report No. 6.
8. *Cf.* W. C. Kvaraceus, *Juvenile Delinquency and the Schools* (Yonkers, N.Y.), 1954; Lane and Witty, "The Educational Attainment of Delinquent Boys," *Journal of Educational Psychology,* Vol. 25, 1934.
9. Miller, Margolin, and Yolles, "Epidemiology of Reading Disabilities," *American Journal of Public Health,* Vol. 47, 1957.

## Chapter 3

1. William Healy and Augusta F. Bronner, *New Light on Delinquency and Its Treatment* (New Haven: Yale), 1936.
2. Fritz Redl and David Wineman, *Children Who Hate* (New York: The Free Press), 1951.
3. William and Joan McCord, *Psychopathy and Delinquency* (New York: Grune & Stratton), 1956.

## Chapter 4

1. William Healy and Augusta F. Bronner, *Delinquents and Criminals* (New York), 1926.
2. See especially E. Greenwood, "New Directions in Delinquency Research, a Commentary on a Study by Bernard Lander," *The Social Service Review,* Vol. 30, June 1956; also David J. Bordua, "Juvenile Delinquency and Anomie, an Attempt at Replication," *Social Problems,* Vol. 6, Winter 1958–1959.

## Chapter 5

1. C. R. Shaw and H. D. McKay, *Juvenile Delinquency and Urban Areas* (Chicago: University of Chicago Press), 1942.
2. William L. Warner and Paul S. Lunt, *Yankee City Series* (New Haven: Yale University Press), 1941, Chapter 6.
3. Milton Barron, *The Juvenile in Delinquent Society* (New York: Knopf), 1954.
4. Albert K. Cohen, *Delinquent Boys: The Structure of the Gang* (New York: The Free Press), 1955.
5. Walter B. Miller, "Lower Class Culture as a Generating Medium of Gang Delinquency," *Journal of Social Issues,* No. 3, 1958.
6. Richard A. Cloward and Lloyd E. Ohlin, *New Perspectives on Juvenile Delinquency* (New York: New York School of Social Work), 1959.
7. Robert K. Merton, *Social Theory and Social Structure* (New York: The Free Press), 1957.
8. Albert J. Reiss and Albert L. Rhodes, "Delinquency and Social Class Structure," *American Sociological Review,* October 1961; Robert Dubois, "Deviant Behavior and Social Structure," *American Sociological Review,* April 1959; John I. Kitsuse and David C. Dietrick,

"Delinquent Boys, A Critique," *ibid.* For a broad-based review of the whole issue see Herbert A. Bloch and Gilbert Geis, *Man, Crime and Society* (New York: Random House), 1961, pp. 433–441; Herbert A. Bloch and Frank T. Flynn, *Delinquency* (New York: Random House), 1956, Chapter 8.

9. The detailed statistics are presented in New York City Juvenile Delinquency Evaluation Project, Final Report No. 2, *Delinquency in the Great City*, 1961, directed by the writer.
10. Reiss and Rhodes, *op. cit.*

## Chapter 6

1. Walter B. Miller, *Social Service Review*, Vol. 33, No. 3, 1959.
2. F. Ivan Nye, James F. Short, Jr., and Virgil J. Olson, "Socio-economic Status and Delinquent Behavior," *American Journal of Sociology*, Vol. 63, January 1958.

## Chapter 7

1. For a brief account of the Mexican system, see A. H. Maslow and R. Diaz-Guerrero, "Adolescence and Juvenile Delinquency in Two Different Cultures," *Festschrift for Gardner Murphy*, Peatman and Hartley, eds. (New York), 1960.
2. J. D. Lohman, "Juvenile Delinquency, Its Dimensions, Its Conditions, Techniques of Control, Proposals for Action," *Juvenile Delinquency Prevention and Control.* Hearings before the Subcommittee on Juvenile Delinquency, U.S. Senate, 86th Congress, First Session, 1959, National Institute of Mental Health, 1960.
3. See, for example, W. C. Kvaraceus, *Juvenile Delinquency and the Schools* (Yonkers, N.Y.), 1954.
4. Albert K. Cohen, *Delinquent Boys: The Culture of the Gang* (New York: The Free Press), 1955, pp. 13, 14.
5. *Ibid.*, p. 150.
6. *Ibid.*, p. 153.
7. Lloyd E. Ohlin and William C. Lawrence, "Social Interaction among Clients as a Treatment Problem," *Social Work*, IV, 1959, pp. 3–13.
8. Ruth Tefferteller, "Delinquency Prevention Through Revitalizing Parent-Child Relationships," *Annals, American Academy of Political and Social Science*, 322, 1959, pp. 69–78; M. Gold and J. A. Winter, *Children, Youth and Family Life* (Ann Arbor: Institute for Social Research, University of Michigan), October 1961.
9. Arthur Hillman, *Neighborhood Centers Today*, National Federation of Settlements, New York, 1960, 239 pp.
10. Melvin Herman, "The Work Group as an Instrument in Enhancing the Employability of Youth," Mobilization for Youth, presented at the National Conference on Social Welfare, Cleveland, Ohio, May 23, 1963 (for staff only).
11. *Ibid.*
12. Lawrence R. Ephron and Irving Piliavin, *A New Approach to Juvenile Delinquency.* A Study of the Youth for Service Program in

San Francisco, Survey Research Center, University of California, Berkeley, California.

## Chapter 8

1. Milton Barron, *The Juvenile in Delinquent Society* (New York: Knopf), 1954.
2. Henry Robert Goddard, *The Kallikak Family* (New York: Macmillan), 1919, Chapter 9; Richard Dugdale, *The Jukes* (New York: Putnam), 1877, Chapter 9.

## Chapter 9

1. Herbert A. Bloch, "The Inadequacies of Research in Delinquency Causation," *National Probation and Parole Association Journal,* Vol. 1, July 1955.

## Chapter 11

1. Frank Reissman, *The Culturally Deprived Child* (New York: Harper & Row), 1962.
2. *The Demonstration Guidance Project: 1957–1962 Pilot Program for Higher Horizons,* Board of Education of the City of New York.
3. Charlotte D. Elmott, Jane Criner, and Ralph Wagner, *The Troublesome Ten Per Cent, A Report of a Demonstration of School Social Work,* Santa Barbara City Schools, Santa Barbara, California, 1961; *Review of the Role of the Schools in Mental Health,* United Federation of Teachers, New York City, December 1963, p. 5.
4. Donald Cook and Seymour Rubenfeld, "Settings and Causes of Juvenile Delinquency," Chapter III, *An Assessment of Current Mental Health and Social Science Knowledge,* Appendix II, National Institute of Mental Health, February 1960, p. 15.
5. Terry Ferrer, "Classroom Revolution," *New York Herald Tribune* 1963 (reprint).
6. Bryce Perkins, "Team Teaching, Current Developments in Education," *Educational Perspectives,* February 1962 (reprint).
7. *Norwalk School Improvement Program,* April 1962–August 1963, Norwalk Board of Education, Norwalk, Conn.
8. Jacob Landers, *Higher Horizons Progress Report,* Board of Education of the City of New York, January 1963.
9. Adele Franklin, "The All-Day Neighborhood Services," *Annals of the American Academy of Political and Social Science,* vol. 322, 1959, pp. 62–68; *The All-Day Neighborhood Schools,* Interim Report XIII, Juvenile Delinquency Evaluation Project of the City of New York, December 1959.
10. *A Cooperative Study for the Better Utilization of Teacher Competencies,* Final Report, Central Michigan College, Mt. Pleasant, Michigan, 1960.
11. James B. Conant, *Education of American Teachers* (New York: McGraw-Hill), 1963.

12. *Students and Their Programs in the "600" Day Schools,* Interim Report VI, Juvenile Delinquency Evaluation Project of the City of New York, December 1959, pp. 7, 8.
13. Gordon P. Liddle, "Relationship of Reading and Delinquency: Role of the School in the Prevention of Delinquency," *Cooperative Research Monograph* #10, p. 50.
14. *Ibid.,* p. 55.
15. *Ibid.,* p. 58.
16. Daniel Schrieber, "Juvenile Delinquency and the School Drop-Out Problem," *Federal Probation,* September 1963, p. 17.
17. *Ibid.,* p. 18.
18. *Annual Report 1962–1963,* Division of Child Welfare, Bureau of Educational and Vocational Guidance, Board of Education of the City of New York, pp. 21–28.
19. *Ibid.,* pp. 28–33.
20. *Ibid.,* pp. 86–88.
21. George T. Donahue and Sol Nitchtern, "A School District Program for Identification and Adaptation to the Needs of Anxiously Disturbed Children."
22. Nathan Glazer, "Out of School, Out of Work," No. 42, July 18, 1963.
23. Tom Wicker, "10,000 Will Return to School After U.S. Drop-Out Campaign," *The New York Times,* Monday, September 19, 1963.
24. *Reducing the School Drop-Out Rate—A Report on the Holding Power Project,* The University of the State of New York, State Education Department, Bureau of Guidance, Albany, 1963.
25. *Annual Report,* Division of Child Welfare, *op. cit.,* p. 38.
26. *Ibid.,* pp. 76–78.
27. *Project: School Drop-outs,* National Education Association, Vol. II, No. 1, September 1963, pp. 2–6 passim.
28. Harold J. Dillon, *Work Experience in Secondary Schools,* National Child Labor Committee, June 1946, pp. 89–92.
29. *Delinquency Prevention through Guidance in the Schools,* Final Report No. 3, Juvenile Delinquency Evaluation Project of the City of New York, August 1961.

# Chapter 12

1. Donald Cook and Seymour Rubenfeld, "Prevention and Treatment in the Community," Chapter VII, *An Assessment of Current Mental Health and Social Science Knowledge Concerning Juvenile Delinquency,* February 1960, p. 3.
2. Martin Gold and Jay Allan Winter, *A Selective Review of Community-Based Programs for Preventing Delinquency,* Institute of Social Research, University of Michigan, Ann Arbor, Michigan, October 1961, pp. 160, 161.
3. *Jobless Youth: A Challenge to Community Organization,* National Social Welfare Assembly, June 1963, p. 9.
4. *Opening Opportunities: New Haven's Comprehensive Program for Community Progress,* New Haven Youth Development Program, April 1962, p. 2; *New Haven Youth Development Program, Part 2,* Community Progress, Inc., New Haven, Connecticut, October 1963,

p. 7; Max Doverman, *New Haven Youth Development Program: Its Contents, Structure and Future Implications.* A Report to the Project's Planning Committee. Community Council of Greater New Haven, October 28, 1963.

5. *Progress Report:* Joint Youth Development Committee, Chicago, Illinois, February 8, 1964; *Gateways for Youth,* A proposal by the St. Louis Human Development Corporation, St. Louis, Missouri, January 8, 1964; *The Boston Program,* Action for Boston Community Development, Inc., Boston, Massachusetts, September 9, 1964, 9 pp.; *Boston Youth Opportunities Program,* Action for Boston Community Development, Inc., Boston, Massachusetts, December 1963, pp. 209, 210.

6. *The All-Day Neighborhood Schools,* Interim Report XIII, Juvenile Delinquency Evaluation Project of the City of New York, December 1959; Adele, Franklin, "The All-Day Neighborhood Services," *Annals of the American Academy of Political and Social Science,* Vol. 322, 1959, pp. 62–68; *The Demonstration Guidance Project: 1957–1962 Pilot Program for Higher Horizons,* Board of Education of the City of New York.

7. *The Chicago Demonstration on Delinquency Control and Prevention, Intentions and Directions,* a summary statement on the Joint Youth Development Committee's Proposal, November 12, 1962, mimeographed statement #630, pp. 4–7.

8. *Gateways for Youth, op. cit.,* pp. 95, 96.

9. *Youth in the Ghetto,* A study of the consequences and a blueprint for change, Harlem Youth Opportunities Unlimited, New York City, 1964.

10. *Action on the Lower East Side,* Progress Report and Proposal, Mobilization for Youth, New York City, July 1962–June 1964.

11. "A Proposal for the Prevention and Control of Delinquency by Expanding Opportunities," Mobilization for Youth, New York City, 1961.


## Chapter 13

1. Jean Selvidge, "The Police Juvenile Bureau's Job," *National Probation Parole Association Journal,* vol. III, no. 1, January 1957, pp. 41–44.

2. Alfred J. Kahn, *Planning Community Services for Children in Trouble* (New York: Columbia University Press), 1963, p. 224.

3. G. A. Mitchell, "The Youth Bureau: A Sociological Study," unpublished Master's thesis, Wayne State University, Detroit, Michigan, 1957.

4. Clyde B. Vedder, *The Juvenile Offender* (Garden City, N.Y.: Doubleday), 1954, p. 193.

5. Saul Bernstein, *Youth on the Streets* (New York: Association Press), 1964, pp. 71–73.

6. Tom V. Waldron, Police-School Liaison Program, Flint, Michigan Police Department, 1962, 42 pp.

7. *Planning Community Services . . . , op. cit.,* p. 24.

8. *The Police Department,* Interim Report No. 11, Juvenile Delinquency

Evaluation Project of the City of New York, December 1956, Table III, p. VI.

## Chapter 14

1. Paul W. Alexander, "Constitutional Rights in Juvenile Court," in *Justice for the Child*, Margaret K. Rosenheim (New York: The Free Press), 1962, p. 92.
2. Elliot Studt, "The Client's Image," in *Justice for the Child, op. cit.*, pp. 206–207.
3. Alfred J. Kahn, "Court and Community," in *Justice for the Child, op. cit.*, pp. 228–229.
4. Sophie M. Robison, *Juvenile Delinquency, Its Nature and Control* (New York: Holt), 1960, p. 334.
5. Howard E. Fradkin, "Dispositions and Dilemmas of American Juvenile Courts," in *Justice for the Child, op. cit.*, pp. 136–137.
6. Negley K. Teeters and John O. Reinemann, *The Challenge of Delinquency* (New York: Prentice-Hall), 1950, pp. 377–378.
7. Harris B. Peck, *et al.*, *A New Pattern for Mental Health Services in Children's Court* (Springfield, Ill.: Charles C Thomas), 1938, pp. 44, 48.
8. Justine W. Polier, *A View from the Bench*, National Council on Crime and Delinquency, New York City, 1964, pp. 8–9.
9. Mary H. Speed, "A Guidance Clinic for Probation," *California Youth Authority Quarterly*, Winter 1961, pp. 30–32.

## Chapter 15

1. Robert Schulman, *This Year in Our Training Schools*, address given at the Second Annual Conference of New York State Training Schools, New Paltz, New York, September 9, 1963.
2. Alfred J. Kahn, *Planning Community Services for Children in Trouble* (New York: Columbia University Press), 1963.
3. Ruth Shonle Cavan, *Juvenile Delinquency, Development, Treatment and Control* (New York: Lippincott), 1962, p. 305.
4. Juvenile Delinquency Evaluation Project, City of New York, *Three Residential Treatment Centers*, New York, 1958.
5. Joseph H. Louchheim, *The Delinquency Problem and Approaches to Its Solution, as Seen from the Standpoint of the Institutions*, November 17, 1958.
6. Juvenile Delinquency Evaluation Project, City of New York, *The Institutionalization of Young Delinquents*, Report No. XI, p. 6, 1958.
7. Clarke, Freeman, and Trent, unpublished report on Warwick Training School.
8. Seymour Rubenfeld, "The Inmate Culture in the Correctional Institute for Mental Health, in Support of Report to the Congress on Juvenile Delinquency," Appendix II, February 1960, Chapter V, pp. 9, 16–20.
9. Howard W. Polsky, *Cottage Six: The Social System of Delinquent Boys in Residential Treatment* (New York: Russell Sage Foundation), 1962, pp. 168–182.

10. Herbert A. Bloch and Frank T. Flynn, *Delinquency: The Juvenile Offender in America Today* (New York: Random House), 1956, p. 453.
11. John W. Mannering, mimeographed memorandum, Department of Public Welfare, Wisconsin, 1957, in *Berkshire Farm Monographs,* December 1962.
12. *Berkshire Farm Monographs,* December 1962, Vol. I, No. 1, p. 19.
13. The Children's Village, Dobbs Ferry, New York, Policies and Procedures, *Handbook for Orientation Seminar,* Fall 1962, pp. 22–25.
14. Rosemary P. Peters, "Treatment Needs of Juvenile Offenders," California State Board of Corrections, Monograph #1, July 1960.
15. North Carolina Board of Corrections and Training, "Second Annual Proceedings Workshop for Cottage Counselors," February 5–7, 1963.
16. Albert Elias, "Highfields After Five Years," *The Welfare Reporter, New Jersey Institutions and Agencies,* Trenton, N.J., January 1958, pp. 3–17; Albert Elias and Jerome Rabow, "Post-Release Adjustment of Highfields Boys, 1955–57," *The Welfare Reporter, New Jersey Institutions and Agencies,* Trenton, N.J., January 1960, pp. 7–12; H. Ashley Weeks, *Youthful Offenders at Highfields* (Ann Arbor: University of Michigan), 1963, p. 49; *General Statement 1964–65 and Annual Report 1962–63,* Highfields Residential Group Center, Hopewell, N.J.
17. H. Ashley Weeks, *op. cit.,* p. 146.
18. Lamar T. Empey and Jerome Rabow, "The Provo Experiment in Delinquency Rehabilitation," *American Sociological Review,* vol. 26, no. 5, October 1961.
19. Robert Schulman, "The Group Residence—Part of a Network of Rehabilitative Services," address delivered at the New York State Welfare Conference, New York City, November 27, 1962, pp. 5–6.

## Chapter 16

1. Donald C. Cook, "Some Evaluative Studies," in *An Assessment of Current Mental Health and Social Science Knowledge Concerning Juvenile Delinquency,* Appendix II, Chapter VI, February 1960, pp. 31, 32.
2. Donald C. Cook and Seymour Rubenfeld, "Settings and Causes of Delinquency," Chapter III, p. 45, and "Some Evaluative Studies," Chapter VI, p. 25, in *An Assessment of Current Mental Health and Social Science Knowledge Concerning Juvenile Delinquency,* Appendix II, February 1960; *Reaching the Unreached,* Monograph #5, New York City Youth Board, 1958.
3. R. C. Wirt and P. F. Briggs, Personality and Environmental Factors in the Development of Delinquency (unpublished manuscript), University of Minnesota, quoted in Donald C. Cook, "Settings and Causes of Delinquency," *op. cit.,* p. 76.
4. Joseph C. Lagey and Beverly Ayres, *Community Treatment Programs for Multi-Problem Families,* a survey of 260 North American Communities Community Chest and Councils of the Greater Vancouver Area, December 1962, pp. 2–8 passim.

5. *Hyde Park Project*, Welfare Council of Metropolitan Chicago, Illinois, May 1955–1958, pp. 65–75.
6. Salvador Minuchin, Edgar Auerswald, Charles King, and Clara Rabinowitz, *The Study and Treatment of Families Who Produce Multiple Acting-out Boys*, Wiltwyck School for Boys, Inc., for presentation at the American Orthopsychiatric Association Convention, March 1963, pp. 2–13 (to be published); Edgar Auerswald, *Developmental Effects of Poverty on Children of Hard-Core Urban Families—Implications for Nosology and Treatment*, Wiltwyck School for Boys, Inc., for presentation at the American Orthopsychiatric Association Convention, March 1964, p. 16 (to be published); Charles H. King and Clara Rabinowitz, *The Impact of Familial Perceptions of Public Welfare Agency Practice on Family Attitudes with Special Reference to Delinquent Children*, Wiltwyck School for Boys, Inc., for presentation at the American Orthopsychiatric Association Convention, March 1964, pp. 11, 12.
7. *Community Treatment Project, First Year Report of Action and Evaluation*, Operation and Research Staff, Department of Youth Authority, Youth and Adult Corrections Agency, State of California, June 1, 1963; *An Evaluation of Community Treatment for Delinquents*, Community Treatment Project Reports #1 through 5, Operation and Research Staff, Department of Youth Authority, Youth and Adult Corrections Agency, State of California, August 1, 1962, pp. 9, 10.
8. *Ibid.*, pp. 21, 22.
9. *Ibid.*, pp. 25, 27.
10. Benjamin S. Bloom, *Stability and Change in Human Characteristics* (New York: Wiley), 1964.
11. Ruth S. Tefferteller, "Delinquency Prevention Through Revitalizing Parent-Child Relationships, *The Annals of the American Academy of Political and Social Science*, vol. 322, 1959, pp. 69–78.
12. Goodwin P. Garfield, United Neighborhood Houses Pre-Teen Delinquency Prevention Project (speech), Institute on Services to Multi-Problem Families, sponsored by the National Federation of Settlements Training Center, March 5–7, 1964.
13. J. H. Reid and H. R. Hagan, *Residential Treatment of Emotionally Disturbed Children;* a descriptive study, New York Child Welfare League, 1952, quoted in Donald C. Cook and Seymour Rubenfeld, "The Nature of Treatment," *op. cit.*, Chapter IV, p. 20.
14. William and Joan McCord, *Psychopathy and Delinquency* (New York: Grune & Stratton), 1956.

# Index

Screening); centers for, 150–51, 157, 173; early, need for, 6, 112–13, 122, 141, 177, 181; juvenile courts and, 5, 141, 149, 150–51, 152, 154–55; treatment and, 177, 181–82

Differential conditions and delinquency, 44, 46–47, 51, 56, 60, 67–69, 83, 86–92 *passim;* treatment and, 96, 189

Dillon, Harold J., 119, 201

Discipline, 15, 75; home (family), 10, 11, 23, 74–78, 83, 86, 96, 178

Discrimination, 13, 20, 22, 56, 61, 68, 95, 99, 187; education and, 104, 110; police and (*see under* Police)

Disorientation: as factor in causation, 73, 86, 87, 178; immigrants and, 20, 61, 62, 63

Disturbed juveniles, custodial institutions and, 162–73; schools for, 110–11, 113; use of term, 31–32, 177

Donahue, George T., 201

Doverman, Max, 202

Drinking, 58, 82, 184

Drop-outs, 22, 73, 78, 79, 133; delinquency, educational process, and, 110, 111, 114–21, 122–23

Drug addiction. *See* Narcotic addiction

Dugdale, Richard, 200

Durkheim, Emile, 70

Economic disabilities, 15–26, 51

Education, 22, 37 (*see also* Schools; Training); class theory of delinquency and, 55–56, 68; causation and, 78–79; delinquency and levels of, 34, 51; delinquency programs and, 98–103, 104–23

Ego, 29, 30, 33, 34

Elias, Albert, 204

Elmott, Charlotte D., 200

Employment, 33, 81; custodial institutions and, 166–67, 168–70, 171; schooling (training) for, 25, 98–99, 115–21, 123, 125–27, 130

Environment, 9–11, 12–26, 28, 52,

91; antidelinquency programs and, 95–103; class theory of delinquency and, 55–72; heredity *vs.*, 37–38, 43–45; physical, 12, 17–26, 28, 46, 55, 97; psychic, 27–38

Ephron, Lawrence R., 199

Escapism, 18, 58, 184

Ethnic groups, 12, 17; delinquency, educational process, and, 110; delinquency rates and, 8–9, 17, 18, 56–72 *passim;* gang culture and, 80; police and, 143–44; programs for, 96

Family, the, 21, 48–52, 59, 64, 85, 116, 140; attitudes and, 22–23, 46, 48–52, 67; cohesion of, 9, 10, 23, 46, 48–51, 66, 67, 76–77, 87, 88, 181; critical situations in causation and, 74, 75–78, 87, 88, 96, 97, 116; guidance (discipline) and, 10, 11, 23, 74–78, 83, 86, 96, 178; psychic environment and, 27–37 *passim,* 44; treatment and, 125, 132, 178, 179, 180–83, 187, 193; values and, 19 (*see also* Values)

Family Court, 111, 140, 149, 152–54, 156

Farm schools, 159–60, 165

Father(s), 44, 47–52, 59, 74–78; absence from home of, 8, 49–50, 59, 74–75

FBI, 42, 141

"Female-based" household, 59

Ferrer, Tony, 200

First graders, identification of problems in, 112–13

Flynn, Frank T., 164, 199, 204

"Focal concerns," delinquent subculture theory and, 58–59, 68, 70

Ford Foundation, 118, 128, 132, 144

Forestry camps, 157, 159–60

Foster homes, 162, 175, 182, 183

Franklin, Adele, 200, 202

Friedlander, Kate, 32

Frustration, 19, 30, 31, 36, 52 (*see also* Aspirations; Strains); crucial factor in causation, 73, 85;

tion and schools, 21–22, 111, 115, 122; programs for, 131; social-class theories of delinquency and, 55–72 *passim*

Insecurity: economic, 19, 20; personality types, 33; schools and, 111; societal, delinquency and, 83–92 *passim*

Institute for Juvenile Research, 34

Institutional commitments (institutionalization), 4, 6, 101–2, 111, 130, 149, 157–75

IQ tests, 104, 106, 111, 187

JDEP. *See* New York City: Juvenile Evaluation Project

Jews, 18, 19, 20, 24; custodial institutions and, 160; family training among, 76

Joint Youth Development Program (Chicago, Ill.), 127, 128

Judges, 101, 148–56; commitments by, 162, 173; diagnosis of delinquency, 6, 101; juvenile courts and, 148–56; school drop-outs and, 115

Juvenile courts, 3–6, 13–14, 42, 60, 101, 102, 111, 139–47 *passim*, 148–56; commitments and, 161–62, 164–66, 170; schools and, 22

Kahn, Alfred J., 140, 150, 162, 203

Kelley, Florence, 154

Kenworthy, Marion, 113

King, Charles H., 205

Kvaraceus, W. C., 61, 198, 199

Lagey, Joseph C., 204

Lander, Bernard, 46, 51, 198

Landers, Jacob, 200

Language difficulties, 18, 21, 104, 133

Laulicht, Jerome, 165

Lawrence, William C., 80, 199

Leisure-time activities, 126–27

Liddle, Gordon P., 201

Lindner, Robert, 32

Louchheim, Joseph H., 161

Love. *See* Affection

Low-delinquency areas, 7–12, 13, 15, 37, 90, 178

Low-income neighborhoods, 13–26, 51, 68, 104, 132

Lower class, delinquency programs for, 95–103; morality (culture), 14, 55–72, 96–97

Lower East Side Neighborhood Association (NYC), 132

Lunt, Paul S., 55, 198

McCord, Joan, 32, 178, 189

McCord, William, 32, 178, 189

McKay, H. D., 55, 198

Mannering, John W., 164, 204

Manpower and Training Act, 126

Marijuana, use of, 82, 185. *See also* Narcotic addiction

Mass media, 8, 9, 36, 37, 83

Mead, Margaret, 38, 197

Merton, Robert K., 58, 71

Mexican in-migrants, 76–77, 115

Middle class, 10–12, 13, 97; delinquency theories and norms of, 52–72, 97

"Milieu" therapy, 30, 168, 189

Miller, Walter B., 57–62, 67–69, 70, 188

Minnesota Multiphasic Personality Inventory, 177

Minuchin, Salvador, 205

Mitchell, G. A., 140, 202

Mobility: physical (geographical), 8, 33, 34, 66; social (vertical), 60, 66, 87

Mobilization for Youth (MFY), 81, 129, 131–34, 137, 194

Morality (morals), 5, 8, 9, 67, 83; codes of, 10–11, 18, 33; "lower-class," 14

Mother(s), 16, 44–45, 48–50; causation and, 73, 74, 75–78; "female-based" household, 59; as volunteer aides, 114; working, 75

Movies, 9, 83, 84

Narcotic addiction, 18, 24, 58, 71; reefer smoking, 82; treatment of, 129, 130, 131, 183–86

Negroes, 13, 17–18, 20, 22, 24, 60, 111, 115; delinquency rate studies, 46, 51; drop-outs among, 115 (*see also* Dropouts); drug addiction among,